PRIVATIZATION, LAW, AND THE
TO FEMINISM

Edited by Brenda Cossman and Judy Fudg

Privatization has caused a major reconfiguration of the relations
between the state, the market, and the family in recent years, and these
changes have in turn had a profound effect on the lives of women. This
collection of essays addresses this important issue by presenting eight
case studies on the role of law in various arenas such as fiscal and labour
market policy, family and immigration policy, the regulation of health
services, and the control of child prostitution.

Starting from the shared assumption that privatization signals a transition from a welfare state to a neo-liberal state, the authors illustrate the
role of law in this process, and its impact on women and the existing
social order. In doing so, they examine the complex interplay between a
globalized political economy, social reproduction, and legal regulation,
providing a significant contribution to feminist political theory and
legal theory.

BRENDA COSSMAN is a professor of law at the University of Toronto.

JUDY FUDGE is an associate professor of law at Osgoode Hall Law
School, York University.

Privatization, Law, and the Challenge to Feminism

Edited by
Brenda Cossman and Judy Fudge

UNIVERSITY OF TORONTO PRESS
Toronto Buffalo London

© University of Toronto Press Incorporated 2002
Toronto Buffalo London
Printed in Canada

ISBN 0-8020-3699-6 (cloth)
ISBN 0-8020-8509-1 (paper)

∞

Printed on acid-free paper

National Library of Canada Cataloguing in Publication

Main entry under title:

Privatization, law, and the challenge to feminism / edited by Brenda Cossman
and Judy Fudge.

Includes bibliographical references.
ISBN 0-8020-3699-6 (bound)   ISBN 0-8020-8509-1 (pbk.)

1. Women – Government policy – Canada.   2. Women – Legal status, laws,
etc. – Canada.   3. Sex discrimination against women – Canada.
4. Privatization – Social aspects – Canada.   5. Privatization – Canada.
I. Cossman, Brenda   II. Fudge, Judy

HD4005.P75 2002   305.42′0971   C2002-901164-7

This book has been published with the help of a grant from the Humanities
and Social Sciences Federation of Canada, using funds provided by the Social
Sciences and Humanities Research Council of Canada.

University of Toronto Press acknowledges the financial assistance to its
publishing program of the Canada Council for the Arts and the Ontario Arts
Council.

University of Toronto Press acknowledges the financial support for its
publishing activities of the Government of Canada through the Book
Publishing Industry Development Program.

For Marlee Kline, 1960–2001
Feminist, scholar, activist, friend, and mother

Contents

Part III: The Self-Reliant Citizen: Social Health and Public Order

Preface

This book began as a collaborative project involving researchers associated with the Institute for Feminist Legal Studies at Osgoode Hall Law School, York University. The goal of the project was to examine how the transition from the welfare to the neo-liberal state in Canada, which began in the early 1980s, affected women, influenced gender relations, and posed a challenge to feminist law reform strategies. Instead of simply documenting the effects of this shift, we wanted to develop a theoretical framework for understanding how the relations between the state, the market, and the family have been reconfigured in Canada and the related transformation in the male breadwinner model gender order.

Drawing upon insights from feminist political economy, Canadian welfare state literature, and legal theory, the eight original case studies collected in this volume examine the complex role of law in privatization projects across policy areas ranging from fiscal and labour policy through family, welfare, and immigration law to laws designed to regulate the provision of health services and new reproductive technologies and to prohibit child prostitution. These policy areas reflect the research interests of the scholars associated with the Institute of Feminist Legal Studies. Some of the case studies however, were commissioned because of the centrality of a specific policy area – such as immigration – to an understanding of the range of social processes and institutions involved in reproducing both the working population and social order. The book concludes by identifying the challenges privatization poses to feminism, evaluating the role of law in achieving substantive equality for women, and assessing the limitations of an equality analysis for evaluating the implications of law and public policy.

All intellectual work is a collective creation and this book is no exception. The collaboration extended beyond the book's two editors to the contributing authors, who helped to develop the theoretical framework and focus as well as to strengthen each other's chapters. We also benefited from the comments of dozens of researchers, activists, lawyers, and students who attended the various workshops, seminars, and conferences at which we presented earlier incarnations of the chapters that make up this book. We learned a great deal from the discussion of our research and ideas, and we are very grateful for this critical engagement.

It is difficult to coordinate and sustain a collaborative research project, especially in an era in which the emphasis is on individual achievement and competition. Thus, we appreciate the public support, both financial and institutional, that provided the infrastructure for our research. In particular, we owe a debt of gratitude to three public institutions: the Social Sciences and Humanities Research Council of Canada for funding the three-year research project, 'Privatization, the Law and Feminism,' from which this book emanated, and for providing an Aid to Scholarly Research Publication grant; to Osgoode Hall Law School for fostering an intellectual community committed to socio-legal research and for furnishing the material supports necessary for scholarly production; and to the Faculty of Law at the University of Toronto, for providing assistance in the final stages of the manuscript preparation and dissemination.

Since institutions are the creations of collective human endeavour, many people played a role in the production of this book. We cannot possibly name everyone here and have thus singled out those who have had a more direct hand in it. The role of our contributing authors is obvious; without them we would not have a book. Joanne Rappaport, with the Institute of Feminist Legal Studies at Osgoode, provided the hidden labour without which any scholarly work would be impossible. She organized workshops, seminars, and conferences, administered the grant, and provided cheerful and efficient assistance throughout the research project. The following people provided able research assistance: Gillian Calder, Nadia Chandra, Stephanie Edwards, Ruth Fletcher, Angela Green-Ingham, Jennifer Guy, Faith Holder, Christine Jenkins, Robert Kelman, Irit Kelman, Gordon Kerr, Freya Kodar, Jason Koskela, Robert Kreklewich, Sarah Loosemore, Munday McLaughlin, Caitlin Morrison, Chantal Morton, Catherine O'Sullivan, Brena Parnes, Karen Pearlston, Cherie Robertson, Vincenzo Rondinelli, Olga San Miguel, Wendy Sutton, Kerry Taylor, Theodora Theodonis, Albert Wallrap, Michael Weisman, and Brian Williams. Numerous librarians at Osgoode Hall Law School Library and the Bora Laskin Library at the University of Toronto gave us unstinting and valuable assistance. Allyn Chudy at the Faculty of Law, University of Toronto, patiently and painstakingly helped us prepare the final manuscript. We would also like to acknowledge the effort of people associated with the University of Toronto Press, especially Virgil Duff, for his help in turning a manuscript into a book, Allyson May, for her meticulous editing of the manuscript, and the two anonymous reviewers (who had the unenviable task of plowing through a much longer version), for their valuable comments and suggestions. Jane Springer helped us to pare the manuscript down.

One of the lessons of feminism is that public work is unsustainable without the private labour that goes into caring for individuals. Our friends and families not only encouraged our intellectual work, they provided the distractions necessary for keeping us human. Our final thanks go to the children of the contributing authors who, throughout the book's long gestation, demonstrated to us over and over again why privatization is a threat to, and not a solution for, social reproduction.

Contributors

MARY CONDON   Osgoode Hall Law School, York University

BRENDA COSSMAN   Faculty of Law, University of Toronto

JUDY FUDGE   Osgoode Hall Law School, York University

JOAN M. GILMOUR   Osgoode Hall Law School, York University

AUDREY MACKLIN   Faculty of Law, University of Toronto

DIANNE L. MARTIN   Osgoode Hall Law School, York University

ROXANNE MYKITIUK   Osgoode Hall Law School, York University

LISA PHILIPPS   Osgoode Hall Law School, York University

PRIVATIZATION, LAW, AND THE CHALLENGE TO FEMINISM

Introduction: Privatization, Law, and the Challenge to Feminism

JUDY FUDGE AND BRENDA COSSMAN

The tragic process of swedenizing Canada must come to a halt ... I am a Canadian and I want to be free, to the extent reasonably possible, of government intrusion and direction and regimentation and bureaucratic overkill ... It is absolutely clear that the private sector is and must continue to be the driving force in the economy ... The role and purpose of government policy will relate to how we can nurture and stimulate the Canadian private sector.

Brian Mulroney

Privatization, along with globalization and restructuring, has become one of the defining terms of the end of the twentieth and the beginning of the twenty-first centuries.[1] While initially the term referred specifically to the sale of government assets to the private sector, best exemplified in England under Thatcher from 1979 through the 1980s, privatization has come to signify a tectonic shift in public policy. In the 1980s it became emblematic of the economic creed that the market was inevitably superior to politics as an allocative mechanism. In 1985, the Royal Commission on the Economic Union and Development Prospects (the Macdonald Commission), appointed to assess Canada's prospects in the global economy, confidently asserted the primacy of the market: 'the presumption must be in the great majority of cases, the market is the best available mechanism for resource allocation. The burden must be on those who propose intervention' (Canada 1985, 260). By the 1990s, privatization also came to signify a broader change in the political orientation of the liberal state, whose role and responsibilities in relation to the life chances of its citizens began to be reconfigured. Responsibility for individual welfare is less and less considered to be a matter of collective, social, or public obligation and is increasingly regarded as a private individual or, at most, a family or charitable matter (Brodie 1994a).

As a general concept, privatization captures the process of transition from welfare state to neo-liberal state as the material base upon which the Keynesian compromise rested has been undermined (Sears 1999) and its mode of governance transformed (Rose 1994). The term was introduced into the Canadian political lexicon by the Conservative government led by Brian Mulroney and it came to represent a broad range of practices, including the sale of government assets, the transfer of government functions to the private sector (contracting out), and the restructuring of government activities to more closely emulate market norms. These practices were all rooted in the assumption that private provision for profit was inevitably more efficient than public service (Cameron 1997, 12). At the same time, governments across Canada attempted to reduce their responsibility for social welfare programs and, correspondingly, to increase the investment of public funds in the private sector to facilitate service delivery (Kline 1997, 332). A growing range of social problems were recast as individual or family failings. Privatization has come to represent a fundamental shift not only in government policy but also in the balance of public and private power, both globally and nationally. It also exemplifies the coincidence of social conservative and family values rhetoric and the neo-liberal goals of self-reliance in public policy.

Feminist theory provides important tools for appreciating and assessing the significance of the restructuring of the Canadian state and economy in the wake of privatization. Feminist scholars have demonstrated that it is crucial to incorporate gender into an analytic framework in order to appreciate the distinctive features of different nations' welfare states (Evans & Wekerle 1997; Lewis 1998; O'Connor 1993; Orloff 1993). Feminist economists have also insisted that the conception of the economy must be expanded to include those aspects of productive life, such as daily maintenance of young children and the household, that are not provided predominantly via the market (Elson 1994, 1998; Folbre 1994; MacDonald 1995). In Canada, feminists have begun to demonstrate not only that privatization has had different impacts on men and women (Luxton & Reiter 1997), but that it undermines the gender order that prevailed under Keynesianism (Bakker 1996a). Constructing a new gender order is a central challenge for the privatization project (Connell 1987).

In liberal societies, law is a crucial mechanism for mediating shifts in state power. The role of law is illustrated in the growth of international law and the significance of international trade and finance treaties under globalization (Picciotto 1998). The enforcement of private property rights on a global level is a key objective of many international agreements and a central component of the World Bank's development strategy (McMichael 1999; Teeple 1995, 77; Tshuma 1999). Such rights are a fundamental achievement of liberal law, but they are always in conflict, to varying degrees, with democratic and human rights, another of liberal law's significant achievements. This tension in liberal capitalist societies is, to a large extent, mediated by legal institutions, since law plays a central role in legitimating power. Law is an important site for the production of discourses that play a powerful role in shaping human consciousness and behaviour. At the same time, its coercive force distinguishes it from other discourses.

Law plays an important role in the privatization project in both shaping and mediating various privatization strategies. Law has institutional and normative dimensions, which operate at a number of different levels. At the macro-level, international agreements have been used to liberate capital from the political constraints of the nation state. This body of international law has given rise to a host of international organizations (most notably the World Trade Organization) that exercise an adjudicative authority (Tshuma 2000). In the macro-economic realm of fiscal policy, provincial governments have sought to use their legislative powers to constrain their successors' ability to raise revenue through borrowing or taxation (Philipps 1996). Law is also important at the intermediate or meso-level, for it shapes the structure of significant institutions such as the labour market and family. At the micro-level, law is not only the preferred mechanism for resolving intractable disputes, it also constitutes the legal subject. The law provides a template for resolving broader social conflict by individualizing disputes. But law does not have only an instrumental value or effect; it has a broader normative import. Regardless of whether law is being used to repress or to foster specific institutional arrangements or social relations, it provides a justificatory framework, defining and redefining values such as equality, liberty, and the rule of law, for the invocation of state power (Cotterrell 1995).

In this introduction we develop three related arguments about privatization, feminism, and the law in order to provide a framework for the case studies provided in the body of the book. First, we argue that privatization signals a shift in state form from the Keynesian welfare state to a neo-liberal state. We develop a theoretical framework, drawing upon feminist work that focuses on the specific role of the state within a capitalist economy, and then we sketch how the Canadian state is involved in a process of restructuring its relations with its citizens. Second, we argue that this shift in state form not only has a distinctively gendered impact, but that it entails a restructuring of the gender order. We also explore the way in which the state's project of revitalizing a flagging gender order is fraught with contradictions. Finally, we argue that law plays a significant role in the restructuring of both the state and gender order. We end by situating the chapters in relation to our established framework.

I. Privatization

Our argument that the Canadian state is currently involved in a process of economic and political restructuring depends upon a particular understanding of the state's role in a distinctive and highly peculiar form of social organization: capitalist society (Fraser 1997a). We focus on two features that distinguish capitalist from other modes of production (Barrett 1988, 164–5). The first is the tendency towards the separation of the site of procreation, daily and generational maintenance (the household) from productive relations (waged work). The second is the creation of a division of labour – based on the capitalist drive to increase profits.

The first tendency accounts for the distinctive role of the state in capitalist social relations. The daily and generational maintenance of the working population (social reproduction) is not directly organized by capitalists, but they are dependent upon this work being performed (Muszynski 1996; Picchio 1992; Seccombe 1992). Social reproduction is typically organized by families in households and, to varying degrees, by the state. While the household is linked to the process of production through the wage, both in influencing the cost of labour power and by providing access to the means of subsistence, it is not subject to the same logic as the production process (Acker 1988). This separation of production from reproduction gives rise to an essential contradiction in capitalist social formations: the conflict between the standard of living of the workers (which is always historical, moral, and institutional and not determined exclusively by the price mechanism of the market) and the drive for accumulation (the need to make profits) (McDowell 1991; Muszynzki 1996; Picchio 1992). The state's role is crucial in mediating this contradiction (Picchio 1992; Ursel 1992). As Jane Jenson (1986, 14) put it, 'a common problem placed on the agenda of all capitalist states since the nineteenth century was the development of a healthy and disciplined labour force.'

The state's role in organizing social reproduction also involves stabilizing a specific gender order (Connell 1987). Social reproduction has predominantly been organized in households through normative families and kin relations, characterized by a gendered division of labour (Acker 1988; Seccombe 1992). Gendering is a process in which social significance is attached to sexual difference which, in turn, 'structures organizations, affects social and political relationships, and becomes intrinsic to the construction of significant social categories and political identities' (Frader & Rose 1996, 22). To a critical albeit limited extent, especially in procreation, sexual differences are material. But while sexual differences are the ontological basis of gender discourses, gender is socially constructed (Barrett 1988; Creese 1999; Lerner 1997; Scott 1986) and sexual differences are thus primarily discursive practices (Butler 1990). In this respect gender is analogous to race; both are processes of social differentiation that attempt to legitimate inequalities in social power by naturalizing differences. Gender discourses naturalize sexual differences through family relations, sexuality, state institutions, and policies that organize procreation and maintain the population (Lerner 1997; Scott 1986). Every gender order encompasses a sexual division of labour and gender discourses that either support or contest that division. The order is stable to the extent that it has been institutionalized in certain key sites such as the family, the labour market, and state policies (Acker 1988; Connell 1987; Laslett & Brenner 1989; Walby 1997). For such institutionalization to occur, there must be some fit, however temporary, fragile, and incomplete, between the processes of reproduction and production.

This conceptualization of gender helps to explain the gender-saturated character of the second distinctive feature of capitalist relations of production: the fragmentation of the labour force along lines of differentiation by levels of skill or need. While there is nothing in the logic of the capitalist drive for increased productivity of labour that inevitably leads to a labour force divided by sex (or race), the drive to accumulate leads to the creation of a labour force divided along the lines in which the labour process is broken down (Barrett 1988; Muszynski 1996). The hierarchical organization of these divisions maximizes competition between workers over their entitlement to a specific level of wages.

Skill is a primary justification for different wage rates and employment conditions. However, skill is ideological to the extent that it ignores certain capacities and talents and is itself the outcome of struggles between capitalists and workers and among different groups of workers. Feminist

scholars have demonstrated the extent to which the social construction
of skill is gendered and how that gendered construction has contributed
to both the creation and the legitimation of a sexually divided labour
market (Cockburn 1983; Steedman 1997). There is also research demonstrating that skill is racialized and the labour market is racially and ethni-
cally segmented (Calliste 1991; Das Gupta 1996; Muszynski 1996). In
Canada, a white settler colony, the subjugation of the First Nations populations and immigration policy were crucial mechanisms used to lower
the costs of reproduction and provide cheap sources of labour. Both processes were racialized and gendered (Avery 1995; Bakan & Stasiulis
1997b; Muszynski 1996; Satzewich 1991).

A second justification for differences in the level of wages and access
to jobs is need. According to Marx, wages depend on the costs of reproduction rather than on the value of the goods produced (Barrett 1988;
Muszynski 1996; Picchio 1992). But, as feminists have argued, need is
socially constructed and depends upon how social reproduction is organized. Gendered consumption norms and family forms have infused
working-class struggles for higher standards of living (Acker 1988; Porter forthcoming). Social differentiation, especially along lines of gender
and race, helped to reduce both the individual and social wage via a
segmented labour market and different, unequal, conceptions of social
citizenship. In all welfare states, employment has been regarded as
more worthy of recognition and entitlement than have the childcare
and domestic duties that women perform. The result is an occupationally based welfare state in which women's labour is systematically undervalued and women receive lower benefits for their labour (Cameron
1995). Social segmentation and differentiation serve to lower the overall standard of living of the population by increasing insecurity and
competition.

The ultimate lever of capitalist control over production is economic
insecurity, and the state assumes the role of dealing with the problems
that this insecurity creates for reproduction of the working population.
The state enforces certain familial obligations of financial support and
provides a social wage, a standard of living, for those members of society
not engaged in labour market activities, primarily by taxing the private
wage. The social wage to which an individual is entitled is typically based
on physical and moral criteria that correspond to different and hierar-
chically organized conceptions of entitlement. Corrigan and Sayer's concept of 'moral regulation' captures how states define acceptable forms
and images of social activity and individual and collective identity. Moral

regulation normalizes, 'rendering natural, taken for granted, in a word "obvious", what are in fact ontological and epistemological premises of a particular and historical form of social order' (Corrigan & Sayer 1985, 4). The state is animated and legitimated by a moral vision produced in contested, conflicting, and reinforcing discourses, that when institutionalized, often through law, can become ideologically hegemonic. In the current restructuring we witness not only a contestation between neo-liberal and neo-conservative discourses of the family, only some of which will become institutionalized (Cossman, this volume), but between formal and substantive conceptions of legal equality (Fudge, this volume). The specific challenge facing the liberal state is how to give a unifying expression to the experience of groups within a society structured unequally along lines of class, gender, physical and mental ability, ethnicity, race, sexuality, age, religion, occupation, and locality.

The liberal challenge is unending, since the state is never able to resolve the contradiction between the aspirations of working people and the drive for profits. Even Keynesianism – which, from the perspective of people who do not have direct access to the means of their own subsistence, was the highest mediation of this contradiction – could not resolve it (Picchio 1992, 119). Indeed, as we discuss in the sections that follow, the Keynesian compromise became unstable as the increased costs of social reproduction came to be seen as undermining capital accumulation and the rate of profit. Changes at the international level, beginning in the late 1960s, rendered the Keynesian compromise to the contradiction between production and reproduction obsolete. Since the 1980s and the advent of free trade regimes, capital is structurally freer from the costs of social reproduction than it has ever been. Not only is it much more mobile, it also has access to a larger, international pool of labour (McMichael 1999; Teeple 1995, 66–7; Ursel 1992, 51). Globalization and economic restructuring have resulted in a conscious retrenchment and realignment of state intervention in the sphere of social reproduction (Elson 1998; Picchio 1999; Sears 1999; Teeple 1995, 5). In the next section, we trace the main contours of this shift in the mode of state regulation in Canada.

A. The Rise of the Keynesian Welfare State

The Keynesian welfare state (KWS) refers to a general set of state policies adopted by Organization of Economic and Cooperation Development (OECD) countries in the aftermath of the Second World War

(Bakker & Scott 1996). It was part of an overall entente, in which 'the state had to take on new (Keynesian) roles and build new institutional powers; corporate capital had to trim its sails in certain respects in order to move more smoothly on the track of secure profitability; and organized labour had to take on new roles and functions with respect to performance in labour markets and in production processes' (Harvey 1989, 133). Using Keynesian demand-management techniques, supply and demand could form a virtuous circle with the state's assistance so long as income was kept in the hands of consumers, through either employment or state welfare benefits and income supplements, thereby sustaining consumer demand, and in turn, economic production. During times of recession and high unemployment governments could use their monetary policy to fight unemployment and their taxing and spending power to offset the loss of private income (Bakker & Scott 1996, 287). In more prosperous times, governments could reduce their activity and accumulate a surplus that could be used when the economic cycle turned downward. Key elements in the KWS came to include government expenditures on social services (education, health, social security, welfare) and income security programs (unemployment insurance, family allowances, old age security). To a large extent, risk of economic insecurity was socialized. 'Securing institutional integration and social cohesion of the social formation' became the central objective of the advanced capitalist welfare state (Jessop 1993, 16).

While the welfare state took different forms in different Western countries, there was a set of shared assumptions about its nature. The KWS was based on a fundamentally new understanding of the role of the state in the economy, and of the responsibility of the state to its citizens. Unlike its precursor, the liberal laissez-faire state, the KWS was explicitly mandated to play an active role in redressing market failures, managing the economy, and ensuring the basic well-being of its citizenry. It was committed, at least in principle, to full employment and to a universal welfare system that provided for its citizens' basic needs.

In Western liberal capitalist societies, 'laws regulating the rights and duties of citizenship constitute formal institutions of basic importance for distributive processes' (Korpi 1998, x). Citizenship, as formulated by T.H. Marshall, has civil, political, and social dimensions and it was the struggle to attain social citizenship that he identified as the new feature of twentieth-century liberalism. Social rights require the state to play a much more redistributive role and include 'a prevailing standard of living and a reduction of the inequalities associated with the market through state provision of some economic goods and services, including education and social services' (Barbalet 1988, 6; Evans & Wekerle 1997, 10). A central component of social rights is the decommodification of labour, the existence of a universal social safety net, and labour standards that ameliorate the harshness of the market (Epsing-Andersen 1990). In this way the welfare state provided a buffer against capital's relentless drive to accumulate by adjusting living standards to the benefit of working people.

The concepts of social rights and decommodification are useful for understanding the balance of forces that gave rise to a particular welfare state (Evans & Wekerle 1997). But as feminist scholars have rightly pointed out, even the best of the traditional welfare state literature is limited by a narrow notion of class, one that has an all-male cast. This has obscured the extent to which welfare states were gendered. Social citizenship has meant different, and typically unequal, things for men and women. The traditional welfare state scholarship has also ignored the extent to which men's and women's labour has been commodified differently (Evans & Wekerle 1997; Lewis 1998; O'Connor 1993; Orloff 1993; Walby 1997).

Feminist scholars have begun to incorporate gender into a framework for evaluating different forms of the welfare state (Lewis 1998; O'Connor 1993; Orloff 1993, 1997). They have gendered the traditional dimensions used for characterizing welfare states – decommodification, stratification, and the division of responsibility between the state and the market – by looking at both the family and women. They have also added two dimensions that probe the extent to which women's subordination to men is inscribed in the gender order: access to paid employment and the associated services to facilitate it (commodification) and the capacity to form and maintain an autonomous household. Moreover, both Orloff (1993) and Porter (1998) stress the significance of juridical norms for understanding how women's subordinate status became institutionalized. Using gender as a lens for analysing the welfare state allows the focus to be broadened beyond the demands of trade unions to include those of the women's movement. For women in particular, equal rights as a political rhetoric and legal challenges and law reform as political strategies have had strong appeal.

At the end of the Second World War, most welfare states subscribed to the idea of a male breadwinner earning a family wage as the norm, although a particular state's ability to achieve that norm has depended upon a host of factors (Fraser 1997a; Lewis 1998). It was based on a specific sexual division of labour in which men's wages would cover the majority of the costs of an economically dependent wife and children while women would shoulder the work of caring for others, much of which, especially the care of young children, would not be paid. Women could also serve as a supply of cheap labour, especially in the service sector (Ursel 1992).

The profound expansion in publicly provided services in the 1960s in Canada and other Western liberal capitalist countries created employment opportunities for women by shifting some of women's traditional caring responsibilities from unpaid labour in the family to paid labour provided by the state. Despite the huge increase in women's participation in the labour market, women's employment was shaped by a sexual division of labour that continued to give them primary responsibility for caring for human beings. Men were regarded as the primary breadwinners and their employment relationships and conditions were superior to those of women. Explicit discrimination against women workers helped to institutionalize both a male breadwinner norm and female economic dependency. Although women benefited from public services and income transfers, their capacity to form and maintain autonomous households was less than men's because of their limited access to childcare and their low wages. On the basis of the Canadian experience, Luxton and Reiter (1997, 215) conclude that 'the welfare state was never able to dissolve the profound contradictions between unpaid and paid work responsibilities of women, nor did legislation or formal policy serve to eliminate discrepancies between men and women workers or even equalize treatment of women workers.'

Social and legal citizenship is also structured unequally according to race and ethnicity, which have been shaped in and through the exercise of violence through war, colonialization, and enslavement (Korpi 1998).[2] In Canada, colonial subjugation of the First Nations' peoples undermined their economic base by imposing a different property rights regime and justified their political, legal, and social subordination through racist ideologies (Muszynski 1996). In First World states, legal citizenship and its associated rights are withheld even to long-term residents of races and/or ethnicities viewed as alien, unassimilable, and undesirable (Bakan & Stasiulis 1996, 218). In the European Community and Canada, this legacy of racial discrimination has continued in the form of guest or migrant worker programs (Sharma 2000). Until the 1960s, Canada's immigration law and policy was explicitly racialized (Jakubowski 1999; Satzewich 1991). Today, racial distinctions are implicit

(Thobani 2000). The extent to which race continues to condition eligibility for legal citizenship entitlements is illustrated by the treatment of foreign domestic workers and foreign agricultural workers in immigration law and policy (Macklin this volume). Foreign domestic workers have been used to meet the increased demand for less expensive live-in childcare occasioned by women's increased labour market participation. The unequal citizenship status of such workers has helped to reduce the costs of private domestic service to women who work outside the home (Arat-Koc 1999; Bakan & Stasiulis 1997b; 1996; Macklin this volume).

B. *The Fall of the Keynesian Welfare State*

The beginning of the end of the KWS can be traced to the late 1960s, when declining levels of profitability impelled capitalists to seek new accumulation strategies (Tshuma 2000; Workman 1999). Nation states began to use monetary policy as a tool to perpetuate the post-war boom in the face of rising inflation and slower growth (Gill & Law 1988, 171-4; Vosko 2000). The pressures intensified in the early 1970s with the world property crash, the increase in energy prices, the breakdown of the Bretton Woods Agreement in favour of floating exchange rates, and emerging debt crises (Harvey 1989, 145). Increased global competition, facilitated by the deployment of new technologies that liberated productive and especially finance capital from the regulatory capacity of the nation state, generated pressure for national restructuring. Canada has historically been vulnerable to global business conditions because of its dependence upon exports (Jenson 1989), and the recent transformation in federal state policy and rhetoric has been profound (Cohen 1997).

Mounting anxieties over economic recessions, the globalization of production, and government deficits clawed away at the key tenets of the KWS. The Keynesian assumptions of the legitimate role of the state in managing the economy that had informed Canadian macro-economic policy were challenged by a new set of assumptions that emphasized the primacy of market relations. Federal macro-economic policies have comprised three broad strands: anti-inflationary monetary policies, trade liberalization, and debt reduction. Their net result has been to lower the wages of the majority of working people in the country and to intensify the demands on women's labour.

By the early 1970s, the KWS emphasis on fighting unemployment and thereby raising demand had given way to a neo-liberal emphasis on fighting inflation through a shift in monetary policy and a new focus on supply and production. In 1975 the Bank of Canada adopted a monetary policy designed to reduce inflation by increasing interest rates and thereby restricting the growth of the supply of money (McBride 1992, 79-82). Monetarism also blamed supply-side factors for the lack of labour flexibility and helped nation states to justify abandoning the post-war objective of full employment for men. The wages of public sector workers were a specific focus of attack in Canada (Fudge this volume). Welfare-oriented social policy became subordinate to demands for labour market flexibility and resonated with the emphasis on individual responsibility found in social policies such as workfare (Jessop 1993, 15; Peck 1996; Vosko 2000).

The Report of the Macdonald Commission marked the beginning of the move towards trade liberalization in Canadian public policy. In 1985 the commission recommended free trade with the United States as the only viable economic strategy for Canada and the federal election of 1988 was fought primarily over this issue. After a bitterly contested campaign and a narrow win, the Conservative government ratified the Canada-U.S. Free Trade Agreement in 1988. By 1994, the Liberal government, which in 1988 had opposed free trade, accepted the inevitability of regional trading blocs and brought Mexico into the North American Free Trade Agreement.

Cutting government expenditures as a way of dealing with Canada's debt became conventional wisdom. To this end, the Macdonald Commission recommended a fundamental redesign of Canada's income support programs. But despite the increasing emphasis on the need for fiscal restraint through the 1980s, the Mulroney government's approach to social policy was one characterized by 'erosion rather than demolition' (McBride & Shields 1993, 66). By the end of the 1980s, however, eliminating the deficit and reducing government debt had risen to the top of the federal government's priorities. The Mulroney government engaged in a massive sell-off of state assets and initiated wide-ranging budget cuts to government programs. Advocacy groups, especially those representing women, Aboriginal people, and people of colour, were among the casualties of the Mulroney government's cuts.[3]

A new, neo-liberal rhetoric about the need to reduce state spending, cut back on state regulation, and maximize exports – all in pursuit of private capital investment – had caught hold of Canada's macro-economic policies (Bakker 1996a). The net effect was to undermine working people's economic position and standard of living by lowering wages and shifting more of the costs of reproduction onto them. In the 1980s the sustained attack on the level of public sector wages in almost every jurisdiction across Canada, combined with the high level of unemployment and increased global competition, resulted in an unprecedented deceleration of wages (Panitch & Swartz 1993, 143). Attention focused on the increased tax burden imposed on the middle class in order to reduce the deficit, obscuring the extent to which social programs were cut and revenues from other sources reduced. Inequality in income, especially from the market, increased and threatens to grow even wider if Canada's social policies continue to be dismantled (Beach & Slotsve 1996; Carey 1998b; Picot 1998; Zyblock 1996).

The restructuring process had a profound effect on men's wages. Times were tougher on working men in the 1980s than they were during the Depression of the 1930s (Fudge this volume). The long-term deterioration in men's wages in Canada was coincident with the profound increase in the labour market participation of married women with young children. As early as the 1970s multiple-earner families were the statistical norm, although the ideal of the male breadwinner earning a family wage was still hegemonic and remained the standard upon which most labour market and labour relations law, institutions, and practices were based (Fudge & Vosko 2001). By the 1980s, however, despite its nostalgic appeal, the male breadwinner norm was no longer an empirical reality for the majority of people in Canada: it took between sixty-five and eighty hours of work each week for a family to earn what it took a single breadwinner, typically a man, to earn in a forty-five-hour work week in the mid-1970s (York 1992). By the 1990s, married women's employment, which since the 1970s had been crucial for maintaining a family's living standard, was essential to prevent that standard from plummeting, let alone declining, and this was especially true for young families (Armstrong 1996a; Fudge 1997).

The Liberals, once the midwives of the Canadian welfare state, took drastic steps in downgrading the social wage and transforming the nature of entitlement. Despite election promises to the contrary, the Chrétien government initiated the most serious financial attack yet on social programs. In his first budget (1994), Minister of Finance Paul Martin began his assault on government spending, announcing a $5.5 billion cut to unemployment insurance between 1994–5, and 1996–7 (Battle & Torjman 1996, 57), as well as massive cuts in federal social transfers to the provinces for welfare, social services, and post-secondary education. In the same year, Lloyd Axworthy, then minister of human resources development, announced a comprehensive reappraisal of

Canada's social security programs, followed by a review of the Immigration Act and policies (Pulkingham & Ternowetsky 1996, 13). But the moment of reckoning came in the 1995 budget; Martin's single-minded focus on deficit reduction delivered a death blow to many of Canada's social programs. He announced a two-year limit to phase out the Canada Assistance Plan (CAP) and Established Program Financing (EPF) and introduced a new block-funding program: Canada Health and Social Transfer (CHST). The cuts amounted to a reduction of $7 billion in 1995–7 alone; altogether the budget proposed federal spending cuts of $25.3 billion over a three-year period. The basis for universal social citizenship was deeply eroded (Day & Brodsky 1998).

A whole new set of assumptions about the role of government and the rights of its citizens is emerging. In the new political and social order, governments are no longer responsible for the social welfare of their citizens but only for helping those citizens to help themselves (Purvis & Hunt 1999). The social citizen is giving way to a new market citizen 'who recognizes the limits and liabilities of state provision and embraces her obligation to ... become more self-reliant' (Brodie 1996a, 131). This new market citizen recognizes and takes responsibility for her own risk and that of her family. She not only creates the possibilities for new markets but is becoming the agent for social well-being. This new conception of citizenship is 'stripped of its notions of social justice and an active state' (Jenson 1997, 637) and is instead based on 'a wholly privatized and marketized notion of rights' (Mooers 1998, 9). Scholars who emphasize govermentality claim that what has emerged is a new mode of governance in which the state creates the conditions under which individuals govern themselves (Purvis & Hunt 1999; Rose 1994). Self-reliance, rather than dependency, is the keyword in contemporary social policy discourse.

The process of restructuring and privatization includes profound social and cultural changes. Moments of social transformation often produce moral panic and the nostalgic appeal to a purer and better past that is the stock-in-trade of social conservatives and family values movements. As Jeffrey Weeks writes, 'moral panic occurs in complex societies when deep rooted and difficult to resolve social anxieties become focused on symbolic agents which can be easily targeted' (Hall et al. 1978; Weeks 1981, 118). The current moment is no exception. The market citizen is also an anxious citizen rocked by the speed of social change. The decline of the KWS has been accompanied by a series of outcries – those proclaiming rising crime rates, out of control immigration, and the demise of the family are simply the most prominent. Although none of these fears has been statistically substantiated – crime rates are down, immigration is heavily regulated, and the family, although changing, is alive and well – anxiety mounts nonetheless. These fears have been incorporated into a new moral vision that legitimates an increasingly coercive role for the state: fear of rising crime rates justifies the intensification of the state's criminal power, anxiety about 'out of control' immigration results in more restrictive immigration policies and strengthened policing of borders, and apprehension about the decline of the family justifies the continued regulation and surveillance of a range of familial relationships. However, the direction of this new moral regulation has been profoundly contradictory (Sears 1999, 105). While the market citizen must take care of herself and her family, the state continues to be called upon to ensure an orderly and stable social order, especially with respect to those individuals who are marginalized by restructuring and neo-liberal policies (Martin this volume). The ideological effects of these discourses of anxiety and risk are in turn partially constitutive of the neo-liberal project of privatization, since they produce a range of 'social problems' to which the neo-liberal state and its experts must respond.

C. Privatization and the Neo-liberal State

The move to highly capital-intensive industries such as computers and electronics has drastically increased productivity and reduced the demand for labour in production. Simultaneously, countries in the Third World are providing new sources of labour that mobile capital can easily and cheaply exploit. The international labour market creates an underclass of displaced and immigrant populations that puts downward pressure on the value of labour power. The rise of international trade over national economic development means there is less need for the state to maintain a high level of wages in order to sustain domestic consumption. The costs of production are pre-eminent and the costs of reproducing the working class have been subordinated to the primary economic goal of attracting global capital (McMichael 1999; Teeple 1995). Moreover, property rights are increasingly privatized as 'nation states have become the authors of a regime which defines and guarantees, through international treaties with constitutional effects, the global and domestic rights of capital' (Marshall 1999, 138). Privatization captures this shift in the alignment between production and reproduction under global capitalism. It reflects the political requirements of internationalized capital in which democracy is subordinated to the requirements of private property and capital accumulation. Privatization is both a means of shifting the costs of social reproduction away from the state to individuals and families and an attempt to carve out new areas of profit taking.

At a general level, privatization can be described as 'a broad policy impulse to change the balance between public and private responsibility in public policy' (Smith & Lipsky 1993, 188 as cited in McFetridge 1997, 3). It involves a fundamental renegotiation in the relationship between the public and private spheres that characterized the KWS (Sears 1999, 104). Privatization includes deregulation of some sectors of economic activity, the marketization (and reregulation) of others, and the selling off of government operations with the goal of increasing opportunities for private profit making, as well as the commercializing of government services. It also involves a fundamental retrenchment of the state in social reproduction, leaving families and charities to shoulder a greater part of the burden of caring for people.

The project of privatization can be usefully broken down into a number of different, but related, strategies. The primary goal of each strategy is to institutionalize the shift in power occasioned by globalization; overall, the project requires a new division of responsibility among the state, the family, and the market for individual and social welfare. This institutional reconfiguration involves a renegotiation of the public/private distinction, a crucial leitmotif of liberalism (Olsen 1983), which Susan Boyd (1997, 4) characterizes as 'an ideological marker that shifts in relation to the role of the state at particular historical moments, in particular contexts and in relation to particular issues.' It also involves a fourth, less well-delineated institutional sphere – the voluntary or charitable sector – which is increasingly being called upon to provide 'public' goods and services. As many feminists have pointed out, where the distinction between the public and private is drawn shifts not only over time and across place, but depends upon the particular group of women involved (Boyd 1997; Thornton 1995). Race, class, and gender influence where and how the boundaries between the public and private are fashioned. For example, in Canada, while the majority of women perform unpaid domestic work in the home as part of their private, family duties, immigrant women have historically worked for wages either in their own homes, for example as garment workers, or in other people's homes as domestic 'servants' (Arat-Koc 1999; Macklin 1994; Ocran 1997).

This does not mean that the distinction between public and private is indeterminate or that it has no utility (Boyd 1997, contra Rose 1987). The nature and direction of the shift in the relationships among the state, the family, and the market are connected to identifiable relations of power (Boyd 1997, 4). Contemporary distinctions between matters of public and private responsibility differ from those made fifty years ago and signal a profound shift in power in capital's favour. The primacy of the market as the 'natural' and privileged sphere for the delivery of goods and services is not only being reasserted, it is also described as 'good' for the political system. A recent report for the C.D. Howe Institute, a major proponent of economic and social policy restructuring in Canada, claimed that '[i]n addition to improving enterprise and market efficiency, privatization may also improve political efficiency. Once completed, it reduces the number of items on the political agenda, thus allowing the political system to focus on the issues requiring the most input (fundamentally political issues), rather than issues that can be dealt with comparatively well by market governance (fundamentally commercial issues)' (McFetridge 1997, 19).

However, contrary to the rhetoric of neo-liberalism, the reconfiguration of public and private spheres of responsibility involves rather more than a simple 'return' to a natural separation. Privatization is not a seamless process of simply shifting goods and services from the public to the private sphere, of hollowing out the public and enlarging the private. It involves a reconfiguration of the form of state regulation rather than deregulation (Brodie 1995). Laissez-faire economic policies rely heavily on common law rules of property, contract, and tort and the common law courts (Cotterrell 1995). Liberalization of commodity and capital markets, the phase of globalization that gained momentum in the 1980s, involved reregulation, not deregulation, at the supra-national and national levels in order to provide for transparent markets (Picciotto 1998). Moreover, in some areas of the Canadian economy there is no call for deregulation at all. For example, the trend in the law regulating securities and mutual funds has been towards an increase in regulation (Condon this volume). And in other areas of social life, privatization actually involves an intensification of surveillance. Criminal regulation, for example, is acquiring a heightened salience at the same time as the significance of social welfare regulation is diminishing (Martin this volume). Even in the area of social welfare law, we see an intensification of surveillance in an effort to 'crack down' on alleged welfare fraud (Martin 1992).

The concept of *reregulation* allows us to highlight better the ways in which privatization is a highly selective process of shifting some public responsibilities to the private sphere while diligently protecting and intensifying the role of the state to regulate in other areas. Reregulation also highlights the continued role of legal regulation in the project of building a neo-liberal state with a disciplined, self-regulated market citizenry. At the same time, it represents a shift in the modalities of regulation, with both quantitative and qualitative dimensions. For example, there is more criminal regulation, responding to social anxieties about allegedly higher crime rates, and that regulation is also displacing the role of social welfare regulation.

In Canada, the decentralization of power at the constitutional level has been a central component of privatization. It has involved a new division of power between the federal government and the provinces, which has undermined the notion of universal social citizenship (Day & Brodsky 1998). Constitutional decentralization has gone hand-in-hand with a devolution in responsibility for social welfare from elected governments to private institutions and charities. But decentralization is more complex and contradictory than the federal government simply ceding its authority and responsibility in the face of global pressures. It is also part of the ongoing process of negotiation and litigation between the federal and provincial governments and First Nation's peoples over social welfare and economic authority.

Reregulation and decentralization are key components of the privatization project which, in turn, involves a range of related strategies that aim to institutionalize a shift in power relations. These strategies typically invoke a number of normative claims about the appropriate role of government in the lives of its citizens, claims that simultaneously attempt to legitimate a shift in the balance of power and to justify a deterioration in living standards for a large proportion of the population. The most prominent among these strategies are reprivatization, commodification, familialization, individualization, delegation, and depoliticization.

Reprivatization refers to the processes whereby once public goods and services are being reconstituted as private, that is, as more appropriately located in the private spheres of market, family, and/or charity. It involves the normative claim not only that these goods and services are better (more efficiently) delivered in the private sphere, but that they 'naturally' belong there (Evans & Wekerle 1997). In this volume, both Philipps and Cossman focus on the processes of reprivatization. Philipps considers the role of tax policy in reconstituting once public goods and services to the market, the family, and the voluntary sector; Cossman examines the role of family and social welfare law in reconstituting these public goods and services to the family, while highlighting the contradictory nature of this process.

Commodification refers to the process whereby once public goods and services are being reconstituted as market goods and services. It involves the normative claim that these goods and services are better delivered in and through the market (Brodie 1996b). Those goods and services that continue to be provided by the state are being reshaped to better conform to market norms (Bakker 1996a, 4). Condon, Gilmour, and Mykitiuk each consider the process of commodification. Condon describes the ways in which pensions are being partially reconstituted as market goods; Gilmour and Mykitiuk look at the commodification of health care in Canada, as health services are being increasingly reconstituted as market services.

Familialization refers to the process whereby once public goods and services are being reconstituted as naturally located within the realm of the family. It involves the normative claim that families ought to take care of their own (Brodie 1996a). While some suggest that the process involves a rearticulation of the so-called traditional family – a nuclear, heterosexual, male breadwinner model – form may be less important than function in this strategy. The neo-liberal state appears to be less concerned with who a family is (traditional/non-traditional) than with what a family does (take care of its members). Philipps, Cossman, and Macklin each illustrate aspects of the familialization strategy. Philipps considers the efforts to reconstitute responsibility for social reproduction as naturally located within the family through tax policy, Cossman examines the often contradictory strategies of familialization being pursed by neo-liberals and neo-conservatives; Macklin explores trends in immigration policy through which the financial responsibility of sponsors to support their family members is being increasingly enforced.

Individualization refers to the process whereby a broad range of social issues is being reconstituted, both with respect to causes and solutions, in highly individualized terms. Health care and poverty are treated as individual shortcomings, products of poor individual choices, to be remedied by emphasizing individual responsibility (Brodie 1996b; Fraser & Gordon 1997; Solinger 1998; Yeatman 1990). The normative claim is that individuals should be more self-reliant and take responsibility for the risks to their own well-being. Social and structural analyses are displaced in favour of individual solutions to individual problems valorizing individual choice and markets. Condon and Mykitiuk both explore this strategy of privatization, particularly in the context of the individualization of risk. Condon examines individualization of risk in Canadian pension policy, as the once partially socialized risk for retirement provision under Keynesianism is now increasingly displaced and recast as an individual responsibility. Mykitiuk considers the individualization of health care, particularly through the new genetics, in which individuals are constructed as responsible for their own reproductive and genetic choices.

Delegation refers to the process whereby decision-making authority is shifted from visible to invisible public agents and from public to private agents, involving a devolution of decision-making power towards less accountable agents and less transparent decision-making processes. Generally, it involves an increase in the discretion of the decision-making authority and a decrease in public accountability. Gilmour and Macklin both consider this strategy of privatization. Gilmour illustrates the increasing delegation of decision-making authority in the context of health care from visible public actors to increasingly invisible public and private actors. Macklin explores a similar process in the context of immigration policy, where private actors are increasingly delegated decision-making authority in relation to temporary workers.

Depoliticization refers to the process whereby a range of issues, goods, and services are removed from political contestation. Encoding a particular good as 'naturally' located within the market or the family removes it from the realm of politics (Brodie 1995). Normative claims about the natural superiority of the market and the family come to trump contrary claims (Yeatman 1990, 173). This position assumes that issues are self-evidently either private or public, 'fundamentally commercial' or 'fundamentally political' (McFetridge 1997, 19). Fudge illustrates how, in the context of the current backlash against substantive equality and feminism, the market is lauded as the only apolitical form of wage determination.

Privatization strategies often overlap and they are mutually reinforcing. Reprivatization, for example, may involve either the commodification or the familialization of goods and services. Commodifying a good or service may also simultaneously individualize it and reinforce the notion that individuals must become responsible for the risks to which they expose themselves. These strategies not only involve a shift in responsibility for a particular service but are often accompanied by a transformation in the nature of the service itself. Childcare, for example, is understood differently by people who support a state-funded and regulated system than by those who believe that a mother's full-time care is best. Privatization involves a complex and contradictory renegotiation and 'recoding' of the relationship between the public and the private (Brodie 1995, 53). As the chapters that follow demonstrate, the restructuring of substantive areas of Canadian public policy involves a complex interplay of privatization strategies and discourses.

The current renegotiation of the public and private spheres requires attention beyond the relationship between the state, the market, and the family and a consideration of the role of a fourth institutional sphere, the voluntary or charitable sector. This institutional sphere has been described more broadly as civil society or 'the public sphere,' which Nancy Fraser, following Habermas, defines as the sphere of political opinion formation and participation (Fraser 1989, 1994). During the KWS the significance of the public sphere declined, as the political relationship of citizens was increasingly channeled through the state, and it became the major site of political contestation (Fraser 1989; Habermas 1989). But with the 'evacuation of politics from the state' (Yeatman 1990), through the strategies of depolitization, delegation, and reprivatization, the neo-liberal state is shrinking the realm of the public political debate by prioritizing the economic realm (Brodie 1996b).

A crucial question to be addressed in the current era of privatization is the relocation of political debate and protest. The increase in popularity of forms of protest such as consumer boycotts or the development of corporate codes of conduct may suggest a slight shift in the locus of political struggle to the market (or at least an effort to effect such a shift) (Fudge 2001). However, the potential for success in this arena is profoundly limited by the foundational claim that the market lies beyond the realm of politics. Given both the limited possibilities of political struggle within the economic realm and the shrinking of the state as the site of political contest, locating and rebuilding political space within the public sphere will be a crucial dimension of any effort to resist the current neo-liberal agenda (Eley 1994; Fraser 1994).

A second and related question involves how the public sphere is being reconstituted. The broader concept of civil society – as a realm of non-governmental or secondary associations that are neither economic nor administrative (Fraser 1997a, 89) – may be helpful in grasping the multiple reconfigurations of the public/private divide. As the KWS gives way to the neo-liberal state, responsibility for the provision of many goods and services once provided by the state is being transferred not only to the family and the market but to the 'not-for-profit' sector as well (Kline 1997). Charitable organizations and a range of other voluntary associations are being called upon to provide everything from food to health research funding; at the same time, they are being transformed by the requirement that they emulate the market sector and market actors. Organizations that operate in terms of business plans, provide client services, and emphasize professionalization appear to be thriving in the era of neo-liberalism, while other advocacy-based groups seem to be under attack. Equality-seeking advocacy groups are increasingly being recast as special interest groups and are no longer regarded as entitled to government funding (Bashevkin 1998; Brodie 1995). Some of the very groups that seek to advance the goals of the original 'bourgeois public sphere' – of political debate and opinion formation – are the ones that are now losing ground within it.

Each of the chapters in this volume explores the varous ways in which privatization strategies are being deployed. Several explore the multiple and contradictory ways the different axes of the public/private distinction are being renegotiated. Lisa Philipps, for example, considers the ways in which tax law and policy is being used to reconstitute once public goods and services in three private spheres: the market, the family, and the private sector. Mary Condon examines the reconfiguration of public and private in the context of pension law and policy, where the Canada Pension Plan is increasingly relying on private markets. Roxanne Mykitiuk explores the ways in which the once primary role of the state in proactively ensuring health and welfare is being recast to promote capital accumulation, while individuals are cast as increasingly responsible for their own health and the health of their families (and families to be). Other chapters focus on strategies used to resist the emergence of a neo-liberal state and its normative claims of the priority of market over state. Joan Gilmour considers the extent to which constitutional claims may be able to impede creeping privatization in the health care system; Brenda Cossman evaluates the efficacy of equality rights discourse in resisting privatizing strategies.

II. Revising the Gender Order

Feminists have begun to argue that a new gender order, premised on a fundamental restructuring of the spheres of production and reproduction, is emerging (McDowell 1991). Several have noted 'a simultaneous intensification and erosion of gender, both literally and metaphorically'

(Bakker 1996a; Haraway 1991). Walby (1997, 2) has identified a convergence and polarization in the contemporary restructuring of gender relations. In some ways, the visibility and relevance of gender difference is disappearing, as the experiences of women and men converge. Yet in other ways, the relevance of gender is increasingly marked. These processes of intensification and erosion, of convergence and polarization, are occurring within the same institutions and discourses. Labour markets and the family, for example, together with welfare policy, are witnessing the simultaneous intensification and erosion of gender.

The restructuring of labour markets in Canada has been a deeply gendered process. The labour market experience of of young men and young women is increasingly similar (Gunderson 1998; Picot & Heisz 2000). In part, this convergence is a result of women's struggle for equality in employment, but to a greater extent it is a consequence of the sharp deterioration in the labour market position of young men (Lipsett & Reesor 1997; Picot & Heisz 2000). At the same time the labour market experience among women, which had been remarkably uniform, has begun to diverge. Women of the baby boom generation, those between forty and fifty-four years old, have benefited from the combined effect of second-wave feminists' struggle to enshrine legal equality in the private sphere and Keynesian economic policies that stressed demand. Younger women have faced a more competitive and more polarized labour market while older women lack the employment history needed to obtain direct access to a good 'retirement' income (Scott & Lochhead 1997; Townson 1995). The growing inequality among women is in part generational. It is also racialized. Roxanne Ng (1990, 107) observes that 'non-English speaking women, particularly those from visible minority groups tend to be concentrated in the bottom rungs of most service and manufacturing sectors in the so-called "non-skilled" and dead end positions.' On average, the employment earnings of visible minority women are lower than those of other women and aboriginal women experience extremely high rates of unemployment (Statistics Canada 2000a). Moreover, the relative success of baby boom women is conditioned in part upon the purchase and availability of low-cost domestic services, much of which is provided by immigrant women of colour. Any assessment of the restructuring of the labour market must also be attentive to race. 'A singular focus on gender not only supports the dominant construction of Canada as white, but also ignores the fact that relations of class, gender, and race are mutually constituting and both shape and structure the subordination of differing groups of women' (Gabriel 1996, 167).

Not only are men's average wages stagnant or declining, there is an increase in the number of jobs historically associated with women, jobs that are part-time, temporary, and/or without benefits (Picot & Heisz 2000). Most women take jobs to stop a sharp decline in standards of living and the labour market employment rate of women is fast approaching that of men (Armstrong 1996a, 234–5; Fudge 1997, 15–16). Yet despite the feminization of the labour market and the 'harmonizing down' of men's work, women are still paid less, work shorter hours, and are disproportionately represented in non-standard jobs (Armstrong 1996a; Drolet 2001; Fudge 1997, 8; Fudge & Vosko 2001; Statistics Canada 2000a). The new employment practices are still gendered (Vosko 2000). These practices '... draw in some ways on existing discourses and practices of gender relations, depend in some ways on their having been altered, and are profoundly implicated in setting out the new limits to gender equality that are being constituted. Just as in the postwar years women's status as a "reserve army" depended on a particular articulation of family forms, gender relations, and production practices, so too does the feminization of non-standard employment' (Jensen 1996, 92, citing Beechy 1988, 54). Although there has been some change in the gender order, what has remained the same is a sexual division of labour in which women perform the vast majority of the labour of social reproduction, most of which is unpaid (Statistics Canada 2000a). Nonstandard employment, such as part-time work, for example, enables women to accommodate the sexual division of labour both within the home and between the home and the labour market. However, these forms of precarious and feminized employment do not challenge, but in fact exacerbate, the inequality that results from the sexual division of labour. Gender, in this respect, is intensifying (Fudge 1997; Vosko 2000).

The changes in the labour market are part of the broader reconfiguration of the gender order, which involves a fundamental shift away from the male breadwinner/family wage norm of the welfare state (Bakker 1996a; Fraser 1997a; Fraser & Gordon 1997). Just as the restructuring of the labour market undermined the material base of the male breadwinner family wage norm, second-wave feminism's struggle for equality challenged the normative basis of women's dependency. Women's demands for equal rights rejected male claims to superiority and contested the patriarchal basis of men's authority. Women won greater legal and political independence from men and made some strides towards gender equality (Bashevkin 1998; Eichler 1997). Improved access to the labour market and social welfare programs, especially for lone mothers, provided a material base for women's independence. So, too, did more effective and reliable mechanisms for reproductive control. Divorce laws were liberalized and marriage breakdown increased. The numbers of women who have given birth to and raised children alone has risen dramatically (Eichler 1997, 30–1). There has also been 'some improvement in the social acceptability of women living alone or with other women. Public attention to violence against women (and children) in intimate relationships has increased, accompanied by a fracturing in the image of the hitherto idealized hetero-patriarchal family' (Boyd 1997, 5).

The problem, however, is that women's greater independence has not been matched by greater economic equality, especially when there are children to care for. Lone mothers and their children are among the most economically disadvantaged groups in Canada. The majority of all families headed by women parenting alone were well below the low-income cut-offs established by Statistics Canada. Only about half of these women were employed, and many of the female lone parents who worked had low-paying jobs (Devereaux & Lindsay 1993, 9; Eichler 1997, 37–8; Statistics Canada 2000a).[4]

The change in the male breadwinner family form has also resulted in an intensification and erosion of gender. Women continue to perform the majority of unpaid work necessary for social reproduction (Eichler 1997, 60–1; Statistics Canada 2000a). Despite some gains in having women's reproductive labour recognized, women's economic situation has not improved (Iyer 1997; Luxton & Vosko 1998). The dismantling of the welfare state through strategies of reprivatization and familialization increases the demands put on women to provide for a range of basic needs, from caring for pre-school children to health care for the elderly and disabled (Armstrong 1996b). Yet the material conditions that allowed women to provide some of these services for the family – namely, the family wage – have almost disappeared. At the same time, the legitimacy of women's (wives) economic dependency on their male partners (husbands) has been challenged by a new emphasis on formal equality and individual self-reliance (Fraser & Gordon 1997).

The contradictory pressures of gender erosion and intensification within the family are part of the reconfiguration of the gender order. The sexual division of labour within the family remains intricately linked with women's precarious employment in the labour market. Women have traditionally worked in nonstandard employment in part because such work has enabled them to accommodate their family responsibilities. As more women took these jobs they were no longer entirely financially dependent on a male breadwinner. However, they were not financially independent either. The loss of a spouse's income as a result of separation or divorce often meant that women and their children risked falling into poverty, even if the women were employed (Lochhead & Scott 2000).

The highly publicized 'discovery' of women and children's impoverishment after divorce meant that formal equality and individual self-reliance made only a limited incursion into the realm of family support law. While in the 1980s there was an increased emphasis on individual self-reliance on family breakdown, the 1990s witnessed an about-face, with a heightened recognition of family support obligations that extend well into the post-divorce family. But this development, too, engendered a backlash; fathers' rights groups are contesting the custody decisions and support obligations that women who have experienced marital breakup have struggled to win (Eichler 1997, 76). Women's groups, such as REAL Women, extol the patriarchal family and women's place within it. Formal equality and an emphasis on individual choice are now gaining ground over substantive equality's attempt to address systemic discrimination.

The simultaneous emphasis on self-reliance and family obligation is a key feature of the current round of welfare reform in North America. The radical reduction of welfare benefits, the expansion of definitions of spouse for the purposes of welfare eligibility, and the shift towards workfare are also part of the reconfiguration of the gender order (Evans 1997). As dependency on state welfare benefits is increasingly pathologized (Fraser & Gordon 1997), women are forced to look either to 'husbands' for support or to the labour market for wages (Evans 1997). The problem is that men's wages are increasingly insufficient to support economic dependents. Welfare rate cuts and restricted eligibility requirements (Battle 1998) are likely to exacerbate women's over-representation in precarious employment. Workfare programs are simply the most visible illustration of the shift in social welfare policy to promoting labour market flexibility (Vosko 2000). Moreover, the ostensible goal of making welfare gender-neutral means that a large and expanding group of single women with children are viewed as workers rather than mothers (Evans 1996; 1997). But the new workfare reforms are failing in the absence of accessible and good quality childcare (Mackie 2000). It is impossible for mothers to be workers unless the very real need for childcare is met.

It is increasingly difficult for public policy to align the norm of the traditional family with contemporary family structure. The variations in families and households – from women-led lone parent to lesbian couples who parent children – are dramatic. While the reassertion of the traditional family may help to legitimize and naturalize the claim that families should take care of their own, the material conditions that supported the patriarchal breadwinner model no longer exist. The gap between the normative ideal of the traditional family and the material conditions of Canadian families is likely to prove too broad for even the most powerful family ideology to resolve.

A new normative claim to legitimate the emerging gender order is thus required. As yet, no model has emerged as hegemonic, although there may be a consensus in the making. Some have suggested that independence and individual self-reliance may provide a new normative basis to family policy (Fraser & Gordon 1997). This strategy appears to accord less importance to the composition of the family and more importance to the functions that a family performs. Although still hotly contested, families are increasingly defined not by nuclear structure but by their support function (Vanier Institute of the Family 1994). The functional approach gives more elasticity to the concept of the family, allowing it to embrace gay and lesbian families, among others, within its fold (Gavigan 1999).

While the family has traditionally been portrayed 'as a rock of private stability in a sea of public storms' (Seccombe 1992, 1), it is taking a battering. The heterosexual child-rearing couple remains pre-eminent normatively, but despite the efforts of pro-family groups to support it, its material basis is being undermined. In Canada, the birthrate has fallen below the replacement rate (Eichler 1997, 30) and the need for labour can be met less expensively through immigration. This leads Ursel (1992, 43) to suggest that the patriarchal family 'has become an essential albatross of the state, indispensable but grossly expensive and decreasingly effective.' The problem is finding a viable alternative to it.

Institutionalizing a new gender order is a difficult challenge. Women's labour has historically functioned as an alternator under capitalism, mediating the tension between reproduction and production (Picchio 1992). But with globalization this tension has increased dramatically. The current process of gender restructuring involves a simultaneous intensification of women's labour market participation and family/ household responsibilities. The discourses of gender neutrality and formal equality do nothing to challenge the state's abdication of its responsibility for its citizens' welfare. Privatization exacerbates the sexual division of labour by shifting more work to women while asserting this is merely a side effect of individual choice (Elson 1998). But a gender order premised upon the elasticity of women's labour will never be stable because there are material constraints upon women's ability to meet the limitless demands placed upon them. Indeed, in the contemporary labour market, employed mothers report the greatest levels of severe time stress (Statistics Canada 2000a, 111).

III. The Role of Law

Privatization involves a shift in power relations that requires the state to intervene in social reproduction on new terms. Law is central to this endeavour. Legal institutions and norms occupy an important role in liberal capitalist societies, for they are central to the exercise and legitimacy of power (Fine 1984). In liberal societies, the state has the exclusive monopoly on the use of legitimate force and to be legitimate this force must be exercised lawfully. Law operates as a principal constraint upon the state's exercise of coercive power against its citizens. Moreover, individuals can call upon the state to assist them in their conflicts with other individuals only if they can establish a legal right. Thus, law is coercive and discursive; it is deeply linked to normative claims, high among them equality, liberty, individualism, and the rule of law, that are used to justify and contest the way in which power relations are organized. As Carol Smart has argued, law's discursive power lies in its distinctive ability to define and pronounce authoritatively on the world around it (Smart 1989). Especially in common law countries like Canada, it is associated with a specific methodology that emphasizes conceptual consistency (Woodiwiss 1990). Legal principles, doctrine, and method provide the normative basis for the authority of the law. Thus while it is the law's close relation to the state that establishes its peculiar force, it is law's legitimacy, its normative appeal, that makes its rule effective (Fine 1984; Hunt 1993; Woodiwiss 1990).

Legal discourse partially constitutes, among other things, legal personality, definitions of spouse and family, the market and property relations, criminals and illegal immigrants. It is the constitutive dimension of law that makes it 'a site of discursive struggle ... a terrain on which competing visions of the world are fought out; on which contesting normative visions struggle for the power to define legal and political concepts that give meaning to our world' (Kapur & Cossman 1996, 41). It is because legal discourses are backed by state coercion in liberal societies that they tend to be dominant or hegemonic. By selecting among competing discourses and then calling upon the state to enforce one over another, legal discourses become institutionalized and have ideological effects (Purvis & Hunt 1993; Woodiwiss 1990). For example, in the current contestation between neo-liberal and neo-conservative visions of the family the law is beginning to privilege neo-liberal claims selectively, though not yet exclusively (Cossman this volume). Yet it is important to acknowledge that law may not be the dominant site for the production of social processes and categories. Gavigan (1999) reminds us that it is necessary to supplement a discursive analysis of law with a relational understanding of law. Law is a social relation (Hunt 1993) and, as such, the relationship between legal form and social content is complex and contradictory (Fudge 1999; Gavigan 1999).

The contribution of law to the privatization project is complex, for law is composed of at least four different elements – legal norms, legal methodology, legal institutions, and legal actors – and it operates at a number of different levels – international, national, institutional, and specific disputes (Gavigan 1999; McCann 1994). The normative element has received the most attention from feminists, and the concept of legal doctrine as embodied in judicial decisions and legislation has been a particular focus of attention (Dawson 1998). Feminist legal theorists have emphasized the gender of law (Lahey 1999; Naffine 1990) and claimed that law is a gendering discourse (Chunn & Lacombe 2000; Smart 1992). Law can usefully be understood as a constellation of state-enunciated discourses that position and constitute individuals, or subjects, in social relations and institutions such as the market, the family, and the prison, for example. Legal institutions draw upon social discourses (medical, moral, scientific) that reflect competing interests for the normative content that must then be fit into specific legal forms (Woodiwiss 1990). For example, the concept of the legal person, the subject of legal rights and duties, has both a legal form and a social content (Fudge 1999; Lahey 1999).

Law also has a specific methodology that serves to distinguish it from politics (Mossman 1994). It emphasizes neutrality and detachment. The ideal of the rule of law, according to which the ordinary courts are to have final say as to the validity of legal decisions, exerts institutional pressure for consistency and coherence across different tribunals and areas of law. Legal methodology is committed to consistency and universality, and this commitment is embodied in the doctrine of precedent and the legal system's adherence to the principle of formal equality. These methodological precepts exercise a dominance or hegemony over other normative traditions; however, the process of closure is never complete since it is always resisted and contested (Woodiwiss 1990).

But law is not exclusively normative; it also has an institutional dimension. The division of powers among levels of government and courts and legislatures is not only a political question, it is increasingly a legal one. Courts and adjudicative tribunals have vied with one another for authority. Thus there are a number of competing legal institutions. Moreover, the long and enduring incorporation of the voluntary sector into the criminal justice system suggests that the relationship between official legal and other social institutions is quite complex and changes over time (Valverde 1991; Martin in this volume). Despite this legal pluralism, state law has historically exercised a centralizing discipline not only institutionally, but normatively (Hunt 1993). At this juncture, however, it is important to be attentive to the ways in which globalization undermines the powers of the nation state and the authority of state law (Tshuma 2000).

It is easy to identify the key legal players at the top of the legal hierarchy; judges stand out, as do cabinet ministers, for their ability directly to make the law. At this level, the absence of women is remarkable, although the gender composition of the bench and legislature is slowly changing (Canadian Bar Association 1993). The numbers of women in the legal profession, the next level in the hierarchy of legal actors, is also increasing; however, the profession continues to be organized around a specific norm of lawyer, one who is male and without childcare responsibilities (Kay 1997; Kay & Brockman 2000). The role of legal actors is crucial in shaping legal discourses, such actors translate social relations into legal categories in order to make claims against the state, institutions, or other people (Gavigan 1999). Feminists have argued that in many areas, especially relating to sexual assault, the law has been shaped by men's experience and the male standpoint (Dawson 1998; MacKinnon 1987).

Law has occupied a privileged site within second-wave feminism. The feminist movement that emerged in the late 1960s fought for the principles of gender neutrality and formal equality in private and public spheres and for an egalitarian model of family (Adamson, Briskin & McPhail 1988; Chunn 1999). But this strategy has resulted in an impasse. It is unable to take into consideration the gendered burden of social reproduction, for it accepts, rather than challenges, the prevailing legal norm in which the legal person is portrayed as a propertied white man. It ignores the disadvantage that women experience on account of a sexual division of labour in which they bear the burden of children by depicting motherhood as a matter of individual choice. The problem with the dominant stream in second-wave feminism, liberal feminism, is that it emphasized individualized solutions to the problem of women's subordination, heightening the differences between women. 'Poor women and/ or women of colour, Aboriginal women, lesbians, and women with disabilities have been disproportionately unable to use legislation and policies based on gender neutrality and formal equality' (Chunn 1999, 254). These women contributed to the broadening of and diversity within feminism.

Since the 1980s the courts have played a crucial role in the struggle for women's rights. In part, this is because of the entrenchment of equality rights in the Canadian Charter of Rights and Freedoms in 1982. Obtaining legal recognition of a substantive conception of equality that attends to the significance of the sexual division of labour and women's subordination has been a central concern of feminist litigation strategy. The outcomes of the litigation strategy have been mixed. The legal form has been able to accommodate changes in social norms, as indicated by the contemporary movement in Canada towards treating gay and lesbian couples the same as opposite-sex cohabitants for the purposes of law (S. Boyd 1999; Gavigan 1999). While women have made strides in having their reproductive labour recognized in the sphere of family law by having legal obligations imposed on specific men as husbands and fathers, they have been unable to challenge the state's attempt to privatize the costs of social reproduction (S. Boyd 1999; Chunn 1999). The tenacity of the public/private distinction has limited the breadth and depth of equality rights, not only in family law but in a broad range of areas of legal regulation, from sexual assault to employment (Boyd 1997; Fudge 1987, 1989). As Gavigan (1999, 157) suggests, it is likely that the legal form defies transcendence through law.

As we argue throughout this volume, law is playing a central role in the project of privatization. The process of globalization has effectively given capital an international charter of rights, chief among which is the extension of private property rights, to curtail the regulatory power of nation states (Mykitiuk, this volume). By contrast, working people have not been able to secure legal rights that are enforceable at the international level. At the national level, legislation is being called upon to implement many of the changes to Canadian public policy. As the chapters that follow illustrate, legal regulation is continuing to play an active role in shaping social relations in the era of privatization. Law is being extensively used to 'recreate a climate of free enterprise' and distribution by market forces (Cotterrell 1995). Cotterrell argues that the dominant ideology of law, grounded in the supporting ideologies of property, liberty, the minimal state, and the rule of law, has been deployed to reinforce the idea that 'law can, by its nature, properly do some things but not others. In particular, it can create conditions to allow certain kinds of enterprise and initiative to flourish; but it must not direct people in the exercise of that enterprise or initiative' (Cotterrell 1995, 254–62).

The role of law in this process is taking on many different and changing forms. Restructuring and privatization is bringing about widespread reform in legal regulation in general, and the legal regulation of women in particular, in a broad range of substantive areas. As the chapters that follow illustrate, family law, labour law, and taxation law, to name but a few areas, are undergoing reforms of a profound nature. Many of the advances made by the women's movement over the last two decades are being undone. In the area of labour, for instance, pay equity and employment equity legislation is being rolled back. The entire landscape of legal regulation is undergoing a profound change. Reprivatization, commodification, and familialization are reconfiguring the legal regulation of women in a broad range of substantive areas. For example, in family law and social welfare law, changing definitions of spouse, increased support obligations, and the intensification of the enforcement of support obligations are all being deployed to redirect women's economic dependency from the public to the private sphere. In tax law, direct social spending is increasingly being replaced with tax concessions to private individuals, while universal social programs are being displaced in favour of programs that target the 'truly needy.' Privatization involves·a fundamental transformation in the form and content of legal regulation.

In this volume, we attempt to reveal the complex role of law in the privatization project of the Canadian state; with a view to illustrating its many gendered implications. The case studies provided here illustrate the ways in which law operates at a number of levels, ranging from international treaties, national and provincial legislation, and municipal by-laws to the micro-regulation of bodies, subjects, and human genomes. They reveal the ways in which law assists with a multiplicity of strategies of privatization, including reprivatization, commodification, familialization, individualization, and depoliticization, and explore how law functions both to legitimate unequal social relations (through for example labour and taxation law) and coerce marginal groups (through immigration law and the regulation of prostitution). Individual chapters also highlight the extent to which law is linked to a number of other discourses, such as the political discourses of neo-liberalism and neo-conservatism; the (neo-liberal) economic discourses of risk and risk management, and the (neo-conservative) moral discourses of 'illegal immigrants,' 'deadbeat dads' and 'welfare mothers.' Finally, the case studies demonstrate that law is located within a number of different institutions and takes a variety of forms, from legislative and judicial to administrative. Some focus on the framing of law, in and through public policy debates and legislative drafting, while others focus on legal argument and legal decisions.

In the first section, the chapters explore the processes of privatization in the context of fiscal and labour market policy. Lisa Philipps focuses on the role of income tax laws – at the macro-level of Canadian fiscal policy – in promoting and enforcing the reprivatization of social reproduction. She illustrates the ways in which governments are revising income tax laws to promote self-reliance, transferring responsibility to the market, the family, and the voluntary sector, and highlights the gendered nature of this process. Judy Fudge focuses on the federal public sector, tracing the transformations in the legal regulation of women's employment with the federal public service in Canada from 1908 to 2001. Located at the meso-level of labour market policy, the chapter illustrates the commodification of women's labour by the Canadian welfare state and the changes brought about as a result of privatization. Mary Condon's chapter on the privatization of retirement income is located at the conjunction of macro- and meso-levels. While much of Canadian pension policy is fiscal, with more capital moving into the private sector, access or entitlement to pensions continues to depend on the labour market. Condon examines the restructuring of Canadian pension policy, focusing on the role of risk governance, individualized risk, and the gendered nature of risk, highlighting the extent to which legal norms and processes are becoming infused with these risk discourses.

In the second section, the chapters focus on social reproduction, especially at the meso-level. Brenda Cossman considers the discourses through which the reprivatization of social reproduction is being pursued, and highlights the contradictions between neo-liberal and neo-conservative visions of the family. Concentrating on recent changes to family and social welfare law, the chapter demonstrates the role of law in selecting and mediating between these competing discourses. While analyses of social reproduction typically look at the institution of the family, Audrey Macklin's chapter considers the extent to which the population is reproduced through immigration policies. Her policy analysis considers the privatizing themes that have seeped into recent changes in Canadian immigration law and policy which, although located at the meso level, is attuned to the macro-level changes of globalization.

In the third section, the chapters consider the enduring problems of social health and order. Under Keynesianism, the state assumed a positive responsibility for social health while reconstructing many issues of crime as issues of social welfare. Joan Gilmour examines privatization in Canadian health law and policy, the ways in which once public health services are increasingly being provided in the private realm through privatized delivery and privatized funding of services, as well the delegation of decision-making authority and processes from public to private actors. Roxanne Mykitiuk considers how macro-changes in global production are driving changes in Canadian reproductive and genetic health policy and the effect of these changes on our notion of the embodied citizen at both the meso- and micro-levels. She examines the role of the new genetics in Canadian industrial strategy, as well as the ways in which the commodification of health through the new genetics is constituting a new gendered subject/citizen of the post-Keynesian order. Dianne Martin focuses on the enduring problems of crime, youth, and prostitution. Her chapter, like many of the others, illustrates that privatization does not mean less state regulation, but rather a shift in the modalities of state regulation. The conclusion identifies the challenges that privatization poses to feminism and evaluates the role of law in achieving substantive equality for women.

Notes

1 The terms 'globalization' and 'restructuring' have a broad range of meanings. We adopt the definitions used by Marjorie Cohen (1997, 30): globalization 'refers to the dramatic increase both in the mobility of capital and in the international organization of production and redistribution ... "Restructuring" is the act of implementing the values of globalization in the nation's economic, social and political systems.'

2 'Social citizenship,' following T.H. Marshall's influential definition, is generally used to describe the range of civil, political, and social rights to which a citizen was entitled from the state, particularly from the KWS (Marshall 1977). Marshall argued that social citizenship rights, including the right to the col-

lective provision of a minimum economic security, were a prerequisite for the effective exercise of civil and political rights. 'Legal citizenship' by contrast, is a more specific concept that describes an individual's membership in a state and operates as a prerequisite for civil, political, and social rights in that state.

3 The beginning of the assault on advocacy groups came in 1989, with a $10 million cut to women's groups, Native groups, and visibly minority groups. The trend continued in 1990, with a further $16 million cut to advocacy groups. In addition, women's centres across the country, as well as national women's organizations, lost their funding. Native groups' programs, ranging from publications to communication programs, also experienced massive funding cuts. In 1991, the Court Challenges Program was eliminated by the Conservatives. It was re-established by the Liberals in 1994.

4 It is important, however, to keep in mind that overall, there are more poor husband-wife families with children than lone-parent families.

PART I

Reproducing the Market

1

Tax Law and Social Reproduction: The Gender of Fiscal Policy in an Age of Privatization

LISA PHILIPPS

The drive towards privatization in Canada has at its heart one central claim: that private choice is better than public regulation as a mechanism for allocating resources and ordering social affairs. The main job of the state, according to neo-liberal wisdom, is just to get out of the way. In the field of fiscal policy this belief often translates into a powerful anti-tax sentiment. Yet a study of income tax reform from the early 1990s belies the image of a leaner, less regulatory state. While governments in Canada are revising their income tax laws to promote and enforce a norm of private self-reliance, privatization is not simply a matter of deregulation (Beneria 1999a, 65–9; Fudge & Cossman this volume; Majone 1990, 3). It is better understood as a new regulatory project, one of the core features of which is to reprivatize social reproduction, the work of sustaining and nurturing human life. In this chapter I argue that recent reforms deepen a historical tendency of the tax system to impose the costs of social reproduction on women, undermining women's economic security, autonomy, and equality.

Focusing on the state's role in regulating social reproduction helps to elucidate the gendered dynamics of tax policy in different historical periods. Part I expands on this idea, arguing that Canadian income tax law has from its inception helped to produce and maintain a gendered economy by conceptualizing unpaid caregiving work as private and non-economic, and by treating women's economic welfare as the private concern of individual men.

Part II turns to developments since 1993 that signal a decisive move to reprivatize social reproduction. In this chapter 'reprivatization' means a renewed emphasis on the responsibility of individuals, families, and communities to secure their own welfare. It is being accomplished in tax law not by a single method but through a variety of strategies (Fudge & Cossman, this volume). I discuss three examples: income tax cuts; tax relief for unpaid caregiving work; and enriched tax benefits for charitable donors. Each of these initiatives promotes the reprivatization of social reproduction by valorizing some form of self-reliance (Young 1997, 307–8). My examples parallel in a rough way the three private sectors that will allegedly supply the resources for self-reliance: the market, the family, and the charitable sector.

Part II also analyses the impact of these tax reforms on women, in their capacities as market actors, caregivers, and contributors to the voluntary sector. While offering immediate fiscal benefits to some individual women, and occasionally even drawing on feminist discourses, the reforms also reinforce the sexual division of labour and the gendered inequalities surrounding both paid and unpaid work. Together these three examples of tax reform expose the contradictions between the formal gender neutrality of market citizenship and its heavy dependence on women's unpaid social reproductive work (Bakker 1996a; Brodie 1996a). In each case I suggest how tax policies could be developed and evaluated in a more gender-aware and equitable fashion. It is necessary to remedy not only the complete lack of attention to gender that has characterized most tax policy making but also a propensity to deploy feminist ideas selectively and superficially in tax reform debates. The conclusion reiterates the general principles I suggest should inform a gender-sensitive analysis of tax policy. Gender analysis of individual fiscal policies, however, while valuable and worth insisting upon, cannot easily resolve inequalities that are rooted deeply in the organization of social reproduction. We must go beyond seeking a few extra income tax cuts for women to examine how the tax reduction and reform agenda overall may impair women's equality and autonomy.

I. Gendering Tax Policy Analysis

The tax system is a key means by which the liberal state mediates the fundamental tension in capitalist societies between production for profit and production to support the living standards of the labouring population (Fudge & Cossman, this volume; Picchio 1992, 112; Ursel 1992, 47–54). Through taxation, resources can be shifted towards accumulation or reproduction, with a view to defusing the political conflicts between the two. Tax policies can be designed to impose more of the costs of reproduction on the owners of capital (to finance a social wage), or on workers and their households. They may also redistribute the costs of reproduction among different segments of the working population, such as between men and women, or between those with higher and lower incomes. The tax system helps to construct a gender order through assumptions and incentives concerning the availability of unpaid caregiving labour in the household and charitable sectors, the extent of economic sharing and support within family households, the ability of primary caregivers to access a breadwinner's wage, and the definitional boundaries of what constitutes a family.

Tax policy's traditional lack of attention to gender can be attributed in part to its close relationship to the conceptual schemes of neoclassical economics (Staudt 1996a). Both have tended to reduce the 'economy' to the private commodity market, and to view the household and public sectors merely as the source of costs that must be absorbed by privately generated wealth. Increasingly, economists are recognizing that the private sector is in fact heavily dependent on the activities of the state and of families. As Bakker and Elson explain, 'The creation of wealth in a country depends on the output of all three domains ... The private commodity economy would be unable to create wealth for use by the government, and by families and communities, if the government and families and communities did not in turn create wealth for use by the private sector. The wealth of a country consists not only of the commodities produced by the private sector, but also the public services produced by the government (law and order, communications networks, health and education) and by the care economy (human capacities, social cohesion)' (Bakker & Elson 1998, 299). Ignoring the productive value of what goes on in households means, essentially, ignoring women's unpaid reproductive work. Feminist revisions of economic analysis have called for greater attention to social reproduction; the links among state, market, and domestic sectors of the economy; and the gendered division of labour and resources within each of these spheres (Bakker forthcoming; 1996b; Elson 1998; Ferber & Nelson 1993b; Folbre 1994; Palmer 1995).

Tax policy traditionally has shared with economics an impoverished understanding of family relations. The fundamental unit of mainstream economic analysis is the utility maximizing individual, and its driving assumption has traditionally been that economic behaviour can be explained and predicted by reference to the rational choices of these independent agents. Because of this commitment to methodological individualism, economic theory has had difficulty grappling with the role of collectivities such as families and business firms in guiding decision making. It has tended to get around these cooperative formations by employing two devices, described by Nelson as 'isolation' and 'engulfment' (Nelson 1996, 99). Both are really flip sides of the same coin, and both enable the theorist to treat families as though they were autonomous individuals. Isolation occurs when the analysis simply focuses on transactions between individual market actors, without regard to the domestic relationships and activities (usually women's) that support or otherwise affect an individual's market activities. Thus Nelson notes that '[t]he most common example of masculine bias concerning families ... is, of course, simply the lack of any attention to families at all' (Nelson 1996, 61). Engulfment occurs when economists 'finesse the private sphere by assuming that the family maximizes a single utility function' (Woolley 1993, 493). That is, the utility of individual family members is collapsed into some measurement of the joint utility of the household or family unit. This is often achieved simply by treating the household 'as if it were an individual itself, consigning all its internal workings to a "black box"' (Nelson 1996, 63). Some economists have attempted to rationalize the black box approach on the basis that family members reach a consensus about their economic interests, or that individuals marry others with the same preferences. However none of these extrapolations adequately addresses family conflict (Beneria 1999b, 296).

The effect of both isolation and engulfment in economic theory is to privatize women's welfare within the patriarchal family, as do many of the income tax provisions considered later in this chapter. First, women's lack of market income and consequent financial dependency on men is assumed as natural rather than problematized. As well, especially in the engulfment models, men are assumed to use their material wealth altruistically to provide for the needs of women and children, though this provision may be hedged by consumption decisions that give some priority to their own individual utility. In this manner economic theory assures us that women's welfare is taken care of outside the market, in the private sphere of the patriarchal family (Folbre & Hartmann 1988). Further, women are portrayed as lacking independent economic agency. In the 'head of household' theories, the power to make consumption decisions is quite explicitly attached to the male breadwinner. In the 'black box' approach women and their individual interests and choices simply disappear into the household unit. Finally, neoclassical economic theory helps to maintain the stark division between market and non-market production, either by completely disregarding anything that goes on outside the market, or by discounting or minimizing the contribution of household labour to the family's welfare. The privatization of women in neoclassical economics is echoed in Canadian income tax policy.

Income tax law is not merely reflective of external economic and social realities, it also produces and alters those realities. The anti-state and anti-tax discourses of neo-liberalism imply that the state must become smaller and less interventionist. But a close look at tax policy from the 1990s indicates that the state is not reducing but rather changing its regulatory role. It is engaged in redefining the boundaries of public and private in a manner that shifts political and economic resources away from social reproduction and towards accumulation.

Tax law must be understood as one of the discourses through which the public/private divide within liberalism is constructed. This divide functions ideologically to draw boundaries around what properly constitutes the subject of politics and what is considered the legitimate scope of political claims. A defining feature of liberalism is the way it divides up social space, separating the 'political' from the 'economic' and the 'personal' and applying different norms and distributional principles to each (Brodie 1997, 228; Walzer 1984). These boundaries, which are shifting, serve to limit arbitrarily the reach of liberal ideals such as democracy, equality, justice, and liberty (Bowles & Gintis 1987, 16). Political claims based on these ideals are effectively confined to a limited public sphere created and defined by marking it off from the family or domestic sphere, and from the market. An expansion of private responsibility for human welfare will therefore tend to depoliticize women's social reproductive labour and to delegitimate any claims to equality based on this work.

The power of tax law to contribute to the reprivatization of social reproduction should not be underestimated. To be sure, the tax system interacts with broader cultural norms and social practices, and we should be cautious about exaggerating its role in creating what is a much larger phenomenon. However, the tax system is one of the primary tools available to governments to effect changes in how resources are allocated to different activities and actors. Its normative power is also significant; tax law has a long reach into the everyday consciousness of most Canadians through the annual tax filing exercise as well as the very public advocacy of organized groups that regularly criticize and propose changes to the system. Eichler has chronicled the evolution of the language used in Revenue Canada's Tax Guide to instruct taxpayers on their entitlement to various family-related deductions and credits (Eichler 1997, Appendix 1).

Her data show that tax discourse squarely marks off which relationships and household financial arrangements are considered typical and worthy of public support and that it has communicated changes in such judgments to taxpayers over the last three decades. This is not to suggest that the state unilaterally creates the normative family through law, but the state-society relation is a mutually constitutive one (Brodie 1997, 226). Tax law interacts with other discourses, including economic theory and such wider currents as neo-liberalism and neo-conservatism, to produce historically changing understandings about what is natural and appropriate in the gender order.

The importance attached to gender roles in the design of the tax system can be traced to the earliest days of the income tax in Canada. Kathleen Lahey's study of the parliamentary debates surrounding the passage of the Income War Tax Act in 1917 reveals that legislators felt strongly that certain domestic relationships should be singled out for more favourable treatment than others (Lahey 1998). The government's bill proposed that the individual should be treated as the unit of taxation. That is, each individual would file a tax return as an individual, and would be taxed only on income legally accruing to him or her, without regard to any income earned by others living in the same household. The government rejected the option of a marital or family unit in which tax rates would be applied to aggregate income reported on a joint return. Furthermore, the government did not propose to allow dependency exemptions for spouses, children, or anyone else. It decided simply to offer the same personal exemption to every individual, preferring to remain neutral about the wide variety of supportive relationships among taxpayers: '... there are many citizens who have not only children to take care of, but other dependents as well. [T]here are many citizens who have not only their own family to take care of, but also the family of a brother or a sister, or perhaps they have to look after an aged father or mother.'[1] Legislators were prepared to accept the basic policy choice of an individual unit, but objected strongly that it was unfair for married men with dependants to receive no greater exemption than singles or childless couples. Lahey's analysis of the parliamentary speeches on this issue reveals an astonishing determination by law makers to withhold tax benefits from those who did not fit the patriarchal family mould. As she writes, '[s]ingle men were described as "escaping too lightly," spinsters were assumed to have no dependants, and married women with no children were accused of being "free," of being able to "go out whenever she wants to," work for wages, or "save a lot of disbursements" by working in the home' (12). The high level of moral anxiety surrounding single men in particular was expressed in the statement of one member that he was 'not in favour' of encouraging men to remain unmarried, because 'a man should get married, if possible, when he reaches a certain age' (12, 13). As a consequence of these protests, the exemption was reduced by half for unmarried individuals.

Marital relationships were treated as significant for other purposes as well in early income tax law, particularly with respect to the matter of income splitting. Provisions known as 'attribution rules' were included from the very outset to prevent (in most cases) a husband from reducing his taxable income by transferring ownership of investments or other income-earning property to his wife (Duff 2001, chapter 8). The attribution rules were designed to maintain the integrity of the individual tax unit by preventing taxpayers from hiving off a portion of their incomes to a spouse. Essentially, they provided that transfers of income-earning property between spouses would be ignored for tax purposes. Regardless of who held title, future earnings from the property would continue to be taxed as income of the transferor spouse, not of the transferee. Income splitting within marriage was originally prohibited even if the wife used her own money to pay fair market value consideration for the property.[2]

The general prohibition on marital income splitting was qualified in 1942, when the law was amended to allow taxpayers to deduct alimony payments following divorce. Almost invariably, this meant that men could claim a deduction for that portion of their incomes paid to an ex-wife. The woman was then required to include the alimony in her income and was responsible for any associated tax liability. It was assumed that women would have no other source of income so that little or no tax would be payable on the alimony. These provisions, known as the 'deduction/inclusion system,' were later extended to apply to child support.[3]

Though diverse in their objectives, all of these policy decisions are linked by certain assumptions about family and gender relations. All three – the higher exemption for married taxpayers, the attribution rules, and the inclusion/deduction system for alimony – drew precise boundaries around what constituted a 'family,' centring tightly on heterosexual marriage and childrearing. The provisions also betray certain expectations about the nature of economic relations inside the patriarchal family. Each tended in slightly different ways to construct women's economic welfare as the private concern of individual men, and to sub-

sume women's economic activities into the tax profiles of their husbands (Philipps & Young 1995, 274–80).

Both the marital exemption and the alimony rules were clearly
designed around an assumption of female dependency on a man's
income. That is, they assumed two separate things: that women did not
have their own incomes, and that a husband would use his income to
provide for his wife. The attribution rules were based on an image of the
family in which women lacked any economic agency. Thus a transfer of
property from husband to wife was understood never as a transaction
between two autonomous individuals but always as a function of the husband's tax planning. Finally, all three provisions drew a stark division
between market and non-market forms of economic production. The
domestic and caregiving labour performed by women outside the market was assumed not to confer any economic benefit on men. A dependent wife or ex-wife was constructed only as a drain on the man's
financial resources, warranting tax relief for him in the form of higher
exemptions or alimony deductions. The value of the goods, services, and
leisure time that the man obtained through the woman's domestic
labour was nowhere included in the law's estimation of his ability to pay
taxes. Indeed, the single man without a stay-at-home wife was viewed as
far better off in economic terms, albeit socially suspect. Implicit here is
the idea that social reproductive labour is provided to men by women
not as a form of economic support but out of a natural affective impulse.
This work is constructed as entirely separate both from the sphere of
rational economic behaviour and from the sphere of politics. In this way,
gendered inequalities of power and material resources within families
are naturalized and depoliticized.

With the rise of the Keynesian welfare state, taxation policy gained a
prominent status as one of the most powerful levers available to government in its new role as active regulator of the market economy. Prevailing wisdom about the purposes of the tax system now included the
promotion of efficient and stable markets, as well as the redistribution of
market incomes. The redistributive function of taxation was seen as both
equitable and efficient; ensuring a basic level of income security was not
only considered fair, it supported demand for consumer goods and
therefore served the purpose of moderating market recessions (Doern,
Maslove & Prince 1991, 2, 3). Welfare state policies, including tax policies, sought to ensure middle-class access to a decent family wage.

The ideal of the family wage was central to the gender order of this
era and ascribed breadwinner and caregiver roles to men and women

respectively (Brodie 1995, 39–41; Fraser 1997b, 41–2). However, the rigid separation of spheres that characterized earlier decades began to be supplanted by an ideal of universal social citizenship. With the expansion of the public realm, the scope for equality claims grew. Women and minority groups enjoyed some success in securing state action to remedy group disadvantages (Brodie 1997, 233). At the same time as it was promoting the family wage system, then, the liberal state had also begun to undertake some affirmative measures to increase women's access to paid labour and participation in public affairs (Schreader 1990, 184–5, 193–6; Vickers, Rankin, & Appelle 1993, 78–80).

These contradictory currents of thought are evidenced in tax policy debates and tax reforms. In the late 1960s debate about the appropriate unit of taxation was reignited by the Report of the Royal Commission on Taxation (the 'Carter Commission'). The report recommended sweeping changes that would make the income tax more redistributive, as well as moving to a system of family unit taxation (Royal Commission on Taxation 1966, 3: 132–3, 142–9). A family would be defined for these purposes as a married couple and their dependent children, if any, or single parents with dependent children. All income received by family members would be aggregated, and intrafamilial transfers of income or property would be disregarded for tax purposes. The commission's assertion that the family as they defined it formed the 'basic economic unit' of Canadian society resonated strongly with prevailing family wage ideology (Royal Commission on Taxation 1966, 3: 123). Carter's recommended family unit was largely endorsed by the Royal Commission on the Status of Women in Canada, established in 1967 to inquire into 'what steps might be taken by the Federal Government to ensure for women equal opportunities in all aspects of Canadian society' (Royal Commission on the Status of Women in Canada 1970, at vii, 303–4). It was not until later that feminist scholars and lobby groups began advocating that women should be taxed as individuals, rather than collapsed into any family-based measure of income.

The federal government implemented portions of the Carter Report in 1972 but rejected the proposed family tax unit. Minister of Finance Benson cited concerns about creating a 'tax on marriage,' in that two earners would pay more tax if they married than if they remained single, and noted the possible unfairness of adding women's wages to their husbands' incomes and so taxing them at higher rates (Benson 1969, 14, 15). Though retained in principle, however, the individual tax unit has been increasingly qualified by a wide range of family-related provisions, many of which have enhanced the tax benefits available to those supporting dependants and some of which impose extra burdens on the assumption that family members share income (Young 2000a). Many of the Act's deductions and credits function in a similar manner to family wage policies by providing tax benefits that cover taxpayer-plus-dependants, often increasing the value of employer-provided benefits such as pension plans and private health and dental plans (Lahey 1998, 21). In other cases tax benefits are reduced or eliminated by basing them on joint household income rather than individual income (Young 1994b). Whether particular family provisions tend to increase or reduce the tax burden, however, the common assumption is that household resources are pooled and shared by a breadwinner and used to support lower-earning members (Young 2000a, 76–105).

Alongside these assumptions of (heterosexual) family dependency some tentative efforts have been made to revise tax policy thinking to advance women's economic status. One of the most prominent examples is the deduction for childcare expenses incurred to enable a parent to earn business or employment income (Income Tax Act, 1985, s. 63). The childcare expense deduction was first introduced in 1972 to recognize the extra costs incurred when two parents (or single parents) enter paid labour, in effect acknowledging women's mass entry into job markets. As many feminist scholars and organizations have pointed out, the deduction is badly flawed as a means of ensuring broad-based access to childcare services (Johnson 2000, 47–61). It is a supply-side response that simply frees up private income, relying heavily on market forces to determine the nature of childcare services that are available and who can access them (Young 1997, 310). The deduction has been criticized for its class and racial biases and its tendency to promote privatized forms of paid childcare work (Macklin 1992b; Young 1994a). What is interesting is the way this provision made visible in the tax code an economic concern of particular importance to women and its overt attempt to promote at least some women's economic autonomy. The valid feminist criticisms of the childcare expense deduction motwithstanding, it can be regarded as a deprivatizing measure relative to the earlier policy of imposing these costs entirely on individual women or their partners. The deduction acknowledged women as both mothers and market actors and signalled that public policy should attempt to facilitate that dual role. Rather than assuming and wholly supporting women's dependency on a male wage it sought, however partially and ineffectually, to support their own income-earning activities.

A second important example of how social reproduction was tentatively deprivatized in the welfare state era relates to the assignment of economic value to household production. Both the Carter Commission and the Royal Commission on the Status of Women asserted that household labour creates value in the form of goods and services provided to family members, and that this value is a form of imputed or non-monetary income (Royal Commission on Taxation 1966, 3: 41, 47, 118, 119; Royal Commission on the Status of Women in Canada 1970, 30–2, 37, 38, 40). Fearing the uncertainties and administrative costs involved in valuing such labour, neither commission recommended taxing imputed income. Yet both served to trouble the conventional boundary between market and non-market forms of production in a very public way. And ironically (since both commissions supported a family unit of taxation), their recognition of women's unpaid labour helped lay the groundwork for later feminist arguments in favour of an individual unit of taxation. Though the effect of an individual unit is generally to tax one-earner couples more heavily than two-earner couples, feminist tax scholars have argued this is justified because of the large amount of imputed income from household labour generated by the stay-at-home partner in a one-earner couple.

This brief historical review of income tax policy and its relation to women's economic status reveals that the income tax system from its earliest origins has been sharply gendered in its assumptions and effects. It also suggests a complex pattern in which tax policy vacillates between treating women's economic welfare and social reproductive labour as matters of private, family responsibility and, less often, of public, state responsibility. In the next section I turn to the 1990s and point to a move away from a redistributive model of the state towards a more market-oriented tax system.

II. Taxing the Market Citizen

The neo-liberal challenge to post-war conceptions of the state has dramatic implications for the tax system. Like other regulatory levers of the welfare state, the use of tax policy to stimulate the economy and redistribute market income is regarded sceptically from a neo-liberal perspective. Such economic activism is frequently derided as inefficient as well as unfair to those individuals who are successful market actors. The solidaristic ideal of universal social citizenship which supplied a normative basis for redistributive taxation is thus being eroded (Marshall 1963,

100). As Teeple explains, the globalization of markets is also eroding the economic base that supplied the fiscal capacity for redistribution: 'As long as capital remained distinctly national, it had an interest in allowing a part of its revenue to be collected as taxes for the purposes of maintaining the national state, or more precisely, the general conditions of production. When capital began to lose its character as a national existence, it began to find fewer advantages in contributing tax revenues to the "nation" ... Their enormous size, economic power, and increased mobility have allowed companies to reduce taxation by playing nations off against nations' (Teeple 1995, 95). International efforts to curtail tax avoidance have been minimal and largely unsuccessful (Picciotto 1999). In addition to the sophisticated tax reduction techniques available to the wealthiest taxpayers, fiscal policy changes in many countries have tended to shift tax burdens downward to middle- and lower-income people. These changes include a trend towards flatter income tax rates and heavier reliance upon non-progressive sources of revenue such as consumption taxes, payroll charges, and user fees (Howard, Ruggeri, & Van Wort 1995, 914–20; OECD 1998a, 160–2). The downward redistribution of the tax burden, combined with the erosion of public services, may contribute to a generalized hostility to taxation and a sense that social programs must be too costly or governments too wasteful (Cohen 1997, 36; Teeple 1995, 96). The political and economic pressures on the tax system can be linked, I suggest, to certain tax reform trends in the 1990s. Income tax policy has been reshaped over the last decade to align it more closely with a market model of citizenship, in which citizens are urged to rely more on private resources and to seek state assistance only in the most desperate circumstances (Brodie 1996a).

Three areas of tax reform illustrate particularly well this shift towards the promotion of self-reliance as the best means of ordering society and fulfilling citizens' basic needs: income tax cuts; new forms of tax relief for unpaid caregiving work; and enrichment of tax benefits for charitable giving. In different ways, each of these tax policy changes encourages or requires citizens to depend less upon state-provided goods and services and more upon their own market incomes, on family members, or if necessary on charitable organizations. These reforms have important privatizing effects in terms of both the distribution of resources and the construction of social norms. Together the reforms identify the self-reliant taxpayer as the new ideal citizen and, paradoxically, the most deserving recipient of government support.

Since one of the central objectives of this chapter is to expose the gendered assumptions and effects of privatizing tax policies, I consider how each of these three tax reforms affects women in their roles as market actors, unpaid caregivers, and contributors to the voluntary sector. Promoting self-reliance entails a reduction or redirection of state support for the social reproduction of people, with powerful implications for the gender order of society. The three tax reforms in question illuminate the contradictory pressures being placed on women to increase their market incomes while simultaneously absorbing more unpaid caregiving responsibilities in the household and voluntary sectors.

A. Cutting Taxes

Both provincial and federal governments are under intense pressure to cut taxes, and especially to reduce the level of personal income tax (Canadian Tax Journal 1999; Policy Options 1998). Notably, personal income taxes are the most progressive element of the Canadian tax system and by far our biggest revenue raiser (Howard et al. 1995; Ruggeri, Van Wort, & Howard 1994; Vermaeten, Gillespie, & Vermaeten 1994). By contrast, other taxes in the system, such as sales taxes and property taxes, are not geared to ability to pay and tend to have a proportional or even regressive incidence, meaning that they consume a constant or declining percentage of a taxpayer's income as that income rises (Ontario Fair Tax Commission 1993, 171–91). The personal income tax is really the only element of the Canadian tax system that gives it significant redistributive potential. Thus the attack on progressive income taxes can be understood as a direct challenge to the redistributive role of the state (Kesselman 2000, 35).

The case for tax cuts is based loosely on a combination of supply-side economics and libertarian politics. It is presented as a means to spur economic growth by increasing private consumption and investment, and by preventing an alleged 'brain drain' of talented (meaning high-income) Canadians to the United States (Brown 1999). Most empirical studies do not support the existence of a serious brain drain, or the notion that income tax rates play a dominant or even significant role in the decision of some individuals to take up opportunities abroad (Brooks 1998, 357–66; Egelton and Szadurski 1999; Murray 1998; Policy Options 1999; Zhao, Drew, & Murray 2000). Tax-cut advocates rely less on empirical evidence, however, than on moral and political claims about the need to reduce government oppression of taxpayers and allow individuals to retain more of their hard-earned income. In his 1997 budget speech, for example, Alberta Treasurer Stockwell Day likened taxation to the beating of slaves (citizens) by a slavemaster (government).

The campaign to reduce progressive income taxes should be understood as a privatizing strategy in that it seeks to bolster the role of market forces in shaping the social and economic order. This is not because governments have significantly reduced their share of the economy. However, income tax cuts are likely to diminish the progressivity of the overall system, so that it will do less than it has in the past to alter market distributions of income and wealth. In addition, their normative impact cannot be discounted. The discourse of tax cutting constructs market income as individually earned and deserved, making the state's claim on that income presumptively illegitimate or at least suspect. It portrays people as better off meeting their needs privately out of market income than having public services and programs made available to them. The effect is to depoliticize the inequalities of income produced in the private sphere of the market.

Personal income taxes can be reduced in a variety of different ways, with different impacts. The progressive rate structure in the Income Tax Act can be broken down into three main components. The basic personal credit removes tax liability on a specified dollar amount of income for all individuals, effectively creating a zero-rate bracket at the bottom of the rate structure (Income Tax Act, 1985, s. 118(1)(c)). The second component is the marginal rates, which apply to income above the basic personal amount (Ibid., s. 117(2)). Finally, surtaxes are levied as a percentage of tax otherwise payable (Ibid., s. 180.1).[4]

In 1997, before the federal government first began cutting income taxes, the total rate structure, incorporating all three of these elements, was as follows:

on taxable income up to $6,459   0%
on taxable income from $6,459 to 29,590   17%
on taxable income from $29,590 to 59,180   26%
on any taxable income exceeding $59,180   29%
+ general surtax of 3% × federal tax payable
+ high income surtax of 5% × federal tax payable
  over $12,500 (applicable to incomes over approximately
  $65,000)

Successive income tax cuts were announced in the 1998, 1999, and

2000 federal budgets, and in the pre-election 'mini-budget' of October 2000 (Canada, Department of Finance 2000b). The overall package includes several tax-cutting strategies: reducing percentage rates, expanding the size of tax brackets so that more of an individual's income is taxed at the lower rates, removing surtaxes, and redefining 'income' so that more capital gains can be received tax free. If this package is fully implemented by 2004 as proposed, the rate structure will most likely be as follows (Canada, Department of Finance 2000c, cl. 58, 59(3.1), 88):

on taxable income up to $8,000	0%
on taxable income from $8,000 to 35,000	16%
on taxable income from $35,000 to 70,000	22%
on taxable income from $70,000 to 113,804	26%
on any taxable income exceeding $113,804	29%

Both the 3 per cent general surtax and the 5 per cent high income surtax will be eliminated. In addition, the October 2000 mini-budget provided that in future only half of any capital gains received by a taxpayer will have to be included in income for tax purposes, down from the two-thirds inclusion rate announced in the 2000 budget, and the three-quarters inclusion rate in effect prior to that budget (Canada, Department of Finance 2000b; Income Tax Act, 1985, s. 38).

What will be the distributional impact of the federal tax-cutting proposals? The proposals were designed carefully to offer something to everyone, including the lowest income taxpayers. On closer study, however, the plan overwhelmingly favours a small minority of people with higher incomes (Mackenzie 2000). Moreover, the federal plan will deliver far greater tax savings to men than to women. In explaining this outcome it is helpful first to focus on those tax filers with less than $30,000 income, roughly the cut-off point for the 17 per cent bracket under the pre-tax-cut system. In 1997 this group comprised 68 per cent of all tax filers (Canada Customs and Revenue Agency 2000, Basic Table 6). Over 58 per cent of the people in this under-$30,000 group were women (Ibid.). Breaking this group down further, Table 1 shows that women were overrepresented among those earning $10,000 or less (63 per cent), and also among those with incomes between $10,000 and $20,000 (58.6 per cent). Tax filers in the $20,000–$30,000 range were quite evenly split by gender, but in all income groups over $30,000 men predominate. Furthermore in all income groups, whether over or under $30,000, men's average income exceeds that of women.[5] Federal income tax cuts will favour men over women both because the most valuable cuts are targeted to those earning over $30,000, who are mostly men, and because women earn less than men in each income group, including the very top group of those earning over $100,000. Class and gender biases intersect in the federal tax-cut plan, in that high-income women will benefit less than high-income men, but far more than lower income women. The large majority of people, those earning $30,000 or less, will receive the least benefit of all.

Tax filers up to $30,000 do benefit from federal tax cuts in three ways. First, the larger basic personal credit increases the amount that can be earned tax free from $6,459 to $8,000. Second, the one point reduction in the lowest marginal rate benefits those earning over $8,000. Finally, the removal of the 3 per cent general surtax provides savings to anyone with federal tax liability. However, the quantum of these benefits is relatively small for lower income earners. For a taxpayer earning exactly $30,000 they would provide total federal tax savings of $639 (these calculations assume the taxpayer claims no personal credits other than the basic amount). For those earning less, say $12,000, the saving is only $330.

The value of federal tax cuts rises quickly as one moves up the income scale. It should be understood that all taxpayers receive the same $639 benefit on their first $30,000 of income. But those earning over $30,000 enjoy additional tax savings. A person earning even $35,000 would save $1,179 in federal taxes, almost doubling their tax cut, because of the steep rate reduction from 26 per cent to 16 per cent on the additional $5,000. At higher incomes, a taxpayer earning $113,804 (in all likelihood a man) would enjoy savings of $5,630, including $748 from eliminating the 5 per cent higher income surtax. The benefits of the 5 per cent surtax elimination continue to rise indefinitely with income over and above $113,804, contrasting sharply with the maximum $639 tax cut on incomes up to $30,000. The tax savings at different income levels are not just unequal in absolute dollar amounts, they are also regressive in proportion to income. Whereas a person with $30,000 will enjoy a federal tax cut equal to 2.1 per cent of his or her income, the $113,804 earner will save taxes equal to 4.9 per cent of income.

Perhaps the most regressive federal tax cut to date is the reduction of the capital gains inclusion rate from three-quarters to one-half, a change that is more obscure than the straightforward reduction of tax rates. Capital gains are essentially the profits earned when capital property such as real estate or corporate shares is sold for more than its orig-

Table 1.1
All returns by income class and sex, 1997 taxation year

Income class	Men		Women	
	Total no.	% of Income class	Total no.	% of Income class
<$10,000	2,099,980	37	3,577,050	63
$10,000–20,000	2,165,850	41.4	3,069,770	58.6
$20,000–30,000	1,673,790	50.4	1,650,050	49.6
$30,000–40,000	1,404,820	56.1	1,097,600	43.9
$40,000–50,000	1,033,410	63.4	596,330	36.6
$50,000–100,000	1,755,070	74.1	613,490	25.9
>$100,000	314,880	81.4	71,730	18.6
Total	10,447,790	49.5	10,676,020	50.5

Source: Data compiled from Canada Customs and Revenue Agency (2000), Basic Table 6. Analysis by author. Revenue Canada's Basic Table 6 desegregates income classes from $10,000 to 50,000 into increments of $5,000. These have been collapsed in the above table to $10,000 increments.

inal cost, and they are received overwhelmingly by a tiny group of high-income taxpayers. In 1997, 59.6 per cent of all capital gains were reported by the 1.8 per cent of taxpayers with incomes of $100,000 and up (Canada Customs and Revenue Agency 2000, Basic Table 6, Basic Table 9). As Table 1.1 indicates, less than 19 per cent of this elite group are women. It is not surprising then that men reported almost 63 per cent of all taxable capital gains in 1997 (Ibid., Basic Table 4). Certainly, some lower- and middle-income taxpayers receive capital gains and will benefit from the reduced inclusion rate, but their benefits will be far more modest. For example, within the female-dominated group earning $20,000 or less, only 5.4 per cent of taxpayers reported any taxable capital gains in 1997, and the amounts they reported comprised only 6.5 per cent of the total taxable capital gains reported (Ibid., Basic Table 2).

The federal rates do not tell the full story, as the provinces also levy personal income taxes, computed as a percentage of an individual's federal tax payable or federal taxable income. Provincial governments have led the way in cutting taxes in Canada. This chapter focuses on Ontario and Alberta, the two most aggressive tax-cutting jurisdictions in the country. Ontario is an excellent case study not only because the Conservative government has defined itself around the issue of reducing taxes, but also because it started cutting earlier than other provinces so that it is possible to observe some actual impacts. Between 1996 and 2000 Ontario's personal income tax rate was reduced by about one-third, from 58 per cent to 38.5 per cent (Ontario Income Tax Act, 1990, s. 4). The rate reduction is the same for all taxpayers but because the provincial tax is computed as a percentage of federal tax owing, which is in turn based on progressive marginal rates, the benefits of the Ontario rate reduction rise with income.

Notably, the tax cuts in Ontario have not translated into smaller government. On the contrary, the government's own statistics show that total revenue as a share of gross domestic product (GDP) was set to increase slightly from 15.0 per cent in 1995, the year the Conservatives were first elected, to 15.3 per cent in 2000 (Ontario Ministry of Finance 1999, 56–7). What has changed, however, is the composition of the revenue stream. Whereas personal income taxes comprised 31.6 per cent of provincial revenues in the 1995–6 fiscal year, that figure was projected to fall to 27 per cent in 1999–2000 (Ibid., 53, 60). The province now draws a larger share of its revenue from sources that have a less progressive or even regressive incidence, such as retail sales taxes (up from 19.1 per cent to 20.8 per cent of total revenue), corporations tax (10.5 to 13.4 per cent), and casino revenues (.85 per cent to 1.71 per cent). It has also relied more heavily on sales and rentals of government assets, a category which represented 1 per cent of total revenue in 1995–6 and was projected to rise to 3.83 per cent in 1999–2000. Thus Ontario has undercut the redistributive capacity of its tax system both by giving the biggest income tax cuts to higher income earners and by changing the fiscal mix so that government relies more heavily on non-progressive sources of revenue.

The Ontario experience with tax cutting shows clearly that privatization is less a matter of deregulation than a new regulatory project to produce a more market-oriented society. While the provincial government is not occupying any less space in the private economy, it now does less to redistribute and more to reinforce the market distribution of income. This dynamic is certainly not limited to Ontario. Many other jurisdictions around the world have experienced a similar trend towards lower marginal income tax rates and heavier reliance on non-progressive sources of revenue, with the result that 'effective tax rates have risen at the low end of the earnings scale' (OECD 1998a, 161). Again, to the extent that women are concentrated in lower income brackets, this shift will tend to exacerbate both class and gender economic inequalities.

The Province of Alberta is undertaking even more dramatic reforms to its income tax rate structure. It has enacted a plan to divorce itself, as of 1 January 2001, from the federal system of progressive rates. Instead, it will impose a flat rate of 10.5 per cent on the taxable income of provincial residents (Alberta Personal Income Tax Act, 2000), a change that will deliver the greatest tax relief to those with high incomes. Importantly, Alberta's scheme does not completely abandon the idea of ability to pay as a criterion for determining relative tax burdens. At the same time as it moves to a flat rate the province has also announced it will increase its basic personal credit amount to $12,900, more than 60 per cent higher than the $8,000 being proposed federally. In effect this means the Alberta system will still have two rates: zero on income up to $12,900 and 10.5 per cent on any excess. As discussed earlier, increasing the basic personal credit benefits all those with taxable income, including the poorest, the majority of whom are women. Despite this faint vestige of progressivity, however, Alberta's proposal represents a historic moment in Canadian fiscal history. Income taxes have been synonymous with graduated rates since the early twentieth-century, when they were first enacted federally (Krever 1981). The explicit rejection of this system in Alberta in favour of a proportional rate is an important shift towards greater acceptance of market-outcomes as just or efficient and a lesser commitment to the state as a moderating influence on social inequalities.

Adding to the downward pressure on income taxes are the tax referendum laws introduced by Ontario and Manitoba (Philipps 1996). These provincial governments are now prohibited from raising tax rates or introducing new taxes unless they first receive approval in a referendum.[6] The creation of extralegislative controls on taxation is unprecedented in Canada. Indeed fiscal policy making has been more tightly controlled by the executive branch of government than almost any other area of policy. The emergence of tax referendum laws suggests a surge of hostility towards taxation, at least among some constituencies. Though in principle they could simply be repealed by a future government, such laws are likely to function as a political disincentive to reversing the tax cuts of earlier years.

The notion that tax referendums will enhance the level of democracy in Canada is highly simplistic. It does not address the many criticisms of referenda identified by political theorists, including their propensity to completely override minority interests and their failure to secure meaningful consent from groups that are disadvantaged in deliberative politics. The U.S. experience with fiscal populism shows that direct democracy mechanisms are just as susceptible as elections to manipulation and domination by powerful and well-organized lobby groups (Garrett 1997; Smith 1998). Especially troubling is the fact that these laws single out tax increases as the one fiscal policy decision that citizens must be able to veto directly. Ironically, they seek to enhance democracy by curtailing the power of the state, the only institution which can counter the undemocratic exercise of private power in markets. Likewise they conceive of the taxpayer, the owner of market resources, as the only citizen who deserves greater voice in government. The laws allow for no public veto of government-imposed user fees or spending cuts, for example, measures that typically impose the greatest burden on those who have low incomes or rely relatively more on public services.

Right-wing populists who advocate for tax referendums rely on a backlash against perceived special treatment for women and minority groups. They purport to seek a return to majority rule and equal (i.e., identical) treatment for all (Patten 1996). However, the privileging of taxation as the defining or most onerous element of the state-society relation reveals the deeply gendered nature of market citizenship. It obscures entirely the role of women's unpaid work in meeting social welfare needs and propping up an ailing public sector. Unpaid work has itself been likened to a tax that women must pay before they are free to engage in income-earning activities in the market (Bakker & Elson 1998, 299; Palmer 1995). The new referendum laws obscure this implicit tax from view because they associate citizenship rights only with the control of market income (Lister 1990, 455–8; Pateman 1998, 199).

The whole agenda of tax cutting coheres well with the new norms of market citizenship, emphasizing the power to express preferences and exercise private property rights in the marketplace over the power to hold governments politically accountable for the quality or accessibility of public services. This is evident in the remarks of the Ontario legislative committee that recommended a tax referendum law for the province: '... taxes bind citizens economically, and ... the level of taxation is fundamental to both the health of the economy ... and to the economic well being of the individual. If citizens are going to be bound in such a fundamental way, they must have a voice' (Standing Committee on the Legislative Assembly 1997, 10). While market citizenship is presented as gender neutral and universally accessible to all those prepared to work in the private economy, it is important to ask who will actually enjoy the benefits of any increased consumption and investment power generated by income tax cuts.

One possible strategy for women's organizations and others concerned with equality in the current fiscal environment is not to resist tax reduction per se, but to insist that it be weighted much more heavily to the lowest income individuals by further increasing the basic personal credit, for example, or even by way of means-tested tax credits. In evaluating and deploying this strategy, however, it is important not to lose sight of the larger implications of a tax-cutting agenda. The redistributive potency of Canada's fiscal system depends not just on the distribution of the tax burden but on the nature and generosity of our spending programs (Smith 1995; Wolfson & Murphy 1998). Any form of income tax cut, no matter how progressively it is designed, may erode government revenues. To the extent that governments replace those revenues through regressive levies such as user fees or sales taxes, for example, they may simply recover the money in a different form. Alternatively, the government may respond to a revenue loss by cutting transfer payments or public services that are of greatest value to the least powerful. The withdrawal of public health, education, and social services often impacts especially harshly on women as public sector employees, as consumers of welfare state services, and as caregivers whose unpaid labour is increasingly called upon to meet the needs of the elderly, children, the ill, and the disabled (Brodie 1995, 54–6; Day & Brodsky 1998, 5–42).

For example, a woman earning $20,000 may benefit from a small income tax cut but then find her disposable income eroded by new or higher fees in the public health care or school systems, or for her childrens' daycare or recreational activities. She may have to miss days of paid work to take care of a sick relative who is sent home early from hospital; she may worry that her children do not have access to the same quality of education as others, or that she may lose her job in the public sector. Groups who tend to be marginalized in markets, including women, are likely to be further disempowered by the overall effects of tax cuts, even if they are successful in demanding a greater share of the immediate benefits. This is not to suggest that women's advocates should not participate in public debates over the appropriate distribution of tax cuts or lobby for a more equality-conscious tax reduction plan. However, there is clearly a need for a two-pronged approach to fiscal reform that does not stop at redesigning tax cuts but tackles the larger problems arising from the exploitation of women's unpaid social reproductive work and lack of market power.

B. Tax Relief for Unpaid Caregiving Work

A second tax policy debate that gathered momentum in Canada in the 1990s is the use of the tax system to value women's unpaid labour. This debate must be viewed in the context of a larger international mobilization around the issue of women's unpaid work. In the last decade the economic importance of household production has received unprecedented levels of attention (Elson 1999; Elson & Cagatay 1999; UNDP 1999, chap. 3). A growing number of economists are making the case that traditional macroeconomic models are inadequate and gender biased because they ignore unpaid social reproductive work, treating it as a naturally chosen function that will continue to occur regardless of changes in the economy or state policy (e.g. Bakker 1998; Colman 1998a; 1998b; Folbre 1994; MacDonald 1998; Nelson 1996, 118–20; Palmer 1995; Waring 1988). Governments are withdrawing public services that support social reproduction on the unstated assumption that the household sector (primarily women) will supply more unpaid caregiving labour to fill the gap. Simultaneously, however, women are under pressure to intensify their market labour in response to workfare policies, declining state transfers, and degraded labour market conditions for men and women alike (Armstrong 1996a; Cossman, this volume; Evans 1996; Fudge 1996b; Scott 1996). Thus women are caught in a contradiction within neo-liberal policy discourse, constructed impossibly as both self-reliant market workers and primary caregivers for the young, the old, the ill, and the disabled, with fewer state supports for either role. Feminist economists have warned that this emerging new gender order is not only exploitative but unsustainable (Elson 1999, 8, 9): 'If the care economy is overburdened, there will be negative feedbacks to the commodity and public service economies which will reduce their productivity and increase their costs, because of inadequate maintenance of human resources and of the social framework.' Empirical research is beginning to document the effects of a tightening double bind on women. Time-use surveys show that women continue to perform about two-thirds of all unpaid work and that this share has remained relatively constant since the 1960s, despite the mass entry of women into paid labour (Statistics Canada 2000a, 97). While non-employed mothers of young children have the heaviest unpaid workload of any group, full-time employed mothers also spend over an hour and a half more per day on unpaid work than full-time employed fathers (Colman 1998b, 67; Statistics Canada 2000a, 111). When paid and unpaid activities are totalled women's total workday is about fifteen minutes longer per day on average than men's (the equivalent of more than two weeks of full-time paid work per year) (W. Clark 2001, 4; Status of Women Canada 2001). Colman's review of historical data reveals an increase in the total workload of women and an absolute decline in leisure time, with corresponding high levels of stress (Colman 1998a, 25, 26; 1998b, 6). The worsening time crunch faced by women helps to explain why the question of unpaid work has come into the foreground of feminist economic research and political struggles (Beneria 1996b, 298–300).

A new wave of international feminist activism around unpaid work has sparked discussion of possible policy responses in Canada (Luxton & Vosko 1998). Earlier efforts to organize feminist lobby groups on this issue were dampened by concerns within the women's movement that state recognition of unpaid work might simply benefit men who enjoyed the fruits of this labour, or might undercut the struggle for women's access to markets (Vickers, Rankin, & Appelle 1993, 255–63). While these concerns have far from disappeared, as discussed below, new efforts are being made to incorporate unpaid work into feminist positions on economic policy. Initially, the focus was on the improvement of quantitative data. The federal government began generating statistics on the quantity and value of unpaid work in the early 1970s (Jackson 1996). In 1996, following an intensive lobbying campaign by women's groups, Statistics Canada for the first time included questions about unpaid work in the census. The challenge now is to move beyond statistics and determine what policy or other changes should be made in response to these data. In Canada much of this debate has centred on the tax system.

First on the table was the federal government's 1998 announcement of a new caregiver tax credit for those with an elderly or infirm relative living in their home. The credit reduces federal tax liability by a maximum of $595 per annum for taxpayers residing with an adult relative who fits into one of two categories: (i) a parent or grandparent who is age sixty-five or older; or (ii) a relative who is dependent on the taxpayer because of a physical or mental infirmity (Income Tax Act, 1985, s. 118(1)(c.1)). The government has presented the caregiver credit as a step towards fulfilling its promises to value women's unpaid work (House of Commons 1999, 12424). However, for a number of reasons, it does this extremely poorly. The trivial amount of the credit, not even approaching the actual value of the services provided, obviously makes it no more than a token gesture towards caregivers. As such it implicitly requires the input of large amounts of unpaid labour. Moreover it is not designed to deliver benefits to caregivers per se. The provision allows any member of the household to claim the credit whether or not they personally helped care for the relative. In fact the provision requires no caregiving work at all, only that the aged or infirm relative is co-resident and has income less than $15,453. Because it is non-refundable the credit can only be claimed by an individual with sufficient tax liability to absorb it. Thus a primary caregiver who has little or no income of her own will have no direct access to the credit. Likewise, households in which all members have very low incomes, or receive only non-taxable forms of income such as social assistance, will gain nothing (Young 2000b, 60). That the government made any budgetary decision with women's unpaid work in mind suggests that feminists have made some progress in raising political awareness of the gender impact of privatizing responsibility for human welfare. However the new credit provides little direct recognition for caregivers' work, nor does it meaningfully increase their access to independent resources. Instead, it relies on the traditional reasoning that primary caregivers will be looked after privately by male breadwinners and legitimizes policy makers' assumptions that public health care, elder care, and other services can be replaced by women's unpaid work.

Aside from the caregiver credit a number of other, more radical proposals for tax reform are in circulation. Almost all originate with social conservative groups such as the Reform Party of Canada, its successor the Canadian Alliance, or REAL Women of Canada, which are distressed by a perceived erosion of (patriarchal) family values and wish to encourage mothers to forego paid labour to care for children. Typically these proposals are aimed at supporting one type of unpaid work – childcare – and are framed as a response to so-called 'tax discrimination' against families with a stay-at-home parent.

The term 'tax discrimination' refers to the relative tax treatment of one-earner and two-earner couples. Because the Income Tax Act uses an individual unit of taxation, a family breadwinner with an income of $60,000, for example, will generally be taxed more heavily under progressive rates than if both spouses were employed with salaries of $30,000 each (Sarlo 1999). The childcare expense deduction may widen this differential, as one member of the two-earner couple can deduct up to $7,000 per annum per child for day care or other child care costs that enable the taxpayer to engage in certain income-earning or educational activities (Income Tax Act, 1985, s. 63). From these facts the conclusion is drawn that the income tax system discriminates against one-earner households, in particular those traditional-type families with a male breadwinner and female full-time homemaker.

The superficial logic of the tax discrimination charge is misleading in several ways. It is mathematically misleading because it compares only the income tax burden and not the full living costs of the one-earner and two-earner couple. The childcare expense deduction, for example, typically compensates for well under half of the real cost of full-time childcare. Once the full expenses of having two parents in the paid workforce are factored in (childcare, transportation, clothing, payroll taxes, etc.), in most cases they will have less take-home pay than the one-earner couple despite bearing a smaller income tax burden (Canada 1999a, 22–3). The complaint of tax discrimination also ignores the compelling policy reasons for choosing an individual unit of taxation, including the basic principle that a person should be taxed only on income that he or she controls, and the need to avoid the high marginal tax rate imposed on secondary (usually women's) earnings if they are taxed on top of the main breadwinner's income on a single return (Brooks 1996; Maloney 1994; McCaffery 1997, 19–26; Nelson 1996). As well, most tax policy commentators have concluded it is appropriate for the one-earner couple to pay somewhat more tax on their market income to offset the substantial tax free economic benefits (i.e. goods and services) generated by the homemaker's unpaid work (Kesselman 2000, 36–7; Nelson 1996, 103, 111).

Despite the weakness of their basic premise and the obvious opprobrium accorded to mothers who work for pay, social conservatives have succeeded in attracting a great deal of interest in several proposals designed to reduce the tax burden on traditional, one-earner families with children. As Cossman (this volume) suggests, this is perhaps because neo-conservative familial ideology happens to coincide on this issue with neo-liberal views about reducing taxes and promoting self-reliance. In the spring of 1999 a parliamentary motion of the Reform Party of Canada that 'the federal tax system should be reformed to end discrimination against single income families with children' (House of Commons 1999e, 12404) generated so much media coverage and political controversy that the government appointed a special parliamentary subcommittee to examine the issues (House of Commons 1999d). A brief review of the main tax reforms under discussion is in order.

Some argue we should increase the tax credit for dependent spouses, especially those who remain out of the paid workforce to care for children. Presently the spousal credit under the federal Income Tax Act does not quite double the basic personal credit available to a breadwinner, but increases it by about 83 per cent (Income Tax Act, 1985, s. 118(1)(a)).[7] The Reform Party of Canada and others have argued that the spousal amount should be raised so that it equals the basic personal credit: 'The spousal exemption is worth about 20% less than the basic personal exemption. What this says to fathers and mothers who decide to stay at home is that they are second class citizens. Their value to society is deemed to be only 80% of the value of somebody who works outside the home. We say enough of this kind of second class status for people who are staying at home to do what is best for their families (House of Commons 1999e, 12405).[8]

The Alberta government has equalized the basic and spousal amounts at $12,900 effective 1 January 2001 (Alberta Personal Income Tax Act, 2000). In announcing this reform Treasurer Stockwell Day echoed the same tax discrimination and family values discourse:

> The choice of whether one or two partners work outside the home should be a personal family choice. But the tax scales are tipped in favour of two-income families, making the choice more difficult for those who choose to live on one income.
>
> ...
>
> By raising the spousal exemption, they get a little relief, and an acknowledgement that taxes should be a little more friendly to the one-income family. Mr. Speaker, my colleagues and I would like to thank Joe and Jenny [a one income family with five children] and thousands like them for strengthening the fabric of this province (Alberta 1999a).

Another proposal popular among social conservatives is to extend the childcare expense deduction to stay-at-home parents. Reform Party MPs have attacked the childcare expense deduction as 'one of the principal offending elements of the tax code,' saying it 'sends the message that parental or extended family care has no value' (House of Commons 1999e, 12405, 12408). The Reform Party proposes to convert the deduction to a refundable tax credit that would be paid to all parents whether or not they are engaged in paid work or purchase childcare services, arguing this would 'end the discrimination against parents who provide child care at home' (Reform Party of Canada undated). The idea has been endorsed by a range of groups, including the federal Conservatives (Progressive Conservative Party of Canada, 1997), Globe and Mail editorial writers (Globe and Mail 1999, A24), the conservative women's group REAL Women (REAL Women of Canada undated), a group calling themselves the Canada Family Tax Coalition,[9] and even New Democratic Party MPs (House of Commons 1999e, 12414).

A more fundamental reform being advocated by some is to move to a joint marital unit of taxation which would allow breadwinners to reduce their tax liability through a fictional or accounting division of income with a non-earning spouse (Progressive Conservative Party of Canada 1997; REAL Women of Canada undated). Others would permit a less dramatic form of income splitting by allowing a breadwinner to transfer some of his income to a stay-at-home spouse, which income could then be deducted from his return and taxed at her lower rate. For example, government backbencher Paul Szabo introduced a private member's bill to allow taxpayers to deduct a maximum of $25,000 per year paid to a spouse with no income, provided the couple has at least one pre-school age child and does not claim any deduction for childcare expenses.[10] In other words, Szabo's income-splitting measure would be specifically designed to target two-parent families where one parent remains out of paid labour to care for a child.

Many of these proposals seem firmly rooted in a nostalgia for the patriarchal family. They often draw upon feminist discourse about the economic value of household labour, while at the same time blaming feminists for its devaluation. Thus MP Paul Szabo published the following defence of his income splitting and other family policy proposals:

Unpaid Work Is Still Work
The gravest social injustice of all time has to be the abandonment of the stay-at-home mother. Managing the family home and caring for our children was and continues to be the most important job in the world. It is an honourable profession which has not been recognized for its value to our society. Any attempt to do so has been discouraged by those who are advocating for women who choose to work outside of the home (Szabo 1997, 49).

It is not surprising that moral conservatives would seek to appropriate knowledge developed by feminists in order to deflect criticisms that they are advocating a move back to rigidly divided gender roles. Feminists need to respond to these tax reform advocates. As Luxton and Vosko have warned, 'neglecting [unpaid work as an] ... area of struggle has the potential to open up a space for the right-wing which already has a clear and well-articulated "family politics"' (Luxton & Vosko 1998, 52). However, developing such a response will be a challenge for feminist tax theorists, who generally have focused more on rooting out tax barriers to women's paid work than on how to support women as unpaid caregivers. Most feminist tax scholars argue that tax law already contains a bias in favour of household production because the value of goods and services produced in the home is not taxed (Lahey 1985, 289–92; Maloney 1994, 129–30; Nelson 1996, 111; Staudt 1996b, 1575–9 and 1589–92). They have most often concluded that one-earner couples should be taxed more heavily as a result. The time is ripe to reconsider whether a feminist tax policy agenda can encompass some form of positive tax relief or recognition of women's unpaid work.

It is clear, however, that the tax reform proposals put forward to date are grossly deficient from a gender equality perspective. In every case they reserve a large degree of control over market income to the breadwinner spouse. All are designed to give tax benefits to breadwinners, leaving them to share the additional resources as they please (or not) with their dependent spouses. There are strong echoes here of the engulfment and privatization of women's economic interests within the family that has characterized Canadian income tax law from its inception. Even under Szabo's proposal, which requires an actual payment of income, the caregiver spouse can only benefit if the breadwinner is financially able and willing to make such a transfer, and to relinquish informal control over the income as well as legal title. Most of the proposals have been framed to exclude non-normative families such as low-income couples, single mothers, or gay and lesbian couples. In addition, all are limited to families where the primary caregiver has little or no market income. The second shift of caregiving work performed by women with paid jobs is completely disregarded. Though sometimes presented as a means of valuing women's unpaid work, therefore, these proposals in their design seem less concerned with gender equality than with resisting women's entry into markets and supporting the shift away from paid childcare and other public services towards greater reliance on women's unpaid work.

The idea of income splitting has also been advocated as a contribution towards gender equality by some scholarly commentators. David Duff, for one, favours a system that would allow income splitting with a caregiver spouse, arguing that by denying deductions for such interspousal payments the Income Tax Act 'ignores the economic partnership underlying this division of labour ...' (Duff 1999, 9). Duff and others would also consider repealing the attribution rules in order to encourage taxpayers to transfer investment properties to a non-earning spouse (Hogg, Magee & Cook 1999, 117; Lahey 1985, 300; Young 2000a, 45–9). Despite the regressivity of such an amendment, which would exclusively benefit a small class of higher income taxpayers in spousal relationships, these authors see the costs as tolerable if they improve at least some women's access to resources. However, it must be recognized that reducing the progressivity of the system would also diminish the resources available for state-funded transfers and services that could more directly promote the economic autonomy of a much wider class of women, including the most marginalized. Rather than facilitating income splitting by higher income men, a more egalitarian approach to recognizing unpaid care work would surely be to provide some kind of refundable credit that would put resources directly in women's hands, without the intermediating control of a breadwinner spouse. The Standing Committee on Finance has tentatively endorsed the idea of such a refundable credit (1999d, 14), but would limit it to parents who entirely forgo market income to raise children. Again, this proposal feeds the myth that employed mothers do not carry the bulk of caregiving and other household work. It would also provide support only to those who severed all ties with the paid labour market for a period of time, an arrangement which may well jeopardize future earning opportunities.

A refundable tax credit to compensate unpaid social reproductive labour might enhance women's economic equality and autonomy, but only if it is designed far more carefully than existing proposals. Certainly the credit would have to be substantial, at least approaching the real value of the work being compensated, and it should be conceived as 'essential social infrastructure for the household economy, rather than as "welfare handouts"' (Colman 1998b, 107). The designers of such a credit would also need to overcome two potential dangers. First, there is a risk of reinforcing the dichotomization of women as either caregivers or paid workers when in fact most women undertake both these roles at some point in their lives, often simultaneously. Rather than isolating one group as society's designated 'caregivers,' such as stay-at-home mothers of preschool children, a refundable tax credit should instead be designed to assist people to balance paid and unpaid work in accordance with their different responsibilities and desires. The meaning of caregiving should therefore include the full range of familial and community care responsibilities that are often assumed by women. And it would be important to deliver the credit not only to those who abstain entirely from market work but also, at least partially, to those who combine paid employment with a primary caregiver role. Finally, any such credit would have to be developed in tandem with far better public services to support caregivers' access to waged labour, including accessible, high quality childcare programs. Women's unpaid work must be recognized in a way that advances, rather than hinders, the related struggle for equal access to markets.

The second potential danger of a refundable caregiver credit is that it could rigidify existing gender divisions of labour. Ideally, such a credit should be designed to encourage a more equal sharing of social reproductive work between women and men. In opposite-sex couples it would be appropriate for the Income Tax Act to presume, as it currently does for the Canada Child Tax Benefit (CCTB), that the woman bears primary responsibility for caregiving unless she files a notice declaring otherwise (s. 122.6; Regs. 6301, 6302). However, unlike the CCTB, it would be important for a refundable caregiver credit to be divisible if the female partner indicates that there is a roughly equal sharing of care work within the relationship. In the case of same-sex couples the presumption could be reversed so that the credit is divided unless the partners file a joint declaration identifying one of them as the primary caregiver, or unless one partner obtains an administrative or judicial determination that he or she is the primary caregiver. The objective of such a scheme is to recognize the current reality that women do the bulk of unpaid caregiving, while at the same time acknowledging and encouraging more egalitarian relationships.

At a time when public transfers and services are being withdrawn it will be tempting to accept tax measures that provide any degree of relief to strained household budgets or a modicum of much-needed political recognition for women's care work. However, the new federal caregiver credit and the various other tax reform proposals being advanced under the banner of valuing unpaid work do less to advance women's economic equality or autonomy than to legitimate the privatization of social reproductive costs to women.

C. Enriched Tax Benefits for Charitable Donors

Discussions of privatization often focus on the changing relationships between state, market, and family. Left out of this familiar triad, however, is the role of the so-called voluntary sector, the myriad community groups and non-profit agencies outside the formal public sector which undertake collective provision of many goods and services essential to the social reproduction of the population. A prominent theme of neoliberal discourse is the need to expand the role of voluntary organizations to encompass many welfare state functions. Among the reasons offered are that governments are incompetent and inefficient providers of public services, that local agencies can be more responsive to diverse and changing local needs, and that a centralized, bureaucratic welfare state has discouraged civic engagement and eroded norms of altruism, social responsibility, and self-reliance (Boaz 1999; Dominque 1996; Waitzer 1996). The promotion of greater voluntarism and community responsibility is not limited to the new right; it has appeal for many progressives as well, who see it as a means of democratizing the public sphere and making the welfare state better serve the goal of egalitarian social change (Barber 1995, 276–88; Salomon 1995, 261–4). These progressive theorists tend not to see the non-profit sector as a replacement for the state, however, but as a supplementary source of popular empowerment that would need to be funded and centrally regulated by governments (Rekart 1993, 20–5). Though neoliberal discourse sometimes blurs into or appropriates progressive critiques of the welfare state, its political vision is very different (Kline 1997, 346–9). In the neo-liberal invocation, 'rather than "community" assuming a public or collective meaning ... it is a tool of privatization' (Boyd 1997, 19).

To promote voluntary sector growth the federal government has enriched the tax benefits provided to charitable donors. This policy trend demonstrates the interdependence of public and private ordering and the indeterminacy of these labels. The cost to the federal government of providing income tax concessions to charities and their donors was estimated at $1.015 billion in 1994, and projected to rise by 67 per cent to $1.693 billion by 2001 (Canada, Department of Finance, 1999). The tax rules also require law makers and public servants to determine which non-profit groups and which donations are worthy of public support, and to police established boundaries. So it is misleading to depict the state as simply relinquishing its role in social reproduction to either voluntary organizations or individual donors.

Despite continued state involvement, the movement away from direct funding of non-profit agencies towards tax subsidization of philanthropy has several privatizing effects. First, it makes government's role in the social welfare system less visible and accountable because tax concessions do not appear explicitly on the public balance sheet, masking their total cost as well as who receives the benefits (Scharf, Cherniawsky, & Hogg 1997, 8). Second, it individualizes decision making about what services should be funded. Private donors not only decide where to send their own money; but in effect they are able to direct a matching amount of government funds to their preferred charity (Brooks forthcoming, 9). Third, it decentralizes service provision to organizations that are spread unevenly throughout the country, are not coordinated centrally, and are not necessarily accountable to those who require social services (Hall & Reed 1998, 4–6; Salamon 1995, 266; Wolpert 1993, 17–19, 24–6). A fourth privatizing effect arises because the distribution of the tax benefits tracks the distribution of market income. As discussed below, the value of the charitable donations tax credit tends to rise with income so that it blunts the redistributive capacity of the income tax and reinforces the market as the predominant distributive mechanism (Bell-Lowther 1988; Brooks, forthcoming; Duff, forthcoming). Finally, all of these privatizing effects operate not only on the distribution of resources but on the construction of social norms. The valorization of charity erodes ideals of equality, collectivism, and universal entitlement to a basic level of human welfare. Individual acts of altruistic sharing are posited as a substitute for a redistributive tax and social security system. Citizens are implicitly urged not to rely on government when they are in need personally, or when social problems need to be addressed in their communities. This reconstruction of citizenship norms is necessary to and inseparable from the reallocation of material resources that is more commonly associated with privatization. For example, Waitzer links the cultivation of voluntaristic values to the creation of a more efficient market economy, as relationships of trust and social obligation can 'reduce transaction costs and permit enterprise to be self-organizing' (Waitzer 1996, 9). When tax policy discourse makes claims about the usefulness and desirability of charity, in other words, it is helping to produce the new market citizens of a neoliberal state (Brodie 1997, 4).

1. Which Voluntary Organizations Are Favoured by the Tax System?

This section examines the implications of the new charitable tax benefits on non-profit groups that focus on advancing women's equality interests or otherwise assisting women. The combination of across-the-board cutbacks in direct government funding of non-profit organizations and the enhancement of charitable tax breaks amounts, in effect, to a policy of favouring that subset of voluntary agencies which qualify as charities under the current legal definition. Two consequences are likely to flow from this policy trend. First, resources within the non-profit sector will most likely be redistributed away from groups and activities defined as non-charitable. And second, among agencies fortunate enough to have registered charity status, those with more experience in private fund-raising and more affluent constituencies will likely fare best. Women's organizations stand to lose out on both counts.

The non-profit sector in Canada is vast and encompasses a diverse range of organizations and activities (Quarter 1992). One basic division within the sector is between those agencies that focus on service provision and those that focus on lobbying or other advocacy functions, with many groups engaging in some combination of the two. The sector can be broken down by major areas of concern, such as religion, health, education, sports and recreation, law and justice, social welfare, arts and culture, and the environment. (Hall et. al. 1998, 19). It can be further subdivided according to client populations, with some groups defining their constituencies geographically and others by reference to particular social groups or interests. Voluntary organizations can also be differentiated by their sources of funding. Many rely heavily on government grants or contracts while others are financed chiefly by membership dues, donations, or other forms of private fund-raising (Bowlby et al. 1994; Canadian Centre for Philanthropy 1994, 24; Francis & Clemens 1999). Finally, the sector includes those organizations that qualify as registered charities for income tax purposes, and those which do not (Income Tax Act, 1985, ss. 249(1), 149.1(1)).

Only those groups designated as registered charities by the Minister of National Revenue are entitled to issue tax receipts which entitle donors to claim the charitable donations tax credit and other tax benefits. In deciding whether to grant this status Revenue officials look to the general law of charity. That is, they apply the definition set out in the Statute of Elizabeth, 1601, as interpreted by the courts through the centuries. Judicial readings of this ancient law have excluded activities with political purposes from the meaning of charity (Michell 1995). As a consequence, non-profit organizations characterized by Revenue Canada as advocacy groups, because they call for legal or policy changes, or publish literature that is deemed propagandistic rather than educational, are routinely denied charitable status (Revenue Canada undated).[11] This excludes the work of many equality seeking groups, including women's organizations, from the definition of charity, and precludes their access to tax-subsidized private donations. Even groups that refrain from active lobbying and focus on public education are at greater risk of being labelled political if they define themselves as feminist or women-centred, though they may speak to the very same issues as other groups which purport not to be concerned with gender or to be gender neutral. Comments on reproductive choice may be within the charitable mandate of a religious organization, for example (Phillips 1995), but viewed as political in the hands of a feminist agency. Similarly, publications by women's groups on the gender impact of economic restructuring or fiscal policy may be viewed as too political to qualify as charitable activity, although the same issues are discussed without attention to gender by bodies like the Fraser Institute or the Canadian Tax Foundation (both of which are registered charities). Feminist or women-focused programs may be perceived as political or controversial simply because they do not reflect currently dominant viewpoints or experiences. Indeed, the very reason for their existence may be invoked to deny them charitable status.

The denial of tax subsidies to women's organizations is especially worrying in light of the larger backlash occurring against interest group advocacy in Canada. Direct funding for advocacy work is growing scarce as governments target their grants increasingly to non-profit organizations engaged in service provision. Women's organizations are receiving less money in the form of general operating grants to fund the day-to-day advocacy work of responding in the media or Parliament to new developments as they arise. Increasingly, they must apply for one-time project funding to carry out narrowly defined objectives that must be identified far in advance, or to conduct research on themes proposed by government agencies. Grant applications and other fund-raising efforts are consuming more time, and project funds must be used for pre-identified purposes. Some commentators have attributed overt political motives to governments in defunding the most vocal critics of restructuring policies, viewing this as part of a larger backlash against the equality-seeking efforts of so-called special interest groups (Cardozo 1996; Floyd 1996).

The combination of direct funding cuts to all non-profit organizations, particularly for advocacy work, with the diversion of greater resources through the tax system to those with registered charity status, effectively starves that portion of the voluntary sector dedicated to promoting egalitarian social change. This trend is likely to have a number of domesticating or deradicalizing effects on women's organizations. Groups dedicated principally to lobbying and advocacy may switch to educational publishing or other activities that might qualify as charitable. One strategy has been to restructure an organization into two bodies, one of which can be registered as a charity because it conducts only the non-political work of the organization as understood by Revenue officials. While this may assist the group in soliciting private donations, those moneys cannot be used to support its advocacy work. Moreover, those who might previously have given money for lobbying activities may now designate their donations for charitable uses only so they can obtain a tax receipt. Groups that focus primarily on delivering front-line services to women can often obtain charitable status and might enjoy an increase in private donations under the new tax rules. However, private fundraising campaigns are time-consuming and provide a less predictable and secure funding base than direct grants. And such agencies are often supported primarily by women, who on average have less private wealth and less capacity to donate than men. There is a danger that service-oriented women's groups will feel pressure to downplay activities aimed at promoting systemic legal or political change and to concentrate exclusively on immediate crisis services, if they wish to obtain or retain charitable status. One long-time feminist activist recounts that following the large cuts to women's shelters and second-stage housing in Ontario in 1995, government officials and political staff cautioned some shelters that fax campaigns to members of Parliament and other forms of protest may be incompatible with their status as charities.[12]

The Supreme Court of Canada's decision in *Vancouver Society of Immigrant and Visible Minority Women v. M.N.R.* (1999) shows how the application of charities law may inhibit activism by women's groups. A majority of the court held that the society did not satisfy the definition of charity for income tax purposes, rebuffing an argument by interveners that the denial of registered charity status violated the constitutional equality rights of immigrant and visible minority women.[13] In answering the equality rights challenge Iacobucci J. simply relied upon the formal equality of the Income Tax Act – whereby 'any organization, by restricting itself to charitable purposes and activities, can qualify for registration' (139). He concluded that the denial of charitable status to the society 'was a consequence of the nature of its purposes and activities, not of the characteristics of its intended beneficiaries' (140). The court avoided the question of adverse impact and whether organizations serving the particular needs of disadvantaged groups may have a higher rate of rejection because they are more likely to be perceived as political or because they may need to engage in advocacy-like work in order to serve the interests of their clientele. Indeed, some of the majority's comments about the society's work tend to underscore this very concern.

Much of the decision is focused on whether the society fit within the 'advancement of education' head of the definition of charity. The society's constituting document described its key purpose as the provision of 'educational forums, classes, workshops and seminars to immigrant women in order that they may be able to find or obtain employment or self-employment' (96). The majority held that these purposes fell out-side the traditional understanding of 'education' within charities law because they did not amount to 'formal training of the mind' or 'the improvement of a useful branch of human knowledge' (113). It singled out certain activities as particularly suspect: 'It is easy to see how the information sessions presented on such topics as human rights, employ-ment equity, violence and abuse against women, and how to start a small business, while probably informative and important, would appear to be more in the nature of "the presentation to the public of selected items of information and opinion" ...' (113–14, quoting Stone J.A. in *Positive Action Against Pornography v. M.N.R.* [1988] 2 F.C. 340 (F.C.A.)). The implication is that because opinions on women's human rights or equal-ity may differ, teaching that addresses these subjects cannot be seen as 'education' for purposes of charitable registration. The problem is that this approach tends to exclude any teaching from a critical or opposi-tional perspective, while treating as neutral and therefore charitable those educational activities that assume or even promote the status quo or dominant perspectives.

Iacobucci J. went on to decide that the traditional meaning of 'educa-tion' should be broadened to embrace 'informal training initiatives, aimed at teaching necessary life skills or providing information toward a practical end' (116), but with the caveat that they must be 'truly geared at the training of the mind and not just the promotion of a particular point of view' (116). His definition expands the meaning of education beyond the typical methodologies and subjects of academic study, but it retains the false distinction between 'education' as an ostensibly value-neutral activity and other ways of informing which are deemed biased or politically loaded. He stressed that a group will not qualify if it is '"edu-cating" people about a particular point of view in a manner that might more aptly be described as persuasion or indoctrination' (118). The majority concluded that the society's purpose of training women to find employment was charitable within its expanded definition of education, but never stated whether the human rights, employment equity- and anti-violence elements of the society's program qualified as such. It did not need to since the appeal was ultimately rejected on the basis of another clause in the constating document which the majority held was too vague and open-ended to ensure the society's purposes and activi-ties would remain exclusively charitable (131–2).

The court was invited to consider whether the elimination of preju-dice and discrimination might itself be recognized as a charitable purpose, but Iacobucci J. declined comment (128–9). He also rejected as too 'radical' the society's argument for a new contextual approach to defining charity which would ask (among other things) whether the activities of an organization are consistent with constitutional values (133–4). Overall, the decision conveys a profound scepticism as to whether the discussion of women's equality issues can be characterized as educational and therefore charitable. Though they did not decide the point conclusively, the court accentuated the worry that such activities may actually disqualify a group which is formed primarily for charitable purposes. This is troubling in light of the court's own recognition that 'the capacity to offer tax benefits to prospective donors can be a major determinant of the success' of a non-profit organization (92–3).

One response to these concerns would be a legislative expansion of the definition of charity to encompass certain forms of advocacy (Panel on Accountability and Governance in the Voluntary Sector 1999, 50–5). Mayo Moran argues, for example, that groups such as the Women's Legal Education and Action Fund (LEAF), formed for the purpose of securing compliance with constitutional norms, should qualify as charitable, as should groups that engage in advocacy or critical public education (Moran forthcoming, 13–22). There is a compelling argument that such a definition of charity would be more consistent with the objective of promoting a pluralistic, democratic society. However, it is critical that policy debate also consider whether providing tax subsidies to private donors adequately supports the work of non-profit organizations that serve the interests of the less powerful. Indirect subsidies are a useful supplement to direct funding by government, but they cannot replace it (Schreader 1990). The reason for publicly funding such organizations is precisely that they represent groups which lack the economic or social power to make their voices heard in the political process. For the same reason, they have limited capacity to raise funds from members or supporters, regardless of how generous a tax credit donors may receive. In short, the enrichment of charitable tax benefits should not be at the expense of direct public funding to support oppositional or equality-oriented work.

2. The Gendered Distribution of Tax Benefits among
   Charitable Donors
This section focuses on the distributive impact of the tax regime on individual donors, explaining why the value of the tax relief provided tends to rise with income and why it is enjoyed disproportionately by men. The amendments made in the 1990s have aggravated this regressivity.

Switching from direct funding of public services to indirect subsidization of charities and their donors through the tax system has two simultaneous effects: (i) government budgetary expenditures appear to be
smaller, because the cost of tax expenditures is not included, and (ii)
more resources are shifted towards those who do well in markets, primarily men but also some women (Table 1, *supra*).

A basic understanding of the tax rules is needed to comprehend their
regressive impact. The main tax benefit available to individuals who
donate to charity is a credit that reduces tax payable by a percentage of
the amount donated (Income Tax Act, 1985, s. 118.1(3)). The credit was
introduced in 1988 to replace the previous deduction for charitable
donations at the same time as a host of other personal deductions were
converted to credits (S.C. 1988, c. 55, s. 92; Duff, forthcoming). The
main purpose of this reform was to improve the equity of the system by
equalizing the value of credits to taxpayers in different brackets. Credits
permit all individuals to reduce their tax payable by 16 per cent (formerly 17 per cent) of a specified dollar figure. Because 16 per cent is the
lowest federal tax rate these credits have the same value to people in the
lowest tax bracket as they do to those in higher brackets (though not for
individuals whose tax liability is too small to absorb the credits). However, in response to concerns that a low-rate credit would provide little
incentive for the affluent to make charitable donations, the government
introduced a unique two-tier credit for charitable giving. The provision
enacted in 1988 allowed a credit equal to 17 per cent of the first $250
donated, plus 29 per cent of amounts exceeding $250. The 1988 reforms
kept in place an income ceiling that limited the value of the donations
claimable in any particular year to 20 per cent of the taxpayer's income
for that year (Income Tax Act, 1985, s. 118.1 'total gifts'). Gifts over the
income ceiling, or which the donor does not wish to claim in the year
they are made, can be carried forward and claimed in any of the next
five years (Ibid., s. 118.1 'total charitable gifts'). The two-tier credit created an incentive to claim all gifts made over a five-year period in a single year in order to maximize the amount credited at the 29 per cent
rate. It also meant that those who could make larger donations received
a more valuable credit than those who made donations under $250.

Several times since 1993 the credit has been amended to make it
more generous. In 1994 the threshold for the 29 per cent credit was
dropped from $250 to $200 (S.C. 1995, c. 3, s. 34). The income ceiling
was raised dramatically to 50 per cent of annual income in 1996 (S.C.
1997, c. 25, s. 26), and to 75 per cent in 1997 (S.C. 1998, c. 19, s. 22(4)).

In addition, special changes were made to encourage testamentary gifts and gifts of capital property. The income ceiling was raised to 100 per cent of annual income for the year of a taxpayer's death and the immediately preceding year (Income Tax Act, 1985, s. 118.1(1) 'total gifts,' subpara.(a)(ii)). This means that an individual's tax liability for the last two years of his or her life may be eliminated entirely by donating a sufficient amount of money or property to a registered charity. Taxpayers who make in-kind donations of capital property such as real estate or shares, rather than cash gifts, also received new concessions. First, the income ceiling for such gifts was raised by a further amount equal to 25 per cent of any taxable capital gain realized on the transfer of property to the charity (Ibid., s. 118.1(1) 'total gifts,' subpara.(a)(iii)). Though such a transfer is made for no consideration the Income Tax Act forces a realization of any accrued capital gains on 'gifted' property (s. 69(1)(b)(ii), s. 70(5)). The income ceiling was amended in response to criticisms that potential donors of property with large accrued gains would be reluctant to pay tax on even 25 per cent of the income resulting from this deemed realization. The '75% + 25%' formula effectively guarantees that any such capital gain will be entirely tax exempt. In fact, in the normal case where the gain does not represent the entire value of the property, the credit will shelter from tax not only the capital gain on the gifted property, but also other income earned by the taxpayer. For example, an individual may donate land worth $1 million that was originally purchased at a cost of $800,000, thereby realizing a taxable capital gain of $100,000 (1/2 x the 200,000 gain on the property: Ibid., s. 38(a), as proposed to be amended by Canada, Department of Finance 2000b). The donor will be issued a charitable tax receipt for the full $1 million value of the property. The first $200 of this donation will be credited at 16 per cent, with the balance credited at the top marginal rate of 29 per cent. The donor will be able to spread the credit over five years, essentially eliminating tax not only on the $200,000 capital gain realized on the gifted land, but on up to $800,000 of other income, from a business, investments, employment, or any other source. Under the 75 per cent income ceiling up to $600,000 of other income could be sheltered from tax immediately in the year of the donation (Mawer 1997).

These benefits have been enhanced even further for taxpayers who donate publicly traded securities (usually shares) to charity. In its 1997 budget, the government announced a 50 per cent reduction in the taxable capital gain realized on a gift of such securities. Only 25 per cent of any capital gain on the gifted securities will now be treated as a taxable

Table 1.2
Charitable credits by sex, 1997

	% of Total returns filed	% of Total income assessed	% of Charitable credits claimed
Men	49.5	62.6	67.5
Women	50.5	37.4	32.5

Source: Data compiled from Canada Customs and Revenue Agency (2000) Basic Table 4. Analysis by author.

capital gain and included in the taxpayer's income, half the normal inclusion rate of 50 per cent (Income Tax Act, 1985, s. 38(a.1)). This change will increase the sheltering effect of the credit, as less of the donation's value will be needed to cover the taxable capital gain on the donated shares, and more will be available to eliminate tax on other income.

The distributive effects of these reforms are bound to be strongly regressive. The one change that may benefit significant numbers of lower- and middle-income people is the application of the 29 per cent credit to donations over $200, rather than the previous $250. However, the credit still has a regressive incidence even after this change. Duff has shown that the value of the credit rises steadily with income because 'average contributions by low-income taxpayers are not much greater than the $200 threshold, while average contributions by high-income taxpayers greatly exceed the $200 threshold, [so that] a significant proportion of the charitable donations by low-income taxpayers are creditable at the 17 [now 16] percent rate, whereas most charitable contributions by high-income taxpayers are creditable at the 29% rate' (Duff, forthcoming, 16). Considering the concentration of women taxpayers at lower incomes (Table 1, supra), it is not surprising to find that the credit also benefits men disproportionately, as illustrated by Table 1.2.

Interestingly, women are slightly more likely to make donations to charitable and non-profit organizations than men. In 1997, 81 per cent of women reported making a donation of some kind, compared to 75 per cent of men (Hall et al. 1998, 15). However, women's average donation ($236) was slightly lower than men's ($243) (Ibid.). Given the similarity in women's and men's donation rates and average donations, the fact that men receive over two-thirds of the tax credits for charitable donations is even more striking. What might explain this pattern? One explanation is that fewer women than men may report their donations for tax purposes. Only 41 per cent of donors indicated they planned to claim a tax credit for their charitable gifts (Ibid., 25). Donations may have been made to non-profit agencies that do not have registered charity status, tax liability may have been insufficient to absorb the credit, or people may simply have neglected to report their donations for tax purposes. Women may also transfer their charitable donations receipts to their spouses more often than men do. Revenue Canada's statistics show that men reported more than four and a half times the amount of personal credits transferred from a spouse in 1997 than women reported.[14] Credits are generally transferred when one spouse cannot claim them due to lack of tax liability.

Some may find the cost and inequity of the charitable donations tax credit to be tolerable if it results in more private resources finding their way into community services that benefit a wide range of people. It should be noted, however, that the tax credit can be claimed for donations to the donor's own private foundation, controlled by the donor and members of his or her family, which provides no goods or services directly but simply makes donations to other registered charities (Income Tax Act, 1985, s. 248(1) 'registered charity'). It is well understood by tax and estate planners that wealthy individuals prefer to make their charitable donations through a private foundation, mainly to avoid having to disclose the details of a large gift (such as the value of private corporation shares) to the entire board of an operating charity (B. Bromley 1997). In addition, private foundations may obtain permission to wait up to ten years before distributing their funds to actual operating charities. Though the policy rationale for this generous deferral is to allow foundations to build up significant endowment funds, it can also be used simply to retain control of property that in formal legal terms has been given away. The new income ceilings and other enhancements to the charitable donations tax credit have created a wide range of new tax-planning opportunities for wealthy individuals. For example, one technique is to have the taxpayer donate private corporation shares to his or her private foundation, and then make a cash gift to his or her children to allow them to purchase the shares from the foundation. Whereas a direct gift or sale to the children would have attracted capital gains tax, completing the transaction through the private foundation not only avoids capital gains tax but likely shelters other income of the donor from tax as well. Instead of generating revenue for government programs or services such a transaction generates resources that ultimately will be used by charitable organizations of the donor's choice, but possibly not for ten years. A recent court decision casts doubt on whether charitable tax planning manoeuvres can be challenged under the general anti-avoidance rule enacted in 1988 (Income Tax Act, 1985, s. 245). In *Jabs Construction Limited v. The Queen* (1999), the Tax Court of Canada held that an avoidance transaction involving a gift to a private foundation did not abuse the provisions or the purpose of the ITA because it simply took advantage of the tax credit granted expressly by the statute. This reasoning begged the question of whether the tax credit was intended to or should properly be interpreted to encompass avoidance transactions of that nature. However, it seems likely that such reasoning will appeal to many courts, especially in light of the mixed charitable and tax avoidance purposes that motivate many such transactions.

The justification most often given for these regressive tax concessions is that they induce high-income earners to make large gifts that are then used to provide services and amenities to the public which government would otherwise have to finance, or which might simply be unavailable. Whether or not the tax benefits significantly increase the total funds available for social services, this chapter has demonstrated that they shift the tax burden away from the more affluent and allow them to control the programs and services their donations are used to finance. Whereas a progressive tax system helps to equalize market outcomes, these tax concessions tend to exacerbate market inequalities without ensuring a fair distribution of funding to organizations that help the less privileged. Some studies indicate that high-income individuals tend to donate more to hospitals, higher education, and cultural charities, for example, while lower income people are more likely to donate to religious organizations and social welfare agencies (Duff forthcoming, 12). Given that men have more income and wealth to donate than women, the services provided by women's organizations, particularly those without registered charity status, may well receive less of the available private resources. When the funding of social services is privatized to individual philanthropists the nature of the services provided and the kinds of claims citizens can make on them is changed. In particular, women's economic disadvantage is deepened, and services essential to women's autonomy and equality are destabilized.

Conclusion

This study of taxation law in the 1990s confirms that privatization cannot be understood simply as a movement to deregulate the market and withdraw the state from economic life. The tax system continues to be busily employed by policy makers to distribute resources and encourage or facilitate certain behaviours, and tax law remains a potent cultivator of gendered norms about ideal social relations. This study does suggest, however, that 'state power has been redeployed from social welfare concerns and economic management to the enforcement of the market model in virtually all aspects of everyday life' (Brodie 1995, 51). Tax law must be viewed as a key contributor to the creation and regulation of a more market-oriented and more unequal society. The rise of market citizenship in the design of the tax system also entails the emergence of a new gender order. While it is still in the process of congealing, a salient feature of this gender order appears to be its contradictory construction of women as both gender-neutral market workers and primary caregivers who can take up the slack for degraded public services. These changes are aggravating the time crunch felt by many women, but as the historical overview in Part I indicates, it is important not to exaggerate the degree of change now taking place. The privatization of social reproduction and of women's economic welfare is embedded in the earliest foundations of Canadian income tax law and has long existed in tension with those few tax provisions that attempt to support women's autonomy and equal access to resources. My analysis points clearly to a need for more feminist interventions in fiscal policy debates, to contest the way the tax system often attributes women's economic inequality to the private workings of the market, family, and charity.

The three case studies presented in this paper illustrate the ways in which current tax reform trends are both producing and enforcing a reprivatization of social reproduction. The tax-cutting agendas sweeping the country call upon all taxpayers, including women, to be more reliant on the market and to expect less from the state, encouraging a more energetic participation in market labour. At the same time, the provision of caregiver credits and larger charitable credits encourages heavier reliance on family and voluntary support for those in need, and much of this support will in practice be provided by women. There is little evidence in the design of the individual tax reforms or the overall direction of tax policy that women's particular economic and social positionings have been carefully considered by policy makers. And there is much evidence that women will not gain the same immediate benefits as men from these three forms of tax reduction. In responding to these and other tax policies, however, feminist researchers and activists need to be wary of accepting small short-term gains for some women at the

cost of entrenching a tax regime that deepens the exploitation of all
women's social reproductive labour.

Notes

Special thanks to Neil Brooks, Brenda Cossman, David Duff, Judy Fudge, and
Miranda Stewart for their detailed comments on earlier versions of the
paper. I am also very grateful to Olga San Miguel, Angela Long, Robert Kreklewich, Freya Kodar, and Karen Pearlston for superb research assistance.

1 Canada, House of Commons, *Debates and Proceedings*, 7th Sess., 12th Parl., IV:
   4102, 4103 (3 August 1917), Thomas White, quoted in Lahey 1998, 12.
2 There is now an exception for transfers at fair market value, subject to certain conditions. See Ibid.: s. 74.5(1),(2), added by S.C. 1986, c. 6, s. 38.
3 The deduction/inclusion rules for child support have been repealed as of
   1 May 1997; the deduction/inclusion system for spousal support remains in
   place. See Ibid.: ss. 56(1)(b), 56.1(4), 60(b), 60.1(4).
4 This discussion does not take into account other complicating factors that
   alter the rate structure for some individuals, such as the availability of other
   personal credits, or the operation of refundable credits which are reduced
   above a certain level of income. See Macnaughton, Mathews, & Pittman
   1998.
5 For example, among those earning 0–$10,000 in 1997, men's average
   income was $4,606 while women's was $4,316. A similar pattern was evident
   at the top of the income range, among those earning over $100,000, where
   men's average income was $216,794 and women's was $187,914. These figures are derived from Canada Customs and Revenue Agency (2000), Basic
   Table 6.
6 See Balanced Budget, Debt Repayment and Taxpayer Protection Act, S.M.
   1995, c. 7, s. 10; and Taxpayer Protection Act, S.O. 1999, c. 7, Sched. A.
7 The lower amount of the spousal credit may be justified on the grounds that
   joint living gives rise to economies of scale so that a couple can live more
   cheaply than two single people maintaining separate households. This rationale does not explain why both members of a two-earner couple can claim
   the full basic personal credit. One possible rationale is that the higher credit
   offsets some of the transportation, clothing, and other costs of having two
   people in the paid labour force.
8 See also Progressive Conservative Party of Canada (1999) at 2.
9 'Family Tax Coalition Calls on Canadians to demand that the federal govern-

ment end tax discrimination against stay-at-home parents' (News Release, 4 March 1999). This coalition is comprised of four groups: Focus on the Family (Canada), REAL Women of Canada, Canada Family Action Coalition, and Home School Legal Defense Association.

10 Bill C-256, An Act to amend the Income Tax Act, was introduced and defeated in 1994.

11 Registered charities are permitted to engage in some political activities so long as those activities are non-partisan and 'ancillary and incidental' to their charitable activities, and provided that 'substantially all' of the charity's resources (at least 90 per cent, as interpreted by Revenue Canada) are devoted to charitable activities. See Income Tax Act, 1985: ss. 149.1(6.1), (6.2); Revenue Canada Information Circular 87-1; Woodman 1988, at 559–67.

12 Personal communication with Eileen Morrow, Lobby Co-ordinator, Ontario Association of Interval and Transition Houses, 8 February 1999.

13 The interveners were the Minority Advocacy and Rights Council, the Canadian Ethnocultural Council, and the Centre for Research Action on Race Relations.

14 $1,428,915,000 for men, versus $311,539,000 for women: Ibid.

2

From Segregation to Privatization: Equality, the Law, and Women Public Servants, 1908–2001

JUDY FUDGE

We dissent from the notion that a woman is naturally the inferior in judgement or intellect. There are men whose disdain for women in business is equalled only by their own inefficiency. With these we shall not attempt argument, realizing that the mind of a bigot is like the pupil of the eye, in that the more light poured upon it, the more it contracts.

Anonymous woman civil servant, The Civilian, 19 June 1908

This chapter focuses on the changing gender order in Canada, exploring the ways in which the privatization process has begun to reconfigure gender relations in an attempt to resolve the deepening contradiction between reproduction and production. It examines the legal regulation of women's employment within the federal public service in Canada from 1908 to 2001. Its goal is to illuminate two elements of twentieth-century Canadian gender: the commodification of women's labour and women's struggle for equality.

An examination of the way in which the federal government treated women as employees throws light on how women's labour was commodified by the Canadian welfare state and how that situation is changing in the current conjuncture. The federal government had a huge workforce (it still is the largest single employer of women in Canada); moreover, its treatment of its employees had a broad symbolic influence. Women's employment in the federal public service also illustrates the extent to which women were treated differently, and worse, than men. This discrimination was initially embodied in different legal norms for men and women. It was not until the mid-1960s that explicit discrimination against women workers in the federal public service on the basis of their sex was eliminated. By that time, the federal government had institutionalized a precise gender order in its workforce in which men were superior and women were subordinate. The federal public service formed a classic pyramid in which women were relegated to the broad base at the bottom.

But at the same time that the male breadwinner norm was institutionalized within the federal public service, the material conditions upon which that institutionalization depended were being eroded. Married men were increasingly unable to sustain a dependent wife and children on their wages alone. This resulted in a profound feminization of the federal public service, beginning in the 1960s, when the percentage of married women in the workforce greatly increased. Employment issues that pertained to women were forcefully brought to the fore, initially by the second wave of the women's movement, and then by the newly established public service union. By the late 1970s, equal pay for work of equal value became the official strategy for improving the situation of women in the federal public service. The present case study thus provides an opportunity to assess how the focus of second-wave feminism on a legal rights and law reform strategy influenced the commodification of women's labour.

In the 1980s 'substantive equality' emerged as a dominant strand of political discourse, especially at the federal level. However, the material conditions for its achievement were undermined by the federal government's embrace of privatization. The contradictions between substantive equality and privatization were especially sharp with respect to the government's treatment of its own employees. This case study therefore allows us to evaluate the success of an equal rights strategy in a privatization context. It also provides some evidence with which to determine how gender relations are currently being reconfigured.

I. Exclusion and Segregation, 1908–1954

In 1908 the Royal Commission on the Civil Service, which had been appointed to recommend measures to prevent patronage from undermining the integrity and efficiency of the expanding federal civil service, warned that one effect of entrenching the merit principle would be to flood the civil service with women, since women performed very well under the competitive examination system.[1] This concern that merit would subvert the gender order of the federal civil service was echoed in the first annual report of the Civil Service Commission in 1908: 'It is freely admitted that there are women who have quite as good executive ability as men, and who might, on the mere ground of personal qualification, fill the higher positions ... There are many other [positions], however, especially those of higher grades, where a number of duties would be quite unsuitable for women. There would be difficulties also, some of them it is true, the result of prejudice, but nonetheless real, were a woman to be appointed to administer an office or section of a department involving the control and direction of a number of male clerks' (Morgan 1988, 5). Despite the threat they posed to the public service, women workers were appealing as a source of cheap labour. According to the Civil Service Commission, 'a much larger number of qualified women than of men are prepared to accept the minimum salary offered' (Morgan 1988, 5).

The solution to the problem that women's merit would undermine men's privileged access to employment in the civil service was embodied in the sex discriminatory classification system implemented as part of the Civil Service Amendment Act, 1908. Women were confined to the third and bottom division of the civil service, where copying and routine work became an almost exclusively female preserve. Deputy heads were told to segregate occupational categories into male and female and women were limited to the lowest levels of appointment, such as 'stenographers and typists.' Sex-stereotyping of occupations and women's job ghettos preserved a gender order that was predominantly male, but could accommodate women in subordinate roles (Archibald 1970, 14–16; Hodgetts et al. 1972, 484–5; Lowe 1987, 72–4; Judeck 1968, 11). The effect of this system was pernicious for women; '[r]estrictions on hiring women gave rise to a caste-like system of employment under which the female civil service had an officially defined inferior status' (Lowe 1987, 73).

Some women in the civil service opposed the policy of occupational sex segregation. One wrote to the *Civilian*, the official newsletter of the Civil Service Association of Ottawa (CSAO): 'So far as the free market is concerned, the day of women is only beginning; as to the civil service, a word to those in authority: Gentlemen, you hold the trump cards at present, and your will is paramount. You may exclude women entirely, thus demonstrating your superiority and, incidentally, adding to the public expense; or you may go as you have been doing, throwing women, efficient and inefficient alike, into a hodge-podge class – a sort of limbo for lost souls. But, gentlemen, you are curiously deceived, and have most mistakenly read the sign of the times, if you think to settle the matter in that fashion' (Doherty 1991, 56, quoting *The Civilian*, 19 June

1908). Similar complaints against sex discrimination were repeatedly raised by women in letters published in the *Civilian* over the years (Doherty 1991, 96, 103, 106), but its editorial line promoted segregation of the sexes when it came to work. In 1911, the editor opposed the admission of women into the second division of the civil service on the ground that it, and other initiatives designed to treat women as equals to men, 'may be unwise or detrimental to the race as a whole' (Doherty 1991, 107 quoting *The Civilian*, 1 December 1911, 416). Undeterred by such attitudes, a group of two hundred women civil servants met in Ottawa in 1914 to establish a Women's Branch of the CSAO. Their demands included: '(a) an adequate initial salary, (b) equal pay for equal work, and (c) the appointment and promotion of women to such of the higher positions as they are qualified to fill with the salary that justly pertains to that position' (Doherty 1991, 107).

The pursuit of equality not only threatened their fellow workers, it was regarded as a broader threat to the gender order. In the House of Commons, Edmund Proulx, MP for Prescott, complained that women in the civil service 'are paid high salaries, are given a holiday in the summer, buy nice clothes and do not think about marrying; and, if they should think about it, they want a man who can afford to keep them in the style to which they have become accustomed' (Doherty 1991, 108, quoting HC Debates, 29 May 1914, 4451.)

The social, political, and labour unrest that erupted at the end of the First World War deepened the federal government's commitment to restoring the social order and preserving the centrality of the male breadwinner. The Civil Service Act was overhauled in 1918 and the most significant new element was the Veterans' Preference Clause, which gave civil service employment first to wounded war veterans, then to able-bodied war veterans, and finally to the widows of veterans. The federal government explicitly relied on the civil service as a mechanism for absorbing surplus labour, especially returning soldiers, who posed a threat to civil order during demobilization. The Veterans' Preference Clause became 'the longest and most powerful affirmative action program ever applied in the federal service, as well as being the least contested' (Morgan 1988, 6).

Sex was mentioned in the 1918 revisions to the Civil Service Act, along with 'age, ... health, habits, residence, moral character' as a characteristic considered to be a limiting factor on individual qualifications. All of these factors could be invoked to trump merit. Less visible, but also important for entrenching the gender order of the civil service, was the new classification scheme implemented about the same time. It was developed by Arthur Young, an American management company which applied scientific management principles to the organization and workings of the growing federal bureaucracy. One effect of the new scheme was the deterioration of the conditions of the women clerical workers (Hodgetts et al. 1972, 486; Lowe 1987, 89–99).

In 1921, barriers against the employment of women in the federal civil service were strengthened. Not only were formal restrictions placed upon the employment of married women, directives allowed deputy ministers to specify the sex of candidates for specific jobs. A married woman who wanted either to obtain or retain employment in the federal civil service had to demonstrate that she was self-supporting and that there were not enough qualified men to fill the position. If a married woman was able to meet these conditions, she could be rehired, but only as a temporary worker who was not entitled to the benefits available to permanent employees, and even then at the minimum rate in the class (Archibald 1970, 16; Hodgetts et al. 1972, 486; Morgan 1988, 6).

The embargo against women in the federal civil service did not withstand the steady demand for women workers. The Civil Service Commission found it necessary to recruit and maintain married women as stenographers, typists, office equipment operators, and clerks (Archibald 1970, 17; Hodgetts et al. 1972, 486). Instead of banning women outright, women were channelled into occupational ghettos that were female-dominated, poorly paid, and offered little chance for advancement. Further, they were treated as temporary workers, and were therefore in a more precarious situation than those (men) who were given permanent jobs. Clerking had been transformed from an occupation which, in 1900, was almost exclusively male to a female job ghetto: by 1941, the majority of clerks were women (Lowe 1987, 47). And although it was increasingly dominated by women, office work retained considerable gender segregation (Creese 1999, 56–7).

Restrictions on the employment of married women were invoked and applied during periods of high unemployment. According to Pierson (1990, 77–8), during the Depression, 'if [a married woman] was employed she was seen as a symbol of the cause of unemployment among men and, if she was dependent, as a symbol of the high cost of male employment in society.' Not surprisingly, 'the Depression was a particularly unhappy and insecure period for women in the public service' (Hodgetts et al. 1972, 487). The vast majority of women appointed during the 1930s were appointed to temporary positions, which meant that their employment could easily be terminated, that they were subject to regular contract renewal, and that they were not entitled to fringe benefits, such as pensions or annual wage increases (Morgan 1986, 20). Invariably, women were classified in positions lower than men's and paid less (Judek 1968, 9, 11).

During the Second World War, when it was a woman's patriotic duty to do a man's job, there was a brief but dramatic disruption of the prevailing gender order in the federal civil service. In 1938, only 16.5 per cent of appointments to the civil service were women; by 1943, women accounted for 65.4 per cent of the appointments. At the war's end, however, the government was quick to re-establish the civil service as a male domain. In 1944, the decision was made to release the approximately seven thousand married women who were employed as civil servants. The only women whose jobs would be saved were those in typing, stenographic, or office appliance operations positions (Hodgetts 1972, 487; Archibald 1970, 17). The Veterans' Preference Clause was renewed, as were restrictions on the employment of married women. Sex-based classifications were reinstituted, despite the fact that women's organizations had complained about the number of job competitions restricted to men (Archibald 1970, 17).

Dr Olive Russell, who had been appointed to the Department of Veterans' Affairs to deal with issues of integrating women into the peacetime economy, opposed the regulations barring women from working in the federal civil service on the ground that they set a bad example for the private sector (Pierson 1986, 83). But such protests did not deter the government from implementing a male breadwinner model in which dependent wives stayed at home (Creese 1999, 4; Pierson 1986; Porter 1993). In 1946, the proportion of women appointed to the civil service was slashed to half of that of the preceding year. Although several deputy ministers resisted the policy on the ground that the married women were very efficient, the Civil Service Commission prodded departments to clear their staffs of them. Married women's marginal status as workers was again officially confirmed, even though the Civil Service Commission complained for the next decade about how hard it was to recruit office staff, who were more commonly known as 'the girls' (Morgan 1986, 18).

In the 1950s, when the flow of veterans diminished, the proportion of women appointed to the civil service began to increase dramatically: between 1950 and 1960 it jumped from 31.9 per cent to 50 per cent

(Morgan 1988, 9). In 1951, the Civil Service Commission lifted its restriction against married women for clerical positions. Even then, however, the overwhelming majority of women's appointments were temporary (Morgan 1988, 10).

In the federal civil service, men's and women's labour was commodified differently. The employment norms and associated rights and obligations were gendered and there was no commitment to equality. Married women were regarded as the most marginal of workers; their position in the labour market was always subordinated to what were considered to be the more compelling needs of men for paid work. Women were tolerated provided that their numbers were limited and that they were confined to clerical positions at the bottom of the hierarchy. In practice, sex segregation was a viable alternative to the exclusion of women from the civil service.

II. Accessible But Unequal, 1955–1966

In 1955 the federal government repealed the regulations prohibiting the employment of married women in the federal civil service. The change in the formal legal status of married women as employees of the federal government was symbolic and material; it encapsulated larger trends within the Canadian labour market and the increasing demand by women and their organizations for equal access to employment. Middle-class women's organizations identified the civil service as a source of employment and advocated equal rights for women. The National Council of Women wanted women appointed to the Civil Service Commission and advocated equal pay legislation, while the Canadian Federation of Business and Professional Women's Clubs demanded the removal of discrimination against women in the federal civil service (Griffiths 1993, 259–61; Porter 1998, 80–2). The repeal of the restrictions on the employment of married women amounted to official recognition of the fact that women were a permanent feature of the civil service, not simply a temporary aberration. It also signalled their access to permanent employment, which provided better benefits and salaries than temporary positions (Morgan 1988, 10). This change in the status of women workers was reflected in the federal bureaucracy with the establishment of the Women's Bureau of the Department of Labour in 1954 and the appointment of the first female Civil Service Commissioner, Ruth Addison (Burt 1990, 196; Hodgetts et al. 1972, 489).

While married women were given access to employment in the federal civil service, they were not treated equally. Pregnant women were routinely fired, and it was not until 1962 that federal public service workers were entitled to maternity leave (Judek 1968, 84). In 1961, when the Civil Service Act was amended to address what was considered to be a broader problem of public management, the explicit mention of 'sex' as a qualification for positions was dropped. The commission, however, retained the discretion to 'prescribe qualifications as to age, residence or any other matters that in [its] opinion are necessary or desirable having regard to the nature of the duties to be performed.' Omitted from the list of prohibited grounds of discrimination, while race, national origin, colour, and religion were included, sex could be a qualification (Hodgetts et al. 1972, 489). The 1960 Glassco Commission, which is held to have heralded the modernization of the federal civil service, devoted only one out of the 1,198 pages in its report to women, stating that 'while there was no official discrimination against women in recruitment, selection or pay – in practice, a number of differences in the treatment of men and women could be considered discriminatory' (Morgan 1988, 13; Hodgetts et al. 1972, 489).

The formal legal treatment of married women in the federal civil service reflected a broader legislative trend in the treatment of women's employment from the mid-1950s through the 1960s. To a certain extent, Canada's international labour commitments drove this push to eradicate sex-discriminatory legislation. In 1964, Canada ratified the 1958 Discrimination (Employment and Occupational) Convention of the International Labour Organization. This instrument committed Canada to eliminating sex discrimination and promoting equal opportunity in access to and the terms and conditions of employment (Archibald 1970, 19; Hodgetts et al. 1972, 489).

Formal legal equality for women who sought employment did not, however, translate into substantive equality. According to Ursel (1992, 246), 'the elimination of women's protected status was accomplished with little debate or controversy. Legislation removing barriers to women's employment was simple and straightforward, while legislation addressing equity was weak and contradictory. This pattern revealed a legislative bias towards access rather than equity.' Basic employment standards, such as minimum wages, which initially applied only to women, were extended to men and the legislative barriers to the employment of women, especially married women, were dismantled. But women were still treated unequally. Between 1950 and 1957 Unemployment Insurance regulations disqualified married women from receiving benefits unless special requirements were met (Porter 1993). In 1956, the federal government embraced the principle of equal pay, but it did not abolish different minimum wages for men and women workers for another nine years (Ursel 1992, 246–7). Thus, employers had access to women as workers regardless of their marital status; however, women did not have access to benefits and wages equal to those of men. The uneven pace of legislative reform furthered the institutionalization of a gender order that was never able to realize fully its male breadwinner family wage norm.

Supply and demand factors account for the increased participation of married women in the labour market in general and the civil service in particular. On the supply side, there was a general increase in married women's employment. In 1955, a third of all working women were married (Hodgetts et al. 1972, 488). By the late 1950s, the value of the male wage had declined and more women sought paid employment because of the increasing need to supplement household income (Porter 1998, 175). In 1961, more married women than single women were employed and women constituted 30 per cent of the total workforce (Archibald 1970, 13). In the early 1960s, married women were making a significant contribution to the family income, preventing an erosion in the family's economic situation (Porter forthcoming).

On the demand side, the public service was expanding, but it had a hard time competing with the private sector for male employees: its wages were lower and benefits no better (Morgan 1988, 9). At the same time, the number of jobs for clerical workers was increasing. Women were the perfect candidates for these jobs, which continued to be poorly paid, were at the bottom of the civil service hierarchy, and offered almost no opportunity for advancement. Women were also more likely than men to be appointed to a temporary position (Judek 1968, 25–8). In 1967, to deal with the shortage of professional workers such as economists, statisticians, and librarians, a pilot project was adopted to encourage 'highly qualified' married women with children to enter the public service on a part-time basis (Archibald 1970, 111–12). But like temporary positions, part-time jobs did not provide the same degree of security associated with full-time positions (Archibald 1970, 118).

In the 1960s women were increasingly being hired into the federal public service, although on a basis that remained inferior to that of men. Between 1960 and 1969, the employment growth rate of women in the federal public service was higher than that of men: the feminization of the federal government's workforce had begun.

III. Feminization and Equality, 1967–1979

Canada's centenary marked several significant changes for federal government workers. First, the federal civil service was formally renamed the public service when the Public Service Employment Act replaced the Civil Service Act. This change in name signified a transformation in employment relations between the federal government and its employees, for it was accompanied by the Public Service Staff Relations Act (PSSRA), which provided the legislative framework for collective bargaining for employees of the federal government. Simultaneously, the employee associations representing the federal government's workers were reborn as the Public Service Alliance of Canada (PSAC), the union representing 78 per cent of unionized federal government employees (Lemelin 1978, 75). These changes in the nature of labour relations and employee representation in the federal public service reflected trends in the labour market as a whole: increased labour militancy in the late 1960s and the third wave of unionization as collective bargaining rights were secured throughout the federal and provincial public sectors. The extension of collective bargaining to the public sector resulted in an increased feminization of the labour movement, a 106 per cent increase in union membership for women compared to a 40 per cent increase for men between 1966 and 1976 (White 1980, 22).

Second, the Public Service Employment Act added sex to the list of prohibited grounds of discrimination, signalling a commitment to formal equality for women in the federal public service. This addition, too, reflected a broader constellation of forces at work in the Canadian political economy. In 1967, following extensive lobbying from women's groups organized through the newly formed Committee on the Equality of Women in Canada and the Fédération des Femmes de Québec, the federal government appointed the Royal Commission on the Status of Women (Findlay 1987; Vickers, Rankin, & Appelle 1993). The appointment marked the beginning of the second wave of the women's movement in Canada and coincided with the growing acceptance by the labour movement of married women who worked for wages (Porter forthcoming). Feminists inside the state, in women's organizations, and in trade unions pressured the federal government to dismantle the last remnants of discriminatory laws, practices, and policies and to develop programs to compensate for structurally entrenched gender biases in a broad range of public institutions.

Third, 1967 was the first year that employment in the public service hit the 200,000 mark, reflecting the expanding Canadian economy and the increased role of the government in the provision of social welfare. In 1968, the government introduced a short-lived freeze on public service employment. During the 1970s, federal public sector employment grew by 25 per cent, although it did not outstrip the rate of growth of either employment generally or the population (Archibald 1970, 118; Bird 1979; Morgan 1986, 61, 75). By 1978, however, the idea that the role of the central government should be limited was accepted by the leadership of the Liberal Party, the midwife of the Canadian welfare state (Vosko 1998).

The 1970s were a period of consolidation of women's position in the workforce. The labour market participation rate of married women, especially those with young children, continued to rise. To an even greater extent, women's employment income was needed to sustain the living standards of the family. The male breadwinner model, although ideologically dominant, was never very strong in Canada, due to the relatively low wages of a large proportion of men. Despite its appeal, by 1974 it was no longer an attainable reality for most working people: married women's employment had become necessary to support the new multiple-earner family (Porter 1998, 300; Ursel 1992, 236).

Despite the huge influx of women into the labour market, women continued to be crowded into a small and generally low-paid range of occupations. More than a third of women performed clerical work, while men captured the lion's share of managerial jobs (Armstrong 1984, 54). Moreover, the female norm of employment departed significantly from that of men. Women were much more likely than men to work part-time and on a temporary basis (Porter forthcoming; Vosko 1998; White 1993); they also remained crowded at the bottom of the occupational hierarchy in jobs with shorter career paths, lower wages, and worse working conditions.

These gendered labour market trends were magnified in the federal public service. Between 1970 and 1976, the rate of growth of women's employment in the federal public service (68.3 per cent) was double that of men (32.4 per cent) (Morgan 1988, 25). But the legacy of the explicitly sex-based classification scheme lived on. In her pathbreaking study on sex and the federal public service in 1970, Kathleen Archibald (1970, 19) concluded that 'these early discriminatory policies were a resounding and still redounding success; they accomplished their purposes so well that their effects are still discernable in today's employment structure.' In 1977, for example, three-quarters of the women in the federal public service performed clerical work, while only 12.5 per cent of the men did. The majority of women continued to be employed in the 'administrative support' category (58.5 per cent), in which 95 per cent of women were classified in the clerical and regulatory or secretarial, stenographic, and typing subcategories (Nichols-Heppner 1984, 61–3). In 1975, over 70 per cent of women earned less than $10,000 per year, while almost 73 per cent of men earned over $10,000 (Townson 1977, 19). Women were also located at the bottom of the public service hierarchy. In 1976, almost one-half of the men working in the federal public service had reached the managerial level, while nine-tenths of the women had not. Moreover, women continued to be overrepresented among temporary workers who were denied coverage under the relevant collective agreement (Archibald 1970, 118). In 1976, women constituted only one-third of permanent public service workers, but 48 per cent of temporary ones (Morgan 1986, 87).

Despite the increasing feminization of the federal public service, the majority of federal employees were men and men continued to dominate the higher echelons of the organizational hierarchy. These features of the federal government's workforce were reflected in the composition and structure of the Public Service Alliance of Canada (PSAC). By 1976, PSAC was the union with the third largest number of women members in Canada (51,761), although women comprised only 36 per cent of its membership. Its national leadership was predominantly male; only two of the nineteen-member national board of directors (11 per cent) were women, although women were slightly overrepresented as local presidents (39 per cent) (Warskett 1997, 188, 212, 251; White 1980, 66).

In the late 1960s and through the 1970s, collective bargaining did not provide a propitious avenue through which to address women's subordinate position in the federal public service. In part, this was due to the conservative orientation and negotiation strategies of the newly formed union (Warskett 1997, 149-52; White 1980, 43), and the dominance of men at the top of its hierarchy. However, the Alliance's failure to address the problem of women's low wages and limited job opportunities was also the result of some stringent restrictions on the scope of third-party arbitration under the Public Service Staff Relations Act (Lemelin 1978; Swimmer 1995). While the majority of federal public service employees had the right to choose between interest arbitration or mediation and conciliation followed by the right to strike as the means of resolving collective bargaining disputes, the classification system fell outside the scope of arbitration. So, too, were promotions, which allegedly were based on merit (Warskett 1997, 147–8). The classification system, while no longer explicitly discriminating against women on the basis of their sex, was founded on deeply entrenched gender biases. The Treasury Board insisted, incorrectly as subsequent legal decisions proved, that these could not be challenged by the union through collective bargaining, even if it wanted to.[2]

In the early 1970s, women's subordinate position in the federal public service was raised as a political, rather than collective bargaining, issue (Morgan 1988, 20). The second wave of the women's movement, signalled by the establishment of the Royal Commission on the Status of Women, took up the banner of equal opportunities for women workers. The Royal Commission's 1970 report was framed in the language of liberalism (Royal Commission on the Status of Women 1970, vii): the concept of equal opportunities for women workers was emphasized and extolled, while the issue of special treatment for women workers was avoided and minimized. Not only did the Royal Commission set the political discourse of the Canadian women's movement until the late 1970s, it also placed the women's movement on the strategic path of elite accommodation and legislative lobbying rather than mass mobilization and direct confrontation (Findlay 1987; Marsden 1980; Vickers et al. 1993; Warskett 1991).

In the late 1960s, the Royal Commission conducted three years of hearings across the country, received briefs, interviewed experts, and commissioned studies. It examined the position of women within the federal public service, declaring that '[t]he position of women employees in the Government of Canada deserves close examination, not only because the government employs a large number of women in a great variety of occupations, but because the government's employment practices should demonstrate its principles' (Royal Commission on the Status of Women, 105). The commission did not find different pay scales for men and women and attributed women's lower earnings in the federal public service to the fact that they were concentrated in support jobs, employed primarily as clerks, secretaries, stenographers, and typists (ibid., 108). Since women were engaged in different kinds of work from men, the commission complained that equal pay for equal work legislation in Canada, which applied only in a limited number of cases in which women's work was the same or identical to men's, was too restrictive. It recommended that the legislation be amended to reflect the intention of the International Labour Organization's (ILO) Convention 100, which speaks of 'work of equal value' (ibid., 76). The commission also noted that federal equal pay legislation did not include workers in the public service and recommended that the existing equal pay legislation be amended to cover them.

On 9 April 1969, before the Royal Commission's report was released, the Public Service Commission issued guidelines for consideration by deputy heads and directors of personnel. This move was provoked by the addition of 'sex' to the list of prohibited grounds of discrimination in the 1967 Public Service Employment Act. The guidelines set out the Public Service Commission's conception of discrimination: '[t]o make an assumption about the capability or lack of capability of a particular individual solely on the basis of group tendencies is prejudice; to act on that assumption is discrimination.' Moreover, discrimination on the basis of marital status was identified as illegitimate and 'protective paternalism' was characterized as a form of sex discrimination (Archibald 1970, 18–19). This expression of good intentions was not enough for the members of the Royal Commission: 'We do not believe that enforcement of the principle of equal pay for equal work should be left to policy or the bargaining table' (Royal Commission on the Status of Women 1970, 71). Instead, it opted for a legislative solution. After the Royal Commission's Report, the government introduced a number of initiatives with respect to its own employees. In 1971, the Office of Equal Opportunities in the Public Service was created, with a mandate not only to remove discriminatory practices in recruitment, selection, and training programs, but to promote equal opportunities for women. The next year, the federal Cabinet issued Directive 44 to all deputy ministers, asking them to take measures to promote the advancement of women to middle and upper positions (CACSW 1979; Morgan 1988, 24). These initiatives were more symbolic than effective. While women were recruited for managerial training, the huge growth rate in women's public service employment, rather than the special efforts of either the government or the Public Service Commission, accounted for their increased representation in managerial positions (Morgan 1988, 25).

Implementing the Royal Commission's recommendations was the primary goal of the Canadian women's movement until the late 1970s. Middle-class professional and highly educated women used their connections with the federal Liberal Party, which had appointed the Royal Commission, to obtain government funding to bring five hundred women from across the country together for a 'Strategy for Change Conference' in Toronto in 1972. The result was the establishment of the National Action

Committee on the Status of Women (NAC), an umbrella organization of women's groups. At its inception, the NAC included both older, middle-class women's groups, such as the National Council of Women (Griffiths 1993), and the newer women's liberation movement, which arose out of the student and anti-war groups of the late 1960s. It was explicitly non-partisan and adopted a lobbying approach (Bashevkin 1998, 39; Marsden 1980; Vickers et al. 1993).

Equal pay for work of equal value was one of the NAC's chief concerns. Support for the principle was also found outside of the women's movement: it had been endorsed by the Royal Commission, had been the official policy of the ILO since 1951 (Convention 100), a March 1971 Gallup poll indicated that 87 per cent of the Canadian population supported equal pay (Warskett 1991, 180), and it was perfectly consistent with the principles of liberal capitalism. In the spring of 1973, the Liberal government revealed that it had quietly ratified Convention 100 in the fall of the preceding year.

International Women's Year, 1975, was a crucial one for women in the federal public service. A number of contradictory policies converged that laid the basis both for the achievement by women workers of legal rights to equal pay and equal job opportunities and for the economic realignment that would undermine their prospects for substantive equality. The NAC mounted a campaign to enshrine the principle of equal pay for work of equal value in the law and the next year the Canadian Labour Congress, the largest organization of unions in Canada, embraced equal rights feminism and endorsed the concept of equal value (Warskett 1993, 253).

The NAC wanted the equal value provision to be put in the Canada Labour Code, since the Department of Labour had monitoring and enforcement powers. More importantly, it demanded a mechanism to overcome the difficulty presented by the fact that men and women performed different jobs. The result of the NAC's intensive lobbying campaign was a compromise and the equal value provisions became a part of the Canadian Human Rights Act. As a means for redressing women's low pay, section 11 of the Canadian Human Rights Act had two structural features: it accepted job evaluation as the mechanism for measuring the value of jobs and it was complaint-based.[3] It did not, however, provide much guidance about how to measure a job's value or to compare different jobs. The legislation, which received royal assent on 14 July 1977, came into force on 1 March 1978 (Warskett 1991, 178–80).

At the same time that the NAC was pursuing a legislative strategy of equal pay for work of equal value, the federal government pushed forward on the equal opportunity front. In November 1975, the president of the Treasury Board, Jean Chrétien, sent a new message to the bureaucracy; 'within a reasonable time frame' the representation of men and women throughout the federal public service should correspond to the proportion of qualified candidates of both sexes. This policy, called Equal Opportunity for Women, emphasized assisting individuals rather than eliminating discriminatory policies (Public Service Commission 1985, 6).

The Public Service Commission's resistance to the Treasury Board directive was immediate and unequivocal, issuing a pre-emptive strike against the adoption of a strong affirmative action policy. In its 1976 Annual Report, the Commission stated that 'it was of the view that this approach would be undesirable and impractical; and that it would conflict with merit and pose unanswerable questions' (Morgan 1988, 40; Townson 1977, 23).

Paradoxically, the most vociferous opposition to the principle of proportional representation of women throughout the public service hierarchy took the form of a defence of the merit principle. The Special Committee on the Review of Personnel Management and the Merit Principle reported in 1979 that many managers could not reconcile the merit principle with directives on equal opportunities (Canada, Special Committee on the Review of Personnel Management and the Merit Principle 1979; Morgan 1988, 40). The history of how merit, which facilitated the employment of women, gave way to explicit discrimination against women seems to have been erased from the Public Service Commission's institutional memory, as merit was now invoked against what were perceived to be policies preferential to women.

The Treasury Board preferred the equal opportunity approach for resolving the problem of women public service workers' low pay to that of equal pay for work of equal value. One benefit of the equal opportunity strategy was that it placed responsibility on the Public Service Commission, the agency in charge of hiring and promotions. As the department responsible for negotiating collective agreements for government workers, the Treasury Board was adverse to any policy which, like equal pay for work of equal value, was likely to result in an increase in the overall government wage bill.

This was especially true in 1975, when the Liberal government identified wage increases as the cause of unacceptably high inflation. In order to break what it portrayed as an inflationary spiral, the Liberal government introduced the Anti-Inflation Act, which imposed wage and price controls throughout the Canadian economy and signalled the adoption of monetarist economic policies (Maslove & Swimmer 1980; Panitch & Swartz 1993, 28). While the wages of federal public service workers were not singled out (the controls also applied to wages in the private sector and to prices generally), their increases were significantly below those of workers in the provincial public sectors and the private sector (Maslove & Swimmer 1980, 9; Nicols-Heppner 1984, 90). Moreover, the Anti-Inflation Program, which extended collective agreements for two years and suspended unions' right to strike during that period, came at a time when federal public service unions, including the PSAC, were increasingly opting for the conciliation and strike mechanism instead of the compulsory arbitration route to resolve collective bargaining disputes (Swimmer 1995, 382).

Broader trends in federal public service employment and the Liberal government's economic orientation boded ill for women workers' claim to improved career chances and equal pay. The expansion of the federal public service ground to a halt; between 1977 and 1978 employment in the federal public service dropped slightly (1.3 per cent), while the following year's decline was even steeper (4.4 per cent). Even more significant was the fact that the Liberal government, long associated with publicly provided services and with playing an interventionist role in the economy and labour market, was beginning to embrace a policy of less government. At the 1978 Group of Seven Economic Summit in Bonn, Prime Minister Trudeau committed the federal government to a policy of reducing government spending and limiting the role of the state in the economy. As part of the reduction program, the federal government announced that it was eliminating 5,000 jobs in the public service. The Liberals began to rein in public service employment, although unlike the Tories, they did not make much of it ideologically (Lee & Hobbs 1996, 339; Sutherland 1987, 58).

The 1978 equal pay for work of equal value provisions in the Canadian Human Rights Act exemplified both the strengths and limits of the second wave of feminism and created an opportunity for PSAC to pursue equal value complaints for its members in the context of wage controls on public sector workers. Lorna Marsden (1980, 257), the NAC's president during its lobbying efforts for equal pay for work of equal value, stated that 'there was no attempt to build mass support for the concept, to sell it to the private sector or even unions. All the focus was on changing the law.' Once the concept was enacted, the NAC considered its job to be done; the question of implementation was left to the specific workplace parties. Nor did the NAC take an official position on the Anti-Inflation Program, despite its potential negative impact on women's wages. According to Vickers et al. (1993, 86), the executive was divided over the NAC's public involvement in this issue, prefiguring what would become a deeper conflict between 'those representing left-ist or working-class feminism and those representing a more traditional status-of-women orientation.'

PSAC was galvanized by the equal pay for work of equal value provisions in the Canadian Human Rights Act to demand wage increases for its women members. Until 1978, the Alliance had taken very little action with respect to the subordinate position of its women members, both in the workplace and in the union. At its 1979 triennial convention, however, PSAC delegates unanimously adopted a policy paper on equal value that identified the problem of women's low pay as a systemic one, requiring a collective rather than an individual response. The policy paper recommended that equal pay for work of equal value be pursued for its women members both through formal complaints to the Canadian Human Rights Commission (CHRC) and by collective bargaining. In February 1979, PSAC filed the first group complaint to the CHRC on behalf of predominantly female librarians, who, it charged, earned an average of 20 per cent less than the predominantly male historical researchers. PSAC argued that the two groups did work of equal value (Cornish 1986, 18–19; Warskett 1991, 181–2).

The Treasury Board opposed bargaining about equal value because it wanted to maintain exclusive managerial control over classifications and evaluation, as it was entitled to do under the relevant collective bargaining legislation. Also, it was concerned that an equal pay settlement with the librarians would have a ripple effect throughout the federal public service, thereby jeopardizing its policy of keeping a lid on federal government workers' wages. Instead of risking a confrontation, PSAC opted to seek redress through a legal avenue (Warskett 1991, 183). This proved remarkably successful. With the CHRC's assistance, PSAC reached a settlement with the Treasury Board which resulted in $2.3 million being distributed to 470 of its members. Individual librarians received salary increases ranging from $500 to $6,000, as well as annual adjustments to ensure that equality was maintained as new collective agreements were negotiated (Cornish 1986, 19; Warskett 1991, 183).

During the 1970s, the Liberal government responded to the demands of the women's movement and to the reconfiguration of the gender order caused by the feminization of labour by introducing the principle of equal pay for work of equal value in legislation and embracing equal opportunities policies for its own women workers. But by the end of the 1970s, it was obvious that formal equality was not enough to remedy the discrimination that continued to disadvantage women in the labour market. CACSW (1980, 1, 40) reported that 'the situation of women in the federal Public Service remains remarkably unchanged,' despite the fact that the relatively buoyant economy and the wide range of new social programs resulted in a 75 per cent growth in the federal public service between 1965 and 1977. Lacking the force of law and without a clear structure of implementation and accountability, such policies had virtually no impact.

Even when women's right to equal treatment in employment was embodied in law, there was no guarantee that this would result in sub-stantive improvements for women workers. Legal rights are not self-enforcing; to be effective they must be backed by significant resources. The Treasury Board refused to negotiate equal pay for work of equal value with the unions representing its employees, forcing them to bring time-consuming and costly legal complaints. Moreover, the prohibitions against discrimination on the basis of sex, while an important political victory, did not address the range of policies and practices that, while not explicitly discriminatory on the basis of sex, had a discriminatory impact on women workers. For example, a 1978 study by the Office of Equal Opportunities for Women in the Public Service Commission examined salary increases awarded to occupational groups within the public service. Although it found no evidence of overt sex discrimina-tion in awarding wage increases over the ten-year period it analysed, it discovered a widening gap between the highest and lowest salary levels in each group, which was a result of the practice of awarding across-the-board percentage increases. On its face, this practice was gender-neu-tral. But as women were disproportionately represented in the lowest pay levels of each group, it increased the wage gap between men and women public service workers. Despite this finding, the practice of per-centage wage increases continued (ibid., 12).

By the late 1970s, there was some indication that the federal govern-ment's new commitment to austerity would have a detrimental impact upon women's struggle for equality in the public service. The federal government began to rely more heavily on temporary help agencies for clerical and secretarial staff, increasing the pool of jobs that were inse-cure and poorly paid. A number of other belt-tightening policies had negative consequences for women workers who already had jobs, as well as threatening the possibility of substantial improvements for women in the public service (CACSW 1979, 19–20, 38, 41; CACSW 1984, 40).

In the face of the limitations of formal equality, the women's movement and its allies within trade unions demanded substantive equality, or equity, to deal with the problem of women's low pay and bad jobs. Systemic and adverse impact, as opposed to explicit discrimination were increasingly the targets of complaints. However, the attack on the public service as one of the primary causes of the federal government's fiscal crisis fell outside traditional legal remedies and threatened to undermine the possibility of future progress.

IV. Privatization and Equity, 1980–1990

The contradiction between equality and monetarist economic policies latent in the late 1970s deepened throughout the 1980s. When the decade began, the Liberals were able to contain it. But their commitment to substantive equality in the face of profound pressure for economic restructuring was not tested; they lost power in 1984. By the time the Conservative government won its second consecutive federal election in 1988, privatization had eclipsed substantive equality as the dominant discourse in Canadian politics.

The Liberal government made good on its promise to promote women's equal rights and the early 1980s mark the apogee of success for the second wave of feminism. The NAC played a crucial role in the legal institutionalization of women's equality rights, the most prominent being the guarantee of sex equality in the Canadian constitution in 1982.[4] The Liberal government appointed Judge Rosalie Abella to head a Royal Commission on Equality of Employment to look at ways to achieve greater equality for groups historically discriminated against in the labour market. Prime Minister Trudeau also appointed the first woman, Bertha Wilson, to the Supreme Court of Canada. As the decade progressed, the highest court adopted a broader, substantive, less formal approach to sex discrimination, overturning outright or limiting a number of decisions from the 1970s that had restricted women's rights. By the 1984 election, the NAC had enough political capital to sponsor a nationally televised all-party leaders' debate on women's issues. The political appeal of women's equal treatment in employment was so strong that during the debate the leaders of the federal Liberal, Tory and New Democratic Parties each endorsed equal pay for work of equal value (Bashevkin 1998, 38, 85–7, 143–4; Bogart 1994, 147, 249; Day & Brodsky 1998, 54–67).

Although equality was prominent in the Liberal government's political agenda, the monetarist economic policies that it had begun to implement struck a deeper chord and had a more profound impact. Business reaction to Finance Minister MacEachen's 1981 reform budget, the last gasp of the already weak Canadian version of Keynesianism, persuaded the Liberal government that it was necessary to take a harder line in restructuring the Canadian economy (Porter forthcoming). It responded to the recession of 1981–2 by targeting its own workers for wage restraint, imposing wage controls, and suspending collective bargaining rights for two years in 1982 (Panitch & Swartz 1988, 85; Swimmer 1995, 382). The Treasury Board also insisted that it had the right to designate a government employee as essential, and thus prohibited from participating in an otherwise lawful strike. PSAC went twice to the Supreme Court of Canada to challenge these restrictions on the rights of its members to engage in collective action and was disappointed both times. In 1982, the court refused to impose any legal limits on the Treasury Board's right to designate public service workers as essential, thereby allowing the government to make a mockery of the right to strike. Later, it upheld the constitutionality of the federal government's wage control legislation, deciding that neither collective bargaining rights nor the freedom to strike were protected by the Charter's guarantee of freedom of association (Panitch & Swartz 1988, 56–66, 73–6). In marked contrast to its decisions on equality rights during the 1980s, the Supreme Court's judgments did not impose legal constraints on the government's ability to roll back workers' rights (Bakan 1997; Mandel 1994).

The deep recession of the early 1980s consolidated concerns about the need for economic restructuring (MacDonald 1995). In 1982, Donald Macdonald, a former Liberal finance minister, was appointed to preside over the Royal Commission on the Economic Union and Development Prospects for Canada, which was asked to assess the country's economic prospects and to suggest how the government should retool the economy to meet the global challenges of the future. As the decade progressed, the Tories would reap the seeds of restructuring sown by the Liberals.

The federal public service encapsulated the tension between the Liberal government's commitments to substantive equality, on the one hand, and to monetarism, on the other. In its 1980 Throne Speech, the

government announced that it was committed to affirmative action programs for women, the disabled, and Aboriginal peoples in public service
(Morgan 1988, 49). Two pilot projects designed to increase the number
of women in specific departments were introduced. In 1983, the Public
Service Commission accepted the need to adopt numerical targets to
ensure that women made it into the ranks of senior management and
Herb Gray, president of the Treasury Board, announced that a formal
affirmative action policy would govern the public service (Knopff 1989,
39; Morgan 1988, 49-51; Swimmer & Gollesch 1986). Finally, the federal government supported proportional representation of designated
groups, including women, as the solution to systemic discrimination.
The problem with this policy was its timing; it was unlikely to be successful in a period the chairman of the Public Service Commission characterized as one of 'continued restraint and cutback in public administration'
(Edgar Gallant, quoted by CACSW 1980, 44).

The decade began with a strike by fifty thousand federal clerks, three-
quarters of whom were women. Although it did not result in any break-
throughs in the clerks' collective agreement, the strike crystallized
women's growing militance within the federal public service. Women's
unequal pay became a major issue for PSAC; women increasingly took
on leadership roles in the union; and women's committees and conferences began to play an important role in formulating the PSAC's general policies (Cuneo 1993, 124; White 1993, 130).

In the early 1980s, winning the legal battle was first on PSAC's list of
pay equity priorities. Its strategy was to lodge group complaints under
the equal pay for work of equal value provisions of the Canadian
Human Rights Act. Wage controls legislation and the Treasury Board's
refusal to negotiate equal pay, combined with the union's success with
several group equal pay complaints – especially the librarians and the
general service workers in cafeterias and laundries – convinced PSAC
that litigation was the best way to improve women members' pay. On 19
December 1984 PSAC filed a complaint with the Canadian Human
Rights Tribunal for its Clerical and Regulatory Group, 80 per cent of
whom were women. By the end of 1984, PSAC was pursuing equal pay
complaints on behalf of approximately 65,000 members (one-third of its
entire membership and two-thirds of its women members) (Warskett
1991, 185).

The union movement also began to pay greater attention to women's
demands for equality. In 1984, the CLC adopted a policy paper on
women and affirmative action that attacked the ideology of the family

wage and the 'myth that men are the breadwinners.' In addition to proposing a wide range of measures to improve women's wages, including equal pay for work of equal value, it argued for the need to break down occupational segregation (Warskett 1993, 253–4).

The election of the Conservative government in 1984 marked an ideological turning point in Canada. For the first time, the public sector, especially the 'swollen bureaucracy,' was targeted as a general political problem. Despite the fact that between 1960 and 1982 the proportion of jobs provided by government employment had changed little in relation either to the share of the total labour force or to the growth in the total population (Bird 1979; Sutherland 1987, 46), Prime Minister Mulroney pledged to give public servants 'pink slips and running shoes' (Lee & Hobbs 1996, 337, 340; Sutherland 1987, 41). Once elected, the Conservative government vowed to hold the line on its workers' wages and announced that the number of federal employees would be reduced by 15,000 over five years (Swimmer 1995, 388). The Tories also introduced 'privatization' into the Canadian political lexicon. While the term initially referred to the selling of government enterprises and services to the private sector, privatization came to represent a much broader range of practices – including commercialization and contracting out – united in the assumption that private provision for profit was more efficient than a public service (Cameron 1997, 12).

The Conservative government's emphasis on reducing the size of the public sector and restricting the role of the state was moderated by a commitment to employment equity, the Canadian term for affirmative action. In part, this was a political legacy of the former Liberal government. In 1985, the equality rights in the Charter of Rights and Freedoms, which specifically permitted affirmative action, came into effect, and Judge Abella issued her report on equality in employment, which coined the term employment equity. The Conservative government responded by implementing most of the employment equity policies recommended in the report. In addition to strengthening the Treasury Board's affirmative action program in the public service, it introduced the Employment Equity Act, which covered federally regulated undertakings and the Federal Contractors Compliance program (Knopff 1989, 63). The legislation monitored the attempts of federal enterprises to achieve proportional representation for target groups through a public reporting mechanism. It did not impose numerical targets or quotas.

The government faced a critical dilemma: how to promote the employment of women and other disadvantaged groups while simultaneously reducing the size of the federal public service. In 1988, Treasury Board President Pat Carney established a Task Force on Barriers to Women in the Public Service, with the goal of finding ways to increase women's representation at all levels in the organizational hierarchy. The problem, however, was no longer discriminatory practices and policies, but the climate of overall restraint. While the promotion rate of women was higher than that of men, the overall promotion rate had declined. As a result of the employment equity policies, women were, to some extent, sheltered from the full impact of the restraint policies (Canada, Task Force on Barriers to Women in the Public Service 1990; Loney 1998, 184–92; Morgan 1988, 53, 50; Swimmer & Gollesch 1986, 246–7).

Pay equity, however, was less popular than employment equity with the federal government. The Macdonald Commission warned that pay equity would simply reduce the number of jobs (Armstrong & Armstrong 1988, 79). The Treasury Board attempted to exert greater control over the pay equity process. On 8 March 1985, International Women's Day, it announced that all thirteen unions within the public service had agreed to work together on achieving pay equity through a joint union-management committee that would undertake a government-wide study of the wage gap. During this process, the equal pay complaints before the Canadian Human Rights Commission would be held in abeyance. However, PSAC insisted on the right to reinstitute the complaints if the Joint Committee process did not work out to its satisfaction (Warskett 1991, 185–6).

The process was riven with conflict in the form both of technical disputes over the evaluation and comparison of specific jobs and more explicit political skirmishes over issues of representation on the evaluation committees and allegations of bias. It took five years for the Treasury Board and public service unions to complete the study. In the meantime, the Human Rights Commission released guidelines for applying equal pay for equal value. But before the unions and the Treasury Board could agree upon a statistical method for analysing the data, PSAC withdrew from the process and reactivated its complaints with the Human Rights Commission. It estimated, based on the study's results, that its members were owed billions of dollars in retroactive equal pay adjustments, as well as an amount that averaged out to a 15 per cent wage increase overall (about $250 million per year in future adjustments) (ibid., 196–7). Litigation looked more promising than negotiation.

The Treasury Board's response was to announce both the results of the study and the pay adjustments it was willing to make ($316 million in back pay and $766 million a year). The retroactive payments were one-quarter of those advocated by PSAC and about one-third of the amount the union claimed was needed to remedy the problem in the future (ibid., 187). PSAC rejected the Treasury Board's offer and insisted on pursuing the legal complaints.

Generally, the Conservative government's bark was worse than its bite when it came to public service workers during the 1980s.[5] But its political rhetoric, especially its emphasis on privatization, prefigured a larger political and economic realignment. This became apparent in the 1988 federal election, which was fought over the need for, and benefits of, free trade with the United States. To its critics in English Canada, free trade signalled both a loss of national sovereignty and the dismantling of the Canadian welfare state. The NAC's intervention during the 1988 election reflected the broader political reconfiguration. Marjorie Cohen challenged free trade orthodoxy on the NAC's behalf, arguing that health care, equal pay, and unemployment insurance benefits were threatened by a more market-driven, privatized economy modelled on that found in the United States. The 1988 election accelerated the NAC's transformation from a liberal lobbying group that deployed the techniques of elite accommodation to achieve equal rights for women to a protest movement that sought to mobilize mass opposition to the Conservative government's policies of privatization and economic restructuring (Bashevkin 1998, 88–9; MacDonald 1995, 2009; Vickers et al. 1993, 143).

The rapidly restructuring economy and the related political collapse of welfare state liberalism brought new hardships for the majority of women. Second-wave feminism caught fire in an expanding economy, but its momentum was difficult to sustain in one that was in decline. As Johanna Brenner (1993, 103) put it, the dilemmas facing women in the new gender order could not be resolved through expanding the definition of sex discrimination. By the end of the 1980s, the women's movement had reached the limits of equality rights and its response was to endorse more radical economic and political demands. However, the combination of economic stagnation and labour market polarization that marked the end of the 1980s and the beginning of the 1990s fuelled competition in the economy and fragmentation of political discourse.

After narrowly winning a majority of seats in the 1988 election, the Tory government was in no mood to forgive earlier slights. The NAC was punished almost immediately; in 1989 the government cut its funding by over 50 per cent in two years and the Tories became the first government in the NAC's fifteen-year history to refuse to meet with NAC representatives during the annual Parliament Hill lobby (Bashevkin 1998, 124; Vickers et al. 1993, 288–9). REAL Women, which since 1984 had advocated the return to a more traditional sexual division of labour in the form of 'family values,' was allocated funding by the federal government in 1989. This organization had close ties with the Family Caucus, a group of thirty five social conservatives who held seats as Tory MPs (Bashevkin 1998, 190). The NAC's status as the pre-eminent organization representing women was thus challenged by groups that rejected an equality rights agenda for women. Not only was the economy being restructured, the backlash against equality rights for women had begun.

On the surface, the federal state's role as an employer changed from a benevolent patriarch in the 1960s to a champion of sexual equality in the 1980s (Ursel 1992, 292). But this characterization is only valid at the level of official legal discourse. Since the mid-1980s, the federal government has contracted work out, reduced the size of its workforce, imposed wage controls, suspended collective bargaining rights, and systematically resisted the equal pay for work of equal value complaints brought by the union representing the largest number of its women workers.

V. The Equity Backlash, 1991–2001

By the 1990s, the pattern of women's labour market participation more closely resembled that of men and the gap between men's and women's wages had narrowed. But this convergence was not a cause for celebration; in part, it was propelled by the deteriorating employment experiences and prospects of men. In the 1980s, for the first time since the early 1930s, men's average annual wages declined as they lost relatively good unionized jobs in the primary labour market. Women did not fare as badly only because they started from a lower position and did not have as much to lose. It was precisely the types of jobs historically associated with women, non-standard (part-time and temporary) jobs in small, non-union firms in the service sector, that proliferated during the 1980s and early 1990s. More women were competing on an equal basis with men, although the majority of women continued to be employed in female-dominated sectors that tended to be low paid with poor benefits and minimal job security. The decline in men's wages and the increase in women's labour market participation meant that dual-earner families were the norm; by the mid-1990s they comprised seven out of ten families. The male breadwinner employment model was no longer viable (Armstrong 1996a; Fudge 1997; Gunderson 1998; Lipsett & Reesor 1997; Picot & Heisz 2000; Rashid 1993; Scott & Lochhead 1997).

These changes did not simply reflect the supply of labour (the increased participation of women, especially those with young children), but involved the structure of the labour market. Throughout the 1980s, workers were taught to accept a deteriorating standard of employment for the sake of increasing flexibility in the face of global competition (Stanford 1996). The need for workers to 'lower their expectations' and for Canadians 'to tighten their belts' was a central theme of the Tories' political rhetoric during Mulroney's second mandate. The recession of the early 1990s underscored the urgency of this message. Moreover, economic restructuring fuelled resentment both against public sector workers and employment equity.

The government targeted its own workers for restraint. Michael Wilson announced in his 26 February 1991 budget speech that the government would not tolerate wage increases for its employees in excess of 3 per cent, and he threatened to legislate the right to contract out public service work (Warskett 1997, 285). The budget made a mockery out of the collective bargaining process. Moreover, the harsh treatment by the government of its employees was unwarranted; since 1985 they had received the lowest wages of any public or private sector grouping of employees (Panitch & Swartz 1993, 92). But the Tories had a great deal of support for the imposition of wage controls on its own employees; not only did the International Monetary Fund endorse it, a January 1991 poll commissioned by the Finance Department indicated that 89 per cent of the respondents supported it (Swimmer & Kinaschuk 1992, 270, 284–7).

In June 1991, the Treasury Board upped the ante by tightening wage controls, claiming that there would be no increase in the first year, to be followed by 3 per cent in each of two subsequent years. On 9 September the union called its first nation-wide strike involving all of its components – the largest strike by a single union in Canadian history. Strike support among PSAC members was high. When Parliament was reconvened on 16 September, the government introduced back-to-work legislation that also imposed wage controls (0 and 3 per cent wage increases) and introduced heavy fines (up to $100,000 a day) for defying the law. The day PSAC held a huge rally on Parliament Hill to protest the legislation, the Public Service Staff Relations Board released its decision ruling

that the government had not bargained in good faith. While this decision had little legal effect, since all the government had to do was
resume negotiations, it contributed to a shift in public opinion. Moreover, it was increasingly difficult to portray government workers as over-
paid, since 30 per cent of PSAC's membership, most of whom were
women, earned below $27,000. Although negotiations resumed briefly,
the government remained intransigent on the issue of wage controls,
offering a $500 signing bonus only to the lowest-paid employees. On 2
October the strike ended when the government's draconian wage control and back-to-work legislation came into effect (Lee & Hobbs 1996,
343; Panitch & Swartz 1993, 93–4; Swimmer 1995, 389, 398–404; Swimmer & Kinaschuk 1992, 287–92).

The deteriorating relations between the federal government and
PSAC spilled over into the pay equity process. Early in 1990, the Treasury Board announced that it was making a down payment on pay
equity, offering about $360 million in back pay to be shared among the
70,000 employees covered by PSAC's largest complaint. In 1991, the government tried to derail PSAC's pay equity complaint by going to the
Federal Court to challenge the jurisdiction of the Canadian Human
Rights Tribunal to hear it (Warskett 1997, 283–4).[6] When this challenge
was unsuccessful and the hearings on the largest of the equal value complaints began, the government demonstrated that it was prepared to
override its employees' legal rights to equal pay in the name of expenditure control. In his 25 February, 1992 budget speech, Finance Minister
Don Mazankowski announced that the government would not make any
retroactive pay equity adjustments beyond November 1990, despite the
fact that several of PSAC's equal value complaints before human rights
tribunals, including the largest, dated back to 1984 (Swimmer & Kinaschuk 1992, 298).

During the 1993 federal election, PSAC joined with other unions and
organizations such as the NAC to fight against the Tories' policies of
privatization and contracting out (Swimmer 1995, 393–8; Warskett
1993). The Liberal Party promised a change from the bellicose stance of
the Tories; in addition to greater prosperity and more jobs, it stressed a
long-term commitment to promoting equality. It also held itself out as a
friend to the public sector. Liberal Party leader Jean Chrétien pledged
that his government would honour the impending Human Rights Tribunal ruling on equal pay for work of equal value for 70,000 government employees (May 1998). The message that it was not necessary to
downsize the federal public service was broadcast by Liberal candidates

in Ottawa ridings that had a high proportion of public servants (Lee & Hobbs 1996, 344).

Political fragmentation along regional lines and within the right, as much as the Liberal Party's social welfare platform, contributed to its victory in the 1993 election. Once in power, Liberal political priorities changed and the government's primary focus became the reduction of the deficit. Although the Tories lost the 1993 election, almost self-destructing in the process, they won the larger ideological battle. The Liberal government reneged on most of its election promises, justifying its deficit-fighting stance by reference to the dictates of the global economy. It turned on its own employees in order to symbolize its determination to cut the deficit. This time, the government not only sacrificed its employees' collective bargaining rights, it invoked the debt and taxes to trump their legal right to equal pay.

In his February 1994 budget, Finance Minister Paul Martin announced that the Conservative government's wage controls, due to expire in 1995, would be extended for another two years. While the controls were largely symbolic as deficit-cutting measures, since personnel costs are a negligible cost of the federal government's budget, they were ideologically crucial: they targeted the public sector as a problem in need of restraint (Swimmer, Hicks, & Milne 1995, 193–4). In its complaint to the ILO that the federal government was violating its members' right to bargain collectively, PSAC documented how the 1994 controls were but the latest instalment in the campaign, first begun in 1981 by the Liberals, to retrench public sector workers' rights (ILO 1995; Panitch & Swartz 1998).

The Liberal government was much more successful than its predecessor at reducing the size of the federal public service workforce. Within sixteen months of taking power it cut employment in the public service by the equivalent of 15,000 full-time positions (compared to the Conservative government's reduction of 3,968 positions between 1985 and 1993). In 1995, the Liberal government broke its 1993 election promise to preserve the size of the public sector when Finance Minster Paul Martin announced in the federal budget that an additional 45,000 jobs in the public service would be eliminated over three years (Lee & Hobbs 1996, 355, 356).

The Liberal government successfully portrayed its primary responsibility as putting the country's economic house in order, which meant, above all else, reducing and eliminating the deficit. In this context, it might be necessary, even legitimate, for the equality rights of some to be compromised on behalf of the greater good, especially if equality entailed government spending. The Supreme Court of Canada accepted this argument in a couple of leading equality rights cases in which it decided that the government's fiscal concerns could limit equality (Day & Brodsky 1998, 82–9). Equality rights had a diminished political and legal currency once government restraint was accepted as orthodoxy. This was even true for women's organizations to which the Liberal Party historically had close ties. The 1995 budget, decried by the NAC for the negative effect that the proposed cut in federal public service employment would have on women workers, also slashed the organization's funding. More dramatically, the Liberal government stopped funding the Advisory Council on the Status of Women, an agency the Liberal Party had established twenty years earlier (Bashevkin 1998, 224–5).

The extent to which economic efficiency and equality were posed as trade-offs, with the former outweighing the latter, is best illustrated by the Liberal government's handling of PSAC's largest equal pay complaint. The union estimated that the legal strategy was the best option and its primary challenge was to persuade its members not to succumb to the government's offers. The government, by contrast, wanted to negotiate a settlement to the complaint, especially after the Human Rights Tribunal ruled that the PSAC-Treasury Board joint committee study initiated in 1985 could be used as the basis for the evaluation of male and female jobs and that any award made would go back to 1983, the year before the complaint was filed.[7]

A month before the writ was dropped for the 1997 election, the Liberal government offered PSAC $1 billion to settle its largest pay equity complaint. The union rejected the offer on the ground that it represented only about 65 per cent of the retroactive pay due under the methodology selected by the Human Rights Tribunal, and it pestered Liberal candidates and cabinet ministers during the 1997 election. After it was returned to office, the Liberal government renewed its offer to settle the complaint. It hired Mary Eberts, a well-known women's rights advocate and lawyer who was active in the campaign to entrench equality rights in the Canadian Charter of Rights, to negotiate on its behalf. The government increased its offer to $1.3 billion, but negotiations broke down. Eberts and the government portrayed the union's demands as outlandishly expensive, claiming that PSAC had upped its demand from $2 billion to more than $5 billion (Bourrie 1998).

On 28 July 1998, thirteen years after PSAC filed the complaint, the Canadian Human Rights Tribunal issued a 200-page decision, the culmination of 295 days of hearings.[8] Together with the Canadian Human

Rights Commission the union was able to convince the tribunal about the appropriate methodology for comparing men and women's work and wages. While the tribunal did not decide the amount of money the government needed to pay its workers in order to meet its obligations under the law, it was obvious that the sum was substantially more than the government had offered. It also ruled that the adjustments would go back to March 1985 and that the federal government was obligated to pay interest on the back pay.

The government was lucky that the decision was released when Parliament was not in session. It had thirty days in which to decide whether or not to appeal, enough time to test the political winds by releasing some trial balloons. Its strategy was twofold: to emphasize both the cost of the decision and its shaky legal foundation. Marcel Massé, the president of the Treasury Board, speculated that the decision could cost $7 billion (May 1998), although PSAC claimed that the pay equity bill was about half that. Darryl Bean, PSAC's national president, said that Ottawa could afford to pay for it out of the anticipated surplus. The Prime Minister waded into the public debate, informing the national press that if his government complied with the pay equity ruling, it would not be able to pump more money into health care: '[T]here's only so much money unless you increase taxes. So you have to decide the priorities' (Greenspon 1998a). The government had reason to believe that when it came to a choice between tax increases and pay equity, few Canadians would opt for the latter. A poll commissioned by the Treasury Board the winter before the tribunal's ruling indicated that although more than three-quarters of respondents said the government must do 'whatever is necessary' to ensure pay equity, support fell to 39 per cent when they were asked how they would feel if pay equity would mean higher taxes (Greenspon 1998b).

The government was also quick to emphasize that the meaning of pay equity was contentious; according to Mr Massé, 'different judges in different courts have given a different definition of equality' (McCarthy & Sallot 1998). Prime Minister Chrétien stressed the need for greater certainty in this area of the law, pointing to the March 1998 decision of Mr Justice Muldoon of the Federal Court in the dispute between Bell and the union representing its predominantly female telephone operators and clerks. In that case the judge adopted a direct comparison methodology that not only reduced Bell's pay equity liability but was similar to that rejected by the Canadian Human Rights Tribunal in the PSAC complaint.[9] The Reform Party critic urged the government to appeal the tribunal's decision, claiming that if Muldoon's methodology was used, the pay equity bill would only be about $100 million (Aubry 1998).

Most of the editorials and columns in the daily press emphasized the cost of the decision, the unfair burden it imposed on taxpayers, and the inutility of any mechanism other than the market to determine the value of work. The *Ottawa Sun* (30 July 1998) complained that 'equal pay for equal work has always been a mug's game'; it punishes taxpayers, who are guilty of nothing, 'for perceived inequities of the past.' According to the *Globe and Mail* (1 August 1998d), 'trying to adjudicate fairness is the fundamental flaw with the decision.' The *Ottawa Citizen* (7 August 1998), however, refused to accept an interpretation of the ruling that pitted pay equity against the taxpayer, asserting that it was in the public interest for the government to live up to legal principles. The union also tried to shame the government into accepting the tribunal's decision by emphasizing the low wages of its women members, contrasting them with high-placed bureaucrats to whom the government had just paid substantial bonuses, and calling upon the prime minister to honour his 1993 election promise to uphold the Human Rights Tribunal's decision (Leblanc 1998d).

On 28 August 1998, an uncomfortable-looking Justice Minister Anne McLellan announced the government's decision to appeal the Human Rights Tribunal's ruling to the Federal Court. She reiterated her government's commitment to 'the principle of paying women and men equally for work of equal value,' but claimed that the government was obligated to go all the way to the Supreme Court of Canada to clarify how the Treasury Board should calculate equal pay. She also promised to review the equal pay legislation. Massé was blunt; he claimed that the decision overcompensated women workers and that it was necessary to appeal in order to protect taxpayers' interests. He invited the union to negotiate and the Justice Minister offered to drop the appeal if the union agreed to a settlement (Eggerton 1998).

The Liberal government simultaneously continued to declare its support for the principle of pay equity while refusing to put that principle into practice. This position simply reflected that of the majority of Canadians. A poll commissioned by the Treasury Board indicated that of the 1,510 people questioned, 85 per cent felt that money was not an issue when it came to providing equal pay for work of equal value in the federal public service. However, almost half of the respondents said that the settlement imposed by the tribunal was 'too much' and agreed with the government's decision to appeal the ruling (Leblanc 1998b).

Once the appeal was underway, the government sweetened its pay equity offer at the negotiating table to $1.3 billion (Leblanc 1998c). The union and the government agreed to special pay equity adjustments for the six predominantly female groups affected by the decision, although the parties agreed that these payments would not be characterized as pay equity. PSAC's determination to give full force and effect to the tribunal's decision was given a boost in November 1998, when a unanimous Federal Court of Appeal overturned Justice Muldoon's decision in the case involving Bell Canada and the union representing the predominantly female telephone operators.[10]

The effect of the Federal Court of Appeal's decision was to undermine the legal rationale for the federal government's decision to appeal the ruling of the Human Rights Tribunal regarding PSAC's complaint. Despite this, Massé insisted that the government would not drop its appeal (Leblanc 1998b). It was not until August 1999, after the Supreme Court of Canada dismissed Bell's final attempt at an appeal, that the government changed its tune. It claimed that the *Bell* case was not relevant to the PSAC case, since the former only dealt with the issue of whether the court or the tribunal had jurisdiction to determine the question of pay equity methodology, whereas it was arguing that the tribunal's methodology was wrong (Treasury Board Secretariat, Pay Equity Page, 13 July 1999). Before the Federal Court, the government's lawyers argued that the tribunal's methodology not only compared jobs of unequal value, but that it made illogical job comparisons: one lawyer exclaimed that the tribunal's method measured clerical work against that of auditors, lawyers, and economists. This complaint ignored the fact that the Treasury Board was in the process of introducing a Universal Classification Standard, which applies one job evaluation system to all public service work, whether requiring professional, university, or trade certificate qualifications (PSAC, Pay Equity Page, 1 June 1999). Adding insult to injury, after appealing the tribunal's decision, the government introduced legislation that would, among other things, ensure that it had complete control of the $28 billion pension surplus in the plan for its own employees (May 1999b). This was more than enough money to pay for equity.

On 19 October 1999, Federal Court Judge John Evans categorically denied every ground for review raised by the government.[11] Although the Federal Court's decision to uphold the tribunal's award was not unexpected in light of the Supreme Court of Canada's refusal to hear Bell's appeal, what was remarkable was the extent to which the federal government's demeanour had changed during the year that had elapsed since the tribunal issued its decision. Gone was Marcel Massé, who had been particularly heavy-handed in his determination to rein in the public service, and in his place as president of the Treasury Board was Lucienne Robillard, a conciliatory politician who repeatedly stressed her government's support for the principle of pay equity. In contrast to the timing of the tribunal's award, the Federal Court issued its decision when Parliament was in session, which forced the government publicly to account for its position without the benefit of polling public opinion and releasing trial balloons. Most significantly, the economic climate had changed; not only had the government racked up a large surplus, in its most recent Throne speech it had committed itself both to cut taxes and to increase social spending. When questioned in the House by the leader of the Reform Party about whether the pay equity ruling would force the government to abandon the promised tax cuts, the Prime Minister contradicted his earlier position and stated that it was possible to do both (Fife & Alberts 1999). The press reported that beginning in 1989, when the Tories were in power, the Department of Finance had set aside an undisclosed amount of money every year to cover the cost of the settlement. According to financial analysts, the government could afford a settlement without foregoing tax cuts, paying the debt, and any new program spending (Little 1999; May 1999a). Moreover, there were also some residual political benefits to maintaining a public commitment to equality. In the House of Commons, the Liberals were careful to emphasize their support for the principle of pay equity and to stress the Reform Party's antipathy to equality (House of Commons Debates, 20 October 1999a, 22 October 1999b).

In a marked departure from Massé's strategy of attacking the pay equity award in the media, within five days of the release of the court decision Robillard began settlement talks, under a news blackout, with PSAC. On 29 October, the parties announced that they had reached a settlement to the dispute: between $3.3 and $3.6 billion would be paid out retroactively to some 230,000 current and former public service employees and the government would forego its right to appeal. Robillard made clear that the fund set aside by the government was sufficient to cover the cost of the settlement and that the tax cuts announced in the Throne Speech would not be jeopardized. She said the agreement signalled 'the new era of partnership we are building with public sector unions' (Treasury Board of Canada Secretariat, Pay Equity Page, 31 October 1999). This part of the strategy was a success; the national president of PSAC echoed the government's sentiment that the settlement heralded a new spirit of cooperation (PSAC, Pay Equity Page, 31 October 1999).

While PSAC won its fourteen-year legal battle to force the government to put the principle of pay equity into practice and pay its employees billions of dollars in back wages, on the larger political front the gap between supporting pay equity in principle and in practice is wide. The appeal of pay equity is on the wane and it appears that the backlash against it is gaining momentum. Justice Minister McLellan's decision to establish a task force to review section 11 of the Canadian Human Rights Act provides an opportunity for the critics of pay equity both to redefine the legal meaning of equality and to help shape equality's social significance in public debate.[12]

The emerging attack on pay equity is playing out along a number of dimensions. At the institutional level, the Canadian Human Rights Commission has been a specific target and its credibility has suffered. The courts, too, have been a focus of attack; according to one national media pundit, '[t]o govern is to choose, but once tribunals or courts rule, governments (read taxpayers) lose the ability to choose ... Tribunals (and courts) rule, governments pay' (Simpson 1999). The equal pay provisions within the Canadian Human Rights Act have also been criticized as inadequate, sometimes by commission members, because they fail to provide a method for the comparison of jobs (Gollam 1998). But according to critics such as the *Globe and Mail* (17 October 1998c), the problem with pay equity is much deeper than institutional or methodological; it is conceptual. 'The rationale for pay equity lies in a hazy concept that fairness is a concrete rather than relative value, one that can be legislated, quantified, and ultimately reduced to mere dollars and cents. But calculating the 'true' comparative value of jobs is impossible. People should be paid according to supply and demand. Philosophy can decide how morally praiseworthy that choice may be, but the market must decide how to pay for it.'

The attack against pay equity is also linked to a broader backlash against substantive equality, fuelled by a defence and celebration of the free market, on the one hand, and declining economic prospects for young men, on the other. These two elements are united by a commitment to an equal opportunities' framework, one that sees the role of the state as limited to prohibiting overt discrimination (Fudge 1996a, 251; 1996b, 82; Loney 1998). Gender-based discrimination in wages is discounted and differences in male and female earnings are attributed to 'the fact that women willingly devote more time than men to child-rearing' (*National Post*, 20 October 1999). Pundits employed or funded by right-wing think tanks or conservative foundations attack the very notion of equal pay for work of equal value on the ground that 'the true value of a job is determined by whatever an employer is willing to pay and an employee is willing to accept' (Basham 1999; Fergusson 1999; Loney 1999). But this position assumes that market outcomes based upon voluntary agreement somehow make discrimination unimpeachable. Attempts to remedy the legacy of past discrimination that have been built into wage structures are now castigated as an invidious form of social engineering (*Ottawa Sun*, 25 October 1998).

So far, the federal government, whether Conservative or Liberal, has been committed to substantive equality in the form of employment equity (i.e., access to jobs). In fact, the government has imposed legal obligations that require it to provide a barrier-free workplace, with the goal of obtaining a workforce that represents the proportion of women (and other designated groups) in the labour force (Baines 2000). But unlike pay equity, which has the potential to be very expensive, employment equity law does not require the government to spend money. This factor helps explain why, historically, the federal government has preferred employment to pay equity as a means of addressing systemic discrimination in the public service.

There is little, however, support for employment equity among federal government employees. The Task Force on Women in the Public Service found that 'numerical targets and quotas received a very bad press both in the interviews and in the questionnaire. Those who apparently had benefited from them resented the implication that they needed them to get ahead, and those who did not qualify for them and who did not get ahead often ascribed their fate to targets and quotas' (Canada, Task Force on Barriers to Women in the Public Service 1990, 128). Nor does employment equity enjoy much popular support as it is regarded as unfair (Antecol and Kuhn 1999; Bakan & Koybashi 2000; Fudge 1996a, 1996b).

Most important is the pragmatic issue of whether employment equity is an effective technique for improving women's access to, and conditions of, employment. The basic problem is that the success of employment equity depends upon an economy that is growing. When the norm of employment is deteriorating, that is, when part-time and temporary jobs are proliferating at the expense of full-time and permanent ones, employment equity is unlikely to improve women's employment conditions, although it may increase their representation in the workplace. Declining recruitment, outsourcing, the sale of public assets to the private sector, and the commercialization of government functions all undermine the capacity of employment equity policies to improve the conditions of, or prospects for, women's employment in the federal public service (Bennett 1995, 142; Luxton & Reiter 1997, 209, 215; McColgan 1997, 393; Warskett 1996, 617).

Privatization, in the sense of the shift of service provision from the public to private sector, also has broader, and generally detrimental, ramifications for women's employment opportunities and conditions (Dantico & Jurik 1986; but see Pendleton 1997). This is because public sector employment in Canada has generally provided more opportunities and better conditions of employment for women than the private sector. Not only are public sector jobs more likely to be unionized than comparable jobs in the private sector, wages at the bottom end of the occupational ladder, where women tend to be crowded, are paid better in the public than the private sector. But now, cuts in federal transfer payments have reduced the amount of money that some of the provinces have to pay for public services. Moreover, the federal government has reduced the size of its own workforce; between 1992 and 1997 it chopped more than 73,000 workers from its payroll. While the private sector may have offset some of these losses, it is unlikely that the quality of jobs it provided was as good as the quality of those that were lost (Bashevkin 1998, 224; Bird 1979; Clark 1997; B. Little 1998; White 1993, 162).

The paradox is that, despite the institutionalization of legal norms of substantive equality in the federal public service by the early 1980s, as the proportion of women in the labour force has grown, employment standards have deteriorated, wages have dropped in real terms, and the proportion of temporary positions has increased (Auditor General 1998, 11–13; Lee & Hobbs 1996, 341; Panitch & Swartz 1993, 92; PSAC 1997, 3). Wage controls and privatization strategies have had an especially deleterious impact on women in the public sector (Gunderson 1998, 156–7). The feminization of labour has been matched by a feminization of employment norms – employment terms and conditions that historically have been associated with women, such as low pay, poor benefits, and part-time or temporary work (Armstrong 1996a; Fudge 1996b; Vosko 1998; 294–304; Warskett 1996, 602). Privatization has exacerbated and accelerated the process of feminization or deterioration in the norms of employment. This, in turn, has fuelled the backlash against substantive equality.

Conclusion

This study of women's employment in the federal public service demonstrates that ideological shifts around the legitimacy of normative claims such as sex equality invariably accompany substantial changes in material conditions. Equality claims by women have less political resonance in an economic climate in which the employment conditions and prospects of men have deteriorated. The last time there was a sustained deterioration in employment norms for men, which was in the 1930s, there was an attack on married women's employment (Hobbs 1993b). Until 1955, married women's rights to employment in the federal public service were explicitly subordinated to men's and this subordination was enshrined in law. Explicit discrimination in the form of occupational segregation, lower pay, and substandard employment norms for women was also legally acceptable.

The gender order has changed considerably since the 1950s. Credible attempts to resurrect the male breadwinner model are a thing of the past, although there is, in some quarters, profound nostalgia for it (Loney 1998). Married women's employment is necessary to sustain household income and it is regarded by most people as perfectly legitimate. According to Brenner (1993, 104), the historic achievement of second-wave feminism 'was to make women fully free sellers of their own labour by substantially dismantling the legal and normative edifice which had mandated women's subservience.' By the early 1970s, formal legal equality in employment for women in the federal public service, regardless of sex or marital status, was the norm.

But formal legal equality did not address the underlying gender order. The edifice of the federal public sector was built on a legacy of explicit sex segregation in occupations, combined with explicit sex discrimination in wages and conditions. In the late 1970s, the NAC ran up against the limits of formal legal equality as a strategy for improving women's situation – it was unable to address systemic social barriers to equality. Both the women's movement and public sector unions took an increasingly militant turn and they joined forces to press for substantive equality. For a brief moment in the early 1980s, substantive equality became dominant in Canadian political discourse. Pay equity and employment equity were official policies of the federal government and greater attention was paid to employment practices which, although they might appear to be neutral, had a negative impact upon women in light of their historical experience.

Pay equity has been one of the primary means of addressing the historic under-valuation of women's work in the federal public service. It requires a gender-neutral re-evaluation of men's and women's work. Not only is this new evaluation extremely contentious, as it raises questions about how to assess the value of work, it is potentially very costly – as PSAC's complaint on behalf of its large Clerical and Regulatory Group has shown. While this is the single largest complaint, it is but one of many that employers in the federal sector, such as Canada Post, are facing.

The Liberal government attempted to characterize pay equity as too expensive. The increased tax burden on working people and the shift in the composition of taxes has combined with deteriorating employment conditions and standards of living to increase resistance to claims of equality, especially if those claims are perceived as imposing any additional tax burden. Despite the fact that the majority of workers who will benefit from the Human Rights Tribunal's ruling are women who earn under $30,000 and who endured wage freezes from 1991 to 1998, the government was able to portray the burden of implementing the decision as unfair to taxpayers. The attack on pay equity is also part and parcel of the attack on the public sector; the decision in the PSAC case was maligned as an income transfer from 'hardworking, underpaid people in the private sector' to 'those in the public sector, who were also poorly paid but at least enjoyed a long period of job security along with benefits and indexed pensions of which others can only dream' (*Ottawa Sun*, 25 October 1999). The 'unfairness' of the equal pay ruling and the resistance to increasing women's wages is reinforced by a perception that feminist demands have gotten out of hand. Moreover, the farther that feminist demands deviate from market norms, the greater the backlash against substantive equality.

Employment equity also illustrates this process. Although it is enshrined in law in the federal sector, it is popularly regarded as unfair. There is some justification for this perception. Under employment equity, young men bear the burden of compensating for past discrimination even though they have neither caused nor directly benefited from that discrimination. While it is true that men are overrepresented in higher level occupations, it is older men who occupy those positions and who have benefited from employment policies that discriminated against women. However, their jobs are not jeopardized by employment equity. Thus, a question of principle arises: does employment equity strike the appropriate balance between competing rights and the public interest (Loney 1998, 186–7; Swinton 1995, 741–2)? Instead of calling on older men who occupy the best positions to account for the inequality in employment conditions and prospects experienced by younger people in the labour market, many of those who criticize employment equity for its unfairness target feminists and other equity activists (Loney 1998). Moreover, they tend to blame politics, rather than economic restructuring, for the deterioration of the employment conditions of men (*Globe and Mail*, 1998a; Philp 1998; Turnbull 1998).

This chapter has shown that the legal norm of women's employment has shifted from exclusion to discrimination to equality. It has also demonstrated that the shift in legal norms has not been teleological, from worse to better treatment; rather, it has been contradictory. Formal legal equality went hand in hand with deteriorating employment norms in the late 1970s. The result was a decline in the gap between women's representation in the workforce and the discrepancy in men's and women's wages. The convergence between men's and women's working situations continued throughout the 1990s, but this owed not to the success of substantive equality so much as the deterioration in or feminization of men's working conditions.

It may be that the contradiction between substantive equality and increasing polarization in the labour market can be sustained. However, the recent backlash against pay equity suggests that the contradiction is deepening and that we are experiencing an ideological shift in the meaning of equality. The question is whether there is a new discourse of equality to replace it. The main contender is the equal opportunity framework, what Ian Forbes (1996) has called 'the privatization of sex equality policy.' Primarily, it involves a celebration of the market on the ground that it produces outcomes that technically cannot be found to be unjust. This framework sees the role of the state not in engineering outcomes, but in outlawing discrimination, and it could result in a retrenchment in the gendered division of labour. Women's responsibility for the bulk of childcare would, according to this policy, simply be seen as an individual choice and women would be solely responsible for its costs (*National Post*, 1 June 1999). The tenor of the majority of responses to the pay equity decision involving the PSAC and the federal government illustrate that in Canada this eviscerated conception of equality may become hegemonic.

Such a privatized notion of sex equality would rest on shaky ground. It assumes that women's labour power is elastic, capable of accommodating the demands of paid employment and of providing care to dependent children and elders. To date, capitalism in Canada has required a healthy and compliant national workforce both to produce and consume the goods and services it needs in order to continue to accumulate. Women's unpaid reproductive labour has been an essential, albeit often ignored, component of the capitalist process. However, in the context of globalization, these relationships are called into question; corporations are increasingly free from political constraints as they seek to exploit the international division of labour. The privatization project embraced by nation states in order to attract internationally mobile capital disrupts the prevailing gender order. Whether men will take on a greater share of the burden of caring responsibilities in order to alleviate women's growing burden remains to be seen. Nancy Fraser (1997a, 59–62) has called for the universal caregiver model as an alternative to the male breadwinner and family wage model that is no longer sustainable. One thing is certain – the gender order has been reconfigured and it is unstable (Brenner 1998, 14; McDowell 1991; Walby 1997).

Notes

1 Report of the Royal Commission 1908 as cited in Hodgetts et al. 1972, 484–5. For a discussion of the employment of women in the federal civil service prior to 1908, see Doherty 1991, 18–23.
2 I would like to thank Elizabeth Millar, pay equity adviser to PSAC, for bringing this point to my attention.
3 While there are a variety of techniques for addressing the gendered wage gap, pay for work of equal value mechanisms that rely upon job evaluation to determine the value of jobs have tended to predominate. Although s. 11 of the Canadian Human Rights Act did not specifically require job evaluation – all the legislation mandated was that the value of a job be determined in light of skill, effort, responsibility, and working conditions – job evaluation was the predominant means of determining the value of jobs in light of these four factors. Pay equity typically refers to an equal pay for work of equal value mechanism that relies on job evaluation as its primary methodology. Moreover, such equity schemes are conventionally divided into two types, depending upon whether they are complaint-based or pro-active. Complaint-based schemes place the onus on employees to lodge a complaint in order to initiate the remedial process. Pro-active schemes, by contrast, place the obligation on employers to determine whether female-dominated jobs receive the same pay as male-dominated jobs of equal value (Fudge & McDermott 1991).

4 According to Vickers et al. (1993, 111–14, 238–41), the NAC was divided over the utility of entrenching equality rights; thus it did not play a prominent role in the patriation and entrenchment process. However, it did play a key role in the interpretation of equality rights, pressing for substantive equality for women as a legal principle.

5 The job cuts were not as massive as the government threatened. But while only the equivalent of 4,684 full-time jobs were lost during the Conservative government's entire rule, thousands of jobs were transformed into part-time and temporary positions (Sutherland 1987; Lee & Hobbs 1996, 341).

6 *Canada (A.G.) v. P.S.A.C.* (1991), 48 F.T.R. 55.

7 *Public Service Alliance of Canada v. Canada (Treasury Board)*, [1996] C.H.R.D. No. 2 (H.R.T.), online: QL (CHRD).

8 In *Public Service Alliance of Canada v. Canada (Treasury Board)*, [1998] C.H.R.D. No. 6 (H.R.T.), online: QL (CHRD), the tribunal endorsed the CHRC's methodology (known as level to segment) for calculating the wage gap

9 In *Bell Canada v. Communications, Energy and Paperworkers Union of Canada*, [1998] F.C.J. No. 312 (T.D.), online: QL (FCJ), Muldoon J.

10 *Bell Canada v. Communications, Energy and Paperworkers Union of Canada*, [1998] 1 F.C. 113 (C.A.). For a discussion of this litigation and Bell's subsequent decision to contract out the operators' work see Fudge 2000.

11 *Public Service Alliance of Canada v. A.G. Canada*, [1999] F.C.J. No. 1531, at paras. 239, 233, 246, Evans J. online: QL (FCJ). For a detailed discussion of that case see Hughes 2000.

12 The establishment of the Task Force proved to be quite controversial. Not until the spring of 2001 did Justice Minister McLellan announced the appointment of Beth Bilson to head the Task Force.

3

Privatizing Pension Risk: Gender, Law, and Financial Markets

MARY CONDON

Introduction: The Gender of Risk

Neo-liberalism is usually characterized as rejecting an active role for the state in either economic activity or the governance of populations.[1] It also supports the enhanced autonomy and responsibility of individuals to define and execute their own well-being (Rose 1999). An important aspect of the project of neo-liberalism is reliance on non-state 'techniques of governance,' which include actuarialism (assessments of the probabilities of harms occuring), 'privatized prudentialism' (risk management through private insurance) (O'Malley 1992), and governance of the self (Hunt 2000, 14; Mykitiuk this volume).[2] One of the most prominent of these governance techniques is the definition, assessment, and management of risk. Ericson and Haggerty (1997, 83) suggest that risk has become a prevailing discourse of governance because it resonates with the neo-liberal project of individual responsibilization (O'Malley 1992, 257), entrepreneurship (Miller & Rose 1990) and the withdrawal of the state. Rose argues that one of the 'subjective conditions' of neo-liberalism involves restructuring 'the provision of security to remove as many as possible of the incitements to passivity and dependency' (1999, 144). Callinicos points out that risk discourses have the effect of depoliticizing 'all the big problems,' which 'turn out to be matters of risk assessment' (1999, 83). Thus risk profiling and the identification of risky populations through surveillance have come to dominate criminal justice policy (Ericson & Haggerty 1997; Hannah-Moffat 1999; O'Malley 1999). Scientific investigations and discoveries have contributed to an enhanced individual consciousness of risk, which can then be managed by science (Beck 1992; Mykitiuk this volume). This consciousness has also, not incidentally, worked to create markets for risk management products (Rose 1999, 159). Meanwhile of course, one of the roles played by the Keynesian state was to socialize various risks (such as those of unemployment and poverty), in order to create a certain sense of security in the population (Rose 1999, 5; Sohrab 1996). A significant implication of the neo-liberal attack on the Keynesian state is that state-based institutions of risk management are being dismantled and risk is being displaced onto the entrepreneurial individual.

The emphasis on the role of risk-based governance in neo-liberalism, however, raises a number of questions. The first is to what extent the claim of a shift to risk-based governance is sufficient to explain specific policy outcomes consequent on the move to the 'neo-liberal state.' For example, the case of the restructuring of retirement income provision is being addressed by a number of countries. While increased privatization is clearly a general trend in these different locations, it is also true that there is variation in the speed and intensity of the move to individualize retirement income provision. Thus, to attempt to explain the extent to which the Canadian state participates in the 'politics of risk' it may be necessary to move beyond the emphasis in the governmentality literature on abstract 'mentalit(ies) of rule' to a focus on politics, contestation and implementation as constitutive of specific outcomes (O'Malley, Weir, & Shearing 1997; Callinicos 1999).

It is equally important to interrogate the idea of the 'individual' who is the target of neo-liberal, risk-based governance. Is the individual governed and responsibilized in neo-liberalism gender-neutral (Cossman this volume; Hannah-Moffat 1999; Philipps this volume)? Part of the answer to this question involves making visible the impact of individualized risk acceptance on men and women. Thus an examination of gender in relation to risk governance may help to illuminate the way in which a focus on risk may serve, as some argue, to obscure inequalities of distribution (Callinicos 1999; Pearce & Tombs 1996, 449). The existence of 'feminist counter discourses' in the politics of risk-based governance must also be recognized (O'Malley et al. 1997, 51). Finally, given that law is ideologically associated with the exercise of state power, one of the animating questions of this collection is, to what extent is it implicated in, and affected by, the restructuring of the state to neo-liberalism (Cotterrell 1995; Simon 1999)? For example, is the current emphasis in legal procedure on 'alternative' methods of dispute resolution involving mediation prompted by a privatizing impulse that shifts dispute resolution away from forms associated with state courts and processes? An associated issue is the extent to which the influence of legal norms and institutions has to cede to, or take on the character of, other forms of governance more closely resonant with neo-liberalism (Hunt 2000). One issue that may be illuminated by this case study of retirement income is the extent to which legal norms and processes themselves become infused with discourses of risk management or work in tandem with such discourses from other sites of governance, such as accounting or investment.

Retirement income or pension provision is a particularly appropriate site to examine because the 'pension promise' was a key component of the Keynesian welfare state's attempt to provide a socialized response to the risk of material disadvantage; it has also recently been the subject of significant reinvention in terms of the role of the state. Pension provision is also significant because, as will be demonstrated, it has been organized around a highly gendered understanding of the nature of the risk being insured against. Accordingly, the chapter will first demonstrate the gendered logic of pension provision in Canada. It will then canvass policy developments taking place in selected countries, in order to place the more detailed discussion of reforms in the Canadian system in a broader perspective. Finally, the chapter will examine in turn the specific components of the Canadian system to elucidate the themes identified above: the role of risk governance, the gendered nature of the risk produced, and the shifting role of law evidenced in these developments.

I. The Gender of Pensions

With the exception of Old Age Security (OAS), the capacity to access specific amounts of pension income upon retirement in Canada is dependent on either a prior connection to the paid labour market or being in a familial relationship with, or a survivor of, a wage earner (Donnelly 1993; Orloff 1993). Both the second and third tiers of Canada's retirement policy, as well as the Guaranteed Income Supplement (GIS) and Spouse's Allowance components of OAS, are linked in various ways to wage earning. This implies that conceptually, as well as in practice, the distribution of the risk of being materially disadvantaged in old age will vary across gender and sexuality, since women's differential relationship to the paid labour market, as well as to the heterosexual family, reflects their particular role in social reproduction (Fudge this volume; MacDonald 1998). Indeed, the very language of 'income replacement,' which is the unproblematized goal of the pension system,

assumes a predominant connection to the labour market. This understanding of the policy goal of the system also serves to perpetuate distinctions between low- and high-income earners. A low-income earner
needs a smaller pension to 'replace' her previously low income.

With respect to the Canadian labour market, Townson has documented the phenomenon whereby women are much more likely than
men to be employed in 'non-standard' work, which she defines as part-
time work, self-employment, temporary work, or multiple jobs with a
series of employers (Townson 1997, 2–3). In 1994, for example, 40 per
cent of women, compared to 27 per cent of men, worked in non-standard jobs (ibid., 13). Specifically, 24 per cent of all women workers,
compared to only 8 per cent of men, were in part-time jobs, most often
in the retail trade and other consumer services (ibid., 5, 8). This is an
issue not just about participation rates but pay. Thus, 'the average earnings of all women, including those who worked part-time or in other
types of work which was not full-time, full-year, were $20,219 in 1995
which was still only 65% of the average earnings of all men at $31,053'
(ibid., 16). The impact of women's earnings on their ability to make
contributions to labour market-based pension schemes, and to receive
benefits on the basis of contributions, is obvious. As Orloff notes,
'Women's inferior status in the work force means that women are disproportionately disadvantaged when benefits reflect work-related inequality' (Orloff 1993, 314). In terms of family status, Statistics Canada
reports that in 1993, 56 per cent of all senior women living alone or with
unrelated persons had 'low incomes.'[3] McDonald's 1997 study of retired
widows, who 'constitute approximately 47% of the senior population,'
and 49 per cent of whom 'lived below the low income cut-offs of Statistics Canada' leads her to support the maxim that 'married women are
one husband away from poverty' (McDonald 1997b, vi–vii).

Townson claims that there are significant differences between male
and female attitudes to retirement (Townson 1995, 6). Her survey of
Canadian women at mid-life showed that, 'women seemed much less
certain than men about the age at which they would retire' (ibid.). She
argues that 'the fact that 41% of women aged 45–54 have no specific
retirement date in mind may reflect their lack of financial planning for
retirement as well as uncertainty about their financial future and what
measures they will have to take to secure it' (ibid.). And of course, in a
demographic sense the extent of the risk of inadequate pension income
is gendered, in that life expectancy rates ensure that women will be
dependent on pension income for a greater proportion of their lives.

The contemporary period of economic restructuring is likely to exacerbate the gendered nature of pension provision in Canada. Despite neo-liberal claims to gender neutrality, a political economy that relies increasingly on the market to produce social policy may well have a differential effect across genders, given women's often more fragile connection to labour and other markets and their greater dependence on the state to recognize the financial implications of their decommodified labour. This possibility necessitates close attention to the gender politics of individualized risk that neo-liberalism entails (Hannah-Moffat 1999), not only in terms of material well-being in the form of social security benefits (Sohrab 1996), but in terms of the operating practices of a market-based delivery system. Are Canadian women well positioned to engage in self-governance to ensure their financial well-being in old age?

II. International Pension Privatization

In his study of comparative forms of the welfare state, Esping-Anderson has pointed out that 'pensions account for more than 10% of GDP in many contemporary nations' (Esping-Anderson 1990, 79). This fact, along with the state's involvement in funding them, has made pensions one of the foremost targets of neo-liberal restructuring (*Economist* 1998). As the 1998 OECD report, *Maintaining Prosperity in an Ageing Society*, put it: 'No two OECD countries have identical pension systems, nor do they face identical fiscal pressures. But in almost all of them, reforms have already had to be introduced to prevent expenditure on public pensions from running ahead of receipts, and in most of them, it is estimated that further significant reforms will need to be implemented in future' (OECD 1998b, 16). Meanwhile, institutions such as the World Bank have identified pension systems in economies in transition as being in need of a privatizing overhaul (Blackburn 1999, 14–15; Rittich 1998). Thus Canada is not the only country to engage in a debate about the future of its pension system. While many countries centre the questions on the need for market solutions to alleged problems caused by a declining workforce and an aging population, there is clear variation in the resulting policy.

In the United States, for example, there is a major debate about ways to 'save Social Security,' a contributory social insurance program to which 96 per cent of American workers contribute, at a rate of 6.2 per cent of their income up to approximately US$68,000 (Leone & Anrig 1999, 13). These contributions are matched by their employers. Like the

Canada Pension Plan (CPP) in Canada, Social Security provides not only retirement but also death and disability benefits and is funded on a pay-as-you-go basis. Reform proposals suggested in the United States can be seen to fall along a continuum from minor alterations to the system that would preserve its basic structure,[4] investing Social Security trust funds in the stock market, to introducing a system of individual retirement accounts, in which an individual's benefits would no longer be guaranteed by the government. A Social Security reform plan proposed by the Clinton administration in early 1999 contained elements both of investing funds in the stock market (US$700 billion over fifteen years) and the establishment of so-called U.S.A.s (universal savings accounts) for individuals. Members of the Republican party have been critical of the proposal to invest Social Security funds in the stock market, largely on the ground that this would turn the U.S. government into a shareholder of U.S. corporations.

It has been a decade since Chile introduced the most radical and oft-cited example of a shift to a financial market-based pension system. There a pay-as-you-go system was abandoned in favour of a scheme requiring workers to pay 10 per cent of their income a year into an individual retirement account of their choice, which they control and invest as they wish (Fazio & Riesco 1997). Other Latin American countries, such as Argentina, Uruguay, Peru, and Columbia, have reformed their pension systems to 'include a greater role for funded, privately managed pensions' (Queisser 1998), though they have maintained a role for a pay-as-you-go system as well.

Edey and Simon argue that recent reforms to Australian pension or superannuation arrangements have brought that country's system into close alignment with the Chilean model (Edey and Simon 1998, 65). However, the building blocks of the system are also similar to those in Canada. They include an age pension, payable from general revenue and awarded on the basis of citizenship and need; a Super Guarantee Charge (SGC), whereby all Australians in the paid workforce must contribute 7 per cent of their gross salary to a superannuation fund, with contributions and lump-sum benefits being earnings-related; and a combination of occupational and personal superannuation schemes (Kingsford Smith 1999, 8-9). The second tier of this system, the CPP-equivalent SGC, was put in place only in the mid-1980s and assumed its current form in 1991 (Edey and Simon 1998, 66–7). From its inception the funds remitted have been placed in superannuation funds that are privately run and managed and the government 'gives no guarantee of safety and soundness of fund assets or returns' (Kingsford Smith 1999, 11). The choice of where to invest the compulsory contributions has usually been made by employers or unions (Edey & Simon 1998, 65), though in 1998 the government introduced the Superannuation Legislation Amendment (Choice of Superannuation Funds) Bill, designed to provide additional member choice (Kingsford Smith 1999, 11). Significant reliance is therefore placed on the private market to provide retirement income funds for Australians, with regulatory supervision being provided by the Australian Prudential Regulatory Authority (APRA) and the Australian Securities and Investments Commission (ASIC) (Freiberg 1996; Kingsford Smith 1999, 12). As Edey and Simon point out, 'the most important distinguishing features of the Australian system are that it is government mandated but privately run and that it has been able to make use of a well-developed financial infrastructure for superannuation, through which the new compulsory contributions could be channeled' (1998, 81).

Britain was one of the first OECD countries to modify its system of pension provision in accordance with the tenets of neo-liberalism. The earliest formulation of its system in the post-war period was, on the one hand, the National Insurance scheme, which pays a flat-rate benefit and is financed by flat-rate contributions, and on the other, occupational pensions voluntarily provided by employers (Waine 1992). In the 1960s initiatives were taken both to introduce a state earnings-related pension scheme (SERPs) and to allow occupational pension schemes to opt out of it, provided equivalent benefits were paid. Two-thirds of full-time workers in Britain are covered by occupational schemes, though 'women have a low rate of coverage, because many work part-time or as carers' (Blackburn 1999, 16, 24). In 1986 a further option, known as a 'personal pension,' was introduced for employees by the Social Security Act. This allowed individuals to contract out of either SERPs or an occupational scheme in favour of a personal pension operated by a private sector provider. Despite the fact that an employer was not required to contribute to a personal pension, as it was to the existing schemes, more than 1.5 million employees during the late 1980s and early 1990s were persuaded by salespersons of private pension schemes to switch out of their occupational plan. As Blackburn describes it, 'the dogma of privatization produced a government-sponsored campaign that propelled hundreds of thousands of employees out of occupational schemes and into the clutches of bonus-hunting salesmen' (Blackburn 1999, 8). Investigation by the Securities and Investment Board in England into the misleading information provided to investors and the sales incentives provided by pension providers to their sales staffs demonstrated the shortcomings of reliance on a system of self-regulation in the financial services industry (Black & Nobles 1998) and led to claims for compensation from many investment houses.

In part as a result of the pension scandal, the Blair government issued further reform proposals in relation to pensions in December 1998. It is proposed to replace SERPS with a state-funded pension for the very low-paid and to encourage by means of tax relief the establishment of funded 'stakeholder pensions,' which would be provided by the pension industry, subject to enhanced regulation. The main difference between these and 'private pensions' appears to be that the former will have a '"collective", rather than individual, structure for cost reasons' (Blackburn 1999, 33).

Finally, the OECD report on pension provision supports 'phased reductions in public pension benefits and anticipatory hikes in contribution rates' (1998b, 19). It suggests that retirement income should be provided by 'a mix of tax-and-transfer systems, funded systems, private savings and earnings. The objective is risk diversification, a better balance of burden-sharing between generations, and to give individuals more flexibility over their retirement decision' (ibid.). Emphasis is placed on the need to strengthen 'the financial market infrastructure, including the establishment of a modern and effective regulatory framework' in order to enhance the capabilities of advance-funded pension systems.[5]

This brief account of comparative developments in pension reform indicates that privatized pensions can take different forms, ranging from those that retain a collective element to those that are more radically individualized, and from those to which voluntary subscriptions are made to those that are mandatory. It is thus important to be attentive to the precise formulation of privatized pension proposals, in part because of the different legal mechanisms that might regulate them. Canada's embrace of neo-liberal philosophies appears to be something of a middle-ground case. To support this characterization, let us first look at the framework of the Canadian system.

III. Tiers and Fears: The Pension System in Canada

Canada's retirement policy is usually characterized as having three 'tiers.' The first tier is represented by a universal state benefit, known as the Old Age Security Program.[6] Funded from general revenue, this is meant as an anti-poverty measure and it is both taxable and repayable, above a threshold amount, by the more well-off. The second, the CPP, has been since 1966 a publicly administered 'paygo' plan (where the contributions of today's workers support today's pensioners) from which all workers and, in some cases their spouses and survivors, will receive benefits. These benefits are financed by mandatory contributions from employers and employees, based on a percentage of income. In the 'income replacement' language of pension policy, CPP benefits are pitched so as to replace about 25 per cent of pre-retirement income, up to the Canadian average income of CAN$35,800 (1997 figures).[7] The contrast with the relevant ceiling for Social Security contributions in the United States, which is a much higher figure of US$68,000, is noteworthy. The third tier is composed of a mixture of employer-sponsored pension plans (RPPs) and individual 'registered retirement savings plans' (RRSPs). With respect to RPPs, it should be pointed out that employers are not required to provide pension plans for their employees. With RRSPs, employees voluntarily deposit money in a variety of investment vehicles provided by financial institutions, and most notably in Canada, by the mutual fund sector. This is facilitated by the fact that employees no longer make contributions to the CPP beyond the average wage (Deaton 1989, 228–9). While Canada is one of the 'developed' countries that has historically relied heavily on the labour and financial markets to provide retirement income for its citizens (Esping-Anderson 1990; Orloff 1993), the state and its laws have been implicated in these tiered retirement sectors at all levels. The state accomplishes the direct provision of income through the OAS; the collection of CPP contributions and, until recently, lending out the modest surplus in the CPP fund to provincial (or local) governments at below-market interest rates; the regulation of employer-sponsored plans; and the provision of generous tax deductions to individuals sheltering income in RRSPs. Even within the most 'private' tier of the system, there is variation from collective (RPPs) to individual (RRSPs) structures. While pensions in Canada have always had a strong private dimension, the significance of recent developments is, on the one hand, the increasing abandonment of the 'public good' element of pension provision, which has been associated with state provision and with the redistributive element of public pensions, and on the other, the shifting of emphasis within the privatized sphere from collective to individual responsibility for providing benefits.

A. Target Practice? Old Age Security (OAS)

As we have seen, the OAS is the only universally available pension in the Canadian system, with the main requirements for eligibility being age (sixty-five or over) and at least ten years of residency as an adult in Canada. Full benefits are payable to those who have lived in Canada for forty years from age eighteen. However, benefits are repayable, on a graduated basis, by seniors whose annual income exceeds $53,215, thus partially removing the universality feature of the pension. In 1999, the maximum benefit available from the OAS was $4,944 ($412 per month), with GIS for a single person being an average of $335 per month (August 1999 figures). The maximum OAS benefit represents about 13 per cent of the average wage, but a higher percentage, obviously, for those who earn less than the average (1995 figures) (Townson 1997, 51).

In the March 1996 budget, the federal government proposed the introduction in 2001 of a pension to be called a 'seniors benefit' to replace the existing OAS, with its accompanying GIS and spouse's allowance. Under this proposal, the maximum benefit payable was to be $120 a year higher than benefits from OAS and GIS combined, but the threshold for receiving maximum benefits was to fall to $25,921 in net indexed family income, down from $53,215 of individual income. Meanwhile, single seniors with income above $52,000 and couples with income above $78,000 would receive no benefits. The proposal had two features that would have transformed the nature of this form of public pension provision. First, it introduced a commitment to 'targeting' those at the very lowest income levels, thus substantially eroding the universality of the system. Second, as payment of benefits would be based on combined family income, the principle of receipt of OAS in one's own right would be abandoned (Baldwin & Townson 1997, 324). Despite the claim in the March 1996 budget document, *The Seniors Benefit: Securing the Future* (Canada 1996a, 38), that nine out of ten single women would receive increased assistance, and that the 'better targeting' of assistance would help this group of seniors, feminist advocates have argued that the receipt of benefits in one's individual capacity is a crucially important principle for women (MacDonald 1998, Philipps, this volume). The shift to targeting was largely justified by the belief that it would 'slow the rate of growth of public pensions, making them more affordable for future generations' (Canada 1996a, 9). As with the CPP reforms, *Securing the Future* pointed to 'demographic changes' involving longer life expectancies and fewer Canadians in the workforce in the future as the chief reasons for the 'sustainability problem.' *Securing the Future* went on to point out that 'slower growth in productivity and wage levels' would compound the demographic problem. However, 'it would simply not be responsible' to count on a return to high wage growth or high labour force growth, in order to make 'public pensions affordable' (ibid., 23–4). Meanwhile, the combined-income testing innovation would 'ensure(s) fairness and equality in the treatment of all couples, regardless of how their income is split between spouses' (ibid., 31).

Two years later, however, in July 1998, the federal government dropped the proposal to replace OAS. The avowed reason was that the deficit which had existed in 1995, when the proposal was introduced, had been replaced by a balanced budget and a declining debt-to-GDP ratio. Thus, 'the inescapable conclusion was that to take money out of the future public pension system at a time when the federal government will be running balanced budgets and surpluses, simply seemed to be the wrong choice' (Canada 1998f, 3). Associated with this improvement in the general finances was the fact that CPP reforms had been implemented in late 1997 (to be discussed in detail below) which would remove 'two-thirds of the long-term cost pressures' on the public pension system. Thus, the legislative reforms to CPP funding were clearly a quid pro quo for maintenance of the OAS. Interestingly, while the finance minister indicated that 'many Canadians' had come forward to 'share their views' about the seniors benefit proposal, Battle asserts that the government 'effectively preclude(d) public debate' on the proposal (1997, 538). He suggests that the government wished to avoid a debate about the OAS, which would be resonant with even more 'emotions and fears' than the one happening around the same time in relation to the CPP. One of the ways the government sought to prevent this debate was by 'grandparenting' existing seniors from receiving the new benefit. He notes that the government was in a better position to circumscribe debate on the OAS than on the CPP because both federal and provincial governments have 'stewardship' over the CPP.

Of course, the fact that saving the OAS was linked explicitly to a turn-around in the government's deficit problem implies that the issue may return to the table. An Association of Canadian Pension Managers (ACPM) position paper attempts to engender a debate about the 'deficiencies' of the current retirement income system in Canada (ACPM 2000). It argues that in order to sustain the OAS, 'it is critical to contain its growth to the minimum rate possible' (ibid., 14). The ACPM claims that the 'typical' middle-income Canadian will get more from OAS/GIS than the disposable income available to them during their working lives, 'without ever having saved a penny for their retirement years' (ibid., 13). Little information is provided to support this claim; what is interesting is that the perceived solution to the incentive problem[8] is not to see public pensions as a deserved reward for a lifetime of work, but rather to reduce them so that there is more likelihood that the post-retirement lives of these 'typical Canadians' will be as straitened as they were before retirement. The position paper rejects the idea that current workers have a socialized responsibility to current pensioners, instead voicing a concern about 'open-ended guarantees to continue these modest incomes after retirement *on the backs of* future taxpayers' (ibid., 13 [my emphasis]).

Since the OAS is available to those who have never, or only intermittently, participated in the labour market, it is clearly animated by a redistributive logic. As we have seen, the proposal for the Senior's Benefit stemmed from the apparent difficulties of funding OAS benefits in their current, albeit clawed-back, form from tax revenues. Yet the funding problem was to be solved not by a shift in the funding mechanism, as with the CPP, but by a reorientation of the benefits payable through the OAS by targeting them to low-income recipients. Battle, however, estimates that the projected Seniors Benefit would have cost $24.5 billion, only $200 million less than the projected $24.7 billion cost of the OAS. By 2030, 'during the peak of the elderly boom, the Seniors Benefit will cost a projected $69.1 billion or $8.2 billion less than what the old system would have cost ($77.3 billion)' (1997, 543). It may be that the demise of the Senior's Benefit owed more to its attack on benefits themselves rather than to the funding mechanism.

B. Demographics, Dependency, and Distribution: Canada Pension Plan Reform

The benefits received by women from the CCP are typically lower than those received by men, since their income-related contributions are lower. However, the CPP's coverage of part-time workers and recognition of time out of the paid labour force because of family responsibilities in the assessment of benefits,[9] as well as the availability of spousal pension sharing and survivor benefits, may all be seen as attempts to recognize the gendered material risk faced by women.

In fall 1997, legislative changes to the operation of CPP (CPP Investment Board Act) were enacted. The major innovations of the legislation were an increase in contribution rates to the plan, along with a change in the method of funding CPP benefits. Proposals to reduce the amounts of benefits payable to CPP recipients were more or less successfully opposed.

Specifically, the 1997 legislative changes have resulted in an increase in the contribution rate from 5.85 per cent of wages, up to the average wage, in 1997, to 9.9 per cent by the year 2003, which rate will be then held steady. They have also frozen the year's basic exemption (the amount below which no contributions are required) at $3,500, instead of indexing it to wages (in contrast, as mentioned earlier, the maximum amount at which contributions are no longer required to be made was not raised from $35,800). The ultimate retirement benefit is now to be based on an average of the last five years' yearly maximum pensionable earnings (YMPE), instead of the last three years.[10] The maximum death benefit payable to survivors has been reduced to $2,500, down from $3,500, which amount was likewise formerly indexed to wages. Collectively, these changes will adversely affect women whose participation in the labour force is low-paying and fragile and will reduce the distributive features of the CPP. As Townson points out, lower-income workers may find it hard to assimilate such a sharp increase in contributions over a short period, since they pay contributions on the whole of their income, compared to workers earning higher than average earnings, who contribute only on a portion. The difficulty will be exacerbated for the self-employed, who have to fund both sets of contributions themselves (Townson 1997, 61–4). Freezing the year's basic exemption will over time draw more very low-income workers into the contributions requirement (National Action Committee on the Status of Women (NAC), House of Commons 1997e, 14; Townson 1997, 62). Reducing the death benefit payable to survivors is also more likely to affect women, given gendered survival figures. Basing the benefit on the last five years of earnings as opposed to three will result in lower pensions generally, with adverse effects for those lower-income earners who rely mainly on the CPP for retirement income.

1. The Demographic Imperative?
The debate that culminated in legislative change began early in 1994, when the Chief Actuary's periodic report on the finances of the CPP, required by its governing legislation, concluded that 'the recession and higher than anticipated disability claims would necessitate increasing contribution rates higher than previously expected' (Townson 1996, 30). The federal and provincial governments issued a discussion paper

in the mid-1990s and held public and 'expert' consultations across Canada[11] for several months preceding the bill's introduction to Parliament. The government's discussion paper set the tone for the debate to follow by asserting a 'crisis of unsustainability' in the operation of the CPP. The root of this crisis was to be found in demographic projections of a declining workforce whose contributions to the CPP could not meet escalating claims by increasing numbers of pensioners. The solutions proposed included a combination of 'early increases in contribution rates and reduced benefits or reduced access to benefits' (Federal/Provincial/Territorial Governments of Canada 1996, 10).

The demographic premise on which these proposals were made was contested by left-leaning politicians and social policy analysts, mainly by pointing to the contribution rates of Canadian workers in relation to workers in European countries with more robust public pension systems, requiring higher contribution rates (*Economist* 1998). The premise can also be contested on other grounds. For example, the gloomy demographic projections on which reform proposals were founded was based on a particular interpretation of an unfavourable 'dependency ratio,' that is, the number of pensioners dependent on the number of workers for contributions. In 1997, Denton and Spencer argued that the 'overall dependency ratio' in Canada would only rise by a 'modest' amount by 2031. This was because while the ratio of workers to pensioners would increase, the dependency ratio between workers and children would decrease because of the declining birth rate. Thus a plausible public policy response might have been a reallocation of resources from, for example, the educational system to support for seniors (Denton and Spencer 1997, 489, 492), or raising above the average wage the ceiling for required contributions to the CPP, thereby increasing the flow of contributions from higher-income earners.

It is also clear that the demographic analysis on which the panic about unsustainability was based was gendered. First, it took no account of the issue of women's unpaid work, so that the only work that counted was 'paid' work (Waring 1988). Nor did it acknowledge the changing nature of work more generally (MacDaniel 1997; McDonald 1997a). The terms of the debate obscured a broader analysis that would recognize not just that in future there may be fewer workers in the paid labour market, but that those workers' earnings are not growing and that workers, especially women, tend no longer to be in stable, continuous employment (Fudge and Cossman, this volume; MacDaniel 1997). The failure to problematize the nature of the labour market beyond a focus on a declining number of workers silenced or discounted a variety of alternative political solutions. These would include: intensifying political efforts at job creation or other ways of increasing labour force participation, especially women's participation; removing or decreasing the tax deduction that favours investing in private RRSPs, mostly by male workers (Young 1997); or even more radically, problematizing the assumed link between labour markets and pension entitlements. Despite the interventions of women's organizations like the NAC (House of Commons 1997e), the political solutions ultimately forged were based on a refusal to recognize the gendered nature of the labour market (Fudge, this volume).

It is also crucial to recognize the link between demographics and redistribution in the debate about the CPP. The reason why the demographic shortfall is significant is because in a pay-as-you-go system, the contributions of current workers are redistributed to current pensioners, with an expectation that the same redistribution will happen for today's workers in the future.[12] Given that the CPP is, in retirement income language, a defined benefit pension (benefit tables are established in advance), it is also redistributive in that individual pensioners may receive more in benefits than the contributions they paid in as workers, depending on the number of years they live post-retirement. This connection between demographics and distribution was expressed by the government as an issue of 'inter-generational fairness,' in the sense that 'early generations did not pay enough' into the plan relative to the amounts of benefits they were receiving (Battle 1996, 6–7). As the Federal/Provincial/Territorial Governments' Consultations Report put it, 'The basic challenge facing Canadians is one of fairness and equity. For the past 30 years, Canadians have paid much less than the benefits they are receiving, or will receive, are worth. Future generations will be asked to pay considerably more for the very same benefits' (Federal/Provincial/Territorial CPP Consultations Secretariat 1996, 9). Some commentators in the CPP debate clearly wished to mount an assault on the redistributive underpinnings of public pension provision. For example, Robson argued that 'These transfers from young to old cannot be excused by casting the CPP as though its primary purpose were redistribution rather than income replacement ... The CPP provides benefits similar to those available from private pension plans and insurance policies but does so in a way that is tilted dramatically against today's children' (Robson 1996, 25). Nor is the construction of oppositional interests between young and old confined to the Canadian debate about the CPP. The OECD's report on ageing asserts that 'a continuation of large public transfers to older generations ... could result in inter-generational conflict, even if there is currently little evidence of it' (OECD 1998b, 52). The report speculates that the current lack of conflict may be due to the fact that 'many young people are themselves dependent (directly or indirectly) on the income their parents or grandparents receive, and do not recognise that the difficulties they encounter in finding employment or in earning adequate takehome pay may be related to the payroll-based taxes which finance the pensions and other social transfers received by their parents and grandparents' (ibid.). The OECD's report is thus explicit about its view that 'blame' for the alleged phenomenon of intergenerational unfairness is appropriately placed on the state, rather than on the changing nature of employment.

The chief innovation of the 1997 legislation was a shift to a financial market-based investment strategy for the CPP, with the aim of maximizing returns to the fund and building up its capital. This was widely viewed by 'business, labour and seniors groups' as a compromise solution to the problems of the CPP's so-called unfunded liability. Indeed, the consensus about the need for a shift to the financial markets extended to women's organizations, which 'supported improved investment of the CPP fund' (Federal/Provincial/Territorial CPP Consultations Secretariat 1996, 22, 25). Previously, any surplus in the fund not needed to meet current obligations to pensioners had been lent to provincial governments at below-market interest rates to accomplish various public finance projects (Deaton 1989, 223–5). Following the passage of the CPP Investment Board Act, CPP funds are now being invested in the equity markets.[13] A new Investment Board has been established to manage any amounts transferred to it 'in the best interests of the contributors and beneficiaries' under the Act. It is to invest its assets 'with a view to achieving a maximum rate of return, without undue risk of loss' (s. 5). The attempts of labour spokespeople to advocate investment objectives such as 'meeting economic goals for the country' or 'secondary objectives to promote economic development' or 'regional economic development' (Federal/Provincial/Territorial CPP Consultations Secretariat 1996, 36) were roundly criticized by the financial planners, investment dealers, and pension experts who appeared in a special consultation session before the legislation was enacted. This position was supported by the government in drafting the legislation. As in the Social Security debate in the United States, a major concern expressed by some participants was the possibility for 'government intervention' in CPP investment decisions (Canadian Youth Federation, House of Commons 1997d, 44; Federal/Provincial/Territorial CPP Consultations Secretariat 1996,

36; Manning, House of Commons 1997a). The legislative solution here was to allow the new CPP Investment Board to 'hire qualified investment professionals to manage the day to day investment decisions at arm's length from governments'(House of Commons 1997c, 2699).

The trade-off for minimizing 'government intervention' in the investment activity of the newly marketized CPP was a variety of governance norms drawn from corporate and trust law. These include: a fiduciary duty to the Investment Board imposed on individual directors and officers who should have 'proven financial ability or relevant work experience'; the ability to hire qualified investment professionals with discretionary authority to manage the fund; and the requirement to invest according to a 'prudent portfolio' standard, as elaborated in a written, publicly available investment policy required by the draft regulations. However, the establishment of a fiduciary duty to act in the best interests of contributors and beneficiaries simply replicates, or submerges, in a depoliticized environment, the apparent interest group antagonisms that prompted the legislative changes in the first place. It also suggests that the way the board operationalizes its obligation to act in the interests of the entire Canadian working population will be significant (Cooper 1997; Jacot 2000, 123).

At the House of Commons Standing Committee on Finance review of the legislation after second reading, the NAC attempted to raise the issues of whether the investment board had to consist entirely of financial professionals, or whether room should be made for representatives of CPP beneficiaries, and why there had been 'no discussion of the possible use of ethical investment criteria' for the fund (House of Commons 1997e, 14). This attempt to broaden the base of participation in running the fund as well as its investment goals was vigorously and successfully resisted by pension experts. With respect to participation, all that the legislation ultimately requires is that there be a biennial public meeting in each participating province. It does not embody the Senate Committee on Banking Trade and Commerce's recommendation that at least one director of the fund attend. Instead, the legislation (s. 52) requires only that 'one or more directors or officers' attend to meet with any of the beneficiaries whose interests they are to maximize. The only issue of major debate with respect to the investment strategy had to do with the more 'technical' question of whether the fund should be invested actively or passively (i.e., replicating an existing stock exchange index). The debate here centred on various pension funds' experience with index-based investing, along with a concern that this particular fund (estimated to be some $60 billion by the year 2006) would be too large to make passive investing viable. The regulations initially required passive investing, though this has been subsequently altered.

Thus, a financial market-based risk management strategy and the employment of financial 'expertise' accompanies the use of legal governance norms derived from corporate and trust law (Miller & Rose 1990). These strategies are employed in an attempt to control the now enhanced, though relatively unacknowledged, market risk resulting from the turn to financial markets for pension funding. In this process, an emphasis is placed on risk management at the expense of a link between pension policy and national economic objectives. In legislating for fund governance, a singular interest in fund maximization, to be accomplished by using a circumscribed fiduciary obligation to govern low-visibility decision making, was privileged and articulated through a discourse of preventing 'government interference' rather than one of attempting to further democratic participation or accountability (Rose 1999, 154; Valverde et al. 1999, 29–30).

The Investment Board has now begun to invest funds transferred to it from the Department of Finance. The amounts transferred increase every few months, and currently stand at $2 billion (March 2000 figures). The amount is projected to increase to $70 billion by 2008. Members of the board have been appointed, as has the CEO, a retired senior executive from Nesbitt Burns. Two investment managers, TD Securities and Barclay's Global Investors, were chosen in March 1999 to invest the funds, domestically and internationally. As we have seen, CPP surplus funds were formerly invested in federal and provincial bonds (which pay an average rate of interest of 11 per cent). Now, as the bonds mature and the principal is repaid, these amounts are transferred to the Investment Board, which has adopted the strategy of investing everything it receives in equities, on the basis that existing funds are invested in bonds. This of course allows little investment diversification within the board's fund. In December 1999, the federal/provincial review of the CPP approved a shift to 'active management' of 50 per cent of the fund. With this strategy investment managers attempt to outperform stock indexes rather than just replicate the index. Active management is obviously a higher risk strategy, since the index is based on a diversified portfolio. It is also more lucrative for investment managers. Interestingly, the ACPM's position paper suggests that there is a 'large body of research which suggests that, on average, actively managed funds underperform index funds by at least the higher fees the active funds charge. Further, there is little evidence to suggest that active funds which perform relatively well in one period will repeat that feat in the next period' (ACPM 2000, note 22). In this connection, it is also somewhat ironic that, according to Blackburn, the present lack of alternatives to equity investment for pension funds in the United Kingdom is 'pushing the fund managers to overreliance on this type of asset' (Blackburn 2000, 134). He reports that 'Gerald Holtham, economic adviser to the Norwich Union, has lamented the scarcity of long-term public bonds and has proposed that the British government float a series of bonds maturing in 25 or 30 years to underwrite improvements in health and education' (ibid.).

The CEO of the Canada Pension Plan Investment Board has given several speeches since he was appointed, all to members of the financial community. His speeches often conclude along the following lines: 'For the directors and management teams of companies, the good news in this development [the fact that pension funds, including the CPP fund, have become the leading owners of corporate Canada] is that it inextricably aligns the retirement income of Canadians with the financial well-being of the private sector. The better Canadian firms perform financially over the long term ... the better off Canadians will be in their retirement years' (MacNaughton 1999, 4). Thus, at least for its CEO, the result of the change to the CPP's funding policy has been explicitly to further an agenda of privatization that links pension policy to the fortunes of private enterprise.

In terms of its accountability to beneficiaries and contributors, the board has so far placed significant reliance on its members to fulfil their fiduciary duty to 'act honestly and in good faith with a view to the best interests of the Investment Board' and to 'exercise the care, diligence and skill that a reasonably prudent person would exercise in comparable circumstances.' A code of conduct on conflicts of interest has been developed to deal with situations where, for example, directors of the Investment Board serve on the boards of companies in which the board owns shares. This code involves disclosure of the conflict and abstention from participating in discussions and voting about transactions in 'which they have a material interest.'

C. The Gender Order of CPP Reform

The increase in contribution rates enacted by the new legislation will have detrimental effects for lower-paid women. However, it is also true that more radical and harmful policy options put forward by the government's information paper – such as eliminating survivor benefits, only partially indexing pensions, reducing the rate at which CPP benefits would replace income from 25 per cent to 22.5 per cent, raising the age of entitlement, reducing the number of non-working or low-income years that could be dropped out – were dropped by the time the debate concluded. What explanation can be offered for this result? Is it attributable to the lobbying by women's groups who participated in the consultation process, or to the strategic mobilization of gender-based arguments by constituencies that do not otherwise welcome feminist arguments (Cossman, this volume; Philipps, this volume)? Representatives of the NAC appeared before the Standing Committee on Finance, to which the CPP bill was referred after second reading in Parliament, and other women's organizations, focusing primarily on the benefits proposals made by the government, participated in the public consultations on the CPP.[14] Indeed, the consequences for women of the government's proposals were highlighted in responses across the political spectrum. Thus, labour spokespersons opposed any reductions in benefits on the grounds that 'they would adversely affect low-income Canadians, fundamentally alter the social insurance side of the plan and adversely affect women' (Federal/Provincial/Territorial CPP Consultations Secretariat 1996, 22). Liberal Parliamentary Secretary Valeri referred in parliamentary debate to the 'gender analysis that was put forward that showed that in fact women would receive $2.56 of benefits for every dollar of contribution' (House of Commons 1997b). Meanwhile, the Official Opposition (Reform) party leader, Preston Manning, said 'When I look at the bill I am reminded that we are dealing with the principal source of income of people who are no longer in a position to add to their income. All of us know of middle aged [and] elderly women who invested most of their lives in raising children in the home and who entered the so-called official workplace, ... late in life or not at all and therefore qualify for little or no CPP benefits ... [We] should keep the needs of these women uppermost as we consider pension reform' (House of Commons 1997a). This attempt on the part of the Reform Party to target specific groups of women – regarded as deserving because of their traditional activities of social reproduction – was not matched by attention to the position of the larger number of women who remain in the paid labour force in marginal and insecure positions (Fudge & Cossman, this volume). No suggestion was made that it might be worth examining the possibilities of restructuring the labour market to allow the enhanced participation of women (Fraser 1998). Nor did the solution offered by the Reform Party involve an uncoupling or de-emphasis of the link between pension entitlements and labour force participation. It supported dismantling the CPP entirely, but in order to move to individual retirement savings accounts to which employers and employees would contribute. The Reform Party called for 'moving ... to a fully funded system based on individual accounts while protecting the benefits of current seniors. This means that individuals will own all the assets in their account and their retirement benefits will be substantially greater. When they die their children and their spouse will inherit the capital. This would go a long way toward eliminating poverty for elderly widows, for example ... Countries from around the world are following the example of Chile in moving from publicly to privately owned and managed pensions ...' (Ablonczy, House of Commons 1997a).

While the Reform Party's proposal was ultimately unsuccessful, it should be noted that it clearly rejects a socially redistributive element in the CPP. The association of a market-based pension delivery system with enhanced financial autonomy should be closely examined by feminists, especially if it is assumed, as the Reform Party did, that women will be recipients of pension income not in their own right, but by the inheritance from their families of market-based pension gains. It must be concluded therefore, that in feminist activist terms, the results of the CPP debate were ambiguous. The most immediately regressive aspects of the government's proposals in relation to benefit issues were successfully resisted by left-leaning politicians, seniors' organizations, and women's organizations, who spoke against them in consultation sessions. Yet the more long-term material and discursive effects of the legislative changes, which included destabilizing the redistributive aspects of the plan, valorizing market-based solutions to pension provision, and introducing norms of private law to support them, were much less effectively contested, with detrimental effects for those women less equipped to thrive in the new gender order of market based social policy.

D. Public Pensions and Neo-liberalism in Canada

The panic about unsustainability which grounded the CPP reform debate is a good example of what Callinicos calls 'a politically constructed risk.' Yet while the debate was prompted by the risk of the failure of the 'public' CPP pension because of demographic projections, the risks associated with investing pension money in the financial market were barely mentioned. The outcome of the CPP debate also suggests the ambiguities associated with a 'privatization' discourse, since the result was that the CPP would retain the features of mandatory labour marketwide contributions paying defined benefits while funds would be raised in private equity markets to supplement contributions.

A move away from a commitment to collective responsibility for pension provision has clearly taken place (Guest 1997, 293), as evidenced partly in the debate about benefit and contribution issues, and partly in the shift to a market-based investment strategy accompanied by governance norms drawing on risk management and fiduciary obligations, according significant discretionary authority to investment decision makers. A major discursive as well as material effect of the 1997 legislative changes was that returns from the financial markets were considered a preferable alternative to socialized reliance on other workers in a pay-as-you-go system (O'Malley 1992, 259, 261). Linked to this preference is diminishing credibility for a redistributive rationale for pension entitlements generally, such that it is now deemed 'unfair' to get more out of a pension plan than you put into it, when what you get out of it came from younger workers, rather than financial markets.

This assault on redistribution is likely to have negative effects for women, whose role in social reproduction tends to produce lower rates of contribution to the CCP. A gendered example of the neo-liberal attack on redistribution from workers to pensioners as the raison d'être for pension policy can be found in the comment of Michael Walker, executive director of a prominent think-tank, the Fraser Institute: '[U]nder the CPP women who live longer collect more in total benefits but do not pay higher premiums. This is, simply put, inequitable.' On being pressed about this, Walker responded, 'You're subsidizing the women's pensions with the contributions of the men ... that's confusing an issue of subsidy with an issue of paying for people's pensions. I don't think we should be doing that either' (House of Commons 1997d). As a result of the CPP legislation, pension contributors and recipients were transformed into stakeholders in an investment fund by means of discourses of financial rectitude and individualized gender-neutral 'fairness,' with little opportunity to render the ensuing decision making democratically accountable. That this transformation continues to be valorized is evident from the ACPM's discussion paper, which exhorts the necessity to 'take steps now to bolster self-reliance rather dependence (sic) as the foundation of the system' (2000, 2).

E. Risky Business: Employer Sponsored Pension Plans (RPPs)

RPPs represent one of the two limbs of the private pension system in Canada, and encompass pension plans organized by an employer for its employees, usually involving contributions from both. RPPs are considered private in the sense that the plan's sponsor is the employer rather than the state, though the state is of course implicated as a result of the regulatory resources it commits to the operation of the system and the tax policy it adopts with respect to it. Most of the biggest employment-based pension funds are found in the public sector itself: for example, the Ontario Teachers' Pension Plan, Ontario Municipal Employees Retirement System (OMERS), and the Caisse de depot et placement du Québec. The latter had over $100 billion in assets under management at the end of 1999 (Press 2000, 7).

While almost 13 million workers contributed to CPP/QPP in 1995, 5.1 million were members of RPPs. Ontario has one of the lowest coverage rates, below the national average of 42 per cent. Men's coverage has declined since 1980, but Statistics Canada reports that the proportion of women covered by these plans has increased in the last decade (Statistics Canada 1997). In 1993, 44 per cent of all employed women (compared to 51 per cent of men), were members of such plans, up from 38 per cent in 1980. This figure fell slightly between 1993 and 1996. The biggest increase is for women in the thirty-five to fifty-four age group, while it has remained fairly constant for younger women. This suggests, as Fudge and Cossman point out, a need to be sensitive to differences in labour market participation by women of different ages. For women in full-time work, coverage has grown from 40 per cent in 1984 to 46 per cent in 1993 (Fudge and Cossman, this volume; Morissette & Drolet 1999). Morissette and Drolet argue that part of the increase in coverage among women overall may result from 'changes in pension legislation which require employers to extend coverage to part-time workers if the employer already had a plan for full-time workers' (1999, 8). But they also argue that 'most of the growth in older women's coverage appears to be related to their movement towards well paid jobs' (ibid., 18). More than half (52 per cent) of the women participating in RPPs belonged to the very large plans, those having 30,000 or more members (Statistics Canada 1997, 39).

Only 21 per cent of part-time employees, however, said in a 1994 survey that they had pension coverage at work (Townson 1997, 35) and Townson argues that the expansion of non-standard employment may, in fact, be a major reason for declining pension coverage of paid workers in total (ibid., 33). Overall, about 24 per cent of workers in non-standard jobs are covered by occupational pension plans, compared with 56 per cent of those in standard jobs. The two employment sectors with the lowest pension coverage are the retail trade and community, business, and personal service. If we turn from coverage to amount of contributions to RPPs, Statistics Canada reports that 'men represented almost three-quarters (72%) of those with a PA[15] of $6,000 or more in 1997' (Statistics Canada 1999, 28). Finally, the number of pension plans is declining (by 24 per cent), with the principal change being in plans with fewer than ten members. This could be because those employers are shifting to group RRSPs (voluntary savings programs, similar to individual RRSPs) or because they are abandoning pension coverage entirely.

The most important trend in the provision of employer-sponsored pensions is the growing shift from 'defined benefit' plans to 'defined contribution' plans. Instead of a plan guaranteeing a worker a particular formula-based pension benefit on retirement, to be paid by the employer even if the plan's investment strategies have resulted in a shortfall, the employer and the worker contribute a defined amount into the plan, but no predetermined benefit is established. The resulting variable amount (again depending on how successful the plan's investment strategies have been) is converted into a retirement plan for the employee. Although a majority of members of RPPs are in defined benefit plans, the number of those belonging to defined contribution plans continues to increase steadily. Between 1996 and 1998, the number of Canadians covered by defined contribution plans grew by almost 20 per cent, the largest increase over the past ten years. However, although defined contribution plans made up 54 per cent of all registered pension plans as of 1 January 1998, they covered just over 636,000 members, or 12.5 per cent of the total (Benefits Canada 2000a, 13).

Defined contribution plans tend to be presented to employees as preferable alternatives to traditional plans on the basis that they provide more 'investment choice' and empowerment to plan members, since they often allow the member to participate in or direct the decision about where the contributions should be invested.[16] They may also provide more flexibility in the event of job changes. Their advantages to employers are clear, in that they make 'their pension contributions stable, predictable and easily managed' (Brown 2000, 6).[17] But it should also be noted that such plans have at least two other major consequences. Discursively, defined contribution plans render illegitimate the idea of an entitlement to a particular pension amount. Materially, they shift the risk of whether an adequate retirement benefit will result onto the employee, away from the employer. Ontario Securities Commission (OSC)[18] Chair David Brown notes that 'it is ... a massive transference of risk from the employer to the employee' (ibid.). The employee becomes more dependent on the success of the investment manager in maximizing returns in the market. This may have the effect of increasing competition within the investment sector, as the focus on fund performance heightens, but it is also an obvious source of revenue for fund managers. Indeed, the development of the defined contribution phenomenon narrows substantially the difference between a 'collective' plan such as an RPP and the more individualized RRSP. Thus Brown argues that 'One of the most important trends that is driving the global convergence of pension management and securities is the shift from defined-benefit plans to defined-contribution plans and group RRSPs' (ibid., 5–6). More generally, the demographic argument mobilized in the context of public pensions is conspicuously absent in relation to financial market investment of retirement income. Blommestein notes somewhat ominously that 'the ageing of OECD populations will tend to increase the price of stocks and bonds, decreasing their rates of return ... After the baby-boomers begin to retire, savings rates would tend to fall, stock and bond prices to decline ... In a protracted period of depressed asset prices and returns, even the most prudently managed pension fund might find itself in difficulty. The danger that large numbers of investors might find themselves deprived of adequate income on retirement might once again generate pressure on governments to intervene ...' (Blackburn 2000, 133; Blommestein 1998, 4–5).

As with the marketized CPP and individual RRSPs, the individualized market risk incurred by worker/investors is managed in part by means of legal rules imposing fiduciary responsibilities on plan sponsors and investment managers, requirements for diversified investments, and investment in Canadian equities. One development occasioned by the increasing popularity of defined contribution plans is that the fiduciary responsibility of the employer sponsor may encompass the requirement to provide the investor 'with enough education to make informed decisions' (Flood 2000, 13). More generally, Brown points out that while individualized pension investment is looking more and more like securities investment, 'many of the requirements that are standard for retail investment don't apply to pensions – in terms of the rules governing advice, the qualifications of advisors, knowledge of client or frequency of reporting' (Brown 2000, 6). This suggests that the enhanced regulatory activity concerning disclosure and proficiency requirements described below in relation to mutual funds will soon be extended to pension plans, at least the defined contribution ones. From a regulatory point of view, Brown asks 'what kind of market discipline is felt by employers who make the decisions but don't take the risks?' (ibid., 8). The ACPM agrees that a 'more efficient prudential/regulatory regime for pensions and investment funds' at both federal and provincial levels is central to its recommendations for reshaping the pension industry to meet the challenge of providing privatized pensions for Canadians (ACPM 2000, 6). It points out in its position paper that

> the [Senate] Committee recommended that ACPM work together with the Pension Investment Association of Canada (PIAC) and the federal Office of the Superintendent of Financial Institutions (OSFI) to develop a common set of governance guidelines for pension fund fiduciaries. The Committee also asked for the development of a 'best practices' framework which would permit governing fiduciaries to assess the quality of their own governance practices.
>
> We are pleased to report that these three organizations, joined by Ontario's FSCO [Financial Services Commission of Ontario], are working together to implement the Senate Committee's recommendations regarding pension fund governance. (ACPM 2000, 17)

Meanwhile, for funds that have remained 'collectivized,' the connection between organized pension funds and the capital markets is obvious. At the end of 1998, the market value of registered pension plan assets stood at $500 billion (ibid., 15). In 1996, the fifteen largest public sector pension funds in Canada had joint assets of over $150 billion, with the fifteen largest private sector pension funds trailing behind at $50 billion (Senate 1997a, 4). A representative of PIAC who appeared before the Senate Committee indicated that its membership consisted of 125 pension fund organizations, which collectively managed 'almost $400 billion of pension assets on behalf of over 6.5 million beneficiaries' (Senate 1997b, 1). However, even the largest pension plans increasingly diversify both the fund management and the investment decision processes (Statistics Canada 1997, 25). Up to now the connection between pension funds and capital markets has largely manifested itself as a debate within corporate law about the pros and cons of the role played by pension funds in the shareholder-governance of individual corporations (MacIntosh 1993). Harmes argues that structural features of institutional investment (such as pay and bonus structures that emphasize 'yield rather than risk exposure,' the 'herd mentality,' leveraging, and hierarchies within institutional investors) have had the effect of 'centralizing investment decision making' and enabling institutional investors to 'coercively reproduce neoliberalism' by means of the power they exercise over commercial corporations and governments (1998, 105; Aglietta 2000).

A broader debate is currently emerging about how to make explicit the connection between individualized and privatized saving for retirement and the role played by institutional investors in the financial markets (Aglietta 2000; Unger 1998). One facet of this debate concerns the pros and cons of 'ethical funds' in the mutual fund sector, where so-called ethical investing is seen as a market niche. Commenting on the current pension reform debate in Britain, Blackburn argues more generally that '[t]he idea that public pension funds could be used to promote wider economic and social objectives will remain central to the pension debate' (1999, 36). He observes that '[t]rade unions should be in the front rank of those seeking to promote a more long-term and socially responsible view, even if it sometimes means asking their members to put group solidarity ahead of immediate personal gain' (ibid., 50), and that 'existing private pension schemes should be required to respect social priorities if they are to enjoy fiscal subsidies and to give proper representation to policyholders' (ibid., 65). Pension reform should be directed to the end of the 'progressive socialization of the accumulation process' (ibid.). These proposals are premised on the idea that pension provision is now inextricably linked to investment in the capital markets, and that ways to render this link more transparent and subject to democratic control are necessary. These ideas are similar to those articulated by Bourdieu, who proposes the development of a 'common investment policy conforming to the general interest and radically different from the orientation towards short-term profit maximization enjoined by the financial markets' (Bourdieu 1998, 94–105; Callinicos 1999, 92; Jacot 2000, 123).

In the Canadian context this debate has not progressed particularly far. Around the same time as the debate over CPP reforms was taking place, the Senate Committee on Banking, Trade and Commerce (SBTC) held hearings into the role of institutional investors in corporate governance. A number of pension fund representatives who appeared before the SBTC hearings were quick to distinguish between ensuring that the 'pension promise' was met and the 'social aspects' of investing. During the CPP debate itself, the NAC proposed that the new investment board operate at least partly on the basis of 'ethical investment criteria,' but this possibility was dismissed in a pre-emptory fashion by other lobbyists and the government. In general the possibilities of a feminist analysis that would investigate the link between payment of pension fund benefits and investment of these funds in the equity markets or other investment vehicles are underdeveloped. Points of departure here might include attempts to develop a broader understanding of the nature of the 'interests' relevant to pension funds, or more generally, market decision making, as suggested by feminist economics (Anderson 1993; Folbre & Hartmann 1988), including attempts to reinvigorate notions of 'collective' interests (Jacot 2000). As Blackburn notes, 'it remains the case that perceptions of interest are socially constructed and open to more generous, enlightened and far-sighted definitions' (Blackburn 1999, 48). Another route might be adaptation of the norms of participation considered necessary for the exercise of citizenship in the 'public' sphere to 'private' institutions (Orloff 1993). This would involve reconceptualizing institutions such as pension funds as components of a wider 'public' sphere. However, as Blackburn suggests and as the *Laflamme* case below foreshadows, such a debate would have to come to terms with existing legal mechanisms for controlling investment decision making, particularly in relation to questions of liability for 'bad' decision making that results in financial loss.

F. Me, Myself, I: Registered Retirement Savings Plans (RRSPs)

In the midst of the panic about the future of the CPP, the significance of RRSPs to Canadian retirement planning is increasing. By 1997, contributions to RRSPs had surpassed that of RRPs (Statistics Canada 1999, 10).[19] However, it is worth noting that of those who contributed to RRSPs over the period 1991 to 1997, only one-quarter did so consistently, that is, every year. Another third contributed only occasionally (in one, two, or three years) (Statistics Canada 1999, 9). In neo-liberal terms, individuals are clearly not 'choosing' to personally invest for their retirement, which bodes ill for privatized pension well-being. Individuals in non-standard jobs are also more likely to use retirement savings accumulated in RRSPs in advance of retirement, for financial support during periods of unemployment or when withdrawing from the paid workforce because of family responsibilities (Townson 1997, 49). The RRSP investment phenomenon is supported by federal government provision of favourable tax treatment to amounts invested in RRSPs as well as the decline noted in employer-sponsored pension coverage (Townson 1997). Up to a current ceiling of some $15,500 of income, amounts contributed to an RRSP may be deducted from income before calculating the tax payable. Further, tax payable on the interest earned on these savings is deferred until the funds are withdrawn, although this withdrawal can occur before the individual retires.

Young has argued, with respect to both occupational pension plans and RRSPs, that investment patterns are gendered, in the sense that women are less likely to work for large employers who offer pension plans and tend to have less 'discretionary income' to contribute to RRSPs (1997, 320–1; Donnelly 1993). She also points out that the possibility for wage earners to contribute to spousal RRSPs (i.e., a transfer of funds into the plan of a lower-income spouse) reinforces traditional gender relations within families. Recent Statistics Canada data supports this conclusion: 'Overall, men saved on average 39% more than women ($6,239 versus $4,509). However, for each income group between $20,000 and $79,999, the average savings of women topped those of men. Average savings of all women were much lower than men's because of the large number of women with incomes under $20,000 who saved relatively little [26.4% of all taxfilers (Statistics Canada 1999, 38)]. In contrast many more men than women had incomes of $80,000 or more' (ibid., 25). Thus, between 1991 and 1997, '35% of women did not save compared with only 23% of men' (ibid., 19). A key point is that 'nearly half of all RRSP deductions are claimed by the 12.5% of tax filers with the highest incomes' (Dickinson 1996, 189; Guest 1997, 283; Townson 1997, 57). Specifically, the 1999 Statistics Canada report indicates that over 70 per cent of the savings in RPPs and RRSPs were accumulated by persons with incomes of $40,000 or more, who represented just slightly more than one-quarter of all tax filers. It is argued that forgone government revenue (which Finance Canada calls 'tax expenditures') as a result of tax exemptions for private pension plans amounts to roughly $12 billion a year, 'about 40% of the total cost of public pension programs such as OAS/GIS and the CPP' (Guest 1997, 283). In this connection, it is interesting to note that the projected tax expenditure for 2001 for RPPs and RRSPs is $15,875 billion. Of this figure, $5,345 billion is the projected expenditure for RPPs, while RRSPs account for $10,530 billion (Canada 1999b, 6).

The popularity of the mutual fund, a collective investment vehicle similar to a unit trust or managed investment, whose value is dependent on the value of the financial instruments it invests in, and which allows for diversification of investment risk, has increased dramatically in Canada in the last decade or so (Stromberg 1998, 24). Mutual fund assets stood at $394 billion at the end of 1998, up from $30 billion in 1989. Seven million Canadian households hold at least one mutual fund (Senate 1997b, 31). There are more than 1,300 mutual funds in Canada, sold by more than 80,000 registrants at brokers, mutual fund dealers, independent distributors, and banks. A 1998 report points out that 'there are now more investment funds in Canada than there are stocks listed on Canadian stock exchanges' (Stromberg 1998, 135).

This phenomenon has resulted in a dramatic upgrading of regulatory oversight of mutual fund operations, which has taken a variety of forms. The link between regulation of investment in mutual funds and saving for retirement has been acknowledged by Chair Brown of the OSC. In one of the first speeches of his tenure, given to the Investment Funds Institute of Canada in July 1998, he said, 'At the present time we do not have the tools to cope with a serious market reversal. Nor would we have answers for investors whose savings comprise these billions of dollars as to why their retirement dreams may have been lost' (Brown 1998, 5). The regulatory initiatives that have been taken in Ontario over the last few years to reduce the market risk faced by individual pension investors include the commissioning by the Canadian Securities Administrators, an umbrella organization for provincial securities commissions, of a member of the OSC to make recommendations for regulating investment funds (Stromberg 1995); the establishment of a self-regulatory organization – the Mutual Fund Dealers Association (MFDA) – to govern mutual fund dealers selling products to the public; new regulatory instruments governing sales practices engaged in by mutual funds (National Instrument 81–105) and a simplified prospectus system for mutual funds (National Instrument 81-101); a variety of enforcement initiatives targeted at mutual funds and their dealers, including a compliance review of twenty-three mutual fund dealers conducted over a two-year period; and hearings against specific fund managers suspected of violating provisions of securities legislation and regulation. Regulatory infractions include failures to disclose conflicts of interest in advice-giving and inappropriate investment advice given to inexperienced investors (*DeLellis*, 1998; *Mersch*, 1998). These regulatory initiatives are premised on the recognition that individuals saving for their retirement through RRSPs and mutual funds do not typically make investment decisions themselves but rely on intermediaries and financial 'experts' of one kind or another.[20]

Still, the presumption is that the investor is ultimately 'in control,' and this is one of the reasons given for the attractiveness of individualized pension investment, in contrast to state-controlled (CPP) or employer-controlled defined benefit schemes (RPPs). Brown points out that investors can always 'fire their broker.' However, the recent *Laflamme* decision of the Supreme Court of Canada, though it dealt with a securities broker rather than a mutual fund dealer or defined contribution pension fund manager, suggests some problems with this supposed advantage. The case dealt with a self-employed business person who transferred management of the proceeds of the sale of his company to a broker, in order to provide himself with a retirement fund. Having learned from his auditor that the broker was managing the portfolio on margin[21] without his knowledge and that a number of the investments being made were speculative, he contacted the broker by letter, setting out his instructions, and sought a meeting to discuss the management of the portfolio. When the account sustained major losses, Laflamme sued the broker and the broker's employer, Prudential-Bache. In its defence the brokerage house sought to reduce the damage award on the basis that the letters sent by the investor and his instructions at the meeting indicated that he had terminated the discretionary management of the portfolio by the broker.

The Supreme Court found that discretionary management had not been terminated, since after receipt of the investor's letter the broker 'bought and sold a number of securities without instructions from the appellant.' Further, he did not advise the investor 'regarding the effect of any such change in the object of the mandate on their respective obligations, as he should have done.' Thus the 'losses caused by the bad advice and grossly negligent management' of the broker 'cannot be laid' at the investor's doorstep. This case is a clear example of legal governance being used, reactively, to perform a risk management function for individual investors. But it also suggests some imperfections in the more pervasive and proactive governance of brokers through the so-called know your client rule imposed by self-regulatory organizations such as the Investment Dealers Association. This example links to the issue of control with much broader implications, namely the capacity of pension and mutual fund beneficiaries to influence the investment decisions made by investment managers on their collective behalf (Blackburn 1999; Harmes 1998). It also links to the concern that a high price may be paid for this supposed control. Thus, as Blackburn argues, 'all "personal" as opposed to "collective" or "group" pension schemes have this defect; at relatively modest levels of contribution, the expense of administering them takes a large bite out of expected benefits' (Blackburn 1999, 22).

The recent frenzy of legal and regulatory activity has culminated to date in another report authored by Commissioner Stromberg, this time for Industry Canada (Stromberg 1998), which is oriented towards 'consumer' protection. This report advocates the recognition of what is described as the 'retailization' of the financial marketplace, and specifically the diffuse nature of the market for investment products. One of its most striking features is the recommendation that individuals be offered the opportunity to learn how to manage investment risks, including the 'risk inherent in being too conservative' (Stromberg 1998, 28), along with support for investor economic education at a young age in the interests of enhancing 'wealth management' (ibid., Appendix D:2). In other words, the report posits that future pensioners need to be educated to accept risks, and it observes that this education would 'facilitate the implementation of a broader range of governmental initiatives in the area of pension and other retirement benefit programs including the increased privatization thereof' (ibid., 68). Should these recommendations be adopted by regulatory authorities, they would clearly further a neo-liberal agenda of individualized acceptance of market risk in pension provision. While the recommendations are presented, as usual, in gender-neutral terms, the data presented above on gender-based differences in RRSP investment suggest that many women are less well positioned to generate adequate retirement income by means of investment in mutual funds. Furthermore, there is interesting empirical work to be done to investigate the extent to which individual investment strategies are gendered and how intermediaries construct the 'risk profiles' of their clients in accordance with self-regulatory codes (*Laflamme*, 2000). The feminist economics literature suggests, in general, that the 'rational actor' model of market decision making may itself be gendered (England 1993; Ferber & Nelson 1993a).

As a result of this regulatory activity the legal relationship between investors and their intermediaries is in the process of being redefined. This redefinition is also occurring through the courts, in the context of civil actions launched by individual investors alleging breach of fiduciary duty (*Hodgkinson*, 1994; *Laflamme*, 2000). The risk of private investing is being actively reshaped by tax, securities, and tort law. Indeed, a plurality of regulatory mechanisms, some familiar from private, corporate law contexts, and others staples of administrative regulation, are being pressed into the service of facilitating financial market-based retirement well-being for those who can afford to avail of it. The existence of this legal code addressing issues of risk management and individualized techniques of investor accountability (Condon 1996; Pearce & Tombs 1996, 448; Rose 1996a, 350–1) amply demonstrates that the investment market is not unfettered, but in fact requires considerable legal resources to support it, resources which may of course themselves fail (Gordon 1987). Deregulation is not at all the order of the day in this sphere.[22] Taking the CPP, defined contribution pension plans, and mutual fund developments together, however, it is possible to see that the role of the state, through legal governance, is shifting towards structuring market risk and away from the direct provision of financial benefits, which will have the effect of producing further material inequality.

Conclusion: The Gender Order of Privatized Pensions

In its focus on individualized risk and its de-emphasis of socialized redistribution, the pension privatization debate in Canada is a classic example of what Rose calls the 'death of the social' (Rose 1996a). Yet the consequences of this demise vary according to gender, sexuality, and class position. Thus, the marketization of the CPP, illustrated by the investment strategy adopted and the inequitable increase in contribution requirements, can be contrasted with the tax revenue-based support of RRSP investment, which helps to ensure that wealthy workers will get wealthy pensions. As Fudge and Cossman suggest, we may be witnessing the development of a new gender order in which women no less than men are expected to provide for their own post-employment well-being, rather than relying on the 'family wage' (Fudge and Cossman, this volume). The Statistics Canada data on workplace pensions also evidence a growing polarization in the positions of richer and poorer women, which seems to reflect access to full-time well-paying jobs. Yet, in terms of specific policy outcomes, at this juncture it appears that the success of the neo-liberal agenda in relation to Canadian pensions lies not so much in concrete withdrawals by the state from providing benefits in an already significantly privatized system, but rather in the discursive developments in relation to 'governance of the self' that both delegitimize the redistributive impulse underlying the Keynesian 'pension promise' and encourage gender-neutral, autonomous individuals to 'embrace risk' and 'financial wellness' (ACPM 2000, 10). We also see the selective mobilization of a risk discourse in which the publicly run CPP is 'unsustainable' but individualized market risk can be managed by enhanced legal regulation. In understanding this outcome, we need to be sensitive to the specificity of the version of privatization being proposed in reform debates in Canada and the role of interest group politics in explaining these outcomes (Deaton 1989).

This picture of the privatization of pensions presents a dilemma for feminist political and legal strategizing, since feminists have historically relied on or exhorted the state to recognize and act upon the need for gender-sensitive decommodification. As Fraser puts it, the 'welfare state is crucial for gender relations' (Fraser 1998, 55). Fraser argues that feminists need to abandon the effort to achieve two competing visions of the 'feminist welfare state,' which she describes as the 'universal breadwinner' model and the 'caregiver parity' model.[23] Fraser claims that neither can ensure gender justice because neither fully integrates redistributive goals with recognition of gender difference. The universal breadwinner model 'valorizes men's traditional sphere,' while the caregiver model would 'entrench gender disparities in income' and institute a 'mommy track' (ibid., 59). Her own blueprint advocates a third alternative, which is to 'deconstruct the gender-based differentiation of breadwinning and caregiving.' Specifically, it would require restructuring the organization of work by 'envisioning a society in which women's current life-patterns are the norm for everyone' (ibid., 63–4). Thus, social and political institutions should be redesigned to ensure that men, like women, combine caregiving with breadwinning, and that the practical difficulty of doing so is eliminated. At a general level, this would imply a recognition of the interdependence of the so-called productive economy and the requirements of social reproduction (Philipps, this volume). Translated into the pension context, it would require pension entitlements to be more fully cognizant of the need to fulfil both roles, the need to take time out of the paid labour force, the need to work part-time, the need to have careers flexible enough to accommodate workplace and caring labour, and in general the need to decrease the link between pensions and the paid labour market.

The problem with Fraser's alternative of course, is that the opportunity for feminists to push the welfare state in the desired direction (Donnelly 1993) is receding under the onslaught of market-oriented policy making, bringing with it new inequalities of gender-based risk. As Rose puts it, 'the state may no longer be assuming responsibility for the management of a whole variety of risks' (Rose 1996a, 338). Feminist strategizers thus face the real dilemma of whether to pursue efforts to reinvigorate the redistributive goals of the welfare state, for example, by moving away from labour market-based benefits to universal ones, or to reorient themselves to engage with the state's new role in relation to pension provision, which is largely to secure the control of market risk through legal and other governance mechanisms. With respect to the first option, it would seem important not to abandon redistribution as a collective commitment, but to keep that normative goal alive. Part of the approach may involve deconstructing the opposition often posed between redistribution and market norms, by pointing out, as some economists have argued, that markets may have a redistributive effect (D. Bromley 1997). This, in essence, is the argument made by Blommestein regarding the possibility that the mass withdrawal of pension assets when members of the baby boom retire may have a depressive effect on the stock markets (Blommestein 1998, 4–5). It may also be possible, in this era of 'post-social politics' (O'Malley et al. 1997), to seek new rationales for redistribution.

With respect to the second option, an aspect of the agenda might be, as I have suggested earlier, to interrogate the techniques and goals of accountability, accomplished via legal mechanisms, of those institutions involved in financial market pension provision, and to invigorate wider discourses of accountability than are countenanced by a focus on individualized risk management (Pearce & Tombs 1996, 446; Valverde et al. 1999). One possibility that might serve to offset the individualizing trend of pension provision via defined contribution schemes and RRSPs is to consider the formation of associations of RRSP investors to monitor the activities of mutual and pension funds. Another broader possibility is to make explicit the connections between the distribution of pension provision by market means and the investment of pension contributions made to mutual funds, pension funds, and the CPP. This would involve no less than the 'politicization' of the economy (Bourdieu 1998; Callinicos 1999). As Blackburn points out, the 'murkiness' of this connection at present is in part due to the private law norms that govern investment by these institutions (1999, 6–7, 36–8). Although the pre-emptory way in which the NAC's proposal for 'ethical investment criteria' was dismissed in the CPP debate may not augur well for this endeavour in Canada, it is a central component of a contemporary feminist analysis of pensions.

Notes

1 However, see Martin's chapter in this collection on the enhanced role of criminal law under neo-liberalism in policing marginal populations.
2 I am drawing here on Hunt's description of Foucault's use of the terms 'gov-

ernment' and 'governmentality,' which Foucault argues do not 'refer only to political structures or the management of states; [but] ... rather [to] the way in which the conduct of individuals or states might be directed: the government of children, of souls, of communities, of families, of the sick ... To govern, in this sense, is to structure the possible field of action of others.' Thus the term 'governance' is used in this paper to describe techniques of ruling populations that have not been associated with the command and control orientation of state-based regulation. The terms 'corporate governance' and 'mutual fund/pension governance' are used to refer to internal mechanisms for governing these institutions. These terms have become widely used in the corporate and business literature, in part, I would argue, because 'governance,' which is not associated with the state, has positive valences, while regulation, which is associated with the state, does not.

3 Statistics Canada does not use the benchmark of 'poverty line,' but rather the term 'low income.' This is defined as spending at least 20 per cent more of pre-tax income than the Canadian average on food, shelter, and clothing.

4 These include (i) increasing the working period over which a retiree's benefits are computed, so as to include more lower earning years, (ii) extending Social Security coverage to state and local government employees who are currently excluded, to bring more revenues into the system, and (iii) raising the age of retirement to sixty-seven by 2011.

5 Specific proposals (at 22) include those of 'reducing the size of public pension benefits where these are now unnecessarily high' and 'reducing benefit levels in pay-as-you-go public plans in order to make room for other sources of retirement income.' The report (at 15) describes the effect that aging will have on 'saving and investment patterns nationally, including through the build up and subsequent unwinding of private pension assets by the retiring baby-boom generation.' It goes on to argue that '[T]hese considerations call for:

– strengthening of financial market infrastructure through improved legislation and codes of conduct and the introduction of rigorous rules of transparency, fiduciary responsibility and disclosure
– improved supervision, an upgrade and modernisation of pension asset investment rules, and better domestic co-ordination among the different regulatory and supervisory agencies involved in the provision of retirement income
– structural reforms in emerging market economies to ensure efficient allocation of savings into the most productive investment opportunities in the mutual interest of OECD and younger, faster growing non-OECD economies.'

6 The program in fact represents a cluster of three benefits: (i) Old Age Security (OAS), based on age (sixty-five) and years of residence in Canada; (ii) Guaranteed Income Supplement (GIS), providing additional benefits to those with low incomes, with the benefits payable varying with marital status; and (iii) Spouse's Allowance, providing further benefits to those who are spouses of OAS recipients, or survivors aged sixty to sixty-four.

7 Note that the CPP also pays disability benefits to those of pre-retirement age who are eligible.

8 Thus the paper asks 'should "typical" Canadians bother saving at all for their retirement ... if the public purse guarantees them almost 100% replacement of the monies they had available for consumption during their working lives.'

9 Time out of the paid labour force to raise children under the age of seven and 15 per cent of the lowest earnings years can be dropped out of the calculation of the 'contributory period' on which benefits are based.

10 This change was apparently made to bring the CPP 'in line with the majority of private plans.'

11 According to the Consultations Secretariat, these consultations were held between 15 April and 10 June 1996 in thirty-three sessions in eighteen cities.

12 A 'pay as you go system' thus differs from a 'funded' or 'advanced funded' system where the pension plan is capable of meeting all future claims on its resources.

13 While the investment figure stands at CAN$11.9 million (as of March 1999), the board is expected to receive CAN$66 billion of funds over the next ten years.

14 The list of women's organizations that participated in the public consultations about the CPP included the Manitoba Action Committee on the Status of Women, the British Columbia Farm Women's Network, the National Association of Women and the Law, Northwest Territories Status of Women, Yukon Status of Women, the Manitoba Women's Advisory Council, the Older Women's Network Metro Toronto and Area Council, the Disabled Women's Network, and l'Association féminine d'éducation et d'action sociale.

15 The PA, or pension adjustment, refers to the value of the pension accrued in the year in an RPP.

16 A survey of defined contribution plans conducted by William Mercer Ltd reports that the average number of investment options in such plans is twelve (Benefits Canada 2000b, 15).

17 A factor that may have influenced the shift from defined benefit to defined contribution plans is the legislative change in the early 1990s relating to the

minimum employer contributions to defined benefit plans. As Morissette and Drolet explain it, prior to the change employers had to contribute only enough to provide the benefits to which workers were entitled. Thus higher rates of return on funds originating from employees could produce lower employer contributions. The legislation now imposes cost sharing, such that employers are required to pay 50 per cent of an employee's pension entitlement (Morissette and Drolet 1999, 4).

18 Regulation of mutual funds in Canada is provincially based, with the main body of governing legislation located in provincial Securities Acts.

19 Thus 'in 1997, the $22.8 billion in contributions to RRSPs by those aged 25 to 64 represented over half (55%) of the savings made through RRPs or RRSPs. This was up from 42% in 1991.'

20 Similar developments are taking place in Australia. See Kingsford Smith 1999, 14.

21 That is, without paying the full amount for the investments made.

22 Indeed the ACPM wants to go even further. It argues, 'we believe that the long term financial interests of Canadians would be better served if investment funds are effectively defined and treated as trust funds governed by independent fiduciaries. These fiduciaries would be required by law to look after the financial interests of the unit holders' (2000, 19).

23 In the first, the 'universal breadwinner' model, the goal is for women's work lives to become the same as men's, while the ideal of 'caregiver parity' would 'revalue feminine life patterns.' These competing visions have manifested themselves in the past in the difficulties experienced by Canadian feminist activists in developing a consistent position on pension reform (Vickers et al. 1993).

PART II

Producing the Social Body

4

Family Feuds: Neo-Liberal and Neo-Conservative Visions of the Reprivatization Project

BRENDA COSSMAN

Family law has always involved the public enforcement of private responsibilities of individual family members. But in an era of privatization, it has acquired a newfound importance. Within the new neo-liberal state – characterized by a reduction of government social spending and a transfer of these responsibilities to the private realms of market and family – family law is becoming a more important regulatory instrument for the enforcement of private support obligations for economically dependent family members. More specifically, family law is being called upon to address the economic needs of women and children at precisely the moment when the welfare state is being dismantled and public financial assistance is becoming scarce. This enhanced role of family law must be seen within the context of a key strategy of the privatization project of the neo-liberal state – namely, the reprivatization of the costs of social reproduction, and the discursive strategies through which this move is being legitimated. By reprivatization, I mean a process whereby the costs of social reproduction are being shifted from the public to the private spheres, in this case, from the state to the family. In the present chapter I examine this reprivatization in the context of the changing regulation of and relationship between family law and social welfare law, with a particular focus on the Ontario experience.

Recent developments in family law and social welfare law in Canada have all the hallmarks of the privatization project. The changing roles and relationship between these two areas of legal regulation embody the shift from public responsibility to private self-reliance and from systemic analyses of social problems to highly individualized solutions. Expanding definitions of spouse within social welfare law, increasing spousal and child support obligations in family law, and an intensification of the enforcement of these private support obligations are all being used to redirect women's economic dependency from the public to the private sphere. The rhetoric within which these reforms are cast is increasingly individualizing. For example, in the area of child support, the problem of child poverty is being reduced to an individualized problem of 'deadbeat dads' (Mossman 1997). If individuals could be made to fulfil their responsibilities to their children, it is implied, the problems would be eliminated. Accordingly, individuals' legal responsibilities toward their children are being increased and the legal remedies for enforcing these responsibilities strengthened. At the same time, the systemic problems associated with poverty are fading from view. For example, a range of children's behavioral problems are increasingly being associated with 'bad parenting' rather than social class, thereby placing the blame on individual parents (*Globe and Mail* 1999a). Similarly, within welfare law, systemic analyses of poverty are being recast in individualized terms, with welfare mothers increasingly seen as blameworthy for their dependency (Brodie 1995; Fraser 1993; Fraser & Gordon 1997).

The shift from public responsibility to private self-reliance, from social welfare rights to individualized support obligations, is not without its contradictions. First, it is important to emphasize that this shift operates at the level of the discursive and not necessarily at the concrete level of women and children's lives. Individual women and children who lose their welfare rights through an expansion of the 'spouse-in-the-house' definition or failure to qualify for workfare do not necessarily obtain enforceable family support entitlements. Indeed, the disjuncture of definitions of spouse for the purposes of welfare and family law means that many women and children fall through the cracks of the support structures of the emergent neo-liberal state (Mossman and MacLean 1997). Nor did social welfare ever fully assume responsibility for addressing these economic needs. While the shift from public responsibility to private self-reliance and from social welfare law to family law is a discursive shift, embodied in legal and political institutions, with real material effects, it does not necessarily operate at the concrete level to actually transfer responsibility for individual women and children from the state to the family.

Second, the privatization of the costs of social reproduction is hardly a new phenomenon in Canada. Family law and social welfare law have long been implicated in constituting a familial ideology that casts women's economic dependency as naturally located within the realm of the nuclear family (Chunn 1992; Gavigan 1993; Ursel 1992). However, as described in the Introduction and argued throughout this volume, there is something distinctive about the current phase of privatization. The project of privatization involves a fundamental retrenchment of the state in social reproduction, with families and charities left to shoulder a greater part of the burden of caring for people. Through the dual strategies of reprivatization and familialization, once-public goods and services are being reconstituted as naturally located within the realm of the family. In the context of family law and social welfare law, this transformation results in an intensification of the demands made on families to support their own. However, this change is not provoking a return to pre-Keynsian welfare state (KWS) gender relations. Feminists continue to make gains in the area of family law, as women's unpaid work in the home is increasingly recognized and valued for the purposes of private support obligations and property entitlements and definitions of family are broadened to include non-traditional families. The current phase of reprivatizing the costs of social reproduction, while at times relying on some of the older 'stories' of gender and family, is resulting in a shift in the gender order, with new and contradictory claims being made on the family.

Neo-liberal and neo-conservative discourses of gender and family are vying for position in this new gender order. While neo-liberalism, with its emphasis on fiscal restraint and individual self-reliance, appears to be in ascendance, its influence is muddied by the continuing influence of moral or social conservatism, which emphasizes the rearticulation of the 'traditional family.' As a result, the discursive struggle over the new gender order is ongoing.

This chapter explores some of the differences between the visions and strategic interventions of neo-liberalism and neo-conservatism and their respective implications for the privatization project in family and social welfare law. It highlights the contradictory implications of these strategic interventions on gender, particularly the ways in which privatizing projects are producing not only 'an intensification and erosion of gender' but an intensification and erosion of the family (Brodie 1995, 76 citing Haraway 1991, 166). The chapter examines the extent to which family, gender, and dependency are sites of intense contestation within the privatizing project.

The first part of this chapter explores the theoretical differences between neo-liberal and neo-conservative visions of the family and the contradictory implications for the regulation of the family. The second part considers three specific areas of family and social welfare law as concrete instances of the contradictions: (1) same-sex challenges to spousal definitions in family law; (2) legislative amendments to child support law; and (3) the restructuring of social welfare for single mothers in Ontario. Each of these examples focuses on a different *form* of law, highlighting not only some of the ways in which the neo-liberal and neo-conservative approaches to family and privatization diverge but also the role of law in mediating and materializing these divergent discourses. Law plays an important role in selecting between competing discourses (Woodiwiss 1990). Although no single model of the family has yet emerged as ideologically dominant, the analysis of these three areas suggests that the neo-liberal discourse on the family is in ascendance in law. At the same time, the neo-conservative discourse remains very much alive, sometimes in concert, but more often in collision with the neo-liberal vision, producing unanticipated fissures and contradictions in the privatization project.

I. Stories of Privatization

A number of different stories are being told about the way in which the reprivatization of the costs of social reproduction is being legitimated and naturalized. According to Janine Brodie, the privatization project in Canada includes a transformation in the 'meso-narrative' of state forms, that is, a rewriting of the stories of governmentality and modernity (Brodie 1997). The meso-narrative of the neo-liberal state involves a fundamental shift in dominant understandings of government and citizenship. A new set of assumptions about the role of government and the rights of its citizens is emerging, in which government responsibility for the social welfare of citizens is being replaced by a political and social order in which governments are only responsible for helping citizens to help themselves. The philosophy of public social responsibility is being displaced in favour of an emphasis on private self-reliance. The new self-reliant citizen – 'the atomized, individual market player' – 'recognizes the limits and liabilities of state provision and embraces her/his obligation to work longer and harder in order to become self reliant' (Brodie 1997; Drache 1992, 221). Difference, social disadvantage, or structural inequality all disappear as the basis for citizenship claims. Social and structural analyses are displaced in favour of highly individualized approaches that identify individual solutions to individual problems. For example, as Fraser and Gordon have argued, economic dependency is recast in individualized terms, reconstituted as personal pathology (Fraser & Gordon 1997).

This narrative resonates with many of the recent changes to family and social welfare law. Family law is displacing social welfare as the primary financial source for persons without market income. Susan Boyd, for example, has argued that '[i]ncreasingly ... courts and administrative arms of the Canadian state are reinforcing certain private familial responsibilities for women's poverty, in the name of feminist values and in part in response to feminist struggle in the courts, while diminishing public societal commitment to alleviating that poverty' (Boyd 1994; see also Eichler 1990; Luxton 1997a; Mossman 1997).[1] Increasing spousal and child support obligations, alongside an intensification of the enforcement of these private support obligations, are accompanying the reintroduction of the spouse-in-the house rule in social welfare law, all with the objective of redirecting women and children's economic needs from the public to the private sphere. Simultaneously, systemic analyses of the underlying problem of poverty are being displaced by an individualized frame of reference, in which 'deadbeat dads' and 'welfare mothers' are blamed for their children's poverty.

A second story about the way in which this reprivatization strategy is legitimated involves the rearticulation of the 'traditional family.' Feminist scholars have observed the mutually constituting relationship between the demise of the welfare state and the resurgence of campaigns around 'family values' and the traditional family (Luxton 1997a). The rearticulation of 'the family' as the most natural and universal of institutions provides ideological support for the transfer of social and economic costs to this private sphere. The family is reconstituted as the 'natural' location for a range of caregiving responsibilities, including health care, elder care, and childcare.

There is much resonance between this rearticulation of the traditional family and recent developments in family and social welfare law. The demonization of both 'welfare mothers' and 'deadbeat dads' can be seen as flip sides of the effort to rearticulate the norm of the traditional nuclear family. The shift in responsibility for dependent persons from the public to the private sphere can similarly be seen to correspond to an effort to renaturalize the family as the appropriate site of women's economic dependency. Along these lines, there are even suggestions from conservative quarters that the best way to deal with child poverty is to toughen up divorce laws, thereby forcing families to remain in their pristine nuclear form (Blackenhorn 1995). The call to shore up the traditional family is heard nowhere more strongly than in opposition to the challenges that same-sex couples have brought to a range of spousal definitions.

Together, a story that has begun to emerge is one of a smooth and seamless web between the fiscally driven project of reprivatizing costs of social reproduction and the meso-discourses providing ideological legitimation of this reprivatization. The dismantling of the KWS has, supposedly, acquired all the ideological legitimation that it needs from these new discourses about the appropriate relationship between citizen and state, and from the rearticulation of traditional familial ideology. What appears is a mutually reinforcing relationship between the neo-liberal fiscal project of reducing state spending and the neo-conservative project of rearticulating the traditional family. But the ideological project of the 'New Right' is not as homogenous as it may appear at first glance, particularly with respect to the reregulation of the family (Somerville 1992). The implications of the dismantling of the welfare state for the family, and for women therein, is more complex and contradictory (Brodie 1995). Both discursively and materially, the family is being reconstituted as a highly contradictory site, in which the various strategies of the privatization project are simultaneously producing an intensification and erosion of the family.

Many commentators have begun to explore the contradictory pressures of privatization on gender – the ways in which the privatization project is simultaneously placing greater demands on women as caregivers in the family and as workers in the labour market (Ursel 1992; Bakker 1996a; Brodie 1995; Haraway 1991). These processes are reflected in the reregulation of the family. The reprivatization of the costs of social reproduction is intensifying the role of the family, and women therein, in the provision of basic needs. From caring for pre-school children to health care for the elderly and disabled (Armstrong 1996b), the state is increasingly attempting to transfer its responsibility under the Keynesian welfare state to the unpaid work of women within the family. In the context of the reforms to family law and social welfare, private family members are increasingly being called upon to provide for economically dependent persons. And the state is becoming voracious in its efforts to enforce these private obligations. The material importance of the family as a caregiving and financial institution is being intensified. The normative and discursive claims on the family are also intensifying, with the rearticulation of so-called 'traditional families' and 'traditional family values.' As Pat Armstrong notes, '[t]he shift of responsibility to communities and families is accompanied by a myth that families have traditionally, and joyfully, taken such responsibilities, and that they have done so effectively' (Armstrong 1996a, 227). Reflecting the discourse of moral or neo-conservatives, the nuclear, heterosexual family is being

Table 4.1
Family earners in Canada

Year	Husband only (%)	Dual income (%)
1967	61	34
1990	15	62
1996	21	68

Source: Lero & Johnson 1994; Vanier Institute
of the Family 1994, 74; 2000, 89

reasserted as the natural and fundamental unit of society, responsible
for the moral and material care of its own members.

At the same time, the privatizing project is leading to an erosion of
the family as a site of caregiving. The restructuring of the Canadian
labour market, with the loss of higher paid 'male' manufacturing jobs
and the decline in men's wages, alongside the increase in women's participation, disproportionately in part-time, non-unionized, precarious
employment, has resulted in the disappearance of the family wage
(Armstrong 1996b; Fudge 1997; Brodie 1995). Few Canadian families
are structured around a single income earner. As Table 4.1 indicates,
there has been a marked increase in dual income earner families. By
1990, only 15 per cent of Canadian families corresponded to the traditional male breadwinner model.

Moreover, women's income increasingly contributes a significant proportion to the family's income. In 1997, wives' earnings represented
31.5 per cent of the income of dual income families, up from 28.7 per
cent in 1989 and 26.4 per cent in 1967 (Statistics Canada 2000a, 145).
Women's participation in the labour market has become essential to the
living standard of families.

At the discursive level, the meso-narrative of market citizenship is also
eroding impositional claims on the family. In the new order of things, the
quintessentially good citizen, devoid of 'special' characteristics or differences, relies only on him/her self for his or her economic well-being.
While dependency on the state is increasingly constructed as pathological, even dependency on the family is falling into disrepute. As Fraser and
Gordon have argued, the 'decentring of the ideal of the family wage' is a
factor contributing to the disappearance of even 'good dependency'
(Fraser & Gordon 1997, 134–5): 'the family wage is no longer hegemonic

but competes with alternative gender norms, family forms, and economic arrangements. It no longer goes without saying that a woman should rely on a man for economic support, nor that mothers should not also be "workers'" (ibid., 135). As a result, 'there is no longer self evidently "good" adult dependency in postindustrial society' (ibid., 135). The new meso-narratives of the neo-liberal state are undermining the normative claims of 'natural' dependency on the family.

Reprivatization is producing highly contradictory pressures on the family, simultaneously intensifying the material and discursive claims made on it while undermining the very material and discursive conditions that could support those claims. At a material level, the family – and women within the family – are being expected to take on a greater role in care-giving while their ability to do so is undermined by greater and greater demands to contribute to the financial support of their families through labour market participation. As Pat Armstrong describes, the process is one that 'means more responsibility for families that have a decreasing ability to carry out the work' (1996a, 227). Similarly, at the normative/discursive level, the family is being rearticulated as the natural site of care-giving for a range of dependent persons (the young, the elderly, the infirm), at the same time as dependency is being pathologized.

These contradictory pressures on the family within the privatization project are reflected in the divergent normative visions of neo-liberals and neo-conservatives. Neo-conservatives' moral claims that family is the natural and fundamental unit of society have often been seen as lending ideological credence to the neo-liberal project of reprivatizing the costs of social reproduction, yet the alliance between these two political forces is precarious (Teghtsoonian 1995, 1997). The family is a site of contestation and contradiction within the privatization project, in which the normative visions and strategies of the neo-liberals and neo-conservatives often clash.

Neo-liberalism and neo-conservatism are often used interchangeably to refer to the policies of restructuring, privatization, and the dismantling of the welfare state, collapsed under the rubric of the 'New Right.' This conflation obscures important differences between the two political philosophies and their respective adherents. There are important differences between social and fiscal conservatives. Lipset and Raab's study of the American Right, for example, found an ongoing alliance between these two groups, the former drawn primarily from lower income brackets, who are attracted to the religious, non-economic issues of conservative politics, and the latter drawn from higher income brackets, who are highly educated and attracted primarily to the economic issues of conservative politics (Lipset & Raab 1970).

Although cast within the language of conservatism (social conservatism versus fiscal conservatism), the divide is really one between conservatism and liberalism. Social conservatives are the true inheritors of a conservative political philosophy, with its emphasis on community, authority, social order, and tradition. Individuals are seen as members of communities, united by common morals, values, and traditions (Klatch 1988; Teghtsoonian 1995). Within this vision, the family is seen as a basic unit of society, forging individuals together through its moral authority, instilling children with values and traditions. By way of contrast, fiscal or laissez-faire conservatism derives from classic liberal theory, with its emphasis on the individual and the liberty to pursue different moral visions of the good. Within classical liberalism, the individual is envisioned as an autonomous, rational, self-interested actor, endowed with free will, whose liberty to pursue his own interest is to be protected above all else (Klatch 1988; Silk Klein 1985; MacPherson 1965). According to classical liberal theory, this liberty is best promoted through the economic liberty of a free market and the political liberty of a minimal state (Elshtain 1981; Olsen 1983; Pateman 1988).

The 'neo' represents the current phase of these political philosophies, both of which have enjoyed a remarkable resurgence in the last two decades. Neo-conservatives see the welfare state as responsible for breaking down the moral basis of society. The decline of the traditional family through welfarism, daycare, divorce, affirmative action, abortion, and gay rights, to name but a few of their favourite targets, is held responsible for the political, economic, and moral decay of society. Neo-conservatives believe that family breakdown and the resulting moral decay have been caused by extensive state intervention in the private spheres of the family and the economy (Klatch 1988; Abbot & Wallace 1992; Herman 1997). Accordingly, the answer for neo-conservatives is simple: strengthen the family and its traditional, hierarchical gender roles.

Neo-liberalism identifies the basic problem of modern society as the erosion of liberty that has accompanied the growth of the KWS (Klatch 1988, 676). Individuals have lost their sense of economic initiative and enterprise through overreliance on the state. The answer for neo-liberals is also simple: restore the economic and political liberty of the individual through the promotion of the free market and the radical reduction of the state. The family does not feature as prominently within neo-liberalism as it does within the neo-conservative vision. Its primary focus is on restoring the individual to his (and now her) place as an autonomous, industrious market actor. But against the back-drop of its concern with the impact of welfarism, neo-liberalism 'promises to restore the state's distance from the family. In short, neo-liberalism suggests and needs the family to take some responsibility for itself' (Bell 1993, 395). The family should be restored to the private sphere, beyond the realm of appropriate state regulation.

These tensions between neo-conservatism and neo-liberalism are visible within the Canadian Right. The Canadian Alliance Party frequently deploys neo-conservative morality in relation to the family and neo-liberal economics in relation to state regulation of the market. On the family values front, its policies include the defence of traditional marriage from the onslaught of gays and lesbians and the recognition of traditional one-earner families through tax (Philipps this volume) and pension relief (Condon this volume). But on the economic front, the Canadian Alliance Party demands tax cuts, free enterprise, and less state intervention in the lives of its citizens. The Ontario and Alberta Progressive Conservative governments are characterized by a similar suturing of neo-conservative and neo-liberal ideas.

Neo-liberalism and neo-conservatism can be seen then, roughly to correspond to the two stories related above about the legitimation of the reprivatization of the costs of social reproduction. The new narrative of individual self-reliance tells a story about neo-liberalism, while the rearticulation of the traditional family tells a story about neo-conservatism. Neo-conservatives and neo-liberals share a contempt for the welfare state, agreeing that it is responsible for a range of social and economic problems. They agree that the solutions to these problems lie in reducing and eliminating welfarism. Further, while neo-liberalism is itself morally agnostic on the issue of the family, much of the moral conservative strategy of rearticulating familial ideology supports the neo-liberal privatization project. The idea of the family as a natural institution, responsible for the welfare of its members, provides considerable ideological support for the renegotiation of the public/private spheres of responsibility. The highly gendered roles and responsibilities within the family also help legitimate the transfer of social and economic responsibilities from the public to the private.

In many ways, however, the normative visions and strategies of the neo-conservatives and neo-liberals diverge. Despite their mutual condemnation of welfarism, their diagnoses of the particular ills of the welfare state differ, as do their prescriptions. Neo-liberalism emphasizes the way the welfare state has undermined individual initiative and enterprise, while moral conservatives stress moral decay and the undermining of the traditional family. Neo-conservatives are not adverse to a continuing role for the state in promoting the family (Herman 1997), whereas neo-liberals deplore state intervention in the 'private' sphere. Neo-conservatives are committed to reinscribing a highly gendered world, in which women and men are constituted as naturally different, and therefore naturally assigned to different roles and responsibilities (Klatch 1988). Neo-liberals, by contrast, deny the relevance of gender and seek to promote an abstracted individual, a disembodied market citizen (Brodie 1997; Klatch 1988). The very nature of the privatization projects can be seen to diverge. Neo-liberalism's project is primarily an economic one of reducing the role of the state and transferring public responsibilities to the private sphere. Conservatism's project is one of reinscribing traditional familial ideology and with it, a traditional, hierarchical family structure.

The conflicts between the privatizing strategies of neo-conservatives and neo-liberals can, in turn, be seen to correspond to the fundamental contradictions of the privatization project for gender and family. Neo-conservatism is intensifying the material and discursive significance of gender and family, while neo-liberalism is eroding their significance. The correspondence is not perfect, because of the internal contradictions of privatization, particularly the neo-liberal strategy. Although neo-liberalism pursues an unapologetically individualizing and degendering strategy, its emphasis on contracting the public sphere and transferring once public responsibilities to the private sphere, mandates an expanded role for the family in meeting these responsibilities. Thus, while neo-liberalism can be seen to be eroding the discursive claims on gender and the family, its policies are nonetheless intensifying their material significance in meeting a range of newly privatized social needs. Here perhaps we can find the appeal of neo-conservative discourse to the neo-liberal project: at least some of the catch-phrases and images of neo-conservatism provide a legitimating rhetoric for the neo-liberal project that neo-liberalism cannot provide for itself. Yet, as the next section explores in more detail, the visions and strategies of neo-liberalism and neo-conservatism are often at odds.[2]

Jennifer Somerville (1992) has explored these differences in the Thatcher era in the United Kingdom. She describes the political constellation of Thatcherism as 'an amalgam of a number of different ideological strands on the right of the political spectrum, for which the family became an important unifying symbol in its capacity to align radical liberal economic policies with traditionalist conservative concerns, and its rhetorical value in translating these into a popular political discourse' (ibid., 105). 'The family ... came to symbolize what both factions within the party, the economic liberals and the moral conservatives, could agree upon: anti-collectivism and anti-egalitarianism. Restoring the power of initiative and choice to the individual by economic deregulation and privatization, the reduction of taxation and the scale of public welfare, enabled individuals to look after their families in the way they chose. Radical liberal economic policy was thus lined up with the moral sibboleths of traditional conservatism' (ibid., 113). Somerville argues that although the focus on the family allowed the New Right to attract a number of different constituencies, 'the uneasy coalition' between traditional conservatives and economic liberals 'was itself a major obstacle to the realization of any consistent and coherent family policy' (ibid., 105). She illustrates that despite the symbolic importance of the family, the Thatcher government, like the Reagan administration in the United States, failed to develop 'any coherent and consistent family policy throughout the decade or so of [its] reign' (ibid., 115).

Somerville's analysis suggests that the internal contradictions within the Right can have significant implications in the development of family law and policy. Liberal economics place a very real restraint on the ability of moral conservatives to reassert the 'traditional family' in law and policy. At the same time, Somerville's study does not consider the continuing legacy of Thatcherism in the deconstruction of the welfare state in the United Kingdom, and the privatization of the costs of social reproduction. Although the neo-conservatives may not have been very successful, the neo-liberals have emerged victorious in the continuing erosion of social welfare and privatization of the family. The contradictions within the Right are not operating to block the project of reprivatization, but they are likely to affect the particular ways in which the project unfolds. The conflicts and contradictions between the visions and strategies of neo-liberalism and neo-conservatism may make some things possible in ways that others are not – from public policy development to strategies of resistance. The next section explores some of these contradictions in the hope of opening up the political imaginary of the Right, revealing some of its gaps and fissures, and creating more discursive space for oppositional strategies within these ruptures.

II. Privatizing Projects in Family/Social Welfare Law

I examine contradictions between the neo-liberal and neo-conservative visions in the privatization project in the context of three areas of public law and policy: gay and lesbian challenges to spousal definitions in family law; legislative reforms to strengthen child support obligations and enforcement; and Ontario's restructuring of social welfare, particularly in relation to single mothers. Each of these issues represents a different form of law. The first focuses on test case constitutional litigation and considers the arguments deployed by litigants as well as the court decisions. The second considers the public policy process of legislative reform and explores the arguments deployed by both proponents and opponents of the child support bill. The third examines enacted legislation and attempts to reveal its underlying assumptions. The goal is to highlight the particular ways in which neo-liberal and neo-conservative approaches to privatization diverge and to explore how these divergent discourses are being materialized in law. Although no single model of the family has yet emerged as dominant in public law or policy, the neo-liberal vision of the family appears to be gaining strength.

A. Gay and Lesbian Challenges to Definitions of Spouse in Family Law

Over the past decade, gay and lesbian couples have resolutely insisted that their exclusion from statutory definitions of spouse violate the equality provisions of human rights codes and the Canadian Charter of Rights and Freedoms. While early challenges were consistently turned down by majority opinions, the tides began to turn, as minority opinions supporting these challenges began to gain judicial support. While no accurate statistical data on gay and lesbian families is available (Lahey 1999), public polls demonstrate a significant transformation in Canadian attitudes towards same-sex families in the last decade, with the majority of Canadians now supporting the extension of benefits to these couples.[3] There is no evidence to suggest an increase in the numbers of same-sex couples, but the legal and political challenges have led not only to an increased visibility of gay and lesbian relationships, but to an increased acceptance of them. As this section demonstrates, however, this acceptance is anything but unanimous.

1. Neo-liberals and Neo-conservatives on Same-Sex Families
The differences in the normative visions and privatizing projects of neo-

liberals and neo-conservatives are revealed most dramatically in the context of gay and lesbian challenges to spousal definitions. Reflecting its generally agnostic position on questions of morality, neo-liberalism is not in principle opposed to gay and lesbian rights. Rather, a general concern with promoting the rights of individuals and a minimalist state would lead neo-liberals to oppose any rules and regulations that would impose special burdens on gay men and lesbians. Similarly, neo-liberalism is generally agnostic in relation to same-sex challenges to spousal definitions, insofar as it is not wedded to any particular family form (Brodie 1995). Given its general impulse towards privatizing costs of social reproduction, neo-liberalism could be expected to support an expanded spousal definition that contributed to the privatization of these costs, while opposing any expanded definition that increased public responsibility for them. The question is largely a cost-benefit one, in which neo-liberals undertake an analysis of the relative costs and benefits of expanding spousal definitions.

By way of contrast, neo-conservatives oppose the recognition of gay and lesbian rights in general, and same-sex spousal rights in particular, at any cost. The rearticulation of the traditional nuclear heterosexual family goes to the very heart of the neo-conservative vision. For neo-conservatives, no group poses a greater threat to that traditional family than gays and lesbians (Herman 1997). Neo-conservatives are unmoved by fiscal arguments about potential cost saving from expanding the definitions of spouse to include same-sex couples. The issue is not economic, but moral, and gay men and lesbians represent all that is wrong with the permissive culture of liberalism and the demise of the traditional moral order.

The script of the neo-conservative/neo-liberal divide was performed in a 1995 debate on gay marriage between two prominent voices of the Canadian Right, Andrew Coyne and David Frum. Andrew Coyne, a voice of fiscal conservatism, spoke in defence of gay marriage: 'A coherent conservative would wish not only to give formal legal recognition to the gay family but to positively encourage it. Think about it: why would a civil society do anything to stand in the way of the most profound expression of love and commitment between two people?' (Coyne & Frum 1995, 69). Coyne's argument focused on individual rights, on the right to non-discrimination and on the right to privacy. Echoing the basic precepts of neo-liberalism, he emphasized the right to be free from state intervention in one's private life (ibid., 68). In Coyne's view 'the sanctity of the family is the sanctity *from* the state' (ibid., 69). The recognition of gay marriage then, fits with the neo-liberal impulse to maximize individual liberty and minimize state intervention. All that is missing in Coyne's neo-liberal argument is the potential for fiscal savings.

In stark contrast, David Frum, the unapologetic voice of social conservatism, spoke against any state recognition of gay marriage. In Frum's view, 'civilization rests on two fundamental institutions; private property and the nuclear family' (Coyne & Frum 1995, 67). Frum argues that 'Canada faces no social problem more urgent and important than the strengthening of the family – reducing the number of births outside marriage and cutting the divorce rate' (ibid., 69). He argues that we have lost sight of the fundamental importance of marriage: 'We have formed the bad habit of thinking of marriage as a private relationship between two people' (ibid., 70). In his view, marriage is in fact a social institution 'which endows husbands and wives with special rights and claims against the rest of society.' This special status is granted because of the unique role of marriage in society: husbands and wives 'create and raise the next generation of humanity' (ibid., 72). Frum argues that although 'homosexuals' may form permanent relationships, their union cannot produce children. There is then, no reason to make their relationships more difficult to exit by allowing them to marry. He further argues that the recognition of gay marriage would fly in the face of what the institution of marriage most desperately needs: revitalization of its time-honoured importance: 'Gay marriage will look to much of the rest of society as a joke upon them, a campy parody of the central institution in their lives. The harm inflicted on the prestige of marriage is likely to prove very great: the last thing an already troubled institution needs' (ibid.). Finally, Frum links the rise of gay rights with the celebration of the demise of the family: 'The restructuring of the family, the weakening of marital ties, the loosening of standards of sexual morality – these form the subtext of the great debate over gay rights. Advocates of gay rights see these social changes as either welcome in themselves or, at any rate, as the inevitable price of liberation from the stultifying morality of a generation and more ago ...' (ibid., 75). Frum's argument is informed by the most basic tenets of neo-conservatism: the erosion of the family in the new 'permissive culture' since the 1960s, the linking of this decline with a range of social problems, the corresponding need to rebuild the traditional family, and above all, the threat that gays and lesbians pose to this traditional family.

2. Privatizing Lesbians

The divergence between neo-liberals and neo-conservatives is brought into sharp relief in a 1999 case involving a constitutional challenge to an

opposite-sex definition of spouse for the purposes of spousal support. In
M. v. H., a woman brought a claim for spousal support against her
female former partner of twelve years. In order to be entitled to support
under the Ontario Family Law Act (FLA), however, an individual must
first establish that he or she is a spouse within the meaning of the Act.
Spouse was defined as a person to whom an individual is married, or a
person of the opposite sex with whom an individual has cohabited in a
conjugal relationship for not less than three years (FLA, s. 29). M, the
woman seeking support, brought a constitutional challenge to this definition, arguing that it constitutes discrimination on the basis of sexual
orientation and violated her rights under section 15 of the Canadian
Charter of Rights and Freedoms. The Ontario Court (General Division)
held that section 29 of the FLA did offend section 15 of the Charter, and
was not a reasonable limit under section 1. By way of remedy, Epstein J.
ordered that the words 'a man and a woman' be severed from the definition of 'spouse' and that the words 'two persons' be read into the definition of 'spouse' in section 29. The majority of the Ontario Court of
Appeal (Charron and Doherty, JJ.A, with Finlayson J. dissenting) dismissed the appeal, and like the court below, ordered that 'two persons'
be read into the definition of spouse in section 29. The case was
appealed to the Supreme Court of Canada.

The case presented a dilemma for a government committed to privatization, particularly one caught somewhere between neo-liberalism and
neo-conservatism. It would, on the one hand, be consistent for a neo-liberal privatization project concerned with fiscal restraint, and with shifting social responsibilities onto private families, to support efforts to
enlarge the category of persons with private support obligations. The
constitutional challenge would have the effect of enlarging the category
of spouse to include same-sex couples, and further contribute to the
strategy of privatizing relationships of economic dependency. On the
other hand, it would be highly inconsistent with the neo-conservative
privatization project rearticulating the traditional heterosexual family.

When the case was initially brought, the NDP government of the time
intervened in support of the constitutional challenge, agreeing with the
claimant that the opposite-sex definition was unconstitutional. But with
a change of government in the intervening years, by the time the case
reached the Ontario Court of Appeal and in turn the Supreme Court of
Canada, the government had changed sides. It was now defending the
constitutionality of the opposite-sex definition of spouse. In so doing,
the Harris Conservative government was showing its neo-conservative

hand. But the government's arguments were not made in explicitly neo-conservative terms, or at least not exclusively so. Admittedly, the attorney general made several references to the family as the basic social unit in which children were produced and raised. The government relied on Justice LaForest's opinion in *Egan*, defining marriage as an inherently heterosexual relationship, and as the basic social unit for raising children, arguing that '(t)he state's intervention in opposite-sex spousal relationships, to the exclusion of other kinds of relationships in society, reflects its underlying concern with children, with the conditions in which children are raised, as well as with the parents who raise them' (Attorney General of Ontario 1998, submission 62; see also submissions 40, 46, 79). But this idea of the family as a basic social unit and its role in reproduction was not the dominant theme in the government's factum. Rather, the arguments of the attorney general before the Supreme Court were made, in large degree, in more feminist and progressive language. Much of the government's argument focused on the objective of the FLA in addressing systemic sexual inequality. For example: 'The Appellant submits that the legislative purpose of spousal support in the *FLA* is to remedy the systemic sexual inequality associated with opposite-sex relationships, including the economic dependence of women on men resulting from women taking on primary responsibility for parenting and from gender-based inequality in earning power' (ibid., submission 49). The attorney general's arguments focused on women's economic dependency within marriage, and on women's economic vulnerability on family breakdown. In so doing, the government borrowed heavily from feminist literature that has illustrated the complex relationship between the family and the market that disadvantages women upon marital breakdown:

> women's economic vulnerability upon separation is a result of their taking on primary responsibility for family related labour in the home and their unequal earning capacity in the workplace. Surveys continue to demonstrate that women bear a disproportionate burden of family and child-care responsibilities, despite the fact that many women are now employed. In particular, women are more likely than men to cease working, to engage in part-time work, to take on irregular work schedules or to work at home as the result of family and child care responsibilities. The economic and career cost of these sacrifices continue to be significant. (ibid., submission 57)

The government argued that the FLA was designed to address the inequality that results from this economic dependency, and that same-sex couples simply do not experience this gender-based inequality: '(t)he sexual inequality often associated with heterosexual relationships and which results both from parenting and gender-based inequality in earning power is absent from most gay and lesbian relationships' (ibid., submission 67). Elaborating on this difference, the government argued:

> Existing research also clearly indicates that same-sex relationships, although they parallel opposite-sex relationships in certain respects, are not characterized by the same economic and other inequalities which affect opposite-sex relationships. Studies have consistently found that same-sex relationships tend to be more egalitarian overall, and that they are not typically characterized by economic dependence. On the contrary, partners tend to be financially self-sufficient, and egalitarian in financial decision-making. Nor do same sex partners assume stereotypical gender roles, and household labour is rarely divided along traditional gender-identified lines. (ibid., submission 70)

Moreover, the government invoked the dissenting voices within the gay and lesbian community on the question of same-sex spousal status, and argued that in light of this difference of opinion it would be inappropriate for the court to intervene in the legislature's effort to mediate between the competing views. These arguments all appealed not to the threat that gay and lesbian relationships presented to the traditional family, but the threat to equality-based norms. The government strategically couched its position in feminist and progressive language, emphasizing the systemic inequality of women in heterosexual relationships and the egalitarian nature of same-sex relationships. Since same-sex relationships were not characterized by inequality and dependency, there was no reason to include them within a statutory scheme intended to remedy this systemic inequality.

Although the government did not deny its concern with the family as the basic social unit, this was not the focus of its arguments. Rather, the neo-conservative position of defending the traditional family was effectively and strategically cast in appropriated feminist/progressive discourse. The more explicit neo-conservative position was left for others to make. REAL Women for example focused on the heterosexual nature of marriage and marriagelike relationships. Its submissions emphasized the established meaning of spouse in 'our history, philosophy and culture' (REAL Women 1998, 5): 'The word "spouse" has a long-established meaning in our cultural lexicon. The Concise Oxford Dictionary defines "spouse" as "husband or wife"; Black's Law Dictionary defines the word as meaning "one's wife or husband". Both definitions accord with our common cultural understanding and use of the word' (ibid., 9–10). According to REAL Women, the meaning of spouse in section 29 of the FLA 'requires that the relationship between the persons must involve physical intimacy of a particular kind – that is, be a conjugal relationship' (ibid., 14). And a conjugal relationship, in its view, is restricted to opposite sexes: 'At its heart, the concept of conjugal rests upon a particular kind of physical intimacy, unique to a man and woman, which has the capacity to beget a child' (ibid., 15). The central importance of biological reproduction to marriage and marriagelike relationships is thus used to exclude same-sex couples: 'a homosexual or lesbian couple are not excluded from the definition of spouse because of a false understanding of the characteristics and capacities of their relationship; they are excluded because their relationship does not, and by its nature cannot, possess the actual characteristics which mark the relationship between a husband or wife, or the "marriage-like" relationship between a man and woman living together in common law. In the words of Gonthier J in Miron, the distinction in the case "rests upon or is the expression of some objective physical or biological reality or fundamental value"' (ibid., 19). The Interfaith Coalition, representing the Evangelical Fellowship of Canada, the Ontario Council of Sikhs, the Islamic Society of North America, and Focus on the Family, was even more emphatic about the role of tradition in the heterosexual nature of marriage:

> Heterosexual spouses have been recognized through our social, legal, political, religious and philosophical traditions, as fulfilling a unique and essential role in the very fabric of our social structure through the procreation, nurturing and raising of children, and require continued social and legislative support. (Evangelical Fellowship 1998, 2)

> The definition of marriage and spouse is grounded in a legal tradition which reflects fundamental philosophical, social and religious considerations. As well, heterosexual spouses fulfil the essential societal functions of procreation and child rearing. (ibid., 13)

Although the Interfaith Coalition considered biological reproduction as a crucial consideration, its arguments explicitly invoke morality and religion in defence of the opposite-sex definition of spouse.

In the coalition's view, there is a 'necessary relationship between law and morality,' and there must be a 'a basis of moral conceptions informed by religious and philosophical traditions underlying the law': 'All of the worlds' major religions recognize that the concept of marriage and spouse should only involve the union of man and woman. This is a basic tenet of the major religious communities which make up the multicultural heritage of Canada and which has been reflected in our legal concept of marriage and spouse' (ibid., 15). Although the interfaith nature of the Coalition prevented its submissions from explicitly deploying the discourse of Christianity, it emphasized the religious and theological importance and basis of the heterosexual definition of spouse.

The arguments defending the constitutionality of the definition of spouse in section 29 of the FLA were all premised on the neo-conservative impulse of defending the traditional family. Although the government did not place much emphasis on the language of family values in its submissions, its intervention had come to represent a neo-conservative performance of family. Its family values constituency had to be satisfied. Neither the government nor any of the other intervenors defending the constitutionality of the spousal definition addressed the fiscal arguments of potential cost savings from expanding the definition of spouse.[4] In other cases, where gay and lesbian couples have challenged spousal definitions that limit access to public and employment benefits, the neo-liberal arguments of excessive public costs could be deployed alongside neo-conservative ones defending the family. But in the case of *M. v. H.*, these neo-liberal concerns of reducing public expenditures whenever and wherever possible simply did not apply, insofar as the expansion of the spousal definition (if accompanied with commensurate amendments to social welfare law) could have resulted in cost savings in social welfare expenditures. It might have been possible to argue that the overall cost savings would not outweigh the increased cost to government from the expansion of the spousal definition in a range of other government programs and benefits. But the government did not even attempt to make these kinds of arguments. Rather, it appeared to relinquish the neo-liberal terrain altogether, as incommensurable with the neo-conservative task at hand.

Ultimately, the Supreme Court came down on the side of equality and, not incidentally, fiscal conservatism. The court held that section 29 of the Ontario Family Law Act discriminated on the basis of sexual orientation by excluding same-sex couples from the definition of spouse.

The principal majority judgment of Cory and Iacobucci JJ. held that the section denied gay men and lesbians the right to apply for spousal support from a same-sex partner. According to the court, section 29 violated the right to equality guaranteed by section 15 of the Canadian Charter of Rights and Freedoms and was not a reasonable limit within the meaning of section 1. The objectives of the FLA were 'the equitable resolution of economic disputes that arise when intimate relationships between individuals who have been financially interdependent break down' and the alleviation of 'the burden on the public purse by shifting the obligation to provide support for needy persons to those parents and spouses who have the capacity to provide support to these individuals' (ibid., paras. 93 and 106). According to Iacobucci J., these objectives would only be furthered if same-sex couples were included within the definition of spouse. The court placed considerable emphasis on the goal of 'reducing the strain on the public purse' by 'shifting the financial burden away from the government and on to those partners with the capacity to provide support for dependent spouses' (ibid., para 98). The arguments of the moral conservatives – of the importance of the traditional family – found little resonance. Only Gonthier J., in his dissenting opinion, endorsed this vision of the family, although it was somewhat tempered by the more 'feminist' discussion of the importance of protecting women from the unique form of disadvantage they have suffered in heterosexual relationships.

In the aftermath of *M. v. H.*, the Conservative government in Ontario was forced to introduce legislation to include same-sex couples. In An Act to Amend Certain Statutes Because of the Supreme Court of Canada decision in M. v. H., the government amended sixty-seven statutes to include 'same sex partners.' As Attorney General Flaherty explained, 'Our proposed legislation complies with the decision while preserving the traditional values of the family by protecting the definition of spouse in Ontario law' (Ontario Ministry of the Attorney General 1999). Flaherty was emphatic that the new law would not in any way affect marriage or the traditional definition of spouse. 'It is important for members to be aware of that fundamental in this debate, that marriage is not affected by this bill. Marriage, as members know, involves a man and a woman in Ontario. We have preserved in the bill the traditional definition of "spouse" and "marital status"' (Ontario Legislative Assembly 1999). Ironically, it was only in defeat that the government acknowledged its neo-conservative vision of the family.

In *M. v. H.*, neo-liberal discourses of formal equality and privatization converged with more egalitarian discourses of eliminating discrimination. It is important to recognize the connections between different forms of law – the success of neo-liberalism in the judicial form feeds into the legislative form, with the Ontario government grudgingly enacting the Act to Amend Certain Statutes Because of the Supreme Court Canada decision in *M. v. H.* While the neo-liberal arguments about formal equality for same-sex couples would not initially have found any support in the legislative arena, the Supreme Court ruling exemplifies the ways in which law operates to mediate and select amongst competing discourses (Herman 1997, Woodiwiss 1990). In affirming the neo-liberal discourse on the family, this discourse was forced onto the legislative stage of a government otherwise committed to a neo-conservative social vision. There may be important limits to the ability of the judicial form of law to do this, particularly with the rise of the judicial activism critique and its allegation that courts are usurping the role of the legislatures. However, the discursive power of formal equality remains powerful in law. Whereas neo-conservative visions of the family collided with the value of formal equality, neo-liberal as well as more egalitarian visions of the family converged with this cornerstone of a liberal legal system. Formal equality was ultimately forced upon the legislative arena.

B. *Toughening Child Support Laws*

The agendas of neo-liberals and neo-conservatives converge in many ways in their approach to child poverty and child support. Both agree that children should not be forced to rely on welfare for their support. To differing degrees, both have targeted the 'deadbeat dad' as responsible for children's poverty and seek to enforce the private support obligations of fathers. But their normative agendas diverge as well. While neo-liberals aim to get tough on deadbeat dads by forcing them to take financial responsibility for their children following divorce, neo-conservatives aim to prevent dads from becoming deadbeat by preventing divorce in the first place. If divorce should occur, neo-conservatives are concerned about legislation that degrades fatherhood.

Although neo-liberalism has been by far the dominant voice in the reform of child support law, neo-conservatism has informed the voice of dissent and resistance to these new reforms. Where child support is concerned, neo-liberals and neo-conservatives sometimes find themselves on opposites sides of the public policy fence. But the controversy surrounding child support reforms in Canada did not simply set neo-liber-

Table 4.2
Incidence of child poverty in Canada

	1980 (%)	1989 (%)	1990 (%)	1996 (%)
All children	15.8	15.3	17.8	21.1
Children in female lone parent families			62.9	65

Source: Canadian Council on Social Development 1998a; 1998b; 1998c

als against neo-conservatives. As the controversy played out, neo-liberals and women's groups lined up against neo-conservatives and fathers' right groups, with some interesting discursive twists and turns along the way.

1. Child Poverty, Divorcing Dads, and Divergent Visions of Family
In recent years, the issue of child poverty has arrived on the public policy stage as the co-star of rising divorce rates. Child poverty has been cast as a problem that results from divorce, and in turn, from the failure of non-custodial parents to adequately provide for their children on marital breakdown (Mossman 1997; Eichler 1990; Pulkingham 1994). Facts and figures are deployed to present a powerful story of irresponsible parents (deadbeat dads) who, intent on pursuing their own happiness, walk away from their families and their familial responsibilities, leaving their children to fall into hard times. In this story, the government had no choice but to respond with tough new child support initiatives to alleviate the growing problem of child poverty. On closer examination, however, the facts and figures present a more complex story.

Child poverty is clearly on the rise. The number of poor children in Canada has increased by 428,000 since 1989. Sixty-eight per cent more Canadian children live in families needing social assistance today than in 1989 (Child and Family Canada 1999). Table 4.2 indicates a steady rise in the percentage of Canadian children living below the poverty line. The rate is dramatically higher for children living in female lone-parent families.

However, it is difficult to make a direct connection between the increase in child poverty and divorce. In recent years, there has been a notable *decrease* in divorce rates in Canada. As Table 4.3 indicates, there

Table 4.3
Divorce rates in Canada

Year	No. of divorces	Rate per 10,000 pop.
1961	6,563	3.6
1968	11, 343	5.5
1981	67, 671	27.2
1985	61,980	25.3
1987	96,200	36.2
1993	78,226	27
1995	77,636	26.2
1997	67,408	22

Source: Bélanger 1999; Ambert 1998

was a dramatic increase in divorce following the enactment of the first federal Divorce Act 1968, which liberalized the grounds of divorce, and another increase following that of the Divorce Act 1985. However, divorce rates appeared to have peaked in 1987, and there has been a slow but steady decrease in the total number of divorces since then.

The years from 1990 to 1996 have thus witnessed both a marked increase in child poverty and a decrease in divorce rates. While many commentators have rightly argued that divorce causes poverty for individual children, it is clear from these figures that only some child poverty is caused by divorce. According to a recent study by Statistics Canada, changing labour market conditions are as important a factor as divorce in child poverty. As Picot et al. note '... for an individual child, a divorce or marriage can have tremendous influence on the likelihood of entering or exiting low-income. At the level of the individual, changes in family composition (when they occur) are more important than changes in jobs held by parents. However, changes in family status are relatively infrequent compared to labour market changes. Parents are much more likely to lose or find jobs, and experience changes in hours worked or wages, than they are to marry or divorce' (Picot, Zyblock, & Pyper 1999, 5).

Notwithstanding the importance of a parent's employment status, divorce came to be singled out in public policy debates as the leading factor in child poverty. A number of facts and figures were used to support this claim. First, studies demonstrated that women's household incomes plummet by approximately 50 per cent within the first year of divorce, while men's incomes decline by only 25 per cent (Finnie 1993). When family size is taken into account, women's incomes drop by approximately 40 per cent, while men's incomes increase slightly. Second, studies revealed the high rate of default of non-custodial parents on their spousal and child support payments. The 'incontrovertible' conclusion drawn from these figures in public policy debates was that divorce is the cause of children's poverty, and that individual fathers are responsible for the poverty of their individual children. Systemic causes of poverty – including the restructuring of the labour market and the significant increase in precarious employment – are obscured, as child poverty is recast as an individualized problem with an individualized solution (Mossman 1997).

A closer examination of the discourses of family and privatization reveal that, once again, neo-liberals and neo-conservatives diverge in their understanding of the problem. The official story was in fact a highly contested one, in which the neo-liberal vision of the family came to prevail. Neo-liberals and neo-conservatives agree that children are financially harmed as a result of divorce, but their strategies for addressing this harm are different. Neo-liberal discourse targets irresponsible parents – a.k.a. 'deadbeat dads' – as the source of post-divorce child poverty and emphasizes strengthening child support laws. Child poverty is recast as an individual pathology, as a problem of fathers who refuse to take responsibility for their children. Deadbeat dads are not only criticized for abdicating their moral obligations to provide for their children but demonized as bad citizens for their flagrant abuse of the Canadian taxpayer, who must subsidize the resulting welfare dependency (Brodie 1997). If individuals could be made to fulfil their responsibilities to their children, the problems would be eliminated. The focus, then, is on individualizing the problem and shifting responsibility from the public to the private sphere (Mossman 1997).

Neo-conservatives seek to get tough on deadbeat dads by preventing divorce in the first place. Divorce, it is said, should be made more difficult, so that families – traditional families – can remain intact. Fathers must become more involved in the lives of their children not after a divorce, but during the marriage (Blankenhorn 1995; Rosen 1996). The desired involvement is the traditional dad, responsible for the child's financial welfare and for providing a good, stable male role model for his children. Child poverty is seen as the result of divorce; the solution is to prevent divorce. Deadbeat dads are often not seen to be responsible for their 'deadbeatness' – rather, with the twist of father's rights rhetoric, dads only become deadbeat because mothers make them so: mothers are blamed for leaving the marriage and rendering fathers obsolete. The solution, again, lies in the rearticulation of the traditional family with the father at its helm.

These different understandings of the nature of the problem have led neo-liberals and neo-conservatives to adopt somewhat contradictory positions on the legal regulation of child support. Neo-liberals are unwavering in their commitment to strengthening child support laws, whereas neo-conservatives are more ambivalent, since, in their view, attempting to improve such laws is to acknowledge defeat in strengthening the family.

2. Legislative Reforms and Divergent Visions of Fatherhood

In May 1997, the federal Divorce Act was amended to introduce new child support guidelines, to revise the rules for the taxation implications of child support orders, and to strengthen the enforcement of child support obligations. The new guidelines set support payments as a share of the non-custodial parent's income. Courts are now required to award the amount set out in the schedules, plus allowable expenses,[5] unless the court finds that the award would result in undue hardship to either parent or to the child. Among the new enforcement measures intended to address the problem of chronic default on child support payments are a federal licence suspension initiative, which includes passport suspension; extended searches to trace defaulters, which will add Revenue Canada to the list of federal departments whose data banks can be searched by provincial enforcement agencies; and broader powers for diversion of federal pensions. The provincial governments moved quickly to bring their laws in line with the new federal guidelines. In Ontario, the Family Law Act was amended by the end of the same year to incorporate the child support payment schedules. But the Harris government had already moved to strengthen the enforcement of child support in the province. In July 1996, the attorney general and the minister responsible for women's issues announced 'new enforcement measures to ensure that children get the support they need' (Ontario Ministry of the Attorney General 1996a). These measures included the suspension of the driver's licences of parents in default of their child support responsibilities.

The reforms at both the federal and provincial levels were sold as a way to get tough on child poverty by getting tough on the private responsibilities of individual parents. At the provincial level, the financial incentive behind these initiatives and the link with the reduction of welfare dependency was made explicit. A government backgrounder described the problem that the measures were intended to address as follows: 'Currently, close to $1 billion in child support payments is outstanding. This forces many recipients onto social assistance and denies children the support they need ... About 95 per cent of recipients of child support are women. When child support isn't paid, women and children are forced into poverty and onto social assistance' (Ontario Ministry of the Attorney General 1996b). The enforcement of child support is expressly linked with reducing welfare dependency. The new measures are justified within the privatizing rhetoric of neo-liberalism of shifting responsibility for dependent persons from the public to the private realm.

While the federal government was somewhat more understated in its rhetoric, focusing instead on the interests of children, the link with reducing public responsibility for private obligations was never far from the surface. Consider, for example, the words of Justice Minister Allan Rock to the House of Commons: 'Refusing to support one's children is a serious breach of the law with consequences that can affect children throughout their lives' (*Toronto Star* 1996). While highlighting the needs of children, the minister was asserting a moral and legal obligation on parents to support their children. The subtle implication is that the impact of poverty on children is a consequence of the failure of parents to fulfil these responsibilities. The responsibility of the state for the financial well-being of these children simply fades away. But the state discourse remains cleverly framed around the best interests of children. The minister of justice continued: 'The record shows that a child who is in a situation where payments are not made by an absent parent bears emotional scars for life and takes the message that the absent parent has abandoned or rejected them and left them behind' (ibid.). The harm to children is not cast as a financial harm, but as an emotional one.

The introduction of the child support guidelines sailed through the House of Commons. But when the reforms to the Divorce Act were sent to the Senate, all hell broke loose. Liberal Senator Anne Cools, who has cultivated a reputation in recent years as an anti-feminist renegade, led the charge against the child support bill, on the grounds that it was too harsh on men. In her words, 'it has a bias against men. It degrades fatherhood' (*Globe and Mail* 1997a). The controversy that erupted in the Senate became a maelstrom of fathers' rights opposition to the bill in particular and to the family justice system in general.

In their submissions to the Senate Committee, the fathers' rights groups emphasized the economic hardships that fathers would endure under the proposed reforms. Much of the focus of their lobbying was on the relationship between child support, custody, and access. A common theme was the alleged unfairness of cracking down on fathers for violating support orders, but not cracking down on mothers for violating access orders. A second and related theme was the perceived unfairness of applying the child support guidelines in situations where custody was shared. The bill had provided that the guidelines would apply unless the child spent more than 50 per cent of his/her time with the payor parent. Throughout their submissions, the fathers' rights groups framed their arguments in the discourse of equality. They argued for the seemingly simple proposition of equality for fathers, and attempted to reveal the ways in which fathers are deprived of this equality in a family justice system that favours women.

Eventually, a number of concessions were made to the opponents of Bill C-41. The shared parenting provision was reduced from 50 per cent to 40 per cent. The bill, as amended, then received Senate approval and was returned to the House of Commons. Despite the eventual passage of the bill, the controversy and its oppositional discourses represented another rupture in the project of privatization. The neo-liberal impulse of privatizing the costs of social reproduction by enforcing the private responsibilities of individual parents collided with a neo-conservative discourse that viewed the initiative as a feminist assault on men and the family. While most of the opposition to the bill was articulated in the rhetoric of the fathers' rights movement – a rhetoric that borrows selectively from conservative and liberal discourse[6] – the controversy represented a moment of alliance between these fathers' rights groups and neo-conservatives.

In opposing the legislation some condemned what they saw as a government 'tax grab' (thereby explicitly opposing the neo-liberal agenda); much of the opposition, however, was articulated in the discourse of fatherhood, family, and anti-feminism. Neo-conservatism could join with fathers' rights groups in this demonization of feminism, blaming feminists for the demise of the family. The crackdown on deadbeat dads was translated into a degrading assault on fatherhood by feminists. Senator Cools led the way, declaring that 'it has been open season on men for too long' (Canadian Press 1997). In questioning a witness who appeared before the committee, Cools asked, 'Do you have any observations that you can share about the penetration of feminist ideology into the field of family law and the practise therein? The damage is so enormous that we are all reeling as we try to heal some of the wounds' (Senate 1997c).

Senator Cools was not the only critic to employ such rhetoric, she was simply more vituperative than most. Fathers' rights groups, from the National Alliance for the Advancement of Non-Custodial Parents (NAANCP), to F.A.C.T. (Fathers are Capable Too) and Fatherhood ... Imagine That, joined in the chorus about the degradation of father-hood at the hands of women's groups. Consider the following exchange in the Senate on the subject of the new guidelines:

SENATOR BOSA: But it took five years to get this to stage. (sic) They con-sulted every Tom, Dick and Harry.
MR BOUCHARD (NAANCP): That is the problem. They did not.
SENATOR COOLS: They did not consult Toms, Dicks and Harrys. It was probably Marys, Janes and Suzies.
BOUCHARD: If you look at the list of people who submitted to the com-mittee, there were only two organizations that did not represent custo-dial mothers. Almost all those organizations were government funded. So, no, they did not speak to every Tom, Dick and Harry.
The guidelines that were proposed by economists were considerably lower than and different from these. They were discarded because they were not politically correct (Senate 1996).

At the prodding of Senator Cools, the representatives of the NAANCP were more than willing to lay the blame of the alleged bias of the child support reforms at the door of women's organizations.

The NAANCP's critique of the 'assault on fatherhood' was explicit throughout their submissions. For example, in Mr Cheriton's words: 'If you have a justice system – that is, lawyers and judges – who firmly believe that getting the fathers out of the family will improve things for children, then providing Bill C-41 as an additional weapon will just cre-ate additional problems' (ibid., 16:29). Similarly, 'Families recognize children's needs for their fathers ... This is done by free choice. Bill C-41 will stop the very thing that children need at the time they most need it' (ibid., 16:32).

The fathers' rights groups were joined by other more conservative organizations, such as REAL Women. Gwen Landolt, appearing on behalf of the organization, expressed REAL Women's position on fami-lies and on fatherhood more generally: 'We are finding that fatherless families are a major cause of problems. The father does have a very important role to play. Of course the mother does too. As the mother of five I am quite strong on that point, but I do think the father has an extremely important role to play. Unfortunately, many of them are not fulfilling the role that they would like to play because of the very stringent legislation that puts them off' (ibid., 17:25). Landolt explained her group's interest in the proceedings. 'Our motto is "Equal rights for women, but not at the expense of human rights." That is why we are here today. We are here to say, "Yes, we do believe in equality for women, but not at the expense of someone else who will suffer as a result of giving extra rights to one element of society"' (ibid.). In these passages, the undercurrent remains the defence of the family – and the role of the father therein – from the attack by those (a.k.a. feminists) who are allegedly attempting to give women more rights than men. At the same time, the passage reveals the underlying objective of the more explicitly neo-conservative forces – namely, keeping the family together.[7]

Neo-conservatives and the fathers' rights groups could join ranks in defending fatherhood from the malicious attacks of their common enemy. Not only did the potential conflict between these allies disappear from view, but the very real conflict between neo-conservatives and neo-liberals could also fade into the shadows, as the public spotlight focused on the antagonism between women and men. The child support reforms were cast as yet another scuffle in the battle of the sexes, a battle in which women were said to be gaining the upper hand, and in which fatherhood and the family were losing out.

The federal government tried to negotiate its way through this explosive terrain. In defending the bill, Allan Rock declared 'this bill is neither anti-mother or anti-father, it's pro-children. It's not driven by ideology, it's driven by the reality of too many children living in poverty of single-parent families' (Canadian Press 1997). Rock was attempting to escape the oppositional discourse created by the neo-conservative/fathers' rights alliance by rearticulating the original legitimating framework – namely, that the child support bill was really about child poverty. Rock's statement is illustrative of the individualizing and degendering nature of neo-liberal strategies. From the point of view of a neo-liberal state, the child support initiative really was neither anti-mother nor anti-father; in fact, it was not really about gender at all. Rather, it was about enforcing the private responsibilities of individual parents. Along the way, however, the federal government got caught in the web of the deeply gendered discourse of the father's rights/neo-conservative alliance.

The susceptibility to the landmine of this gendered discourse lay in the paradox of the neo-liberal position on child support. Despite neo-liberalism's tendency to pursue strategies that erode material and discursive claims on the family, the child support initiative ultimately intensified the family as a site of dependency. The fiscal impulse of shifting dependency from the public to the private realm led neo-liberals to a child support strategy that intensified both the material and discursive claims on the family. The family (in this case, the post-divorce family) was rearticulated as the appropriate site for the support of dependent children. The federal government could not escape the gendered discourse of the opponents of child support because of the extent to which its privatizing strategy relied on the same underlying familial ideology. Despite the government's efforts to mask its discursive claims to the family in gender-neutral language (speaking of 'deadbeat parents' or 'best interests of children'), the underlying vision of the family remains so deeply gendered that a degendering strategy was unsustainable.

The neo-liberal strategies on child support exemplify the internal contradictions of the neo-liberal project. The child support laws illustrate the way in which neo-liberalism's contraction of the public sphere relies on an expanded role for the family in meeting these responsibilities. Despite neo-liberalism's tendency to pursue individualizing and degendering strategies which erode both the material and discursive significance of family, the child support initiative exemplifies the extent to which its policies often implicitly rely on the family to provide for newly privatized social needs. Neo-liberalism does not itself have legitimating resources for this move, and thereby may have to rely on the familial discourse of neo-conservatism. But in so doing, it runs the risk of igniting the fundamental differences between these two normative visions. Contained at the provincial level, at the federal level the intervention of the fathers' rights groups seemed to provide the spark that ignited these contradictions.

Although the privatizing project of neo-liberalism did win out, its discourse was not uncontested. Child support guidelines have been enacted, with tough new enforcement procedures against those who default, though at the federal level this was not accomplished without concessions to Bill C-41's opponents. The neo-conservative impulse of rearticulating the traditional family was an undercurrent of the opposition to the bill, and these deeper conflicts remain unresolved. Some neo-conservatives continue to work in alliance with the fathers' rights movement, defending the moral integrity of fatherhood and the family, while others argue for stronger divorce laws to keep families together in the first place. Yet, paradoxically, the neo-conservative vision of the family remains an important constitutive element of the neo-liberal performance of privatization. The child support initiative would itself be unsustainable but for the continuing viability of the family as an acceptable, indeed natural site of dependency.

At the same time, more conservative visions of family remain alive in public policy debates regarding children. Part of the compromise in the Bill C-41 controversy was the promise by the minister of justice to establish a special joint parliamentary committee to consider reforms to child custody and access. As the Special Joint Committee on Custody and Access held public hearings across the country, both fathers' rights groups and conservative pro-family organizations continued to push for a reform of child custody laws, stressing the importance of the traditional nuclear family, and of the importance of fathers in children's lives. The hearings before the committee were yet another site of this intense contestation, with Senator Cools once again at the helm of the precarious alliance between neo-conservatives and fathers' groups, united in their opposition to mothers and feminists, once again defending fatherhood from the malicious attacks of their common enemy (Special Joint Committee on Custody and Access 1999). While neo-conservatives and fathers' rights groups may have been defeated in the child support initiatives by the neo-liberal impulse to privatize support obligations, they are not down for the count. Their conflicting visions of family, parenthood, and parental responsibilities will continue to clash in the public policy debates on children and divorce.

The child support guidelines, like the debate on same-sex relationship recognition, illustrates the divergence between neo-liberal and neo-conservative visions of the family, the role of law in mediating and selecting amongst these competing discourses, and the extent to which neo-liberal discourses appear to be in ascendance. While neo-conservative arguments were powerful in the public policy debates, and have remained powerful voices of dissent and contestation, neo-liberalism continues to win the day, in both legislative and judicial arenas. Further, the case study of the child support guidelines suggests that the outcomes in the debates between neo-liberal and neo-conservative visions of the family are shaped by underlying material conditions. Regardless of the extent to which it can be attributed to divorce, the neo-conservative/fathers' rights discourse could not adequately respond to the phenomenon of child poverty. Nor could it adequately respond to the statistics about child support orders in default. Neo-liberalism, on the other hand, played powerfully into these underlying material conditions, and offered a marketable solution.

C. Social Welfare Law

In recent years, welfare dependency has also arrived on the public policy stage as a demon of neo-liberals and neo-conservatives alike. Both share a loathing of welfare dependency, and both tell a tale of the need to crack down on welfare abuse. Facts and figures are deployed to present a very different kind of irresponsible citizen than in the child support context. The story in this instance is one of welfare mothers responsible for a chronic drain on public resources and on the Canadian taxpayer. The political agenda of the Right is united in its uncompromising assault on welfare, and this convergence has in large part made the assault devastatingly successful.

Although both neo-liberals and neo-conservatives have sought to demonize the 'welfare mother' to justify their assault on the welfare system, their prescriptions for the problem are somewhat different. Neo-conservatives want the welfare mother to be 'properly' dependent – that is, to find a spouse and make him pay. By contrast, the neo-liberal wants to put the welfare mother to work, redefining 'single mother' as a potentially employable worker. Both seek an end to her reliance on the state, but their vision of her fate is radically different. This section explores these subtle differences between neo-conservative and neo-liberal approaches to welfare mothers, and argues that both approaches can be found in the Ontario government's restructuring of social welfare.

1. Sole Support Parents and the Attack on Welfare Dependency

Over the last decade, neo-liberals and neo-conservatives have successfully reconstituted 'welfare dependency' as a chronic problem in need of a radically new approach. Rising child poverty is not part of this discursive strategy. Rather, the figures showing swelling welfare rates and the increasing cost of welfare dependency are deemed to give the governments no choice but to respond with a radical restructuring of welfare aimed at reducing this dependency. Welfare mothers were the target of much of this discourse. In the early years of his government, Ontario's Premier Harris did not mince words. When asked why his government was cutting a $222 food allowance ($37 a month for six months) for pregnant women on welfare, Harris responded, 'We are making sure that those dollars don't go to beer' (*Hamilton Spectator* 1998). More recently, the Ontario government has flaunted figures that demonstrate the alleged success of their policies: decreasing welfare cases and an increasing number of employment placements through its workfare program (Ontario Ministry of Community and Social Services 2000). As with child poverty, however, a closer look at the facts and figures suggests a more complex story, in which the impact of welfare reforms on women and children is much more problematic.

An increasing number of Canadian families are single parent families. In 1971, single parent families comprised 9 per cent of all families, a figure that had increased to 13 per cent in 1991 and to 14.5 per cent by 1996 (La Novara 1993, 10; Statistics Canada 1996). The overwhelming majority of these families are headed by women: in 1996, 83 per cent of single parent families were female headed (Statistics Canada 2000, 43). Families headed by female lone parents are also disproportionately represented within Canada's poor (La Novara 1993, 35; Statistics Canada 1992, 2000). In 1997, 56 per cent of all families headed by female lone parents had incomes below the poverty line (Statistics Canada 2000, 139). The 1997 *Poverty Profile* issued by the National Council of Welfare found that the overall poverty rate for single mothers was 57.1 per cent, and the rate for single mothers under eighteen was 93 per cent (National Council of Welfare 1997). These figures indicate the extent to which poverty in Canada is both gendered and related to family structure: single mothers and their children are disproportionately represented amongst Canada's poor.

Studies have also indicated that attempts to overcome poverty and reliance on social assistance through work in the labour force are limited for single mothers, particularly those with young children. In 1999 only 38 per cent of single mothers whose children were less than three years of age, and 55 per cent of those with children aged three to five, were employed (Statistics Canada 1992, 22). However, when the youngest child was between the ages of six and fifteen, the percentage of single mothers in the labour force rose to 69 per cent (ibid.). The presence of young children is thus a critical factor; without affordable childcare, women are unable to participate in the labour market.

Welfare dependency did increase in the early 1990s. In 1987, approximately 84,300 sole support parents comprised nearly 30 per cent of all recipients of social assistance. By 1994, nearly 200,000 single parents relied on social assistance (Ontario Social Safety Network Backgrounder 1998). In Toronto, new social assistance cases grew from 5,500 in 1989 to

12,000 in 1991 (Community Services Committee of the City of Toronto 1999). In the same period, the caseload more than doubled, from 38,000 to 87,000 cases. By 1993, the caseload had reached 120,000 and it attained a high of 126,500 in March 1994 (ibid.). While these kinds of figures were used by the Ontario government to paint a picture of a crisis in welfare dependency, the rise in caseload reflected the length and depth of the economic recession in Toronto, as well as significant cuts to unemployment insurance through the early 1990s (ibid.). Since the peak in 1994, welfare caseloads in Toronto have fallen dramatically, to approximately 71,300 cases in April 1999. The Ontario government takes credit for this reduction in welfare, pointing to the 21.6 per cent reduction in social assistance rates in October 1995, the restriction in eligibility rules, and the introduction of *Ontario Works* in 1997. But other changes are also significant. Changes to the Immigration Act in 1996, for example, reduced the number of sponsored immigrants applying for assistance (Macklin this volume). There was a sustained improvement in the economy, and a decrease in the unemployment rate in Toronto and Ontario more generally.

Of particular significance is the change in the nature of the social assistance cases. In Toronto, the proportion of families on social assistance has increased dramatically (26 per cent in 1991 and 58 per cent in 1999), while the number of individuals receiving assistance has declined (Community Services Committee of the City of Toronto 1999). By July 1999, the number of single individuals on welfare had returned to levels last seen in the early 1990s, at the onset of the recession. However, the number of families in receipt of assistance in July 1999 was nearly four times higher than in the early 1990s (ibid). There has been a corresponding increase in the number of children in receipt of social assistance (from 31,000 in 1991 to 87,000 in 1999, ibid.). The increase in single parent cases is consistent with demographic trends, in which single parent families continue to grow as a percentage of total families. The reduction of caseloads thus reflects the increased employment of single individuals while masking the increase in single families cases, particularly single women and their children.

The figures illustrate that neither the increase in the early 1990s nor the now celebrated decrease in welfare cases had anything to do with 'welfare mothers.' The problem was very clearly an economic recession that created high levels of unemployment. The unique problems that single mothers and children on welfare assistance confront – of systemic poverty and lack of available childcare – have not only *not* been addressed by recent welfare reforms, they have been exacerbated by these reforms. Moreover, the complex relationship between female lone parent families and poverty has disappeared from view, as the problem of welfare dependency has been recast as an individualized problem with an individualized solution. According to neo-liberals and neo-conservatives alike, it was time to break the cycle of welfare dependency and get welfare mothers off welfare. This entirely constructed 'social problem' became the official story informing the provincial government's initiatives in reforming social assistance.

Once again, a closer look at the discourses of family and privatization reveal that neo-liberals and neo-conservatives diverge in their prescriptions for the ills of welfare dependency. Within neo-liberal discourse, the emphasis has tended to be placed on transforming welfare recipients into workers, and in particular, on transforming single mothers dependent on welfare into self-reliant, employable individuals (Teghtsoonian 1995; Brodie 1997). The strategy is an individualizing and degendering one – emphasis is placed on individual self-reliance. Single mothers are thus being redefined as employable individuals, their dependency no long a 'natural' feature of their status as mothers, but rather a temporary problem that needs to be fixed through a welfare system that provides appropriate work incentives, training, and employment opportunities (Evans 1996).

Neo-conservative discourse on welfare dependency, although generally supporting a shift from welfare to work for employable individuals, approaches the problem of single mothers somewhat differently. In this vision, single mothers are not so easily redefined as employable workers. Neo-conservative discourse, consistent with its emphasis on rearticulating the traditional family and traditional gender norms, seeks to strengthen the role of the family in supporting dependent persons. Neo-conservatives seek to transform single welfare mothers into appropriately dependent mothers – that is, mothers who are dependent on husbands/male partners for their economic support. The strategy is a familializing and gendering one, focusing on the family as the appropriate unit for support and on the importance of traditional gender roles within this unit.

At one level, these policies do not appear to be entirely inconsistent. Neo-liberalism is not so much *opposed* to shifting dependency from state to family as it is agnostic. The ultimate neo-liberal goal is to reduce welfare dependency. Although it pursues this goal with its normative vision of the market as the primary mechanism for allocating wealth, it can accommodate other strategies provided that these strategies help reduce welfare dependency. In the context of child support, neo-liberalism supported the individualization and familialization of support obligations in order to reduce welfare dependency. At this level, neo-liberal and neo-conservative approaches to welfare reform are mutually reinforcing. But, at a deeper level, we can see that these two distinct, privatizing strategies have contradictory implications. Neo-liberal approaches to reforming welfare are eroding the significance of gender and family, while neo-conservative approaches are intensifying gender and family.

These distinctive approaches to welfare reform are simultaneously being pursued by the Harris government in Ontario. On the one hand, the government has sought to shift single mothers' dependency from state to family, by returning to the quest for a spouse-in-the-house. On the other hand, the government has also sought to redefine single mothers as employable. Both policies share the objective of disentitling women and their children from their welfare benefits. Beyond this shared objective, the political imaginary of these policies diverge.

Spouses in Houses: Social assistance programs have long been informed by a male breadwinner model, and women in need of state assistance have long been subject to moral regulation and legal surveillance. From its inception in 1920, Ontario Mothers' Allowance provided assistance only to mothers who had no male breadwinner and who were deemed 'worthy.' While initially only widows were considered to be worthy, over time a variety of single mothers, including unwed mothers, were covered, which in turn created more anxiety and surveillance of these women's behaviour (Little 1998). The state was always concerned that there was no male breadwinner to whom these mothers could more appropriately turn to for support. In 1965, Mothers' Allowance was replaced by the Family Benefits Act. While single mothers were not targeted as a distinct group and moral criteria were deleted in favour of criteria based on need, this program continued to be based on a male breadwinner model, and the conduct of single mothers continued to be subject to intense scrutiny. Both of these features of social assistance programs were particularly evident in the 'man in the house' rule. The rule automatically deemed a woman to be ineligible for social assistance in her own right if she was living with a man, even if that man was under no legal obligation to support her. The assumption underlying the 'man in the house' rule was the assumption of the male breadwinner model – that is, any woman living with a man ought to be supported by him

(Evans 1997, 98–9; Little 1998). The man in the house rule resulted in highly intrusive investigations into the intimate lives of single mothers who applied for and were receiving family benefits (Little 1998). While the 'man in the house' rule became the 'spouse in the house' rule under the new regime of formal equality ushered in by section 15 of the Charter of Rights and Freedoms in 1985, the substance remained unchanged: welfare authorities vigilantly scrutinized the private lives of single mothers and cut off their benefits if the authorities found a spouse in their house (Gavigan 1993).

In 1987, the Ontario Liberal government introduced a new definition of 'spouse' under the General Welfare Assistance Act and the Family Benefits Act.[8] The new definition corresponded with the one in the Family Law Act, treating individuals as spouses only in situations where there would be an actual support obligation in law between them. Individuals would be treated as spouses if they were married, if they were the parents of a child, if there was a contract or court-ordered support obligation between them, or if they had lived together in a conjugal relationship for at least three years. As a result, a man and a woman living together for less than three years were no longer automatically assumed to be financially interdependent, and women were no longer automatically disentitled from welfare benefits simply by cohabiting with a man.

In October 1995, the Progressive Conservative government reintroduced the spouse-in-the-house rule, by reforming the definition of spouse in the General Welfare Assistance Act and the Family Benefits Act. Spouse was defined in section 1(1) as:

> (d) a person of the opposite sex to the applicant or recipient who is residing in the same dwelling place as the applicant or recipient if, (i) the person is providing financial support to the applicant or recipient, (ii) the applicant or recipient is providing support to the person, or (iii) the person and the applicant or recipient have a mutual agreement regarding their financial affairs, and the social and familial aspects of the relationship between the person and the applicant or recipient amount to cohabitation.[9]

Section 1(3) further provides that for the purposes of the definition of spouse in section 1(1), 'unless the applicant or recipient provides evidence to satisfy the Director to the contrary, it is presumed that if a person of the opposite sex to the applicant or recipient is residing in the same dwelling place as the applicant or recipient, the person is the spouse of the applicant or recipient.'

The effect of the section is to reintroduce the assumptions of women's financial dependency on men, in the absence of an actual legal obligation under family law. Under the new rule, a woman will be disentitled from her social welfare benefits by virtue of cohabiting with a man, even though that man will not have a legally enforceable obligation to support her until they have cohabited for three years or have borne a child. The spouse-in-the-house rule is, as Pat Evans notes, a return to gender-specific social welfare policies (Evans 1997). The reintensification of the spouse-in-the-house rule can be seen as an effort to reconstitute the dependency of single mothers. It revives the assumption of women's financial dependency within a traditional sexual division of labour, the assumption that women should not be looking to the state for their financial support, but rather to the men in their lives. The spouse-in-the-house rule can thus be seen to reflect neo-conservative efforts to revive the material and discursive significance of family by transforming single welfare mothers into appropriately dependent mothers – that is, mothers who are dependent on husbands/male partners for their economic support. It is an example of a familializing and gendering strategy that seeks to establish the family as the appropriate unit for support, and to re-emphasize the importance of traditional gender roles within this unit.

Shortly after its reintroduction, the constitutionality of the new spouse-in-the-house rule was challenged. In *Falkiner et al. v. Attorney General (Ontario)*, the applicants sought an order declaring section 1 of the regulation defining spouse as unconstitutional (*Falkiner*, 1996).[10]

The Social Assistance Review Board (SARB) ruled that the definition of spouse in the house violated the applicant's constitutional rights under sections 7 and 15 of the Charter (SARB, 11 August 1998). The Ontario government appealed the SARB decision to Divisional Court and continued to try to deploy the discourse of formal equality to justify the rule. According to Minister of Community and Social Services Janet Ecker, 'couples who live together and have a spousal relationship should be treated the same as married couples when they apply for welfare. The income of both individuals must be taken into account when deciding if they are eligible for welfare' (Ontario Ministry of Community and Social Services 1998). In the government's view the old rule, which allowed one member of a cohabiting couple to receive welfare assistance for three years while living with a spouse who might have a good income, effectively discriminated against married couples, who could not receive such assistance. The government was adopting a neo-conservative position not only in its assumption of appropriate dependency for women, but in its arguments about not imposing burdens on married couples that are not imposed on cohabitants. Since marriage is the preferred family form, it is altogether inappropriate for cohabiting couples to receive preferential treatment in law. The government thus attempted to cast its neo-conservative position within the language of formal equality.

The Divisional Court dismissed the government's appeal and agreed with the SARB ruling that the definition of spouse was unconstitutional (*Falkiner*, 2000). Throughout the ruling, Justices Land and Haley rejected the government's arguments about the regulation promoting the formal equality of married couples and unmarried couples (ibid., paras. 63–74, 113, 130–2). In the court's view, 'the impugned legislation does not just treat common-law couples the same as married couples, but it catches a large number of relationships which do not resemble married, where there is no "couple" and no "family unit" involved' (ibid., para. 132). The fact that roommates who share nothing but accommodation could become 'spouses' within the meaning of the regulation, in the court's words, 'makes nonsense of the claim that the pressing concern on the part of the government is to ensure equality between common-law and married couples' (ibid.). Although the court did not discuss the underlying moral vision of gender and family of the spouse-in-the-house rule in any detail, it did not entirely escape scrutiny. In the context of the section 1 argument, the court noted, for example, that '[t]he Regulation is based on "false stereotypes and myths" and appears to owe a good deal to the view of some in society that a woman on social assistance should refrain from intimacy with a man' (ibid., para 142).

The government again appealed the ruling. While the constitutionality of the regulation will remain contested for some time to come, the litigation to date illustrates that the government's attempt to deploy the discourse of formal equality in defence of the spouse-in-the-house rule has been difficult to sustain. The rule is too broad; it includes individuals who live together in non-marriagelike units and individuals who have no legal obligations to support one another. While the government is attempting to use the language of law, its efforts to rely on the discourse of equality sit uncomfortably with the neo-conservative vision that underlies the spouse-in-the-house rule. A neo-conservative vision of the family is not premised on equality but rather on an explicit hierarchy of marriage over non-marriage, and on a naturalized sexual division of labour in which women are economically dependent on men, particularly on those men with whom they have a sexual relationship. At least so far, the legal discourse of formal equality has favoured those progressive voices seeking to challenge the neo-conservative vision rather than those seeking to promote it. Without attempting to predict the outcome of this constitutional challenge, it seems unlikely that the government will be successful casting its neo-conservative agenda in the language of formal equality. Rather, it is more likely to operate to limit the neo-conservative vision.

Mothers in Markets: An altogether different trend can be seen in other reforms to social welfare introduced by the Ontario government, in which neo-liberal discourse is seeking to eliminate welfare dependency by a series of policies designed to reintegrate welfare recipients into the labour market. Sole support parents, whose entitlements to welfare were previously determined under the Family Benefits Act, now fall within the jurisdiction of the Ontario Works Act, 1997. According to the Ministry of Community and Social Services, the Ontario Works Act is intended to 'restore the welfare system to its original purpose: a transitional program of last resort that provides people on welfare with a stepping stone back into the workforce' (Ontario Ministry of Community and Social Services 1997). Section 1 of the Act provides a statement of the purpose of the Ontario Works Act, namely, the establishment of a program that:

(a) recognizes individual responsibility and promotes self-reliance through employment;
(b) provides temporary financial assistance to those most in need while they satisfy obligations to become and stay employed;
(c) effectively serves people needing assistance;
(d) is accountable to the taxpayers of Ontario.

The statement of purpose is deeply imbued with the discourse of neo-liberalism, with its emphasis on individual responsibility, the priority of work over welfare, and creation of financial incentives for individuals to break their welfare dependency, all the while ensuring against welfare fraud and abuse. The neo-liberal impulse of restoring individual initiative through market-based incentives runs throughout government policy statements. The Minister of Community and Social Services, Janet Ecker, has stated, for example, 'As a government, we owe it to people on social assistance to provide them with opportunities to help them become self-sufficient, Equally, we owe it to taxpayers to ensure that their dollars are going to help people truly in need' (Ontario Ministry of Community and Social Services 1997).

The main plank of the welfare reforms, in keeping with this neo-liberal impulse, is the introduction of mandatory workfare for welfare recipients. According to section 7(4) of the Ontario Works Act, in order to receive basic financial assistance, a recipient may be required to:

(a) satisfy community participation requirements;
(b) participate in employment measures;
(c) accept and undertake basic education and job specific skills training; and
(d) accept and maintain employment.

Sole support parents are included within the scope of the Act, and the regulations provide that only parents with very young children, that is, 'sole support parents with at least one dependant child for whom publicly funded education is not available' may be exempted from the mandatory work program (Ontario Works Act, O. Reg. 134/98, s. 27(2)).

Although nothing in the Ontario Works Act specifically names welfare mothers, the government's message is clear. Only welfare mothers with pre-school and thus very young children are exempt from the mandatory workfare program. According to Pat Evans, these welfare reforms reflect the general trend in Canada, in which 'single mothers on social assistance are increasingly subjected to the same work requirements that pertain to married men and single women' and in which social assistance 'has become increasingly gender-neutral and single mothers, a large and expanding group of recipients, are increasingly viewed as "workers" rather than mothers' (Evans 1997, 100; Mosher 2000).

The privatizing strategy of the Ontario Works Act is an individualizing and degendering one. Consistent with the basic precepts of neo-liberalism, emphasis is placed on individual self-reliance, and on erasing the significance of gender for the purpose of achieving it. The welfare dependency of single mothers is not cast as a 'natural' feature of their maternal role within the family, but as a pathological dependency that needs to be fixed (Fraser & Gordon 1997). Indeed, their familial roles are being rendered all but invisible, as single mothers are reconstituted as abstract, disembodied market citizens.

The contradictions inherent in this strategy are brought to the surface in a 1999 study commissioned by the Ministry of Community and Social Services. The consulting firm KPMG concluded that the Ontario government would need to spend $133 million to fund additional child-care services in Toronto alone in order to expand its workfare program. 'Without additional resources, child care will almost certainly prove to be a barrier to the achievement of future [Ontario Works] objectives' (KPMG Report as cited in *Globe and Mail* 1999b).[11] The report reveals the obvious – that single mothers cannot be reconstituted as abstract, disembodied market citizens without considerable attention paid to the care of children. But neo-liberalism, with its individualizing and degendering strategies, has no obvious solution. Its notion of market citizenship implicitly relies on the unpaid or low paid social reproductive work of women.

In the current round of reforms to social welfare law and policy the neo-liberal impulse, with its unapologetic agenda of reconstituting women as market citizens, seems dominant. But this neo-liberal discourse is neither exclusive nor uncontested. The neo-conservative impulse of rearticulating the traditional family is very much alive in the revival of the spouse-in-the-house rules, which disentitle women from welfare benefits altogether. Despite the apparent dominance of neo-liberal approaches in the most recent round of reforms, the way in which the spouse-in-the-house rule operates as an a priori exclusion suggests that for women in financial need, the family remains the place of first resort. The neo-liberal emphasis on mandatory workfare is only triggered if there is no spouse-in-the-house. The spouse-in-the-house regulations and the mandatory workfare program are, in effect, a two-step process, in which social welfare authorities must first determine whether a woman is ineligible by virtue of her spousal status, and if not, then whether she is required to participate in a workfare program in order to remain eligible for her basic financial assistance. Within this process, the family continues to be cast as the first stop of appropriate dependency for financially dependent women and their children. The law has not yet been called upon to mediate and select between these competing discourses, because at the policy level the two are being pursued separately and simultaneously.

However, these two privatizing strategies are at a deeper level contradictory. The neo-liberal strategy is defamilializing, it is eroding the significance of family and constructing individualized, degendered market citizens responsible for their own well-being. The neo-conservative strategy is familializing; it is intensifying the significance of family and constructing gendered subjects, economically dependent on a male breadwinner. It is not clear that these two visions of the family can be sustained. However, each of the visions of family and welfare is also subject to its own internal contradictions. Neo-liberalism, in denying the significance of gender and women's continuing responsibility for childcare, is encountering a structural obstacle in operationalizing workfare. Without the supporting material conditions – adequate childcare – single mothers cannot simply be recast into employable market citizens. Neo-conservatism is similarly encountering dissonance with underlying material conditions, insofar as the male breadwinner vision of the family is no longer a sustainable family form for the vast majority of Canadians. The neo-conservative vision is also being contested by the discourse of equality. Although it is unclear how the courts will resolve this conflict, the experience to date suggests that law's mediating role will select formal equality over neo-conservatism. At the public policy level, however, it appears that for the moment these contradictions are being ignored, with the Ontario government boldly pursuing both neo-liberal and neo-conservative privatizing strategies. Social welfare reforms exemplify some of the ways in which the Right attempts to suture together these two divergent visions within its ranks – a suturing that remains fragile.

Conclusion

An important part of the state's current privatization project involves the effort to fashion a viable new gender order. Yet as analysis reveals in the context of family and social welfare law, no single model of the family has yet emerged as dominant. The new neo-liberal discourse around the family – that families are responsible for their own – appears to be gaining strength. Recent legislative enactments, as well as decisions of the Supreme Court of Canada, continue to expand the scope and content of familial support obligations. Unlike the claims around the traditional family, the neo-liberal discursive strategy appears to be according less importance to the normative structure of the family and more importance to its actual support function. In other words, within this discourse, a family is defined less in terms of who it is and more in terms of what it does. This new functional understanding of the family allows systemic gender inequalities to disappear from view, emphasizing instead a gender-neutral model of familial responsibility. Within this model, women and men are equally responsible for their families' wellbeing, and any division of labour within the family can be seen as a matter of individual choice, effectively a private matter. If and when a relationship breaks down – also a matter of individual and private choice –

this model is only concerned that families continue to take care of their own in the new post-divorce family. Family law within this model is intended to reflect and respect the private choices of individual families while protecting the public purse.

Despite the increasingly powerful ideological claim of this new neo-liberal family, conservative claims to a traditional male breadwinner model are very much alive in the political and legal discourse. The Alliance Party, the *National Post*, and the *Alberta Report*, alongside a range of conservative family organizations and fathers' rights groups, have kept the traditional family flame burning. Ultimately, the conservative vision of the traditional family may prove to be unsustainable, given that few Canadian families can afford to live on the income of a single wage earner. But in the meantime, its normative claims continue to cause problems for the neo-liberal vision of the family, in unanticipated and uncontrollable ways. Moreover, as seen in the context of the spouse-in-the-house rule, the neo-liberal agenda of fiscal conservatism sometimes deploys the conservative vision of the family. The neo-liberal project of privatization, with its strategies of reprivatization and familialization, keeps the contradictions alive by relying on the conservative vision of the family when it serves its ideological purposes.

One of the questions that feminists need to ask at this juncture is how they can intervene in any of these public policy debates and legal controversies. To what extent, if at all, can feminists act to mitigate the harshest impact of these privatizing strategies in family law and social welfare law? To what extent, if at all, might we use the contradictions between neo-liberals and neo-conservatives to challenge the economic, political, and normative agendas of privatization? Should feminists work to highlight the fissures, frictions, and contradictions and propose new and alternative ways of conceptualizing problems such as child poverty? Is it possible to use the neo-liberal language of efficiency against moral conservative moves to strengthen the family? Or conversely, is it possible to deploy the language of family values against policies that erode the small advances that have been achieved in family policy, such as subsidizing childcare?

For example, in the case of gay and lesbian struggles over family recognition, should arguments about the economic efficacy of recognizing same-sex families be used? Not all same-sex spousal or parental cases will lend themselves to these arguments, since many have involved couples seeking additional government benefits. But cases in which the remedy sought is one that can be cast as privatizing social costs, such as *M. v. H.*, could rely on the neo-liberal discourse of fiscal restraint. Arguments in favour of better public enforcement of private support obligations could similarly rely on these neo-liberal arguments. By way of contrast, cases challenging the dismantling of social welfare programs could attempt to deploy the neo-conservative discourse of family values. In a reversal of its ordinary deployment, 'family values' might be used to challenge the elimination of daycare subsidies or perhaps even the harsh attacks on welfare mothers. Conservatives have similarly appropriated bits and pieces of feminist discourse in support of their otherwise reactionary law and order agendas (Cossman et al. 1997; Martin & Mosher 1995).

But appropriation is a risky strategy. The deployment of the discourse of fiscal restraint on the one hand, or traditional family values on the other, risks reinforcing the political purchase of that very discourse and the possibility that neo-liberals or neo-conservatives may, in the next round, win on the same discursive terrain. It runs similar risks to those posed by feminist alignment with conservative forces in the context of campaigns around pornography and violence against women. In both instances, these strategies have been criticized for the failure to consider the dangerous implications of an alliance with the Right.

However, it may be that the dangerous terrain of appropriation needs to be reconsidered. Appropriation has long been a strategy of both neo-liberals and neo-conservatives (Kline 1997). It is admittedly easier for those in positions of political and ideological power to appropriate and rearticulate the meanings of particular discourses. But most discursive moves are easier for those in positions of power. Feminists may need to reconsider whether there are any potentially subversive possibilities lying within the gaps and fissures of these dominant discourses. We might at least consider the possibility that playing both sides of this discursive divide might help destabilize the imaginary coherence of the Right.

These strategic questions are heightened by a sense of both urgency and despair. While the neo-liberal state continues to undermine many of the advances made by the women's movement through the 1970s and 1980s, feminist arguments appear to be losing their purchase in the public sphere, in the face of an aggressive and intensifying backlash. Through the effective discursive strategies of both neo-conservatives and neo-liberals, 'women's groups' have become a marginal, special interest group who do not speak on behalf of Canadian women (Brodie 1995). Legislatures are no longer even remotely feminist-friendly, and even the Supreme Court appears to be reacting to the neo-conservative attacks on judicial activism (Cossman & Ryder 1999).

If old arguments are losing their political purchase, then it is incumbent on feminists and others committed to social justice to develop new ones that respond to or at least have some degree of resonance with the new political and ideological order. Recognizing the currency of the political imaginary of the Right – that is, ' the catch phrases, images and assumptions' of their rhetoric and reasoning around family and social welfare (Fraser 1993, 9) – may be a way of reinvigorating our legal and political strategies, just as conservative forces reinvigorated their own political claims a few years ago by appropriating elements of the political imaginary of progressives. We may need to think harder about how we might appropriate, shape shift, and redeploy these catch words and images in pursuit of our own reinvigorated political imaginary.

A politics of resistance needs a language with resonance. Appropriation of the key words and catch phrases of the Right is but one way of trying to reinfuse our politics with a language that has some resonance and political purchase. We may have to find new ways to advance our claims, armed with the language of family values, or child-centred approaches, or even the efficiency of distribution. If this is our goal, we may need to invent new concepts and language. However, while these discursive strategies may help advance the goals of affirmation and recognition, they may have limited effectiveness in changing the underlying material conditions that are fueling inequality and exclusion.

Notes

1 It should be emphasized that social welfare never fully assumed responsibility for the economic needs of women and children. Rather, welfare schemes have enforced the private responsibilities of family members (Ursel 1992). However, with the rise of the Keynesian welfare state, there was at least a claim to be made for income support from the state, and this claim found discursive support in family law. For example, in *Pelech v. Pelech*, the Supreme Court of Canada, in articulating a narrow test for varying spousal support agreements, stated that absent a causal connection between a radical change in circumstances and economic dependency within the marriage, 'the obligation to support the former spouse should be, as in the case of any other citizen, the communal responsibility of the state.'

2 It is important to recognize that the distinctions set out here between neo-conservatism and neo-liberalism are intended to provide an analytical model, rather than a description of the views of particular individuals or

groups. In practice, a particular political party may (and often does) adopt a neo-conservative position on one issue, and a neo-liberal view on another. For example, the Progressive Conservatives in Ontario and the federal Canadian Alliance Party take a neo-liberal stand on child support (in favour of tougher laws cracking down on deadbeat parents), while adopting a resolutely anti-gay position in terms of same-sex relationships. The analytical distinctions are intended to illuminate the internal contradictions within the Right in general, as well as the contradictions that may inhere in individual actors and groups within the Right.

3 For example, an Angus Reid poll conducted for the Department of Justice in 1998 found that 74 per cent of respondents supported the extension of federal social benefits to gay couples. An Angus Reid poll conducted in 1999 found that 53 per cent of Canadian support same-sex marriage.

4 While acknowledging that decreasing welfare costs was one of the objectives of the legislation (Attorney General of Ontario 1998, submission 21, 55), the attorney general did not address the potential cost savings of a definition of spouse expanded to include same-sex couples. Rather, in addressing the legislative history, the attorney general focused on the economic dependency and needs of women in common-law relationships. Further, in trying to argue that *Egan* could not be meaningfully distinguished, the attorney general noted that 'the fact that there would be little or no additional cost to government entailed in expanding the definition of "spouse" in the *Family Law Act*, as compared to the *OAS Act*, is not a meaningful distinction,' since in its submission, Sopinka J. did not place heavy reliance on the cost argument (ibid., 44).

5 The guidelines set out the kinds of special child-related expenses that can be added to the Schedule amount, provided that these expenses are reasonable and necessary in light of the needs of the children and the means of the parents. These include net childcare expenses for children who are not in full-time school, or for whom extraordinary arrangements are required; medical and health-related expenses over $200 per year per child not covered by provincial or territorial health insurance; educational expenses for primary, secondary, or postsecondary education, or for an educational program that meets a child's particular needs; and extraordinary expenses for extracurricular activities that allow a child to pursue a special interest or talent.

6 For example, the discourse of the fathers' rights movement places greater emphasis on the right of an individual to leave a marriage and to remarry. The importance of individual choice owes more to liberalism and diverges from the neo-conservative emphasis on keeping families together. But the fathers' rights movements borrows from the neo-conservative emphasis on the importance of fathers in the lives of their children.

7 The alliance between neo-conservatives and fathers' rights groups could
   have destabilized on this point, since many within the fathers' rights camp
   would defend their right to divorce and remarriage. But the alliance was at
   least temporarily maintained, with fathers' rights representatives emphasizing the importance of the family and fatherhood, despite divorce. For example, in the words of Mr Bouchard (NAANCP) 'the "best interest" of a child is
   not just money, it is having both parents – that is, the closest thing to having
   the intact family model continue after divorce' (Senate 1996, 16:27).
8 0. Reg. 589/87, s. 1(1), (2) and O. Reg. 590/87, s. 1(1), (2). The amendment
   followed a constitutional challenge by the Women's Legal Education and
   Action Fund (LEAF), who argued that the spouse-in-the-house definition
   violated women's equality rights under the Charter.
9 As a result of An Act to Amend Certain Statutes because of the Supreme
   Court of Canada decision in M. v. H., and subsequent amendments to the
   regulations, 'same sex partner' has since been added to the regulations on
   the same basis as spouse. O. Reg. 32100.
10 The applicants were four women who had been deemed 'spouses' under the
   Family Benefits Act, and had thus been disentitled to their family benefits
   allowances. Each of the applicants had been living with a person of the
   opposite sex for less than a year, none of whom were the fathers of the applicants' children, nor had any legal obligation to support the applicants or
   their children. Each had made the decision to reside with the men prior to
   the change in the definition.
11 The KPMG study was commissioned to help resolve an ongoing dispute
   between officials in the Ministry of Community and Social Services and the
   City of Toronto in implementing Ontario Works. The key problem identified by the report was the shortage of subsidized childcare spaces and the
   bureaucratic difficulties faced by individuals who are trying to leave welfare
   by using childcare subsidies. According to the report, 'clients who become
   employed and are able to leave social assistance before they reach the top of
   conventional waiting lists [for childcare subsidies] lose their Ontario Works
   child-care subsidies by virtue of leaving social assistance, but are not necessarily immediately entitled to a conventional subsidy. In consequence they
   could be forced to remove their children from care, forced to give up their
   job, and forced to return to social assistance ... Ironically, they would then
   be again eligible for an [Ontario works] child care subsidy' (*Globe and Mail*
   1999b).

5

Public Entrance / Private Member

AUDREY MACKLIN

Immigration policy seems an unpromising place to look for evidence of privatization, if by this one means the retraction of the state. As sociologist Robert Miles remarks, 'immigration is a social process that is widely considered to require state regulation (especially by governments otherwise ideologically committed to "rolling back the state")' (Miles 1993, 11). Indeed, the real and imagined lines dividing insider and outsider, citizen and foreigner, 'us' and 'them,' are constituted by and constitutive of the modern nation state. Policing territorial borders against people – as opposed to trade and investment – symbolizes the site, if not the last outpost, of national sovereignty.

For over a century, the periodic arrival of uninvited sea-borne migrants has nourished the spectre of a nation state inundated by waves of humanity washing up on our shores. At various historical moments, South Asians, European Jews, and Chinese have in turn been cast in the role of the desperate and vilified alien clamouring for admission. The moral panic fomented in 1999 by the arrival of six hundred Fujian migrants off the coast of Vancouver Island signals the latest eruption of this anxiety over so-called illegal immigrants.

The fact that only weeks before the arrival of the first ship, Canada admitted to falling short of its immigration target by some 26 per cent in 1998 attracted little mention in the media. With an aging population and low birth rate, Canada depends on immigration to achieve the demographic equilibrium required for economic growth and for social reproduction. Canada's current problem is not too many immigrants, but too few. Nevertheless, capitalizing on the role of the state as 'protector' of law-abiding Canadians against 'illegal migrants' deflects attention from the state's diminishing role as protector of all Canadians from 'unpredictable market forces' (Brodie 1999, 6) and the place that migration occupies in stabilizing social reproduction. Canadian immigration law is designed to regulate the phenomenon. Policies of interdiction, deflection, and criminalization attempt to deter and punish those who circumvent Canada's entry rules. Although discretion to determine 'who gets in' is constrained by an international obligation not to turn back refugees who reach our shores, Canada attempts to evade its duty by including political refugees in the category of those whose arrival should be deterred. Enforcement is not only effected at ports of entry: foreign airports, the high seas, and the territory of other states all become sites for the extra-territorial extension of Canadian border control. Carrier sanctions for improperly documented migrants mean that even private airline personnel are conscripted into quasi-public service.[1] These employees can refuse to board passengers holding valid tickets for Canada if they deem the travel documents suspicious. When it comes to restricting and regulating entry, the state's geographical and functional reach is expanding, not receding. What does not extend across borders so readily is the reach of domestic legal protections available to those who are wrongly or unfairly rejected, interdicted, or turned back.[2]

Despite the apparent political consensus affirming the state's monopoly to police borders, immigration policy is not immune from the transformation signified by privatization. After all, Canadian immigration policy is driven largely by the objective of enriching the Canadian economy. In this sense, immigration policy is a quintessentially public form of regulation serving ends defined by the private realm of the market. Allocation of responsibility between state, family, and market will reverberate in the immigration context at two levels: immigrants may be the targets of privatization strategies; they may also constitute embodied instruments of privatization.

This chapter explores those aspects of Canadian immigration policy that affect migrant women disproportionately or distinctively. The first part examines how temporary worker schemes for male-and female-dominated occupations articulate differently with economic globalization to 'promote, control and maximize returns from the market forces in the international setting' (Cerney 1990, 230, quoted in Brodie & Gabriel 1998, 6). Using 'high-tech' professionals, live-in caregivers, and garment workers as case studies, I reveal the way in which the state selectively delegates decision-making authority to private actors, while simultaneously manipulating terms of entry in order to secure a labour supply that accommodates the demands of private employers. The second part examines the regulation of family reunification under Canadian immigration law as a site of past and present 'familialization.' It draws out strands of historical continuity and interweaves them with contemporary shifts in discourse and in enforcement of family support obligations. This section also highlights the right of landing fee (the so-called head tax) as a counter-example to privatization. The final section reviews the evolution in government funding of immigrant settlement and integration in order to assess the gendered impact of commodification on the provision of language training and other settlement services.

In the course of the chapter, I also refer to legislative changes contained in the new Immigration and Refugee Protection Act (IRPA), passed in October 2001. To the extent that certain provisions involve a renegotiation of responsibility, they offer a timely roadmap of policy trends. However, since the IRPA takes the form of framework legislation, many of the crucial operational aspects remain to be fleshed out in subordinate legislation or guidelines.

A few notes of caution. First, the mere existence of an immigration law or policy says little about implementation and enforcement, owing to the enormous scope for discretion and political intervention. One recent example concerns 'exotic dancers' (strippers) admitted to Canada on temporary work visas in response to an apparent shortage of Canadian women willing to do the job. When it emerged that many women were being exploited and/or engaging in prostitution, immigration authorities did not eliminate the exotic dancer visa, they simply manipulated the levers of discretion and rejected all applicants as unqualified. Immigration policy is notorious for conveying multiple, conflicting and contradictory messages: doors that look open on paper swing shut in reality and vice versa. The disjuncture between theory and practice demands an analysis that addresses the endemic, institutionalized deception embedded in Canada's migration regime.

Second, we must always take into account the interactive impact of 'race' and ethnicity on the character and consequences of Canadian immigration policy for women. Canadian immigration policy formally discarded explicitly racist selection criteria almost forty years ago and the majority of recent immigrants to Canada are characterized as racialized or ethnic minorities. While 'race' and ethnicity now play a lesser role in determining physical exclusion than in the past, they remain powerful markers of socio-economic marginalization. The persistent segmentation of the labour market along racialized and ethnic lines operates in tandem with the gender hierarchy to locate migrant women disproportionately on the lower rungs of the economic ladder, especially in low-wage, precarious, female job ghettos (Shamsuddin 1997). This chapter does not undertake of a critique of privatization per se. I do not argue that privatization is inherently good or bad for immigrants in general or for migrant women in particular. A fully realized program of privatization in immigration would presumably deliver benefits to some migrants and impose burdens on others. One could attempt to articulate a normative claim about who ought to get in and how they ought to be treated, and then measure how well an idealized privatization scheme would fulfil these objectives. That is not the project of this chapter, however, because that is not the project of the state. My present interest is in uncovering where, how, and why strategies of privatization are deployed in the field of immigration, and how these strategies affect women. As Fudge and Cossman note, privatization is partial, selective, and inconsistent. In the domain of immigration, its impact may also vary according to context. Certain practices associated with privatization may operate to the detriment of migrant women, while some immigration policies appear to ignore the putative logic of the market model, also to the detriment of women. Indeed, a truly 'free market' model of migration would mean open borders, which would surely offer greater opportunities to prospective migrants around the world. Conversely, most versions of the modern welfare state presume a territorially bounded polity where benefits extend only to a determinate set of members. At a theoretical level, the exclusionary impulse challenges a romanticized conception of the welfare state, at least from a migration perspective.

The complexities of immigration policy suggest that simply tallying up examples of 'privatization' against counter-examples will reveal less about the normative implications of the evolving role of the state, the market, the family, and the non-profit sector in migration policy than will a critical inquiry into when, how, and why the state chooses to regulate, restrict, or delegate control over entry and settlement.

I. Globalization and Temporary Workers

This section examines three categories of temporary workers to illustrate the profoundly gendered impacts of privatization in the context of immigration law and policy. While admission of temporary workers in general is motivated by the state's desire to reduce the costs of reproducing specific sectors of the labour force, the particulars of the schemes vary dramatically. The federal government delegates its supervisory and selection authority to the private sector to a greater or lesser extent for both 'high-skill' (paradigmatically male) and 'low-skill' (traditionally female) occupations.³ However, where the Canadian state supplements the private sector's efforts to recruit 'high-skill' workers by encouraging workers to acquire permanent residence, it does not offer incentives to attract 'low-skill' workers in the competitive global market, but instead erects barriers to discourage permanent settlement.

Whether workers are designated 'high' or 'low' skill, Canada reaps the benefits of the education, training, and experience the workers acquired elsewhere. Temporary workers are taxed on their income, but have restricted access to various social welfare benefits and public services while residing in Canada.⁴ Foreign workers thus subsidize the resident Canadian population.

The dynamics of privatization interact with gender to influence temporary worker policies at two sites. On the global level, economic restructuring in sending countries often entails an array of privatization strategies. The short- and long-term negative impact of these mechanisms on employment, living conditions, and social benefits function as a significant 'push' factor propelling emigration. At the domestic level, where I focus my argument, the delegation of selection authority over temporary workers from Citizenship and Immigration (CIC) to the private sector is an example of the shift from public to private ordering within Canada, with a concomitant loss of visibility and public accountability. A comparison of the salient differences in the recruitment and settlement policies governing male-dominated occupations and female-dominated occupations reveals the gendered impact of delegation as a strategy of privatization.

Globalization figures at least as prominently as privatization in the lexicon of contemporary social, political, and economic transformation. The two terms share more than ubiquity. Cable argues that economic globalization should be understood as privatization writ global: 'Globalization is largely private sector driven. It represents, therefore, a shift in the locus of decision-making not only from the nation-state to transnational actors, but also from national governments to the private sector. For this reason, economic liberalization and globalization have often gone hand in hand' (Cable 1995, 37).

What is the relationship between economic globalization and migration? Although the movement of people is frequently invoked as an instance of globalization, contemporary migration to settler societies is, in fact, less intensive in size and velocity than it was in the late nineteenth century (Held 1999). In 1913, Canada received over 400,000 immigrants; in 1999, we admitted less than half that number (CIC 2000c, 2). This statistic would hardly assuage the anxieties of those for whom immigration is like the crime rate: always increasing and always bad. Indeed, the more globalization is credited with or blamed for dissolving borders for capital and goods, the louder the clamour to fortify those same borders against people. This contemporary assertion of territoriality regarding the movement of people across borders has been dubbed counter-globalization (Sutcliffe 1998, 325). Yet, as Saskia Sassen argues, '[t]he idea that international migrations, now directed largely to the center from former colonial territories, ... might be the correlate of the internationalization of capital that began with capitalism is simply not part of the mainstream interpretation of that past and the present' (Sassen 1996, 142).

How does the dynamic of globalization and counter-globalization affect women? Perhaps the most obvious manifestation of the globalized workplace is the 'offshoring' of manufacturing and services to export processing zones, where young women serve as low-wage, 'docile' labour for transnational companies. Sex tourism is another facet of taking the work to where labour is cheap. On the other side of the equation, bringing low-cost female labour to the work represents a variation on traditional migration patterns. The extent to which the entry of this labour force is formally restricted or subject to strict temporal limits evinces the 'counter-globalization' impulse. In Canada, exotic dancers and garment workers, among others, embody the conjunction of a global demand for commodified gender roles with migration policies that ensure their performance at low cost by women whose foreignness and ethnic/racialized identity is deployed both as marketing device and as justification for subordination. Not infrequently, these women appear on the losing side of the international, sexual, and racialized division of labour (Pettman 1996).

Membership in the nation state is a public good, and it is distributed to migrants to Canada via permanent residence or 'landed immigrant' status. Permanent residence creates a qualified entitlement to enter and remain in Canada and is the precursor to legal citizenship, which in turn confers a virtually unqualified right to enter and remain in Canada. Immigrants and most refugees acquire permanent resident status. They are prospective members of the nation state and are free to choose their abodes and occupations. In contrast, migrant workers who seek temporary employment in Canada must obtain a Temporary Employment

Authorization (TEA), which allows them to remain in Canada for the duration of the permit and typically ties them to a particular employer. Domestic workers and seasonal agricultural workers are compelled to live in particular locations.

The TEA system is a more privatized system of choosing migrants than immigrant selection and the criteria for selection are entirely labour-market driven. The employer chooses the worker, and CIC issues the visa once minimal health and security checks are done. A TEA binds the worker to a specific job with a specific employer. In political terms, immigrants are admitted to Canada as parties to an ongoing, open-ended, and theoretically renegotiable social contract; temporary workers on TEAs enter as parties to a private employment contract. The terms may vary, but the end of the work relationship signals the end of the worker's relationship with Canada. Temporary workers have a place in the economy, but not in the nation.

The ostensible purpose of Canada's temporary foreign worker policy is to admit foreign workers to meet domestic labour market needs without displacing qualified and available Canadians and permanent residents (CIC, *Immigration Manual* Chapter FW2, 1.1). Temporary workers are not supposed to displace Canadian workers or drive down wages, working conditions, and benefits for Canadian workers. They are also meant to fill only temporary needs. The state attempts to monitor compliance with these criteria by requiring employers to seek and obtain an employment validation from a local Human Resources and Development Canada (HRDC) office before a prospective foreign worker is issued a TEA.

In practice, foreign workers are admitted temporarily to do jobs that Canadians are either unable *or* unwilling to do under prevailing wages and working conditions. Despite the theory that TEAs are intended to meet temporary needs, they have also evolved into instruments for enabling rapid recruitment to fill immediate but not necessarily temporary needs, and into mechanisms to fill chronic gaps in devalued and low pay sectors – such as live-in domestic work, 'exotic dancing,' and the garment industry – which are almost exclusively female domains.

A. 'High-skill' Temporary Workers

Two recent developments suggest an increased willingness by Canada to relinquish its supervisory role and permit the private sector to exercise greater autonomy over the selection of temporary workers. Significantly, both involve 'high-skill' occupational categories where males predominate, and both arise in a context where the discourse of free trade and competitiveness in the 'global market' are asserted to justify the freer movement of certain classes of worker across the Canadian border.

The first example is the insertion of facilitated entry provisions into transnational trade agreements. Both the North American Free Trade Agreement (NAFTA) and the General Agreement on Trade in Services (GATS) exempt employers from the requirement to obtain an employment validation prior to issuance of a TEA for a small retinue of nationals from signatory countries.

NAFTA applies to Mexican and U.S. nationals, and includes professionals, intra-company transferees, business persons, and traders/investors. Some need not obtain a TEA prior to entry, and may apply for it from within Canada. Designated 'business visitors' do not require a TEA at all, as long as their primary source of remuneration is outside Canada (*Immigration Manual*: Chapter FW8).

As Gal-Or indicates (1998, 397, 411), the NAFTA labour mobility provisions are unlikely to become the 'thin end of the wedge' of freer trade in labour. Rather, it appears that the class of eligible migrants under NAFTA are conceptualized less as workers than as trade and investment's personal escorts, who cross the border with approximately the same ease as the capital, trade and investment they ostensibly deliver. As a recent paper by two CIC analysts asserts, 'It is recognized that facilitated entry through trade agreements benefits businesses that operate around the globe with a high-skill workforce. This trend toward international migration of high-skill workers is becoming an increasingly important ingredient for a firm's competitiveness ... [and] carries benefits such as job creation and skill transfer to Canadians' (Pascoe & Davis 1999, 6).

It is also important to observe that neither NAFTA nor GATS replace CIC with a supra-national governance mechanism. Rather, they establish the legal framework within which certain private companies can move their workers across borders with little scrutiny from any public institution or entity.

The Software Development Workers Pilot Project ('Software Pilot Project') introduced in May 1997 implements an even broader, sector-wide delegation of selection authority to the market. Since the mid-1990s, Canadian employers in high-tech industries have complained about the shortage of information technology (IT) workers and the impediments to securing prompt validation for qualified foreign candidates. The terms of the Software Pilot Project allow employers to hire foreign workers who meet one of seven designated job descriptions without requiring a job validation. Once the employer has located a foreign worker who fits one of the job descriptions, the worker can obtain a TEA from the nearest Canadian visa office abroad. The involvement of the state in this process is confined to screening the worker for health and security risks. This has reduced the turnaround time in some cases to less than a week.[5] From May 1997 to January 2000, about 3,000 workers entered under the program (CIC 2000c).

Despite their mode of entry, software professionals (80–90 per cent of whom are male) and other 'highly skilled' workers would be considered desirable immigrants to Canada. They enter on TEAs on the assumption that expediting their entry will give Canada an edge over other countries competing for their skills. Although they enter on a temporary basis, software professionals are greeted with a welcome that encourages them to stay.

In 1998, CIC launched a pilot project to enable spouses of 'highly skilled' workers on TEAs to work legally in Canada without prior labour market testing. Certain other 'less skilled' classes of temporary workers are not even allowed to bring their spouses, and in no other case are spouses permitted to work. As I discuss in Part II, even some spouses of citizens and permanent residents are not permitted to work until they regularize their status.

I contend that the pilot project for spouses of highly skilled temporary workers is designed to make Canada a more attractive short- *and* long-term option for the high-skill foreign worker. The United States, for example, does not offer work permits to spouses of high-skill workers admitted under its H1-B work visa program. Canadian policy makers anticipate that once the spouse of the worker is admitted on terms that facilitate social and economic incorporation of the family unit, at least some workers will apply to remain permanently as immigrants. Most are from South Asia and Western Europe (Pascoe 1999a).

Viewed as a package of policies, the NAFTA and GATS labour mobility provisions, the Software Pilot Project, and the spousal work permit pilot project signal a creeping marketization of the form and content of worker selection practices, combined with public incentives aimed at encouraging permanent settlement. The net effect is that the class of temporary workers over whom the state has delegated greatest selection authority to private employers is also the class for whom permanent resident status will be most facilitated. This gives new meaning to the phrase 'market citizen,' as the scheme is explicitly designed to place those selected by the market on a fast track to political membership.

B. *Live-in Caregivers*

Foreign workers who take jobs Canadians are unwilling as opposed to unqualified to do find themselves in a dramatically different position from high-skill workers. In these cases, work authorizations are temporary not because demand is temporary, the workers desire to remain only temporarily, or because of the relative celerity of the TEA process: the insecurity created by linking permission to remain in Canada with continued employment ensures that workers tolerate wages and working conditions Canadians and permanent residents find unacceptable.

Throughout the history of Canadian immigration, female migrant workers have traditionally been admitted through the servant's entrance. Though the source countries and the terms of admission have evolved over time, one enduring feature is the objective of privatizing the cost of social reproduction, and keeping that cost low. Foreign domestic workers constitute the instrument of that privatization.

At present, the Philippines is the largest Asian exporter of migrant labour and dominates the global supply of domestic workers. In many less developed countries (LDCs), including the Philippines, IMF and World Bank global debt and restructuring policies mandate export-oriented development, deregulation of capital and industry, privatization of the public sector, and cuts to government spending. These policies often result in decline in health education and social services, increases in un- and underemployment, shrinkage in public sector employment, price jumps when subsidies are reduced, a deterioration in the status of women, and an expanding gap between rich and poor (Bakan & Stasiulis 1996; 1997a, 1997b; Brodie 1999, 4). Migration of nationals who will send back foreign currency remittances thus emerges as a crucial strategy for both family and state debt relief (Sutcliffe 1998, 332).

Half a million Filipinos leave annually; 40 per cent of these migrants are women, and most are employed in the 'service-sector' as domestic workers (Tyner 1996, 39, 45). The state aggressively markets its nationals via the Philippines Overseas Employment Administration (POEA) in order to secure a niche in the highly competitive global market for temporary labour. Part of that marketing strategy entails selling gendered representations of Filipinos that appeal to racialized sex stereotypes. This means that many Filipino women are employed well below their skill level, revealing both a gendered and racialized structuring of opportunity (Tyner 1996, 45). As Tyner states, 'At the risk of over generalizing, labour-importing countries prefer to hire Philippine women as baby-sitters rather than pediatricians, or as hostesses rather than hotel managers' (ibid.).

Within the Canadian context, if market principles of supply and demand were permitted to operate freely, wages and working conditions for live-in domestic work would have to improve significantly to attract and retain employees. If supply still failed to meet demand, or if the cost were prohibitive for too many Canadians, some prospective employers might be driven to make a choice they would not otherwise make, and exit the full-time workplace in favour of unpaid work in the home. Given the gendered division of labour within Canada, that employer would in most cases be the mother, not the father. Alternatively, the paucity of cheap, live-in childcare might stimulate more vigorous demands for a national, public childcare program. A more radical possibility is that it might mobilize public demands to reconfigure the professional workplace, which remains premised on the obsolete model of a full-time breadwinner with a stay-at-home wife. It would be an understatement to say that such a transformation is unlikely in the short run.

The privatization agenda is decidedly incompatible with publicly funded childcare. The gender order promoted by the state manages to exalt both the virtue of women caring for children in the home and market self-sufficiency for both sexes. These apparently irreconcilable objectives create an intractable dilemma for Canadian working women. However, middle- and upper-class parents can be placated ideologically and materially by supplying them with cheap, private, live-in childcare. This can only be achieved by strategic public intervention via immigration law to pre-empt private market forces. The Live-In Caregiver Program (LCP) is the latest scheme designed to secure a pool of labour whose immigration status compels workers to accept conditions which they, like Canadian and permanent resident workers, would otherwise reject (Macklin 1992a; 1994). Live-in caregivers thus serve as a safety-valve mediating the contradictions of the new gender order.[6] Increasingly, the LCP is also being deployed to supply qualified Filipino nurses as live-in home support workers for elderly and disabled people. Privatization of health care has replicated the logic of childcare in the domain of 'home care.'

Until nearly the middle of the twentieth century, the majority of domestic workers were white, working-class British and Northern European women whose migration was organized, encouraged and financed by emigration societies, the Canadian government, and railway and shipping companies. After serving for a suitable time as domestics, these women were expected to marry Canadian men and assume their reproductive role in the nation-building enterprise of a white settler society. As the institution of domestic service waned in Britain and Europe, the supply of white women petered out and employers turned to women of colour from LDCs (Macklin 1992a). Given racist entry restrictions in the 1952 Immigration Act, the supply could not be secured without program-specific government intervention. In the mid-1950s, the Government of Canada negotiated agreements with several Caribbean nations to permit the entry of a designated number of women 'of exceptional merit' to serve as live-in domestic workers. The women entered as permanent residents. Racism in the labour market supplied an effective brake on their ability to exit the occupation, but by the 1960s it was no longer adequate to suppress a high rate of mobility (Arat-Koc 1997).

By 1967, the government had replaced explicitly discriminatory selection criteria with a superficially neutral 'point system', that appraised prospective migrants against a checklist emphasizing language ability, formal education and training, and occupational demand. The operating assumption of the point system is that Canada neither needs nor wants immigrants to fill 'low skill' jobs, and domestic work was one such example. The result was that domestic workers were ineligible as immigrants under the points system. In 1973, the advent of TEAs turned domestic workers into long-term, European-style guest workers, with no entitlement to settle in Canada permanently and no right to bring their families. Unlike their white predecessors, domestic workers from the Caribbean (and later, the Philippines) were not viewed as future members and reproducers of the nation. Their predicament is one example of how structural racism persists in immigration policy long after the demise of explicitly racist restrictions.

The fact that domestic workers could labour in Canada for years under exploitative conditions with no prospect of permanent residence sparked a successful campaign by those workers and their allies, which culminated in 1981 in a unique immigration program known as the Foreign Domestic Movement (FDM) Program. The FDM gave live-in domestic workers the opportunity to become permanent residents after completion of two years of live-in domestic service on TEAs. Although workers could change employers during that time, they required a new employment authorization for each employer. The system effectively extracted two years of minimum-wage[7] live-in labour in exchange for likely (though not assured) permanent resident status.

In effect, live-in domestic workers are indentured to the state by the positive incentive of permanent residence. While this situation is not optimal, the recent case of *Baker v. Canada* (1999) recalls the harshness of the situation the FDM replaced. Mavis Baker worked as an undocumented live-in domestic worker for eleven years.[8] In the course of rejecting her application for landing based on humanitarian and compassionate considerations, the visa officer tersely summed up the value he attached to her occupation and past service: 'She has no qualifications other than as a domestic' (*Baker,* para. 5).

By the mid-1980s, the Philippines had largely supplanted the Caribbean as the major source region for domestic workers. Familiar clichés about domestic workers ('Filipina women are so docile, so good with children, so willing to do all the cleaning'), along with class arrogance ('Canada really does these women a favour because they wouldn't be able to earn that amount of money back home') and private sphere ideology ('she's like one of the family' ... 'this work is a labour of love'), operate synergistically to enable the physical, financial, and occasional sexual exploitation of foreign domestic workers (Arat-Koc 1999; Macklin 1992a). Moreover, because the live-in caregiver is confined to the 'private sphere' of the home, she is typically un- or underprotected by provincial employment and labour legislation regarding maximum hours of work, minimum wage, and overtime (Macklin 1992a; 1994; Nemiroff 1999, 10, 12). Her precarious immigration status confines her to a work setting that potentiates mistreatment, and also gives her an incentive not to complain about it.

Unlike the pilot project for spouses of high-skill temporary workers, CIC ignores the fact that live-in caregivers on TEAs have spouses or children. After all, the unpaid labour the caregiver might provide to her own family if they were in Canada would distract her from devoting her labour power to providing childcare and household labour to other people's families. Live-in caregivers are explicitly prohibited from bringing any dependants with them, even if their employer consents. Giving birth to a child in Canada may jeopardize the live-in caregiver's application for permanent residence and lead to removal.[9]

In 1992, the FDM program was modified and renamed the Live-In Caregiver Program (LCP), but the essential element of two years' live-in domestic work in exchange for permanent resident status remained unchanged. The changes made it tougher for applicants to qualify for

entry to the program by raising educational and experience requirements, but easier to obtain permanent resident status after completion
of the two-year period of live-in work. Indeed, under the FDM and the
LCP, the overwhelming majority of workers do acquire permanent resident status. Nevertheless, both live-in caregivers and their employers
know that the workers are 'on probation' for at least two years. This creates a disincentive for live-in caregivers to insist on their employment
rights.

The LCP ensures that childcare continues to be provided at low cost
by women in the home. The constitution of childcare as 'women's work'
of low economic value remains unchanged. What has changed are the
women doing it: racialized non-citizens who may well be mothers – but
not of the children to whom they provide childcare. The LCP furnishes
a rich illustration of how migrants propelled by the gendered and racialized impact of privatization strategies in the South become instruments
of privatization in the North.[10] Their availability permits the Canadian
government to elude, or at least diffuse, demands to place childcare on
the roster of public responsibility. As an elaborate regulatory instrument
designed to intervene on the supply side of the labour market, the LCP
demonstrates how keeping childcare a private matter in Canada
requires considerable state intervention.

C. Sewing Machine Operators

The garment industry also reveals many of the global gender dynamics
of economic restructuring and national projects of privatization (Fudge
1993). As a 1999 report about the Canadian and international garment
industry states, 'Globalization and trade liberalization policies have
caused profound changes not only in the international division and global organization of labour, but also in how, by whom and under what
conditions our clothes are made in Canada and in other countries'
(Yanz et al. 1999, ix). Historically, there was no need to import migrant
workers to supply inexpensive female labour for the garment industry.
The structural inequities in the Canadian labour market have long generated enough Canadian workers – mostly immigrant, mostly women of
colour – to meet demand. Today, 76 per cent of all Canadian garment
workers are women, half are immigrants, and almost 30 per cent are
members of a visible minority. Men predominate in cutting and pressing, women in sewing. Immigrant women comprise 94 per cent of sewing machine operators in Toronto (Yanz et al. 1999, 14).

In the 1990s, globalization and NAFTA eliminated the tariff and quota protections insulating the Canadian garment industry. From 1988 to 1995, between a third and half of all Canadian garment workers lost their jobs as Canadian factories downsized, shut down, or relocated (Yanz et al. 1999, 13). Nevertheless, Canadian manufacturers still require a small pool of local labour to deal with 'quick turnover.' The impact of restructuring on remaining employment opportunities in Canada precipitated the emergence of contract-shop and home-work (Yanz et al. 1999). Like live-in caregivers, home-workers in the garment trade experience the deterioration of legal recognition and protection of their status qua workers that accompanies the relocation of their workplace to the feminized 'private sphere' of the home. The garment-making workplace, reconstituted in atomized, isolated, and privatized form presents serious impediments to union organizing and enforcement of employment standards (Ocran 1997; Ng 1990; Fudge 1993). On the other side of the global equation, Less Developed Countries (LDCs) anxious to attract foreign investment and work establish export-processing zones 'which offer cheap labour, favourable terms and investment prohibitions on unionizing and tax environment and labour standards' (Yanz et al. 1999, 111). China has emerged as the world's main garment manufacturer, and is the top garment exporter to the Canadian market. The industry is staffed by some four million workers, mostly female, many of whom have migrated from rural areas in search of work in the factories (Yanz et al. 1999, 13). The similar profile of garment workers in Canada and abroad seems to belie the prediction that the current model of export-based development will suppress emigration by boosting local economies. Many garment workers in Canada originate from Asian countries, including China. As Yanz et al. comment, 'Many come to Canada seeking opportunities or fleeing repression, and find themselves competing against workers in their countries of origin and watching standards fall toward those they thought they had left behind' (Yanz et al. 1999, 14).

Despite the general decline in the garment industry in Canada, Winnipeg is in the anomalous position of lacking adequate numbers of workers to meet demand. The drive to lower production costs in order to remain competitive may be one reason. Given that one can be trained on the job as a sewing machine operator, I surmise that the shortage of workers must be due to wages and working conditions insufficient to attract and retain Canadian citizens or permanent residents. The story of importing sewing machine operators to Manitoba is brief and regionally specific, but provides a quirky illustration of the contradictions produced by globalization of production and counter-globalization in immigration policy.

In 1996, in response to pressure from the apparel industry, the Province of Manitoba and the federal government entered into a 'Sewing Machine Operators Agreement,' which permitted Manitoba to nominate up to two hundred experienced sewing machine operators (CIC 1996b) as prospective immigrants. Under ordinary conditions, the low skill level attributed to sewing machine operation would preclude this category of workers from accumulating enough points to qualify as immigrants. The agreement created a window for 160 female sewing machine operators who, along with their dependants, migrated to Winnipeg as Canadian permanent residents. An intriguing term of the agreement was the imposition of a sponsorship-style relationship on employers and employees similar to the sponsorship arrangement between family members. Article 6.3 of the *Canada-Manitoba Sewing Machine Operators Agreement* stated that

> Manitoba shall obtain ... from a relative residing in Manitoba *or the Manitoba employer* ... a written undertaking to provide financial support for the principal applicant and his or her accompanying dependants for a *period of ten years* from the date of landing of the principal applicant. The undertaking ... will include the following provisions:
> (a) The relative *or employer* shall agree to provide for the essential needs of the principal applicant and his or her accompanying dependants while the undertaking is in effect;
> (b) The Government of Manitoba shall be entitled to recover directly from the relative *or the employer* entering into the undertaking the equivalent of all income support or social assistance provided by the Government of Manitoba to the principal applicant and/or his or her accompanying dependent, including (without limitation) benefits, supports or assistance provided under *The Social Allowance Act of Manitoba* (CIC 1996b, emphasis added)

Although the agreement obliged the governments of Canada and Manitoba to track the economic performance of the sewing machine operators and the integration of their dependants, no formal assessment has ever been made public. One suspects that the program did not achieve its goal of redressing the chronic shortage of sewing machine operators. First, the shortage of workers in Manitoba continued unabated long after the arrival of the 160 workers, but the agreement was not renewed or extended. An unconfirmed rumour indicated that employers 'skimmed off' the most proficient sewing machine operators, leaving the rest to find other jobs or resort to social assistance. There is no evidence that Manitoba attempted to enforce the sponsorship undertaking against employers. To my knowledge, CIC has never attempted to bind employers to a ten-year sponsorship undertaking. Since employment relationships in the garment industry typically feature high turnover rates, the sponsorship undertaking seems unrealistic. It represents a novel, if impractical, attempt to graft familial responsibilities onto market relationships.

In any event, by 1999, representatives of Manitoba's garment industry had hired a private recruiter to go to China to locate qualified sewing machine operators to fill some of the thousand job vacancies with temporary workers (Janzen 1999b, A3). Federal, provincial, and even union officials collaborated on a proposal to issue one-year TEAs to experienced sewing machine operators. The recruiter identified seventy-four Chinese sewing machine operators with prior overseas work experience. In June 1999, Canadian embassy officials in Beijing interviewed five applicants and refused to issue TEAs to all seventy-four applicants. The reason? According to a letter from an immigration official to the recruiter, 'Our checks and interviews revealed the applicants are all earning very low salaries (in China). Moreover, they all come from a region of China that is economically depressed' (Janzen 1999b). Therefore, the visa officer was not satisfied that the workers would return to China after termination of their TEAs. The unarticulated and probably unsupportable premise appears to be that the workers would neither extend nor renew the TEAs when they expired, but would instead go 'underground.' This scenario is a classic Catch-22: foreign workers are motivated to accept jobs that Canadians will not do for the same reason used to deny them entry – the bleakness of life opportunities at home.

At least one factory owner warned that if the government continued to block efforts to import cheap labour to fill his demand, he would consider relocating production to Mexico (Janzen 1999b). Less than a year later, the same recruiter succeeded in obtaining TEAs for thirty-seven female sewing machine operators from Thailand. Within weeks of their arrival, local newspapers reported that the women had been 'cheated and exploited' by the recruiter, prompting the intervention of the Thai Embassy, CIC, and provincial authorities (Guttormson 2000). CIC and the Thai embassy immediately announced a moratorium on arrivals of foreign sewing machine operators.

The story of sewing machine operators in Winnipeg will doubtless continue. While the dynamics of economic globalization, Canadian immigration policy, and the international division of labour may clash over how to supply Winnipeg garment manufacturers with cheap sewing machine operators, they synchronize enough to ensure that sewing machines will be operated for Canadian companies by racialized women from poor countries labouring in substandard conditions, whether in Canada or abroad.

D. Temporary Worker Regimes and Gender

Liberalized trade and investment practices across borders have yielded transnational agreements which, as a subsidiary to facilitating trade, also ease the movement of certain 'high-skill' workers. The mobility provisions of NAFTA and GATS represent the purest extension of free trade logic from goods to labour.

Political motives for resorting to temporary worker schemes vary. Experience precipitated the Software Pilot Program. Had CIC been able to process applications for permanent residence promptly, I suspect that software professionals would have been admitted as immigrants through existing channels. Yet, even the conventional TEA system ultimately proved too sluggish for employers. To the extent that the market is promoted as more efficient than the state, the Software Pilot Program appears to validate claims advanced in favour of private ordering. At the same time, the state aids the private sector's recruitment strategies with public inducements, particularly the spousal work permit, which encourage these workers to settle permanently in Canada.

The situation for live-in domestic workers is very different. Unlike software professionals, domestic workers do jobs Canadians will not do, at least not under prevailing wages and working conditions. Without external pressure, it is doubtful that the government would have reformed the 'guest worker' regime, which effectively extracts maximum value at minimal cost to employers and to the state. The campaign by advocacy groups, NGOs, civil libertarians, and others to vindicate the rights of domestic workers mobilized around the slogan 'good enough to work, good enough to stay.' The result was not a complete victory, but rather the hybrid regulatory scheme now known as the Live-in Caregiver Program. The treatment of domestic workers under this program stands in stark contrast to the treatment of IT professionals. The prohibition on bringing family members and the ultimate 'pay-off' of permanent resident status operates to discipline live-in caregivers during their two-year stint of compulsory live-in work.

As for sewing-machine operators in Winnipeg, the lack of coordination and cooperation between different institutional actors speaks to the lack of coherence in Canadian immigration policy. The institutional discord between local bureaucrats committed to appeasing employers' demand for low-cost labour, and visa officers committed to border control demonstrates the inability of the neo-liberal state to resolve the contradictions of managing borders in an era of economic globalization.

The implications of delegating increased selection authority over temporary workers to employers will vary according to the location of the worker and the employer in the global marketplace. For example, software professionals operate in a seller's market vis-à-vis Canadian employers. High-tech workers are in demand all over the industrialized world, and most workers (especially in the computer industry) consider the United States the preferred destination. In 1996, three Canadian workers entered the United States under NAFTA for every American entering Canada (DeVoretz 1999, 5–6). Canadian employers offer prospective employees incentives to lure and retain them. For its part, the state intervenes to supplement market incentives with public inducements: spousal work permits and the prospect of permanent residence. Software professionals' strong bargaining position in Canada suggests that the efficiency gains of delegation to the private sector do not expose workers to the risk of exploitation. These workers can take care of themselves as long as employers believe that their foreign employees will head south (or home) if conditions in Canada do not meet expectations. The same outcomes would not obtain, however, where the parties do not believe that the workers have alternatives of equal or greater preference. Thus, the material significance of temporary immigration status depends in large measure on the economic opportunities and social citizenship entitlements available to the worker in her country of origin or elsewhere.

Given a profoundly uneven distribution of global wealth, coupled with a burgeoning demand for 'women's work,' considerable numbers of women are willing to enter states on any terms, even if it involves occupational de-skilling and restrictive conditions. The perceived reward is eventual access to a range of economic, social, and political opportunities that their impoverished countries of origin cannot match, even considering the additional race and class barriers facing them in countries such as Canada (Bakan & Stasiulis 1997a, 46). Despite worldwide demand for women's work, women who migrate as caregivers or sewing machine operators lack meaningful bargaining power anywhere.

The revised point system under the IRPA will award up to ten points for at least one year's full-time authorized employment. However, other elements of the point system diminish the likelihood that a temporary worker in a low-skill occupation will acquire the requisite point total. This means that so-called low-skill temporary workers will remain excluded from the prospect of permanent residence. In any event, the Live-In Caregiver Program exposes the option of delayed permanent residence as an imperfect solution to the problem of using temporary worker regimes to secure 'cheap labour' for the 3D jobs (difficult, dirty, dangerous). In part, the defects of the Live-In Caregiver Program are attributable to the combination of state intervention to create a market for low-paid, live-in domestic labour with state non-intervention in the protection of workers' interests and rights. Offering permanent residence as a reward for performance of socially and economically devalued labour amounts to public compensation for assumption of a publicly created risk of private exploitation.[11] In other words, access to citizenship becomes the remedy for the worker's past vulnerability caused by her non-citizen status.

In principle, this dilemma could be overcome by vigilant state supervision and enforcement of relevant employment standards, the ability to change employers within the sector without jeopardizing immigration status, and information and support services to workers – all of which require more, not less, state regulation. The experience of domestic workers indicates that in practice, these measures are either not undertaken or are insufficient to countervail the vulnerability created by the live-in requirement. Once again, the selectivity of government regulation in this field illustrates the partial, instrumental nature of privatization strategies as mechanisms of actualizing the normative objectives of the neo-liberal state.

II. Immigrants, Markets, and Families

From its inception, Canada's nation-building project has been guided by two key objectives: building an economy and building a citizenry (Avery 1995). Canada needs workers for the former and mothers for the latter. In pursuing the economic goal, the state acts as an agent for the market. From attracting nineteenth-century farmers with free passage and land grants, to entering twenty first-century software programmers with free flights and spousal work visas, tuning immigration policy to maximize labour market return has been a defining feature of Canadian immigration policy.

As a colonial, settler society, the imagined nation excluded Aboriginal people. Among potential settlers, the state preferred white people of English, French, or northern European descent. As long as Canada could attract sufficient numbers of male workers who met this description, their wives and children were welcome. Unmarried women from preferred countries were actively recruited as servants to supply cheap domestic labour until they married. As wives and mothers, they would provide unpaid domestic labour, thereby reproducing both citizenry and labour force. In general, immigration policy conceived of men as workers and women as housewives or housewives-in-training.

As the labour supply from 'preferred' countries failed to meet demand, the emerging incongruity between economic and demographic ambitions was manifested in the treatment of migrants from 'non-preferred' countries and racialized groups. The demand for labour – especially cheap labour – could not be met with British and northern Europeans. Eventually, the state grudgingly broadened the concept of 'nation' to encompass southern and eastern Europeans, but resolutely excluded racialized minorities deemed undesirable and unassimilable, such as blacks, South Asians, and Southeast Asians. An array of regulatory instruments, including formal but unenforced exclusion, guest worker schemes, prohibition on family reunification, and denial of citizenship, facilitated the insertion of racialized minorities (and women qua workers) into the economy as exploitable labour, while barring them from membership in the nation (Avery 1995).

The legacy of these practices resonates in the modern immigration categories of 'independent' immigrant and the 'family class.' While evaluating newcomers as future market citizens is not new in immigration policy, perhaps the most significant postwar development was the abandonment of explicitly racist criteria and the adoption of a 'point system' in the 1960s (incorporated into the 1976 Immigration Act). The point system disaggregated the assessment into various categories and required the applicant to obtain a minimum number of points to qualify. The more liquid one's capital, the fewer points required. 'Skilled workers' trading on their human capital require seventy points. Investors and entrepreneurs with a high enough net worth and willingness to invest hundreds of thousands of dollars, or start up a business venture in Canada, require only twenty-five points. These elite immigrants are

often 'closely connected to international trade and international financial institutions' that typify the globalized economy (Simmons 1999, 64).
Skilled workers and business persons are known as 'economic' or 'independent' immigrants.

Public documents insist that today's immigrants (from wherever they
come) are valued not only for their labour market potential, but for
their contribution to social and cultural 'nation building.' However, the
state tacitly treats the latter as a dependent variable of the former. As a
recent government report stated: '*Highly skilled* immigrants make an
invaluable contribution to Canadian society. As they integrate into communities, these immigrants become integral parts of all facets of Canadian society. They enrich the cultural and social fabric of Canada' (CIC
1999c: 28, emphasis added). Even the seven to eight thousand government-sponsored refugees chosen each year are assessed for their ability
to establish themselves successfully in Canada; those who have suffered
most will be passed over in favour of those likely to perform best in the
labour force.

The point system formally eliminated race and ethnicity from the
selection process and focused almost entirely on education, training,
language ability, and experience as indicators of future labour market
performance. In contrast to the explicitly racist criteria for selection in
the past, China/Hong Kong, the Philippines, and the Indian sub-conti-
nent are the top three regional sources for recent immigrants (CIC
1999a, 7). Unfortunately, discrimination and protectionism persist in
the labour market, with the result that many high-skilled immigrants do
not find work commensurate with their abilities or expectations because
their foreign qualifications go unrecognized. In other words, the points
system operates as an idealized representation of how the market ought
to work. Unlike temporary workers, immigrants need not obtain a job
offer from a specific employer as a precondition to entry. Therefore, the
job validation process does not apply and there is no assurance that prospective employers will recognize an immigrant's foreign qualifications.

The discrepancy between how the point system imagines the labour
market should work and how the labour market really works ensures
that Canada retains a highly educated and skilled reserve of cab drivers,
pizza delivery people, homecare givers, and factory workers. On the
other hand, the point system accurately mirrors the market's devaluation of skills traditionally associated with women, which is one of the
reasons why women are relatively less likely to apply and to qualify as
independent immigrants. The point system attempts to mimic the mar-

ket's evaluation of skills and places a premium on educational attainment, advanced technical qualifications, and work experience. When one takes into account differential access to education and training for girls and boys in many foreign countries, it is predictable that fewer women than men 'have what it takes' to succeed under the point system. Anecdotal reports also relate that CIC discourages qualified married women from applying as independent immigrants if their spouse also qualified. Between 1996 and 1998, men comprised 70 per cent of principal applicants in the economic class (CIC 1999a).

Family reunification is the other pillar of Canadian immigration policy. Nation building has always meant creating future generations of Canadians. The obverse is that certain migrants considered unworthy of membership in the nation are denied the right to reunite with their families or penalized for having families at all. Up until 1967, sponsorship provisions still discriminated on the basis of nationality (Kelley & Trebilcock 1999, 333). The fact that Mavis Baker, an undocumented, unmarried Jamaican domestic worker, gave birth to four children while in Canada was hardly viewed as a positive contribution to the future of Canadian society by the visa officer assessing her application to be landed on humanitarian and compassionate grounds.[12] The confluence of racialization and family ideology in this context is particularly stark.

Immediate family members (spouses and dependant children)[13] who immigrate with the principal applicant in the independent class are known as 'accompanying dependants.' Close relatives (spouses, dependant children, parents, and grandparents, etc.) living abroad who wish to join a permanent resident or Canadian citizen in Canada are labelled 'members of the family class.'[14] Accompanying dependants and members of the family class are exempt from evaluation under the points system, as they are presumably not entering the labour market. Insofar as this assumption applies to female spouses, it is counter-factual. Immigrant women have higher labour force participation than native-born women, albeit in more precarious, poorly paid jobs.

We should not sentimentalize the rationale for exempting accompanying dependants and the family class from the points system. Admission of family members is conceptualized as ancillary to the economic objectives of immigration policy overall (Hathaway 1994, 6). The family constitutes both a social and economic unit. To use a contemporary example, wages remitted by an immigrant to family members abroad is money withdrawn from the Canadian economy. More generally, the family is also the site for the social and physical reproduction required to sustain the market citizen, traditionally furnished by the unpaid labour of women in exchange for material support.

The obverse to male overrepresentation in the independent class is female overrepresentation in the family class. In the period 1996–8, at least 60 per cent of accompanying dependant spouses were female, and women comprised approximately 64 per cent of spouses and fiancées entering as members of the family class. Monica Boyd (1999a, 15) reports that for the ten-year period 1985–94, the ratio of females to males immigrating as spouses was almost 7:1.

The bottom line is that despite the growing number of female migrant workers, most adult women still immigrate to Canada as spouses, and most spouses who immigrate to Canada are women. The admission of wives to Canada as accompanying dependants or members of the family class effectively inscribes onto immigration law a gender order that identifies male as independent/economic/producer and female as dependant/family/reproducer.

The rigidity of these categories does not necessarily reflect women's labour force capabilities or actual participation. Nevertheless, rules regarding the eligibility of sponsors, the admissibility of sponsored family members, and the imposition of a sponsorship undertaking all operate from the tacit assumption that the members of the family class are economic dependants. At the level of discourse, the sharp distinction between independent and dependent immigrants created and enforced by these categories also contributes to a cultural construction of immigrants as wedded to a static, traditional, patriarchal family structure, whereas Canadian men and women are seen as increasingly adopting more egalitarian, flexible, and 'progressive' family forms (Lutz 1997a, 105).

In practice, men and women enter Canada as immigrants in roughly equal numbers. The combined number of accompanying dependants and members of the family class exceeds the number of independent immigrants, with the result that females comprise about 51 per cent of immigrants to Canada each year.

A. Enforcement of Family Sponsorship Undertakings

Perhaps the strongest indication of the economic underpinnings of the family class is the sponsorship undertaking. A permanent resident or citizen may sponsor an applicant member of the family class by first demonstrating sufficient income to support the applicant.[15] Next, the sponsor must provide an unconditional undertaking to provide for the financial needs of the applicant for up to ten years. From the outset, the objective is to ensure that the sponsored member of the family class will not become a burden on the state.

What legal difference does it make if permanent resident status is acquired on the basis of evaluation under the point system or on familial relationship? If a woman successfully applies to immigrate and enters Canada with her spouse and children, the short answer is 'not much.' The spouses' respective legal statuses as permanent residents and entitlements are identical, whether the individual entered as an accompanying dependent or as an independent immigrant. No sponsorship undertaking applies. However, if the would-be immigrant applies to be sponsored as a member of the family class by a person who is already a permanent resident or citizen, the scenario changes.

Some spouses of Canadian citizens or permanent residents apply to immigrate from within Canada. They may have come to Canada on temporary visas (student, visitor, worker) or they may be unsuccessful refugee claimants. Their Canadian/permanent resident spouse must apply to sponsor them, and the applicant is usually permitted to remain in Canada pending processing of the sponsorship application. Until such time as the application is 'approved in principle,' the applicant (unlike the spouse of a 'highly skilled' temporary worker) cannot work legally. She is also ineligible for public health care, settlement assistance, or social assistance.[16] Due to persistent delays in the processing of applications, an applicant can spend as long as two years in limbo awaiting approval in principle. During this time, she is financially dependent on her husband, who may withdraw his sponsorship application at any time. If he does so, processing ceases and the applicant becomes liable to removal from Canada.

A superb study on the impact of sponsorship on francophone migrant women in Ontario (Côté, Kérisit, & Côté 1999) demonstrates how these restrictions on inland applicants structures the very dependency that the neo-liberal state both disdains and expects in women in the family class (Cossman, this volume). Much like foreign domestic workers, women in the family class know that their continued presence in Canada depends on their relationship to a private actor. Women living in these conditions are especially vulnerable to financial, physical, and sexual abuse from men who choose to exploit this imbalance of power. Despite depictions of gender relations among migrant communities that attribute domestic violence to 'cultural norms,' immigrant women point out a connection between immigration status and abuse of power:

'Dans mon pays, il n'avait pas l'occasion de me faire sentir dépendre de lui et comme on lui avait offert cette occasion sur un plateau en or, il en a abusé' (Côté et al. 1999, 114).[17]

Women who are sponsored from abroad enter Canada as permanent residents, enabling them to seek work immediately. The sponsorship undertaking binds their sponsor to a ten-year support obligation. The first regulation formally imposing a duty to 'receive and care' for sponsored family members appeared in 1946 (Kelley & Trebilcock 1999, 321), and was incorporated into the 1952 Immigration Act. Still, provincial and municipal governments complained that sponsorship default left them providing social assistance to sponsored immigrants. The 1976 Immigration Act responded by stipulating that any social assistance/welfare expenditures paid to a member of the family class within ten years of landing are recoverable from the sponsor. The intent of the undertaking is to privatize any costs associated with supporting a family member that the state would otherwise bear. The obligation persists regardless of any deterioration in the financial circumstances of the sponsor or the relationship between the parties during the ten-year period.

The sponsorship undertaking can hardly be traced to the revival of the neo-liberal state. Arguably, its introduction should be attributed to the rise (rather than decline) of the Keynesian welfare state in the postwar era, and a concomitant political decision to exclude immigrant families from membership in it. While this may appear anomalous, the sponsorship undertaking is consistent with historical trends in Europe which co-relate the growth of the welfare state to the consolidation of territorial nation states in the last 150 years. Stated briefly, the more responsibility governments undertook to ensure the welfare of those over whom they exercised authority, the greater the perceived need to circumscribe the social and geographical boundaries of eligibility for those benefits and perquisites. Or to put it another way, the more membership has its privileges, the more important it becomes to deny membership, whether legal or social.

We cannot assess how immigration policy works without appreciating the disjuncture between law and its administration. The sponsorship undertaking binds the federal government and the sponsor, but it is the provincial government that distributes welfare and many other forms of social assistance. Neither the applicant nor, until recently, the provincial government were parties to the sponsorship undertaking. The result was that undertakings existed on paper, but were rarely monitored or enforced.

A development which can be attributed to a neo-liberal revival is more aggressive enforcement of the sponsorship undertaking. Borrowing from the contemporary discourse in family policy about 'deadbeat fathers,' the 'deadbeat sponsor' has now entered the immigration vernacular to describe the sponsor who neglects his or her sponsorship obligation, callously abandoning sponsored family members or wilfully colluding with them to cheat Canada's welfare system.

Although the undertaking is only enforceable against the sponsor for recovery of social assistance payments to the sponsored family member, sponsors and sponsored immigrants of both sexes are affected by the enforcement measures, across the full range of relationships between sponsors and family members (children, parents, siblings, grandchildren, and spouses). My comments focus on spousal sponsorships, though sponsorship of other family members may raise separate concerns.

Quebec and Ontario take the lead in this area. Quebec exercises greater control over immigration selection and settlement than do other provinces. Unlike the federal government, Quebec spousal sponsorship undertakings last three years, terminating with eligibility for citizenship. In 1996, the Quebec government began enforcing sponsorship obligations; between 1 April 1996 and 31 December 1997 the Quebec Ombudsperson received 396 complaints in respect of this new policy (Jacoby 1998, 1).

The complaints centred on poor communication of information, the failure to take into account reasons for non-payment beyond the sponsor's control (e.g., un- or underemployment, lay-off, illness) or deterioration in the relationship between sponsor and sponsored family member (i.e., marriage breakdown, estrangement between parents and children). For example, the Quebec government obliges sponsors on social assistance to forego part of their benefits to reimburse amounts paid to the sponsored recipient. While Quebec authorities claimed to be sensitive to situations of domestic violence by suspending debt collection from sponsors where the sponsoree was the aggressor, the debt continued to accumulate. In response to the array of problems in the system, the Quebec Ombudsman issued several recommendations for reform.

While the Quebec enforcement scheme targets sponsors, the Ontario strategy thus far has targeted sponsored recipients of social assistance. Under a regulation passed pursuant to the 1997 Ontario Works Act[18] (O. Reg. 134/98) the Ontario government automatically deducts a minimum of $100 from the monthly benefit payable to sponsored immigrants living apart from the sponsor regardless of whether any financial support is actually available or forthcoming from the sponsor. Payment can be reduced by more than $100 or even refused entirely if the social worker decides that the sponsor is able to pay and the sponsored family member has made insufficient efforts to obtain support from the sponsor (O. Reg. 134/98, s. 13). The only exceptions to the deduction are in cases where the parties live together and both are on social assistance, or where the recipient of social assistance can furnish proof in the form of police reports or health/community service providers that she was the victim of domestic violence (O. Reg. 134/98, s. 51). Given the legal, social, and personal barriers that immigrant and racialized women encounter inside and outside their communities in accessing protection from domestic violence, the evidentiary burden imposed on them by the Ministry of Community and Social Services erects a significant obstacle to acquiring social assistance (Côté et al. 1999, 204–7).

The strategy of familialization has been a key ideological and fiscal instrument for the dismantling of the welfare state (Brodie 1997, 236). In the context of immigration, however, recent initiatives by provincial governments are simply activating commitments already encoded in federal law. In Quebec, this redounds primarily to the detriment of sponsors, whatever their prior understanding of their obligations or the reasons for their default. Ontario targets the recipients, presumably because it is easier to save money by not paying it in the first place than by trying to recover it. In the process, the Ontario government effectively deems permanent residents who happen to be members of the family class less deserving of public assistance solely because of the legal category in which they immigrated to Canada. Given the constitution of the family class, the policy has an obvious discriminatory impact on women, non-citizens, and racialized minorities.

One should not lose sight of the fact that in recent years the Ontario government has diminished the range of entitlements constituting social citizenship for all Ontarians. It is critical to realize, however, that sponsored women in Ontario are restricted to an even smaller slice of that shrinking pie because they entered as members of the family class. This development is not restricted to welfare. A similar trend can be detected in respect of access to health care coverage, where cost-saving measures adopted by the provincial government narrowed the definition of an Ontario resident, imposed a three-month waiting period on eligibility, and changed the basis of entitlement from family to individual. Eight immigrants unsuccessfully challenged the new regulations as violating Charter-protected rights. At present, the combined effect of federal immigration law and Ontario provincial social welfare legislation explicitly denies sponsored immigrants (many of whom are women) equal social citizenship long after and despite the acquisition of legal citizenship. Côté et al. (1999, 222) aptly describe sponsored spouses under this regime as 'citoyennes de deuxieme classe.' Viewed through the optic of familialization, the IRPA offers an ambiguous response to the current situation. Assessing the meaning or impact of immigration legislation is often futile in the absence of regulations, administrative guidelines, and data about implementation. In general, however, the new legislation eases some of the current entry rules for family members abroad, while imposing more stringent requirements on their Canadian sponsors. The federal government will follow Quebec's lead and reduce the sponsorship undertaking from ten to three years for spouses. It will also exempt sponsored spouses and dependent children from the current admission bar on grounds of 'excessive demands on health or social services,' thereby loosening restrictions on family class admissibility.

These initiatives, which enlarge the possibility of access to state support by non-citizens, do not sustain a thesis of creeping privatization. However, they are met with countervailing initiatives directing at tightening sponsor eligibility requirements. These include plans to deny sponsorship to persons currently in receipt of social assistance (unless it is for reasons of disability), with some flexibility 'to facilitate the entry of some family members on compassionate grounds if their presence in Canada is likely to improve the financial situation of the family' (CIC 2001).[19] Those in default of court-ordered spousal or child support payments are also ineligible to sponsor. The new legislation further intends to strengthen the federal government's ability to enforce sponsorship undertakings. The minister of immigration, Elinor Caplan, proposed requiring prospective sponsors whose income falls below the 'Low Income Cut-off' to post a bond as a precondition to admitting family members, to be set off against future social assistance payments (CIC 2000a). Each of these measures is designed to ensure that members of the family class do not access public income support.

One unsolved mystery of the family sponsorship regime is the rationale behind imposing sponsorship undertakings on immigrant families whose members arrive at different times while families who arrive together as principal applicant and accompanying dependants are not similarly encumbered. The putative justification for sponsorship undertakings is that immigrants are beholden to Canada for receiving them. The state extends to them the privilege of entry, but only on condition that they do not exploit Canada's beneficence by drawing on public services. As a pragmatic matter, the fact that non-citizens are disenfranchised means that the government can impose burdens on them at low political cost. Yet these factors cannot explain the disparity in treatment of accompanying dependants versus members of the family class. Nor is it apparent why immigrant families (especially nuclear families) warrant greater surveillance of their mutual support obligations than do Canadian families. Do policy makers suspect that, absent the sponsorship undertaking, immigrants are more likely to abandon family members? Do they consider the family support provisions under the Criminal Code and family law legislation inadequate with respect to immigrant families?

Perhaps the state imposes the sponsorship undertaking as a precondition to admission of family class members simply because it *can*. The desire of separated family members to reunite and the need to secure the state's permission to accomplish this goal gives the Canadian government leverage to 'familialize' social costs that it lacks in other domains. After all, it would be virtually unthinkable to demand that prospective parents sign an undertaking prior to the admission of a child into Canada via birth, or to prohibit Canadian parents on welfare from having children. And, as noted earlier, the state does not insist on a sponsorship undertaking from principal applicants arriving with accompanying dependants, presumably because such a move might deter the migration of the primary applicant, the economic immigrant. The imposition of a sponsorship obligation on family class immigration may be as much a matter of political and practical feasibility as an indicator of the normative distinction between [legal] members and non-members. After all, as Fudge and Cossman argue (Introduction, this volume), the state does utilize other (albeit less draconian) devices to familialize costs among citizens. Moreover, while section 27(1)(f) of the Immigration Act permitted the state to strip permanent resident status from a holder who 'wilfully fails to support himself or any dependent members of his family in Canada,' the provision was rarely used and does not appear in the new legislation. Deportation of 'public charges' at the present stage of liberal democratic governance in Canada would come at too high a political and bureaucratic cost.

The family class is the least favoured category of immigrants from the perspective both of policy makers and many critics of immigration policy (Stoffman 1993). Admisson of the family class is supply driven. Applicants do not have to audition under the points system and are therefore constructed as B actors in the labour market. Until recently, the family class was also the single largest class by a wide margin. This owes primarily to the absence of quotas and the fact that eligibility is ascriptive, not performative. In theory, anyone who proves the requisite relationship to the sponsor and passes the various medical and security screens is entitled to immigrate as a member of the family class.

Although there has been some tinkering over the years with the range of eligible relationships in the family class, definitional modification alone cannot account for the precipitous decline in the family class relative to the economic class. The ratio of family class to economic class immigrants admitted to Canada reversed from almost 3:2 in 1993 to slightly more than 1:2 in 1998 (CIC 1999a, 3; 1996a, 26). Anecdotal reports suggest at least two additional factors are at work. First, a reduction in staff in the CIC has led to greater delays and inefficiencies in processing applications. Priorizing among classes of immigrants means allocating some applications to the bottom of the pile, which in turn may result in a decline in the number of sponsorship applications processed in any given year and a growth in the backlog. Second, the exercise of discretionary power by immigration officials locally and abroad can make it tougher for family class applicants to qualify. Bureaucratic obstacles may include rejecting the probity of identity documents establishing the requisite relationship to the sponsor, demanding expensive DNA testing, or challenging the adequacy of arrangements made by the sponsor to support the applicants. Each of these 'low visibility' mechanisms of adjusting admission rates may have the effect of stalling family reunification for months or years, if not indefinitely. In the meantime, the state continues to benefit from the contribution of the preferred economic migrant.

B. Right of Landing Fee

Another source of delay in family reunification is the Right of Landing Fee (ROLF) imposed on persons seeking permanent resident status. The cost is $975 per adult. This so-called head tax is not a cost recovery device – immigrants and inland refugees pay an additional $500 ($100 for children) to defray the expense of processing the application for permanent residence. If and when they wish to become citizens, they must pay $100 for the 'Right of Citizenship Fee' in addition to processing fees of $100 to $200. Like the Chinese head tax, the fees paid by newcomers generate significant revenue for the Canadian government.

In 1997–8, immigration and citizenship fees netted over $360 million (CCR, 1999). The Canadian Council for Refugees calculates that the average burden on newcomers from entry to citizenship has more than trebled from $460 in 1993 to $1,526 in 1998 (CCR 1999). The CIC website dubs the ROLF a 'privilege fee,' and justifies it in the following terms: 'These fees provide partial compensation for the many intangible economic, social and legal rights and privileges that citizenship and permanent resident status confer. They are designed to increase equity in the revenue system by shifting a greater proportion of the financial responsibility from general taxpayers to the principal beneficiaries of the services' (http://www.cic.gc.ca/english/info/fees-e.html).

In general, the principle of equal citizenship militates against selective taxation: we do not tax old people more even though they consume a disproportionate share of health care services, nor do we tax parents more than childless people to cover the cost of public education. Available data suggests that in the long run, immigrants as a whole contribute more than the native-born to the public fisc than they draw out of it (Kelley & Trebilcock, 1999; Akbari 1995, 1999). Over time, they utilize public assistance at a lower rate than native-born Canadians. Moreover, Canada benefits (to the extent that it chooses to do so) from the education, skills, and experience immigrants acquire in their countries of origin at no cost to Canada. Labelling ROLF a 'privilege fee' reinforces the deeply entrenched notion that the state's right to exclude is unqualified. The corollary is that admission is a privilege which, in turn, translates into a debt that immigrants 'owe' Canada, trading on the unsubstantiated proposition that the burdens of immigration exceed the benefits. In any case, the 'head tax' is paid into the general revenue fund of the federal government. It is not allocated to subsidizing the 'up-front' social costs of integration and settlement, which have been increasingly downloaded to provincial and municipal governments.

The arrival of the Kosovar refugees in 1999 generated substantial public pressure to exempt refugees from the head tax,[20] which materialized in a laudable decision not only to exempt refugees from paying the ROLF, but to refund amounts paid in the past by all refugees. Immigrants, however, must still pay. Maintenance of the ROLF appears especially incongruous since 1999, when the government first boasted of paying off the deficit. Similarly, various pundits and politicians (including Finance Minister Paul Martin) have endorsed cuts to income tax as a means of stopping an alleged 'brain drain' of highly skilled Canadians to the United States (many of whom gain admission under the NAFTA labour provisions); meanwhile, immigrants to Canada merit no relief from the additional tax burden they bear (*National Post* 1999c).[21] Like the live-in caregiver program, the ROLF suggests that neo-liberal logic loses its charm for policy makers at approximately the point when it might actually benefit migrants, especially those from the South.

The principal impact of the ROLF is to increase the cost to each person who immigrates, meaning that families may elect not to migrate together as principal applicant and accompanying dependants and/or be forced to live apart longer in order to amass the resources to be reunited in Canada. And, of course, money spent on the head tax is money unavailable to the immigrant family to 'look after their own,' as the neo-liberal state instructs them to do.

C. Same-Sex Partners

Fudge and Cossman (Introduction this volume) argue that the 'neo-liberal state seems less concerned with who a family is (traditional/non-traditional) than with what a family does (take care of its members).' Changes under the IRPA substantiate this hypothesis by expanding eligibility for the family class in various ways. For present purposes, the most interesting proposal involves the addition of same-sex partners to the family class. Since the early 1990s, CIC tacitly conceded that the Immigration Act's definition of spouse as 'the party of the opposite sex to whom that person is joined in marriage' (s. 2) would not withstand a section 15 Charter challenge. Indeed, almost any time a Canadian citizen or permanent resident threatened to attack the exclusion via litigation, CIC found a discretionary route to facilitate the entry of that person's same-sex partner.

In 1994, an enterprising visa officer devised a systematic method of dealing with such applications. It involved advising the non-Canadian partner to apply as an independent (economic) immigrant. Under the points system, visa officers possess residual discretion to award an applicant up to ten points for 'personal suitability' (Immigration Regulations 1978, Schedule I) or to issue an immigrant visa to 'an immigrant who is not awarded the number of units of assessment required' under the points system if 'there are good reasons why the number of units of assessment awarded do not reflect the chances of the particular immigrant ... becoming successfully established in Canada' (s. 11(3)(b)). Furthermore, Immigration Regulations, 1978, section 2.1 permits a program manager at a visa office to exempt an applicant from the points assessment but issue an immigrant visa anyway where 'the person's admission should be facilitated owing to the existence of compassionate and humanitarian considerations.' Independent immigrant applications made by same-sex partners benefit from the favourable exercise of discretion on one or more of these bases, with the result that they eventually receive visas qua independent immigrant. The *Immigration Manual* incorporates the process in guidelines which visa officers are expected (though not mandated) to apply.

According to Lesbian and Gay Immigration Taskforce (LEGIT) advocate Christine Morrissey, the policy has proved enormously successful. She estimates that about seven hundred people have entered on this basis since 1994, and that the success rate among applicants is virtually 100 per cent. Of course, LEGIT continue to advocate for inclusion of same-sex relationships in the family class, and the Minister of Citizenship and Immigration complied by adding a gender-neutral category of 'common-law partner' to the family class. How will the material situation of lesbian and gay couples change if processed under the family class? First, CIC will scrutinize the couple to assess the bona fides of the relationship. Proposed regulations under the IRPA require that the couple prove cohabitation 'in a conjugal relationship' for at least one year unless cohabitation is precluded by 'persecution or any form of penal control.' Anecdotal reports from within the bureaucracy suggest that the factors will more or less mimic the indicia of conjugality drawn from heterosexual relationships (*M. v. H.* 1999). The nature and quantum of evidence required to prove persecution or penal control must await elaboration.

Without the spectre of Charter litigation hanging over visa officers, there is little risk to rejecting same-sex applicants in the family class on grounds that their relationship to the sponsor is one of convenience entered into for purposes of immigration. Rejection of heterosexual spouses on these grounds is not uncommon (though it varies dramatically by region).[22] A certain number of same-sex sponsorships may also be refused as 'relationships of convenience.' Finally and most importantly, lesbian and gay couples will be subject to the same sponsorship obligations as other members of the family class. Given the application of the undertaking to same-sex sponsors, the willingness of the government to recognize same-sex couples under the family class comports with a neo-liberal/functionalist rather than neo-conservative/ideological approach to defining family. Its effect is to expand the range of relationships recognized as familial, and thereby to subject members to the expectation of mutual financial support (Cossman, this volume).

Ironically, lesbian and gay immigrants currently enjoy the most advantageous position possible. Their relationship to a citizen or permanent resident facilitates entry, but they 'cross the threshold' as members of the economic class, with relatively little of the invasive scrutiny and none of the sponsorship obligations borne by spouses in the family class. Arguably, this anomalous situation arose because the bureaucracy anticipated (rightly or wrongly) that the courts, if given the opportunity, would opt for a neo-liberal definition of family and strike down the exclusion of same-sex partners as a violation of equality rights under the Charter. Whether owing to neo-conservative conviction or lack of political will, legislators seemed unlikely to take the initiative to pre-empt a Charter challenge by amending the law. CIC's solution shrewdly steered a middle course that allowed it to avoid litigation in the absence of legislative change, albeit at the cost of transparency and accountability. It bears mentioning that the majority of applicants thus far have also been white people from the North, a group not otherwise strongly represented in the immigrant pool (Morrissey 1999).[23]

While the foregoing is not an argument against expansion of the family class definition to include same-sex couples, it is a reminder that what is being sought by recognition as family is access to a regime that offers the benefit of relatively easy entry at the cost of intensified surveillance of the relationship. It also imposes a particularly robust privatized model of financial support in the form of the sponsorship undertaking. Though the categories of independent immigrant, accompanying dependent, and family class immigrant are formally gender-neutral, they codify and replicate a family model premised on a male-breadwinner model with dependent spouse and children. Consequently, while incorporation of same-sex partners as members of the family class looks like victory on an ideological level, the practical implications are ambiguous and uncertain.

III. Settlement and Integration

Settlement and integration services began as private ventures, supplemented by inducements (e.g., free or subsidized passage, land grants) proffered by the state to preferred immigrants. Long before the rise of the welfare state, local charities and religious and ethno-cultural community organizations furnished settlement services to newcomers on a volunteer basis. While the state eventually recognized a public interest in and responsibility for facilitating the integration of newcomers, both the federal and provincial governments avoided playing a dominant role in service delivery, leaving it to educational institutions and local associations and ethno-cultural/racial groups affiliated with the various immigrant communities. Not only was this decision practical for the government, it was probably wise insofar as community-run initiatives were, in principle, more likely to be culturally sensitive than programs formulated and imposed by bureaucrats.

The central role played by non-profit, community-based immigrant service agencies (ISAs) does not result from a devolution of responsibility from the public to the private sector, but reflects a government decision to underwrite activities previously consigned to the volunteer sector. As the government came to recognize that facilitating their full social, cultural, economic, and linguistic participation in Canadian society enables Canada to realize maximum benefit from newcomers, it expanded the range and scope of services available to them. As Lisa Philipps observes, neo-liberal discourses of voluntarism and community responsibility lubricate the slide by which public services are downloaded to the non-profit sector and community groups (Philipps, this volume).

ISAs provide a wide range of services, including language training, reception and settlement, health care, housing, employment, mental health services, skills training for refugee women, and shelters for abused women from specific ethno-racial communities. Because they are institutionally independent of government, many ISAs also maintain an activist mandate and engage in lobbying and advocacy, anti-racism initiatives, coalition building, and public education. However, as the recent case of *Vancouver Society of Immigrant and Visible Minority Women v. Canada* illustrates (see Philipps, this volume), these organizations pay a price for their equality and social justice orientation insofar as Revenue Canada narrowly interprets the term 'charitable purposes' under the Income Tax Act. This limits the ability of non-profit ISAs to attract private donations. In addition, when administering specific government programs ISAs are constrained by federal or provincial policies dictating eligibility and content.

A. Language Training

Language training is a critical component of settlement services, and language facility is key to liberating the other forms of social and human capital that immigrants possess. Language ability among immigrants is also highly gendered: recent female immigrants are less likely to speak one of Canada's host languages (English and French) than recent male immigrants (Boyd 1992, 357). Visible minority immigrant women who do not speak English or French have the highest unemployment rate and lowest earnings of all sex and language fluency groups (Boyd 1992, 351; 1996, 158). Surprisingly, 40 per cent of immigrant women with low or no host language skills are nonetheless employed, usually in service or manufacturing, especially the garment industry. They work longer hours, but more irregularly than other foreign-born women. Though many of these women were poorly educated in their countries of origin, others are well educated but unable to exploit their human capital because of weak host language ability. In addition to the impact of language on labour market performance, inability to converse in a host language limits access to information, opportunities, and autonomy and heightens 'the potential for intensified isolation and dependency on those who act as linguistic brokers' (Boyd 1992, 362). A person who cannot communicate in the host language is disenfranchised as a public citizen in almost every way imaginable.

In 1997, the Immigration Legislative Review Advisory Group (ILRAG) struck by then Citizenship and Immigration Minister Lucienne Robillard imported an explicit neo-liberal agenda into its analysis of immigration policy. At the outset, it identified 'tax fatigue' and 'increased fiscal constraints' as influencing their subsequent analysis and recommendations (ILRAG 1997, 8). The authors later noted the correlation between language ability and labour market performance and 'successful integration' (58). It translated this observation into a recommendation that independent (economic) immigrants possess basic proficiency in one of the official languages as a prerequisite to admission, and that 'no other attribute ... be able to substitute for this lack of ability' (58).

Of course, the majority of potential economic immigrants come from non-English and non-French speaking countries. This did not trouble the authors, who asserted that '[o]fficial language ability can be acquired [overseas] by a motivated person who wants not only to qualify for immigration to Canada, but to succeed and to participate fully in Canadian society' (58). The authors also observed that metropolitan areas receiving the bulk of new immigrants 'must cope with the strain exerted on their classrooms by the lack of official language skills – and the lack of adequately funded language training.' The solution to inadequate funding, they declared, was to impose a tuition fee 'reflecting the cost of basic language training in Canada [on] all sponsored Family Class immigrants who are six years of age or older and have not achieved a basic knowledge of English or French' (45).

These language recommendations are a bald attempt to reprivatize settlement by compelling immigrants to internalize the cost of language training. Seen in this light, the ILRAG proposals are the logical end-point of a fiscally driven immigration policy less interested in maximizing long-term social and economic returns from newcomers than in minimizing short-term investment in language and labour market training. Implementation of the ILRAG proposals would probably disable Canada from attracting enough immigrants to meet its annual immigration targets, and would inevitably increase the debt burden on immigrant families. It would also render language training an unaffordable luxury for many sponsored spouses, who would remain unemployed or trapped in the low-wage occupations reserved for those with little or no facility in the host language. Commentators denounced the proposals so swiftly and so vehemently that then Minister Robillard disavowed them almost immediately.

Quite apart from ILRAG, federally funded language training programs have evolved from a gendered model of unequal access to a gender-neutral model of equal inaccessibility. As Monica Boyd explains, from 1986 to 1992, federal funding for language training allocated most resources to those immigrants 'destined immediately for the labour force,' a group deemed to exclude sponsored immigrants who had no language skills and/or no past labour force participation. Furthermore, family class participants in the program were ineligible for the living allowance available to other participants. The assumption was that sponsors would assume financial responsibility for the sponsored immigrant. In practice, of course, migrant households depended on the income from the 'dependent' spouse, meaning that women working in the low-skill, low-paying jobs where requisite language ability was minimal could not afford to forgo their income to attend job market language training. A smaller budget was reserved to provide basic linguistic coping skills to adults not destined for the labour force, namely immigrant women caring for children (Boyd 1992, 360). Thus, the older system preferred to invest public funds in those deemed likely to produce the greatest return in productivity as market actors. Members of the family class were assumed to represent a poor investment risk, and treated accordingly.

In 1992, the government reversed its emphasis and allocated approximately 80 per cent of its language training budget to 'Language Instruction for Newcomers to Canada (LINC),' which is open to adult immigrants (though not to refugee claimants) regardless of their projected labour market destination. The remaining funds are channelled into a job-specific 'Labour Market Language Training Program' (LMLT). The government financed this expansion of service in part by abolishing living allowances for all participants. Participants in the LINC program thus rely on employment insurance, social assistance, or family members for financial support.

The reallocation of funds in the current system improved upon its predecessor by directing more funds at those most lacking in language skills. The program also provides a childcare service to facilitate attendance by women with children. It would be churlish not to credit the government with making these positive changes to the system. Nevertheless, it should be noted that the present arrangement does not diminish the pressure on women whose husbands are employed (meaning the family is not in receipt of social assistance) to forgo language training in favour of a second paycheque. It also disqualifies persons who have become Canadian citizens on grounds that they must have acquired proficiency in the host language to pass the citizenship test. Given that citizenship judges have discretion to waive the language requirement on humanitarian grounds, (Citizenship Act, s. 5(3)(a)), this inference is no more valid than the assumption that sponsored spouses are not destined for the labour market. Moreover, Boyd (1996, 158) indicates that women are more likely than men to be both Canadian citizens *and* lacking proficiency in English or French. Thus, the citizenship disqualification likely has a gendered impact on access to language training.

While the framework of the language training programs remains in place the IRPA increases the relative weight granted to official language ability under the points system. This may reduce demand for language training by independent immigrants, but it does not necessarily follow that consumption of language training by family members would also drop.[24] It is clear that increasing the weight attributed to language ability is designed to reduce public investment in immigrant settlement by shifting more of the cost of language acquisition onto the prospective immigrant. From the perspective of government, this privatization strategy has the political advantage of being less visible than functional analogs such as cutting funding, restricting access, or imposing user-pay systems for language training within Canada.

B. *Commodification in the Non-profit Sector*

Although settlement services for immigrant populations have always been partially privatized (in that they were provided by the voluntary or non-profit sector), the basis upon which these services are provided is shifting. Settlement services are evaluated not only in terms of integrating newcomers into Canadian society, they are increasingly measured against market-based norms. This is particularly evident in Ontario, where the provincial government has enthusiastically embraced privatization, and especially in Toronto, which now bears much of the responsibility shed by the provincial government.

In 1998, 53 per cent of immigrants and refugees settled in Ontario and 42 per cent of all newcomers to Canada headed for Toronto. Close to half of Toronto's population was born outside Canada. In 1994, about 35 per cent of settlement funding came from the federal government and 42 per cent from the province (T. Richmond 1996). Government restructuring in the last five years has meant, quite simply, massive budget cuts at the federal and provincial levels in immigration settlement services, as well as progressive downloading of responsibilities from the federal to provincial and municipal governments, and eventually to the Immigrant Settlement Agencies (ISAs).

A 1996 research project estimated that from 1993 to 1996, federal funding of programs was cut by about 10 per cent per year, while provincial funding was frozen (T. Richmond 1996, 4). More recently, the Ontario Coalition of Agencies Serving Immigrants (OCASI) reported that between 1995 and 1999, provincial funding declined by over a third and that it will be reduced again in the next fiscal year (OCASI 1999).

Deficit reduction has provided the rationale for cost-cutting in government, and privatization furnishes a strategy. In Ontario, slogans such as 'from demand driven to affordability ... from state responsibility to personal and community responsibility' (Ontario Ministry of Community and Social Services 1996, 2) provide an ideological justification for the state's abdication from social services. With respect to immigrants, the province (and now municipalities) can also invoke the standard constitutional complaint that since the federal government is responsible for admitting immigrants, it should pay a greater share of expenses associated with their settlement (Spears 1999). Finally, demonization of newcomers – cultivated and exploited all too often by mainstream media and right-wing politicians – create a climate of public opinion that makes ISAs soft targets for budget slashing.

One of the first programs eliminated in Ontario was the Ministry of Community and Social Service's Multicultural Access to Social Assistance Initiative (MASAI), which supported ISA clients. A government that is busy figuring out how to chase down 'deadbeat sponsors' and penalize family class recipients of social assistance is not likely to allocate resources to help immigrants locate social assistance in the first place. Since 1995, at least forty programs for newcomers have been cancelled; about half of these programs provided settlement services.

Commodification of settlement services includes a variety of strategies beyond budget cutting. One technique is to download delivery of services from government to ISAs. Some of these services had been initiated and retained by government because they were money-losers. Devolving them to ISAs becomes problematic because the agencies do not have the capacity to run deficits, meaning that program delivery suffers. Some service providers also express discomfort with increased pressure to play a policing role, wherein they are expected to monitor and report attendance of program participants in receipt of social assistance.

Another move is the displacement of ongoing funding with short-term market-based delivery models where specific service contracts are allocated on a competitive tendering process. In addition, the non-profit sector now competes with for-profit providers who may lack immigration-related experience or commitment. Community-based ISAs experience greater pressure to enter into 'partnerships' within and without the ISA sector. One of the risks is a loss of focus on immigrant and refugee needs, as mainstream organizations assume a greater degree of involvement and control. In addition, small specialized ISAs, including those that serve women, tend to get squeezed out because they lack the resources and infrastructure required to compete effectively for contracts.

Many settlement workers are migrant women themselves. Commodification of the settlements sector affects them both as clients and as service providers. As Jo-Anne Lee reports (1999, 97), restructuring in the front-line settlement sector contributes to 'working conditions for immigrant and visible minority women [that are] characterized by part-time, low waged, term-limited, and unstable employment' (98), arising from short-term, contract-based funding. This process is also racialized, insofar as white, Canadian-born women predominate in the better paid and more stable jobs related to ESL and employment training (Lee 1999, 98). Funding cutbacks and contraction of services have cost women jobs or required them to assume the additional work of former colleagues. Some are also expected to 'volunteer' without pay to fundraise, provide outreach or community development, and to keep programs afloat during periods of transitional funding (Lee 1999, 99–100). This ethic of voluntarism is, of course, highly gendered and ethnicized, insofar as it plays on assumptions about women's traditional roles and cultural 'differences' in racialized ethnic minority communities' responses to their members' social welfare needs' (Lee 1999, 103).

The effect of the pressure on the non-profit immigrant settlement sector 'to transform itself to operate according to market principles' (Brodie 1999, 6) is difficult to disentangle from the general impact of massive budget cuts. It is not self-evident that devolution, the tendering process, or comparable measures are inherently detrimental. Nevertheless, the convergence of commodification and budget slashing certainly diminishes the range and quality of settlement-related services available to migrant women. To the extent that the Ontario government opposes affirmative action and employment equity, organizations serving people who stand at the intersection of multiple forms of marginalization – race, gender, class, ethnicity, language, disability – are most likely to be hit by budget cuts. It follows that many programs serving migrant women, including initiatives related to physical and mental health, domestic violence, and anti-racism, would be (and have been) eliminated (T. Richmond 1996, 5).

The impact of restructuring and commodification in the settlement and integration sector is twofold. First, the contraction of government funding narrows the scope of social citizenship available to newcomers. Second, as financial responsibility is increasingly devolved onto immigrant communities, and then onto women within those communities, migrant women increasingly perform the underpaid and unpaid labour of 'civic reproduction' not only for their own families, but for their ethno-cultural community at large.

Conclusion

Paradoxically, immigration policy has always been and will never be privatized. Deregulation of borders in its purest sense is the subject of academic debate and activist aspiration; few seriously expect to see a global regime of open borders and a free flow of labour across territorial frontiers in accordance with market-driven supply and demand. On the other hand, the state always has and will continue to assess prospective members based on a short- and long-term economic valuation of human capital. Increasingly, the state is also delegating selection of temporary workers to the private sector; to the extent that the state encourages 'high-skill' workers to immigrate, the private sector plays a critical role in choosing new Canadians. At the same time, the state reserves its most intensive regulation and intervention in the market for those migrants deemed 'low-skill,' in order either to keep them out or to ensure that their labour remains cheap and available to private employers on favourable terms. Privatization is a selective, uneven process both in application and impact.

Within this landscape, female migrants are both object and instrument of privatization strategies. Historically, they have been depicted primarily as dependants doing women's work for free within the family, or as temporary workers doing women's work for cheap in the market. In either case, immigration policies hinder them from making certain claims on the state that might actually mitigate their dependence or increase their market value. Access to legal and social citizenship is either contingent (domestic workers), compromised (sponsored spouses), or denied (exotic dancers). Immigration rules and conditions are designed to extract as much as possible from migrants (in the form of labour and taxes) while minimizing investment in their integration or claims to public benefits. In general, the state can extract more for less from migrants than from the native-born, to the extent that much of the cost of social reproduction has already been borne by the country of origin. The operation of the global economy and the gendered division of labour arguably enable the state to extract more for less from female temporary workers, and more from families that migrate separately (often for financial reasons) than from those who migrate together.

One of the ironies exposed by investigating the link between migration and privatization is that many trends attributed to privatization with respect to Canadian-born women have long been standard fare for migrant women. Migrant women were disproportionately represented in low-wage, precarious, irregular work well before 'restructuring' entered public discourse. Family law in the 1990s may have discursively revived an ethic of 'reliance on one's family, even after that family has broken down' (Cossman, this volume), but that principle has been explicit in immigration legislation since the sponsorship undertaking appeared in 1946. Immigrants' contingent claims to membership, along with nativist rhetoric that depicts them as opportunistic welfare cheats, converge with neo-liberal family ideology to intensify the enforcement of familial support obligations on migrants. The gatekeeping function of immigration policy permits the state to impose contractual terms of entry on migrants that it cannot impose on citizens. These conditions may limit access to the welfare state, as in the sponsorship undertaking, or compel performance of certain undesirable jobs that female citizens of the welfare state increasingly reject, as in the garment industry or live-in domestic work. Migrants have, in a sense, always been expected to rely more on the market and on their families than Canadian-born citizens.

The privatization trend may entail some quantitative reduction in entitlements for migrants in general and for women in particular, but it manifests itself chiefly in the qualitative reallocation of resources to surveillance, apprehension, and criminalization in order to police migrants' physical exclusion from the state or social exclusion from the welfare state. This pattern fits with a wider phenomenon that Dutch scholar Sarah van Walsum describes as a new form of official nationalism: 'While relinquishing its central role in dealing with inequality and social risks, the nation state can now profile itself as protector of citizens' property against violence, defender of the taxpayers against fraud. While no longer attempting to contain or control the export of capital or production activities, the state can claim a role in protecting its borders and repressing international crime' (van Walsum 1994, 207). The emphasis in the IRPA on mechanisms of deterrence, detention, and criminalization of migrants bears testimony to this phenomenon.

Migrants have always been partially excluded from the welfare state in Canada (and elsewhere); this chapter has proceeded from the thesis that the exacerbating effect of 'privatization' in its neo-liberal incarnation is best framed in terms of its historical continuity with, or disjuncture from, the discursive and material practices that preceded it. Looking to the future, we might query whether the experience of migrant women habitually living on the margins of social citizenship yields important clues about where Canadian-born women are headed as the borders of the welfare state are redrawn under their feet.

Notes

I am grateful to several people who kindly shared their time, knowledge, and insights with me: Tim Owen, COSTI; the late Amina Malko; the Ontario Coalition of Associations Serving Immigrants; Bradley Pascoe, Citizenship and Immigration Canada; Christine Morissey, LEGIT; Mary Taylor and Christina Alcivar, Exotic Dancers Alliance; and numerous participants at the 1999 Canadian Council for Refugees Spring Consultation. I also wish to thank Ruth Fletcher for her invaluable research assistance.

1 Airlines are coerced into this role by virtue of $7,000 carrier sanctions for transporting undocumented or improperly documented passengers. There

is no recourse for the person falsely accused of travelling illegally. (Immigration Act, Part V).

2 A partial exception concerns situations in which a Canadian citizen or permanent resident may challenge a decision not to permit the sponsorship of an overseas family member. Technically, the legal rights accrue to the sponsor who is in Canada, though the benefits of a favourable decision extend to the overseas applicant. Legal scholar Donald Galloway has argued persuasively that the Charter ought to apply to the actions of Canadian immigration officials overseas, but the courts have so far been unreceptive (Galloway 1991).

3 The main exception is male seasonal agricultural workers, for whom demand is regular but intermittent (Morton 1999).

4 Temporary workers who cannot or do not bring their families do not utilize public education. Spouses and dependent children of temporary workers are eligible for health care in Ontario only if the employer intends to employ the worker for at least three years. Temporary workers cannot collect employment insurance (though they pay premiums) or social assistance (Lindberg 1999).

5 Bradley Pascoe, Citizenship and Immigration Canada, Personal Interview, 18 June 1999.

6 A recent media account of the bureaucratic delays in processing live-in caregiver applications is typical in its construction of a mother-nanny dyad. The article depicts the hardship imposed on affluent professional women who are 'plunged into the hell of holding down a high-powered management job ... while caring full time for a curious toddler,' or 'reluctantly playing the role of stay-at-home mother.' Fathers are not mentioned in the article (Philp 2000).

7 Depending on the applicable provincial employment standard legislation, and the scruples of the employer, the actual salary may sink below minimum wage.

8 Since Mavis Baker did not have a TEA in the first place, she was probably ineligible for the FDM program when it was introduced.

9 One woman, not realizing she was pregnant when she came to Canada, was unable to secure steady employment as a live-in domestic worker after giving birth. Though she did not access public assistance and eventually did find employment, she did not accumulate the requisite twenty-four months of employment in the previous three years and was ordered to leave Canada (Curran 2000).

10 Domestic workers have drawn attention to the linkages between globalization, privatization, migration, and gender. A 1993 brief by the Coalition for

Visible Minority Women to an Ontario Cabinet Committee on NAFTA contained the following trenchant comment: 'Many women were casualties of free trade in their home countries – that's why they left. Filipino domestic workers have told us, "We've been squeezed dry once and now it is happening again"' (Gabriel & Macdonald 1996, 168).

11 NGOs advocating for the rights of live-in caregivers struggle with this dilemma. Some support retaining but modifying the program in order to better protect workers from exploitation, because it is the only means for women from the Philippines and elsewhere to acquire permanent resident status in Canada. Others object to a system of indentured labour and insist that live-in caregivers be admitted as permanent residents from the outset. If the workers choose to exit the occupation at the first opportunity, then that is the price the state pays for sustaining an occupation that inherently tends towards exploitation. I have elsewhere advocated that the live-in requirement be removed from the domestic worker regime (Macklin 1992a). My reasoning is that if (as the government insists) there is no shortage of Canadian women willing to work on a live-out basis, then participants in the program will perforce live in. If there is a labour market for live-out work, however, foreign domestic workers ought to be able to exercise whichever option they prefer.

12 Baker's family status was only one factor animating the visa officer's decision. Her recent mental illness and the fact that she had been a welfare recipient also weighed heavily against her, to the point where they obliterated the fact that she had actually supported herself and her children for eleven years as a domestic worker.

13 Dependent children are defined as unmarried sons or daughters who are under nineteen, or are full-time students, or by reason of physical or mental disability, are financially dependent on their parents. Immigration Regulations, 1978, s. 2.

14 Other categories of the family class include children under nineteen the sponsor intends to adopt; orphaned siblings; nieces, nephews, and grandchildren under nineteen; and the so-called wild card relative, who is the sponsor's only relative.

15 This requirement is waived in respect of spouses and children.

16 In Ontario, a person who has applied for landing from within Canada may be eligible for social assistance, on a discretionary basis (Ontario Works, Directive #13.0-8).

17 'In my country, he didn't have the opportunity to make me feel dependent on him but as they have handed it to him [here] on a silver platter, he abuses it' (author's translation).

18 O. Reg 134/98.
19 Citizenship and Immigration Canada 2001. Bill C-11: Immigration and Refugee Protection Act, Explanation of Proposed Regulations. http://www.cic.gc.ca/english/about/policy/c-11-regs.html.
20 Government-sponsored refugees fleeing persecution are exempt from the Right of Landing Fee but must repay the cost of transporting them to Canada before they are permitted to sponsor any family members.
21 Alan Simmons (1999, 64) makes the important point that Canadian tax policy lacks the strong redistributive elements required to adequately support settlement and training.
22 The Beijing visa office rejected 18 per cent of spousal sponsorship applications from January to August 1997. Currently, China is also the single largest source country for immigrants to Canada. The rejection rates at other visa offices for the same period was much lower (New Delhi, 8%; Hong Kong, 3%; Manila, 0.1%) (Sarick 1997).
23 The top ten source countries for immigrants to Canada in 1999 were China, India, Pakistan, the Philippines, Korea, Iran, the United States, Taiwan, Sri Lanka, and the United Kingdom (Canada 2000c, 7).

PART III

The Self-Reliant Citizen: Social Health and Public Order

6

Creeping Privatization in Health Care: Implications for Women as the State Redraws Its Role

JOAN M. GILMOUR

Entitlement to health care funded by public health insurance is often identified as a defining marker of Canadian society. Access to insured services is based on need rather than ability to pay, while the costs of health care – that is, the financial risks of illness – are spread among taxpayers. It is a system that has worked to increase equitable access to needed health care. Many in both the public and government view it as one of Canada's major national accomplishments (National Forum on Health 1997c; 1, 3). Despite growing concerns about the system's ability to meet health care needs, most Canadians continue to express satisfaction with the health care they receive (Conference Board of Canada 2000; Picard 2000), and while there are clearly serious areas of unmet need and undercapacity, the Canadian medicare system continues to enjoy wide-spread and strong public support. Politicians perceived as attacking or undermining it thus do so at their peril: the public expects deficiencies to be addressed in a way that maintains both the system and access to it (Conference Board of Canada 2000).

At the same time, a contrary discourse, marked by claims that health care costs are out of control, has made rapid gains in the past decade. The system is said to be unnecessarily expensive, and failing to provide needed care. These arguments are typically accompanied by assertions that Canadians will have to reduce their expectations of a publicly funded health care system that has become unaffordable and assume more responsibility as individuals for the cost of the health care they use. Indeed, the rhetoric of individual responsibility is extended even to falling sick itself, with greater emphasis placed on disease as the result of personal lifestyle choices, rather than acknowledging the important influence on health status of social, economic, and environmental factors beyond individual control (Federal, Provincial and Territorial Advisory Committee on Population Health 1999b, 1-10, 39-67; Lock 1998; National Forum on Health 1997a). The twin themes of unaffordability and individual responsibility are relied on to justify a transfer of health care responsibilities from the public realm to the private. Our individualized social and cultural understandings of health and illness feed into and support the prescriptions of individual responsibility that are gaining popularity. They are used to justify a shifting of costs from the single payer, government, to multiple other payers. Yet given the continuing high level of public support for medicare, overtly adopting a policy agenda espousing privatization carries with it unacceptable political risks (Conference Board of Canada 2000, 4; Gee 2000). Consequently, shifts in this direction are being accomplished obliquely, either without acknowledging the end result or by focusing attention on other, more palatable consequences. It is creeping privatization of health care, achieved through a variety of means.

Of the many different meanings and strategies that 'privatization' encompasses (Cossman & Fudge in this volume; Starr 1989), my focus is on reprivatization and commodification, that is, the processes by which goods formerly provided by the state are now being provided in the private realm through privatized delivery and funding of services. I also focus on delegation: privatization in the identity of decision makers and the nature of the decision-making process.

In the early 1990s, the rhetoric of fiscal crisis combined with economic recession to make fighting deficits a political priority for both federal and provincial governments. The federal government significantly reduced transfer payments to fund social programs, including health care, leaving provinces with restricted resources to meet their obligations. Restoration of federal funding at the end of the decade and since has been partial and piecemeal,[1] and the provincial response of cutting social programs has not been abandoned despite the generalized though 'muted' economic recovery (Sonnen & McCracken 1999, 228). We should remember, however, that arguments about the need to control the costs of health care by adopting various forms of privatization are not new. They were central to the debate about health care policy in this country even before the inception of a publicly funded health insurance system (Barer et al. 1994; Evans 1984). What is new and particularly evident in Ontario is the unprecedented barrage of legislation, regulation, and policy changes, notable not only for its breadth but for the lack of public consultation prior to its imposition or in its implementation. While much of that activity may not directly privatize the organization and delivery of health care (indeed it may be promoted as improving the publicly funded system), its effect is to do just that or to set the stage for further privatization.

Health care, income transfers to the disadvantaged, and the construction and maintenance of a public infrastructure are some of the crucial contributions made by modern welfare states to smooth the fraught process of social reproduction. However, beginning in the 1980s and accelerating during the 1990s, the Canadian state significantly reduced its responsibility for the reproduction of a healthy population that enjoys equitable living standards. Significant downsizing and restructuring in the publicly funded health care system have been accompanied by deep cuts in other social services and programs designed to transfer income and resources to the least well off in Canada. The deterioration in redistributive social programs and policies can be expected to cause the greatest harm to the vulnerable and marginalized in society, whose health is already the most precarious (Federal, Provincial, and Territorial Advisory Committee on Population Health 1999a, 58–61; 1999b, 39–67; National Forum on Health 1997a). The National Forum on Health observed, 'the bottom line is that distributing money and power is the same as distributing health status' (National Forum on Health 1997d, 2). It is now recognized that not only absolute disparities but the scale of relative income inequities and social and economic differences within a society act as a significant determinant of population health (Federal, Provincial, and Territorial Advisory Committee on Population Health 1999a, 184–5). International research has confirmed the link between equity in a society and health: the greater the inequality, the more profound the effect on the health of the population (Wilkinson 1996). In Canada, it can be anticipated that the effects on citizens' health of the multiple assaults on the welfare state through social welfare, labour market, tax, pension, and other policy changes will be not merely cumulative but synergistic. Changes in the labour market and cuts in social services are felt particularly harshly by women, who already experience disproportionately high rates of poverty, head the largest percentage of lone parent households with limited economic resources, and take on the burden of becoming caregivers to those no longer cared for by the health and social services systems (Morris et al. 1999).

Reductions in health care and social service spending have taken place against the backdrop of the repeated observation that increased funding for health care as it is presently structured results in little discernible improvement in the health status of populations, although it can and does improve the health of some individuals (Burgess 1996;

Starr 1982; Wilkinson 1996, 17). This view is shared by a curious confluence of fiscal conservatives and those with a more progressive social
agenda, although the conclusions they draw from it differ widely. The
former rely on it as justification for reducing public resources allotted to
health care and leaving more decisions about such 'discretionary'
expenditures to private choice and payment. The latter argue it is reason to revamp the organization and delivery of health care, to move
away from the medically dominated model, with its emphasis on acute
care and tendency to medicalize normal life processes such as childbirth
and menopause, towards a model more focused on prevention and on
altering social and economic relations and conditions to reduce inequalities.

In much of the rhetoric surrounding changes made to the health care
system the government presents its role not as formative but as a con-
duit implementing reformers' proposals to increase the well-being of
those affected (e.g., through deinstitutionalization, emphasizing health
promotion, and reorganizing services to increase the provision of community and home care). The government portrays itself as an 'arbitrator
between the interests of the health care system and the care needs of ...
citizens' (i.e., weighing in on the side of citizens against a powerful and
self-interested health care sector), rather than acknowledging that it
acts as 'an initiator of important dynamics' in setting the agenda and
direction for health care reform (Neysmith 1997, 233). In the result,
'public officials rely on progressive discourse to legitimate regressive
practice' in health care reform; bureaucratization, rather than being
diminished, is transferred to and even intensified in the segments of the
private sector now responsible for delivering care (P. Armstrong 1996c,
129; Luxton & Reiter 1997, 214). The changes are driven by cost consciousness and an ideological commitment to a sharply limited view of
the role of the state, but they often appropriate the language of feminists and community activists with respect to achieving better delivery of
better services. Legislative change, interpretation, and implementation
have all been deployed to facilitate further privatization.

Because women are disproportionately represented among patients,
workers in the health care sector, and informal unpaid caregivers within
households and in the wider community, they are inordinately affected
by changes in laws, practices, and policies that shift the burden of health
care to private provision and private payment. Women are often primarily responsible for obtaining health care for members of their families,
and also for providing care when the public system no longer does, as
occurs more frequently in the wake of hospital policies of early dis-

charge, day surgery, outpatient visits, limited stays in acute care beds, and other measures designed to restrict and decrease use (Armstrong & Armstrong 1999; Aronson & Neysmith 1997). As the state increasingly shifts the costs of social reproduction from public to private responsibility, the expectation that women will continue to provide caregiving and housework for others without pay continues. The social and emotional toll can be onerous. Even more significantly, the negative financial implications for women increase the likelihood and extent of economic dependency, at a time when being dependent has itself come to be portrayed as individual pathology rather than an appropriate social role (Fraser & Gordon 1997).

A number of Canadian writers, feminists in particular, have begun to examine privatization in health care (see e.g. P. Armstrong 1996c, Aronson & Neysmith 1997, Fuller 1998; and Neysmith 1997). The present chapter explores the meaning and impact of specific changes in the legal framework governing the organization and delivery of health care, highlighting the implications for women. In keeping with the theme of creeping privatization, I analyse some of the less apparent but nonetheless significant privatizing tendencies in changes ostensibly made to improve publicly funded health care. The effects of privatization initiatives on Canada's ability to maintain a publicly funded health care system in light of its commitments under the North American Free Trade Agreement, while of great significance, are beyond the scope of this analysis.[2] My focus of study is Ontario because, along with Alberta, it has proceeded farthest down the privatization road.[3] In the first part, I outline the legal backdrop against which the process of privatization has occurred. In Part II, I concentrate on three areas exemplifying the process: decision making resulting in selective de-insurance of health care services; the potential of the Independent Health Facilities Act, 1989, to allow and encourage not just privatization but increased commercialization and commodification in health care; and the implications of hospital restructuring for women's access to abortion. In Part III, I examine litigation strategies and assess their ability to impede or reverse increasing privatization in health care.

I. Setting the Stage

A. *The Canadian Health Insurance System*

While a patchwork of state-sponsored and private medical insurance plans developed in Canada through the 1940s and 1950s, Canada's universal health insurance system had its genesis in the system first adopted by the Cooperative Commonwealth Federation government (the predecessor to the New Democrats) in Saskatchewan (Taylor 1987). It began with the Hospital Insurance and Diagnostic Services Act, 1957, a cost-sharing arrangement the federal government undertook with provinces that established insurance programs for residents to cover hospital care and services associated with hospitalization and medical testing. Following the Report of the Royal Commission on Health Services in 1964, this arrangement was augmented by the Medical Care Act, 1966, in which the federal government committed to pay provincial governments 50 per cent of average provincial costs incurred in insuring physician services, adjusted for population. There were four conditions for eligibility: universal coverage (stipulated by the federal government to be at least 95 per cent of the population within two years); portability among provinces; comprehensive coverage of all necessary medical services on uniform terms; and public, non-profit administration (Medical Care Act, 1966, s. 4). By 1972, all provinces had universal hospital and medical insurance plans eligible for federal cost-sharing. Federal grants continued to be matching and open-ended, and costs were to be shared in such a way as to redistribute income from richer to poorer provinces (Naylor 1986; Taylor 1987).

Even in the early days, provincial and federal governments chafed at the cost-sharing arrangements, the former because of jurisdictional concerns and the latter because of the potentially unlimited nature of its financial commitment. The result was a major change in federal-provincial fiscal arrangements. In 1977, with the Federal-Provincial Fiscal Arrangements and Federal Post-Secondary Education and Health Contribution Act, 1977, generally referred to as Established Programs Financing (EPF), shared-cost programs for health and post-secondary education were integrated into a block grant program. While the federal government achieved the certainty of a fixed annual contribution not tied in any way to provincial expenditures, it relinquished a measure of control over how funds were spent. Provincial health insurance plans still had to meet the criteria for eligibility, but the provinces were free to decide on the allocation of funds, as long as programs in post-secondary education, hospital, and medical insurance were maintained. Transfers consisted of a combination of tax points and cash, with equalization payments to less fiscally strong provinces and initial adjustments each year in accordance with an escalator that took into consideration per capita growth rate in the GDP and changes in population of a province

(Maslove 1995). Transfers for welfare and social assistance were dealt with separately under the Canada Assistance Plan (CAP).

Health care costs continued to grow and charges to patients over and above the amount covered by the provincial health insurance plans became a flashpoint. While never a significant part of total physician billings, they were becoming more frequent and attracting negative publicity and concern (Tuohy 1994, 225). By the early 1980s, all participants were dissatisfied with the system, and debates raged over hospital daily charges and physician extra billing (Barer et al. 1994). The upshot was another federally sponsored review to re-evaluate medicare (Canada, Health Services Review 1980). Among other findings, it concluded that without a ban on extra billing, Canada's publicly funded health care system could not survive. The federal government responded with the Canada Health Act, 1985, which consolidated and expanded previous legislation. Passed in 1984, that Act remains in place. A provincial health insurance plan must meet five criteria for eligibility: accessibility, portability, comprehensiveness, universality, and public administration. In addition, a province cannot allow physicians or hospitals to bill patients for fees or charges beyond the amounts authorized under the provincial health insurance plan for insured services. If a province does not comply with the program criteria, the federal government can reduce the amount of its cash contribution, or in the case of extra billing or user charges, deduct from its contribution an amount equivalent to the total of what was charged (ss. 15, 20). Pursuant to the Budget Implementation Act, 1991, the federal government can take those deductions against any federal cash payments to provinces not in compliance with the Canada Health Act, 1985.

Over the subsequent few years, all provinces complied with the new requirements of the Canada Health Act, 1985. With the exception of Ontario, where physicians struck over the issue, agreements between provincial governments and the medical profession over the ban on extra billing were negotiated, with the medical profession achieving substantial fee schedule increases, future binding arbitration over fees and other gains (Tuohy 1994, 226–7; 1999, 94). In Ontario, extra billing was banned by the Health Care Accessibility Act, 1986. Again, debates about user charges 'fell off the policy radar' for a few years (Barer et al. 1994, 20). They were revived with a vengeance in the 1990s, as provinces responded to decreasing federal cash transfers, sagging economies, and continually escalating health care costs with caps, freezes, and clawbacks on physician payments, major decreases in hospital funding, and significant restructuring in the health care system (Barer et al. 1994; Evans et al. 1994a, 1994b; Stoddart et al. 1993; Stoddart, Barer, & Evans 1994). EPF financing remained in place through the changes introduced with the Canada Health Act, but in 1986 the federal government unilaterally altered the funding formula in an effort to control its spiralling deficit. It first decreased the rate of growth in and then froze federal contributions, with allowance only for increases based on population growth (Canadian Bar Association 1994, 111-12; Maslove 1995).

In 1995 the federal government combined EPF and CAP into a new block funding mechanism, the Canada Health and Social Transfer (CHST), with a structure analogous to EPF. The pattern of reducing transfer payments continued, with significant reductions in the cash portion (O'Neill 1997; Maslove 1995). While the federal government restored a floor to annual cash transfers of $11 billion (later increased to $12.5 billion), and in its February 1999 budget announced an infusion of new funds into health care (an additional $11.5 billion by 2004), it was estimated these funds would only restore federal transfers to 1995 levels (Morris et al. 1999, 7–8). This was followed by an announcement of a one-time payment to the provinces of $2.5 billion for health care in the February 2000 budget (Canada, Department of Finance 2000a). Provincial response to both the 1999 and 2000 federal budgets and the surpluses being realized at the federal level was to demand that Ottawa restore and increase funding (McCarthy & McKinnon 2000; P. Adams 2000; Provincial and Territorial Ministers of Health 2000). 1999 also saw the establishment of a Social Union Framework by the federal government and all provinces and territories except Quebec. The federal government agreed in principle to obtain the consent of a majority of provinces before introducing new Canada-wide programs in health, education, or social assistance and services. Additionally, it agreed to notify and consult provinces before making significant funding changes in existing social transfers. This was followed by a new health accord signed by all First Ministers in September 2000, with a federal commitment of an additional $23.4 billion in funding over a five-year period (Canada, Intergovernmental Affairs 2000; McCarthy & Mackie, 2000).

One result of federal and provincial cost-cutting was a marked decline in the growth rate of Canada's publicly insured health care expenditures, which fell from 11.1 per cent annually between 1975 and 1991 to 2.5 per cent annually between 1991 and 1996 (Federal, Provincial and Territorial Advisory Committee on Population Health 1999a, 137, 139). The public share of total health spending declined overall, from approximately 75 per cent in 1986 to 70 per cent in 1996 (Canadian Institute for Health Information 2000). Private expenditures on health, such as those for pharmaceutical products and other medications, have increased significantly.[4] In Ontario, the forecasted private sector share of total health expenditures in 1999 had risen to 34 per cent (ibid). Changes have also occurred in how funds are spent. In 1997, drug costs (public and private) overtook spending on physician services for the first time, making them the second largest component in health care expenditures. By 2000, drug costs were forecast to constitute 15.5 per cent of total health spending, compared to 13.5 per cent for physicians (Canadian Institute for Health Information 2001, 75). The total amount spent on drugs has been increasing rapidly as well, with an annual percentage growth between 1985 and 1999 more than double that for overall health expenditures (ibid., 76). National health expenditures have begun to reflect increases in government spending for health care in the last few years, but the increasing significance of the private sector and changing emphases in health care spending, particularly for drugs, are continuing trends (ibid., 72, Table 63).

The five conditions set out in the Canada Health Act continue to apply to provincial health insurance plans. Yet with the reductions in federal transfers, the withholding of the federal contribution that comprised both the carrot and the stick driving the statutory scheme and much of the federal power over health care became more illusory. With it, many commentators argued, would go the federal government's ability to enforce national standards in health care (O'Neill 1997; Madore 1995). Meanwhile, the provincial response to limitations on federal transfers, at least in Ontario, has been to look not only for ways to reduce costs in the publicly funded health care system, but for ways out of the system itself, a response in keeping with the province's ideological commitments. One route has been to continue to narrow the list of insured services. While that may seem to involve a shrinking of the state's role and presence, in fact, the state has redrawn its role so as to regulate in other ways.

B. Medically Necessary Services

In reflecting on the structure of the Canadian health insurance system, it is important to remember that, as Carolyn Tuohy has noted, 'the advent of national health insurance in Canada essentially froze in place the delivery system that existed in the 1960's ... organizational change was forestalled by the introduction of a system of financing which essentially underwrote the costs of the existing delivery system without changing its structure' (Tuohy 1994, 209–10). The Canadian health insurance system is not state or socialized health care, but rather a publicly organized and funded system to pay for existing forms of service, often privately provided (Evans 1984). At the time of its adoption (and in important respects continuing to the present), that meant hospital services in non-profit institutions that might be public or private, medical services provided by physicians in private practice who billed on a fee-for-service basis, and extended care facilities owned by a mix of non-profit and for-profit entities (Taylor 1987; Naylor 1986; Maslove 1995).

The Canada Health Act (CHA) does not prohibit public reimbursement of private or for-profit providers for provincially insured health services, as long as patients are not subject to extra billing or user charges. Nor does it prevent health care providers from operating entirely outside the publicly funded health care system (Flood & Archibald 2001). What it does require is that in order to qualify for full federal transfers, the five criteria for eligibility must be met: a provincial plan must be universal, comprehensive, portable, accessible, and publicly administered. Comprehensiveness and accessibility are conditioned on provincial coverage of all 'insured health services' provided by hospitals, medical practitioners, or dentists (Canada Health Act, 1985, ss. 9, 12). A province may also insure similar or additional services by other health care practitioners such as physiotherapists and chiropractors (ibid., s. 9). In addition, the federal government contributes to the cost of extended care. Provincial health insurance plans typically go beyond the minimum required to satisfy the CHA criteria. Additional coverage varies from province to province and is generally subject to caps, limitations on the number of services funded, and other conditions (Maslove 1995; Naylor 1999).

The Canada Health Act defines 'insured health services' to mean 'hospital services, physician services and surgical-dental services provided to insured persons ...' (ibid., s. 2). Each of those terms is in turn defined with reference to the service being 'medically (or dentally) required' or in the case of hospitals, 'medically necessary for the purpose of maintaining health, preventing disease or diagnosing or treating an injury, illness or disability' (ibid.). However, there is no definition of 'medically necessary' or 'medically required' in the Act. There is some guidance in the objectives of the CHA set out in the preamble and the 'primary objective' of Canadian health care policy incorporated in the legislation itself ('to protect, promote and restore the physical and mental well-being of residents of Canada and to facilitate reasonable access to health services without financial or other barriers' (ibid., s. 3)). But the history of the adoption of the CHA (public insurance to pay for an already established system of health care focused on physician services and acute care in hospitals) and the legislative focus on medical judgment have had the greatest influence on understandings of these terms. As Timothy Caulfield has noted, the lack of operational definition for the term 'medically necessary' has meant that 'it has historically amounted to any service which physicians believe should be provided' (Caulfield 1996, 64). In practical terms, lists of insured services are generally formulated through negotiations between the provincial medical associations and government, and they have largely followed fee schedules (Deber, Ross, & Catz 1993, 10). Provincial health insurance legislation, while varying in the type and extent of additional services covered, tends either to track the CHA by requiring that 'medically necessary' services be provided (while leaving the term undefined) or to define it tautologically as those services listed as insured in the regulations (Canadian Bar Association 1994, 37–9; Canadian Medical Association 1994a, 12–13).

Attempts to define what is meant by 'medically necessary' or 'medically required' have occupied little judicial attention, with a few recent exceptions (*Cameron v. Nova Scotia (A.G.)*, 1999; *Auton v. British Columbia (Minister of Health)*, 2000).[5] The terms have, however, been the subject of considerable academic commentary. With growing costs and shrinking ability to meet them, the concept of medical necessity has also attracted extraordinary attention from an ever-expanding number of government committees and task forces and their policy advisers. Several different approaches have been proposed, ranging from defined lists of services, as in Oregon, through an evidence-based approach, to applying sequential policy filters (Health Action Lobby 1994) or dividing core from comprehensive services based on considerations of quality of care, ethics, and economics (Canadian Medical Association 1994a). Not surprisingly, the various proposals have in turn given rise to critical analysis and counter-proposals (see e.g. Charles, Lomas, & Giacomini 1997, concluding that the focus on medical necessity locks the status quo in place and is therefore counter-productive in attempts at reform; Caulfield 1996, suggesting a 'practical, operational and meaningful definition' is likely impossible). It is notable that these processes and submissions have been public or made available to the public. While not always easily accessible, they have resulted in a relatively open debate about the values underlying the Canadian health care system and the policies most congruent with them, although there has been little government action in response to this debate.

II. Creeping Privatization

A. *Selective Deinsuring of Services*

Despite the public discourse, the policy process employed by provincial governments to make decisions about what is medically necessary – that is, the scope of their health insurance plans – has been neither public nor transparent. This is evident from the manner in which decisions are made about deinsuring services. What began as negotiations between provincial governments and the respective medical associations over fee schedules (see e.g. Health Care Accessibility Act, 1986, 1990, s. 3) have expanded considerably, fundamentally changing the character of the activities. As fiscal pressures increased, negotiations came to include the establishment of caps on expenditures for physician services, as well as agreement on structures that would be employed to make decisions about coverage (Tuohy 1994, 230–1; 1999, 218–19). Joint Management Committees (JMC) comprised of representatives of the provincial government and the medical association have been put in place in several provinces to develop policies on a wide range of medical and other health care–related services, including practice guidelines, physician resource planning and technology assessment (Health Action Lobby 1994, 5; Canadian Bar Association 1994, 39; Tuohy 1999, 221, 226–9). The result is that decisions about continued access to public goods (insured health services) are delegated to a private setting that affords one set of private stakeholders a privileged position. In Ontario, the process initially included a review by an expert panel with public members and wider public consultation (Rusk 1993; Borsellino 1994; Giacomini, Hurley, & Stoddart 2000). By 1997–8, when the Schedule of Benefits was culled for delisting, the review was conducted by a joint medical association / Ministry of Health Working Group (Physician Services Committee), which in turn had obtained the endorsement of an expert panel, equally divided among association and government members (Ontario 1998b, 2). As the external facilitator appointed by the parties noted, in this process options are 'developed with the assistance of an expert joint staff' and evaluated 'according to principle and party interests' before solutions are recommended; 'ultimately, the OMA [Ontario Medical Association] and the government must be the judge of the process and its outputs' (G. Adams 1999). The most recent agreement between the government and the OMA anticipates this process continuing, committing the parties to achieving savings of an additional $50 million annually in the Schedule of Benefits by a combination of 'tightening and modernization' (OMA/MOHLTC Agreement 2000). Both public participation and openness in the process appear to have been left aside. That would be less troubling if there was clear policy in place to guide the decision making, but there is not.

JMCs have been assigned the task of selective deinsurance of services, sometimes with a set dollar volume of reductions in billing to be achieved (Blum 1997, 380; Tuohy 1994, 231; Ontario 1998a; 1998b; OMA/MOHLTC Agreement 2000). Deinsurance generally requires only a change in regulation; public consultation is not mandatory, and while the JMC recommendation is not binding (Blum 1997; Moulton 1997), it is influential. As Deber et al. noted in their report to the National Health Forum, 'Most such decisions are based on input from a limited number of stakeholders – primarily government and the provincial medical association. Participation on the part of other groups, including affected members of the public is rarely extensive, though lip service is paid to the concept' (1996, 7–7). The most common pattern has been one of deinsuring services where another province has already taken the lead (ibid. 7–5). While one consistent theme in public statements is that the public plan should only pay for services of proven efficacy – that is, evidence-based medicine (National Forum on Health 1997b) – this precept has often not guided decisions in fact (Giacomini, Hurley, & Stoddart 2000). Deber's study established that 'Neither insurance nor de-insurance decisions are commonly based upon evidence, usually because decisions must be made too quickly for such evidence to be obtained. Neither is there systematic monitoring of the impact of coverage decisions' (Deber et al. 1996, 7–7).

Conceptually, deinsuring a health service must mean that it is not 'medically necessary,' at least in the eyes of the provincial government and medical association, because the CHA definition of comprehensiveness requires coverage for all medically necessary services.[6] In times of economic expansion there was less concern about controlling spending on health care and more receptiveness to funding physician services without much analysis of need or efficacy. The result was expansive and expanding lists of insured services.

That climate has changed. Cost control is a significant concern, but the assertion that deinsuring services reduces costs is not as self-evident as it may at first appear. The economic interests of both the provincial government and the medical association are affected by a conclusion that a service is not medically necessary. In that event, provincial governments no longer have to pay for it, and providers can offer it privately on a for-profit basis. For the government, deinsuring shifts costs to individuals who obtain the services privately if at all. While it may reduce costs for government, deinsuring does not contain health care costs overall (Evans 1990; Griffith 1999). Indeed, the limited evidence available indicates costs may increase (Deber et al. 1996, 5–11). For the medical association, whose members have been subject to caps, clawbacks, sliding scale reimbursement, and freezes on payments for their activities within the publicly insured system, the appeal of being able to offer services outside the plan in addition to insured services is obvious: deinsurance has the potential to increase incomes (Evans et al. 2000). The same motivation underlies physicians' increasingly frequent 'unbundling' of the services they provide; these are broken down into insured and uninsured components and patients are charged for the latter on a per service basis, or on the administratively more efficient and less costly (for the provider) requirement of payment of a block fee in advance (College of Physicians and Surgeons of Ontario, 1997; Coutts 1998). The utility of this form of analysis as a rhetorical device is certainly understood by those advocating essentially a two-tier system. The Canadian Medical Association's review of the legal issues arising from its proposal to divide health care services into 'core' (publicly insured) and 'comprehensive' (uninsured) services concluded that 'the safest course' was to characterize deinsured services as medically unnecessary rather than unaffordable, because to do otherwise 'would clearly violate the *Canada Health Act*' (Canadian Medical Association 1994b, 30). The decision makers' interests are not, of course, singular. Concern for patients' well-being and their own professional obligations, as well as for the political consequences of decisions taken, act as checks on decisions about deinsurance. They do so, though, in a way quite opaque to the public. And despite the clear interests of the participants, little attention seems to have been given to their agendas. A private process (private in the sense that the process is not open and that it favours the input of one set of private actors, the medical profession) has resulted in further privatization in the health care system (in that the state ceases to fund provision of certain services as a public good, shifting both payment and provision to the private sphere), under the rubric of reducing costs and purging the public system of inappropriate expenditures. Through the dual strategies of delegation and commodification, privatization is gradually working its way into the health care system.

A review of the lists of services deinsured by the various provinces reveals that procedures are not being dropped only when non-economic or when there is no or insufficient evidence that they are effective (Deber et al. 1993, 11; Giacomini et al. 2000; Canadian Medical Association 1997; *Cameron*, 1999, para. 151). While deinsurance has affected coverage for drugs, vision, dental, and laboratory services, many of the services are concerned with reproductive health care, mental health, cosmetic surgery and recently in Ontario, gender reassignment surgery (O. Reg. 528/98 made under the Health Insurance Act, 1990). The political nature of deinsurance decisions was apparent in *R. v. Morgentaler:* as the Supreme Court of Canada noted, Nova Scotia had put regulations and then legislation in place requiring abortions to be performed in hospital with the 'direct and exclusive aim' of stopping the Morgentaler clinic as a 'public evil which should be eliminated,' despite evidence of these clinics' safety and cost effectiveness (*R. v. Morgentaler*, 1993, 503, 506, 510). The series of cases challenging provincial funding refusals for abortions arose in unique circumstances, but they clearly indicate the vulnerability of the process to political and partisan considerations unrelated to health or the purposes of the enabling statute. As Carolyn Tuohy has observed, 'the selection of .... procedures for consideration has resulted in part from the ideological agendas of governments, and in part from a consideration of income differentials within the medical profession' (Tuohy 1994, 229). In Tuohy's view, the confluence of those interests was exemplified by the manner in which the Alberta Conservative government's decision to deinsure family planning, counselling, tubal ligations, vasectomies, and mammoplasty in 1985 dovetailed with its conservative social policy, as well as with the interests of medical practitioners in being able to bill privately for lucrative procedures. Alberta's was a short-lived decision; insurance coverage was largely reinstated in the face of concerted public opposition (Martin 1989, 6). Elsewhere, in a move perhaps motivated more by the concerns of fiscal rather than social conservatives, a number of other provinces have deinsured reversals of tubal ligations and vasectomies, while still insuring the original sterilization (Canadian Medical Association 1997)!

What of economic considerations, then? Deber et al. note that deinsurance has been limited and has taken place 'around the margins of insured services, with physician co-operation' (Deber et al. 1996, 7-5). Lists of deinsured services in various provinces include breast reduction surgery, artificial insemination, in vitro fertilization, repair of earlobe torn by earring traction, and gender reassignment surgery. Are these marginal in that they do not account for a significant proportion of health care spending and so will not arouse much public protest (or lead to significant savings)? Or are they marginal in that they edge too close to being frivolous, constitute not health care but consumer choice, or affect largely marginal (powerless) populations, at least in the view of government and provider stakeholders? Tuohy notes that target savings through delisting in 1997 were '2% or less of the respective provincial governments' expenditures on physician services' (Tuohy 1999, 220). Critics of the process argue convincingly that selective deinsurance is unlikely to achieve substantial savings (Rachlis 1995; Charles et al. 1997, 377). To the extent that that is true and known to the decision makers, the ideological commitments underlying the choice of services to be deinsured loom even larger.

Were there an effective public presence in the decision-making process and articulated goals that included attention to broader repercussions, it would be more difficult to discount the interests of those relegated to the margins. If deinsurance is to be retained as a strategy, public representation would result in a better and fairer process overall. However, that would still leave unanswered the criticism that deinsurance is not only the wrong approach but that it does not and cannot achieve significant cost savings.

B. Free-Standing Health Care Facilities

The Independent Health Facilities Act, 1989 (the IHFA), which was introduced by the Liberal government, came into force in Ontario in 1990. It was meant to enable government to regulate existing undertakings but also to facilitate and even promote a new form of delivery of health services. It.gave the minister power through a licensing system to control the establishment and operation of selected free-standing diagnostic and surgical health facilities outside hospitals (hereafter, IHFs) and to ensure services performed in these facilities were of acceptable quality and standards (Sharpe & Weisstub 1996). With independent health facilities legislation, the state promotes change in both the location of services and the form and extent of regulation. The legislation was in part reactive, a response to the rapid expansion in the provision of various medical and surgical procedures outside hospitals. However, it was also proactive, as it set directions and policy for further expansion. The types of procedures performed at IHFs continue to expand, as medical advances and health care budget cutbacks mean that more and more services are provided outside hospitals. Most services in these settings provide access to technology or consist of high volume, short-stay surgical procedures (National Forum on Health 1995, 11–12). In Ontario the list, which includes anaesthesia, induced abortion, dermatological laser procedures, gynaecologic procedures, haemodialysis, nuclear medicine, ophthalmologic procedures, peripheral vascular surgery, plastic surgery procedures, pulmonary function studies, radiology, sleep medicine, and ultrasound, continues to grow (College of Physicians and Surgeons of Ontario 1998, 31; 2000). Of the almost one thousand IHFs in Ontario, the majority provide what the College of Physicians and Surgeons of Ontario characterizes as diagnostic services; only a small number provide surgical procedures such as induced abortion and cataract surgery (College of Physicians and Surgeons of Ontario 1999).

Other than exempting existing facilities, which were grandfathered, the Act combined a mandatory request for proposal process with a policy requirement for the participation of local district health councils (MacMillan & Barnes 1991). New facilities would have to be licensed by the ministry and would be subject to ongoing quality assurance review overseen by the College of Physicians and Surgeons of Ontario. It was anticipated that local district health councils would be among the groups that could define a need and recommend establishment of a facility, or that the Ministry of Health would do so and ask district health councils to respond with recommendations (Ontario Ministry of Health n.d.). Physicians providing insured services in an IHF bill the health insurance plan for those services; facility fees can also be charged. Where the latter are incurred in connection with insured services, in Ontario they are generally determined through negotiation between the government and the IHF owner or operator (Lavis et al. 1998). That is not necessarily the case in all provinces. New Brunswick, for instance, has long refused to pay for abortions performed in private clinics, although it does pay for those performed in a hospital with the approval of two physicians (C. Clark 2001). Facility fees are meant to reflect the overhead and operating costs of providing a service (e.g., the costs incurred in staffing, operating, and maintaining an operating room or paying a technician to operate laser equipment; the capital cost of equipment; the cost of some medical devices used). When that same service is provided in a hospital, generally no separate charge is made. Provision for facility fees required rewriting the Schedule of Benefits under the Ontario Health Insurance Plan: '[s]ervices which would become facility fees under the new Act were removed, and constituent elements of insured services which form the basis of the IHFA had to be more clearly defined' (MacMillan & Barnes 1991). Charges to patients are to be limited to services that are neither part of a covered facility fee nor insured services under the provincial plan (Lavis et al. 1998).

The IHFA changed significantly with the Conservative government's Bill 26, the omnibus Savings and Restructuring Act, 1996. Initially, the IHFA had given a preference to non-profit and Canadian-owned providers. While not a strong commitment, that preference nonetheless represented an ideological choice to continue to favour the non-profit nature of the health care system.[7] Bill 26 removed this preference. The rationale offered for the change was to ensure provision 'at the least cost by the most qualified operator in the most appropriate setting' (Sharpe & Weisstub 1996). Additionally, the section dealing with district health council involvement was revised to eliminate the council's role in the independent health facilities development process, despite the initial commitment to use the IHF process to develop a 'more community-based health care system' (Ontario Ministry of Health n.d.). Bill 26 also removed the reference to 'insured' in the definition of 'health facilities,' making it clear they can also provide non-insured, for-profit services. The definition of 'facility fee' was similarly changed.

One result of these changes is that the ability and temptation to redefine the services deemed 'medically necessary' (and therefore covered by the provincial health insurance plan and subject to a ban on extra billing) are increased. Independent health facilities, licensed by the ministry and subject to a statutorily mandated quality assurance program operated by the College of Physicians and Surgeons of Ontario, are now explicitly envisaged as providing non-insured services. The Ontario government recently announced its intention to increase the use of for-profit firms (Mackie 2001).

In jurisdictions where physicians can have 'private' patients and charge for them, experience has shown that waiting lists for needed medical procedures for patients in the public system are significantly lengthened (W. Armstrong 2000; Parkland Institute 1999; De Coster et al. 1998, 54; Light 1996; C. Richmond 1996). A two-tier system does not ease the pressure on publicly funded services and institutions, as some proponents claim. Nor do users self-select such that only the relatively affluent who can absorb the cost will avail themselves of private services (De Coster et al 1998). A two-tier system does, however, set up competition between public institutions (hospitals) and the parallel system of independent health facilities providing the same services. Robert Evans suggests this competition will in fact lead to increased costs, most obviously from the larger numbers of 'administrations' to support, and also from the fragmentation leading to a loss of bargaining power inherent in a single payer system (Evans 1990; 1999). Private care can also drain resources from the public system, as physicians choose to focus on providing privately paid services (Guyatt 2001). Quality of care can be affected too, particularly with the introduction of for-profit facilities. Recently, American researchers concluded after an extensive review that patients treated with dialysis at for-profit facilities in the United States had a 20 per cent higher mortality rate and a 26 per cent lower rate of placement on waiting lists for transplant; these findings are suggestive of a 'more aggressive response' to incentives to economize in the former instance and to maintain the income stream associated with continued dialysis in the latter (Pushkal et al. 1999, 1658). Similar unfavourable comparisons resulted when American investor-owned health maintenance organizations were compared to non-profit HMOs on quality of care variables (Himmelstein et al. 1999). The small number of for-profit dialysis centres in Ontario remain to be examined (Wysong 1999). Since the regulatory and insurance environments differ, it cannot simply be assumed that American results will be replicated in this country. However, some information is available about IHF operations. The College of Physicians and Surgeons of Ontario reported that it made recommendations to correct serious quality of care deficiencies (deficiencies severe enough to recommend suspension or removal of service from the licence) in 15 per cent of the 186 facilities selected for assessment in 1997/8, 10 per cent of the 159 assessed in 1998/9, and 7.3 per cent of the 219 assessed in 1999/2000 (College of Physicians and Surgeons of Ontario 1998, 1999, 2000).

The potential of independent health facilities to affect women's access to appropriate health care is mixed and will be determined by the regulatory regime adopted and how it is applied, as well as whether the policy and payment frameworks foster the preservation of the publicly funded system and the provision of needed services. The increasingly complex and extensive health care services delivered outside hospitals must be provided in a regulated environment to ensure safety and quality of care without imposing unnecessary barriers. The IHFA puts in place provision for licensing and monitoring that, if rigorously implemented, could ensure that proper regulation occurs. However, in comparison with public hospitals, the regulatory framework is sketchy. Supervision and quality assurance activities are only referenced briefly in the enabling legislation. The adequacy of the system in practice will depend on the resources and commitment government is prepared to devote to that end.

The IHFA might have provided a framework for increased availability of and choice in abortion services. Owing to political pressures, fears of harassment and violence, limited resources and personnel, and disapproval or indifference, abortions are not available at many hospitals (Ferris et al. 1998). Often a free-standing clinic is women's only option.[8] While the statute could have been employed to facilitate the establishment of independent health facilities performing the procedure, it was not (Farid 1997, para. 38). Despite its medical orientation, the IHFA could also have allowed for community initiatives to identify health needs and how they might best be met (Sutton 1996). In practice, however, the financial, organizational, political, bureaucratic and now legislative barriers are likely to prove too formidable for community groups.

Ontario has witnessed a move away from both a non-profit orientation and community input through district health councils. The shift in orientation in the regulatory environment has also made evident the potential threat posed by independent health facilities to the publicly funded health care system and the quality of care delivered. The delivery of uninsured services in these facilities is potentially associated not only with the negative consequences noted above, but with conflicts of interest, 'cream-skimming' both higher paying and lower cost patients, opportunities for extra billing, pressure to buy 'enhanced' services, and inappropriate services (Evans et al. 2000). When legislative and policy changes facilitating IHFs are structured in such a way that care available through the public system is diminished, while opportunities and incentives to maximize uninsured services offered or to minimize insured services are encouraged, there is cause for serious concern.

C. Access to Reproductive Services

Through Bill 26 the Ministry of Health Act was amended by the Conservative government to allow Cabinet to create the Health Services Restructuring Commission (HSRC), a non-profit corporation established for a period of four years to restructure the health care system, and in particular, hospital services in Ontario.[9] The Public Hospitals Act was also amended to give the minister comprehensive funding authority, including the power to reduce, suspend, or terminate funding to a hospital, inter alia, if it is in the 'public interest' to do so (Savings and Restructuring Act, 1996, Sch. F.). The HSRC was to make decisions about hospital restructuring and to advise the minister of health on other aspects of the health care system. While the process appears to remove these decisions from political influence, it also removes them from political accountability by rendering them bureaucratic and largely untouchable in the legislature or the courts.[10]

Lack of accountability has been a uniform theme in the decisions involving challenges to hospital closures, mergers and amalgamations. In a frequently cited passage from *Pembroke Civic Hospital v. Ontario (Health Services Restructuring Commission)*, the Divisional Court commented on its restricted role in reviewing decisions of the commission: 'The court's role is very limited in these cases. The court has no power to inquire into the rights and wrongs of hospital restructuring laws or policies, the wisdom or folly of decisions to close particular hospitals, or decisions to direct particular hospital governance structures. It is not for the court to agree or disagree with the decision of the Commission. The law provides no right of appeal from the Commission to the court. The court has no power to review the merits of the Commission's decisions. The only role of the court is to decide whether the Commission acted according to law in arriving at its decision' (*Pembroke Civic Hospital*, 1997, 44). Restructuring is treated as a technical matter, with decisions left to administrators and experts charged with the theoretically neutral task of rationalizing the health care system, beginning with hospitals. The result has been essentially unchallengable HSRC decisions which, through lack of commitment, inattention, or a narrow interpretation of its mandate to focus on cost efficiency to the exclusion of other rights and interests, have maintained and sometimes increased barriers to women's access to reproductive health services, most notably abortion.

In some instances in Ontario, HSRC decisions resulted in the 'winning' hospitals (the survivors) being those with Roman Catholic affiliations. Thus the Pembroke Civic Hospital was directed to merge with the Roman Catholic Pembroke General while, in Toronto, the Wellesley Central Hospital was directed to transfer its assets and programs to St Michael's Hospital, a Roman Catholic institution. The effect of the latter order was to eliminate access to a number of reproductive health

care services previously available at the Wellesley. Abortions, vasectomies, tubal ligation as a form of birth control, and even the distribution
of condoms in waiting rooms and other public spaces were halted
(Wellesley had served a high-needs, low-income population with a high
incidence of HIV/AIDS infection) (*Wellesley Central Hospital*, 1997, para.
60; *Globe and Mail* 1998e, A5).[11] Although St Michael's was directed to
appoint one-third of its board of directors from nominees provided by
Wellesley for three years and to develop '... a governance structure that
is representative of the communities served with regard to the demographic, linguistic, cultural, economic, geographic, ethnic, religious,
and social characteristics' (para 36), these provisions did not alter the
reality that these services would no longer be available at that site. In
Pembroke, to be eligible to be a member of the newly constituted board
of directors, one had to formally commit to '... comply with the obligation to ... respect the mission, values and goals of the Pembroke General
Hospital' (Health Services Restructuring Commission 1997d, 15).

A Charter equality rights challenge made in *Wellesley Central Hospital*,
1997, failed because, in the court's view, women (and those personal
applicants who were HIV+ gay men) had other options. The court did
not even call on the respondents on this issue. Nowhere does the court
explicitly consider the implications of a public hospital deciding not to
offer reproductive health care services on the basis not of resource availability but rather as the result of a moral judgment that those services
(which are for the most part insured and therefore by definition medically necessary), are wrong. In *Pembroke Civic Hospital*, Archie Campbell
J. commented on the lack of coercion in the 'silent presence of crosses
and crucifixes' as they neither constrain nor compel particular religious
practices (*Pembroke Civic Hospital*, 1997, para. 56). That observation
misses the point. These are cases about access to health care, not about
patients being compelled to 'engage in religious ... observances' (ibid.).
The institutional policies dictated by adherence to the Catholic faith are
in themselves coercive, because they prohibit the provision of certain
types of health care on the basis that a particular religion condemns
them as morally wrong. They carry with them an inherent judgment, the
judgment of a publicly funded institution charged with carrying out government policy to provide comprehensive health care, that those seeking such services – primarily women – are also morally in the wrong, or
at best misguided.[12] That is not a silent presence but an active judgment
with real consequences and ramifications, particularly when other hos-

pitals and health care are not easily accessed, either because of geography or owing to lack of individual resources or institutional capacity. The policy does not simply reduce the number of treatment choices available at a particular institution, it also narrows the number of people who will benefit from the health care offered there. In the absence of open counselling and ready referral, it also restricts decisions about health care options to a range dictated by religious belief rather than leaving those decisions with the patient, as the law requires.

Only one hospital was successful in challenging the HSRC's directions that it substantially reduce its operations and fold them into those of other hospitals. The Divisional Court quashed the directions to L'Hôpital Montfort in Ottawa and remitted the matter to the HSRC for reconsideration, on the basis that the destruction of the Montfort's ability to provide francophone medical services and medical training violated constitutional rights to francophone minority protection (*Lalonde* 2001). Neither the HSRC nor the court remarked on the hospital's policies on reproductive services. The Montfort did not provide abortion services nor did it make available prescriptions for the morning-after pill (Table feministe de concertation provinciale de l'Ontario, no date).

Even before the hospital restructuring process, research indicated that despite the Supreme Court of Canada's 1988 decision in *R. v. Morgentaler*, access to abortion was limited and controversial in many areas (Ferris et al. 1998; 1995). Gavigan has commented on the paradox that a medicalized concept of abortion once resisted by Canadian feminists and pro-choice activists as tending to privatize, and hence depoliticize, a struggle over equality has been employed since *Morgentaler* to support arguments that access to abortion is part of women's right of access to health care generally (Gavigan 1992, 127). Despite judicial recognition of women's constitutional rights, ensuring the ability of women to access abortion services has remained a struggle, both in the courts, given some provincial governments' refusal to allow or fund this type of care (see e.g. *Morgentaler*, 1993; *Lexogest*, 1993; *Morgentaler*, 1995), and in the less obviously political realm of local hospitals' decisions. The shift to a focus on abortion access as a matter of health care administration has meant that denials of access that occur when a hospital board decides the facility will not offer that form of health care 'get recast as stories about self-regulation by local communities rather than about the gendered nature of power within those communities' (Lessard 1997, 85; 1993). Such narratives can in turn assume a life and power of their own.

In *Pembroke Civic Hospital,* the court relied on the fact that abortions had not been performed at the secular hospital or elsewhere in the county for more than fourteen years to bolster its conclusion that there was no breach of women's Charter equality rights in requiring a transfer of that hospital's assets to the Roman Catholic Pembroke General, which prohibited abortions as morally wrong. In the court's view, since nothing would change there was no basis for complaint.

The absence of any specific consideration of women's access to abortion in most of the HSRC Directions and Reports is disturbing. Neither the St Michael's/Wellesley Central nor the Pembroke materials make specific reference to abortion and when the HSRC identified gaps in service in Pembroke, abortion services were not among them (Health Services Restructuring Commission 1997f). In its final Directions for Metropolitan Toronto the HSRC claimed 'there will be no reduction in patient services as a result of restructuring' (Health Services Restructuring Commission 1997a); even though the loss of capacity at the Wellesley was known, no explicit mention of or provision for ensuring access to abortion was made. The push towards privatization however, surfaces time and again: hospitals are specifically directed to explore 'alternative delivery systems, including services that can be provided by the private sector' (Health Services Restructuring Commission 1997b, no. 9).

The notable exception to the silence on abortion is found in the HSRC's 1998 'Stormont, Dundas & Glengarry, Prescott & Russell Counties Health Services Restructuring Report,' which includes a section on 'Access to Women's Reproductive Health Care Services.' The commission rejected suggestions that women's reproductive health care services could all be referred out of the area or to a free-standing clinic (a new twist to the 'Not In My Backyard' syndrome familiar from environmental disputes). It recognized the importance of maintaining local access to reproductive health care services that 'may include therapeutic abortion, rape counselling, sterilization, artificial insemination and genetic counselling,' noting the 'current Ministry of Health policy ... that hospital-based services ... are clearly superior to those received in stand-alone clinics.' It stated that 'women's reproductive health services [for the area] must meet local needs ... [and] like all health care services, should be provided in a manner that respects both local access and patient choice' (Health Services Restructuring Commission 1998, 18–19). That type of express commitment is largely missing in the HSRC's other Reports and Directions. They had tended to perpetuate the approach Adams J. identified in *Ontario (A.G.) v. Dieleman:* 'Public hospitals have not always given priority to the interests of women seeking access to abortion services ... The need for free-standing clinics in Ontario is pronounced because of the politics which pervaded the abortion issue and the impact of political forces on hospitals throughout the province ... In effect, the free-standing clinics are a response to the uncertain delivery of abortion services at Ontario's public hospitals notwithstanding that hospitals provide the greatest protection against the harmful effects of protest activity' (1994, 315–16).

Despite major differences in health care system financing, the American experience, which since the 1980s has been marked by widespread mergers and other types of alliances among hospitals and managed care plans, is instructive of what may happen to women's access to reproductive health care in the aftermath of amalgamations between Catholic and secular hospitals. Observers conclude that where Catholic organizations have been involved, health care access has been compromised by the institution's religious affiliation, with particularly onerous effects for women. While the most obvious curtailment of services is an end to performing abortions in the new entity, prohibitions have extended to tubal ligations, vasectomies, in vitro fertilization, prescribing or dispensing contraceptives, use of the morning-after pill even for victims of rape, and limitations on honouring advance directives at the end of life that include refusals of artificial nutrition and hydration (Bucar 1998, 10–11; Boozang 1995, 1147–51; Ikemoto 1996, 1107–8; Paine 1999, 380). Physicians and employees working in clinics and other entities owned by Catholic institutions have been required to adhere to Catholic precepts (Gallagher 1997, 67; Hochberg 1996, 945).

Some American commentators suggest that extensive and increasing government regulation and financing will erode religious providers' ability to limit the care offered (Boozang 1995, 1430). Others, however, conclude that the ability of Catholic health care institutions to restrict the care offered, particularly reproductive health services, is strong and growing (Bucar 1998, 16–17). The elimination of reproductive health services is felt especially by low-income women who lack the resources or mobility to seek those services elsewhere (Ikemoto 1996; Bucar 1998; McDaniel 2000, 45). Restructuring, promoted as increasing efficiency and even enhancing services, has in fact operated to limit both the care and the choices available to the least powerful and most marginalized in the United States. In Ontario proposals are being made to promote further integration of care among community and hospital facilities and to restructure the provision of primary care into group practices, which

are in turn envisaged as entering into service arrangements with particular hospitals (Health Services Restructuring Commission 1999). The
American experience raises disturbing questions about whether similar
'extraterritorial' effect will be given to Catholic policies in Ontario.

III. Using Legal Strategies to Resist Privatization

Privatization diminishes both the publicly funded health care system
and what the public expects of it. Public acceptance of reduced norms
and standards in turn attenuates the will to oppose restructuring. The
Ontario government has sought to implement an incremental policy of
privatization by shrouding its decisions from public scrutiny, transforming political decisions that affect the health of Ontario residents into
technical decisions concerned chiefly with the bottom line. Another
strategy of privatization is thus apparent, namely, depoliticization,
through which the government is attempting to remove health care services from the realm of political contestation. One crucial means by
which it has advanced this agenda has been to shield the restructuring
process from legal scrutiny or challenge. This part explores the extent
to which the government's efforts to repel legal challenges have been
successful and legal remedies that may be employed to affirm and
enforce the state's obligations with respect to health care. There are a
number of possible avenues to challenge government action and inaction, among them civil lawsuits, coroner's inquests, and public inquiries.
My focus is on three types of legal claims: those based on the Canada
Health Act, administrative law grounds, and breaches of the Canadian
Charter of Rights and Freedoms, respectively.

A. The Canada Health Act

As discussed above, the Canada Health Act, 1985 (CHA) requires each
province to ensure that its public health insurance plan is accessible,
publicly administered, comprehensive, universal, and portable in order
to qualify for full cash contributions from the federal government. Even
with reduced transfer payments, the federal government can take steps
to control provincial non-compliance. In the past, however, it has not
withheld payments for failure to comply with program requirements,
although instances of extra billing or user fees have sometimes resulted
in the imposition of penalties (Choudhry 1996). In New Brunswick, for
instance, which has consistently refused to pay for abortions performed

in private clinics and insures only those performed in public hospitals with the approval of two physicians, the federal government has merely warned the province that its policy violates the CHA. No sanctions have been imposed (Priest 2001). It announced an intention to be more pro-active in the face of Alberta legislation broadening private clinics' scope of practice, but its commitment to following through on this promise is as yet uncertain (Choudhry 2000; Harper 2000). Perceiving a lack of political will on the part of the federal government or, more simply, viewing the CHA as providing assurances directly enforceable by them as citizens, some individuals have attempted to rely on this Act to attack provincial limits on access to, provision of, or payment for health services. Jurisprudence on this point is not well developed, but courts to date have not been receptive.

In both Ontario and British Columbia, provincial limits on reimbursement for out-of-country hospital charges have been challenged on the ground that they contravene the CHA requirement that health insurance benefits be portable. In *Collett v. Ontario (Attorney General)*, the majority of the Divisional Court dismissed the application on the basis that the CHA anticipated intergovernmental consultation as to whether the Act had been breached and the federal government's response. As that had not occurred, the matter was not yet justiciable. In *Brown v. B.C. (A.G.)*, the court held that the CHA itself provided a complete code of remedies, which did not include lawsuits by aggrieved individuals (*Brown*, 1998, 282–3). Similarly in *B.C. Civil Liberties Association v. B.C. (A.G.)*, McEachern C.J.S.C. noted that whether or not a provincial regulation purporting to define when abortions were medically required breached the accessibility requirements of the CHA, it was for Cabinet to assess the risk of losing federal funds. The matter was a political responsibility, to be addressed by political steps. The challenged regulation was, however, struck down on other grounds. The issue was also decided against the individual applicants in *Cameron v. Nova Scotia (A.G.)*, an unsuccessful claim that the provincial government was required to include coverage for in vitro fertilization and intracytoplasmic sperm injection (ICSI) under the provincial health insurance plan (*Cameron*, 1999, para. 97; leave to appeal refused 29 June 2000, S.C.C.; see also *Lexogest*, 1993). The Nova Scotia Court of Appeal characterized the alleged breach of the CHA (in this instance, the requirement of comprehensiveness) as a political and not a justiciable issue.

Reliance was also placed on the CHA to support a challenge to a province's decisions about the organization of the publicly funded health care system in the context of provider payments in *Waldman v. British Columbia (Medical Services Commission)*. The provincial legislation at issue required compliance with the CHA in order to maintain eligibility for full federal cash contributions. In an attempt to control costs, the Medical Services Commission had instituted a system that sharply limited reimbursement to new medical practitioners in the province unless they met stringent conditions with respect to the location and type of their practices. Although it struck down the restrictions on other grounds, the Court of Appeal held that the CHA's requirement of 'reasonable compensation' to providers referred to the compensation system as a whole, not to whether individual practitioners were adequately compensated.[13]

The few attempts by individuals to use the courts to attack provincial regulations or policy for failure to comply with the CHA have thus failed. While individuals can satisfy the test for direct or public interest standing in appropriate circumstances (*Finlay*, 1986), the courts are clearly loath to enter what is obviously a highly political and contested arena. Although the question has not yet been considered by the Supreme Court of Canada, the decision in *Finlay v. Canada (Minister of Finance)*, 1993 suggests that that court is likely to adopt a deferential approach to provincial decisions about how to meet federal funding requirements in the context of a challenge brought by an individual.[14]

The room to manoeuvre allowed provinces in *Finlay* renders it difficult to be optimistic about successful use of litigation to enforce the CHA, and the 1999 Social Union Framework Agreement (SUFA) entered into between the federal government and all provinces except Quebec reinforces the conclusion that provincial breaches of the CHA will generally not be justiciable at the instance of individuals. Not only does the CHA provide for intergovernmental consultation, but the parties to the Social Union all agree to adopt 'dispute avoidance and resolution' as the leitmotif of intergovernmental relations, a commitment that is specifically extended to interpreting the principles of the CHA (SUFA, s. 6). Interpretation of norms in this area is envisaged as a joint federal-provincial undertaking, although this would not prevent federal enforcement of CHA provisions if the alternative dispute resolution contemplated had failed. While the agreement refers in general terms to governments ensuring effective mechanisms for citizen participation in developing social priorities and reviewing outcomes (SUFA, s. 10), it is difficult to reconcile the framework as a whole, a hallmark of which is to be cooperation and collaboration, with the possibility that privately instituted lawsuits against either or both levels of government could proceed simultaneously with governmental negotiations or a resolution on the same matter.

That leaves potential for a significant disjunction between Canadians' beliefs about their entitlement to health care and their ability to do anything about it when the system does not meet their expectations, at least through the vehicle of legal action seeking to enforce government obligations under the CHA. The CHA in and of itself is not a Health Charter that Canadians can enforce in the same way as the Canadian Charter of Rights and Freedoms, though many may wish and believe it to be so.[15] The federal government may choose not to take action when a province fails to comply with the CHA program criteria; it may be satisfied with less than users of the health care system consider to be required; or it may be unaware of provincial deficiencies. While *Finlay* implies a bottom line of enforceable rights, it also affirms considerable flexibility in provincial arrangements, a flexibility augmented in the area of health care by mandated intergovernmental consultation. The CHA can usefully be relied on as an interpretive guide, especially when its statements of principle are emphasized over its context, the governance of cash contributions by the federal government to provinces meeting criteria for their health insurance plans (see e.g., *Auton*, 2000, para. 89). However, the Act alone will not serve to underpin an action against government at the instance of individuals. That being the case, are there more promising remedies?

B. Administrative Law Grounds

Decisions about the overall shape of the publicly funded health care system – what types of services will be insured, in what settings they should be provided, and for patients in what circumstances – have generally been considered to be policy decisions properly made by government, at least at a macro-level, although they will be fleshed out and implemented by the many providers and institutions in the system. As such, these decisions have for the most part been beyond the supervisory power of the courts. It was on this basis that the applicants in *Re Metropolitan General Hospital and the Minister of Health,* who sought judicial review to compel the minister of health to remedy a claimed emergency situation at a Windsor hospital and reinstate twenty-five beds and the attendant funding for them, failed. Although the evidence established that the hospital failed to meet the ministry's target ratio of beds to population for its catchment area, the court held that, provided the minister was acting in accordance with his duties, departmental expenditures were within his discretion. The minister need not spend the money allocated to his department in any specific way, or indeed at all, and as between the minister and the applicant, no legal duty existed that would require any particular expenditure to be made. The court concluded, 'the wisdom of the decision can never be the subject of judicial review. It is a political and not a judicial problem' (*Re Metropolitan General Hospital*, 1979, 705).[16]

As noted above, the same reliance on the division between political and judicial spheres was evident in cases challenging decisions made by the Ontario Health Services Restructuring Commission. In the course of judicial review, the courts consistently described the scope of their power as highly circumscribed and indicated that the merits of the directions and orders that had been given were beyond their purview (*Pembroke Civic Hospital*, 1997, para. 4). The minister was authorized by various statutes to make decisions requiring hospitals to amalgamate or to cease operations and while he had arguably insulated himself from political accountability by delegating the decision making to an administrative body, he (and it) were also largely immune from question in a legal forum. Other than ensuring that the commission had acted within the broad confines of the law – that its members were not biased or controlled by government, and that it had not exceeded its jurisdiction, contravened constitutional rights, considered extraneous matters or acted in a way that was procedurally unfair – such decisions were not subject to supervision by the courts.[17]

Legislative functions, which can include ministerial decisions made on broad grounds of public policy, have generally been exempt from obligations of procedural fairness. However, as David Mullan notes, there 'is still considerable uncertainty over where the exception for broadly-based policy decisions actually engages' (Mullan 1996, 200, 202). This traditional insulation from scrutiny has been weakening in any event. The Supreme Court of Canada in *Baker v. Canada (Minister of Citizenship and Immigration)* applied the 'pragmatic and functional' approach familiar from procedural fairness cases to judicial review for abuse in the exercise of ministerial powers, expanding the obligation at least when individual rights and interests are at stake (*Baker*, 1999; Mullan, 1999).

Discretionary power is not unlimited. Decisions must be made within the bounds authorized, although both the choices made and determination of the scope of jurisdiction are treated with a significant degree of deference (*Baker*, 1999, para. 53). A body exercising delegated but nonetheless legislative power cannot discriminate among people unless authorized to do so by the empowering statute, and cannot in any event violate constitutional rights or human rights legislation (*Brown*, 1998).[18] The minister cannot misinterpret his or her duties so as to refuse to make payments that are due, nor can he or she use a statute designed for one purpose for another (*Re Doctors Hospital*, 1976). Further, the minister cannot exercise a statutory power on extraneous and irrelevant considerations (*Re Multi-Malls*, 1976; *Re Wittman*, 1990; *C.U.P.E. v. Ontario*, 2000).

On this point, it is instructive to compare the reasoning in *Toronto Birth Centre Inc. v. Ontario (Minister of Health)* and *Ottawa Carleton Dialysis Services v. Ontario (Minister of Health)*, two of the few cases to have considered the licensing process in the Independent Health Facilities Act. The Toronto Birth Centre, a community-based, non-profit organization, had been selected as a short-list bidder to enter into negotiations with the ministry to be licensed as an independent health facility. Following a change in government from the New Democrats to the Conservatives, the new minister decided, for political reasons, not to issue a licence. Although the decision constituted an exercise of a statutory power, the Divisional Court held that, because it involved ministerial discretion, the decision would only be impeachable if it clearly departed from the objects and purposes of the statute or if the minister had failed to comply with the statutorily prescribed conditions. The court accepted the minister's assertions that he had considered the statutory factors and ended the process on the grounds of fiscal responsibility, despite the applicant's contention that there was no factual basis for that conclusion. In contrast, in *Ottawa Carleton Dialysis Services*, the court rejected the minister's rationale for his decision not to issue a licence and directed the process to continue. This organization had similarly been selected to enter into negotiations with the ministry for issuance of a licence as an independent health facility; the minister had subsequently decided not to issue the licence. The reasons were again political, in this instance involving media reports and questions in the legislature about ongoing investigation of the American parent for fraud and the sale of defective products. The Divisional Court overturned the minister's rejection of the dialysis centre's bid, holding that, given the course of events, these were improper considerations and ought to have been addressed in negotiations surrounding the anticipated agreement. The court's conclusion was reinforced by the doctrine of legitimate expectations. While not creating substantive rights, when coupled with the government's choice of procedures, the doctrine augmented the duty of fairness owed the applicant (see also: *Baker*, 1999). The latter consideration had not contributed to the determination in *Toronto Birth Centre Inc.* at all, although the applicant, a non-profit community organization focused on reproductive health care, had reached the same stage in the licensing procedure, had also been led to expect negotiations with the ministry, and was under no cloud of suspicion.

Where the decision challenged is that of a tribunal rather than an exercise of ministerial discretion, additional grounds may be available and the scrutiny to which the decision is subject may be more intense (Cherniawsky 1996). Even advisory or investigatory bodies empowered solely to make recommendations can be subject to duties of procedural fairness. Aside from any appeal mechanisms set out in the legislation, on an application for judicial review a court may consider whether the tribunal acted outside its authority or on extraneous or irrelevant considerations, whether it misinterpreted its enabling legislation, and whether it was biased. In sum, it is to consider whether the duty of procedural fairness owed in the circumstances was met (*Stein v. Quebec,* 1999; *Re Isabey,* 1986).

Administrative law remedies can thus be used to challenge public bodies that restrict access to health care. The nature of the grounds that may be relied on and the intensity of judicial scrutiny vary considerably according to the decision, action, or omission as well as the nature of the decision maker. However, because of the nature of judicial review, the discretionary nature of many macro-level decisions in health care, and the difficulty of obtaining evidence of the considerations on which decisions were taken, the utility of such remedies is likely to be limited.

C. Canadian Charter of Rights and Freedoms and Human Rights Legislation

1. The Scope of the Charter

While the CHA may not provide a justiciable Health Charter for individual Canadians and the availability of administrative law grounds for challenge is likely to be quite narrow, the Charter and human rights legislation can be enforced at the instance of individuals.[19] Human rights legislation applies to both government and private actors. The Charter is more limited; hospitals are not directly subject to Charter scrutiny, as they are not considered part of 'government.' However, in *Eldridge v. B.C.(A.G.)* the Supreme Court of Canada held that where the state has provided for the delivery of a comprehensive social program through the vehicle of public hospitals, it remains responsible for defining the content of the services to be delivered. Decisions about health insurance are even more clearly subject to the Charter, since they are made pursuant to statute and subordinate legislation (*Eldridge*, 1997). Prior to *Eldridge*, the judicial characterization of hospitals as private institutions enabled government and hospitals faced with politically difficult or unacceptable choices either to avoid confronting or to excuse the consequences of decisions taken by administrators and hospital boards that limited women's access to a full range of reproductive health care, including abortion. That approach is no longer tenable. As Adams J. noted in *Ontario (A.G.) v. Dieleman*, 'medical care has constitutional implications' (*Dieleman*, 1994, 229). Where the Charter applies, decisions must comply with it.

Even a finding of a constitutionally protected right may not be enough to counteract policies that restrict access to abortion, however. Whether a facility provides abortions is the result of a complex mix of private and public decisions. Doctors and other health care workers, for instance, must be willing to perform the service: access to abortion decreases as the physical safety of physicians and other health care workers is increasingly threatened (*Pembroke Civic Hospital*, 1997).[20] In *Wellesley Central Hospital v. Ontario (H.S.R.C.)*, the court noted that because any Charter breach was only prospective, the applicants had failed to meet the higher threshold required – substantial evidence of anticipated violations. The better approach, it is suggested, is that taken by the Supreme Court of Canada in *R. v. Morgentaler*, 1993, where in rejecting provincial attempts to limit abortions to hospitals, it noted that women's free access to abortion is clearly vulnerable to 'administrative erosion' (*Morgentaler*, 1993, 514). The reality of the circumstances in which abortion is (or more often, is not) provided led the court to conclude it was not necessary to decide whether access had in fact been reduced by the province's actions. The likelihood was all too apparent. Relevant circumstances would now include not only administrative inertia or opposition but also violence, harassment of providers and patients, reduced physical facilities and capacity, and fee caps. Given the complex set of factors discouraging the provision of abortion, what is required in response is a web of public policies and initiatives to ensure safe, timely, and widespread access (see e.g., British Columbia's Abortion Services Statutes Amendment Act, 2001).

2. Interpreting Charter Rights

Eldridge not only extended the scope of the Charter to non-governmental institutions to which the government had delegated its decision-making authority regarding health care, it also established when equality rights had been violated. In *Eldridge*, the claimants, who were deaf, sought a declaration that the failure by hospitals and the provincial Medical Services Commission to provide sign language interpreters as insured benefits for deaf persons seeking medical services violated their equality rights under subsection 15(1) of the Charter.[21] The Supreme Court rejected the British Columbia Court of Appeal's suggestion that any inequality in ability to benefit from insured health services was the result of the applicants' pre-existing disability rather than the law, characterizing it as a 'thin and impoverished' view of equality. Instead, the court engaged in a contextual analysis to ground its conclusion that 'medical services' had to incorporate the ability to effectively access those services. That requirement must in turn include the ability to communicate, a precondition so fundamental in a world structured on the basis that everyone can hear that, as the court noted, the need would not even occur to most of us. It is simply taken for granted. Without effective access, people with hearing impairments are denied equal benefit of the law – here, laws requiring the provision of needed insured medical care without charge. Further, once the state provides a benefit, it must do so equally. In *Eldridge*, that meant special provisions to ensure that the disadvantaged group was able to benefit equally from government services and benefits. Any limitations on the obligation to accommodate would have to be justified by the government under section 1 of the Charter.

While the court has not yet addressed the full extent of positive obligations imposed by the Charter on government, a number of its decisions include promising developments. In *Eldridge* and other cases it has clearly affirmed that achieving a constitutionally sound result may require the state to take positive measures. Nor is legislative silence necessarily 'neutral'; the selective exclusion of protected classes from otherwise comprehensive coverage can result in impermissible underinclusiveness (*Vriend v. Alberta*, 1998). Further, the duty to accommodate in equality and human rights jurisprudence requires that rather than adopting a mainstream standard based on majority requirements and capabilities and then trying to accommodate the applicant to those norms, conceptions of equality must be built into standards (*B.C. Government and Services Employees Union v. B.C. (Public Service Employee Relations Commission)*, 1999; *B.C. (Superintendent of Motor Vehicles) v. B.C. (Human Rights Commission)*, 1999). Health services too, can be denied or not offered on prima facie discriminatory grounds – for instance, on the basis of judgments about an individual's 'inability to benefit' or services that are 'not medically required.' In some instances those conclusions will not withstand scrutiny, particularly in light of the court's recognition that 'handicap' and 'disability' must be understood in a multidimensional fashion that takes into account the socio-political dimensions of these terms rather than conceptualizing them simply as unmediated biological fact (*Quebec*, 2000, paras. 76–81). The focus in subsection 15(1) disability analysis is to be on the problematic response of the state to impairment or associated limitations, rather than on the impairment itself (*Granovsky*, 2000).

It must be acknowledged that arguments to the effect that the Charter imposes positive obligations on government have been more often rejected than accepted (see, e.g., *Thibaudeau*, 1995; *Ferrel*, 1998, leave to appeal denied, 6 December 1999, S.C.C.). Lower courts are particularly hesitant, as the Divisional Court noted in *Masse v. Ontario (Minister of Community and Social Services)*: 'The intractable economic, social and even philosophical problems presented by public programs are not the business of this court' (*Masse*, 1996). And absent a finding of discrimination contrary to the Charter or provincial human rights codes, it is unlikely that an exercise of discretion by a government official who is under no duty to implement a particular program or benefit package that is otherwise unexceptional on administrative law grounds would be disallowed (*R. v. S.S.*, 1990).[22]

The *Eldridge* decision did not add to the list of services insured; it involved unbundling already insured services such that the element of communication, which had always been included by implication, was made explicit and hence recognized as an essential part of the service. The decision was also made in a very specific context, involving persons with disabilities who could be accommodated in ways neither particularly costly nor resulting in the provision of radically different services. Some commentators have concluded that while the decision is important, it may too easily be confined to its own facts (Grant & Mosoff 1998; Young 1998). The court explicitly left open questions about the wider applicability of the decision to persons with disabilities in other situations where medical care is required to non-disabled persons unable effectively to access health services, or more generally.

Nonetheless, *Eldridge* is a positive, significant expansion of the scope of the state's constitutional responsibilities. Arguments for an expansive reading and application of the case are bolstered by the nature of health care in Canada. Publicly funded universal health insurance, while not without its faults, is highly and widely valued. As Adams J. noted in *Ontario (Attorney General) v. Dieleman*, health care in this country is a public resource, and medical services have constitutional implications (*Dieleman*, 1994, 229). A strong reading of government responsibilities vis-à-vis health care is strengthened by section 36 of the Constitution Act, which provides that the federal and provincial governments are committed to promoting equal opportunities for the well-being of Canadians and to providing essential public services of reasonable quality to all. Even if section 36 is understood more as an objective than a presently enforceable obligation, it should at the very least act as a compelling interpretative guide to the extent of government obligations under the Charter and in general (see Nader 1997, proposing a stronger reading of s. 36). For all these reasons, at the macro-level of decision making about the form and extent of health services, initiatives and omissions should be understood to constitute 'government action' and attract Charter scrutiny regardless of the setting. Health care is most certainly regarded by government and public alike as the business of government, at least where its overall form and the resources that will be devoted to it are concerned. That said, the very different nature of the decisions that may be at issue in health care makes singular answers about the import of the Charter an impossibility in the abstract.

Attracting Charter scrutiny is only the beginning. The fact of a breach and that the breach cannot be justified under section 1, must still be established. In *Cameron v. Nova Scotia (A.G.)*, for instance, while a majority of the Court of Appeal was prepared to regard infertility as a disability engaging section 15, Bateman J.A., who dissented on this point, was not. In any event, the majority held that, given the legislative objective of providing the best possible health care coverage in the context of limited financial resources, the decision not to insure this service was justified under section 1. The plaintiffs' loss makes it clear that the fact that decisions about access to publicly funded health care must comply with the Charter is not in and of itself sufficient to carry the day for those asserting a Charter breach when insurance coverage is denied or a treatment is not available.

3. Claiming the Benefit of the Charter

A claim that falls within one of the enumerated or analogous grounds under subsection 15(1) is likely to be among the strongest that can be advanced. Exclusion of same-sex partners from the spousal coverage provisions of a provincial health insurance plan has been held to violate section 15 (*Knodel*, 1991). Impermissible age-based distinctions among persons with disabilities used to determine entitlement to assistive devices contravened provincial human rights legislation and were not saved by the statutory provision protecting affirmative action programs (*Ontario Human Rights Commission*, 1994; see now *Lovelace*, 2000). As discussed above, denial of health insurance coverage for sign language interpreters required in connection with medical care was found to breach Charter equality rights on the grounds of disability (*Eldridge* 1997). Clearly, many conditions and illnesses could potentially constitute a disability within the meaning of subsection 15(1) or provincial human rights legislation, giving rise to a successful Charter claim or human rights complaint if associated with discriminatory treatment in the provision or availability of health services (Bickenbach 1994; *Auton*, 2000). However, there is little jurisprudence on the meaning of disability or discrimination in the context of health care and equality rights, or on how to assess justifications under section 1. Consequently, there is little certainty in predicting the approach courts will take (*Quebec v. Montreal*, 2000, alluding to a distinction between 'handicap' and 'personal characteristics' or 'normal' ailments; *Granovsky*, 2000, focusing analysis on inappropriate legislative or administrative responses). Boundaries on what can appropriately be considered health care rather than social services and limits on providers, although expansively treated in *Auton*, also remain largely unconsidered.

People who do not readily fall within one of the enumerated or analogous grounds under subsection 15(1) are likely to have considerable difficulty in relying on Charter rights to argue for greater access to health services. Lower courts have held that poverty is not an analogous ground under subsection 15(1) of the Charter and does not attract protection per se under section 7, as the Charter does not extend to what courts have characterized as economic rights (*Masse*, 1996). The Nova Scotia Court of Appeal recognized that provisions denying public housing tenants the security of tenure afforded tenants in the private sector constituted a breach of their equality rights on the basis of gender, race, and age (*Dartmouth*, 1993; see also *Federated Anti-Poverty*, 1991). Yet later cases have generally refused to recognize that government action targeted at or affecting poor people engages equality rights. When the Ontario government cut welfare benefits by more than 20 per cent, and when it repealed legislation that had ended agricultural workers' exclusion from the protections of labour relations legislation, the courts found no breach of section 15 (*Masse*, 1996, *Dunmore*, 1999, reversed on other grounds, 2001, SCC).[23] While those affected were poor and suffered social, political, and economic disadvantage and marginalization, they were characterized as a disparate and heterogeneous group. Since they were not united by the requisite personal traits, section 15 was not triggered. Women and other groups enumerated in subsection 15(1) are most severely affected by this harsh reality. Their social and economic situations are often the most fragile and precarious; disproportionate numbers live in poverty. It is again a thin and impoverished view of equality that cannot grasp that reality and take it into account in constitutional jurisprudence.

The discouraging results in cases challenging reductions in welfare and other programs make the attraction of categorizing the benefits or services at issue as health care all the more evident. Not only have litigants begun to establish a track record in Charter claims for health services, but the claims are for access to a system Canadians view as an entitlement for all, rather than for discretionary benefits of a type more easily subject to disparagement and distancing. When needed services affecting health have not been provided, the courts have been more receptive to claims that such denials should be redressed. This was evident in *Auton*, 2000 in which the British Columbia Supreme Court firmly identified the services sought (a demonstrably effective treatment program for autism in young children) as health care, regardless of whether the government had allocated responsibility to other ministries and regardless of provider. In the result, the government was ordered to ensure that effective treatment was made available; decisions about specific treatment, funding and access criteria were left to government to resolve (*Auton* 2000). The case does not examine the broader implications of courts adopting a medicalized view of both disability and required state responses, but it does make apparent the artificiality of the 'silo' model of funding.

Not all distinctions in the availability of insured health services will contravene section 15 of the Charter or human rights legislation, even when strongly associated with an enumerated or analogous ground. In *Brown v. B.C. (Minister of Health)*, the British Columbia Supreme Court held that the decision of the provincial government to include AZT in the provincial Pharmacare plan, which meant that individuals with AIDS (90 per cent of whom were homosexual or bisexual males) would have to pay a portion of the cost of the drug up to $2,000 per year, did not contravene section 7 or 15 of the Charter (*Brown*, 1990). The court was satisfied that it was acceptable to classify AZT in the same manner as drugs used to treat other catastrophic diseases for which co-payment was also required, rather than fully fund them in the same way as drugs for cancer treatments and organ transplants.[24] *Brown* makes starkly evident how difficult it is to balance multiple claims and interests in health care funding decisions that are constrained by limited financial resources. Whether addressed under section 15 or section 1, the issues raised seldom admit of self-evident answers.

Section 7 of the Charter (the right to life, liberty, and security of the person, and the right not to be deprived thereof except in accordance with the principles of fundamental justice), may also be available to found a Charter claim challenging lack of access to needed health care. In *R. v. Morgentaler*, the Supreme Court of Canada held that Criminal Code restrictions on access to abortion infringed women's section 7 rights and could not be justified under section 1 of the Charter (*Morgentaler*, 1988). Though its parameters, and in particular the question of the need for direct engagement of the justice system, have not been finally determined, it is clear that the section itself is not limited to the criminal law context (*Blencoe*, 2000, paras. 45, 46; *N.B. (Minister of Health and Community Services) v. G.C.J.*, 1999). In a number of cases and a variety of contexts since *Morgentaler*, individuals' physical and psychological integrity have been identified as important interests protected by section 7 from state-imposed harm (*R. v. Dyment*, 1988; *Canadian AIDS Society*, 1996; *R. v. Mills*, 1999; *N.B. v. G.C.J.*, 1999). Bodily integrity – mental and physical – as well as autonomy and liberty interests can be greatly affected by access to needed health services or the lack thereof. Both access and the extent of health care services available are matters for which government assumes a major share of responsibility. Some commentators have argued that Supreme Court jurisprudence on section 7 recognizes that the section includes 'certain minimal substantive requirements, the absence of which would be inherently incompatible with the *Charter*' (see, e.g., Sossin 1998, 169). The parameters of any such requirements vis-à-vis health services have yet to be mapped, but given the state's pervasive presence and power in so many areas of health care, there are strong arguments to be made that some forms of state action or inaction could breach section 7.[25]

Conclusion

While there are obstacles to scrutinizing decisions about the organization of the health care system under the Charter or human rights legislation, *Eldridge* has considerable potential to broaden the concept of 'benefit of the law' in subsection 15(1) of the Charter in ways that are significant to questions of access to health services, as well as enlarging the type of entities and activities that can be subject to the Charter. *Eld-*

ridge dispels the notion that decisions about publicly funded health care and access to health care services are purely local and private in nature or can be rendered such by the simple expedient of removing them to the private realm. Privatization without public scrutiny is no longer tenable. *Eldridge* is particularly significant in the face of the ongoing strategies of delegation and commodification, with government increasingly divesting itself of services and programs and transferring responsibility for formerly public resources to private sector providers. The case makes it clear that despite the form of the provider organization, to the extent such entities carry out specific government policies and are subject to significant government control in providing health care, they can still be subject to direct Charter scrutiny. Further, even where the Charter is not directly applicable, equitable access to needed health care without financial burden is deeply resonant with Charter values as well as being a touchstone of the Canadian health care system. The Charter should, therefore, influence decisions made in these contexts as well.

Canadians may not have a Health Charter per se, but by involving itself in the health care area so extensively both materially and discursively, the state has ensured that Charter rights will often be engaged when decisions are taken. Charter challenges, while they may be insufficient to repel privatization of the health care system provide an opportunity to publicly scrutinize decisions governments would prefer to make privately and without accountability. The Charter may, in other words, be used to fight the depoliticization of health care services. Moreover, litigation can serve as a rallying point for public opposition to a political process cast by governments as the inevitable outcome of economic and technical decisions. Feminist organizations have successfully used the Charter to mobilize opposition to government decisions and policies that detrimentally affect women (Hein 1999). If they have not always prevailed in their legal arguments, they have at least succeeded in keeping feminist ideals on the public agenda. And while Charter rights may not answer in every case, both Charter rights and values can serve as a strong force to support continued and renewed equity and access to health care in Canada.

Notes

I am grateful for the research assistance of Wendy Sutton, Faith Holder, Theodora Theodonis, Nadia Chandra, and Stephanie Edwards.

1 While the federal government did increase the amount allocated for health

care in its 1999 budget, estimates at that time were that it would be several years before funding would be restored even to 1995 levels (Morris et al., 1999). In its February 2000 budget, the federal government announced an additional one-time payment to the provinces of $2.5 billion for health care (McIlroy 2000a). In September 2000, the First Ministers signed a new health accord that was supported by an additional $23.4 billion in federal funding over the next five years (Canada, Intergovernmental Affairs 2000; McCarthy & Mackie 2000).

2 See generally, Appleton 1999 and Schwartz 1997.

3 Despite vehement opposition, Alberta recently passed legislation allowing significant expansion in the types of surgical services and other treatment that can be provided outside hospitals (and outside the publicly funded system) (Klein 1999, 52; Health Care Protection Act, 2000).

4 Between 1991 and 1996, hospital expenditures declined by 0.1 per cent annually to $25.9 billion in 1996, spending on physicians increased by 1.0 per cent annually to $10.7 billion in 1996, and spending on drugs increased by 5.9 per cent annually to $10.2 billion in 1996 (Federal, Provincial and Territorial Advisory Committee on Population Health 1999a, 140). Data on increases in expenditure on publicly funded home care is conflicting. However, it is clear that many people who need assistance to carry out the activities of daily living do not receive publicly funded care. Some individuals receive informal support; for others, the needs are simply not met (ibid. 1999a, 143–4; Aronson & Neysmith 1997).

5 *Cameron v. Nova Scotia (A.G.)* (1999), 177 D.L.R. (4th) 611 (N.S.C.A.), leave to appeal denied (29 June 2000), [1999] S.C.C.A. No. 531; *Auton (Guardian ad litem of) v. British Columbia (Minister of Health)*, [2000] 8 W.W.R. 227 (B.C.S.C.). See also *Morgentaler v. P.E.I. (Minister of Health and Social Services)*, 1995, and generally Canadian Medical Association 1994a, 11, n.31 and cases cited therein.

6 Although see *Lexogest*, 1993, per Helper J.A. at 37 and Scott C.J.M. (dissenting) at 21, both noting that Manitoba's health insurance legislation authorized the province to exclude coverage for medically necessary services (cited to Man. R.).

7 The 'Canadian operator' requirement, however, seems to have been easy to circumvent. In *Ottawa Carleton Dialysis Services*, 1996, an American for-profit provider simply set up a Canadian subsidiary in partnership with a Canadian physician and proposed to contract with the American parent for consulting advice on setting up and managing the Ontario dialysis facilities.

8 Just over one-third of abortions in Canada in 1997 were performed in clinics (Statistics Canada 2000b).

9 As of 29 April 1999, the duties of the commission changed to advising the

minister, and its power to issue directions under the Public Hospitals Act has been revoked (O. Reg. 272/99; O. Reg 273/99). See also the Ministry of Health and Long Term Care Statute Law Amendment Act, 1999.

10 However, the recent decision of the Divisional Court (affirmed by the Ontario Court of Appeal) rescinding the HSRC's Directions to the Hôpital Montfort to curtail its operations, on the ground that such severe restrictions on the activities of the only francophone teaching hospital in the province contravened constitutional rights, indicates that at least in limited instances, the commission is not entirely insulated from the political and legal fray (*Lalonde*, 2000).

11 Individual physicians report they can discuss reproductive health and sexual behaviour with patients, and that they continue to make referrals (Milne 2000a).

12 The Royal College of Obstetricians and Gynecologists in the United Kingdom identifies abortion as part of basic health care and strongly supports the concept that abortion services should be provided as an integral part of broader sexual health services (Royal College of Obstetricians and Gynecologists 2000). In Ontario, see *Russell v. Ontario (Health Services Restructuring Commission)*, 1998, in which the HSRC's Direction to the Roman Catholic Hôtel Dieu Hospital in Kingston to relinquish the operation and management of the programs and services of the hospital to the Kingston General Hospital was upheld. The court noted that historically, when Hôtel Dieu became a public hospital and accepted substantial public funding, it gave up certain rights of alienation. The religious order affected could still carry out its mission to minister to the poor elsewhere, even though not as a public hospital. The court added that '*freedom of religion cannot be taken to require state support of one's religion*' (*Russell*, 1998, paras. 29, 33) (emphasis added).

13 See contra O'Leary J. in *Collett*, 1995 (dissenting), who viewed the issue not as a politically charged inter-governmental dispute, but rather, as a determination of the effect of Ontario's failure to comply with its own Health Insurance Act, which similarly required that regulations could not be such as to disqualify the province for federal contributions under the CHA. The difficulty with the latter interpretation is that it assumes the outcome of the required intergovernmental consultation – that is, that the province was in breach of the CHA, and further, not entitled to full federal transfers. The court in *Waldman* did not address this issue, since it effectively read the Canada Health Act as a macro-level and not a micro-level requirement, at least vis-à-vis practitioners. See also *Rombaut v. N.B. (Minister of Health and Community Services)*, 2001 (provincial restrictions on billing numbers for new physicians did not breach their Charter rights).

14 The individual's challenge to the legality of provincial deductions from his social assistance payments made in order to recoup earlier overpayments failed. Conditions attached to the federal government's contributions to provinces under the Canada Assistance Plan still allowed provinces flexibility in meeting standards imposed, and thus had not been breached. Although provinces must comply with the general purpose of the statute, giving rise to an enforceable entitlement to benefits, entitlement had not been triggered in this case, *Finlay*, 1993, 1125–6 (per Sopinka J.); 1107 (per McLachlin J., dissenting). See also *Hughes v. Canada (A.G.)*, 1994.

15 The Royal Commission on Health Services in its 1964 *Report on Health Services* called on Canada to adopt a Health Charter for Canadians as a primary objective of national policy, aimed at 'The achievement of the highest possible health standards for all ...' (Royal Commission on Health Services 1964, 1: 10–15). It proposed a statement of rights and responsibilities for all sectors in the health care system, from governments to individuals. Both the legislation that resulted and the successor CHA, while incorporating a number of the elements proposed, had more modest goals: '... to protect, promote and restore the physical and mental well-being of residents of Canada and to facilitate reasonable access to health services without financial or other barriers' (s. 3, CHA).

16 A similar approach is evident in *Cameron v. Nova Scotia (A.G.)*, 1999, where the decision to allow the Health Services and Insurance Commission to lapse some years previously (it having, inter alia, considered appeals from decisions not to pay particular claims for health services), was held not to give rise to any rights or entitlement in the applicants, as no appellate procedure was required by law. It was simply a discretionary decision.

17 As to constitutional rights, see *Lalonde*, 2000; as to bias, see *Association of Optometrists (B.C.)*, 1996.

18 In the constitutional context, see *Irshad*, 2001.

19 See, e.g., the Ontario Human Rights Code, 1990.

20 Access likely became even more compromised in April 1998, when the agreement reached earlier between the government and the Ontario Medical Association imposing a soft cap on fees for physician services was extended to include performance of abortions (Ontario 1998a). Although not in the same order of magnitude as threats to personal safety and harassment at work and home, and while allowing exemptions, the cap provides one more disincentive to providing the service at all (Mackie 1998).

21 The legislation at issue neither prohibited nor required funding for sign language interpreters, but in exercising their discretion, neither the hospitals nor the Medical Services Commission had funded the service. A non-profit

agency had previously provided interpreters, but when it too was hit by government cutbacks, it could no longer do so. The applicants in this case had needed interpreters in connection with childbirth and ongoing medical care for diabetes and other conditions.

22 The provincial attorney general's exercise of discretion not to implement an alternative measures program under the Young Offenders Act was acceptable; geographic diversity is a positive attribute in Canada's federal system.

23 See also *Dunmore v. Ontario (A.G.)*, 1997; but see *S.E.I.U. Local 204 v. Ontario*, 1997.

24 The court was swayed by evidence of a distinction in treatment protocols at the time – those for cancer and organ transplants were complex and rapidly changing, while those for AZT were not.

25 Any such claim would, however, have to address the argument that was dispositive of the section 7 claim in *Brown v. B.C. (Minister of Health)*, 1999, that unlike *Morgentaler*, where the Criminal Code had directly affected women's security of the person, decisions to fund or not to fund particular health services (in that case AZT, a pharmaceutical product) affected economic interests and only indirectly impinged on section 7 rights. That argument has at least partially been answered by *Eldridge*, which required provincial funding for services. However, drawing the line where the measure challenged has an economic aspect but also affects life, liberty, or security of the person will remain difficult, whether the analysis is carried out under section 7 or with government bearing the onus under section 1.

7

Public Bodies, Private Parts: Genetics in a Post-Keynesian Era

ROXANNE MYKITIUK

Genetics is a branch of biology that deals with the heredity and variation of organisms and understands such variation to be located in one's genes.[1] It is aligned with the realm of the natural, the empirically verifiable, and the material essence of the individual organism. It is ahistorical and apolitical. Privatization, as understood in this project, refers to the process of state restructuring attendant on the economic and political forces set off by globalization, and stands on the opposite side of the nature/culture divide. Privatization is a politically inspired project, the creation of human design. However, there is a significant affinity between the new genetics and the recent projects of privatization and neo-liberalism.

I use the phrase 'new genetics' to refer both to a world-view that shapes understandings of human characteristics and approaches to health and disease and to the various technologies that now influence clinical and policy decisions related to reproductive and other health services. The new genetics is both a 'way of thinking' about human characteristics, health, disease, and normalcy, and a 'way of doing' – a technology employed to produce genetically based goods and services characterized primarily by the knowledge or information they reveal. Moreover, given their intimate link to understandings of heredity and relatedness, genes are inextricably linked with biological reproduction and the process of procreation.

The privatization project is largely political and economic, entailing a shift in state form from Keynesianism to neo-liberalism (Cohen 1997; P. Evans 1997; Leonard 1997) as well as a shift in governing practices (Brodie 1997; Rose 1996b). Its economic momentum is rooted in the beliefs that the Canadian state must reduce the fiscal burden of social welfare programs that have become too costly and that the state is an inefficient provider of services for its citizens. Services characterized as social or public goods and previously provided by the welfare state have thus been eliminated, scaled back, or transferred to the private realm. As Brodie suggests, in this process 'the very distinction between the public and the private is eroded. Public goods are privatized while the public sphere embraces as its governing logic market practices and rationales' (Brodie 1997, 239). At a discursive level, privatization is also about privacy, individual choice, and self-reliance. One of its core ideas is that the preferred mode of social arrangement is one that allows individuals to control their lives as they see fit without interference from others or from government. It is a view that distrusts collective solutions with respect either to economic arrangements or normative social relations. Within neo-liberalism the best form of regulation is self-governing; the governance of individual subjects promotes processes of self-regulation and provides the circumstances under which people may effectively govern themselves (Petersen 1999; Rose 1996b).

Genetic discourse and its associated medical practices and technologies have come to dominate health and medicine at a time when state support for health care and social services is decreasing and the privatization of health services is increasing (Gilmour this volume). This chapter explores the role played by the geneticization of health and medicine in the ongoing process of the dismantling and restructuring of the welfare state in Canada, together with the associated privatization of values and institutions in the age of globalization. It examines the recent Canadian Biotechnology Strategy, the federal government's proposed changes to health protection, and the lack of state regulation of the social and health effects of the new reproductive and genetic technologies. It shows how the changing discourse of health is integral to the state project of privatization and neo-liberalism: discursive shifts in the meaning of health are used to legitimate the interests of privatization in both the spheres of production and social reproduction. Using genetics as a focal point also demonstrates the range and shifting forms of governance deployed in order to carry out the privatization project. Law and state policy remain dominant forms of regulation in accordance with the aims of privatization. However, less direct and accountable forms of governance, such as professional regulation and self-governance, are also used, suggesting that the forces of privatization are not confined to state institutions but are more diffuse and pervasive.

This chapter is divided into four sections. Part I sets out the theoretical framework for my analysis of the new genetics in the context of privatization. In Part II, I examine changes in conceptions of health as the Keynesian welfare state gives way to neo-liberalism, demonstrating that health and health care are increasingly constituted as commodities with a corresponding decline in the notion of health as a social good. A new discourse of health has emerged where responsibility for the social risk of disease is transferred from the public state to the private individual and the management of this risk is viewed as a marker of individual responsibility. In the third part I examine three recent policy initiatives of the Canadian government: the Canadian Biotechnology Strategy, health protection, and new reproductive and genetic technologies. I suggest that the new genetics, as one form of knowledge in the information and knowledge-based economy, constitutes an integral part of the capital accumulation strategies of the state. Moreover, in the Canadian state's response to regulating the new genetics we see a shift in paradigms of legal regulation, from one in which the state assumes the role of protector of the public and social interest to forms of private ordering, including international trade and intellectual property law. In the final section of the chapter, the focus moves to procreation as a central aspect of the process of social reproduction. Here, the individualist discourse of neoliberalism can be contrasted with the eugenic discourses of the mid-twentieth century. By allocating the risk of disease on the basis of genetic predisposition, the new genetic discourses discipline the body through the process of biological reproduction, with women acting as the principal gatekeepers of social cost. Thus, genetic discourse informs and constructs a new gendered subject/citizen of the post-Keynesian order.

I. Social Reproduction and Biological Reproduction

Configurations of the relationship among the state, the market, and the family are historically specific and associated with particular technologies of production. The demise of the Keynesian welfare state was occasioned by a prolonged economic crisis and the collapse of public finances; both crisis and collapse are generally attributed to the rise of 'globalization,' the integration of production processes by transnational corporations that has effectively destroyed the national market as an economic space, and with it, the power of the nation state to manage the national economy. The advance of globalization has shifted responsibilities previously consigned to the state and the market to the family, as well as restructuring state institutuions to favour the market and private investment. Thus, globalization and privatization in the neo-liberal era have been contingent on new and different industrial structures and technological processes: investment in high technology has been promoted in order to offset job losses in old industrial sectors. And in recent years the most prominent areas of high technology have been information technology and biotechnology. Not only are these technologies transforming the class structure of industrial societies, they are transforming the meaning of property through developments to intellectual property rights that grant new forms of ownership over biological entities and processes. By changing the relationships involved in biological reproduction, the very meanings and definitions of family and kinship relations are being contested.

Overlooked by the state in its single-minded quest for global competitiveness in the sphere of production is the fact that genetic technologies are as much or more about reproduction as about production. Biological reproduction has often been regarded as an immutable fact of nature (Franklin 1995, 333), albeit controllable through technological developments including abortion and contraception. Feminists have hesitated to address the subject, in part because biological explanations were used to subordinate women's roles and to legitimate the gendered division of labour. They are understandably reluctant to essentialize women by focusing on the reproductive role of motherhood. Feminist political economy has instead followed the insights of Engels to illustrate the hidden and undervalued contributions of women's role in social reproduction within capitalist modes of production. Social reproduction, or the creation of human life, as defined by Ursel, involves three processes: *procreation, socialization* and *daily maintenance and care giving* (Ursel 1992, 5).

By emphasizing women's roles in social reproduction, as opposed to strictly biological reproduction (or procreation), feminists have called attention to the social implications of gender and of unpaid female labour. Nevertheless, gender roles have been closely tied to cultural understanding and definitions of roles in biological reproduction. Therefore, any redefinition of biological reproduction through the introduction and utilization of new genetic and reproductive technologies is bound to have an impact on cultural understandings of reproduction and consequently on gender.

The role of biological technologies may be seen as both symptomatic and as an important constitutive factor in the transformation of the state in the post-Keynesian era (Loeppky 1999). Examination of the legal issues that surround the introduction of the new genetic and reproductive technologies provides access to the forces driving contemporary social and economic changes as well as 'fleshing out' the shape of the new social relations emerging in their wake. Gender not only affects the ways in which these new technologies are being applied and adopted, it is also reshaped as a result of the biological entities created and the legal definitions that accompany them. In sum, it is literally correct to speak of the new post-Keynesian state as being inscribed on our bodies. Perhaps never before have the 'body politic' and the biological body been so dramatically reshaped by the same social forces.

The new biological and reproductive technologies have promoted the commodification of reproductive arrangements via surrogacy contracts and the sale of gametes, ova, and sperm. It is not far-fetched to say that the introduction of these new technologies is driven by commercial interest and the redefinition of childbearing as a consumer good (Basen 1994). Thus, reproduction becomes 'a site for capital investment and profit through the proliferation of commodified reproductive services and goods' (Singer 1993, 87). In this context, biological reproduction is being removed from the private realm, and human reproduction is becoming increasingly public. The emergence of reproduction as a public process is at the same time shaping and being shaped by novel forms of property arrangements, 'privatizing' to the market various elements and functions of human biological reproduction. I have looked at the role of law in the fragmentation of reproductive and biological processes elsewhere (Mykitiuk 1994); here, I examine the political and economic forces that play a significant role in the reconstitution of legal norms. Whereas the new reproductive technologies disassemble and reassemble the procreative processes in ways that facilitate the commodification of the reproductive process, the new genetic technologies, by linking specific reproductive outcomes to specific genetic traits that can now be revealed though genetic tests, make possible the appropriation of traits. What was formerly opaque and immune to human intervention can now be revealed and manipulated so that an element of choice can – at a price – be introduced with respect not only to bearing offspring but to which *kinds* of offspring to bear.

II. The Discourse of Health in an Era of Privatization

Discourses on health are never just about health. Specific discourses emerge at particular historical moments and gain acceptance primarily because they are more or less congruent with the prevailing economic, political, and social order (Robertson 2000). Moreover, discourses about health function as repositories of ideas and beliefs – they are profoundly normative and not merely descriptive of the current state of scientific fact.

Canada's universal health insurance program developed under the Keynesian welfare state regime during the post–Second World War era. The introduction of National Health Grants in the 1940s, the Hospital Insurance Schemes in the 1950s, and Medicaid in the 1960s all contributed to the construction of health and health care as a basic social good, to be distributed equally on the basis of need without regard to ability to pay. Under the welfare state, state planning and state funding meant that medical services were accessible and less expensive than if they had been privately organized. Private actors, however, were not denied the opportunity to profit through the health sector.

The decline of the welfare state and the rise of privatization and neoliberal ideology have redefined health and called into question the provision of health care as a right of citizenship. In the post–welfare state era, health is increasingly conceptualized as an individual responsibility and health care as a commodity. This transformation in the nature of health and health care is produced via a shift in the concept of health embedded and implicit in the new genetics and a shift in public policy with respect to the meaning of health and the location of responsibility for the provision of health-related goods and services in the restructured state.

A. The Changing Concept of Health

The anthropologist Margaret Lock reminds us that the idea of health is not self-evident; its meaning has changed over time and social, cultural, and political factors are inevitably implicated in how it is conceptualized (Lock 1998, 48). According to the dominant concept in North America, health is an individual biological state or condition characterized primarily by the absence of disease (Lock 1998, 48). Illness, for its part, is equated with a recognizable pathology that can be detected, measured, and managed through the application of various technologies to individual bodies. As a consequence, a biomedical concept of health emerges in which responsibility and agency for health is located with individuals, who are made responsible for safeguarding, monitoring, and regulating their own physical conditions.

Identifying health with factors that lie within individual bodies obscures the fact of external determinants of health. Physical, social, and economic factors – the presence of environmental and workplace toxins, income and social status, levels of education, and social support networks – have been proven to affect individual and population health status. However, these social determinants are increasingly viewed as less significant than genes and detectable changes in the material body as indicators of health.

The privileging of a biomedical concept of health carries with it certain political implications (Lippman 1998, 69). It empowers specific people and institutions with the ability to define health and manage health care and simultaneously excludes others. Concomitant with government cutbacks in health care funding has been the promotion of 'healthism,' which emphasizes individual health practices and consists primarily of exhorting individuals to change their behaviour and manage their own health. Initially, this change was touted as a shift towards 'health promotion' and 'disease prevention.' An emphasis on individual responsibility for health, corresponding as it does with a reduction of state expenditures on health care and other social policies, protects those institutions that – 'perversely – threaten individual health through discrimination, exploitation, pollution and iatrogenisis' (inadvertent physician-induced illness) (Lippman 1998, 72). 'Victim' or patient treatment, in this instance, takes precedence over workplace or institutional 'treatment' or cleanup (Lippman 1998, 72). 'Healthism' bears a certain affinity to other state policies characterized by a decrease in government spending for social welfare and a rise in strategies that lead to increased profits for the biomedical and pharmaceutical industries (Lock 1998, 49).

The rhetoric of 'individual empowerment' found in the area of health and health care over the past two decades encompasses stronger protection of informed consent and a social rejection of health care paternalism at one end of the spectrum, while at the other end lies an explosion of popular interest in healthy lifestyle choices, diet, exercise, and alternative therapies. Behind the rhetoric of individual empowerment, however, lurks the shadow of individualized responsibility for health and an unwillingness to acknowledge the social causes of illness.

Individual empowerment is manifested, in part, through the ability to make personal choices concerning health and well-being. When individuals, rather than health professionals, shoulder the responsibilities for personal health maintenance and the prevention of illness, the principle of informed consent has been invoked to allow patients to accept, decline, or withdraw from particular treatment or preventative options. Choice, with respect to the provision of health, has been fashioned as an integral aspect of women's individual autonomy. Championed by feminists, choice provides a means to escape the paternalism that has characterized women's health care provision under medical models of care and encompasses the notion that every individual has the right to determine what is done to his or her body.

Choice, however, as part of an emergent discourse of health within the neo-liberal political regime, has been effectively appropriated by politicians and industry in order to accomplish the goals of privatization. 'Choice' is utilized as representative of the array of options available to the individual through the procurement of biomedical goods and services (Lippman 2000, 1). Lippman insists that 'this market-driven approach to health care co-opts and manipulates concepts of choice to rationalize industry-driven health care' (Lippman 2000, 1). In the neo-liberal era, government agendas are focused on budget reduction and the development of profitable global industry. Industry is encouraged to develop, market, and sell new pharmaceuticals, health-related technologies, and services which are then presented as additional health care 'choices' available to the individual. Constructing choice in this manner leads to an obvious shift in the balance of relations among the state, the individual, and the market – one in which health care choices are increasingly relegated to, and regulated by, the market – encouraging the individual or patient to take on the role of consumer. Under neo-liberalism, autonomy, understood as greater patient choice, is perceived to encompass the right of access to health-related goods and services. The existence of a wide array of preventative and treatment options feeds into this perception as those options become desired, whether provided by the state or through the market (Caulfield & Feasby 1998, 384). Choice, constructed in this manner, coupled with notions of individual responsibility for health, serves to privatize need and to reframe it as want.

While the commercialization and further privatization of health care presents favourable financial incentives for private sector industry, it also presents particular risks for women. Women's demands for heightened choice have been translated into one of the most profitable areas of private sector health-related expansion. As women are the predominant managers of health within the domestic sphere, they are primarily responsible for the access to and use of health-related goods and services, and are therefore increasingly targeted as consumers. Commercially influenced notions of autonomy, individual responsibility for health, and the extent to which choice is created and constrained by the state will result in further inequalities for women. The market approach 'reinforces libertarian self-reliance without promoting true self-determination and choice' (Lippman 2000, 2). It is thus essential that we be scrupulous about the way in which 'choice' is deployed within the context of health, as it is not necessarily consistent with the *type* of choice advocated by feminists. As Sherwin cautions, 'it is a mistake ... to believe that expressions of choice always represent expressions of autonomy' (Sherwin 1998b, 6).

B. Shifting Priorities in Public Policy

The Lalonde Report of 1974 drew attention for the first time to the role of social determinants of health (Lalonde 1974). In 1981, the World Health Organization (WHO) incorporated these notions into its position that 'health related issues should not fall primarily into the medical domain; that limited resources for health care should be better distributed, and that the individual is not necessarily the unit around which the concept of health should be organized' (Lock 1998, 49). Although these principles were adopted by the Canadian government in 1986, in the Ottawa *Charter on Health Promotion,* increasingly they are *not* being used to direct governmental activities with respect to health in Canada (Lippman 1998, 75). In the same year, under the Progressive Conservative government, the Epp report identified the following as major challenges to health policy: a reduction of inequalities in health and health care; an increase in the prevention effort; and the enhancement of people's capacity to cope with chronic conditions, disabilities, and mental health problems (Epp 1986). This recognition of non-medical determinants of health went far in acknowledging that Canadian health policy had in the past emphasized the role of medical, curative, and acute-care hospital-based approaches to health at the expense of non-medical, preventative, and community-based approaches. Widely hailed as progressive and forward looking both nationally and internationally, the Epp report reflected a shift away from a narrow focus on medicine towards a broader focus on health. This shift was indicated by the reference in the 1984 Canada Health Act to 'health practitioners,' opening the door to billing under medicare by health professionals other than medical doctors. One side effect of the focus on non-medical determinants of health, however, was an increased emphasis on the responsibility of the individual to look after his or her health.

When health policy shifted its focus away from medicine, it turned towards an emphasis on self-care and lifestyle as primary determinants of health. The Epp report, for example, identified three mechanisms as intrinsic to health promotion: *self-care*, which 'refers to the decisions taken and practices adopted by an individual specifically for the preservation of his or her health'; *mutual aid*, which refers to the support of people working together to deal with health issues; and *healthy environments* (Epp 1986, 401). While the creation of healthy environments was recognized as the most complex and difficult of the three mechanisms, it received very little attention in the report. Factors within the individual's sphere of control were emphasized at the expense of environmental factors requiring societal or state intervention. In short, a process which began as a renewed examination of the societal determinants of health was subtly transformed into one that pinpointed individual responsibility for health.

As health promotion policy began to encourage people to lead healthy lives though exercise, nutrition, and the avoidance of risky habits, those who persisted in following perceived 'unhealthy' lifestyles became the focus of social disapproval (Lippman 1998, 72). For example, arising from the Epp report, the government created initiatives to 'encourage moderation in drinking, promote breast feeding, discourage smoking, and to assist voluntary groups committed to undertaking health promotion activities' (Townson 1999, 2). Under such policies, moral choice is eventually substituted for societal and environmental factors and systemic explanations for unhealthy practices are lost. Not only are socio-economic influences on a person's habits downplayed, but the relationship between poverty and ill health is also obscured. Health status becomes associated with personal preference. Moreover, as Pat Armstrong points out, an emphasis on the role of non-medical determinants of health is held out as a rationale for cutting hospital funding at the same time that the funding of social determinants of health, such as housing, are cut (Armstrong & Armstrong 1996, 66; Townson 1999, 40–3). Policy that once focused on 'population health,' an approach that addresses the entire range of factors that determine health now focuses on 'health promotion,' a process for enabling people to take control over, and improve their health (Townson 1999, 5).

From this perspective, if we want to improve public health by taking action against those social determinants that have a negative impact on health, we instruct individuals how to live so as to maximize their health outcome. If individuals refuse to act on that instruction, their bad health becomes their fault. One of the ideological effects of health promotion has thus been to persuade the citizen that he or she has a responsibility to minimize behaviour that might have a negative impact on his or her health and increase the cost to the public purse. Once people believe that they are personally responsible for their health status they are less likely to identify poverty as a primary determinant of ill health, even though statistics support that link (Lock 1998, 56; Townson 1999, 55–63, 98–9).

As publicly funded health care was reduced and the range and scale of services provided by the state cut back, there was a move to make conditions of access to services more rigorous, to promote private health insurance and the provision of private medical services. At the same time, new regimes and routines of the body came into play, founded on the assumption that subjects of risk would opt to participate in a self-imposed program of health and fitness. Voluntary participation in risk management has since become an essential precondition of responsible selfhood (Petersen 1999, 123).

Since the 1980s, government policy has increasingly come to regard health as a commodity. While health had been commodified, to some extent, under the post-war health care system through the adoption of such measures as fee for service arrangements, we are now witnessing the expansion of the market within the state rather than alongside it; health is actually becoming explicitly regulated as a commodity. The commodification of health used to be implicit: health was regulated as a commodity through the effects of capitalism on state administration. Contemporary health policy at both the federal and provincial levels, however, is characterized by explicit adherence to market mechanisms as the means by which government policy ought to be achieved. As Pat Armstrong argues, Canadians now live under a regime that has collapsed the distinct governmental functions of accumulation and legitimation into each other so that accumulation has become the sole legitimate goal of government (Armstrong & Armstrong 1996).

In the health sector, privatization is effected through such measures as the adoption of private sector techniques, the transfer of responsibility for payment from the collective to individuals, the shift to for-profit provision, and the move to transfer care from public facilities to the private household (Armstrong et al. 1997; Gilmour this volume). These moves are justified by the government as means to save the social safety net. Left critiques of the health care system have been appropriated by the government in the task of persuading the people that the public good is being served by the privatization agenda (Armstrong et al. 1997).

While the cultural construction of health as a public good is still very much with us, the socio-economic conditions that gave rise to that construction are changing. The notion of 'public good' is being redefined as market mechanisms are promoted as the appropriate means to achieve that good. Determinants of health, such as secure employment and secure income, are increasingly being used as an argument for cost reduction (Armstrong & Armstrong 1996, 17). Various government reports that outline the determinants of health explicitly call for cost reductions in health care (ibid.). Yet health care costs are no greater now than they were forty years ago (Armstrong 1997, 10). Federal spending on health care has actually decreased over the last twenty years (Armstrong 1997). The decline in economic growth, however, has meant that a greater portion of the gross domestic product is taken up with health care costs. In spite of the priority placed upon cost reduction by the state, 'cutbacks are bound to increase inequality in access and thus contribute to reducing the possibilities for health' (Armstrong & Armstrong 1996, 17).

C. Individualizing Health Risks and the Impact of Genetic Technologies

The fairly recent proliferation of human genetic research and medicine, sustained in large part by the publicly and privately financed International Human Genome Project, is consistent with, and indeed further entrenches, a concept of health that is located in individual bodies and that encourages individual responsibility for health and health improvement. Lippman has coined the term 'geneticization' to capture the growing tendency to distinguish people on the basis of genetics and to define most disorders, behaviours, and variations as wholly or in part, genetic in origin (Lippman 1998, 68–70). Geneticization is both an emerging ideology and a set of practices, and it has enormous potential to divert attention from structural changes necessary to improve health by reinforcing individual responsibility for the maintenance, and indeed the improvement, of health (Lippman 1998, 68). It is likely to present a formidable challenge to maintaining health issues as collective and political rather than individual and medical (Lippman 1998, 69). At the same time, the development of the new genetics is tightly linked to financial markets and the interests of private biotechnology companies, and it becomes part of a structural change in which health care is increasingly regulated as a business.

   Currently, genetic medicine is carried out primarily through genetic testing and screening involving prenatal, neonatal, and presymptomatic testing. Genetic testing is used to identify genetic susceptibility to a disease – it is a predictive model and in many cases one method of identifying increased risk to a particular condition. In certain cases, such as some breast cancers, this susceptibility indicates a higher risk of developing the disease. In others, it indicates a certainty that the disease will develop; however, genetic testing cannot predict the severity of the manifestation of disease, nor in the case of diseases of late onset, such as Huntingtons, when the disease will manifest itself (Lippman 1998, 69). At present, there is no way of 'fixing' or treating most genetic mutations.

The alleged predictive ability of genetic testing is problematic because it takes for granted that awareness of personal risk status is important to the individual, and that that awareness will encourage behavioural changes to prevent the future development of the predicted condition. Framing genetic testing as educating individuals about their health risks – when cost containment is a primary criterion for governments in considering health policies and practices – is especially problematic. Individuals with a genetic susceptibility to a disease have their physiology opened up to professional observation and are possibly subjected to medical intervention prior to the actual onset of ill health. They may be subject to increased regulation on the basis of this difference and their increased dependence on the public purse. Not only does geneticization turn some healthy individuals into patients, it creates the possibility that they will become bad patients if they do not follow advice about managing their health and taking 'genetic responsibility' (Lippman 1998, 72).

Genetic technologies constitute a significant departure from conventional medical technologies in that they do not, for the most part, treat an existing condition or diagnose a disease in progress. As such, they challenge an already burdened health care system and symbolize the pressures which new technology places on the universal and comprehensive aspects of the publicly funded system. The advent of genetic technologies, whether we like it or not, is changing our definition of health and disease. Increasing awareness of the fiscal pressures on the public health care system makes those who have experienced delays and cutbacks in receiving health services become more conscious and possibly more critical of those who can be perceived to be abusing the health care system (Lippman 1998, 72). In this context it is important to question the results of individualizing health care risks through the application of genetic testing. Might this information be used to ration publicly funded health care and contain costs? (Clarke 1990). Alternately, in a climate where individuals are asked to assume more individual responsibility, will genetic testing be viewed as an aspect of preventive health care?

Under the former welfare state regime, the cost of providing health care to individuals in need was largely borne by society. However, when the individual is required to 'manage' and 'minimize' risks to health on an increasingly personal basis, the social nature of both costs and risk disintegrate. Because genetic risk is located in individual bodies, it deflects attention from the social risks and determinants of health, apportioning responsibility for that risk, and its associated costs, with the individual. Since women's bodies are the predominant site of prenatal genetic testing and screening, the process of biological production will likely render women the principal gatekeepers of 'social' cost.

The commercial providers of private genetic tests will naturally exaggerate the risks of genetic factors in order to expand their market (Harper 1995; Kirk 1997). These claims are likely to reshape the public's conception of what is necessary as part of heath care and they will expand the share of health care dollars spent privately. Without a concerted policy decision, we may quickly face a bifurcated health care system. Moreover, once genetic information becomes more widely available, would it not be reasonable to expect that public policy decisions concerning health care will be made on the basis of known genetic risk factors? In other words, we may as a matter of public policy refuse to routinely fund genetic tests. However, we cannot pretend that genetic information does not exist, as the very availability of such information has profound policy consequences.

As patients are exhorted to take greater responsibility for their own health, they are demanding more information on which to base their decisions. In a publicly funded health care system, they will insist that the government fund the tests on which to base these decisions.[2] Ironically, the more responsibility is placed on individuals to look after their own health status, the more politicized the question of the provision of health care services becomes, and the less deferential individuals will be towards health providers and government officials. Whether genetic technologies are utilized in our publicly funded health care system or not, they are likely to become an example of the 'creeping privatization' of our health care system.

III. The Political Economy of New Technology

A. Biotechnology and Genetics in the 'Knowledge-Based Economy'

One key response to globalization in advanced economies has been to promote investment in high technology in order to offset job losses in old industrial sectors. The development of a Canadian biotechnology is a key component of a strategy aimed at reaping the benefits of a 'knowledge-based economy.' The Organization for Economic Cooperation and Development (OECD) defines knowledge in the knowledge-based economy as 'the acquisition of intellectual property through learning or research' (OECD 1989). The appropriation of research as intellectual property is integral to the knowledge-based economy in general and to an industrial strategy focused on biotechnology in particular.

Knowledge-based capital accumulation, defined broadly, entails not only research and development but also design, advertising, marketing, and management (Marshall 1999, 117). A prime example is the pharmaceutical industry, in which the costs of the applied knowledge and information required for maximum productivity greatly outweigh the manufacturing costs of pharmaceutical goods. This industry is currently transforming its chemical base into a biotechnology-driven foundation. Technology, in this sense, acts as an 'engine of transition,' facilitating the transformation of the capitalist state (Marshall 1999, 116).

Biotechnology – 'the application of scientific, and engineering principles to the processing of materials by biological agents to provide goods and services' (OECD 1989) – advances the notion of an information age to new levels. The information captured and developed in the context of biotechnology is the genetic information contained within all living things. Given the ability of this information to provide insight into the complex workings of living organisms, biotechnology has widespread and potentially revolutionary importance with respect to the creation of new processes, systems of knowledge, and products in the medical, scientific, and industrial sectors. Biotechnology therefore, not only promises revolutionary implications in the context of science and medicine, it will enable Canada to achieve competitiveness in the globalized, international economy.

The growth of biotechnology within the high technology sector has involved the creation of new forms of intellectual property and new forms of ownership in biological entities and processes. This has been justified as allowing those who have invested in research, development, and creation to recoup their investment. Efforts to promote investment in biotechnology have been stimulated by the emergence of the health sector as a source of corporate profit making. Given that the health sector is a potential source of private profit and at the same time forms a major part of the state budget, biotechnology occupies a critical position in the transformation of the role of the state. Even in Canada, where health care is still regarded as a public good, patients are increasingly encouraged to view themselves as consumers and health is increasingly seen as a commodity in the marketplace.

Analysis of Canadian government policies with respect to biotechnology, health, and new reproductive and genetic technologies demonstrates that efforts to promote biotechnology as a sector of production underemphasize its potential and actual impacts on social (including biological) reproduction. State promotion of the productive aspect of new genetic technology has taken precedence over the regulation of such impact.

Government policies on biotechnology have undergone a dramatic shift and pharmaceuticals, in particular, have received specific government attention in Canada. An alteration of the objectives behind patent protection can be detected, from providing pharmaceutical drugs to Canadians on an accessible, affordable basis, to encouraging technical innovation, competition, and the growth of domestic industry.

Early patent protection in Canada was extended only to the process by which a product was made, not to the chemical product itself. High drug prices, a result of the nature of Canadian patent law, were perceived by a series of federal commissions from the late 1950s to the mid-1960s to inhibit competition (Marshall 1999, 125). Rather than choosing to implement policies such as limiting selling costs, prices, or profits, the Canadian government decided to alter the conditions of competition at the manufacturers' level. Thus, increased competition was promoted 'by easing the conditions under which new competitors entered the market for finished pharmaceutical products' (Marshall 1999, 126). Canada's policies took the form of compulsory licensing of imported prescription drugs. Proprietary drug companies voiced strong opposition, on the grounds that such licensing affected their ability to recoup investments and that drug companies would be reluctant to invest in research, development, and manufacturing in Canada (Marshall 1999, 127). These companies are predominantly foreign-owned and mostly American (Marshall 1999, 129). The effects of compulsory licensing were controversial: while Canadian companies documented large savings on pharmaceutical costs, foreign investment in Canada remained low. By the late 1970s and early 1980s, low levels of investment in biotechnology in Canada led to the incorporation of research and development as the primary objectives relative to the pharmaceutical sector. Growth was to be stimulated by changes to intellectual property incentives.

Policy choices at the nation-state level, however, are effectively restricted by international trade agreements. As will be demonstrated in the following analysis, the policies adopted by the Canadian state respecting biotechnology and the NRGTs have imposed and ensured neo-liberal reform. Fractions of capital, such as the pharmaceutical and biotechnology industries, have aligned themselves so as to enable reorganization of the state's infrastructure to accommodate the changing international economic regime (Marshall 1999, 146, n. 57). In so doing, they have also maintained their policy dominance. Within government, decision-making centres have been placed within 'opaque' sites (Marshall 1999, 146). In other words, 'internationalization changed the nature of nation-states policies and functions, by intensifying the pressure to remove key regulatory functions from popular scrutiny' (Marshall 1999, 146, n. 57).

The Canadian government codified its intentions to become an international biotechnological player with the passage of Bill C-91, the Patent Act Amendment Act 1992. The bill was intended to bring Canadian patent law into line with international standards.[3] Formerly, Canadian law only permitted the issuing of patents on unicellular biological materials (Marshall 1999, 133), whereas the United States granted patents on plants and animals – higher life forms. In addition, the bill eliminated outright compulsory licensing and extended patent protection to twenty years (ibid.). Buttressed by the presence and acceptance of a public discourse of globalization, the political environment surrounding the legislation was accepting. As a means to increase the private appropriation of intellectual property resulting from research and development, such reform was intended to be 'the key to the creation of a competitive and dynamic regime of private accumulation' (ibid., 135). Within an 'innovative' economy, intellectual property rights are essential to the maintenance of the commodity status of knowledge as well as the provision of a continued incentive for private capital investment (ibid., 142).

B. The Canadian Biotechnology Strategy

The Canadian Biotechnology Strategy (CBS), created in 1998, is the most recent version of the twenty-year-old federal policy concerning biotechnology (Canada 1998e, 1–5; National Biotechnology Advisory Committee 1998, 12). The main purpose of the CBS is to define the role of the federal government in managing the biotechnology industry and the development and use of biotechnology in Canada. Building on recent developments in molecular genetics and the international human genome project, the CBS is intended to facilitate new industry regarded as having national and global significance (Canada 1998e, 8). The strategy seeks to situate Canada as a world leader in biotechnology by harnessing molecular genetics, other biological technologies, and social technologies such as intellectual property protection to attain market advantage. The process of renewing Canada's national biotechnology strategy is being carried out by the Biotechnology Ministerial Coordinating Committee (BMCC), under the leadership of Industry Canada, in collaboration with seven federal departments (Health, Agriculture, Natural Resources, Environment, Fisheries and Oceans, Foreign Affairs, and International Trade and Human Resources Development).

Biotechnology is defined as 'an umbrella term that covers a broad spectrum of scientific tools. Biotechnology uses living organisms, or parts of living organisms, to make new products or provide new methods of production' (Canada 1998c, 1). This broad description covers all organisms and their parts and products, whether developed traditionally or through the newer molecular techniques such as genetic engineering (Canada 1998c, 1). Specifically, the biotechnology strategy focuses upon the development of new innovations and products in sectors as diverse as agriculture, health care, aquaculture, forestry, mining, energy, and environmental services (Canada 1998e, 4). Public opinion as to the desirability of biotechnological goods varies in relation to different processes, uses, and countries. For example, there has been widespread public scepticism of the merits of agricultural technology, in particular, in relation to genetically modified foods and the alteration of seed crops that would require farmers to purchase seeds on a yearly basis (Abergel 1999). This led to mandatory labelling in many jurisdictions.[4] At the same time, there is public acceptance and excitement in Canada about the potential health benefits of genetics for human beings including, for example, the development of processes that allow better tracking of pathogens through rapid tracking and detection of DNA sequences (Canadian Biotechnology Strategy Task Force 1998b, 3; Johnston 2000).

Aside from stressing its economic benefits, the government is promoting biotechnology to a sceptical publicly by emphasizing the anticipated *health benefits* (Canada 1998a, 1). The policy literature emphasizes that 90 per cent of the current uses of biotechnology worldwide are related to human health, and it is projected that health will continue to be an important part of the biotechnology strategy and framework (Canadian Biotechnology Strategy Task Force 1998b, 1). Thus, the CBS is promoted as a strategy that will help to develop the tools to improve the health and well-being of Canadians through 'improved disease surveillance, diagnosis, treatment and prevention' (Canadian Biotechnology Strategy Task Force 1998b, 3).

The CBS mandates the creation of an expert, arm's-length committee to advise the BMCC on biotechnology issues, raise public awareness, and engage Canadians in discussions regarding biotechnology (Canada 1998e, 7). The Canadian Biotechnology Advisory Committee (CBAC) is to advise the government, independently and impartially, on crucial policy issues associated with the ethical, social, regulatory, economic, scientific, environmental, and health aspects of biotechnology (Canada 1998e, 8, emphasis added). The addition of the CBAC to the strategy was effected in order to ensure increased public participation. The CBAC is presently composed of senior executives from the industry and finance communities, representatives from consumer interest groups, and academics. Within its first workplan, CBAC has made public its intention to undertake five special projects: the regulation of genetically modified foods; the protection and exploitation of biotechnological intellectual property (including the patenting of higher life forms); the incorporation of social and ethical concerns into biotechnology; the use of novel genetically based interventions; and genetic privacy (Canadian Biotechnology Advisory Committee, 2000c). Each project will be evaluated using the following thematic structure: stewardship, including the social, ethical, legal environmental, and regulatory dimensions; economic and social development, focusing on scientific development and its application to health, the environment, and the economy; and citizen engagement, where discussions of the public policy implications of the development and application of biotechnological innovations will focus on the concerns of both present and future generations (*Workplan for Biotechnology Review*, 2000).

Statements made during the first CBAC meeting, which identify the moral and ethical issues associated with biotechnology as ones to be 'managed' by the committee, raise doubt as to whether the CBAC investigations will effectively address public concerns (Canadian Biotechnology Advisory Committee 2000b). Further, in determining 'areas of interest' within the membership of the CBAC, it was stated that one of the main objectives of the committee ought to be the 'building [of] public acceptance of biotechnology where the balance between benefits and harms is positive' (Canadian Biotechnology Advisory Committee 2000a). A closer examination of the CBAC's membership reveals not only that parties close to industry are well represented but communications experts are also prominent, suggesting that the committee's role is to 'spin' or finesse issues of public interest rather than to incorporate the concerns of society as a whole (http://cbac.gc.ca).

The CBS is a prime example of the form of privatization in which, the state actively intervenes to facilitate market rationality, which, in the context of biotechnology, includes the licensing of new forms of appropriation. It is significant that the strategy is being coordinated by Industry Canada rather than Health Canada. Inherent in this shift is the relativization of the role of Health Canada, including the Health Protection Branch, within the interministerial structure of an initiative whose explicit purpose is industrial promotion. As a result, the CBS has been couched within an economic paradigm (Sherwin 1998a, 1). In the CBS workplan, health protection is but one aim; others include economic expansion, promotion of development, modernization of intellectual property laws, facilitation of commercialization of new technologies, creation of international leadership and stewardship, and the management of data and sectoral action plans. 'Responsible leadership' within the vision statement is coupled with 'market access,' providing a clear indication of actual priorities.

Clearly, although its role is shifting with globalization, the Canadian government has responsibilities in both the economic and health spheres. Where it was once more confined to the promotion and protection of health, as intended within the CBS, the role of the government has shifted so that its primary function is now the development of the tools necessary to improve the health and well-being of Canadians. The CBS is an industrial strategy aimed at capitalizing genetic knowledge. It is about wealth: new commodities, new markets, and the social forms that can maintain these forms of accumulation, including law. Two examples, as proposed by the National Biotechnology Advisory Committee (NBAC), illustrate the potential role of law within this shift. First, the NBAC recommends the strengthening of Canadian intellectual property protections to bring them into conformity with global standards (i.e., those of the World Trade Organization), in order to promote regulatory efficiency, expanded international cooperation and increased international market access (National Biotechnology Advisory Committee 1998, 46–8). Biotechnology patent issues include, among others, whether and to what extent patent claims covering plants, animals, and human body parts should be allowed, what exemptions and safeguards are needed to protect the public interest, and whether or not ethical and moral aspects should be considered in granting patents (Canada 1998e, 6). Second, the NBAC recommends that the commercialization of biotechnology be facilitated through increased access to experienced management and scientific personnel (National Biotechnology Advisory Committee 1998, 14). This would necessitate an easing of immigration legislation in order to grant timely recruitment of such individuals, harmonization of salary and income tax rates with those of Canada's major trading partners, and improved access to capital and the flow of funds through alterations to corporate tax provisions (National Biotechnology Advisory Committee 1998, 14–16).

The relationship between the health and economic areas of governance and the development of biotechnology policy in Canada has arguably been skewed in favour of economic prosperity, as it is assumed that prosperity alone will have positive impacts upon health. It is by no means obvious that development and sale of profitable biotechnology is a particularly effective way to promote the health of Canadians (Sherwin 1998a, 2). Economic development contributes to health only when its benefits are widely distributed throughout the community (Sherwin 1998a, 2). Health needs in relation to social determinants such as gender, class, region, race, language, and ethnicity are minimized within the CBS. There is presently nothing in the biotechnology strategy to suggest that its economic benefits will be extended to those citizens whose health is most threatened by economic insecurity. Rather, it promises to make a contribution through the development of new products that will foster the overall health of citizens – for example, vaccines, pharmaceuticals, and nutraceuticals (Sherwin 1998a, 2). Some of these developments may indeed foster the overall health of citizens if the products in question are made available to them. Others, however, may detract from health. Prudent financial planning requires that government policy consider carefully its use of limited health care dollars and be wary of the development of technologies that will generate individual demand without making a positive contribution to the overall health of the population (Sherwin 1998a, 4). Moreover, the adoption of the goals of both promotion and protection by the government brings the role of consumer choice into question. The dilemma is articulated as follows: 'It is fairly clear why industry would be guided by consumer choice – after all, manufacturers have reason to produce all and only products that can be effectively marketed. But it is essential that government agencies responsible for the health of Canadians not make the mistake of believing themselves bound by the notion that consumer choice is an adequate criterion for determining product development and availability because *it is not the only relevant ethical value*' (Sherwin 1998a, 3, emphasis added). The CBS will not be an effective strategy for meeting the challenge of globalization unless the government can ensure that there is indeed something to sell. This necessarily entails the creation of increased opportunities for the commodification of health products and their sale on national and international markets. While the benefits of health and health care are touted as a public good, what we are actually seeing is a further extension of privatization. One suggestion made in a CBS policy document on research and development, a suggestion that is particularly alarming for those of us in the academic community, is that universities change promotion and tenure standards to promote patenting as a substitute for publication (Canada 1998d, 3–4). There is no greater indication of the shift in government priorities than movement away from the public dissemination of knowledge towards its private appropriation for commercial purposes.

Despite the federal policy mandate that identifies the need for gender-specific analysis of Canadian policy developments, the dimensions of gender as they relate to health and molecular biotechnology are presently unexamined within the CBS (Status of Women Canada 1998).[5] Framed in gender-neutral language, the CBS is silent regarding the gender contours and the potential effects genetic biotechnologies may have on women. Ultimately, whether issues of gender and health are integrated into the CBS in an effective manner will be a telling example of the ability (and desire) of commercially based strategies to incorporate 'social' and ethical concerns. This type of analysis will be important in demonstrating how policies such as the CBS act as containers of genetic knowledge, shaping and limiting their gendered effects.

C. The Health Protection Branch of Health Canada

Nowhere has the shift in governmental roles from social protection to industrial promotion been so apparent as in the recently proposed transformations of the Health Protection Branch (HPB), which is responsible for regulating the approval and safety of aspects of the new health-related technologies (Health Canada 1998d). Arguing in part that the new reproductive, and especially the new genetic, technologies do not correspond physically or conceptually to the medical devices and pharmaceuticals traditionally licensed and regulated by the HPB, Health Canada has stated that its regulatory and legislative framework is inadequate and launched a so-called transitions program (Caulfield & Feasby 1998, 377; Health Canada 1998c).

This process, articulated by Health Canada as a 'modernizing of the health protection system' and framed as a transition rather than a 'cutback' or 'downsizing' (Health Canada 1998b, 3) corresponds to the restructuring of the Canadian state in a climate of privatization. Not surprisingly, the transitions program includes strategies to externalize the costs of regulation by enhancing cost-recovery and the development of stronger relations with industry (Health Canada 1998a). The effort to externalize the costs of regulation corresponds with an increase in extra-governmental research and scientific activity. In this transition not only would outdated methods and ideals become 'modern,' but the protection of health would increasingly be carried out by actors other than the Canadian government. Citing the inadequate number of government laboratory and testing systems, Health Canada has signalled its intention to embrace the increasing capacity of non-governmental organizations, universities, and industry to 'strengthen the science that underlies decision making' and carry out health protection work (Health Canada 1998b, 3, 8–9). This is an example of active state restructuring in the context of the promotion of health.

One of the central safeguards proposed under the Health Protection Branch Transition Program is legislation which would, in principle, prohibit manufacturers from placing dangerous products on the market (Health Canada 1998c, 35). This 'umbrella' health protection legislation would replace four existing statutes: the Food and Drugs Act, the Hazardous Products Act, the Radiation Emitting Devices Act, and the Quarantine Act. Such prohibitions are expected to force manufacturers to be more explicitly responsible for ensuring product safety via the imposition upon them of enhanced and more rigorous liability.[6] Currently, it is the government that is primarily accountable to the public for safety and the protection of the health of the public. Under the proposed legislation, primary responsibility for ensuring product safety prior to public exposure would lie with industry and Health Canada's interventions would be activated after a danger has been detected by market use. One readily apparent disadvantage would be the potential for dangerous goods to enter the market before government intervention, in the form of punishment, occurs. Incidences in which women have suffered serious harm from the introduction of unsafe drugs and devices such as DES (diethylstilboestrol), Thalidomide, breast implants, and the Dalkon Shield illustrate the disasters that can occur as a result of releasing unsafe drugs and medical devices onto the market (Working Group on Women and Health Protection 1999). Moreover, the HPB

is presently considering allowing private individuals to bring enforcement actions, such as injunctions, against companies (Health Canada
1998c, 33). This raises questions as to whether the HPB is, in fact, envisioning the replacement of federal enforcement with civil enforcement
by private parties (MacIntosh 1999, 23).[7]

Health Canada acknowledges that its regulatory system is shifting
away from a model where assessments of risk are made in-house towards
what it calls a 'networked' model, which includes universities and industry (Health Canada 1998b, 5, 8). The new model is defended as being
more consistent with access to the best scientific knowledge and expertise. But look, for example, at the restructuring of funding proposed by
the transition in the Therapeutic Products Directorate, which is responsible for licensing new drugs and medical devices and for banning or
restricting drugs and devices that prove to be unsafe. Its costs were previously covered by general tax revenues, in a manner similar to other
public agencies. This division now relies on industry user fees to cover
approximately 70 percent of its operating costs (Simand 1998, 3).
Therefore, industry must pay to have its product reviewed for potential
market approval regardless of whether the submission is approved or
rejected. A proposal to formalize this practice by integrating it into legislation would place industry, not the public, in the position of being
Health Canada's client for the purposes of product review (MacIntosh
1999, 13).

Yet another illustration of the shifting role of the state can be found
in one of the primary objectives of the transitions process – the promotion of 'efficiency.' The goal of efficiency highlights the distinction
between privatization as simple deregulation and privatization as regulation in the service of private industry. This goal, under a health protection system characterized by increasing levels of industry involvement,
will likely be manifested through the championing of shorter time
frames for regulatory approvals.[8] More rapid introduction of new pharmaceuticals is obviously in the interests of industry but glosses over the
potential trade-offs between accelerated introduction of new products
and the assessment of possible risks. In the long term, the HPB has
agreed in principle to implement a suggestion of the pharmaceutical
industry which would tie the amount of fees collected each year to the
'performance targets' of the branch (Working Group on Women and
Health, 1998: 2). If this type of proposal were to be implemented, the
potential for even greater conflicts of interest would arise. The
increased potential for collection of industry fees could negatively influ-

ence the quality of HPB reviews of applications for the marketing of goods or services.

There is little evidence that Health Canada or the federal government seeks to abandon its mandate to protect health, or that it is blind to the ethical concerns which have been raised. Rather, the renewal of the mandate for health protection occurs in a context where the role and meaning of the state is shifting, and where the autonomy of the Canadian state has been reduced by international trade agreements and the demands of multinational corporations.[9] For example, the transition strategy addresses the extent to which Canada's drug regulations should be harmonized with those in Europe, the United States, and other industrialized countries (Health Canada 1998c, 22). Concerns have been raised that harmonization will be used as a cost-cutting tool of deregulation, which will encourage Health Canada to adopt the weakest of the member states' regulations (Working Group on Women and Health 1998, 5). The lack of representation of women's groups at industry-led international fora on this issue illustrates the potential for economic concerns to take precedence over the gender, ethical, and health implications of change (ibid.). The implementation of the privatization agenda is not bringing about the deregulation of health; rather, the manner in which health is being regulated is changing. Health is increasingly being regulated as a commodity rather than a public good, health care as a business rather than a public service. The federal government is positioning itself to manage the risk inherent in unsafe pharmaceuticals and medical devices and to mediate between the interests of industry and the citizen public. Where formerly it characterized social reproduction as a central issue, the state now balances this concern with the requirements of production, and often privileges production in the process.

D. Efforts to Regulate New Reproductive and Genetic Technologies

One of the functions of the Keynesian welfare state in mediating the tension between production and social reproduction has been to monitor and regulate technologies of production in the interests of the social good. The profit of innovation was balanced by the potential social harms of innovation. In the current context of globalized capital and state restructuring, the capacity, or indeed priority, of the state to regulate in relation to the social good is called into question. While the federal government has signalled its intention to regulate reproductive and genetic technologies, the slow pace at which this has been effected – in contrast with the speed at which policies related to the Canadian Biotechnology Strategy and the Health Protection Branch transition have been implemented – suggest a shift in state priorities from social democratic concerns to technocratic management and economic development and efficiency.

There has been a significant demand in Canada for federal legislation pertaining to the regulation of reproductive and genetic technologies, on the basis that the use of these technologies will have important ethical, social, and health impacts for citizens. Canadian legislation would exist within the greater international regulatory framework, including that imposed by international trade agreements. The North American Free Trade Agreement (NAFTA), for example, contains provisions that can be used to limit the capacity of a member state to regulate commercial activity within its territory with respect to new reproductive and genetic technologies (NRGTs). Yet the potential for national regulation is not entirely precluded.[10] In response to growing public concerns about developments in reproductive and genetic technologies, the Government of Canada appointed the Royal Commission on New Reproductive Technologies (RCNRT) in October 1989. In November 1993, the commission made public 293 recommendations, concluding that 'decisive, timely, and comprehensive national action is required with respect to the regulation of new reproductive technologies' (Royal Commission on New Reproductive Technologies 1993, 107).

In particular, the commission called for legislation to set clear boundaries around acceptable and non-acceptable uses of NRGTs and to regulate and monitor the use of practices and developments in this field. The commission stated that the federal government should use its power under the Criminal Code to prohibit practices that 'because of their unsafe or unethical character [are] considered unacceptable under any circumstances' (Royal Commission on New Reproductive Technologies 1993, 108). In addition, the commission recommended the establishment of a National Regulatory Commission charged with setting and enforcing standards for those practices deemed acceptable. The major functions of the proposed National Commission were to be 'licensing and monitoring; guideline and standard setting; information collection, evaluation, and dissemination; records storage; consultation, coordination, and intergovernmental cooperation; and monitoring of future technologies and practices' (Royal Commission on New Reproductive Technologies 1993, 115–16).

In July 1995, the then federal Minister of Health, Diane Marleau, called for an interim moratorium on specific applications of NRGTs and announced the appointment of an advisory committee to monitor compliance with the moratorium (Health Canada 1996). In June 1996, the federal government introduced Bill C-47, An Act Respecting Human Reproductive Technologies and Commercial Transactions Relating to Human Reproduction (the Human Reproductive and Genetic Technologies Act), providing for criminal sanctions for the most serious practices, including those named in the moratorium. The bill would prohibit 'practices that commercialize reproduction or are inconsistent with the principles of human dignity, including the buying and selling of eggs and sperm, sex selection for non-medical reasons, and commercial surrogacy.'

Bill C-47, if enacted, would have prohibited specific genetic manipulation, the payment of surrogate mothers, the purchase and sale of reproductive materials, and the use of ovum without consent. The offering, or giving of, consideration for any of the illegal procedures was also prohibited (ss. 4(2) and (3)). This prohibition was extended to preclude the offering or giving of consideration to a woman to act as a surrogate mother, or to any person acting as an intermediary in obtaining such services (s. 5). In acknowledgment of the health and ethical dangers inherent in the commercialization of human reproduction, the selling, purchasing, bartering, or exchanging of gametes, embryos, and foetuses were included within the prohibitions of the bill (s. 6(1)).

The prohibitions contained within Bill C-47 were intended to signal state recognition of health and safety, the dignity of all persons (particularly women and children), and the inherent potential of reproductive materials as human life. Attached to the prohibitions were to be punishments ranging from serious fines to imprisonment for a term not exceeding ten years (ss. 8 to 11).

At the same time as the introduction of Bill C-47, the federal government published a White Paper entitled *New Reproductive Technologies: Setting Boundaries, Enhancing Health*, in which it promised to establish a regulatory body and framework for acceptable practices. The White Paper identified several guiding ethical principles for a policy framework: balancing individual and collective interests; equality; protecting the vulnerable; appropriate use of medical treatment; non-commercialization of reproduction and reproductive materials; and accountability (Canada 1996, 15–17). A two-step enactment process was proposed for legislation that would eventually combine prohibitions (under Bill C-47) and regulatory controls to provide for 'a comprehensive management regime for NRGTs' (Canada 1996, 27). Any such regime would promote a multidisciplinary approach and would be established under an agency removed from central government (Canada 1996, 27). The proposed regime would centre on the issuance of licences for various NRGTs and related practices and the establishment of appropriate standards by a range of enforcement mechanisms, as well as the creation of information registries and health surveillance procedures. Under the various pressures of an upcoming federal election, however, this regime failed to materialize. Bill C-47 died on the order paper when the June 1997 federal election was called.

In December 1999, the minister of health again expressed a commitment to pursuing a legislative approach to the regulation of NRGTs, which 'could provide the statutory basis for regulation of human reproductive and genetic technologies through the enforcement of prohibitions (where technologies are unacceptable) and the regulation of other technologies through the development of standards, licensing, information registries, health surveillance, and enforcement and compliance' (Health Canada 1999, 5). Health Canada, in citing the values of dignity, equality, health and safety, and the 'best interests of children born of reproductive technology,' situates the proposed legislation within the broad context of 'sexual and reproductive health.'

The portion of the new proposal pertaining to prohibited procedures clarifies the provisions of Bill C-47 in attempting to prevent commercialization and the exploitation of vulnerable persons (predominantly children). Advertisement for any of the proscribed procedures is to become a prohibited activity and qualifications have been added to the restrictions against use of reproductive materials in the creation of an embryo, foetus, or person to further condemn the use of 'anyone under eighteen years of age' (Health Canada 1999, 11).

The regulatory procedures for the management of new reproductive and genetic technologies would apply to all activities involving the manipulation of human sperm, eggs, and embryos. Thus, there has been a shift in emphasis from reproductive technologies to one concerned also with genetic technologies. Health Canada foresees the creation of a national multifaceted regulatory body, which would take on administrative, developmental, and policing responsibilities. The body would develop national standards for the use of human reproductive materials in medical research and practice; create and circulate requirements for counselling and informed choice; review relevant developments and research in the approval process for new medical and research practices; develop and maintain data registries; and monitor new national and international research developments. It would also create and submit recommendations to the minister of health regarding the development of regulations. With respect to monitoring and enforcement, the body would license individuals or facilities offering or providing for the collection, processing, distribution, and use of human reproductive materials and inspect practices, procedures, and treatments (Health Canada 1999, 12–15). The proposed regulatory framework represents an attempt to govern the uses of NRGT in a timely, systematic, and accountable fashion.

Since the RCNRT reported in response to public concern about the social, ethical, and health consequences of new reproductive and genetic technologies, virtually no new legislation has been passed. Regulation of the social and medical impacts of the technologies has principally been left to standard setting by 'private' professional bodies such as the Canadian College of Medical Geneticists and the Canadian Society of Obstetricians and Gynaecologists and is overseen by the advisory committee monitoring the voluntary moratorium. The effect of government inactivity in this area has thus been to cede regulatory authority to private or quasi-private actors – professional associations or the market. While it might be reasonable to defer to professional regulation in relation to some of the medical implications of reproductive or genetic technologies, professional medical bodies are not best placed to monitor, regulate, and enforce the innumerous social and ethical consequences. Moreover, deferring regulatory authority to a quasi-private body reduces, even eliminates, mechanisms of public accountability. The absence of legislation prohibiting or regulating practices involving reproductive and genetic technologies signals a preference for market norms and mechanisms as means of governing in this area.

Considering the range of federal government initiatives that relate to biotechnology and the new genetics, the phenomenon we are witnessing is not 'deregulation' in the service of the market, but rather a different kind of state regulation and a shift in the legal paradigm of regulation. Instead of deregulating, the state regulates with a view to promoting investment and capital accumulation in biotechnology, making possible the greater appropriation of intellectual property and its capitalization. At the same time, however, the Canadian Biotechnology Strategy and the restructuring of the Health Protection Branch illustrate not merely the promotion of the biotechnology industry but a redefinition of the public interest such that it becomes aligned with or subsumed by private corporate interests. The economy is no longer managed by the state for social purposes; rather, the social interest is redefined and governed in the service of economic interests.

Within this new regulatory framework, the state sees itself as promoting the interests of private actors as the potential benefactors of the public through their production of health commodities, whereas in the welfare state era the state sought to protect, or at least to balance, public and private interests. Changes such as those to the Health Protection Branch are justified on the basis that they provide rapid access to new therapies, rather than as an outright regulatory bias in favour of the owners of capital. While demonstrably furthering the rights of property and capital owners, the discourse of choice and freedom of access mollifies a public which might otherwise be concerned about the erosion of citizenship rights. In moving from defining and representing the public interest to promoting product liability and intellectual property, the state is also shifting the arena of adjudication into the area of private, commercial law and away from public and constitutional law.

Changes to the nature of state regulation and adjudication are accompanied by a transformation of the governing normative ideals. Equality and social justice concerns have given way to competitive fairness, protection of proprietary interests, and the creation of conditions for wealth accumulation (Fudge and Cossman this volume). In the absence of a legislative template articulating the public interest concerns in genetic technology, when courts are brought in to adjudicate disputes involving NRGTs they will interpret problems and render decisions based on analogy to a familiar context or category, in which the discourses of individual choice and liberty prevail. This entails not only a different set of concerns, expertise, and evidentiary rules, but also a shift into a socio-legal arena with its own gendered hierarchy. The shift from a paradigm of the state as the guardian of public interest to the state as guardian of private ordering may involve a movement toward the recognition of the interests of organized parties (such as multinational corporations or professional bodies), where women are notably absent, disempowered, or otherwise lack authoritative representation.

IV. Genetic Technologies and the Production of the Neo-Liberal Subject

The qualities and characteristics of the citizen are historically contingent; that is, citizens are shaped by and contribute to contemporary ideology and practices. Whereas under the Keynesian welfare state, the citizen was the beneficiary of social rights and civil protections and risk was, to a large degree, socialized, the neo-liberal citizen is self-reliant and individually responsible for the risks to his or her well-being; he or she also has reduced expectations about the state's provision of social welfare. Neo-liberal practices and the accompanying strategies of privatization operate not only to justify the decrease in government activity in economic terms, they signify as well an ideological commitment to recognizing and rewarding individual choice and personal decision making. Neo-liberal governance operates at arm's length from its subjects (Rose 1996b). Integral to the neo-liberal project is the notion that the best forms of governance create the conditions that facilitate autonomous self-regulation; the individual is rendered an active entrepreneur of his or her self (Petersen 1999, 33). Thus, a range of strategies for the regulation of the conduct of individuals are employed by a variety of agencies, including organizations, professional bodies, families, and individuals themselves, which enhance the distance between the apparatus of rule and individual regulation (Rose 1996b). The new genetic technologies are one means through which the neo-liberal citizen is governed and materially produced.

The shift to a neo-liberal discourse of risk and choice is predicated on a distinct politics of knowledge. Individual risk and choice occur within the context of the provision of 'information' by experts. However, the provision of this information is itself contingent on the production and sanctioning of new forms of knowledge, including knowledge about health. The knowledge economy at the macro-level is dependent on a knowledge economy at the micro-level, where individuals consume genetic information to ensure against risks. While federal and provincial governments may not directly regulate the use of this information in the health care system, the state actively encourages its production within the biotechnological sector and medical research. By encouraging the production of such knowledge, the state implicitly certifies the expertise of the providers of genetic information and indirectly legitimizes the risk categories they create.

In the absence of legislation, at present prenatal diagnosis, a form of genetic testing, is primarily regulated by the disciplines of medicine and ethics. Lack of explicit guidelines turns the practice of prenatal diagnosis into an individual matter between patient and physician, facilitating its emergence as a site of self-surveillance. '[N]eo-liberal notions of individual autonomy, the free market and limited government are related, in a mutually producing and sustaining way, to the imperatives of "self-care" – in the form of self-surveillance and self-regulation – which themselves are a consequence of the phenomenological experience of being "at risk"' (Robertson 2000, 7–8). Prenatal diagnosis becomes the means through which individuals are able to literally construct the post-Keynesian citizen, through the exercise of choice. Within neo-liberal rationalities of privatization, health and health risks are individualized and depoliticized. Embodying risk represents the embodiment of a neo-liberal rationality. By selecting the qualities of an embryo, or choosing to abort those with undesirable characteristics, risk is translated into 'desirability' – which in the neo-liberal context centres on the ability to be an autonomous, competitive, self-reliant individual.

Many fear that the new genetics will usher in a new wave of eugenics. It is important, however, to distinguish the social context and social implications of the kinds of eugenic practices fostered by the new genetics in a climate of neo-liberalism from the eugenics movements of the early twentieth century. Analysis of the new genetic practices embedded in neo-liberalism reveals the material links between the discursive practice of neo-liberalism and the reorganization of social reproduction attendant on the new genetics. What this entails is a technological splicing of biological reproductive processes with the political requirements of neo-liberal governance. In effect, the new genetics disciplines biology in order to create the neo-liberal subject.

A. The New Genetics: Are They Eugenic?

It is better for the world, if instead of waiting to execute degenerate offspring for crime, or to let them starve for their imbecility, society can prevent those who are manifestly unfit from continuing their kind. The principle that sustains compulsory vaccination is broad enough to cover cutting the Fallopian tubes ... Three generations of imbeciles are enough.

Buck v. Bell (1927)

Eugenic philosophy has historically been translated into legal imperatives which not only permitted but mandated the sexual sterilization, institutionalization, and segregation of a designate population: the prostitute, the mentally ill, the poor, the criminally deviant, and the 'non-white' (Law Reform Commission of Canada 1979; Press & Browner 1995, 307). Efforts were also made to encourage the reproduction of those who did not fall within these social categories. Negative eugenic practices were largely rationalized on the basis of decreasing the 'costs to society' attendant upon the existence of such individuals. Thus, the old eugenics situated society as the subject of state directives regarding interference with reproduction and was constructed around an ideology of 'social protection and improvement' (Caulfield & Robertson 1996, 72). While the means to achieve desired eugenic goals still involves the manipulation of the reproductive capacities of the body, the site of the struggle for social protection and improvement has shifted. In part as a result of feminist struggles, it is no longer acceptable for the state to directly discipline reproductive capacity. Due largely to the existence of genetic technologies, such as prenatal testing, the individual has become the 'gatekeeper' of healthy offspring and is increasingly imparted the ability to 'manage' these issues (Roy, Williams, & Dickens 1994, 187). To identify differences between current practice and the eugenic policies of the early twentieth century, we must carefully examine the context and rhetoric surrounding the new genetics. The twentieth century was haunted by the racist approach to eugenics that culminated in the Nazi-directed genocide of the Holocaust. Thus, the mere mention of genetics tends to raise alarms about its possible consequences for social policy (Caulfield & Robertson 1996, 72). The promoters of new genetic technologies are well aware of the shadow that hangs over any discussion of eugenics and therefore carefully craft their message in terms of 'choice.'

As eugenic arguments are founded on the premise that negative traits are inherited, reproduction is perceived to be the means for controlling the propagation of undesirable traits. What counts as a negative trait, however, and the techniques for controlling reproduction have changed over time. Previous eugenic policies assumed, wrongly, that behavioural attributes such as criminality, laziness, and homosexuality were genetically transmitted to future generations. Despite the lack of scientific grounding, these assumptions were generally accepted and reinforced notions of normalcy.

In Canada, the eugenic movement dates to the early part of the twentieth century and culminated in the introduction of the Sexual Sterilization Act in Alberta, passed in 1928 and revised in 1937 and 1942. During the forty-four years in which the Alberta act was in effect, the Eugenics Board, as it was widely referred to, authorized 4,725 sterilizations, of which 2,822 were actually carried out (Caulfield & Robertson 1996, 61). Those who were sterilized were disproportionately female[11] and people who were unemployed, of minority ethnic backgrounds – particularly eastern and southern Europeans and Asians – and from lower socio-economic classes; many of them were children (Caulfield & Robertson 1996, 61). Newspaper accounts of the legislative debates about the Sexual Sterilization Act make its eugenic objectives very clear.[12] This Act, together with restrictions affecting procreation within marriage statutes,[13] demonstrates that the state, in adopting policies of negative eugenics, had assumed the role of deciding whether or not particular individuals had the right to reproduce.

Early eugenics programs, which sought to purge the social body of unwanted or undesirable characteristics, designated categories of people unfit to reproduce and subjected them to involuntary sterilization. The goal is evident in the language of the Alberta statute, which stated that a patient about to be discharged from a mental hospital 'might safely be discharged *if* the danger of procreation with its attendant risk of multiplication of the evil by transmission of the disability to progeny were eliminated.'[14] Among the characteristics that many eugenicists regarded as almost exclusively hereditary were mental retardation, mental illness, pauperism, criminality, prostitution, and sexual perversion (Caulfield & Robertson 1996, 65). While some of the attraction of eugenic practices was the reduction of the financial burden on the state arising from families with 'defective offspring,' the primary motivation was the prevention of social delinquency and crime attributed to inherited conditions (ibid.). The absence of scientific grounding and the increasing opprobrium of eugenics in light of human rights concerns led to the repeal of the Act in 1972.

The new genetics, by contrast, is individual rather than state-centred, and purports to be about both individual 'choice' and individual 'health.' Its language is that of the informed consumer rather than a state-directed ideology of social protection and social improvement. Negative eugenic policies are extremely unlikely in most, if not all democratic societies. Indeed, since the adoption of the Canadian Charter of Rights and Freedoms in 1982, the Supreme Court of Canada has moved to effectively outlaw the forms of state action upon which the old eugenics depended (*Re Eve*, 1986). Moreover, some of the individuals wrongfully sterilized under this regime have been able to claim retroactive compensation.[15] The advocates of the new genetics do not make explicitly eugenic claims and scrupulously avoid the slightest suggestion of state coercion. Ironically, however, the same individualistic calculus used to outlaw past eugenic practices is presently employed to promote the new genetic practices.

In the context of reproduction, the new genetics is promoted as offering prospective parents information upon which to make choices. The primary rationales for contemporary use of prenatal genetic testing or screening is to provide pregnant women with information they can use to make decisions about whether to terminate an affected pregnancy; to take measures while the foetus is in utero to reduce the 'negative' effects on a future child, where these are available; or to prepare for the birth of a disabled child or one with a genetic disease. Where former eugenic practices involved coercive activities designed and implemented by the state to 'improve the quality' of future generations for the benefit of society, current programs of prenatal diagnosis operate at the level of the individual pregnancy, and compliance is voluntary.

Browner and Press argue that the success of contemporary prenatal diagnosis programs rests upon the willingness of individual women to take personal responsibility for deciding whether to bear a disabled child (Press & Browner 1995, 308). But why do so many women accept this responsibility? As a society we already accept quantitative mastery over procreation, and find it acceptable to control the number of children we have through the use of contraception (Testart 1995, 305). In a culture of increased commodification, the issue of qualitative mastery arises. Prenatal diagnosis is promoted as a service or technology that can be used to reassure a pregnant woman that her foetus is healthy. The technology is offered in a cultural and social context which mandates that pregnant women (in judicial intervention cases, through the coercive power of the state, but also in the media and pop culture), abstain from all behaviours that might pose risks to the developing foetus. 'Women view pregnancy as supremely risky because society imposes nearly total responsibility on them as prospective mothers for assuring a favourable birth' (Press & Browner 1995, 309). In order to reduce this risk, pregnant women are often willing to defer to medical or scientific knowledge as insurance of the health of their foetus (Oakley 1981). Moreover, once a test exists, whether a woman uses it is not a neutral act – refusal implies her reluctance to do everything in her power to assure the health and well-being of the developing foetus (Beck-Gernsheim 1991, 47; Press & Browner 1995; 1997; Sandelowski & Carson Jones 1996). There is societal and cultural approbation for giving a child a head start and all the opportunities one can. In this way, the use of genetic technologies becomes, along with reading to him or her, extracurricular activities, sound education, and proper nourishment, another form of doing what is best for a child.

The success of contemporary prenatal diagnosis programs also rests upon society's endorsement of abortion as a legitimate course of action in the event of a 'defective' pregnancy.[16] Often using a cost/benefit analysis, it is argued that it is less costly for a woman to abort her disabled fetus than for the public to provide a lifetime of social services, or increasingly in the context of privatization, for individual families to incur the financial responsibility of caring for a disabled child, as this function is shifted from the state to the family. The risk of bearing an unhealthy child results in more than the dependency of the offspring; it often implicates the parent, usually the mother, in caring for the child. This has a profound bearing not only on the economic status of the family, but on the social and political status of the caregiver in a society in which participation in the labour force is the mark of full citizenship.

The growth of genetic testing and the prevalence of its marketing suggests that we are witnessing a shifting rationality regarding child-bearing, one that may have an explicitly eugenic slant to it. Genetic testing and counselling practices 'reinforce the message that not only do individuals have a right to "healthy" genes, they also have a right to information that will assist them to minimize their own contribution to disease and disability' (Petersen 1998, 64). In addition, the new reproductive and genetic technologies provide increased opportunities not only for selective abortion of 'undesirable foetuses' (a form of negative eugenics) but also for the choice of gametes with specific traits or characteristics and the preferential treatment of pre-embryos with such characteristics for implantation and gestation (a form of positive eugenics). A new eugenics – one which, unlike older versions, is acceptable to our developed and democratic sensibilities – is emerging. It consists in the selection of the genome, not its manipulation, through embryo selection and prenatal diagnosis (Testart 1995).

The deployment of new genetic technologies in the context of reproduction is an important site where the construction and rearticulation of the neo-liberal citizen takes place. The new 'eugenic' practices leave pregnant women, and their health care providers personally responsible for deciding what kind of life is worth living; in an era of increasing cutbacks in the provision of health care and social services, they also force women (and the family) to assume the costs of care if the choice is made to proceed with a 'risky' pregnancy. This is a form of privatization. In contrast to the old eugenics, the state is only indirectly implicated in the creation of the conditions where private actors – professionals, industry – enable individuals to make personal choices and exercise their autonomy in the procreative context. Under neo-liberal governance, while experts act as advisers and define norms, individuals are called upon to take an active role in decision making, and to exercise their right to know, so that they can make informed and responsible decisions about their health and that of their progeny (Petersen 1999). Information pertaining to the health of the foetus obtained through the employment of genetic technologies is the basis upon which procreative and 'eugenic' choices are made. Risk, characterized as the possibility of genetically inherited disease or traits, becomes a crucial factor in the decision-making process arising from genetic testing.

In the age of neo-liberalism, risk management becomes an everyday practice of the self (O'Malley in Petersen 1999, 123). In order to be independent and to avoid becoming a burden upon others, the individual takes rational steps to avoid and insure against risk. A new prudentialism also arises in which insurance against eventualities such as ill health, unemployment, and old age become a private choice rather than a communal responsibility (O'Malley in Petersen 1999, 123). Rose suggests that 'social insurance as a principle of social solidarity, gives way to a kind of privatization of risk management' (Rose 1996b, 58). As the state disengages from providing or monitoring insurance schemes, the individual is left to make his or her own choices (Harris 1999, 45). Thus, the impetus behind selecting the qualities or traits of offspring, deciding which foetuses to terminate and which to carry to term, or controlling the quality of one's progeny through the use of genetic and reproductive technologies must be set in the context of a neo-liberal ideology and political order in which risk consciousness and freedom of choice prevail.

The discursive and material effects of the new genetics in the context of privatization have restrictive implications for women, for people with disabilities, for historically disenfranchised groups, and for our understanding of social good. The routine availability of genetic testing fosters an ideology according to which the birth of individuals with certain diseases and traits should be avoided. In addition, it leads to more restrictive notions of normalcy and humanity. The individualist rationale also constitutes an effort to deny that there are social consequences pursuant to the adoption of the new genetic technologies. This effort is situated within the general context of privatization and the drive to make social policy conform to the needs of the market. By highlighting individual well-being and choice, promoters of the new genetic technologies seek to entice the individual as consumer to purchase their products. The new forms of appropriation and private property these new technologies require are 'sold' as a way to promote the public good. Social responsibility is privatized, as the onus for the consequences of choices is placed squarely on the shoulders of the individuals making the decisions, rather than on the state. The state merely regulates the availability of the technologies and licenses the forms of private appropriation required to make investing in them viable.

Active citizenship is a key mechanism by which individuals engage in risk management and regulate themselves through exercising their freedom of choice (Petersen 1999). Implicitly, and in some cases explicitly, genetic testing is looked upon as a form of responsible behaviour. King predicts that 'we are going to be told that if we know that certain genes cause disease and we can test for them, then we are being irresponsible leaving things to chance; and we are being irresponsible and cruel if we even consider bringing a disabled child into the world' (D. King 1995, 25–6). Within the political rationality of neo-liberalism, in order to act responsibly individuals are expected to govern themselves through processes of endless self-examination, self-care, and self-improvement (Petersen 1999). The consumer who chooses to know and behave prudently where genetic health risk is concerned is therefore the self-reliant citizen who actively works to avoid becoming a burden on society and to maximize her or his productive potential. The genetically responsible health care consumer is the ideal new citizen of the post-Keynesian state. The choice to become informed about genetic risk also provides an individual with the knowledge upon which to make decisions about reproductive choices. In the neo-liberal context these choices are shaped by the desire to produce offspring who conform with neo-liberal rationality. Genetic technology becomes a quintessential tool of neo-liberal governance, one which simultaneously enables and disciplines, through the categories of risk and choice, permitting the state to govern from a distance. As eloquently stated by King: 'One way or the other, we are all going to be dragged into the regime of gene management, that will, in essence, be eugenic. It will all be in the name of individual health rather than for the overall fitness of the population, and the managers will be you and me and our doctors, not the state. Genetic change will be managed by the invisible hand of individual choice, but the overall result will be the same, a co-ordinated attempt to "improve" the genes of the next generation on the way' (D. King 1995, 25–6).

B. Disciplining Women's Bodies

The effects of the new genetics are predominantly borne by women, in part because of the historically gendered nature of procreation. The ideology of geneticization purports to be gender neutral: the health benefits produced by genetic technology and practice are considered to be good for all human beings. However, men and women are situated differently in relation to the production and reproduction of these health effects. Unlike the eugenic practices of the early twentieth century, which were enacted upon the bodies of both men and women, current genetic interventions in the reproductive context occur predominantly upon and within the bodies of women.

The concept of choice and the process of decision making are problematic for women as pregnancy and motherhood are increasingly subject to control through the category of risk (Weir 1996). 'The growing availability of supposedly risk free genetic testing technology' (testing techniques that do not create a physical risk for the foetus or the pregnant woman), 'combined with the imperatives of responsible healthy citizenship, compromise the exercise of free choice in relation to genetic testing' (Petersen 1999, 126). Choosing not to know about genetic risk becomes less of an option.

Women are the gatekeepers of genetic risk and social cost in two overlapping and complementary senses. First, as the gender disproportionately burdened with the costs and responsibilities of social reproduction, women are the primary 'managers' of the risks of dependency (Mahowald 1996; Stacey 1996). Second, women, as the gestational sex, carry the foetus whose 'risks' to the family and society are rendered transparent through the use of genetic technologies. In this sense, women literally embody genetic risk. Genetic knowledge and 'genetic responsibility' transform the subjectivity of child-bearing women, and to the extent that child rearing and child bearing construct women as a gender, all women are affected by the reconstruction of subjective embodiment surrounding the issues of genetic risk.

Self-surveillance has particular effects on women. Women's bodies have become the predominant site of testing and screening (especially in the prenatal context); therefore they become the dominant agents through which this kind of governance is achieved. Subjective feelings of well-being are juxtaposed against 'objective knowledge' provided by genetic technologies. Through these acts of surveillance the body is continually produced as a potential source of danger to the subject (Kavanagh & Broom 1998). The purported 'choice' associated with genetic knowledge and genetic testing presupposes a profound alienation from personal embodied experience and places a particular burden on women as the site of 'responsible citizenship.' In particular, prenatal diagnosis involves a calculated alienation of the woman from the foetus and from her own body.

Both forms of alienation are a result of the way in which genetic technologies have been developed and subsumed within the neo-liberal

imperative. Genetic counselling is based upon a model of rational decision making which assumes that, when properly advised about the risk of
genetic disease, individuals will weigh up all available information and
arrive at the most appropriate decision (Petersen 1998, 65). However,
this model fails to acknowledge that genetic information is complex and
difficult to interpret and that, 'except for a few diagnostic tests, most fall
into a gray area where the results can be more confusing than helpful'
(Feldman in Petersen 1998, 65). Decisions, including those about
whether to terminate a pregnancy, are often made on the basis of partial
information, without knowing whether or how seriously a condition will
manifest itself. This decision-making model also overlooks the fact that
many other factors may influence an individual's behaviour when she is
confronted with the choice of whether or not to reproduce. Further,
women's choices are limited by available treatment options: no effective
therapies exist for many genetic disorders for which they or their foetus
have been screened or tested. Often, the only reproductive option for
women is to choose whether or not to abort. Reproductive choice, in a
context where the social safety net has been dismantled and self-reliance
and autonomy are the hallmarks of citizenship, is not a choice at all.

Conclusion

This chapter has addressed the gendered impact of the relationship
between privatization and the new genetics. The Canadian state has
played a central role in promoting the production and dissemination of
genetic knowledge; by failing to regulate the use of genetic technologies
in the context of procreation, it has also facilitated the emergence of the
new active citizen responsible for her own risks. Law operates on a number of different levels and in a variety of ways in this process. Most visibly,
at the instrumental level, new forms of property and opportunities for
accumulation are legally constituted through supra-national agreements
and state law. However, state restructuring and supra-national agreements have also weakened the role of law as an instrument of a democratically organized society acting through the state to impart norms of
social justice and substantive equality. This diminishes the potential for
women's collective action and their ability to shape and limit the gendered effects of NRGTs. At the same time, the normative role of law, by
underscoring and sanctioning the discourse of individual autonomy and
choice, supports and guides the acceptance of the normative categories
which the marketing of NRGTs requires. Moreover, law's emphasis on

individual autonomy and informed choice, which are central elements of neo-liberal discourse, help to legitimize a professional-client model for the regulation of genetic testing in the context of procreation. Explicitly and implicitly, law has sanctioned the contribution of genetic technologies to the gendered and unequal burden of social reproduction. Although women now have more information on which to base reproductive choices, they are disproportionately burdened if the 'wrong' choices are made.

The discourse of genetic risk and the practices of genetic testing have created an environment in which women increasingly understand themselves, and their pregnancies, in terms of embodied risks. Internalization of genetic risks has forced women, individually, to incur the responsibility for social reproduction. Resistance to this political imperative could be effected by recognition and re-emphasis of the fact that human beings and 'normalcy' involve tremendous variation. The construction of disability and disease as costs to the individual (and greater society) relies upon a purposeful obstruction of the social determinants of health. Insisting upon a recognition of the relationship between genetic expression and social, political, and physical environments will lead to an equal recognition that individual health and the health of future generations cannot be ensured solely through reliance upon genetic information. Contrary to the tenets of neo-liberalism, interdependence and dependence are facts of life. Even if procreation is controlled in the effort to pre-empt future dependency, people will continue to display 'difference,' and dependence: no amount of individualization of responsibility will eradicate the social facts of life attendant upon social risks. Genetic knowledge may help us to recognize that each individual is different, and infinitely varied and allow us to begin to embrace those differences. When facing reproductive decisions we can use genetic technologies to highlight genetic variation and diversity rather than genetic risk.

Individual prudence and knowledge comes with great social risk and potentially great social cost. While genetic knowledge may inform individual choices concerning procreation, it renders more obscure or opaque the shape of future society, including the very individualistic values of metaphysical life and personhood on which the ideology of genetic choice is founded. The dilemma we face is that the current ideological climate diminishes the effectiveness of the regulatory tools we require to order and to better control the consequences of our own productive and reproductive activities.

Notes

This chapter was written in partial fulfilment of the requirements of the degree of Doctor of the Science of Law in the Faculty of Law, Columbia University. I would like to thank Judy Fudge, Brenda Cossman, Lisa Philipps, Jeremy Paltiel, and Isabel Karpin for being generous readers and collaborators. Wendy Sutton, Cailin Morrison, and Ruth Fletcher provided wonderful research assistance. I am extremely indebted to Kerry Taylor for her diligent assistance in completing the chapter.

1 Victor McKusick, whose catalogue of human genetic conditions is a classic in the field, defines 'genetics' in the following way: '[T]he science of biological variation; *human genetics*: the science of biological variation in humans; *medical genetics*: the science of biological variation as it relates to health and disease; and *clinical genetics*: the part of medical genetics concerned with health and disease in individuals and their families or the science and practice (art) of diagnosis, prevention, and management of genetic disorders' (McKusick 1993).
2 See e.g. Abraham 1999 for a discussion of the case of Fiona Webster. Webster was successful in her appeal to the Health Services Appeal and Review Board of Ontario of a decision of the Ontario Health Insurance Plan (OHIP) that denied coverage of the fee for private BRCA 1 and 2 testing through Myriad Genetics. Webster argued that given her high-risk status for breast cancer, OHIP should cover the cost of having the test done privately as she would otherwise have had to wait approximately a year for the testing to be done in a local laboratory.
3 In the context of patents and intellectual property rights regimes, the Canadian state, by entering into both NAFTA and the GATT agreement (the Uruguay Round), has ensured the entrenchment of intellectual property rights (Marshall 1999, 139). The protectionist provisions for intellectual property rights grant a monopoly for a period of twenty years to those corporations holding patents on inventions. The entrenchment of intellectual property rights has ensured that future democratically elected governments will be restrained from implementing policies favourable to generic pharmaceutical companies (Marshall 1999, 139–40). This is accomplished through the threat of trade sanctions: future Canadian governments cannot reinstate compulsory licensing without violating trade obligations under the threat of reprisal (Marshall 1999, 137).
4 Internationally, these fears have been voiced through a growing movement in the European Union and are the subject of the 1998 EU Council Regula-

tion 1139/98, which requires that products containing modified corn and soybeans carry information on the food label or ingredient list stating that the product contains genetically modified materials (*International Trade Reporter* 1999). Similarly, in 1999, Australia and New Zealand proposed legislative measures regarding labelling requirements for genetically modified foods (ibid.).

5 In 1995, the Government of Canada adopted a policy requiring the application of gender-based analysis in the policy development and analysis process. All federal departments and agencies are now required to analyse their policies and legislation to take into account their differing impacts on women and men (Status of Women Canada 1998).

6 Currently, for example, under s. 31(b) of the Food and Drugs Act. R.S.C. 1985, c. F-27, the maximum fine that can be imposed on a drug manufacturer is a mere $5,000.

7 A number of public interest groups have expressed concern that new health protection legislation may do away with accountability under the Criminal Code. They argue that any new health protection legislation should maintain its status as criminal legislation. The scope of the federal criminal law power in relation to health was addressed in *RJR-MacDonald Inc. v. Canada* (A.G.) [1995] 3 S.C.R. 199, a case involving the constitutionality of the federal Tobacco Products Control Act.

8 In February 2000, the Science Advisory Board submitted a report to the minister of health criticizing the approval process for its lack of transparency, timeliness, efficiency, and effectiveness (Science Advisory Board 2000). Later that month, in memoranda obtained by the CBC under the Freedom of Information Act, reference was made to the introduction of a Health Canada policy for the fast-tracking of drug approvals (Canadian Broadcasting Corporation 2000).

9 According to *Shared Responsibilities,* a Health Canada discussion paper, health protection legislation must 'meet Canada's international obligations including free trade agreements' (Health Canada 1998c, 22).

10 NAFTA does allow a state to exclude from patentability diagnostic, therapeutic, and surgical methods for the treatment of human beings, as this was a provision within the Canadian Patent Act at the time the agreement came into effect (Cameron 1996, 121). In addition, the Canadian government placed a reservation in Annex II to NAFTA with respect to social services. This reservation is directed at excluding existing and future measures of Canadian governments related to certain public and social services from coverage by important clauses of NAFTA (Cameron 1996, 122). While there is some ambiguity about the precise definition of 'social service' under the

agreement, the provision of such services in Canada may occur pursuant to it. Also, the Canadian government retained the right to impose standards to be met by the producers of goods and services entering the Canadian market (Cameron 1996, 121). Standards-related measures apply the notion of 'safety' – the protection of human, animal, or plant life or health, the environment, or consumers and sustainable development – as legitimate objectives (Cameron 1996, 121). For example, a fertility drug deemed unsafe could be excluded from the Canadian market on this basis (ibid.).

11 At the time some women who held themselves out to be 'feminists' or 'progressives' did support eugenic initiatives. Legendary suffragettes and feminists Nellie McLung and Emily Murphy promoted sterilization, as, in the words of Murphy, 'the sterilization of the unfit was needed to produce "human thoroughbreds"' (*Western Report* 1995, 1).

12 See, for example, *Edmonton Journal* 1928a; *Edmonton Journal* 1928b; *Medicine Hat News* 1928.

13 In Alberta, the Solemnization of Marriage Act, R.S.A. 1925, c. 39, s. 29 prohibited the issuing of a marriage licence where one party was, 'an idiot, insane or mentally incompetent.' A similar prohibition was enacted in British Columbia.

14 R.S.A. 1942, c. 194, s. 5

15 See, *Muir v. Alberta* (1996), 132 D.L.R. (4th) 695 (Alta. Q.B.), in which damages of approximately $750,000 were awarded to a woman who was wrongfully sterilized under the Alberta Sexual Sterilization Act in 1959.

16 The practice of rejecting 'defective' babies has a long history. Even in many jurisdictions where abortion is subject to criminal sanctions, a woman may have access to an abortion when there is a substantial risk that if the child were born, he or she would suffer from such physical or mental abnormalities as to be seriously handicapped. See (Clayton 1993) for a discussion of legislative examples in the United States. Abortion laws, as well as prenatal diagnosis and other foetal screening programs, have been defended against eugenic claims on the ground that they reflect compassion for the child who would be born and its potential pain and suffering. Others, however, assert that such laws, programs and techniques really relate to the welfare of the parents, or to the public purse.

8

Both Pitied and Scorned: Child Prostitution in an Era of Privatization

DIANNE L. MARTIN

Privatization, used here to refer to the amalgam of neo-liberal and neo-conservative strategies that mark the dismantling of the welfare state (Fudge & Cossman this volume), is fundamentally paradoxical. People are consenting to policies and practices that consistently enhance state coercion while undercutting state supports – practices which, although essential to privatization, are harmful to most people. Resolutions to this paradox inevitably include a consideration not only of privatization and refamilialization practices, but also of the criminal justice 'system,' the most significant institution of state coercion. As Douglas Hay has demonstrated, periods marked by increases in social inequality also demonstrate increased state reliance on the coercive instruments of criminal law, as crime control strategies serve privilege, control dissent, and provide effective paradigms for explaining social dysfunction (Hay 1992, 1975). Fear of crime and of those constructed as criminals tends to be enhanced, even promoted in such periods. Indeed, fear of crime and a harsh response to it may have less to do with the actual incidence of crime than with justifying increasing disparity in income and well-being among classes and people.

Women have complex relationships with the processes of the criminal law, and feminists have struggled to reconcile competing interests – for effective and respectful treatment of women as crime victims, and for equal and just treatment of defendants, to name but two (Abell 1992). The paradox inherent in entering into partnerships with the institutions of criminal justice as a means of achieving social justice has been of particular concern to feminists, who have argued that state concern with the preservation of privilege, and not the interests of women, tend to triumph (Currie 1990; Daly 1994; Martin 1998; Snider 1994, 1990).

These questions have renewed significance in the current period of aggressive privatization, as traditional avenues to social justice are being restructured and dismantled while the apparatuses of the coercive process expand, both into the private realm and inside state institutions. However, that expansion is itself paradoxical. At times, it is simply an expansion of familiar state processes intended to control the 'dangerous classes' through criminal and quasi-criminal instruments. At other times, however, coercive strategies are developed and promoted by reformers who are persuaded that they are the only means to obtain some measure of social justice. Regardless of the motives of those using or seeking new crime control methods, the end result is similar: status quo power relations and distinctions based on race, class, age, and gender are preserved and reinforced (Cole et al. 1995; Martin 1998).

Youth have been particularly disadvantaged under privatization, as witnessed by the disturbing and visible increase in homeless and disenfranchised children and youth on city streets. Their increased presence is clearly a by-product of privatization (N. Fraser 1993, 9; Gordon et al. 1988, 609). Under welfare reform campaigns such as those waged in Alberta and Ontario, for example, social assistance for youth who leave the family home has been eliminated or sharply narrowed, and entitlements have been diminished in most provinces (National Anti-Poverty Organization 1996). Social assistance, which allowed young people to live independently while enrolled full time in school did not survive welfare reform because it was an affront to the prerogatives and the responsibilities of families: kids should not be 'encouraged' to leave home by the availability of social assistance.[1] Most of those who leave home today have very few options available for the basics of survival: food, clothing, and shelter. Cuts to budgets for child welfare programs have weakened another strand in the safety net that used to be available to catch some children, some of the time. Although the cuts have affected programs generally, the harshest have decimated those for teens and youth (Alberta's Official Opposition 1997; Ontario Association of Children's Aid Societies 1993–8).[2] Most of the resources of staff, time, and money available to child welfare agencies are directed to very young children, a choice mandated by limited budgets, changing priorities, and a loss of legitimacy. The education system has also been 'reformed' in ways that adversely affect the most disadvantaged youth. Students with special needs find fewer qualified teachers and reduced resources for specialized programs. Alternative schools and alternative programs have been cut and publicly provided adult education is much reduced. School funding formulas are changing so that the dropout child is a liability, ensuring the death of part-time, flexible programs that were the last safety net for some kids (Ontario Secondary School Teachers Federation 2000). Given the loss of these supports it was inevitable that a significant number of youth who leave home turn to or are captured by street prostitution (Department of Justice 1998). The rest either juggle part-time minimum wage jobs, panhandle, wash windshields, engage in crime, or starve. For some, the reasons to leave home are so serious that life on or nearly on the street, with all its dangers and degradation, is an improvement. For others, the route home is much longer if drugs, prostitution, or crime have intervened.

The shrinking of supports has been matched by increasingly authoritarian and punitive measures directed at youth who do not 'measure up' or whose presence on city streets is considered to be disturbing. Current 'zero tolerance' policies to school violence for example, guarantee that certain demonized and marginalized young people have nowhere to go but the street (Blouin & Martino 1986, 81; Murphy & Cool 1990). Once there, they encounter not only the dangers of street life but also harsh anti-begging laws like Ontario's Safe Streets Act, which targets street youth in particular with fines and jail terms. Other laws are directed at the youth who have been coerced and seduced into the sex trade. Ostensibly both girls and boys are included in both types of legislation, but the new laws aimed at 'child prostitutes' (Alberta) and 'children sexually exploited for commercial purposes' (Ontario) focus on young women and girls[3] while the anti-begging statutes and by-laws primarily target young men and boys.

This chapter is concerned with young women working or constructed as child prostitutes, and who are thus victims and offenders at the same time. The methodology is qualitative, drawing on interviews with volunteer street workers and social workers, on analysis (in terms of both content and tone) of popular media sources and legislative debates and hearings, and on review of the relevant literature, legislation, and case law. What emerges is a map of the ways in which communities and legislators are responding to a particular group of young women, a map that demonstrates that selling crime – as if it were a commodity – is intimately linked to privatization. The techniques and practices employed in the maintenance of a status quo social order have intensified the commodification of crime and exacerbated the tensions inherent in women's relationship to the criminal justice system and the state. These techniques and practices are examined, and this tension is explored, in the context of the treatment of (female) child prostitution in the two jurisdictions in Canada most aggressively committed to restructuring: Alberta and Ontario. The first section examines the commodification of crime and the intensification of criminal regulation in an era of privatization. The existing legal structure and the discourse claiming that the law is inadequate and in need of 'reform,' is then described. Analysis of the ways that legal approaches to youth deviance and youth prostitution have altered under privatization follows, together with examination of the means: legislation that permits police to arrest and detain child prostitutes (in 'safe houses') in order to 'protect' them. Finally, the discourse that accompanies these sharp shifts is explored in the context of the city of Calgary, Alberta, where citizens, agencies, and government responded aggressively to a perceived crisis of (female) child exploitation. The chapter concludes with an examination of the impact of similar thinking in Ontario, where the Alberta model has been adapted and similar legislation is expected to be proclaimed in 2001.

I. The Commodification of Crime and the Intensification of Surveillance

The use of crime as a device for advancing a political agenda has become increasingly deliberate and sophisticated under privatization. Crime has always been a commodity to some extent, if only as a means to 'sell newspapers.' Lurid, sensational, titillating, terrifying, crime stories touch something in us, and crime (and its punishment) have been capitalized upon to teach, entertain and manipulate for centuries (Hay 1975). The strategies used for these purposes inevitably reflect and serve their own times (appearing quaint and obvious to later times), and not surprisingly, in this period of privatization, crime and its control is literally being marketed, like other products or services. One need only reflect on the remarkably successful campaign that persuaded millions of women, and those who loved them, that a cell phone 'for the car' was essential to their safety, in a country where crime against the occupants of motor vehicles is almost non-existent, to appreciate the marketing power of crime.

The commodification of crime control is somewhat different from the discursive strategy of commodification described in the Introduction as reconstituting goods and services once provided by the state as goods and services now provided by the market. While examples of this kind of commodification can be found, for instance in the privatization of prisons, in crime control, the state continues to provide the goods and services but actively markets them as well. Demand is created, markets fostered, brand names developed, and new products promoted. In the case of criminal justice, the demand is for more safety, more control, more order, and more punishment. The markets are the middle classes whose support (or apathy) must be maintained. The products that service the newly experienced demand are usually laws or campaigns for laws to resolve a successfully marketed 'crisis.' In the last provincial election in Ontario, for example, an aggressive and punitive approach to young offenders was identified by a political pollster as 'a good issue for the "PC"s to trot out as an election issue because it tends to appeal more to the PC voters ... Everybody likes a tough stance on crime ... If the PC's want to make it an issue and say, "Look, the place has gone to hell in a hand basket," they could possibly do that' (Rusk 1998).

The same techniques shape common perceptions about what 'crime' is, so that 'crime' is understood to be street crime and disorder and random acts of violence. It would not do to recognize that corporate or so-called white collar deviance cause considerably more social harm than street crime ever can (Pearce & Snider 1992). Linked to this perception is the belief that the criminal justice system is 'broken,' that crime is 'out of control,' that criminals are 'getting away with murder,' which in turn reinforces exaggerated fear of crime, irrespective of actual rates (Keane 1995).

There is no doubt that fear of crime persists in the face of significant declines in its rate (Carey 2000b; Roberts & Doob 1990), nor that it features in all political campaigns. Fear of crime and lack of faith in existing institutions diverts attention away from more politically volatile and concretely based fear, legitimating politically expedient promises of 'get tough,' law and order 'solutions' that pose little threat to entrenched interests. The corollary is that perceptions about social well-being and security are also shaped, with the result that 'reforms' to the processes of criminal sanctions are perceived and experienced as both necessary and effective.

At the same time, social divisions are reinforced and legitimated. Unruly, 'low-value' women, youth, and minorities are demonized and eroticized. Race, class, gender, and social location generally play a pivotal role in whether or not police, the system's gatekeepers, observe and police a particular individual. Once brought in to the criminal justice system, few escape. Conduct that is widespread across class and social location, such as truancy, use of soft drugs, and various acts of 'disorder,' is only criminalized among those who are being intensively policed, and race and gender operate as particularly discriminatory filters. In a racialized society like Canada it is visible minority youth who command most police interest and surveillance (Cole et al. 1995).

The criminal justice system is also deeply gendered. Women have been intensely concerned with the enterprise of making the system more effective; thus the high level of corporate and state support made available to campaigns that focus on women's role as crime victims is not surprising (Martin 1998; Martin & Mosher 1995). Nor is it surprising that only some crimes against women and some victims receive attention (Martin 1998; Valverde 1991, 44; Walkowitz 1992, 81). 'Good' women and 'innocent' children (the pairing and the depiction is deliberate) are represented as the ultimate beneficiaries of the protection and safety of the criminal justice system. At the same time, women as good citizens and good mothers participate as partners in the many criminal law 'reforms' which strengthen the coercive power of the state. The criminal justice system is a significant resource, and often the only resource that women who have been victims of crime can access. Thus women, as crime's victims, are posed appositionally to crime's perpetrators and silenced as allies to those constructed as criminal: – the poor, the young, members of a minority, and the male. Women in conflict with the law, on the other hand, are rendered both invisible and impotent while being objectified and eroticized (Adelberg & Currie 1987; Faith 1993).

Privatization does not always involve deregulation (Fudge & Cossman, this volume). When the criminal sanction is invoked in its aid, both the scope and the reach of retributive influences increase. Under a neo-liberal fiscal agenda private security, policing, and correctional services expand and treatment and social services are privatized while public institutions face cuts and private charities remain the preferred means to deliver services to offenders and victims. In aid of a neo-conservative moral agenda, a 'law and order' retributive approach to social disorder and dysfunction is used to reinforce hierarchical/patriarchal social organization. While neo-liberalism claims to celebrate the autonomous individual, arguing for the elimination of all but the most essential intrusions of the state, neo-conservatism insists on a combination of punishment and the charitable 'rescue and reform' model. However, even when advanced as a way to cut costs and to restore governance to individuals, these policies have only selectively curtailed the reach of the state. Deregulation may be apparent in decisions to close half-way houses, to shut down beds in treatment centres, and to cut the budgets of agencies such as Children's Aid Societies. But the retributive agencies – courts and police – remain firmly in place (Ismael & Vaillancourt 1988; Mays 1995, 41; Wright 1993, 1).

The role of what Dorothy Chunn and others have identifed as 'familial ideology' – to describe the location of an idealized white, Christian, heterosexual, bourgeois, patriarchically organized family at the centre of crime control policies – is central in neo-conservative ideology and justifies an aggressive legislative role in restoring this family to its 'proper' place in the social order (Daly 1989). In aid of this vision, state expenditure on crime has, in fact, increased under privatization with crime commissions, more police, more prosecutors and more prisons, while private enterprise provides 'strict treatment facilities' and 'boot camps.'[4]

The two approaches are not inconsistent if criminal law is recognized as a device for the preservation and reinforcement of existing power relations. The combined effect of cuts and new initiatives is to reduce the state's ameliorative role while expanding its coercive power. The justification is that these steps have been taken in the service of a return to an idealized past when the streets were safe, families were intact, and demands on the state were humble and modest. The real purpose, conscious or not, is to strengthen the reach of the criminal justice system and extend its scope against selected targets, particularly the 'dangerous classes' (Silver 1992). The scope and content of the criminal law is being reconstituted. While the regulation of corporate deviance (and risky behaviour) is diminished as investigative and prosecutorial infrastructures are dismantled in the name of 'cutting red tape' and 'getting government out of the boardrooms of the nation, homeless people, beggars and street youth are increasingly demonized and criminalized' (Snider 1990; Cavaluzzo 2000).

One of the more obvious manifestations of the intensification of surveillance and the commodification of crime control is the proliferation of criminal and quasi-criminal legislation and the way that these laws are presented to the public. They are increasingly brand-named – clear evidence of the work of marketers in the guise of policy makers. In the United States, for example, 'Megan's Laws' are being passed to enact sex-offender notification laws. In Ontario we have, among several brand-named statutes, a 'Christopher's Law' to create a registry of known sex offenders and a 'Brian's Law' to force mentally ill persons into treatment

(Mallan 2000). These laws are identified with a victim's name – in effect a brand name – not by their content. Crime victims and their survivors are encouraged to promote new legislation to find significance for the harm done to them in this way, some tangible evidence that their loss was not in vain. More often than not, however, the law they have brought into being is at best speculative and at worst utterly empty. In fact, the failure of many of these reforms is itself a form of planned obsolescence, effective for fuelling new demand for more law. A similar strategy names a piece of legislation with its message, such as Ontario's 'Safe Streets Act,' aimed at criminalizing begging and street life, or the Protection of Children Involved in Prostitution Act (Alberta) and the Protecting Children from Sexual Exploitation Act (Ontario), both aimed at the coerced removal of young prostitutes from the street. Once again, there is instant identification, at an emotional level, with the issue. Debate or critique becomes almost impossible. Who wishes to re-victimize Brian or Christopher or their families? Who wants unsafe streets?

The current 'crisis' of child prostitution similarly contains elements of a 'moral panic' (such as exaggeration of the phenomenon and the required response) (Cohen 1972; Hall et al. 1978), but the response involves a much more deliberately structured proactive strategy. The child prostitution 'crisis' is more helpfully understood as a marketing campaign selling fear, crime control, and obfuscation of issues as well as crafting partial and individualized solutions to complex social issues and garnering scarce resources to that end. Street prostitution is framed not as a problem arising out of systemic influences and deliberate social policy choices, but increasingly as the result of individualized choice. That is, the presence of women and girls on city streets is not explained in terms of economic pressures but as a decline in moral values and an increase in sexual and other disorder. At the same time, these young women represent crime victims and act as lightning rods for anxieties generated by the rapid social and economic changes associated with restructuring. The stories of individual girls are told and retold as tragic, sordid morality tales, offered as incontrovertible 'proof' that a crisis exists. The solution provided to the crisis, a punitive coercive mechanism with social welfare overtones, answers the needs of both crime fighters and victim saviours.

On the one hand, 'law and order' language and institutions are deployed. The police are empowered to detain and convey girls and young women to secure 'safe' facilities and new provincial offences are created to punish pimps and purchasers. On the other hand, a new vocabulary becomes part of the reform strategy[5] as the young women are framed as subjects of pity or victims of child abuse rather than as prostitutes. Resources are generated and allocated to 'rehabilitation' and support. But the appropriated discourse and the reform agenda are no more than superficially ameliorative. The child prostitution initiatives reflect a law and order campaign that has engineered a 'crisis' and deployed a highly individualized and coercive solution to it. The language (or goal) of child protection notwithstanding, surveillance and coercion of women and girls has increased, echoing regimes long past.

II. The Existing Regime

With rare exceptions, the women most likely to be in conflict with the law have either been involved in the sex trade or in some way constructed as prostitutes, the quintessentially gendered criminals. Whether prostitutes or not, women in conflict with the criminal law are cast as immoral, sexually loose, irresponsible breeders of poverty and disorder and punished accordingly (Adelberg & Currie 1987; Faith 1993). They are also the exception within the criminal justice system. Prostitution is the only category of offence under which more women than men are convicted (Duchesne 1995). Although the act of exchanging sexual services for money is not itself illegal, and the law is technically gender neutral, most law enforcement devoted to prostitution is expended on the conduct of women who sell sexual services to men.

There is considerable ambiguity about prostitution, both in popular terms and among feminists. On the one hand, prostitution is posited as the 'victimless crime' and an improper target for criminal sanction. According to this reading, the predominant social interest is in managing the 'trade' from the perspectives of health, nuisance, and urban planning and curbing the occasional excesses. Otherwise it is unworthy of much, if any, interference by the state (Roach 1999). But prostitution is also about sex, almost exclusively heterosexual sex, although always both squalid and subversive. The popular images are vivid: fallen or debauched women, rakish or compulsive men. Prostitution is rendered as the ultimate act of moral degradation of both prostitute and her purchaser, but with the greater level of concern expressed for the 'fallen' woman. Eradication of the sex trade is pursued as a moral crusade, and both historically and in contemporary contexts these missions are often religiously based. The pattern has been consistent: adult prostitutes can expect at best pity as degraded workers, at worst, scorn and punishment as moral failures (Backhouse 1991, 1984; Brock 1999; Brock & Kinsman 1986; Hunt 1999).

Feminists have not resolved these conflicts, although feminist texts have expressed the tensions differently and identified the gendered nature of the issues. There is consensus that criminalization strategies unfairly stigmatize women. Many feminists have argued that in a patriarchal society prostitution represents the ultimate commodification of the female body. In this analysis, prostitution is fundamentally a matter of gender politics and its eradication a goal of sexual liberation (Bell 1994; Dworkin 1987; Pateman 1988). Other feminists have argued that through this approach feminists have privileged a single sexual standard (Rubin 1984) and failed to account for racialization (Razack 1993), when what is required is openness to multiple discourses about sexuality, and the choices women make (Bell 1994; Jaggar 1994).

These conflicts are much less evident when the prostitutes are, or are framed as, 'children.' Regardless of the position taken on consenting adults in the sex trade, there is considerable unanimity of concern over the employment of children in any of its aspects (Diduck 1999, 129, Stainton Rogers & Stainton Rogers 1999, 183–7). That unanimity, however, can overwhelm care about precision in regard to age and conduct definitions. For example, contrary to much popular rhetoric about increasing numbers, measuring child prostitution and determining whether or not it is increasing or decreasing is very difficult. The lack of uniform definition as to who is a 'child' for these purposes, or even what constitutes prostitution, renders the data speculative at best.

Some studies, which not surprisingly report the highest number of 'children' in the sex trade, include all young women and men under twenty-one (House of Commons 1984). Others, which report fewer numbers, restrict their definition to youth under fourteen (Brannigan & Fleishman 1989; Department of Justice 1998). Similar disparity is found in the ways of measuring the conduct that constitutes prostitution. Some consider the occasional trading of sex for favours or a place to sleep to be 'engaging in the sex trade' and include these girls as child prostitutes when compiling their service statistics. Others limit the definition to the more usual commercial transaction of sex for money (Brannigan & Fleischman 1989; Department of Justice 1998).

The interests involved and reasons for this disparity vary, but it does highlight a disturbing hypocrisy according to which some young people under eighteen are vilified as fully adult 'criminals' for some purposes but placed on pedestals as abused 'children' for others (Martin 1998).

The public debate that takes place when prostitution involves young people tends to be about approaches and techniques of rescue and interdiction, not about whether or not child prostitution is wrong, increasing, and harmful (Department of Justice 1998). The rare dissenting voices are almost exclusively found in the male gay community.[6]

Both federal and provincial governments have jurisdiction to respond to child prostitution. Provincial jurisdiction over matters of child welfare and child protection empowers police and child protection workers to apprehend, detain, and even to impose medical treatment on children 'in need of protection.' The devil, as always, is in the details: who is a 'child,' when is she or he 'in need of protection,' and what resources are available for his or her care and treatment? Child protection competency enables provincial governments to craft remedial responses to child prostitution. The federal power over criminal law means that the apprehension, prosecution, and punishment of prostitutes, pimps, purveyors, and purchasers of sexual services falls within federal competency. The federal government has been active in this area, and the Criminal Code has an entire scheme of prohibitions and procedural provisions dealing specifically with the purchase of sex from persons (apparently or actually) under the age of eighteen. Provincial interest is more recent and closely linked to the politics of privatization.

The deep ambivalence associated with this quintessentially woman's work has ensured that some level of control has always been in place. Justification for the regulation of prostitution, however, has varied at different times and under different social and economic conditions. Three rationales have dominated: an interest in protecting or saving prostitutes from themselves, the need to regulate an unseemly but inevitable nuisance, and the need to express moral outrage against the activity. In any given regime, these three rationales are intricately intertwined. As feminist scholars have effectively documented, the legislation of every era has had elements of rescue, control, and sanction, so that no approach seems satisfactory for long (Backhouse 1984; Walkowitz 1992). The next section sketches that history and sets out the legal structure in place today in regard to prostitution in general and child prostitution in particular.

A. Regulating Prostitution

Prostitution laws seem to be particularly prone to changing social conditions. The legislative scheme that currently governs prostitution came into effect in December 1985 and was a political response to public pressure to do 'something' about the problem of street prostitution. The perceived crisis of the 1980s was itself a product of law reform efforts in the 1970s that resulted in the repeal of a prohibition- era law, which had operated on the basis that a woman who could not account for her presence on the street was presumed to be a 'common prostitute' (The same regulation captured begging and loitering.)

In 1972, paragraphs (a), (b), and the notorious 'Vagrancy "C"' paragraph of section 175(1) were repealed and replaced with a summary conviction offence (s. 195), which simply made it an offence to solicit in a public place for the purpose of prostitution. This amendment also removed the gender distinction, making it possible for the first time to arrest purchasers of sexual services (who by asking were 'soliciting') and to recognize that men and boys also work as prostitutes.

The seeds of the failure of this reform were imbedded within it. The liberalization of attitudes towards all sexual behaviour, including prostitution, which marked the 1970s, was not universally shared. The police seemed to resent the loss of arbitrary arrest powers over street prostitutes and applied the new soliciting laws aggressively. Undercover officers made arrests on the basis of a mere 'wink or nod' or other low key communication and charged liquor licence holders for permitting prostitution on their premises, driving many women out of such traditional locales and onto the street. Prostitutes fought back, successfully challenging the prostitution and bawdy-house laws in court. When the meaning of soliciting under the new section 195 was interpreted by the Supreme Court in 1978 to mean 'pressing or persistent' conduct (*Hutt*, 1978), the police began to refuse to apply it at all. In a tactic to maximize their claim that they needed stronger laws, the police allowed street prostitution to flourish, in sometimes flagrant ways (i.e., they ignored soliciting that was clearly 'pressing and persistent').[7] Community pressure mounted, often with overt police support, most of it concerned with the 'nuisance' effects of street prostitution and the adverse impact on property values, but concerns about child prostitution and the high risk and demeaning lives of street prostitutes were also voiced.

In June 1983, Parliament responded by establishing the Special Committee on Pornography and Prostitution (House of Commons 1985, 'Fraser'). A year earlier Parliament had established the Committee on Sexual Offences Against Children and Youths (House of Commons 1984, 'Badgley'); this committee was also concerned with child prostitution, demonstrating the essential ambivalence these questions generate.

Badgley and Fraser reported in 1984 and 1985, respectively, on many overlapping issues, including the circumstance of child prostitution, but they took sharply different positions.

The Fraser Report identified prostitution as symptomatic of women's inequality and recommended partial decriminalization along with improved strategies to reduce social and economic inequities between men and women. The Badgley Report, on the other hand, identified young prostitutes as victims of individually abusive homes but favoured criminal law strategies that would allow authorities to 'help' the arrested women and girls, who were seen as being otherwise 'incorrigible' or beyond reach. The Badgley position won the day, and the Justice and Legal Affairs Committee of the House recommended stronger sanctions against prostitution. The Fraser Committee recommendations were ignored and the current law that criminalizes literally all aspects of street prostitution was enacted.

Following a review of their operation three years after implementation (Department of Justice 1989) the new provisions were made permanent. They amount to a ban on all street prostitution. Civil libertarians and those feminists[8] outraged by the discriminatory and punitive underpinnings of the 'reform' raised these issues when the Supreme Court of Canada reviewed the legislation (*Reference re Sections 193, 195*, 1990). The court concluded, in a split decision, that it imposed a justifiable infringement on freedom of speech. A related challenge, to the presumption that being in the company of prostitutes or living with a prostitute implies living off the avails of prostitution, also failed (*R. v. Downey*, 1990). Cory J. writing for the majority in *Downey*, recognized that the presumption infringes the presumption of innocence provided in section 11(d) of the Charter but concluded that it constitutes a demonstrably justified limitation on that right within section 1. The objective of the provision was framed as a laudable attempt to deal with the cruel and pervasive social evil of pimping without requiring the testimony of prostitutes, who are easily threatened by pimps. Expressing a more sophisticated gender analysis, the dissent (Justices Laforest, McLachlin, and Iacobucci) argued that the presumption cast its net far too broadly to have a rational connection and recognized the legitimacy of the claim that the provision compels prostitutes to live and work alone, deprived of human relationships save those who are prepared to run the risk of criminal charges.

In the end, both Parliament and the Supreme Court of Canada stamped their seal of approval on a regime that treats street prostitutes very harshly, but also, in the name of equality and concern for the prostitute's well-being, extends the net more broadly. The regulation of prostitution has always included the prosecution of pimps and procurers, but with the repeal of 'Vag C' purchasers were included as well. Just as attitudes towards prostitutes vary over time and with changing social conditions, so too do attitudes towards the men who purchase sexual services. Whether seen as 'real men' exercising 'natural' urges or as degraded self-indulgent abusers in regard to adult female prostitutes, those who seek to purchase sexual services from young women and girls are no longer tolerated (Roach 1999, 122–4).[9]

In 1985 the 'communicating' law was amended to create a separate offence of communicating for the purpose of obtaining the sexual services of a minor (Criminal Code, s. 212(4)). However, the section was almost never used and law enforcement as well as community groups were frustrated by the problems of proof it raised. In order to obtain a conviction it was almost essential that the young prostitute testify against her 'customer' – and few did (Daum 1999). This lacuna was corrected in 1997 with Bill C-27. Subsection 214(5) now makes it an offence to solicit a person one believes to be under eighteen, making the use of undercover operatives posing as youthful prostitutes a law enforcement tool. It also appears that when prosecutions are actually brought and convictions won, the sentences imposed are substantial, in contrast to those imposed for soliciting an adult (Department of Justice 1998).

It soon becomes apparent, however, that dissatisfaction sets in rapidly even when the desired reforms are enacted. Selective enforcement of the provisions, and the limits of the criminal law as a tool for changing behaviour generally, will once more set the stage for disappointment. As the social and economic forces underlying street prostitution begin to push large numbers of women and youth onto the streets, pressures mount to intensify law enforcement and to introduce even harsher measures. In recent years, the centre of reform momentum has moved to include provincial governments, which have become increasingly active in pursuing the political advantages of crime. In the result, much of the recent crisis response to child prostitution has been provincially based.

B. Regulating Youth

The underlying assumption of provincial child welfare administrations is that in circumstances in which private, familial responsibility has broken down the state has an interest in and responsibility for the child. Such laws also reflect the constantly contested and revised assumption of a social responsibility for the welfare of children; thus the dominant legal principle is 'the best interest of the child.' If one is prepared to acknowledge that the sexual exploitation of young people by adults is an issue of child welfare, then child welfare regimes naturally include the exploitation dubbed 'child prostitution.' Different assumptions predominate in the criminal law, and even in regard to youthful offenders the 'welfare' of the child is subordinate and individual culpability and social responsibility predominate. Here the fact that the 'child' 'chooses' to disobey the laws against public solicitation for purposes of prostitution, for example, justifies the intervention of state actors to 'correct' the deviant child. Who should be or will be subject to which regime is a matter of considerable variation. The discretion of law enforcement officers and child welfare workers, the availability of resources, prevailing public opinion, gender, class, and race all play a role in determining the fate of girls and youth in conflict with the law.

The discursive construction of 'child prostitute' is indeterminate and indiscriminate in most respects. The popular impression of a 'child prostitute' is a very young adolescent, thirteen or fourteen years of age or younger. Coercive regimes such as those imposed by the Criminal Code and the Young Offenders Act 'define' child as a person under the age of eighteen. However, in child welfare contexts, the fairly widespread definition is that full child protection services apply only to youth under fourteen, with differing degrees of involvement for youth under sixteen and eighteen years of age, respectivlely. These distinctions have considerable significance in the debates over responses to youthful prostitutes. They are muted, however, in the language of child protection legislation.

1. Child Welfare Approaches

Each province has legislation concerned with child welfare administered by a child protection agency, which in most provinces are quasi-independent agencies or children's aid societies, organized regionally. Although the precise statutory language of what constitutes a child in need of protection varies, there is a shared core meaning. For a child to be found 'in need of protection' there must be a significant departure from the standard of care one would generally expect for a child of a given age. A minimum parental standard is set, as well as a secondary standard, which take into consideration the age of the parents and the community in which they live. The definitions in the legislation tend to be quite precise, offering a 'shopping list' range of harms and risks, any one of which might warrant intervention. A number of the defined harms overlap with criminal provisions and with new legislation aimed specifically at child prostitution. Typically, the child must be found to fit within one or more of the provisions,[10] which usually include proof that a child has suffered physical harm or is at substantial risk of physical harm; has suffered emotional harm or is at substantial risk of emotional harm; has been sexually molested/exploited or is at substantial risk of sexual molestation/exploitation. A child would also be in need of protection when he or she requires but does not receive medical treatment or consent to treatment is refused; when the child's development is being impaired; where there is parental abandonment or absence or an inability to care for the child; or where the child has engaged in criminal-like behaviour (Wilson 1997). One would expect that 'children' involved in prostitution, or at risk of such involvement, would clearly fall within these definitions, but there has been reluctance to utilize this strategy, and indeed few resources to do so. The delinquency approach, that of scorn, perhaps tempered with pity, certainly dominated historically.

2. Delinquency Approaches

Ever since the introduction of the Juvenile Delinquents Act in 1929, young persons in conflict with the criminal law have been treated differently from adults committing the same offences or engaging in the same conduct. The reform wave, which resulted in the enactment of that statute, was concerned with distinguishing between youth who were in need of reform and correction and adults who merited punishment. The new law relied on a finding of 'delinquency,' a status that could be imposed whenever a person under sixteen and over nine committed an offence against the Criminal Code or was otherwise found to be 'delinquent.' With young men, non-criminal conduct that would sustain a finding of delinquency often involved truancy and running. With young women, sexual precocity was often enough. In Ontario alone, where 'schools for delinquents' were opened in the 1930s, hundreds of young women were subjected to abuse and imprisonment in discredited institutions like the Grandview Institution for Girls, for nothing more than running away from abuse at home or exhibiting rebelliousness and/or sexually precocious behaviour (Bala & Mahoney 1995; Brannigan & Fleischman 1989). The situation was similar in other provinces. Rarely would a young person be brought into the Child Welfare Process for truancy or prostitution. Instead, they were treated as 'juvenile delinquents.' Until the introduction of the Young Offenders Act in 1984, youthful prostitutes were treated legally as delinquent; in need of correction more than punishment, perhaps, but delinquent all the same. Indeed, all young women who demonstrated sexual precocity were treated as delinquent, and the connection between the sexual exploitation of girls by adult men and their own deviance was explicit.

In the late 1970s and early 1980s an attempt to remedy these patronizing and increasingly discredited approaches to youth gained purchase. The approach to child prostitution began to change as the women's movement achieved success in uncovering the hidden crimes of child sexual abuse and forced changes to child protection laws. The spirit of these changes was the protection of individual rights; an underlying motivation was reduction of state support for children, the mentally ill and others who had earlier been seen as state responsibilities. Regardless of the stated, laudable motives, the stage was being set for the ultimate withdrawal of the state from social responsibility for the disadvantaged.

In the case of the Young Offenders Act, the new legislation was clear about its purpose and rationale. Young persons were to be held accountable for their actions, but responsibility would be decided in accordance with due process. That is, youth were no longer to be subject to intrusive interventions in their lives on the basis solely of their status as young people in conflict with, or alleged to be in conflict with, their school, parents, or community. At the same time, amendments to child welfare legislation restricted the right of child protection workers to have children removed from their homes. The paternalistic, class and race–biased interventions of the 1960s, which had resulted in countless harmful child apprehensions, coupled with an inadequate and poorly supervised foster care system had discredited child welfare initiatives. The 'new' approach, introduced in one form or another in most jurisdictions, was to put the onus on the state to justify an apprehension and for courts to make 'minimally intrusive' orders.

III. The Processes of Re-Regulation

Reforms to child protection, delinquency, and mental health laws, despite their emphasis on protection for the rights and dignity of individuals and their families, set the stage for what was to come – the devolution of social justice claims and entitlements to little more than a hope for charity. At their best, de-institutionalization and similar reforms were barely funded; as funding cuts became the norm, the legal structures governing the new approaches were ripe for discreditation. Economic restructuring had already begun during what is now seen as the height of the modern liberal welfare state – the mid-1970s – and the discursive strategies of privatization such as refamilialization, individualization, and the intensification of law and order campaigns were starting to gain currency.

This is particularly apparent in the history of the campaign to discredit the more forward-looking provisions of the Young Offenders Act, which began almost as soon as the Act was proclaimed (Bala 1994; Corrado & Markwar 1994; Leschied 1995; Mcguire 1997). In provinces such as Alberta and Ontario, which opposed the change in the definition of 'child' to young persons under eighteen from the Juvenile Delinquents Act definition of under sixteen, two interrelated factors are particularly important. First, the demonization of youth made it politically viable to introduce increasingly harsh measures against young offenders. Second, the discrediting of the existing legal structure set the stage for introducing more 'effective' legal instruments. The discrediting of provincial child welfare schemes made it politically viable to defund and privatize them, and the discrediting of the federal criminal law generally, and the Young Offenders Act specifically, as 'liberal,' 'soft on crime,' and unrealistic made it politically viable to 'get tough on crime.' These ideas were successfully promoted by a loose coalition of police forces and officials, right-wing and religious/conservative groups, crime victims, and (particularly provincial) politicians, and they were given wide media coverage. In Alberta first and then in Ontario, quasi-criminalization emerged as the approach to child prostitutes and in Ontario punitive legislation aimed at street youth generally has been enacted (Safe Streets Act). Other provinces are following suit.

A. Demonizing Youth

Young runaways and prostitutes receive at least a measure of pity and sometimes considerable compassion from courts and commentators. The young people in conflict with the reviled Young Offenders Act are not as fortunate. Lurid and sensationalized stories about young killers and gang members are widespread in all forms of media. Particular attention is focused on the criminality of girls – there is something not only 'unnatural' but titillating and frightening about violence perpetrated by adolescent girls. The case of the murder of fourteen-year-old Reena Virk, of Victoria, exemplifies most of these themes, as both young women and young men were implicated in the beating that led to her death. One theme saw Reena as the cause of her own misfortune, rejecting the 'safety' of her own home. This is an important subtext in much of the discourse concerning street youth; young people must be returned home to the safety and the control of parents and not encouraged to reject family values by 'soft' social welfare policies or the contamination of peers (*Toronto Star*, 29 November 1997).

Other stories fuel a belief that 'violent teens' are 'out of control.' In 'The New Lawman in Town' (*Toronto Sun*, 14 February 2000) Julian Fantino, the incoming police chief, is quoted as cautioning a Progressive Conservative party convention that '[w]e must be extremely concerned about the growing number of young people who are out of control and seem to be accountable to no one.' Citing Canada as having a reputation of being 'soft on crime,' Fantino proposed that violent teens be held accountable for their criminal conduct by trying them in adult court.

The media has almost entirely accepted this version of youth and danger (*Globe and Mail* 1997b; *Toronto Star* 1997). Falling crime rates cannot, in the short term at least, dislodge it, as demonstrated in a study by several experienced reporters for the *Globe and Mail*, given this headline: 'Shakedowns in the schoolyard. Youth crime may not be rising but bullies are getting more sophisticated and brutal' (Campbell et al. 1997). These images and language become internalized and normalized. No other understanding is possible as rough play becomes assault and bullies become criminals (Roberts & Doob 1990).

Outcomes are also affected. It may be easier to treat harshly someone who has been so effectively demonized. Certainly the past decade has seen significant increases in the numbers of youth in custody (Canadian Centre for Justice Statistics 1996, Figure 6.12, 146–7). The inevitable race and class biases of law enforcement strategies such as the drug 'war' and the focus on street activities ensure that racialized youth comprise a disproportionate number in that increase (Cole et al. 1995, 82, 83, 101, 185).

B. *Discrediting Existing Legislation*

1. Lack of Jurisdiction

Child welfare and criminal legislation have both been subject to intense pressure and to loss of legitimacy in the privatization era. Police forces supported by right-wing politicians initially led the attack on the Young Offenders Act. They focused on the new limits imposed on their discretion to arrest and detain in general (the same limits that existed in regard to the arrest of adults), and in particular on the loss of criminal jurisdiction over children under age twelve. For example, under the Juvenile Delinquents Act, police could arrest and detain youth, from age seven, not only on reasonable suspicion that they were committing crimes but when they were reported as being incorrigible. The police had unfettered discretion to detain young persons 'for questioning' and then to release, to refer to a social agency, to release into the custody of a parent with a reprimand, or to refer them to a juvenile court. These powers not only served law enforcement requirements, they were also used to maintain class, race, and gender boundaries (Gandy 1970; Houston 1972). With this type of power, the police had little reason to learn the scope of child welfare law, and they tended to ignore the apprehension and detention measures available under that regime, except as a backup to a Juvenile Delinquents Act arrest.

One of the most publicized limits on police powers was the change in the age of youth subject to the criminal law. Where children as young as seven could be dealt with under the Juvenile Delinquents Act, with the introduction of the Young Offenders Act jurisdiction was narrowed to youth between twelve and eighteen years of age. Police persistently complained that they were powerless to intervene to arrest or protect youngsters under twelve who were in trouble. This was of course not true (Bala & Mahoney 1995). In Ontario, for example, section 21(1) (a) of the Child Welfare Act permits a police officer to apprehend and detain in a 'place of safety' a child who is apparently 'in need of protection' within the terms of the Act. That is, they may arrest and detain a child of any age for dangerous, harmful, or criminal behaviour. While there are other problems inherent in these provisions (Bala & Mahoney 1995), police complaints that 'nothing can be done' are unfounded.

Detention for being 'out of place,' however, is no longer within the police prerogative. In Toronto that 'place' is described as follows: 'The intersection of Yonge and Dundas Streets and the north-east entrance to the Eaton Centre in downtown Toronto have a certain notoriety founded upon fact. The area described generates an almost magnetic appeal for children who have run away from home, some of whom become the so-called 'street kids' and acts as a focal point for many persons involved in prostitution and drug trafficking. The mix is undesirable, unhealthy and dangerous' (R. v. I.C.V., 1985). I.C.V., a fifteen-year-old girl found hanging around in the Eaton Centre, was charged with assault police when she resisted police 'rescue' attempts: 'she was forcibly dragged, kicking and screaming, out to the sidewalk and to a police vehicle which had been summoned from 52 Division.' Youth Court Judge D.R. Main notes that I.C.V. 'was sitting quietly and chatting with a friend inside the north-east entrance to the Eaton Centre when she was approached by two uniformed police officers.' In the opinion of the officers, because I.C.V. had remained where she was for approximately five minutes, she was either loitering or a possible runaway.

The two six-foot tall officers forcibly searched the 5'2" girl and her bags and then arrested her. As Judge Main describes it, the force involved was considerable: '... this young lady was lifted into the air and slammed face down onto the sidewalk, handcuffed and with the assistance of a passing ambulance driver, forced into the cruiser and driven to 52 Division ... at approximately 11:45 pm., she was taken to Toronto Sick Children's Hospital for examination as a result of an injury to her ankle which was swollen and painful enough to impede normal walking ... In addition, I.C.V. suffered bruises to her arms, wrists and legs, her knees were scraped and her right pant leg was torn.' He dismissed the assault police charge (based on a kick to Constable Scudd's groin) and identified the 'confusion' surrounding the approaches being taken to young people by quoting Judge Nasmith, in the decision of *R. v. D.E.M.*: 'In my experience there has been considerable confusion concerning the approach the police and others have taken towards young persons. The boundaries are often blurred as between criminal investigations on the one hand and forms of benevolent service on the other. This has not been a particularly good situation for young persons. There are very important distinctions to be made between a criminal investigation and the role of the police and others in child welfare matters. There are defined procedures for dealing with children in need of protection under the Child Welfare Act which no doubt would have been more suitable for dealing with D.E.M. as a "missing person."' (*D.E.M.*, 12)

Although a police officer is empowered, pursuant to section 21(1)(a) of the Ontario Child Welfare Act, to apprehend and take to a place of safety a child apparently in need of protection, Judge Main expected more than '[t]he mere suspicion that a child is loitering in a public place or a "missing person" based solely upon five minutes of observation and the knowledge that the area is one in which missing children congregate' before an apprehension could be justified.

In a similar vein, the case of T.C., an appeal from Family Court to the General Division, illustrates the attempts made to use the Young Offenders Act to detain runaways for their own good (*R. v. C. (T.)*, 1988). Justice

Salhaney resisted the plea to interpret the Act for that purpose and over-turned a sentence of six months' closed custody imposed at trial on a thirteen-and-a-half year-old girl 'to protect her from returning to a life of prostitution on the streets of Toronto or Vancouver.' He framed the issue in terms of the changed philosophy with respect to youthful offend-ers, the shift from paternalism to 'accountability,' and concluded that the trial judge had to deal with the law as it was written and leave the inadequacies of child welfare law to the legislatures.

Whether or not there is a gap in the legislation dealing with young persons, there is certainly ambivalence about whether engaging in pros-titution merits intervention. In *Re A.C.* an application was brought by the Children's Aid Society to the Alberta Family Court for a secure treat-ment order on the grounds that the sixteen-year-old child was involved in prostitution, drugs, and a violent lifestyle while out of control of her parents, and on her expressed wish to escape from secure treatment. In issue was whether her behaviour amounted to a 'mental or behavioural disorder' justifying secure treatment, which would be 'in the best inter-ests of the child' (*A.C.*, 1990). The court refused to interpret disorder in light of the best interests principle and decided that secure treatment may only be considered once a determination has been made on the issue of 'disorder. In making that determination, Judge Russell rejected a psychologist's opinion that the young woman's lifestyle constituted a behavioural disorder. In effect, he found that her life as a prostitute rep-resented a 'choice,' not a problem justifying state intervention:

> The psychologist is of the opinion that this child suffers from a mental dis-order because of her lack of affect in describing her violent lifestyle, and because as a 16 year old she should be living at home, going to school and not engaging in this type of sexual activity.
>
> ...
>
> The psychologist's opinion that the child should be at school, living at home and not engaging in this type of sexual activity, is not in my view, a matter falling within the range of matters requiring expert testimony, and is not a matter on which this expert has been qualified to express opinions.

Judge Russell's rejection of the expert opinion appears to be based on the view that sixteen-year-old prostitutes have chosen a lifestyle and there should be no further state intervention (other than criminal law intervention presumably.) This attitude explains in part the movement to develop new legislation, but it is also helpful in demonstrating how widespread the discrediting of child welfare approaches had become. The rationalizations are also significant. He went on to say:

> Further, legislation and common law in effect in this province reflect social norms of behaviour in young persons which are in conflict with the psychologist's opinion. The School Act provides that mandatory school attendance ceases at age 16; the Maintenance Order Act provides that parents' responsibility to support children ceases at age 16 unless the child is incapacitated. Under the common law parents are not able to legally compel their children to remain at home beyond age 16; the age of discretion was generally set at 16 for girls and 14 for boys and was the age at which a child could legally consent to sexual relations. Recent amendments to the Criminal Code may now have reduced that to 14 for both boys and girls, though consent for some forms of sexual activity may be 18 years. (Sections 150.1 and 159 of the Criminal Code of Canada)

The Crown attempted to persuade Judge Russell that the court must 'accept its duty to provide protection for her [A.C.]' and that it could not 'abandon' her 'to adult standards and adult expectations at this stage in her life.' However, the judge concluded that child welfare law was not intended to solve this type of problem:

> These Courts are daily confronted with the sordid reality that prostitution and drug involvement is the dreadful way of life for shocking numbers of sad and lonely children. *Though none would condone that choice of lifestyle for any child* the Court must apply the law as it finds it. *If the legislature in this province intends that children below the age of 18 and over the age of 16 who engage in prostitution and who are out of control of their parents should be confined for their own protection, the legislation should specifically address this issue.*
>
> I cannot conclude however, in the absence of any definition of that term or expert opinion thereon, that a history of prostitution and drug involvement and an attempted escape from secure treatment constitutes a behaviour disorder in a 16 year old child. (emphasis added)

These three cases are not definitive but they illustrate the thinking of many courts across the country. More importantly, the judgments demonstrate the basis for the frustration of many police officers and members of the community, indicating that in essence, nothing can be done about troubled rebellious adolescents, whether they are a danger to others or harming themselves through prostitution.

Many in the media were certainly convinced. In 1996 the CBC aired, to great acclaim, a made-for-television movie called *Little Criminals*. Its theme was the absence of any legal resource for an eleven-year-old boy who was out of control and a danger both to himself and others. The fictional police officer, social workers, and distraught mother all asserted that nothing could be done unless the child consented to enter treatment. He refused to do so. The premise was utterly false in legal terms, but it had become as true for the author, the CBC, and the media as it was for the police officers who arrested I.C.V., T.C., or A.C.

2. Lack of Resources

The Alberta and Ontario decisions discussed above, which stress individual rights and a sort of positivist legality, are not the only approach Canadian courts have taken. The aggressive cutting of resources has also undermined the legitimacy of child protection regimes. In Nova Scotia, for example, a series of related judgments demonstrate the jurisdictional gaps that have frustrated service providers and others who want a 'solution' for runaway girls. They also detail the individual stories of young prostitutes. In these cases, judges sought to hold the state accountable for the lack of resources. In *T.M.* and *B.F.*, Family Court Judge Neidermayer considered an apprehension request in regard to young girls who were already involved in prostitution (*Nova Scotia (Minister of Community Services) v. T.M.*, 1992). Pimps allegedly make contact at the group homes where troubled girls are placed and assist them to run away. He specifically commented on the legislative 'gap' (which is in effect the same across the country). More significantly, perhaps, he clearly identified the lack of appropriate resources:

> The increasing problem of prostitution is well-known in this community. Safe and secure facilities are required for the protection of these girls. Under the previous legislation, the Children's Services Act, the courts had the power to order children to a place of safety, which had the element of security. Now, however, the current legislation does not permit the courts to make such an order and no such facilities are available in this province for these very vulnerable individuals.
>
> ...
>
> However, the jurisdiction under the provisions of the Act is limited. The court can only order the return of the child to the legal guardian. It is with severe apprehension that the order is to issue. Their long-term safety and welfare cannot be adequately protected because of the practical inadequa-

cies, as well as the legal limits, which are placed on the courts and the child welfare agencies.

Judge Neidermayer developed the theme further in a later decision, *A.A.*, first describing a troubling case of a sexually exploited child (*Minister of Community Services and A.A.*, 1995). He was, in effect, attempting to generate a crisis that would produce more substantive solutions: 'She is a young girl, only 12 years of age. She has involved herself with persons known to be involved in prostitution and the fact that she has put herself at risk by being sexually active and contracting a sexually transmitted disease. Under these circumstances I am not reluctant to authorize the order which has been requested.'

He was clearly frustrated, however, by the reality that such orders were meaningless in the absence of any secure facilities for such children. Previous legislation had designated 'places of safety' for seriously disturbed children where 'erratic and dangerous behaviour' could be stabilized. However, no such 'secure treatment facilities' were currently available; thus 'the only place where A. can be given a bed is the very place from which she ran.' ' Whether because the child in question is younger than A.C., or because Judge Neidermayer holds different views about when a child is in need of protection than Judge Russell is difficult to say; however, he had no difficulty concluding that intervention was justified: 'I think it is patently obvious that 12 year old girls who are involved in prostitution, use drugs and have no home to go to need to be provided a safe, secure environment which can commence remediating the situation. Luring young girls into and maintaining them in the prostitution industry is a well-known activity in the Halifax metropolitan area.' Judge Neidermayer was not prepared to view the child's conduct as a 'choice': 'Twelve year old children cannot be expected to make rational adult decisions. There are many decisions adults or society have to make for children. Placing them in a secure environment when prostitution and drug abuse are the issues is the responsibility of society. Under the current legislative scheme society is abdicating its responsibilities.'

The issue has not been resolved, except that in Nova Scotia the child protection option has been utterly discredited by cuts to staffing and the absence of any secure treatment facilities. In *M.G.* the Family Court reviewed Neidermayer's judgments and the current 'crisis' (*Family and Children's Services of Kings County, applicant, and T.G. and R.G,* 1998), setting out the litany of abandonment, running, drugs, and prostitution that constitute the life of a thirteen-year-old prostitute. The police role is fairly consistent with reports from across the country about similar cases: 'Specifically, the court was told that on the very afternoon of the first appearance, an R.C.M.P. officer in the Windsor area came across M.G. and two other girls, one of whom was unclothed below the waist and crying, in a pickup truck with a 47 year old male. This person is so well known to the police for such matters that on his being observed by the officer in the presence of these young females, the officer felt compelled to stop his vehicle and check it out. The officer returned M.G. to the care of the applicant right away.' In a wide-ranging judgment, Judge Levy reviewed the legislative history of apprehension and arrest powers relating to children and youth and identified why past procedures have been discredited: 'Few would argue for a return to indeterminate committals for vague transgressions of some ill-defined moral code. Equally we could note the absence of any express requirement in the Acts for the child to receive treatment while so detained. Lastly, there would appear, over the years, to have been a great many problems experienced by a number of youth while in Shelburne or other institutions, which caused untold and permanent damage to some of these children.' The scandals and failures of past efforts were no excuse, however, for failing to do anything. 'No doubt these laws went further than most people would see as appropriate today, or maybe not far enough so as to assure professional help. But at least there was a mechanism, Dickensian though it may have been, that gave the courts the power to get a child off the streets and into, in theory at least, a place where she or he could be safe and potentially receive some help.' His review of M.G.'s life and personality is exhaustive, touching on the facts that while she refers to herself as a 'slut' or 'whore' and has had literally uncountable sexual partners, her favourite television program is 'Sailor Moon' and she still experiences enuresis at night. A Calgary street worker, or any frustrated police officer or social worker in the country, might have written his concluding comments: 'There are, tragically, as any judge on our court knows, far too many children with situations comparable to those of the girls like M.G. or the child that Judge Niedermayer was speaking of ... I know of no one who is unaware of the seriousness of suspending a youth's freedom so that she or he may be treated ... I know this however: these children in care are the legal responsibility of the State, they desperately need protection and help, and they aren't getting it.'

3. The Political Context
It is difficult to ignore the congruence of drastically diminished resources to assist youth with the strategy of discrediting the legislative

schemes surrounding them. The attack on the Young Offenders Act is as overtly political as the defunding of child welfare facilities, although the tone is different. The defunding has been quiet, rationalized when challenged as 'necessary in a time of budgetary restraint.' The approach to the federal criminal sanction has been different. Politicians, police, anyone with an interest in playing the 'crime card,' have all taken critical stances against the Young Offenders Act. Most have strengthened their position through strategic alliances with segments of the victim's rights movement (Keane 1995, 431; Skurka 1993, 334).

In Ontario, the government has been particularly astute in capitalizing on an undercurrent of fear of and anger against youthful offenders. Tough measures against young offenders are commonplace, and in 1997 a Crime Control Commission was established, headed by three backbenchers (Jim Brown, Gerry Martiniuk, and Bob Wood), all of whom described experiences with young offenders that frightened them (J. Armstrong 1997b; Duncanson 1998; Ruimy 1998). This was the message advanced in a *Toronto Star* article by the parents of Jonathon Wamback, a fifteen-year-old boy who was beaten into a coma by a group of youth, and the Toronto Police Association: adult sentences for violent youth. Ontario Solicitor-General David Tsubouchi expressed a similar sentiment at a related news conference, stating, 'If you do commit adult crimes, I think there should be adult penalties involved.' According to the *Star* article, 400,000 signatures had been collected by families critical of the Young Offenders Act (*Toronto Star*, 11 January 2000.)

In a similar piece, 'Law, Order High on Conservative Agenda' (*Toronto Star*, 31 December 1999), Ontario Attorney-General Jim Flaherty demanded that government reform the proposed Youth Criminal Justice Act to impose 'more effective sentencing' of criminals. Using the frequently misused statistic of a 77 per cent increase in violent youth crime nationwide over the past decade, Flaherty criticized Ottawa's 'weak response, the Youth Criminal Justice Act,' which 'would allow rapists, armed robbers and drug traffickers to get away with just a slap on the wrist.' The statistic is misleading because it only measures charges laid. The bulk of the charges involve level one assault and threatening and reflect a changed attitude towards schoolyard bullying. The introduction of 'zero tolerance' policies on schoolyard violence plays a significant part in the increase. But this information has become muted and discredited, while the proposition that laws and courts are 'soft' on crime has gained currency (Doob, Marianos, & Varma 1995).

Flaherty promoted Ontario's law to control squeegee kids, which he considered 'solid progress towards giving families peace of mind.'

According to Ontario Solicitor-General David Tsubouchi, the reasoning behind the proposed tougher measures against youth crime is that 'people have the right to not only be safe, but also to feel safe in their communities.'

Fear of crime is an essential component of a law and order strategy, which is an essential component of privatization. Neo-conservative politicians have been successful in playing on the propositions that 'crime is out of control' and the 'criminal justice system doesn't work.' The now-defunct Reform Party in their 1997 policy statement issued under the name of then leader, Preston Manning, hit them all: 'Canadians deserve to feel that they and their families are safe in their homes, at work, at school, on the street and in their communities. We want to live in a country where our children can play in the park, go to school, and grow up without fear. And we want a justice system that does more to protect law-abiding citizens than it does criminals. Canadians want a country where we can look to the future, instead of over our shoulders' (Manning 1997, 4).

The text seems benign, the subtext, however, is quite clear. Canadians do not feel safe anywhere – not at home, not at work, not in the streets. Our children are not safe in parks or in their schools. Our children live in fear. The (federal Liberal) justice system does nothing to keep the public safe. Rather, it coddles criminals and leaves us in fear. The solution, according to this reasoning, is 'get tough' provincial legislation.

C. Developing a New Legislative 'Solution'

With the delegitimization of existing legal instruments and a form of panic on the issue of child prostitution in place, the stage is set for government to 'solve' the crisis. The solution brought forward in Alberta, pending in Ontario, and under consideration elsewhere is to give police wide powers to apprehend and detain, without warrant, if necessary, 'children' under the age of eighteen (in practical terms, female children) who they believe are engaged in or attempting to engage in prostitution. The discretion placed in the hands of police and the faith in their ability to exercise it properly is substantial. While the language of the legislation is that of child protection, the mechanisms are coercive. Indeed it is difficult to distinguish this approach from sympathetic use of the Young Offenders Act, except that these laws are within provincial competence and garner provincial credit.

Existing law is not effective in removing prostitutes and their customers from city streets. That, being largely symbolic, it was never intended to do so is not the point. Throughout the 1990s, citizen anger and frustration with street prostitution flared up. The law, particularly the criminal law, was apparently even less successful at reducing the trade in young prostitutes. In 1997 Kimberly Daum, a social worker with Downtown Eastside Youth Activities Society, Vancouver, British Columbia, analysed the use of the Criminal Code provision prohibiting purchase of sex from a minor (section 212 (4)) and concluded that young prostitutes were significantly more likely to be charged than the men who solicited them. She reports that on a typical night, between 350 and 525 prostitutes sell sex on downtown Vancouver streets, a number which includes about forty juveniles. Police charged a total of eight men with buying sex from juveniles in the eight years between 1988 and 1996. Only two were convicted and neither was sentenced to jail. Seven more charges were laid later. In contrast, 354 juveniles were charged with communicating for the purpose of prostitution in the six years between 1988 and 1994. Weak federal legislation, slack enforcement, and inadequate community resources were cited and Daum is quoted as saying that 'the Canadian government's track record on this issue remains one of incompetence, bias and neglect' (Matas 1997). The section was amended to permit charging based solely on the belief of the sex trade customer. However, Daum's next report. 'Painting by Numbers' (1999), was equally damning. The volume of street prostitution had not decreased, and the improvement in the prosecution record was modest. Only twenty charges were laid under section 212(4) in British Columbia between 1 April 1997 and 31 March 1998 (Daum 1999). The report contrasts these numbers with the numbers of charges laid in Ontario and Quebec: forty-one and sixty-seven, respectively. Only forty charges were laid in British Columbia in the preceding ten years versus forty per year in Quebec (Daum 1999). A *Globe and Mail* story on the report quotes Commander Andre Bouchard of the Montreal Urban Community's Morality and Narcotics Division as saying that juvenile prostitution is not a problem in the city. 'I'm not saying we're better that anyone else. But it's a priority here, and if we get any information about juveniles, we just drop everything and deal with it.' He said the police are helped by strict laws and by adult prostitutes who cooperate with the police in trying to keep children off the streets (Matas 1999).

Daum's 1999 report does not, unfortunately, address the problem inherent in the assumption that criminal prosecution of customers will reduce the use of young people for sexual services. Indeed, there is substantial evidence that suggests that these strategies tend rather to move the problem around or underground (Bagley, Burrows, & Yaworski 1991; Brannigan & Fleischman 1989). Moreover, youth continue to be charged as prostitutes, despite the rhetoric about their victimization (Lines 1998; Shephard 1999a). The significant question, then, is why did Alberta and Ontario choose to revitalize a coercive strategy? Part of the answer is found in Calgary.

1. Calgary

The level of prostitution activity in Calgary prior to the late 1980s was considered by residents to be moderate and relatively tolerable, in terms of its scope and the presence of children (Brannigan & Fleischman 1989; Valpy 1990). That perception changed. Increased levels of street prostitution and increased citizen concern have some of the qualities of a canary in a mine – they signal social disjunction. Such disjunction was apparently the case in Calgary, a wealthy city with a long history of support for right-wing 'free enterprise' politicians. Support for privatization in Calgary was early and strong. Alberta's Conservative premier, Ralph Klein, had been a popular mayor in that city before he revolutionized the provincial government in the early 1990s with a mix of neo-conservative and neo-liberal policies. Although Klein is given credit for it, privatization was well advanced when he took power (Ismail & Vaillancourt 1988). His political skills ensured that the project continued. When the recession of the 1980s ended and massive oil revenues launched an era of significant wealth and prosperity, it became clear that the tattered remnants of the social 'safety net' were insufficient to cope with unprecedented levels of homelessness, poverty, and street prostitution. The climate was ripe for the kind of grassroots charitable response Calgarians like to claim is typical of their city.[11] Solutions were not immediately found, however. It took eight years before issue-specific, quasi- criminal legislation targeted on these youth emerged as the approach of choice, winning community, activist, and political support. First, citizens rallied around the issue of street prostitution generally. For example, a much-publicized web site, 'Calgary Ho-down,' threatened to post the licence plate numbers of the men who visited the 'stroll' to pick up women; it expressed the frustration of middle-class citizens with street prostitution in their neighbourhoods and with the apparent impotence of the criminal process to deal with it.[12]

Next, attention turned to the more complex issue of the presence of children and youth in the sex trade. The material circumstance was that a small, relatively constant percentage of young prostitutes are females under the age of eighteen. That previously tolerated abuse became a target for reform. The story, as it is now told, begins in 1990 when a frantic mother drove Heather Forsyth, who was to enter provincial politics shortly after, to a Calgary street corner to watch a fourteen-year-old hooker – her daughter – turn tricks (Canadian Press 1999b). The experience galvanized Forsyth into action. She was instrumental in bringing about and chairing the Task Force on Child Prostitution, which was set up in June 1996 and held consultations across the province. Although the task force made many recommendations dealing with prevention and supports for children, it stressed the need for more powers to intervene in children's lives and greater punishment of customers and pimps (Alberta Task Force on Juvenile Prostitution 1997). The task force became the authority for Alberta's quasi-criminal response and was influential in Ontario and other provinces as well (Lines 1998).

The Discourse: Successful marketing campaigns revolve around vivid, simple themes and a memorable message. In this instance, all were contributed by Ross MacInnes, a now retired police officer, who helped to found Street Teams, one of several Calgary agencies inspired by an expressly religious (Christian) mission to rescue street prostitutes.[13] MacInnes and Street Teams were profiled in an *Alberta Report* article in 1995 (Sillars 1995, 11). The piece is a classic example of the type of writing associated with the commodification of crime and the intensification of surveillance. It poses the issue of prostitution as an unaddressed problem of lost innocence and debauched morals and MacInnes and Street Teams as heroic Christian crusaders. MacInnes is cited as the authority for the inflated claim that between Calgary and Edmonton four hundred child prostitutes, aged from eleven to fifteen, are serving a largely middle-class clientele of paedophiles and hebophiles. Firsthand stories about 'baby-faced rebels of 12, fresh from the suburbs' reinforce the danger to middle-class families, while racist labels demonize immigrants and minorities as pimps and procurers. Pimps are described as 'Asian,' 'often Vietnamese,' and as being 'considered the most vicious.' The text and subtext are clear. The situation is so grave that exceptional measures are called for.

Although the article acknowledges that 'three out of five' girls are runaways from group homes and 'four out of five' have been sexually abused, the real focus is the girls who have *chosen* to 'run with the wrong crowd.' 'Leanne, for instance, was gradually pulled away from home.

Now 16, she revelled in street life as a never-ending series of parties, drugs and cool friends. Best of all, there was no parental authority. "She would be out all night," says Leanne's mother, "then for three nights, then a week at a time. Then I found out she was into prostitution.'" However, these girls are 'doomed.' Their feckless adventure will rapidly turn sour. A 'real' pimp will enter her life, enslaving her and brutalizing her: 'When she has "fallen in love" with this predator (all pimps are pathological liars, according to Mr. MacInnes), he will allow some "friends" to rape her, possibly for free.' The description of the 'inevitable' outcome of this youthful adventuring is vivid, even pornographic: 'Within months a teen-aged prostitute, whether or not she is being pimped, will be badly malnourished, underweight and addicted to drugs or alcohol. She will have one or more sexually transmitted diseases to complement her body lice. The young whore will be emotionally unstable and her memory could be impaired – important dates and names have simply vanished from her mind. She could also be pregnant and have collected a criminal record for petty theft and other minor crimes.' This outcome is then presented as posing a significant risk to other (middle-class) youngsters, a message which will become government policy within a few years. 'The cycle is constantly being played out in malls (where pimps prowl among rebellious students who skip classes by the score in Calgary), parks, pool halls and streets of every North American city.'

The need for urgent, even extreme rescue missions has been established. Degradation, abuse, even death are waiting for Alberta's middle-class rebellious girls, and it is almost impossible to save them by existing means. They do not trust the 'system' (the discredited social assistance and child welfare regime that Street Teams despises); they have not been taught values or principles that might save them; and they are incapable of adult choices: 'Sometimes the girls take a long time to get desperate, no matter how appalling their situation. Many, having run away from an abusive home or "the system" of social workers and treatment centres, see no point in returning. Most are paralysed by fear of their pimp ... "At 13, even girls raised in a loving home often have horrible judgment. Add on trauma, sexual and physical abuse, and then you want her to make a good decision?" "Half these kids haven't been told prostitution is wrong," adds Barb.'

Street Teams has the solution. 'Point of Departure' or POD, is a six-client residential facility that will 'groom' selected girls for 're-entry' to the normal world. The approach is one of structure and strict discipline, themes frequently sounded by neo-conservatives: 'Instead of sleeping until early afternoon and then hanging around the streets until 4:00 am, they will be up at 6:45 a.m. and in martial arts class from 7:15 to 8:15. Breakfast is at nine. Girls will spend two hours on "life-planning," where they decide on an attainable goal (go home, get into a foster home, independence, etc.) and take steps to achieve it. Lunch at noon is followed by correspondence schoolwork until 6:00, then supper, some recreation time and lights out at 10:15.' At the same time, 'family values' are being recreated and reinforced. 'Daddy' provides everything a girl might need, including a curling iron and cosmetics:

> Last week Jody, 14, bounced into Street Teams' downtown office. 'Hi, Daddy,' she says brightly to Mr. MacInnes. 'How are you doing, sweetie,' he replies, squeezing her around the shoulders.
>
> ...
>
> She came to the office to bum some smokes and hints that it's her birthday. She gets her present – cosmetics and a curling iron – and reassures Mr. MacInnes that she hasn't been working. 'We are the largest dysfunctional family in Calgary,' the ex-cop sometimes jokes with his staff.

MacInnes preaches his message assiduously through media contacts and a seminar he offers with the evocatively erotic title 'High Heels and Teddy Bears.' The neo-conservative message is complete with the information that although the media attention is 'jarring' to some, it helped fund Street Teams' 1996 budget of $373,000. Excluding a $23,000 grant from the city, all is privately donated (Sillars 1995).

The Outcome. Early in 1997, the newly re-elected government of Alberta released the report of the Task Force on Children Involved in Prostitution and announced that it was amending the Child Welfare Act to make it an act of child abuse to use a prostitute under the age of eighteen. No reference was made to the fact that this had been a criminal offence for some time. Six months later, on 27 January 1998, the premier selected the Protection of Children Involved in Prostitution Act (PCHIP) as his Bill One for 1998. One year later, on 1 February 1999, Bill One was proclaimed into law.

The new law was promoted as a radical reform of the problem of child prostitution. Described in the government's press release as 'the first of its kind worldwide,' several discursive claims are made supporting the new act (Alberta 1999b). The first claim, one that is adopted by most involved in the issue in Ontario and elsewhere (Lines 1998), is that children involved in prostitution are victims of sexual abuse. The next, however, belies any commitment to the proposition that prostitution is not, for children, a 'choice.' These child 'victims' are specifically presented in the release as 'choosing' whether or not they wish to end their 'victimhood,' a 'choice' that justifies their imprisonment (it is for their own good): 'A child who wants to end his or her involvement in prostitution may access community support programs. *A child who does not want to end his or her involvement in prostitution can be apprehended by police.* Police will then take the child to a protective safe house, where he or she can be confined for up to 72 hours. At this safe, secure facility, the child receives emergency care, treatment and an assessment' (emphasis added). The Alberta government has not been shy about making misleading claims for its new legislation. The website leaves the impression that Alberta has reformed the punitive nature of the criminal law approach to the prostitutes: '*Previously*, children involved in prostitution could be charged with solicitation' (emphasis added). The site also claims that Alberta has reformed a presumed leniency towards customers and procurers, which might lead a person unfamiliar with the criminal law to believe that previously 'johns and pimps' could not be charged (and punished far more harshly than the redundant provincial charges permit) (Alberta, Child and Family Services Authority 1999). Finally, that middle-class runaways are the real issue is reinforced by a section that tells concerned parents how to determine whether their 'child could be involved in prostitution.' The list of suspicious behaviours includes demanding 'more freedom,' 'coming home 'later than usual for unexplained reasons,' 'hanging around with an older crowd,' and talking about moving into his or her own place to have 'more freedom.'

The Solution in Action: The first girls were 'rescued' and the first safe houses opened shortly after the 1 February 1999 proclamation. No safe houses were established for boys. Calgary's Safe Haven, which accommodates seven girls at a time, is described as a cozy, comfortable, lime-coloured cottage overlooking the Bow River. In a touch both poignant and somehow repellent, a teddy bear and slippers are provided in every bedroom (Shephard 1999a). Public forums for street youth have been held; not surprisingly, youth have responded with mixed reviews. Many resent the arrests and detention. Others have been clear that their stay in the house helped, but they want to remain longer than seventy-two hours. Randy Diddams of Exit Youth Services reports that there was a sharp, visible decline in the numbers of young women on the streets

Table 8.1
Total number of prostitutes (female) met by Exit staff, per month

Number	July 1997	August 1997	July 1998	August 1998	July 1999	August 1999
Total (all ages)	115	104	243	186	200	165
Total 8 + under	23	15	30	21	4	10
By age:						
12	1	0	0	0	0	0
13	0	0	0	0	0	0
14	0	2	1	1	0	0
15	0	0	1	2	0	0
16	2	1	0	2	0	0
17	11	4	11	5	0	3
18	9	10	17	11	4	7

since proclamation.[14] Three months after proclamation, there was speculation that these young women have moved inside to so-called 'trick pads,' moved out of province, or returned home (Shephard 1999a).

Exit has a drop-in centre and a van that patrols the streets each evening. The organization keeps records of the numbers of individuals it has contact with as well as the number of 'contacts' (including repeated contacts with individual youth); as the agency managing Calgary's safe house, it also records the numbers of girls taken into custody. The Calgary statistics suggest that there has been a decline in the numbers of younger women on the streets. The decline in the summer of 1999 from the previous two years, is obvious – there are no girls under sixteen at all. However, the total numbers of very young girls in prior years is also very small. The epidemic numbers of thirteen- and fourteen-year-old hookers may never have existed.

Street prostitution is most prevalent during the summer months, and during the summers of 1997 to 1999, Exit Staff met only one twelve-year-old, no thirteen-year-old, and four fourteen-year-old girls who they identified as being involved with prostitution. The majority were seventeen or eighteen and even they represented no more than 10 per cent of the women involved in prostitution who made any contact with Exit at all.

These figures are consistent with the detentions made by police under PCHIP from 1 February to 1 September 1999. Fifty-nine young women and girls were brought by police into the Safe Haven Program in the first seven months. Six were fourteen, six were fifteen, eleven were sixteen, and twelve were seventeen. Of the fifty-nine apprehended, fifty-three were discharged after an average time in the program of forty-eight days: two to 'independent living;' one to live in a group home; six to return to their family home; six to live in the home operated by Exit; and six to live independently with support from Exit. Seven more were remanded into custody and five were referred to a City shelter. Almost one third, or fifteen, returned to the streets, while five were resident in the 'Safe House' and six remained in the program receiving other services.

The Solution Challenged: On 13 September 1999, Calgary police forcibly removed two seventeen-year-old girls, without a warrant, from a premises described by the police as a 'trick pad' and by the girls as their home. They were held in a 'protective safehouse' for an initial seventy-two hours for assessment, which included 'questioning by a staff member about activity related to prostitution, drug use and child protection history' (*Alberta v. K.B.*, 2000, paras. 13, 14, 15). More than 350 similar apprehensions had already been made, involving a hundred or so young women in Calgary and Edmonton (one girl was apprehended seventeen times) (Cotter 2000; Mahoney 2000b).[15] Through counsel Bina Borders and Harry Van Harten, the girls brought a Charter challenge to the legislation and to their confinement. Alberta Provincial Court, Family Division, Judge Karen Jordan delivered judgment on 22 July 2000, holding that Alberta's Protection of Children Involved in Prostitution Act (PCHIP) infringed sections 7, 8, and 9 of the Charter, and could not be saved by section 1.

Judge Jordan accepted the good intent of the legislature but held that the absence of any due process safeguards, most importantly any judicial review of the police officer's discretion to search, apprehend, and detain, could not be justified.

The response of PCHIP's supporters was swift. Children's Services Minister Iris Evans stated, 'It's a black day because the protection we've had isn't there' (Mahoney 2000a). MLA Heather Forsyth, one of original proponents of the Act, said, 'I will go to my grave knowing this law was the right thing to do. They should take the Charter of Rights and shove it. I am absolutely sick' (Canadian Press 2000a, 2000b). Justifying a decision to ignore the ruling and continue making apprehensions, Alberta's Justice Minister Dave Hancock said that directives to police with respect to advising youth that they have the right to counsel and the right to appear before a judge had been issued. However, the appearance need not be immediate: 'we're interested in using resources to protect children, not to fill the courts' (Mahoney 2000b).

There was no public comment on Judge Jordan's most fundamental criticism, however. As she pointed out, the procedural safeguards would be relatively easy to remedy; it would be much more difficult to actually make a case that this approach is effective at doing what it purports to do. That critique was reserved to her reasons for concluding that the legislation was intra vires the provincial legislature and for rejecting the applicants' argument that PCHIP is, in effect, criminal law. Judge Jordan's obiter comments, however, exposed the degree to which this legislation is political, not remedial, punitive, not restorative. At paragraph 36 she points out, accepting the argument of the applicants, that nothing in the Act ensures treatment or rehabilitation beyond the seventy-two hour 'assessment,' and at paragraph 37, she exposes the circularity of the claim that PCHIP helps children:

> ... The Director would have the public believe that because hundreds of apprehensions are accomplished in a given period the Act is achieving its stated goal of protecting children. Yet we are left not knowing anything, except by way of anecdotal evidence, of the lives of the children after their periods of confinement are completed. How many accept the services offered? How many return to the same lifestyle? How many gradually escape from that world?
>
> ...
>
> The questions go on and on, but the Government of Alberta has not made a commitment to provide us with answers even though the liberty of children is being curtailed.

The Crown elected to call no evidence to justify the legislation pursuant to section 1 of the Charter – in all likelihood they had no answers. Politically, however, the government was on good ground. Justice Rooke of Alberta's Court of Queen's Bench reversed the decision on review. The procedural flaws were corrected in any event (*Alberta v. K.B.* 2000).

2. Ontario

The story of prostitution in Calgary is replicated, with local variations, across Canada. In Toronto, concern becomes of public interest when the neighbourhoods where street prostitution flourishes are 'gentrified,' or when the scale of the activity increases significantly (Martin & Kuszelewski 1997; Moyer & Carrington 1989). As in other cities, patrols

392 Dianne L. Martin

of citizens have made attempts to drive the business out of their neighbourhoods, complaining bitterly about the trolling cars soliciting female
residents, the presence of used condoms and discarded syringes in
parks and yards, and the increased trafficking in crack cocaine associated with street prostitution.[16] More recent efforts have concentrated on
influencing law enforcement and the courts.[17]

In February 1997, shortly after the release of the Alberta Task Force
report, the (former) Toronto Board of Health initiated a meeting with
police and the relevant social service agencies to develop a report on the
prevention of prostitution involving children and youth. The 'Toronto
Roundtable on Prostitution Involving Children and Youth' was released
on 28 September 1998, after a series of three meetings in the summer
and fall of 1997. The Toronto Roundtable relied on the Alberta Task
Force recommendations to provide a general framework for their discussions (Lines 1998). However in Ontario, the government chose not
to amend child welfare laws so that youth between sixteen and eighteen
could be considered 'children in need of protection' and thus the frustration that police in Calgary described was heightened in Toronto.

In April, two months after proclamation of PCHIP in Alberta, the *Toronto Star* published a major piece on the legislation and on child prostitution in Toronto. The front page carried a night-time photo shot of a
man holding a large hunting knife; in the background another man is
frisking a young blonde woman wearing jeans and a baggy sweat shirt.
The photo was taken on Isabella Street in Toronto, salaciously described
as the 'kiddy track.' Detectives Mike Dicosola and Kevin White question
Becky (a pseudonym for the young woman in the picture). She is
described as looking like a teenage student caught skipping classes, with
her baggy sweat shirt and backpack, and as 'whining': 'I'm here from
New Brunswick. I'm going back in the morning. I haven't done anything so why are you talking to me? I can't believe you think I might be a
prostitute.' Police learn that Becky has outstanding charges (theft under
(six CD's), and fail to appear). She is arrested and detained. A search
uncovers coloured condoms, straws described as 'used for crack
cocaine' and a fifteen-centimetre knife. The police sound sympathetic;
'I've never met anyone out here who enjoys what they're doing,' [Detec-
tive] White says. 'We treat these girls as victims because they are victims.'
Victim or not, 'Becky' is arrested and charged. She is detained in the
young offender 'lock up' at 311 Jarvis Street until she pleads guilty to
concealing a weapon, theft, and failing to appear in court. She receives
a one-day sentence to reflect the eight days she has already served. This

addition to her record will ensure more harsh treatment in the future, but the fact that Becky is released after eight days in custody is treated in the story as a failure in the law. There is no mention of whether she received any counselling or a needs assessment, or if not why not. That Alberta's legislation permits only three days in detention is not raised (Shephard 1999a).

A law such as the PCHIP has an obvious appeal to parents, police, and others troubled by the recalcitrance of the child prostitution issue. It allows authorities to detain and apprehend girls like 'Becky,' whether they are in possession of a small knife or not. It offers a seductively simple solution: define the girls as victims of child abuse and incapable of accepting help voluntarily, and empower police to detain them so that they can be helped, literally in spite of themselves. In Ontario, the plight of a middle-class father and his daughter (identified at the subsequent committee hearings as Alan and Mallory) motivated Rick Bartolucci, Liberal member of the Provincial Parliament for Sudbury, to present a private member's bill (Bill 18) for the 'Protection of Children involved in Prostitution Act' on 12 May 1998, which is identical to Alberta's PCHIP Act. In an unusual, apparently non- partisan, move, the bill was referred to the Standing Committee on Social Development on 29 June 1998. The standing committee, in the same spirit, unanimously agreed to hearings, which were held in August and September in Sudbury, London, and Toronto.

The Dominant Discourse: Alan and Mallory both spoke at the first day of hearings in Sudbury, 17 August 1998. Mallory, nineteen was particularly eloquent about the 'young kids' on the streets and the predators who used them, and about the drugs, pain and degradation of street prostitution.

> I didn't prepare a speech. I don't have a lot of education, but I came here for those kids. There were 12-year-olds, when I used to work that corner, standing on that corner. It's sad, it really is. It's really sad having to be a cocaine addict. I've got tracks, man. I was nuts.

> Those girls have nothing. They don't have dads; they don't have moms. They don't care any more. They feel probably much like I did, like I'm a loser, I'm a bottom-feeder. I'm not good in school. I'm good at making money and I'm good at doing drugs. That's what I'm good at.
> ...
> But who cares, right? They're just kids. No, they've got to be taken care of. This is sad. These are little girls who are having grown men who have money

and cocaine take over their lives, making them feel wanted. Those are idiots. Those aren't nice people, man. I've seen what those guys do to those young girls. They have sex with them. They do some pretty disgusting things. They make them feel dirty. They make them grow up before their time.

...

When you get in that car, you don't know if you're getting back out. Us older girls – man, I knew what I was doing. Those younger girls are naive, they're stupid, they're not using condoms ...

Those girls, they're selling their bodies and it isn't fair. You've got to help them out. That's all I'm saying. They really need to be helped. They're asking you. They're never going to be cool; they're never going to be able to go to school. These kids aren't going to ever develop. They're never going to be like you guys – citizens. They're never going to be that. They'll always be like that.

That's really all I have to say.

The theme of lost innocence and an inability to help themselves was developed by several speakers over the four days of hearings. The picture painted by Beverley Crockford, executive director of Sudbury Youth Services, a young offender facility for twelve- to fifteen-year-old boys and girls where convicted youth serve sentences of both open and secure detention and custody, was particularly vivid.

I can recite, chapter and verse, stories of children as young as 12 years old who are involved in the sex trade in this community. You would be reduced to tears to know of the poor physical condition they arrive in, most often needing immediate medical attention. They lack even the most basic awareness of the dangerous circumstances from which they have been removed. They think they are invincible and they do not fully comprehend the negative ramifications of the high-risk lifestyle they have been leading, even in the short term. Aside from the STDs they are being exposed to that are life-altering and the drugs they use to feel good about themselves, they have been somehow convinced that their pimps will protect them and keep them safe.

They also believe they are in control of their customers. Everyone here knows that nothing could be further from the truth. In fact, we all know that they are considered quite expendable. Their only value to their pimp is economic, and to their customers, sexual gratification. We genuinely fear for these kids upon their release from the detention facility.

The Counter Narrative: Although all speakers commended Mr Bartolucci for raising the issue and gave the benefit of the doubt to the intent of the Bill, the need for such legislation was repeatedly challenged. When Mallory's father Alan testified, he described the despair and frustration he and his wife experienced in trying to find help for their daughter. Mallory was presented as the perfect child until she reached high school, when her behaviour changed dramatically. She was diagnosed with a major mood disorder, which did not respond to medication, and gradually turned to street drugs and street life. A cocaine addiction contributed to her eventual involvement in prostitution. Alan went to his provincial member when he realized that there was almost nothing more he as a parent could do after his daughter turned eighteen.

The theme of a middle-class kid lost to the 'street' parallels the *Alberta Report* article, except that we know more about Mallory and her father. No one asks either of them what difference a PCHIP would have made to their situation – because it would have made no difference. Mallory was receiving help as she struggled with mental illness and drug addiction. The 'system' was assisting her and her family to deal with the devastation of mental illness and drug addiction. The 'crisis' arose because after Mallory turned eighteen, her parents could do little more.

The picture alters as well when an attempt is made to assess the actual scope of the problem, in the sense of determining how many twelve to fifteen year olds are involved. Chief McCauley of the Sudbury Police testified: 'In April of this year, [1998] about 30 prostitutes were working our downtown core of the city. At least 10 of them were teenagers and at least one, as I mentioned earlier, was 12 years of age.' Even one is too many. However, implementing a legislative solution with 'draconian' powers that some youth at least resent bitterly (*Alberta v. K.B.*, 2000) because of one twelve year old, or even ten teenagers, requires some justification.

That justification turns out to be based on a political assessment of the best way to deal with the fact that in Ontario, youth between the ages of sixteen and eighteen cannot be 'children in need of protection' unless they were wards before they reached sixteen, and are ineligible for assistance more generally. In contrast, Alberta Child Welfare legislation defines 'child' as a person under eighteen years of age. Even in regard to girls who are wards, agencies frequently seek to terminate the orders when they learn that sixteen or seventeen year olds are involved in prostitution or are otherwise becoming unruly (Patty Taylor, Cecil Facer Youth Centre, Sudbury, 17 August 1998).

Many speakers argued that appropriate amendments to the Child and

Family Services Act should replace the PCHIP or at least supplement it. However, in response to a compelling argument from Diane Cresswell of the Ontario Association of Children's Aid Societies at the hearings held in Toronto on 29 September 1998, Mr Bartolucci acknowledged the extent to which the medium of reformed legislation had become the message: '*There's a conscious effort here on my part* – I have to be honest, I had the option of doing an amendment to the Child and Family Services Act or a stand-alone bill. I chose a stand-alone bill because of the perception out there – and I say "perception" because in 30 years in teaching I spent a lot of time talking to children's aid society workers, so I appreciate the dilemma and the role you have and you fulfill for society and for children. But *the perception out there is that the act is ineffective, that the people who are charged with fulfilling the perception don't do the job we want*' (Emphasis added).

Other speakers raised many of the due process and abuse of the process issues that were successfully argued in Alberta in *K.B.* Most powerfully, Velma Demerson reminded the committee in Toronto on 28 September 1998 that these were lessons already learned:

> The title of my talk today is Bill 18, Traces of the Past. You can see by the title that I am bringing up the point that we haven't really gone that far in the past 50 years or so ...
>
> The title of the proposed act, *An Act to Protect Children involved in Prostitution*, may be new but the contents are similar to past legislation directed against females for immorality or anticipated immorality ...
>
> Bill 18 is proposed in a climate of fear. This same fear can be seen in an article entitled 'Protective Bureau for Young Girls,' which is attached, which appeared in the Mail and Empire on January 8, 1919 ... The girls were arrested for being idle and dissolute. This act lasted for 50 years and it was repealed in 1964, so you may have some idea of how many girls and women were unlawfully arrested.

Demerson paralleled her own experience with imprisonment for being 'incorrigible' (she wished to marry a man of Chinese descent, against her father's wishes) under the Female Refugees Act with forced detention in a 'safe house' under the proposed legislation. She was asked no questions. The only critique that prompted a response came when Patty Taylor raised the issue of police use and abuse of prostitutes: 'If there were no demand, they say there would be no supply. Some of the girls laugh at this and say: "The very people using the services are the ones that are arresting us. How do we cope with that? How do we answer to that? We don't have very much control.'" Reaction was swift:

> Mr Jim Brown: Good morning. I just have clarification on one point you made. You said that the girls said that the people who are arresting them are using their services.
> Ms Taylor: Yes, that's what they have said. They don't say those are the only people who are –
> Mr Jim Brown: But the people who are arresting them would be the police.
> Ms Taylor: That's what they're inferring.

Tamara Bodnaruk-Wide, appearing as a representative of the Council of Elizabeth Fry Societies of Ontario, said in Toronto on 28 September 1998: 'In sum, we believe Bill 18 brings about more questions than it answers at this point. We are deeply concerned that the way it is worded and read criminalizes those who are victims. We fear that this perception is not ours alone and that it will become that of the police, community agencies and, most importantly, the children themselves.'

The Outcome. Bill 18 died on the order paper when an election was called. However, in their second term in office, the Conservatives introduced a two-pronged approach to street youth that drew heavily on neo-conservative values. In 1999 the Safe Streets Act, which criminalizes begging, loitering, and 'squeegee kid' work, was enacted. A year later the Protecting Children from Sexual Exploitation Act (PCSEA) was given first reading and the promise of support from all sides of the house. It is essentially an improved PCHIP, with an even more well-articulated child abuse theme. The operating assumption is 'that prostitution involving children and youth [should] be defined as commercialized child sexual abuse' and 'that children and youth involved in prostitution [should] be treated as victims of sexual abuse.' The bill authorizes the apprehension and forced detention for up to thirty days of any youth under eighteen who seems to be 'a child who is sexually exploited for commercial purposes or is at risk of sexual exploitation for commercial purposes.' In other words, the child can be arrested and detained if she is being sexually exploited or to prevent her sexual exploitation – for example, if the police believe that she will in the future attempt to engage in prostitution. The police are empowered to use force to enter residences or other places to apprehend children and youth at risk of exploitation. Once in custody, the young victim may then be detained in a 'place of safety,' which could be the section of an adult jail reserved for young offenders, to a total maximum of thirty days. She has two opportunities to challenge her detention.

This legislation is more attentive to due process concerns. Within twenty-four hours of apprehension, the child will be given a notice with information about her detention and the phone number of a legal aid office, ostensibly to prepare for an initial hearing 'before' a justice of the peace. At this first 'show cause' hearing a decision is made as to whether to release her or to hold her for a five-day assessment. After the five-day detention, a more formal hearing is held to decide whether 'continued confinement will assist the child to end his or her sexual exploitation or will lessen the risk that the child will be sexually exploited.' If the answer is yes, the confinement can continue for the balance of the thirty days. If it is no, she will be released. Even if detention is ordered, the child will be released at the end of the thirty days – apparently protected. However, if she escapes or runs away, she can be rearrested without a warrant, and the thirty day 'clock' starts over, with no credit for the time already served.

The intention driving PCSEA is not an interest in child protection but rather the politics of crime. Once again a crisis is identified that cannot be resolved by existing means. There are, of course, some very young people being exploited in the sex trade. There are some very young people being abused and suffering from substance abuse. It is certainly the case that some police, youth workers, teachers, and parents have become convinced that the short-term pain of arrest and detention is justified by the long-term gain of 'assist[ing] the child to end his or her sexual exploitation.' However, even judged on its own terms, PCSEA is a bad, or at best partial, solution to an issue that was deliberately manufactured into a crisis. This legislation's claim to protect children is exaggerated. PCSEA does not address the reasons why children run to the street and it does not deal with why, when they do, more children than before are harmed when they get there. While both prostitution and the exploitation of children have long been with us, the numbers of homeless street youth vulnerable to that exploitation are a product of government and corporate strategies, both recent and historic. The strategies that have generated unprecedented disparities between rich and poor have consequences – and we see those consequences sleeping under bridges, begging on the street, and selling their bodies every day. The arrest and detain tactic ignores the recent history of failure when similar, equally punitive approaches placed sexually exploited and street-involved youth into institutions like Grandview Training School for Girls or St Johns Training School for Boys. And it simply assumes that 'sex is different.' Runaways defined as beggars and 'squeegee kids' are scorned as 'young offenders;' they are only to be pitied as victims when their exploitation is sexual.

The current interest in child prostitution is not new. First-wave feminists launched rescue operations in early Victorian times and 'white slavery' scares have titillated the masses in recurring cycles of concern with prostitution generally, while in every era there has been enduring concern for exploited children (Hunt 1999; Walkowitz 1992). Indeed, each period has used the iconic power of the child in its own interest and in its own frame (Piper 1999). It therefore comes as no surprise that the child prostitute has again become a player in this era of privatization; she is the perfect victim for crime control and family values advocates: young, innocent, defiled. So long as she maintains the victim façade, the child prostitute is almost a poster child of privatization politics.

Her story here has illustrated the extent to which the current era of privatization is marked by reregulation, not deregulation – a shift in state resources and powers, not their diminution. While state regulation is receding in the area of social welfare, it is intensifying in the criminal justice system. The state is abandoning public responsibility for social problems as it increasingly individualizes issues like child prostitution and then relies on the coercive powers of the criminal justice system to address this (now) individualized problem.

Ultimately, this study demonstrates that solutions for feminists concerned to expose the paradoxes of privatization and to assist the children and youth abandoned to the street are, as always, the slow and difficult path of truth telling, coalition building and equality-enhancing efforts. The men, women, and youth who testified before the legislative committee considering PCHIP for Ontario were at least partially successful. Ontario did not enact PCHIP: the PCSEA has a semblance of a due process structure and far more precision concerning who might be caught in its net. The risk of utterly arbitrary abuse of police power has been decreased. Moreover, the members of a coalition who might decide to challenge PCSEA more directly can be found among those who testified about the risks of such an approach. That coalition would begin with street youth themselves, who could tell us what is needed beyond a granola bar, a kind word, and condoms. It would add parents, social workers, teachers, lawyers, and activists, and they would speak often and clearly to politicians, police, and business.

This coalition would also consider litigation strategies. Although the danger that litigation can swallow all the energy and resources of a political movement is well known, it is sometimes the only way to hold the state accountable, as reaction to the initially successful Charter challenge to PCHIP in Alberta demonstrated. The active intervention strategy initiated by LEAF (Women's Legal Education and Action Fund) has opened the way for others who seek to bring an alternate view into a public arena, one that helps to generate a counter-narrative against coercion and reregulation discourse. Generating and preserving a record of challenge and dissent provides a basis for fighting another day, when the way may be more open. In short, feminist strategies will succeed where coercion fails once more.

Notes

1 Ruth Patterson of Street Teams (a private Christian rescue organization in Calgary, discussed below) sees the presence of young prostitutes on Calgary streets as a product of 'working mothers and social services (welfare).' In her view, social services contribute money that serves as an incentive to leave home but does not provide the training, guidance, or values that many young people no longer receive from their absent (because working) mothers (Interview 1998). Federal Liberal MP Paul Szabo echoes her views in a story by *Toronto Star* columnist William Walker. Szabo released a 120-page report entitled *The Child Poverty Solution*, to argue that Canada's divorce rate is a root cause of child poverty. He acknowledged that his views on reducing marital break-ups might not be considered 'politically correct' (W. Walker 1999).
2 The newspaper headlines paint a clear picture of the grim situation for teens. See, e.g., 'Program to stop runaways chopped. Children's aid blames provincial changes in welfare funding' (Harvey 1999); 'Alberta's abused children wait-listed for aid' (Laghi 1997); 'We need cash and workers not studies, CAS staff say' (Welsh & Donovan 1997).
3 The dynamics surrounding the lives and treatment of young male prostitutes are beyond the scope of this paper and are considerably different from the discourse and assumptions about young females (Sas & Hurley 1997).
4 Crime generally is a growth industry. Spending on police services in Canada between 1988–9 and 1992–3 rose from $4.39 to $5.72 billion. In 1992/3, spending on policing was one and a half times greater than all other justice costs combined (Canadian Centre for Justice Statistics 1996, 152). Even

more significantly, a corrections 'market' is expanding rapidly as communities vie for more prisons and private corporations bid for the lucrative contracts. The headlines alone tell much of the story: 'Firms to bid on offender centres. Government seeks new youth facility operators' (Girard 1998); 'Penetang, Lindsay chosen for mega-jails. Each will house 1,200 prisoners and bring in 300 new jobs' (J. Armstrong 1997a); 'Town's lust to host jails is desperate' (Findlay 1997).

5 The appropriated references to abuse, victimization, and empowerment are both contemporary and reminiscent of the 'rescue' language of earlier movements (Hunt 1999; Valverde 1991; Walkowitz, 1992). The current strategy uses terms such as 'sex trade offender' rather than 'john' in reference to the purchasers of sex from young prostitutes, and 'sex trade offence location' rather than 'stroll,' for example (Interview, 1 October 1999, Randy Diddams, Exit Youth Services, Calgary Alberta).

6 Such as those expressed by HALO (Homophile Association of London, Ontario), dubbed 'Project Guardian' by London police (Sas & Hurley 1997).

7 The documentary, *Hookers on Davie Street* (directed by Janice Cole and Holly Dale, Spectrum Films, Toronto 1983), filmed in Vancouver, captures the kind of soliciting that offended the public but was ignored by the police. In some cases women were grabbing men by the arm, in others, they repeatedly 'came on.' The conduct is quite clearly both 'pressing *and* persistent'.

8 No mainstream feminist organization intervened at the Supreme Court (interventions were made by the Canadian Organization for the Rights of Prostitutes (CORE), as well as by attorney generals of Canada, Ontario, Saskatchewan, Alberta, and British Columbia), which demonstrates the ambivalence feminists feel about prostitution (McGinnis 1994).

9 That there is a strong heterosexist bias operating here is obvious. The attitudes towards the purchase of sexual services of boys by adult men is popularly constructed quite differently (Sas & Hurley 1997).

10 See e.g. the Alberta test from the Child Welfare Act, S.A. 1984, c-8.1. *S.A.* section 1(2) provides that a child is in need of protection if there are reasonable and probable grounds to believe that the survival, security, or development of the child is endangered because of any of the following: the child is abandoned; the guardian is dead and there is no other guardian; the guardian is unable/unwilling to provide the child with necessities of life; there is substantial risk of physical and sexual abuse by the guardian; the guardian is unwilling to protect the child from such abuse; there is evidence of emotional injury by the guardian; the guardian is unwilling to protect the child from such injury; the child is subjected to unusual treatment/punishment by the guardian or the guardian is unwilling/unable to protect the child from

such treatment; the condition/behaviour of the child prevents the guardian from providing adequate care. In Alberta, children under eighteen years of age are included (Child Welfare Act, 1984). Ontario uses a similar definition, and has taken care to include children under twelve who have caused serious injury or death, but specifically excludes children sixteen and over unless they are already wards (Child and Family Services Act, 1990). The latter issue provoked considerable discussion at the hearings into Ontario's proposed Act to Protect Children Involved in Prostitution, discussed below (Ontario Legislative Assembly 1998).

11 Calgary interviews, 26, 28 April 1998, above.
12 www.calgaryhodown.tsx.org. Last accessed 20 April 2000. Other cities have used similar strategies (Robinson 1992; Canadian Press 1992).
13 Ruth Patterson, Street Teams, Interview 24 April 1998.
14 Interview, 1 October 1999. Exit is the street services component of a well-established social service agency (Wood's Homes).
15 Interview, Bina Borders, 26 June 2000.
16 The battle posed ratepayers and other residents' groups who wanted the trade out of their neighbourhood against prostitutes and the community workers, law students, and lawyers of Parkdale Community Legal Services who supported and defended them. The headlines capture the tone of the media coverage: 'Parkdale Fights Sex Trade: Prostitutes Weigh Legal Action to Get Residents off Streets;' 'People of Parkdale Taking Back Their Neighbourhood' and 'Dear "John," We Know Your Licence No. We'll Write Soon! Addressed to John Everyman, Toronto' (Abbate 1992; Mallan 1992).
17 The residents of downtown Toronto's upscale Cabbagetown were allowed to give a 'victim impact' statement to the court sentencing a woman labelled the 'big momma' of Cabbagetown prostitutes. They blamed her for the break-ins, crack deals, and discarded condoms and syringes in the area. She has a record with sixty-seven convictions, including five of fail to comply. An eighteen-month order to stay out of Cabbagetown/Regent Park was imposed; a six-month conditional sentence of imprisonment was followed by twelve months probation (Darroch 1997).

Conclusion: Privatization, Polarization, and Policy: Feminism and the Future

JUDY FUDGE AND BRENDA COSSMAN

Beginning in the early 1980s and broadening and deepening throughout the 1990s, the project of privatization was institutionalized in Canada. Economic restructuring and the mantra of deficit and debt reduction have been the twin rationales for clawing back the state's redistributive role. The market was liberated from restrictive regulation and its jurisdiction expanded throughout social life. The primacy of private ordering was given a constitutional boost through various supranational treaties, of which NAFTA was the most prominent. With globalization, neo-classical economic theory was elevated to an article of faith and private accumulation and increased competition were applauded as the only reliable mechanisms for achieving prosperity. While the forces of neo-liberalism and social conservatism fought for political ascendancy, social democracy fell victim to a shift in public opinion and public policy from an emphasis on social responsibility to one on self-reliance. Institutionally, political parties fragmented on a regional basis, legislative power was devolved from the federal to provincial governments and from the latter to municipalities, and democratic forms of governance were sidelined as political power was increasingly concentrated in an executive elite within the cabinet (Savoie 1999). The power of state law was transformed through processes of privatization, marketization, and reregulation and the state accordingly lost its privileged status as the central unit of political, economic, and cultural analysis (de Sousa Santos 1995).

As the chapters in this volume have demonstrated, this shift in state forms and norms has been achieved through a variety of related privatization strategies in which law has been deeply implicated. From reprivatization strategies in taxation, family, and social welfare law, which seek to reconstitute once public goods and services into completely private ones, 'naturally' located within the private spheres of market, family, and/or charity, to commodification strategies in health, reproductive, and genetic technologies and pension law that insist that these public goods and services are better delivered in and through the market, normative claims are made that are intended to naturalize and legitimate the renegotiation of public and private spheres in the new neo-liberal state.

Privatization presents a formidable challenge to feminist theory and practice. First, as several of the contributions to this volume have argued, it has been accompanied by a change in the gender order, once premised on the male breadwinner family. But while the old gender order is no longer stable and unlikely to be restored to its former glory, there is no new alignment of gender relations on the horizon that is likely to become hegemonic. In part, this is because the process of privatization subjects women to contradictory demands and pressures. Several chapters (Cossman, Fudge, Mykitiuk, Philipps) explore how gender is being simultaneously intensified and eroded. For example, while women are increasingly depicted for welfare policy purposes as workers rather than mothers, they are simultaneously cast as traditional caregivers who will pick up the slack that results from cutbacks in social programs.

Second, privatization has been accompanied by a backlash against feminism. Although subject to multiple meanings, feminism as a political movement and theoretical analysis contested the conventional patterns of order, hierarchy, and decision making in public and private institutions (Bashevkin 1998, 7). The contemporary challenge to feminism has played out along a number of dimensions. The resurgence of social conservatism and family values campaigns has called into question the legitimacy of women's struggle for equality, asserting that women have different values and goals than men and that their social and private roles should reflect these differences (Cossman this volume). The increase in material differences among women and greater awareness of these differences has shaken the assumption that women constitute a group united by a commonality of interest, while a renewed emphasis on the differences between men and women has undermined the normative appeal of equality as the basis for women's political and legal struggles (Fudge this volume). Moreover, feminist discourses are being appropriated and transformed both by neo-liberals and neo-conservatives alike. As Mykitiuk's contribution to this volume has shown, neo-liberals emphasize a woman's right to reproductive choice in their attempt to market a wide range of genetic tests, while neo-conservatives, according to Philipps, have emphasized the value of women's unpaid labour and the sacrifices women make in order to justify tax benefits for the economically beleaguered male breadwinner family.

Third, privatization presents a serious challenge to the strategies for social change that feminists have used over the last three decades. The Royal Commission on the Status of Women, which issued its path-breaking report some thirty years ago, marked the second wave of the women's movement in Canada, in which law reform was adopted as the primary means of achieving the goal of equality. The feminist movement won formal legal equality as explicit legal discrimination against women and explicitly sex-based standards were, by and large, eradicated and gender neutrality was embraced. Simultaneously, but with less success, feminists pressed for recognition of the burden of domestic responsibilities, primarily childcare, which disadvantaged women when it came to competing with men in the labour market and detrimentally affected their ability to reap the benefits of the occupationally based welfare state. However, by the 1980s it was obvious that the strategy of formal legal equality, epitomized by the explicit inclusion of women's equality rights in the Charter of Rights and Freedoms, had reached its limit, as it failed to account for the different roles and responsibilities assumed by women and men. Increasingly, feminists called for substantive equality. This marked the third wave of the women's movement, in which feminists demanded that rather than ignoring the patterns of social inequality that shaped men's and women's roles and responsibilities, law and social policy should actively compensate women for the legacy of historical discrimination. Moreover, greater attention and emphasis was given to the differences among women (Razack 1991). Organizations like the Women's Legal Education and Action Fund (LEAF) began to develop complex understandings of equality designed to account for the intersection of historical relations of disadvantage, such as sex and race (Jhappan 1998). Key feminist organizations like LEAF and the National Action Committee on the Status of Women (NAC) made efforts to ensure the representation of lesbians, visible minority women, women from the First Nations, and disabled women in their governing structures, policy development, and litigation strategies. This both strengthened and complicated feminist legal strategizing. The NAC also developed a gender analysis of economic and social policies which attempted both to reveal the gendered assumptions of macro-economic policies such as free trade and to assess their gendered impact (Bashevkin 1998).

I. The Future of Equality Litigation?

Several chapters in this collection have touched upon the use of litigation by feminists and others to achieve substantive equality. There have
been some notable successes. The Public Service Alliance of Canada
was able to use the federal equal pay for work of equal value legislation
to contest male wage norms and achieve millions of dollars in back pay
for its women members (Fudge this volume). Moreover, as Gilmour
indicated, in *B.C. Government and Services Employees Union v. B.C. (Public
Services Employees Relations Commission)* the Supreme Court of Canada
condemned the use of the male norm when it came to setting employment performance standards. And while litigation has not reversed
many of the political decisions that have resulted in the creeping privatization of health care, Gilmour's discussion demonstrated that several
cases have had the positive effect of subjecting such decisions to public
scrutiny. In the broad arena of family policy, Cossman has shown how
equality litigation has been an important prophylactic against the worst
excesses of social conservatives who seek to continue to deny legal recognition and protection to gays and lesbians. But while courts have
grudgingly forced legislatures to protect gays and lesbians from discrimination and to recognize their intimate relationships, they have
stopped short of requiring that same-sex relationships be granted the
same status as marriage. Nor have the courts been willing to develop
equality jurisprudence to address systemic gender biases in the tax system that disadvantage women (Philipps this volume). This suggests
that while equality litigation strategies are helpful in promoting social
recognition of previously ignored or despised identities, they are not
especially useful when it comes to promoting economic redistribution
(Fraser 1997a; Hein 2000).

Jhappan (1998) notes that one of the difficulties with an equality litigation strategy for feminists is operationalizing the concept of equality
in a way that avoids both horns of the sameness/difference dilemma.
This dilemma arises from the fact that the male norm is accepted, more
implicitly than explicitly, as the legal standard against which women's
equality claims are measured. Thus, women must claim either that they
are the same as men in all relevant respects, thereby running the risk of
ignoring salient differences – pregnancy being the most obvious example – or that they are different from men, thereby sacrificing the goal of
equality. LEAF has made great strides in developing a contextualized
approach to equality that rejects a formal model and recognizes that

substantively equal outcomes may require different treatment (Jhappan 2001). This approach avoids some of the problems of the sameness/difference dilemma by conceptualizing women's inequality as rooted not in nature but in gendered social relations in which women are subordinated. But while LEAF has successfully operationalized a contextualized account of equality, it has had mixed success in persuading the courts to adopt it. Similarly, although LEAF has begun to develop an account of equality that addresses multiple bases of discrimination, such as sex, race, and disability, the courts have been unable or unwilling to deal with intersecting equality claims (Jhappan 1998; Razack 1991). Jhappan argues that it is impossible to eradicate essentialism (the positing of a norm against which other claims are measured) from equality claims, leading her to conclude that the 'discourse of *legal* equality as an overarching goal and strategy is an idea whose time may have passed' (Jhappan 1998, 63). Instead of forcing justice claims through the narrow aperture of equality, she proposes that they be asserted directly, forcing the courts to shift attention from the identity of the claimant to the nature of the relationship that oppresses them.

While there is considerable merit in this critique of equality litigation, particularly regarding the impossibility of avoiding the assertion of some standard against which equality is to be measured, it is difficult to see how embracing a justice-based approach to Charter litigation would be much of an improvement for feminists. To a large extent, as Jhappan acknowledges, the ascendancy of equality as the primary basis of feminist litigation was facilitated by the Charter's equality rights guarantees. But it is also important to recognize that formal equality has a place of honour within legal discourse. It continues to have resonance precisely because it is one of the fundamental values of a liberal legal system. The same cannot be said of justice claims. Moreover, many of the limitations of feminist litigation are rooted in the structure of the adversarial common law system, with its stylized rhetoric and reasoning; narrow rules of evidence; inequitably distributed legal resources; and doctrines and principles, such as property and individualism, supportive of unequal social relations. These features of the legal system, more than shortcomings in the theory of equality, account for feminists' lack of litigation success, and they will also plague a justice-based litigation strategy. As hard as it is to operationalize a feminist version of equality through litigation, it is likely easier than operationalizing a feminist version of justice.

To the extent that law remains an important site of discursive struggle, where competing visions of the world are fought out, equality remains an important tool in the feminist arsenal. In the face of the resounding backlash against substantive equality expressed in the popular press and some provincial legislatures, the courts remain one of the last bastions in which substantive equality has some purchase. Despite its limitations, formal legal equality continues to be a powerful discourse. At a time when the forces of social conservativism are gaining ground, it may be more important than ever to fight equality battles in the courts to ensure that subordinated identities are provided with legal recognition and protection. While litigation strategies cannot be expected to transform social relations or modes of governance, they can remain an important defensive strategy, challenging some of the most egregious examples of intolerance and chipping away at some isolated examples of privatization. Moreover, the defence of equality in law may function as a brake against the logic of privatization within feminism. Zillah Eisenstein has argued that privatization undermines the transformative potential of feminism: 'Western feminism is itself being privatized by the market and reduced to self-help strategies, while women, especially poor women, are losing all forms of public help as government programs are dismantled. The market has to transform the militancy of this feminist individualism into a privatized consumerism. It attempts to do this by focusing on freedom – which the mass market absorbs – instead of equality – which the market rejects' (Eisenstein 1996, 59).

Despite its limitations, feminists cannot afford to abandon equality litigation. They must, however, be attentive to how the legal form and dominant social discourses influence legal strategies, creating a range of dilemmas to be negotiated. As Susan Boyd (1999, 380) points out, 'the dilemmas reveal the limits of seeking cultural recognition through law as well as the disciplining effects of engaging with law as a tool of social change.'

II. Beyond Equality

The difficulty in transcending the sameness/difference dilemma goes well beyond litigation strategies. Gendered understandings of the appropriate social roles and entitlements of men and women, upon which the sameness/difference dichotomy hinges, are deeply inscribed into economic and social policies and laws. Over the past three decades there has been much debate, both theoretical and strategic, among feminists over how to achieve economic independence for women in relation to the family, the labour market, and the state, the two poles of which have been summarized by Lochhead and Scott: 'Should women organize to support women in the role of mother and caregiver, legitimizing and facilitating the claims and labour of caregivers on the state and on the family/household (e.g., wages for housework)? Or, should women abandon family-based policies altogether, social assistance being a prime example, and seek to establish parity in the labour market as individuals (e.g., employment equity, child care)' (Lochhead & Scott 2000, 47)? The problem with the debate, which Nancy Fraser (1997a) has stylized as the universal-breadwinner model versus the caregiver-parity model, is that it challenges neither capitalist relations of production, which privilege a narrow and alienating conception of employment, nor the sexual division of labour in the home, which promotes individual women's responsibility for child rearing. Moreover, as Condon (this volume) concludes, neither model adequately addresses the enduring problem of women's poverty.

Today, despite the success of institutionalizing formal equality for women and the legacy of the welfare state, women, especially those at either end of the age spectrum, continue to experience a greater risk of poverty than men. Visible minority women, women who are recent immigrants to Canada, First Nations' women, and disabled women are more likely to be persistently poor than other women. Although 'family structure plays a significant role in determining one's poverty status independent of one's gender' (single-adult households fare poorly compared to two-adult households), the incidence of poverty among single-adult households 'is greatest for women regardless of their age or status as a parent' (Lochhead & Scott 2000, 41). In the era of privatization, rather than alleviating women's poverty, economic and social policies, with the exception of those targeting elderly Canadians, have deepened women's economic insecurity. The restructuring of the Canadian economy to increase its global competitiveness has polarized employment opportunities and deepened income inequality (Townson 2000). At the same time, attacks on social assistance, which include reducing benefit rates, tightening eligibility rules, and harassing recipients, have resulted in a deterioration of the standards of living of those who rely on social assistance (Lochhead & Scott 2000; Townson 2000). The combined effect of these privatization policies has been to widen the gap in the living situations and life chances between women who are white, born in Canada, well-educated, able-bodied, and live with another adult and those who are members of visible minorities, recent immigrants, or disabled, those who lack higher level education, labour market skills, and an adult partner, deepening poverty for women already on the bottom of the income ladder. Traditional notions of social citizenship and access to legal citizenship (Macklin this volume) have been narrowed and increasingly conditioned upon meeting the model of the independent market actor at the same time as feminized and precarious forms of employment have grown.

Privatization strategies have not improved the economic situation and living standards of the majority of women, although some women, those already closest to the top of the income hierarchy, have benefited from them. Philipps's analysis of the gendered assumptions and implications of recent changes in the Canadian tax system has demonstrated their regressive impact on income distribution and how this is likely to exacerbate the situation of people, many of whom are women, who are already marginalized in capital and labour markets. Condon's discussion of the changing logic of retirement income provision from a mixture of universal and occupational citizenship to private sector conceptions of return on investment is likely to increase older women's risk of poverty unless they have enjoyed a full-time, uninterrupted, and well-paid career in the labour market. Moreover, Martin has demonstrated how young women, often the victims of cutbacks in the child welfare net and social benefits, are increasingly subjected to the power of the criminal law in order to force them to take responsibility for their lives.

The belief that the capitalist market combined with individual responsibility for life chances will result in the greatest good for all has informed the privatization project. But this belief has turned into dogma as the proselytizers of privatization have failed to address, let alone resolve, ugly and deeply rooted problems that arise under this regime. First, while it is true that unrestricted production for profit produces great wealth, it also produces great inequality globally, nationally, and locally. The retrenchment of mechanisms of redistribution has increased the social marginalization of groups of people, often identified on invidious bases such as race, and the numbers of people homeless (City of Toronto 2000) or in jail have risen (Correctional Services of Canada 2000). Second, there is no necessary correlation between production for profit and production for social need. Increasing profits do not translate transparently into improved standards of living for the working population (Picchio 1998). Capitalism is rapacious. The role of the liberal state has been to align the requirements of capital accumulation with those of social reproduction. Third, the gender order which has underpinned the welfare state is unsustainable and the extension of the male employment norm to women is no solution. While it is true that men have greater economic resources than women, they also incur costs. Not only is men's life expectancy lower than women's (Statistics Canada 2000a, 54), men have little choice in how to spend their lives, being forced into the full-time continuous lifelong employment career whether they like it or not. In any event, it is clear that an unbridled emphasis on waged work and profit cannot address the needs of children and the elderly. Ultimately, the polarization of privatization will likely prove to be unsustainable (Picchio 1998).

III. From Polarization to Paralysis in Public Policy

At the beginning of the twenty-first century the contradictions generated by privatization are increasingly apparent and there is some evidence that its central tenets are being questioned. The economic crisis in Mexico in 1994 followed by that in Asia in 1997 has highlighted the need for finance capitalism to be regulated at the national and supranational levels (Tshuma 2000). Even the World Bank is entertaining the idea that national regulatory authorities can exert some control over international financial flows (Weiss 1999, 139). In Canada, at the federal level, the deficit crisis is over and the key political question is what to do with the surplus (Little 2000a): pay down the debt, lower taxes, or increase spending? The answer to this question, not surprisingly, is controversial. CEOs of Canada's largest corporations demand the first option (Toulin 2000), while public opinion polls taken before the 2000 federal budget indicated that Canadians would prefer increased government spending, especially on health, rather than tax cuts (*Toronto Star* 2000; Whittington 2000). Since 1997, the performance of the labour market has improved dramatically, generating more full-time employment than non-standard jobs; however, real wage growth has remained stagnant (Canadian Labour Congress 1999–2000). This suggests that the rate of overall growth has been uncoupled from income growth of working-class households. By contrast, in 2000 corporate profits reached their highest level relative to the GDP in almost twenty years (Little 2000b). According to Judith Maxwell (2000a), former head of the Economic Council of Canada and now leader of a new 'civil society' think tank, the problem is that 'the rising tide has not lifted all boats.' Prosperity, polarization, and a paralysis in public policy are the three contradictory forces that characterize this stage of privatization (Maxwell 2000b).

In Canada, as well as internationally, policy makers and analysts are increasingly concerned with issues of social cohesion, inclusion and investment (Jenson 1998; OECD 1997). In the 1980s and 1990s social policy was subordinated and sacrificed to the dictates of economic restructuring, but increased attention is now being directed at putting the social house in order. Emphasis is once again placed on the recurring dilemma in liberal capitalist societies: what to do about social reproduction. Significantly, health care and childcare, crucial aspects in the reproduction of a population, are two of the most prominent topics of current social policy discussion. It is particularly with respect to the latter issue that the clash between neo-liberals, who emphasize individual choice, and neo-conservatives, with their specific vision of what constitutes the social good, is creating a paralysis. Yet some provinces have managed to break this impasse in specific areas and have embarked on new policy initiatives. Alberta, reflecting the dominance of economic neo-liberalism, has introduced changes to the funding and delivery of health care that many predict is the first step along the road to wholesale privatization (Health Care Protection Act, S.A. 2000). By contrast, Quebec has implemented childcare programs that help to socialize the costs of raising children (Jenson & Maxwell 1999; Bailey 2000). In this jurisdictions, social democracy still resonates, albeit faintly, in social policy.

In general, however, the tensions and contradictions between neo-liberalism and neo-conservatism remain unresolved. Indeed, they are again in the public spotlight with the emergence of the Canadian Alliance and that party's internal struggle to define its agenda. This new federal political party is trying to unit the Right and straddle the divide between its neo-liberal and neo-conservative constituencies. While the allegiance of Canada's business community is dependent on an agenda of fiscal responsibility, much grassroots support is dependent on one of social conservatism, from abortion and gay rights to religious schooling. As Cossman and Martin illustrate in their chapters, the coalition between these two visions is often unstable, producing at times diametrically opposed positions on concrete issues of governance and public policy. Social conservatism has not yet run its course in Canada; however, its appeal is not growing. The public debate over such divisive issues as gay rights may provide an opportunity to expose the cracks and fissures within and among the Right. At the level of public policy, however, this instability may do little more than breed further paralysis.

The policy impasse over how the neo-liberal state should deal with the contradictory demands of production and reproduction generated by capitalism is exemplified by the conflict over the appropriate family policy for the new economy. How to balance the competing demands of employment and domestic responsibilities – of work and family – is moving to the top of the policy agenda (McIlroy 2000b). It is precisely here that the advantages of a feminist analysis are the most obvious. In Ontario, workfare policies designed to transform women who are lone parents from social benefit recipients to labour market participants have run aground because of the lack of accessible and affordable childcare (Mackie 2000). Changes to the Employment Insurance Act have had a particularly detrimental impact on women workers, contributing to further increases in women's poverty (Townson 2000, 10). When the number of hours required to qualify for benefits nearly tripled during the 1990s, many incumbents in part-time and temporary jobs, the majority of whom were women, failed to qualify (Canadian Labour Congress 1999). These are but two examples of the pernicious impact of policies that fail to take into account the sexual division of labour.

In pointing out the importance of the sexual division of labour, feminists find themselves in strange company. Neo-conservatives are also concerned about the failure of public policy to take women's roles as mothers and caregivers into account (Philipps this volume), although they elevate this sexual division of labour to a natural and ordained status. While neo-conservatives seek to resolve the contradictions between production and reproduction by returning to a male breadwinner gender order, they join and appropriate feminist discourse in recognizing the importance of women's unpaid labour. Feminists might try to reappropriate this neo-conservative discourse, but the risks are multiple. Deploying neo-conservative discourse against neo-liberal policies risks reinforcing the strategies of familialization and its naturalization of familial ideology. And in playing the fissures and tensions between neo-liberal and neo-conservative discourses, feminists may only succeed in further institutionalizing the paralysis while succumbing to the drift to the right.

It is not only feminists and neo-conservatives who are talking about women. Paradoxically, at the same time that the National Action Committee on the Status of Women has declined as a political institution, the gender analysis it brought to bear on economic and social policy in the 1980s has flourished. The Beijing International Women's Conference in 1995 marked the apogee of a gender-based analysis, as it forced governments around the world and national systems of economic accounting to focus on the contribution of women's unpaid work to economic growth and development (Luxton & Vosko 1998). That year, the federal government in Canada resolved to incorporate gender-based analysis of future policies and legislation, where appropriate, and in 1997, together with the provincial and territorial governments, it came up with a multifaceted equality indicator (Federal-Provincial/Territorial Ministers Responsible for the Status of Women 1997; Status of Women Canada 1996). Moreover, in 1996, for the first time, the Canadian census contained a series of questions designed to measure the contribution of unpaid work in the household made by women and men (Luxton & Vosko 1998).

Simply asserting the need for a gender-based policy analysis does not mean either that the government will follow through on it or that the implications of the analysis will be acted upon. The same year that it endorsed integrating a gender-based analysis into public policy, the federal government radically altered the nature and amount of its commitment to funding social programs, a change that had especially harsh consequences for women (Day & Brodsky 1998). Moreover, as the chapters in this volume have illustrated, many of the privatization strategies in a broad range of public areas are undercutting the potential relevance of gender analysis. As gender disappears from view in the discourse of the neo-liberal citizen – as the citizen is degendered and individualized – the apparent need for a gender-based analysis also fades from view. Yet, as we have argued, gender is being subjected to the contradictory forces of erosion and intensification. Gender may be disappearing from view, but the impact of the project of privatization is, as we have argued, anything but gender-neutral. The political resonance of gender-based analysis may be dissipating just as it is becoming more urgent.

At the same time, and in other circles, gender-based analysis of economic policy is gaining ground and moving beyond a narrow equality framework. For example, with regard to unpaid domestic work performed by women, the first stage of feminist analysis emphasized the inequitable distribution of such work, the second called for its social recognition (often through wages for housework campaigns), while the third stage is beginning to articulate its links with the macro-economy (Bakker 1998). As Diane Elson (1998, 204) cautions, the absence of representation in 'financial flows of unpaid domestic labour and the costs of maintaining human and social assets ... [creates] problems in macro-economic management, as privatization and restrictive fiscal and monetary policies can turn out to have hidden costs – or at least costs which are invisible to macroeconomic policy makers, though they are felt by the poor mothers struggling to make ends meet.'

The essays in this collection demonstrate the need for a feminist analysis that problematicizes and seeks to understand the linkages between production for profit; the social reproduction of the population; relations of income distribution through the wage, family, and social transfers; and how these processes and institutions are both conditioned by and condition the gender order. While each of the chapters is animated by an ethical commitment that women are worthy of equal respect to men, together they demonstrate the need to move beyond an equality analysis that emphasizes the situation of women to one that focuses on how gender is implicated at the macro-, meso- and micro-levels in social and productive relations and modes of governance.

IV. Re-imaging Resistance

It is time to exploit the contradictions in privatization and to begin to develop a new vision and new strategies to achieve it. This is a daunting task, but paradigm shifts have occurred before. Not so long ago in Canada, women were not considered to be legal persons and were denied many of the entitlements of legal and social citizenship available to men. The same was true, although in different ways, at different times, and in different areas, with respect to Aboriginal people, gays and lesbians, and racialized groups not of British stock (Lahey 1999). Legal strategies played an important, though not exclusive, role in the paradigm shift for women. Feminists then as now were targets of a backlash against the new gender paradigm they sought to institutionalize. History has not ended.

What, then, is the way forward? What strategies should feminists and others committed to social democracy be using? What legal strategies should be deployed to counter the forces of privatization? The essays in this collection do not provide a blueprint. Indeed, in much of our analysis in this volume, we may appear as the prophets of doom and gloom – illustrating, as we have, the complicity of the law in the dismantling of the welfare state and the rebuilding of the leaner, meaner neo-liberal state, with its devastating effects on the lives of marginalized groups. Privatization risks appearing as an unstoppable force, a juggernaut, against which resistance is futile. But the essays in this volume are all animated by an ethical commitment to resistance, and a sense that the first step in this resistance is understanding the changes around us. The authors share the belief that it is time to grapple with difficult theoretical problems, too long ignored. They are also united by the belief that there is no return to a golden age of a Keynesian welfare state and its promise of equality for women. The golden age never delivered on its promise in any event. Part of the way forward is recognizing the fundamental structural changes that privatization has brought about and grappling with their implications. Each of the essays in this volume has sought to bring these changes into sharper focus, as a first step in coming to terms with the new challenges.

And those challenges are formidable. Privatization has institutionalized a new vision of citizenship and governance, in which the market has firmly displaced the state as the primary mechanism of distributing goods and services. The contributors to this volume emphasized the central role that law has played in institutionalizing the project of privatization. In light of this fact, how can law be expected to play a role in challenging it? The answer lies in the contradictory nature of the law. Law has long played a contradictory role in progressive struggles, simultaneously supporting an edifice of inequality while providing the very discourse that has allowed marginalized groups to challenge this inequality. As we have argued, law is deeply linked to normative claims, high among them equality, liberty, individualism, and the rule of law. Law continues to provide a site where claims based on these normative visions can be made, if not always won. Moreover, law remains the preeminent modality for the deployment of coercive power in liberal states. Defensive battles must continue to be fought in the courts.

By challenging the normative authority of the courts and their traditional forms of reasoning, feminists have an opportunity to make controversial policy choices apparent. As several of the chapters in this collection have demonstrated (Condon, Fudge, Philipps), the carving up of economic and social policies into discrete analytic and legal categories has created barriers to developing integrated policies that deal with the complex interconnections of our world. The continued separation of tax and pension policy from employment and family law and policy simply replicates the unhelpful separate spheres model (household versus market) of neo-classical economics (Philipps this volume). As Martin has shown, child welfare regimes and criminal law are not separate forms of regulation but deeply interconnected and mutually conditioning. We have tried to illustrate some of the connections in this volume, but feminist analysis needs to continue to rethink traditional legal categories.

Law is a crucial part of any counter-hegemonic struggle. But the role of law must be linked with a broader project of political revisioning and revitalization. These essays have demonstrated that feminist frameworks and methodologies have been and continue to be invaluable in making links between what have been considered to be autonomous social fields. Greater attention must be given to the entire process of social reproduction – procreation, socialization, immigration, health – and its links to the economy must be articulated. This stage of analysis is crucial for developing an alternative social vision and devising the strategies needed to institutionalize it. For example, new conceptions of citizenship must be imagined. As Macklin (this volume) has shown, the universalist conception of citizenship has obscured the extent to which it is gendered and racialized. But we should not abandon the project of re-imagining a world in which citizenship involves a collective sense of responsibility. While the new market citizens – defined in terms of self-reliance – may seem antithetical to the idea of collective social responsibility, they may provide a location to begin to chip away at the neo-liberal mode of governance and citizenship. From the apparent crisis in Canadian health care to the tragedy in Walkerton, Ontario, in the spring of 2000, where the failure of water purification and testing systems led to several deaths from a virulent form of E-coli bacteria, there are signs of a growing unease on the part of these market citizens. Despite the Ontario government's insistence that its cutbacks in the number of government water inspectors and its transfer of water testing to the private sector did not contribute to the Walkerton tragedy, it seems unable to close down the public debate (Bourette 2000a, 2000b; Harris 2000). These kinds of political crises – and there is no reason to believe that they will stop – are creating the possibility for a re-evaluation of the impact of tax cuts, as ordinary market citizens begin to see their own well-being and the well-being of their families implicated and compromised in the project of privatization. These crises may provide moments in which the ideological effects of the discourses of privatization – the celebration of markets as the most efficient way of distributing goods and services, and of families as natural providers for the needs of its members – become unstable.

There are signs of a new politics of opposition. People with a diverse range of interests have begun to coalesce in their opposition to the agendas of globalization and privatization, collectively seeking to rebuild a political space in which it is possible to voice opposition. Naomi Klein, for example, has argued that anti-corporate activism 'is the new brand of politics' (Klein 2000, xix). While her predictions may be overly optimistic, she traces the emergence of this new anti-corporate politics through a range of developments since the early 1990s: from the politics of culture jamming, in which artists and computer hackers are reclaiming public spaces by transforming corporate ads, to the Reclaim the Streets movements, in which ravers, self-described anti-capitalists, anti-corporate activists, and radical environmentalists have sought to reclaim public spaces such as busy intersections for spontaneous gatherings, to the more explicitly political anti-corporate activism in which activists have targeted the exploitative labour practices of multinational labels. Activists have sought to reveal the exploitative practices behind the brand name, from Nike and Wal-mart to Starbucks and Shell: 'A handful of non-governmental organizations and groups of progressive intellectuals have been developing a political strategy that recognizes that multinational brands, because of their high profile, can be far more galvanizing targets than the politicians' (ibid., at 342).

The events in Seattle in 1999 suggest that there may be something brewing with this anti-globalization, anti-capitalist activism. Tens of thousands of activists of many stripes, including members of labour movements, human rights groups, and environmental organizations, as well as a disenchanted youth movement, took to the streets in one of the largest protests witnessed in North America in recent years. This activism bypassed national governments, going straight to the new supra-national organizations. The target was the World Trade Organization. The protests have continued, first, several months later, in Washington, DC, where the targets were the World Bank and the International Monetary Fund, and subsequently in Quebec City and Gottenburg. Both followed on the heels of the 1998 defeat of the Multilateral Agreement on Investment, which was characterized as the constitution for a single global economy, by popular groups (Tabb 1999a). Some commentators have embraced Seattle as the dawning of a new era of resistance and of the burgeoning of civil society (Studies in Political Economy 2000; Tabb 1999b). Others are more sceptical. The mainstream media attempted to play on the fears and anxieties of the new market citizen by representing the events in Seattle as riots, crime, vandalism, and the actions 'out of control' youth (Solomon 2000). While the meaning of Seattle will no doubt remain contested, at a minimum it suggests that the neo-liberal consensus is not without its cracks and its increasingly vocal detractors.

However, the tragic events of 11 September 2001, and the subsequent 'war against terrorism' have, at least for the short term, shifted attention away from the social justice, anti-globalization protests. Whether the events of September 11 will continue to dominate political priorities and quell other forms of protest and politics is an open question. Efforts to resist the forces of globalization and the neo-liberal agenda through labour and human rights campaigns that include consumer boycotts and a demand for corporate codes of conduct may be revitalized and may signal the emergence of a new politics that contests the very idea that the market is a realm beyond politics. This form of resistance is taking its political message to the market, insisting on the transparency of the market's politics (Fudge 2001). While this form of politics is limited by the logic of the capitalist market itself – it will not result in a significant restructuring of the relations of production and reproduction – so too were its social democratic predecessors, which were based on engagement with the Keynesian state. The politics of the KWS was limited by the role of the state in mediating the conflicts between production and reproduction. This new anti-corporatist politics may be criticized for ceding too much to the role of market and accepting the new vision of citizenship as consumption (Fudge 2001), but it may offer a place to stand in the effort to reclaim politics and political contestation in an age of neo-liberalism. The crucial questions are whether it can be linked with the key protest movements of the twentieth century – anti-war, labour, women and civil rights (anti-racism) – and whether these movements can be revitalized.

Feminists need to find ways to participate in the reclaiming of public space and in the rebuilding of politics. The gendered impact of privatization must be brought into public view and the ways in which privatization further marginalizes already disenfranchised groups must be brought into sharper focus. If the discourse of substantive equality is not up to this task, feminists need to construct a new political language through which we can illustrate the devastating impact of privatization on the lives of many women and children.

As part of the counter-hegemonic struggle, it is important, for example, to insist that individual self-reliance – so resonant in the brave new world of neo-liberalism – is in fact an individual good and long a demand of feminists. As feminists have argued (Fraser & Gordon 1997), for too long women have been characterized as dependent upon either a man's wage or the state's helping hand. We need to find creative ways to argue that this individual self-reliance is not an alternative to social responsibility and redistribution, as neo-liberals and social conservatives would have us believe. The question is how to create the conditions in which individuals can self-determine and be self-reliant. Similarly, we need to find ways to insist that supporting families – so resonant in the world of neo-conservatives – has also long been a demand of feminists. Yet, contrary to the claims of neo-conservatives, supporting families means supporting the diversity of emotionally and economically inter-dependent relationships, and recognizing the real and often gendered consequences of those relationships. The question is, once again, how to create the conditions in which relationships and the individuals within them can thrive. These are social questions and, as feminists have consistently argued, any solution to them will require the concerted effort of the collective resources of society for human beings to flourish.

References

Books, Articles, and Theses

Abbate, Gay. 1992. 'Parkdale Fights Sex Trade: Prostitutes Weigh Legal Action to Get Residents Off Streets.' *Globe and Mail,* 4 September, A11.

Abbot, Pamela, and Claire Wallace. 1992. *The Family and the New Right.* Boulder, CO: Pluto Press.

Abell, Jennie. 1992. 'Women, Violence, and the Criminal Law: "It's the Fundamentals of Being a Lawyer That Are at Stake Here."' *Queen's Law Journal* 17(1), 147–73.

Abergel, Elisabeth. 1999. 'Genetic Food Fight.' *National Post,* 29 July, B6.

Abraham, C. 1999. 'Tenacious Woman Scores Medical Victory.' *Globe and Mail,* 27 August, A1.

Acker, Joan. 1988. 'Class, Gender, and the Relation of Distribution.' *Signs* 13, 473–97.

Adams, G. 1999. 'The Physician Services Committee.' *Ontario Medical Review,* March, 12–13.

Adams, P. 2000. 'Premiers Set to Fight for Health Care.' *Globe and Mail,* 1 March, A1, A4.

Adamson, Nancy, Linda Briskin, and Margaret McPhail. 1988. *Feminist Organizing for Change: The Contemporary Women's Movement in Canada.* Toronto: Oxford University Press.

Adelberg, Ellen, and Claudia Currie, eds. 1987. *Too Few to Count: Canadian Women in Conflict with the Law.* Vancouver: Press Gang Publishers.

Aglietta, Michel. 2000. 'Shareholder Value and Corporate Governance: A Comment and Some Tricky Questions.' *Economy and Society* 29(1), 146–59.

Akbari, Ather. 1999. 'Immigrant "Quality" in Canada: More Direct Evidence of Human Capital Content, 1956–1994.' *International Migration Review* 33, 156.

– 1995. 'The Impact of Immigrants on Canada's Treasury, circa 1990.' In Don Devoretz, ed., *Diminishing Returns: The Economics of Canada's Recent Immigration Policy.* Toronto: C.D. Howe Institute.

Alberta. 2000a. News Release. *Alberta Prepares the Way for a Bold New Tax System with Bill 118.* 16 March.

– 2000b. News Release. *Amended Bill 18 Increases Alberta Advantage over Other Provinces.* 23 May.

– 1999a. *Provincial Treasurer Stockwell Day's Budget '99 Speech.* 11 March.

– 1999b. 'Protection of Children Involved in Prostitution Act.' Edmonton: Government of Alberta. http://www.gov.ab.ca/cs/initiatives/prostitution/pros_main.htm (11 July 2000).

Alberta. Child and Family Services Authority. 1999. 'Protection of Children Involved in Prostitution Act Information.' http://www.assembly.ab.ca/lao/mla/mlabio.asp?RNumber=10 (11 July 2000).

Alberta Family and Social Services. 1993–1998. *Annual Reports.* Edmonton: Office of the Minister.

Alberta Task Force on Juvenile Prostitution. 1997. *Children Involved in Prostitution: The Forsyth Report.* Edmonton: Ministry of Alberta Family and Social Services.

Alberta's Official Opposition. 1997. *To Fend for Themselves: Alberta's Approach to Reforming Child Welfare.* Edmonton: Office of the Official Opposition.

Ambert, Anne-Marie. 1998. *Divorce: Facts, Figures and Consequences.* Ottawa: Vanier Institute of the Family. http://www.vifamily.ca/dft/divorce/divorce.htm

Amin, Nuzhat. 1987. *A Preliminary History of Settlement Work in Ontario, 1900–Present.* Toronto: Joint Centre for Excellence for Research on Immigration and Settlement.

Anderson, Elizabeth. 1993. *Value in Ethics and Economics.* Cambridge: Harvard University Press.

Antecol, Heather, and Peter Kuhn. 1999. 'Employment Equity Programs and the Job Search Outcomes of Unemployed Men and Women: Actual and Perceived Effects.' *Canadian Public Policy* 25 (Supplement), 727–45.

Appelby, Timothy. 1999. 'Toronto Police Bust Prostitution Ring.' *Globe and Mail,* 21 July, A5.

Appleton, B. 1999. 'International Agreements and National Health Plans: NAFTA.' In Daniel Drache and Terry Sullivan, eds., *Market Limits in Health Reform: Public Success, Private Failure.* London: Routledge, 87–104.

Arat-Koc, Sedef. 1999. '"Good Enough to Work but Not Good Enough to Stay:" Foreign Domestic Workers and the Law.' In Elizabeth Comack, ed., *Locating Law: Race/Class/Gender Connections.* Halifax: Fernwood, 125–52.

- 1997. 'From "Mothers of the Nation" to Migrant Workers.' In Abigail Bakan and Daiva Stasiulis, eds., *Not One of the Family: Foreign Domestic Workers in Canada*. Toronto: University of Toronto Press, 53–79.

Archibald, Kathleen. 1970. *Sex and the Public Service*. Ottawa: Queen's Printer.

Armstrong, Jane. 1997a. 'Penetang, Lindsay Chosen for Mega-jails. Each Will House 1,200 Prisoners and Bring in 300 New Jobs.' *Toronto Star*, 9 October, A8.

- 1997b. 'Tough Boot Camp Rules to Spread. Young Offenders to Face Stricter Conditions.' *Toronto Star*, 9 December, A1.

Armstrong, Patricia. 1997. 'Privatizing Care.' In Patricia Armstrong, Hugh Armstrong, Jacqueline Choiniere, Eric Mykhalovskiy, and Jerry P. White, *Medical Alert: New Organizations in Health Care*. Toronto: Garamond Press.

- 1996a. 'The Feminization of the Labour Force: Harmonizing Down in a Global Economy.' In Isabella Bakker, ed., *Rethinking Restructuring: Gender and Change in Canada*. Toronto: University of Toronto Press, 29–54.

- 1996b. 'Resurrecting "The Family": Interring "The State."' *Journal of Comparative Family Studies*, 27(2) (Summer), 221–47.

- 1996c. 'Unravelling the Safety Net: Transformations in Health Care and their Impact on Women.' In Janine Brodie, ed., *Women in Canadian Public Policy*. Toronto: Harcourt Brace, 129–150.

- 1984. *Labour Pains: Women's Work in Crisis*. Toronto: Women's Press.

Armstrong, Patricia, and Hugh Armstrong. 1999. *Women, Privatization and Health Care Reform: The Ontario Scan*. Toronto: National Network on Environments and Women's Health.

- 1996. *Wasting Away: The Undermining of Canadian Health Care*. Toronto: Oxford University Press.

- 1994. *The Double Ghetto*, 3rd ed. Toronto: McClelland and Stewart.

- 1988. 'Taking Women into Account: Redefining and Intensifying Employment in Canada.' In Jane Jensen, Elizabeth Hagen, and Ceallaigh Reddy, eds., *Feminization of the Labor Force*. New York: Oxford University Press, 65–84.

Armstrong, Patricia, Hugh Armstrong, Jacqueline Choiniere, Gina Feldberg, and Jerry White. 1994. *Take Care: Warning Signals for Canada's Health System*. Toronto: Garamond Press.

Armstrong, W. 2000. *Canada's Canary in the Mine Shaft: The Consumer's Experience with Cataract Surgery and Private Clinics in Alberta*. Edmonton: Alberta Chapter of Consumers Association of Canada.

Aronson, Jane, and Sheila M. Neysmith. 1997. 'The Retreat of the State and Long-Term Care Provision: Implications for Frail Elderly People, Unpaid Family Carers and Paid Home Care Workers.' *Studies in Political Economy* 53, 37–66.

Association of Canadian Pension Management (ACPM). 2000. *A Retirement*

Income Strategy for Canada: Dependence or Self-reliance: Which Way for Canada's Retirement Income System? Toronto: Association of Canadian Pension Management.

Attorney General of Ontario. 1998. *In the Supreme Court of Canada between The Attorney General of Ontario and M and H, Factum of the Appellant.*

Aubry, Jack. 1998. 'Pay Equity Win Worth Billions.' *Ottawa Citizen*, 30 July, A1, A2.

Auditor General. 1998. *1998 Report of the Auditor General of Canada.* Expenditure and Work Force Reductions in the Public Service, April. Ottawa: Auditor General.

Ausili, Peter J. 1988. 'Withholding or Withdrawing Artificial Nutrition and Hydration from Terminally Ill and Permanently Unconscious Patients: Some Recent Case Law and Contemporary Catholic Theology.' *Catholic Law* 32, 55–88.

Avery, Donald. 1995. *A Reluctant Host: Canada's Response to Immigrant Workers, 1896–1994.* Toronto: McClelland and Stewart.

Backhouse, Constance. 1991. *Petticoats and Prejudice: Women and the Law in Nineteenth-Century Canada.* Toronto: Women's Press.

– 1985. 'Nineteenth-Century Canadian Prostitution Law: Reflection of a Discriminatory Society.' *Social History* 53, 387–423.

– 1984. *Prostitution in Canada.* Ottawa: Canadian Advisory Council on the Status of Women.

Bagley, C. 1985. 'Child Sexual Abuse and Juvenile Prostitution: A Comment on the Badgley Report on Sexual Offences Against Children and Youth.' *Canadian Journal of Public Health* 76, 65–6.

Bagley, C., B.A. Burrows, and C. Yaworski. 1991. 'Street Kids and Adolescent Prostitution: A Challenge for Legal and Social Services.' In N. Bala, J.P. Hornick, and R. Vogl, eds., *Canadian Child Welfare Law.* Toronto: Thompson.

Bagley, C., and L. Young. 1987. 'Juvenile Prostitution and Child Sexual Abuse: A Controlled Study.' *Canadian Journal of Community Mental Health* 6(1), 5–26.

Bailey, Ian. 2000. 'B.C. Launches Ambitious Childcare Program.' *National Post*, 6 June, A1.

Baines, Beverley. 2000. 'Occupational Sex Segregation and Employment Equity: Lessons from Canada.' *Canadian Labour and Employment Law Journal* 8, 291–324.

Bakan, Abigail, and Audrey Koyabashi. 2000. *Employment Equity Policy in Canada: An Interprovincial Comparison.* Ottawa: Status of Women Canada.

Bakan, Abigail, and Daiva Stasiulis. 1997a. *Not One of the Family.* Toronto: University of Toronto Press.

– 1997b. 'Foreign Domestic Worker Policy in Canada and the Social Boundaries of Modern Citizenship.' In Abigail Bakan and Daiva Stasiulis, eds., *Not One of the Family*. Toronto: University of Toronto Press, 29.

- 1996. 'Structural Adjustment, Citizenship, and Foreign Domestic Labour: The Canadian Case.' In Isabella Bakker, ed., *Rethinking Restructuring: Gender and Change in Canada*. Toronto: University of Toronto Press, 217–42.

Bakan, Joel. 1997. *Just Words: Constitutional Rights and Social Change*. Toronto: University of Toronto Press.

Bakker, Isabella. Forthcoming. 'Engendering Economics: Sites and Processes.' In Jim Stanford, Lance Taylor, and Ellen Houston, eds., *Power, Employment and Accumulation: Social Structures in Economic Theory and Policy*. Armonk, NY: M.E. Sharpe.

- 1999. 'Can an Engendered Macroeconomics Discipline "Disciplinary" Neo-Liberalism?' Paper delivered at the Conference on Feminist Perspectives on the Paradoxes of Globalization, Free University of Berlin, 5–6 November. Copy on file with the author.

- 1998. *Unpaid Work and Macroeconomics: New Discourses, New Tools for Action*. Ottawa: Status of Women Canada.

- 1996a. 'Introduction: The Gendered Foundations of Restructuring in Canada.' In Isabella Bakker, ed., *Rethinking Restructuring: Gender and Change in Canada*. Toronto: University of Toronto Press, 3–25.

- 1996b. 'Deconstructing Macro-economics through a Feminist Lens.' In Janine Brodie, ed., *Women and Canadian Public Policy*. Toronto: Harcourt, Brace and Company, 31–56.

Bakker, Isabella, and Diane Elson. 1998. 'Towards Engendering Budgets.' In *Alternative Federal Budget Papers 1998*. Ottawa: Canadian Centre for Policy Alternatives, 297–324.

Bakker, Isabella, and Riel Miller. 1996. 'Escape from Fordism.' In Daniel Drache and Robert Boyer, eds., *States against Markets: The Limits of Globalization*. London: Routledge.

Bakker, Isabella, and Katherine Scott. 1996. 'From the Postwar to the Postliberal Keynesian Welfare State.' In Wallace Clement, ed., *Understanding Canada: Building on the New Canadian Political Economy*. Montreal: McGill-Queen's University Press.

Bala, Nicholas. 1994. 'What's Wrong with YOA bashing? What's Wrong with the YOA? Recognizing the Limits of the Law.' *Canadian Journal of Criminology* 36, 247–70.

Bala, Nicholas, and D'Arcy Mahoney. 1995. 'Responding to Criminal Behaviour of Children Under 12: An Analysis of Canadian Law and Practice.' Submitted to the House of Commons Committee on Justice and Legal Affairs for Phase II of Young Offenders Study, July. Ottawa: Justice of Canada.

Baldwin, Bob, and Monica Townson. 1997. 'Public Pensions.' In Canadian Centre for Policy Alternatives/Choices: A Coalition for Social Justice, *Alternative Federal Budget Papers 1997*. Ottawa: Canadian Centre for Policy Alternatives.

Barbalet, J.M. 1988. *Citizenship Rights, Struggle and Class Inequality*. Minneapolis: University of Minnesota Press.

Barber, Benjamin R. 1995. *Jihad vs. McWorld*. New York: Time Books.

Barer, M., V. Bhatia, G. Stoddart, and R. Evans. 1994. *The Remarkable Tenacity of User Charges*. Prepared for the Ontario Premier's Council on Health, Well-being and Social Justice. Toronto: Queen's Printer.

Barrett, Michele. 1992. 'Words and Things: Materialism and Method in Contemporary Feminist Analysis.' In Michele Barrett and Anne Phillips, eds., *Destabilizing Theory: Contemporary Feminist Debates*. Stanford: Stanford University Press, 201–19.

– 1988. *Women's Oppression Today: The Marxist/Feminist Encounter*. Rev. ed. London: Verso.

Basen, Gwynne. 1994. 'The New Reproductive Technologies: Genetics, Manipulation and the Corporate Connection.' *Herizons* 8(1), 42–4.

Basham, Partick. 1999. 'Equity or Social Engineering?' *Montreal Gazette*, 26 October, B3.

Bashevkin, Sylvia. 1998. *Women on the Defensive: Living through Conservative Times*. Toronto: University of Toronto Press.

Battle, Ken. 1998. 'Poverty and the Welfare State.' In Les Samuelson and Wayne Antony, eds., *Power and Resistance: Critical Thinking about Canadian Social Policies*. 2nd ed. Halifax: Fernwood.

– 1997. 'Pension Reform in Canada.' *Canadian Journal on Aging* 16(3), 519–52.

– 1996. 'Summary.' *Experts' Forum on Canada Pension Plan Reform*. Ottawa: Caledon Institute of Social Policy.

Battle, Ken, and Sherri Torjman. 1996. 'Desperately Seeking Substance: Commentary on the Social Security Review.' In Jane Pulkingham and Gordon Ternowetsky, eds., *Remaking Canadian Social Policy: Social Security in the Late 1990s*. Halifax: Fernwood.

Beach, C.M., and G.A. Slotsve. 1996. *Are We Becoming Two Societies?* Toronto: C.D. Howe Institute.

Beck, Ulrich. 1992. *Risk Society*. London: Sage Publications.

Beck-Gernsheim, Elisabeth. 1991. *The Social Implications of Bioengineering*. Atlantic Highlands: New Jersey: Humanities Press.

Beechy, Veronica. 1988. 'Rethinking the Definition of Work: Gender and Work.' In Jane Jenson et al., eds., *The Feminization of the Labour Market: Paradoxes and Promises*. Oxford: Polity Press.

Bélanger, A. 1999. *Report on the Demographic Situation in Canada, 1998–1999: Current Demographic Analysis.* Ottawa: Statistics Canada.

Bell, Shannon. 1994. *Reading, Writing, and Rewriting the Prostitute Body.* Indianapolis: Indiana University Press.

Bell, Vikki. 1993. 'Governing Childhood: Neo-liberalism and the Law.' *Economy and Society* 22(3), 390–405.

Bell-Lowther, Erica. 1988. 'Privatization: Increasing Government Efficiency or Dismantling the Welfare State?' *Social Worker* 56(3), 101–4.

Benefits Canada. 2000a. 'The DC Century.' *Benefits Canada,* 13 February.

– 2000b. 'In Fact.' *Benefits Canada,* 15 February.

Beneria, Lourdes. 1999a. 'Globalization, Gender and the Davos Man.' *Feminist Economics* 5(3), 61–83.

– 1999b. 'The Enduring Debate over Unpaid Labour.' *International Labour Review* 138(3), 287–309.

Bennett, Laura. 1995. 'Women and Enterprise Bargaining: The Legal and Institutional Framework.' In Margaret Thornton, ed., *Public and Private: Feminist Legal Debates.* Melbourne: Oxford University Press, 112–43.

Benson, Edgar J. 1969. *Proposals for Tax Reform.* Ottawa: Queen's Printer.

Bickenbach, Jerome. 1994. 'Voluntary Disabilities and Everyday Illnesses.' In Marcia Rioux and Michael Bach, eds., *Disability Is not Measels: New Research Paradigms in Disability.* Toronto: Roeher Institute, 109–26.

Bird, Richard M. 1979. *The Growth of Public Employment in Canada.* Toronto: Institute for Research on Public Policy.

Black, Julia, and Richard Nobles. 1998. 'Personal Pensions Misselling: The Causes and Lessons of Regulatory Failure.' *Modern Law Review* 61, 789–820.

Blackburn, Robin. 2000. 'Reply to Henri Jacot.' *New Left Review* 1, 130–6.

– 1999. 'The New Collectivism: Pension Reform, Grey Capitalism and Complex Socialism.' *New Left Review* 233, 3–65.

Blankenhorn, David. 1995. *Fatherless America: Confronting Our Most Urgent Social Problem.* New York: Basic Books.

Blommestein, Hans J. 1998. 'Pension Funds and Financial Markets.' *OECD Observer* 212, June/July, online: OECD Homepage http://www.oecd.org//publications/observer/212/Article6_eng.htm (12 April 2000).

Blouin, J., and M.J. Martino. 1986. 'Drop Out.' *L'Actualité* 11, 81–4.

Blum, John D. 1997. 'Balancing Regional Government Health Mandates with Federal Economic Imperatives: Perspectives from Nova Scotia and Illinois.' *Dalhousie Law Journal* 20, 359–99.

Boaz, David. 1999. 'Charity and Mutual Aid.' *Fraser Forum,* June, online: Fraser Institute Homepage http:www.fraserinstitute.ca/publications/forum/1999/06/01_mutual_aid.htm (13 August 1999).

Boessenkool, Kenneth J., and James B. Davies. 1998. *Giving Mom and Dad a Break: Returning Fairness to Families in Canada's Tax and Transfer System.* Toronto: C.D. Howe Institute.

Bogart, W.A. 1994. *Courts and Country: The Limits of Litigation and the Social and Political Life of Canada.* Toronto: Oxford University Press.

Boozang, Kathleen M. 1995. 'Deciding the Fate of Religious Hospitals in the Emerging Health Care Market.' *Houston Law Review* 31, 1429–1516.

Borsellino, M. 1994. 'OHIP Cuts Eight Unnecessary Services.' *Medical Post,* 8 March, 44.

Bosniak, Linda. 2000. 'Citizenship Denationalized.' *Indiana Journal of Global Legal Studies* 7, 447–509.

Bourdieu, Pierre. 1998. *Acts of Resistance: Against the Tyranny of the Market.* New York: New Press.

Bourette, Susan. 2000a. 'Ontario Ignored Water Alert.' *Globe and Mail,* 8 June.

– 2000b. 'Provincial "Cover-Up" Alleged in Water Tragedy.' *Globe and Mail,* 9 June.

Bourrie, Mark. 1998. 'Pay Equity Ruling Will Cost Canadian Taxpayers Billions.' *Workplace News,* September, 2.

Bowlby, Ken, Peter C. McMahon, Pat Bradshaw, and Victor Murray. 1994. 'Privatization and the Delivery of Personal Social Services: Is the Voluntary Board of Directors Up to the Task?' *Philanthropist* 12(1), 21–43.

Bowles, Samuel, and Herbert Gintis. 1987. *Democracy and Capitalism: Property, Community, and the Contradictions of Modern Social Thought.* New York: Basic Books.

Boyd, Monica. 1999a. 'Gender, Refugee Status and Permanent Settlement.' *Gender Issues* 17, 5–23.

– 1999b. 'Integrating Gender, Language, and Race.' In Shiva Halli and Leo Driedger, *Immigrant Canada: Demographic, Economic and Social Challenges.* Toronto: University of Toronto Press, 282–306.

– 1996. 'Migration Policy, Female Dependency and Family Membership: Canada and Germany.' In Patricia Evans and Gerda Wekerle, eds., *Women and the Canadian Welfare State: Changes and Challenges.* Toronto: University of Toronto Press, 142–69.

– 1992. 'Gender Issues in Immigration and Language Fluency.' In Barry R. Chiswick, ed., *Immigration, Language and Ethnicity: Canada and the United States.* Washington, DC: AEI Press, 305–72.

– 1989. 'Family and Personal Networks in International Migration: Recent Developments and New Agendas.' *International Migration Review* 23, 638–71.

Boyd, Monica, and Elizabeth Grieco. 1998. 'Triumphant Transitions: Socioeconomic Achievements of the Second Generation in Canada.' *International Migration Review* 32, 853.

Boyd, Susan B. 1999. 'Family, Law and Sexuality: Feminist Engagements.' *Social and Legal Studies* 8(3), 369–90.

– 1997. 'Challenging the Public/Private Divide: An Overview.' In Susan B. Boyd, ed., *Challenging the Public/Private Divide: Feminism, Law and Public Policy.* Toronto: University of Toronto Press, 3–33.

– 1994. '(Re)Placing the State: Family, Law and Oppression.' *Canadian Journal of Law and Society* 9(1), 39–174.

Boyle, Philip. 1996. 'Genetic Services, Social Context, and Public Priorities.' In Stanley Aronowitz, ed., *Technoscience and Cyberculture.* New York: Routledge.

Brannigan, Augustine, and John Fleischman. 1989. 'Juvenile Prostitution and Mental Health: Policing Delinquency or Treating Pathology?' *Canadian Journal of Law and Society* 4, 77–98.

Brantingham, Paul, and Stephen T. Easton. 1999. *The Crime Bill: Who Pays and How Much?* Economic Freedom Network, Fraser Institute. http://www.fraserinstitute.ca/publications/critical_issues/1996/crime/ (8 August 2000).

Brenner, Johanna. 1998. 'On Gender and Class in U.S. Labor History.' *Monthly Review* 50(6), 1–15.

– 1993. 'The Best of Times, the Worst of Times: U.S. Feminism Today.' *New Left Review* 20, 101–60.

Brock, D.R. 1999. 'Victim, Nuisance, Fallen Woman, Outlaw, Worker? Making the Identity *Prostitute* in Canadian Criminal Law.' In Dorothy Chunn and Dany Lacombe, eds., *Law as a Gendering Practice.* Toronto: Oxford University Press.

Brock, D.R., and G. Kinsman. 1986. 'Patriarchal Relations Ignored: A Critique of the Badgely Report on Sexual Offences against Children and Youths.' In J. Lowman, M.A. Jackson, T.S. Palys, and S. Gavigan, eds., *Regulating Sex: An Anthology of Commentaries on the Badgley and Fraser Reports.* Vancouver: School of Criminology, Simon Fraser University, 107–25.

Brode, P. 1993. *Streets of Fear: The Failure of the Canadian Criminal Justice System.* Toronto: Mackenzie Institute occasional paper.

Brodie, Janine. 1999. 'The Politics of Social Policy in the 21st Century.' In David Broad, ed., *Citizenship and Social Policy: Neo-liberalism and Beyond.* Halifax: Fernwood Press.

– 1997. 'Meso-Discourses, State Forms and the Gendering of Liberal-Democratic Citizenship.' *Citizen Studies* 1(2), 223–42.

– 1996a. 'Restructuring and the New Citizenship.' In I. Bakker, ed., *Rethinking Restructuring: Gender and Change in Canada.* Toronto: University of Toronto Press, 126–40.

– 1996b. 'Canadian Women, Changing State Forms, and Public Policy.' In Janine Brodie, ed., *Women and Canadian Public Policy.* Toronto: Harcourt Brace, 1–28.

– 1996c. 'New State Forms, New Political Spaces.' In Daniel Drache and Robert Boyer, eds., *States against Markets: The Limits of Globalization*. London and New York: Routledge.

– 1995. *Politics on the Margins: Restructuring and the Canadian Women's Movement*. Halifax: Fernwood.

– 1994. 'Shifting Public Spaces: A Reconsideration of Women and the State in the Era of Global Restructuring.' In Isabella Bakker, ed., *The Strategic Silence: Gender and Economic Policy*. London: Zed Books, 46–60.

Brodie, Janine, and Christina Gabriel. 1998. 'Canadian Immigration Policy and the Emergence of the Neo-Liberal State.' *Journal of Contemporary International Issues*. http://www.yorku.ca/research/cii/journal/issues/vol1no1/article_3.html

Bromley, Blake. 1997. 'New Rules for Charitable Giving.' *Report of Proceedings of the Annual Tax Conference Convened by the Canadian Tax Foundation* 49, 27:1–27:11.

Bromley, Daniel. 1997. 'Rethinking Markets.' Address to Annual Meeting of American Agricultural Economics Association, Toronto, July (Copy on file with the author).

Brooks, Neil. Forthcoming. 'The Role and Financing of the Voluntary Sector in a Modern Welfare State.' In Bruce Chapman, Jim Phillips, and David Stevens, eds., *Charities: Between State and Market*. Montreal: McGill-Queen's University Press (draft on file with the author).

– 1998. 'Flattening the Claims of the Flat Taxers.' *Dalhousie Law Journal* 21(2), 287–369.

– 1996. 'The Irrelevance of Conjugal Relationships in Assessing Tax Liability.' In John G. Head and Richard Krever, eds., *Tax Units and the Tax Rate Scale*. Sidney: Australian Tax Research Foundation, 35–80.

Brown, David A. 2000. 'The Canadian Securities Administrators – Concept Paper on Market Regulation: What Will It Mean for the Pension Industry?' Address to the Association of Canadian Pension Management, 16 February, online: Ontario Securities Commission Homepage http://www.osc.gov.on.ca/en/About/News/Speeches/Brown_marketreg_20000216.html (20 August).

– 1998. 'The Ontario Securities Commission and the Mutual Fund Industry: Milestones and Challenges for Mutual Funds in the Coming Years.' Address to the Association of Canadian Pension Management, 6 July, online: Ontario Securities Commission Homepage http://www.osc.gov.on.ca/en/About/News/Speeches/mutualfund_19980706.html (20 August).

Brown, Robert D. 1999. 'Tax Reform and Tax Reduction: Let's Do the Job Right.' *Canadian Tax Journal* 47(2), 182–205.

Bucar, Liz. 1998. *When Catholic and Non-Catholic Hospitals Merge Reproductive Health Compromised*. Washington: Catholics for a Free Choice.

Burgess, M. 1996. 'Health Care Reform: Whitewashing a Conflict between Health Promotion and Treating Illness?' In Michael Stingl and Donna Wilson, eds., *Efficiency vs. Equality: Health Reform in Canada*. Halifax: Fernwood Publishing, 153–62.

Burt, Sandra. 1990. 'Organized Women's Groups and the State.' In William D. Coleman and Gale Skogstad, eds., *Policy Communities and Public Policy*. Toronto: Copp Clark Pitman, 191–211.

Butler, Judith. 1990. *Gender Trouble: Feminism and the Subversion of Identity*. New York: Routledge.

Cable, Vincent. 1995. 'The Diminished Nation-State: A Study in the Loss of Economic Power.' *Daedalus* 124(2), 123.

Caddick, Alison. 1995. 'Making Babies, Making Sense: Reproductive Technologies, Postmodernity, and the Ambiguities of Feminism.' In Paul Komaseroff, ed., *Troubled Bodies: Critical Perspectives on Postmodernism, Medical Ethics and the Body*. Durham: Duke University Press, 142–67.

Callinicos, Alex. 1999. 'Social Theory Put to the Test of Politics: Pierre Bourdieu and Anthony Giddens.' *New Left Review* 236, 77–102.

Calliste, Agnes. 1991. 'Canada's Immigration Policy and Domestic Blacks from the Caribbean: The Second Domestic Scheme.' In Elizabeth Comack and Stephen Brickey, eds., *The Social Basis of Law: Critical Readings in the Sociology of Law*. 2nd ed. Halifax: Garamond Press.

Cameron, Barbara. 1996. 'Brave New Worlds for Women: NAFTA and New Reproductive Technologies.' In Janine Brodie, ed., *Women and Canadian Public Policy*. Toronto: Harcourt Brace, 105–25.

– 1995. 'From Segmentation to Solidarity: A New Framework for Labour Market Regulation.' In Daniel Drache and Andrew Ranachan, eds., *Warm Heart, Cold Country: Fiscal and Social Policy Reform in Canada*. Ottawa: Caledon Institute of Social Policy / Roberts Centre for Canadian Studies, 193.

Cameron, Duncan. 1997. 'Selling the House to Pay the Mortgage: What Is Behind Privatization.' *Studies in Political Economy* 53, 11–36.

Campbell, Murray, Michaeil Grange, Miro Cernetig, Tu Thanh Ha, and Virginia Galt. 1997. 'Shakedowns in the Schoolyard. Youth Crime May Not Be Rising but Bullies Are Getting More Sophisticated and Brutal.' *Globe and Mail*, 4 October, A1.

Canada. 1999a. *Response of the Government of Canada to the Communication of Beverley Smith to the United Nations Commission on the Status of Women*. (On file with the author).

– 1999b. Ministry of Finance. 'Estimates and Projections.' In *Tax Expenditures*

1999. online: Ministry of Finance Homepage http://www.fin.gc.ca/taxexp/taxexp99_2e.html (21 August 2000).

– 1999c. *Response to the Report of the Special Joint Committee on Custody and Access: Strategies for Reform.* Ottawa: Department of Justice.

– 1998a. *Factsheet: Key Elements of the Renewed Canadian Biotechnology Strategy.* (Bio-Industries Branch). http://strategis.ic.gc.ca/SSG/bh0029e.html

– 1998b. *Factsheet: National Biotechnology Advisory Committee, Sixth Report.* (Bio-Industries Branch). http://strategis.ic.gc.ca/SSG

– 1998c. *Factsheet: The Federal Regulatory System.* (Bio-Industries Branch). http://strategis.ic.gc.ca/SSG/bh00232e.html

– 1998d. *CBS: Roundtable Document, Related Resource Documents: Research and Development.* CBS Renewal Online. http//strategis.ic.gc.ca/SSG/bh00191e.html

– 1998e. *The 1998 Canadian Biotechnology Strategy: An Ongoing Renewal Process.* Ottawa: Distribution Services, Industry Canada.

– 1998f. Ministry of Finance. *Finance Minister's Statement on the Seniors Benefit.* News Release, 28 February, online: Ministry of Finance Homepage http://www.fin.gc.ca/newse98/98-071e.html (18 May 2000).

– 1996a. Ministry of Finance. *The Seniors Benefits: Securing the Future.* (Budget 1996 Document). Ottawa: Department of Supply and Services.

– 1996b. Ministry of Finance. 'The Seniors Benefit: Questions and Answers.' Budget 1996 Document, March, online: Ministry of Finance Homepage http://www.fin.gc.ca/budget96/retince/retq&ae.htm (18 May 2000).

– 1985. *Royal Commission* on the *Economic Union and Development Prospects for Canada.* Ottawa: Ministry of Supply and Services.

– 1964–5. *Report of the Royal Commission on Health Services.* Ottawa: Queen's Printer.

Canada Customs and Revenue Agency. 2000. *Income Statistics – 1999 Edition (1997 tax year).* Ottawa: Canada Customs and Revenue Agency.

Canada. Department of Finance. 2000a. *Budget 2000: The Budget Plan.* 28 February.

– 2000b. *Economic Statement and Budget Update.* 18 October.

– 2000c. *Legislative Proposals and Explanatory Notes Relating to Income Tax.* December.

– 1999. *Government of Canada Tax Expenditures.*

Canada. Health Services Review. 1980. *Canada's National-Provincial Health Program for the 1980s: A Commitment for Renewal.* Ottawa: Department of National Health and Welfare.

Canada. Intergovernmental Affairs. 2000. News Release: 'New Federal Investments to Accompany the Agreements on Health Renewal and Early Childhood Development,' 11 September http://www.pco-bcp.gc.ca/aia/docs/English/press/release/20000911.htm.

Canada. Special Committee on the Review of Personnel Management and the Merit Principle. 1979. *Report of the Special Committee on the Review of Personnel Management and the Merit Principle (D'Avignon Report)*. Ottawa: Department of Supply and Services.

Canada. Task Force on Barriers to Women in the Public Service. 1990. *Beneath the Veneer: The Report of the Task Force on Barriers to Women in the Public Service*. Ottawa: Minister of Supply and Services.

Canadian Advisory Council on the Status of Women (CACSW). 1980. *Women in the Public Service Overlooked and Undervalued*. Ottawa: Canadian Advisory Council on the Status of Women.

– 1979. *Women in the Public Service: Barriers to Equality*. Ottawa: Canadian Advisory Council on the Status of Women.

Canadian Bar Association. 1994. *What's Law Got to Do With It? Health Care Reform in Canada*. Ottawa: Canadian Bar Association.

– 1993. *Touchstones for Change: Equality, Diversity and Accountability*. Ottawa: Canadian Bar Association Task Force Report.

Canadian Biotechnology Advisory Committee. 2000a. *Minutes: CBAC Meeting, 17–18 November 1999*. http://www.cbac-cccb.ca.

– 2000b. *Minutes: CBAC Meeting, 13–15 October, 1999*. http://www.cbac-cccb.ca.

– 2000c. *Program Plan 2000*. http:www.cbac-cccb.ca.

Canadian Biotechnology Strategy Task Force. 1998a. *Renewal of the Canadian Biotechnology Strategy Resource Documents*. Ottawa: Industry Canada.

– 1998b. *Health Sector Consultation Document: Renewal of the Canadian Biotechnology Strategy*. Ottawa: Industry Canada.

Canadian Broadcasting Corporation. 2000. 'Health Protection Branch Needs More Evaluators.' www.cbc.ca/cgi-bin/templates/view.cgi?/news/1999/12/15/health991215 17 February.

Canadian Centre for Justice Statistics. 1996. *A Graphical Overview of Crime and the Administration of Justice in Canada*. Ottawa: Statistics Canada.

Canadian Centre for Philanthropy. 1994. *A Portrait of Canada's Charities: The Size, Scope and Financing of Registered Charities*. Toronto: Canadian Centre for Philanthropy.

Canadian Council for Refugees. 2000a. *Migrant Smuggling and Trafficking in Persons*. http://www.web.net/~ccr/traffick.htm. 20 February.

– 2000b. *Report on Systemic Racism and Discrimination in Canadian Refugee and Immigration Policies*. www.web.net/~ccr/antiracrep.htm. November.

– 1999. 'CCR Decries Heavy Fees Imposed on Refugees and Immigrants' (Press Release). 15 February.

Canadian Council on Social Development. 1998a. 'Incidence of Child Poverty among Children in Female Lone Parent Families.' Fact Sheets on Child Poverty. www.ccsd.ca/factsheets/fscp90s.htm (last visited 10/20/1999)

434 References

- 1998b. 'Child Poverty Rates by Province, Canada, 1980–1989.' www.ccsd.ca/factsheets/fscphist.htm (last visited 10/20/1999)
- 1998c. 'Incidence of Child Poverty by Province, Canada, 1990–1996.' www.ccsd.ca/factsheet/fscphis2.htm (last visited 10/20/1999)

Canadian Human Rights Commission. 2001. *Time for Action: Special Report to Parliament on Pay Equity.* http://www.chrc-ccdp.ca/pe-ps (21 March).

Canadian Institute for Health Information. 2000. 'Health Care in Canada 2000: A First Annual Report.' http://www.cihi.ca/Roadmap/Health_Rep/healthreport2000/toc.html.

Canadian Institute for Health Information. 2001. Health Expenditures Data. http://www.cihi.ca/facts/nhex/hexdata.shtml.

Canadian Labour Congress. 1999–2000. 'Economic review.' *The Economy* 11(1), 1–9.
- 1999. *Left Out in the Cold: The End of UI for Canadian Workers.* Ottawa: Canadian Labour Congress.

Canadian Medical Association. 1997. *Uninsured Medical Services: A Canadian Perspective.* Ottawa: Canadian Medical Association
- 1994a. *Core and Comprehensive Health Care Services: A Framework for Decision Making.* Ottawa: Canadian Medical Association.
- 1994b. *Core and Comprehensive Health Care Services: The Legal Issues.* Ottawa: Canadian Medical Association.

Canadian Press. 2000a. 'Alberta Won't Back Down on Prostitution Law: Calgary MLA Vows Action to Keep on Protecting Children.' *Toronto Star,* 31 July, A6.
- 2000b. 'MLA Defends Quashed Child-sex Law: Alberta Bill Aimed at Helping Young Prostitutes "Was the Right Thing to Do."' *Globe and Mail,* 31 July, A4.
- 2000c. 'Ontario Set to Appeal Court Ruling Barring Province from Denying Welfare to Common Law Moms.' *Canadian Press,* 29 June.
- 1999a. 'Provinces Tiring of Deadbeat Sponsors.' Canadian Press Newswire, 4 October.
- 1999b. 'New Law Aims to Break Hold of the Streets on Child Prostitutes.' *Canadian News Digest,* 31 January. http://search.canoe.ca/NewsArchiveJan99/candigest_jan31.html (September 20, 1999).
- 1997. 'Child-support Bill Closer to Becoming Law after Deadlock Broken.' *Canadian Press,* 11 February.
- 1992. 'Citizen Patrol Protects Teen Hookers.' *Toronto Star,* 27 December, A26.

Canadian Tax Journal. 1999. 'Special Report, Parts I and II: Proceedings of a Conference on Personal Income Tax Reform – The Framework for Reform.' *Canadian Tax Journal* 47(2) & (3).

Caputo, T., R. Weiler, and K. Kelly. 1994a. *Phase II of the Runaways and Street*

Youth Project: The Ottawa Case Study. Ottawa: Ministry of Supply and Services Canada.

– 1994b. *Phase II of the Runaways and Street Youth Project: The Saskatoon Case Study.* Ottawa: Ministry of Supply and Services Canada.

Cardozo, Andrew. 1996. 'Lion Taming: Downsizing the Opponents of Downsizing.' In Gene Swimmer, ed., *How Ottawa Spends, 1996–97: Life under the Knife.* Ottawa: Carleton University Press, 303–36.

Carey, Elaine. 2000a. 'GTA Leads Way as Crime Drops across Canada. Offences on Slide Nationwide, but Especially in T.O.' *Toronto Star,* 19 July, A1.

– 2000b. 'Stats Show Crime Is Down – So Why Don't We Believe Them?' *Toronto Star,* 23 July, A1.

– 1998a. 'Immigrant Kids Better Adjusted, Study Says.' *Toronto Star,* 27 October, A3.

– 1998b. 'Record-high Income Taxes Gobble Fifth of Family Pay.' *Toronto Star,* 23 June, A1.

Caruso, B.J. 2000. 'Why Is There a Shortage of Donors? Peeling Away at the Truth.' *Immigration & Citizenship Bulletin* 11(10), 31–3.

Caulfield, Timothy A. 1996. 'Wishful Thinking: Defining "Medically Necessary" in Canada.' *Health Law Journal* 4, 63–85.

Caulfield, T., and C. Feasby. 1998. 'The Commercialization of Human Genetics in Canada: An Overview of Policy and Legal Issues.' In Bartha Maria Knoppers, ed., *Socio-Ethical Issues in Human Genetics.* Cowansville, QC: Les Éditions Yvon Blais, 343–401.

Caulfield, T., and G. Robertson. 1996. 'Eugenic Policies in Alberta: From the Systematic to the Systemic?' *Alberta Law Review* 35, 59–79.

Cavaluzzo, Jean Smith. 2000. 'Ontario's System of Two-tier Justice.' *Toronto Star,* 7 August, A9.

Cerney, P. 1990. *The Changing Architecture of Power: Structure, Agency and the Future of the State.* London: Sage.

Charles, C., J. Lomas, and M. Giacomini. 1997. 'Medical Necessity in Canadian Health Policy: Four Meanings and ... a Funeral?' *Millbank Quarterly* 75, 365–94.

Cherniawsky, Katherine. 1996. 'Enforcement of Health Care Rights and Administrative Law.' *Health Law Journal* 4, 35–61.

Child and Family Canada. 1999. 'Children and Poverty.' www.cfc-efc.ca/docs/00000764.htm (last visited 10/20/1999).

Choudhry, Sujit. 2000. 'Bill 11, the *Canada Health Act* and the Social Union: The Need for Institutions.' *Osgoode Hall Law Journal* 38, 39–100.

– 1996. 'The Enforcement of the Canada Health Act.' *McGill Law Journal* 41, 461–508.

Chronicle Herald. 2000. 'Coalition Criticizes Health Canada's Juggling Proposal.' *Chronicle Herald,* 26 April.

Chunn, Dorothy. 1999. 'Feminism, Law and "the Family": Assessing the Reform Legacy.' In Elizabeth Comack, ed., *Locating Law: Race/Class/Gender Connections.* Halifax: Fernwood, 236–58.

– 1992. *From Punishment to Doing Good: Family Courts and Socialized Justice in Ontario, 1880–1940.* Toronto: University of Toronto Press.

– 1987. 'Regulating the Poor in Ontario: From Police Courts to Family Courts.' *Canadian Journal of Family Law* 6, 85–102.

Chunn, Dorothy, and Dany Lacombe. 2000. *Law as a Gendering Practice.* Toronto: Oxford University Press.

Citizenship and Immigration Canada (CIC). 2001a. *Bill C-11: Immigration and Refugee Protection Act. Explanation of Proposed Regulations.* http://www.cic.gc.ca/english/about/policy/c-11-regs.html.

– 2001b. *Immigration Manual.* Available online http://www.cic.gc.ca/manuals-guides/english/FW-e/index.html. Accessed 14 March 2001.

– 2000. *Backgrounder #1: Closing the Back Door … (News Release* 2000–9).

– 2000a. *Backgrounder #2: Opening the Front Door Wider … (News Release* 2000–9).

– 2000b. 'Landing Fee Eliminated for Refugees.' News Release, 28 February.

– 2000c. *Facts and Figures 1999: Immigration Overview.* Ottawa: Ministry of Public Works and Government Services.

– 2000d. *Immigration and Refugee Protection Act:* Bill C-11 Online: Citizenship and Immigration Canada Homepage. http://www.cic.gc.ca/english/about/policy/legrev_e.html (15 June 2000).

– 1999a. Statistics Requested by Author. Run Date 13 August.

– 1999b. *Facts and Figures 1998: Immigration Overview.* Ottawa: Ministry of Public Works and Government Services.

– 1999c. *Canada … The Place to Be, 2000 Annual Immigration Plan.* Ottawa: Minister of Public Works and Government Services.

– 1998a. *Building on a Strong Foundation for the 21st Century: New Directions for Immigration and Refugee Policy and Legislation.* Ottawa: Minister of Public Works and Government Services Canada.

– 1998b. 'Pilot Project to Help Canadian Employers Attract Highly Skilled Temporary Workers.' News Release, 30 September.

– 1998c. 'Exotic Dancers.' *Operations Memorandum* IP 98, IS 98, 15 July.

– 1998d. *Canada – A Welcoming Land, 1999 Annual Immigration Plan.* Ottawa: Minister of Public Works and Government Services.

– 1997. 'Exotic Dancers – VEC E99.' *Operations Memorandum* OP97–13, PE 97–09, IP 97–05, 11 April.

– 1996a. *Staying the Course, 1997 Annual Immigration Plan*. Ottawa: Ottawa: Minister of Public Works and Government Services.
– 1996b. 'Implementation of Canada-Manitoba Sewing Machine Operators Agreement.' *Operations Memorandum* OP96–11e, 13 May.
– 1995a. *A Broader Vision*. 1996 Immigration Plan. Ottawa: Ottawa: Minister of Public Works and Government Services.
– 1995b. 'Strengthening Family Sponsorship.' News Release, 14 December.
– 1995c. *A Broader Vision*. Immigration and Citizenship Plan 1995–2000. Ottawa: Ottawa: Minister of Public Works and Government Services.
– 1994. *Into the 21st Century: A Strategy for Immigration and Citizenship*. Ottawa: Ministry of Supply and Services.
City of Toronto. 2000. *The Toronto Report Card on Homelessness 2000*. http://www.city.Toronto.on.ca/homelessness/ (last accessed 12 March 2001).
Clark, Campbell. 2001. 'Ottawa Girds for Battle on Abortion.' *Globe and Mail*, 5 January, A1, A5.
Clark, Christopher. 1997. *Public Sector Downsizing: The Impact on Job Quality*. Ottawa: Canadian Council on Social Development.
Clark, Warren. 2001. *Gender Economic Equality Indicators 2000*. Ottawa: Statistics Canada.
Clarke, A. 1990. 'Genetics, Ethics and Audit.' *Lancet* 336, 120.
Clayton, Ellen Wright. 1993. 'Reproductive Genetic Testing: Regulatory and Liability Issues.' 8 (suppl 1) *Journal of Fetal Diagnostic Therapy* 8, 39–59.
Cockburn, Cynthia. 1983. *Brothers: Male Dominance and Technological Change*. London: Pluto Press.
Cohen, Marjorie Griffin. 1997. 'From the Welfare State to Vampire Capitalism.' In Patricia M. Evans and Gerda R. Wekerle, eds., *Women and the Canadian Welfare State: Challenges and Change*. Toronto: University of Toronto Press, 28–67.
Cohen, Stanley. 1972. *Folk Devils and Moral Panics*. London: MacGibbon & Kee.
Cole, D.P., M. Tan, M. Gittens, T. Williams, E. Ratushwy, and S.S. Rajah, Commissioners. 1995. *Report of the Commission on Systemic Racism in the Ontario Criminal Justice System*. Toronto: Queen's Printer for Ontario.
College of Physicians and Surgeons of Ontario. 2000. 'Independent Health Facilities Program Status Report.' *Members Dialogue*, July–August. http://www.cpso.on.ca/articles.asp?Article Id = 120049033
– 1999. The Independent Health Facilities Program – Status Report 1998/1999.' *Member's Dialogue* July/August, 14–16.
– 1998. 'Independent Health Facilities Status for 1997/98.' *Member's Dialogue* July/August, 30–32.

– 1997. 'CPSO Policy on Fees for Uninsured Services.' *Members' Dialogue* May/June, 8.

Collier, Jane, Michelle Z. Rosaldo, and Sylvia Yanagisako. 1997. 'Is There a Family? New Anthropological Views.' In Roger N. Lancaster and Micaela di Leonardo, eds., *The Gender/Sexuality Reader: Culture, History, Political Economy.* New York: Routledge, 71–81.

Colman, Ronald. 1998a. *Measuring Sustainable Development: Application of the Genuine Progress Index to Nova Scotia – Module One: The Economic Value of Civic & Voluntary Work in Nova Scotia.* Halifax: GPI Atlantic.

– 1998b. *Measuring Sustainable Development: Application of the Genuine Progress Index to Nova Scotia – Module Two: The Economic Value of Unpaid Housework and Child Care in Nova Scotia.* Halifax: GPI Atlantic.

Community Services Committee of the City of Toronto. 1999. *Ontario Works Caseload Profile,* 23 August. www.city.toronto.on.ca/legdocs/1999/agendas/committees/cms/cms990909/it007.htm (last visited 6/26/2000).

Condon, Mary. 1996. 'Alternative Accountabilities: Examples from Securities Regulation.' In P. Stenning, ed., *Accountability for Criminal Justice.* Toronto: University of Toronto Press, 239–67.

Conference Board of Canada. 2000. *Canadians' Values and Attitudes on Canada's Health Systems: A Synthesis of Survey Results.* http://www.oma.org/pcomm/cha/values/pdf.

Connell, R.W. 1987. *Gender and Power.* Cambridge: Polity Press.

Cooper, Davina. 1997. 'Fiduciary Government: Decentring Property and Taxpayers' Interests.' *Social and Legal Studies* 6(2), 235–57.

Cornish, Mary. 1986. *Equal Pay: Collective Bargaining and the Law.* Ottawa: Minister of Supply Services.

Corrado, Raymond, and Alan Markwar. 1994. 'The Need to Reform the YOA in Response to Violent Young Offenders: Confusion, Reality or Myth?' *Canadian Journal of Criminology* 36, 343–78.

Correctional Services of Canada. 2000. The Safe Return of Offender to the Community. Statistical Overview, Research Branch, April. http://www.csc-scc.gc.ca/text/faits/facts08_e.shtml (last accessed March 12, 2001).

Corrigan, Phillip, and Derek Sayer. 1985. *The Great Arch: English State Formation as Cultural Revolution.* Oxford: Blackwell.

Cossman, Brenda. 2000. 'Developments in Family Law: The 1998–99 Term.' *Supreme Court Law Review* 11, 433–81.

Cossman, Brenda, and Bruce Ryder. 1999. 'M. v. H.: Time to Clean Up Your Acts.' *Constitutional Forum* 10, 59–64.

Cossman, Brenda, Shannon Bell, Lise Gotell, and Becki Ross. 1997. *Bad Attitude/s on Trial: Pornography, Feminism and the Butler Decision.* Toronto: University of Toronto Press.

Côté, Andrée, Michèle Kérisit, and Marie-Louise Côté. 1999. '*Qui Prend Pays ...*', *L'impact du parrainage sur les droits des femmes immigrantes*. Ottawa: Status of Women Canada.

Cotter, John. 2000. 'Alberta Ignores Prostitute Ruling. Children Turning Tricks Will Be Apprehended, Government Says.' *Toronto Star*, 1 August, A10.

Cotterrell, Roger. 1995. *Law's Community: Legal Theory in Sociological Perspective*. Oxford: Clarendon Press.

Coutts, J. 1998. 'Pay First, Surgeons Tell Patients.' *Globe and Mail*, 24 June, A1, A8.

Coyne, Andrew, and David Frum. 1995. 'How Far Do We Take Gay Rights?' *Saturday Night*, 66–75.

Creese, Gillian. 1999. *Contracting Masculinity: Gender, Class and Race in a White-Collar Union, 1944–1994*. Toronto: Oxford University Press.

Culbert, L. 1999. 'Child Prostitutes Pimps Targeted.' *Vancouver Sun*, 4 May.

Cuneo, Carl. 1993. 'Trade Union Leadership: Sexism and Affirmative Action.' In Linda Briskin and Patricia McDermott, eds., *Women Challenging Unions: Feminism, Democracy and Militancy*. Toronto: University of Toronto Press, 109–36.

Curran, Peggy. 2000. 'Ottawa Set to Kick Out Pregnant Caregiver.' *Montreal Gazette*, 28 August.

Currie, Dawn H. 1990. 'Battered Women and the State: From the Failure of Theory to a Theory of Failure.' *Journal of Human Justice* 1(2), 77–96.

Currie, S., et al. 1994. *Assessing the Violence against Street Involved Women in the Downtown Eastside/Strathcona Community: A Needs Assessment*. Vancouver: Mimeo.

D'Emilio, John. 1997. 'Capitalism and Gay Identity.' In Roger N. Lancaster and Micaela di Leonardo, eds., *The Gender/Sexuality Reader: Culture, History, Political Economy*. New York: Routledge, 169–78.

Daly, Kathleen. 1994. 'Men's Violence, Victim Advocacy and Feminist Redress.' *Law and Society Review* 28, 777–85.

Dantico, Marilyn, and Nancy Jurik. 1986. 'Where Have all the Good Jobs Gone? The Effect of Government Service Privatization on Women Workers.' *Contemporary Crisis* 10(4), 421–39.

Darroch, Wendy. 1997. 'Prostitute Ordered out of Community: Residents in Court to Bolster Case against "Oldest" Hooker.' *Toronto Star*, 8 August, A26.

Das Gupta, Tania. 1996. *Racism and Paid Work*. Toronto: Garamond.

Daum, Kimberly. 1999. *Painting by Numbers*. Vancouver: Downtown Eastside Youth Activities Society.

Davies, Margaret. 1996. *Delimiting the Law: 'Postmodernism' and the Politics of Law*. London: Pluto Press.

Dawson, Brettel. 1998. *Women, Law and Social Change: Core Readings and Current Issues*. 3rd ed. North York, ON: Captus Press.

Day, Shelagh, and Gwen Brodsky. 1998. *Women and the Equality Deficit: The Impact of Restructuring Canada's Social Programs.* Ottawa: Status of Women Canada.

De Coster, C., K. Carriere, S. Peterson, R. Walld, and L. MacWilliam. 1998. *Waiting Times for Surgery in Manitoba.* Winnipeg: Manitoba Centre for Health Policy and Evaluation.

de Sousa Santos, Boaventura. 1995. *Toward a New Common Sense: Law, Science and Politics in Paradigmatic Transition.* New York: Routledge.

Deaton, Richard. 1989. *Political Economy of Pensions.* Vancouver: UBC Press.

Deber, R. et al. 1996. *The Public-Private Mix in Health Care.* Report to the National Health Forum. Ottawa: National Health Forum.

Deber, R., E. Ross, and M. Catz. 1993. *Comprehensiveness in Health Care.* A Report to the Health Action Lobby.

Denton, Frank T., and Byron G. Spencer. 1997. 'Population Aging and the Maintenance of Social Support Systems.' *Canadian Journal on Aging* 16(3), 485–98.

Department of Justice. 1998. Federal/Provincial/Territorial Working Group on Prostitution. *Report and Recommendations in respect of legislation, Policy and Practices Concerning Prostitution-Related Activities.* Ottawa: Department of Justice.

– 1989. *Street Prostitution: Assessing the Impact of the Law, Synthesis Report.* Ottawa: Department of Justice.

Devereaux, Mary Sue, and Colin Lindsay. 1993. 'Female Lone Parents in the Labour Market.' *Perspectives on Labour and Income* 5(1), 9–15.

DeVoretz, Don. 1999. 'Temporary Canadian Migration: Quo Vadis?' Third International Metropolis Conference, Zichron Yaacov, Israel, 30 November–3 December 1998 (Revised 5 December 1999).

Dickinson, Paul. 1996. 'Six Common Misperceptions about the Canada Pension Plan.' In John B. Burbidge et al., eds., *When We're 65: Reforming Canada's Retirement Income System.* Toronto: C.D. Howe Institute, 171–222.

Diduck, Alison. 1999. 'Justice and Childhood: Reflections in Refashioned Boundaries.' In Michael King, ed., *Moral Agendas for Children's Welfare.* London: Routledge.

Doern, G.B., A.M. Maslove, and M.J. Prince. 1991. *Public Budgeting in Canada: Politics, Economics and Management.* Ottawa: Carlton University Press.

Doherty, Bill. 1991. *Slaves of the Lamp: A History of the Federal Civil Service Organizations, 1865–1924.* Victoria, BC: Orca.

Dominque, Richard. 1996. *The Charity 'Industry' and Its Tax Treatment.* Ottawa: Library of Parliament.

Donnelly, Maureen. 1993. 'The Disparate Impact of Pension Reform on Women.' *Canadian Journal of Women and the Law* 6, 419–54.

Doob, A., Voula Marianos, and Kimberley Varma. 1995. *Youth Crime and the Youth Justice System in Canada: A Research Perspective.* Toronto: Centre of Criminology, University of Toronto.

Drache, Daniel. 1992. 'Conclusion.' In Daniel Drache, ed., *Getting on Track: Social Democratic Strategies for Ontario.* Montreal: McGill-Queen's University Press.

Drolet, Marie. 2001. *The Persistent Gap: New Evidence on the Canadian Gender Wage Gap.* Ottawa: Statistics Canada, Analytic Studies Branch, Research Paper Series, No. 157.

Duchene, Doreen. 1995. 'Street Prostitution in Canada.' In *Juristat* 17(2). Ottawa: Statistics Canada, Catalogue No. 85-002XPE.

Duff, David. Forthcoming. 'Charitable Contributions and the Personal Income Tax: Evaluating the Canadian Credit.' In Bruce Chapman, Jim Phillips, and David Stevens, eds., *Charities: Between State and Market.* Montreal: McGill-Queen's University Press (draft on file with the author).

– 2001. *Canadian Income Tax Law: Cases, Text and Materials* (draft manuscript on file with the author).

– 1999. *Written Submission to the House of Commons Committee on Finance, Sub-Committee on Tax Equity for Canadian Families with Dependent Children.* (Unpublished – on file with the author).

Duffy, Andrew. 1999. 'Canada Attracts 24% Fewer Skilled Immigrants Than Expected.' *Ottawa Citizen,* 15 July.

Duncanson, John. 2000. 'Toronto Crime Rate Lowest Since' 70's.' *Toronto Star,* 27 June, A1.

– 1998. 'Three Welcome Debate on Crime: Tory MPPs Stand Behind Get-tough Stance.' *Toronto Star,* 23 March, E5.

Durnford, John W., and Stephen J. Toope. 1994. 'Spousal Support in Family Law and Alimony in the Law of Taxation.' *Canadian Tax Journal* 42, 1–107.

Dworkin, Andrea. 1987. *Intercourse.* New York: Free Press.

Economist. 1999. 'Where the Grass Is Greener.' *The Economist,* 27 July.

– 1998. 'A Survey of Social Insurance.' *The Economist,* 24 October.

Edey, Malcolm, and John Simon. 1998. 'Australia's Retirement Income System.' In Martin S. Feldstein, ed., *Privatizing Social Security.* Chicago: University of Chicago Press, 63–97.

Editorial. 2000. 'Take Them Before a Judge.' *Globe and Mail,* 4 August, A14.

Edmonton Journal. 1928a. 'Lengthy Discussion Ensues in House on Sterilization Bill.' *Edmonton Journal,* 24 February.

– 1928b. 'Sterilization Bill Finally Adopted in House.' *Edmonton Journal,* 7 March.

Egelton, Rick, and Wojciech Szadurski. 1999. 'Trends in Canada–U.S. Migration: Where's the Flood?' *Bank of Montreal Economic Analysis*, 24 March, online: Bank of Montreal Homepage http://www.bmo.com/economic/econ.htm (19 July 2000).

Eggerton, Laura. 1998. 'Ottawa Appeals Pay-equity Ruling.' *Globe and Mail*, 28 August, A2.

Eichler, Margrit. 1997. *Family Shifts: Families, Policies, and Gender Equality*. Toronto: Oxford University Press.

– 1990. 'The Limits of Family Law Reform or, The Privatization of Female and Child Poverty.' *Canadian Family Law Quarterly* 7, 59–84.

Eisenstein, Zillah. 1996. 'Stop Stomping on the Rest of Us: Retrieving Publicness from the Privatization of the Globe.' *Indiana Journal of Global Legal Studies* 4(1), 59–96.

Eley, Geoff. 1994. 'Nations, Publics and Public Cultures.' In Craig Calhoun, ed., *Habermas and the Public Sphere*. Cambrige, MA: MIT Press.

Ellis, Elizabeth. 1996. Note, 'Bordering on Disaster: A New Attempt to Control the Transboundary Effects of Maquiladora Pollution,' 30 *Valparaiso University Law Review* 621, 629–30.

Elshtain, Jean Bethke. 1981. *Public Man, Private Woman: Women in Social and Political Thought*. Princeton: Princeton University Press.

Elson, Diane. 1999. *Gender Budget Initiative: Background Papers*. London: Commonwealth Secretariat.

– 1998. 'The Economic, the Political and the Domestic: Businesses, States and Households in the Organization of Production.' *New Political Economy* 3(2), 189–208.

– 1994. 'Micro, Meso, Macro: Gender and Economic Analysis in the Context of Policy Reform.' In Isabella Bakker, ed., *The Strategic Silence*. London: Zed Books.

Elson, Diane, and Nilufer Cagatay. 1999. 'Engendering Macroeconomic Policy and Budgets for Sustainable Human Development.' Paper delivered at First Global Forum on Human Development, New York, 29–31 July.

England, Paula. 1993. 'The Separative Self: Androcentric Bias in Neoclassical Assumptions.' In Marianne A. Ferber and Julie A. Nelson, eds., *Beyond Economic Man: Feminist Theory and Economics*. Chicago: University of Chicago Press, 37–53.

Epp, Jake. 1986. *Achieving Health for All: A Framework for Health Promotion*. Ottawa: Health Canada.

Ericson, Richard, and Kevin Haggerty. 1997. *Policing the Risk Society*. Toronto: University of Toronto Press.

Esping-Anderson, Gosta. 1990. *Three Worlds of Welfare Capitalism*. Princeton: Princeton University Press.

Ettorre, Elizabeth. 1998. 'Review Article: Re-shaping the Space Between Bodies and Culture: Embodying the Biomedicalised Body.' *Sociology of Health and Illness* 20(4), 548–55.

Evangelical Fellowship. 1998. In the Supreme Court of Canada between The Attorney General of Ontario and M and H, Factum of the Intervenor.

Evans, Patricia. 1997. 'Divided Citizenship? Gender, Income, Security, and the Welfare State.' In Patricia M. Evans and Gerda R. Wekerle, eds., *Women and the Canadian Welfare State*. Toronto: University of Toronto Press, 91–116.

– 1996. 'Single Mothers and Ontario's Welfare Policy: Restructuring the Debate.' In Janine Brodie, ed., *Women and Canadian Public Policy*. Toronto: Harcourt Brace and Company, 151–71.

Evans, Patricia, and Karen Swift. 2000. 'Single Mothers and the Press: Rising Tides, Moral Panic, and Restructuring Discourses.' In Sheila Neysmith, ed., *Restructuring Caring Labour: Discourse, State Practice, and Everyday Life.* Toronto: Oxford University Press.

Evans, Patricia, and Gerda Wekerle. 1997. 'The Shifting Terrain of Women's Welfare: Theory, Discourse and Activism.' In Patricia Evans and Gerda Wekerle, eds., *Women and the Canadian Welfare State: Challenges and Change.* Toronto: University of Toronto Press, 3–27.

Evans, Robert G. 1999. 'Health Reform: What "Business" Is it of Business?' In Daniel Drache, and Terry Sullivan, eds., *Market Limits in Health Reform: Public Success, Private Failure.* London: Routledge, 25–47.

– 1992. *What Seems to Be the Problem? The International Movement to Restructure Health Care Systems.* Vancouver: Centre for Health Services and Policy Research, University of British Columbia.

– 1990. 'Tension, Compression and Shear: Directions, Stresses and Outcomes of Health Care Cost Control.' *Health Politics, Policy and Law* 15, 101–28.

– 1984. *Strained Mercy: The Economics of Canadian Health Care.* Toronto: Butterworths.

Evans, R., M. Barer, and G. Stoddart. 1994. *Charging Peter to Pay Paul: Accounting for the Financial Effects of User Charges.* Report prepared for the Ontario Premier's Council on Health, Well-being and Social Justice. Toronto: Queen's Printer.

Evans, R., M. Barer, G. Stoddart, and V. Bhatia. 1994a. *Who Are the Zombie Masters and What Do They Want?* Report prepared for the Ontario Premier's Council on Health, Well-being and Social Justice. Toronto: Queen's Printer.

– 1994b. *It's Not the Money, It's the Principle: Why User Charges for Some Services and Not Others?* Report prepared for the Ontario Premier's Council on Health, Well-being and Social Justice. Toronto: Queen's Printer.

Evans, R., M. Barer, S. Lewis, M. Rachlis, and G. Stoddart. 2000. *Private Highway,*

One Way Street: The DeKlein and Fall of Canadian Medicare? Vancouver: UBC Centre for Health Services and Policy Research.

Faith, Karlene. 1993. *Unruly Women: The Politics of Confinement and Resistance.* Vancouver: Press Gang Publishers.

Falcon, N. 1989. *Street Prostitution: Assessing the Impact of the Law: Halifax.* Ottawa: Minister of Supply and Services Canada.

Farid, Claire. 1997. 'Access to Abortion in Ontario: From Morgentaler 1998 to the Savings and Restructuring Act'. *Health Law Journal* 5, 119–45.

Farquhar, Dion. 1996. *The Other Machine: Discourse and Reproductive Technologies.* New York: Routledge.

Fazio, Hugo, and Manuel Riesco. 1997. 'The Chilean Pension Fund Associations.' *New Left Review* 223, 90–100.

Federal, Provincial and Territorial Advisory Committee on Population Health. 1999a. *Toward a Healthy Future: Second Report on the Health of Canadians.* September. http://www.hc-sc.gc.ca

– 1999b. *Statistical Report on the Health of Canadians.* September http://www.hc-sc.gc.ca or http://www.statcan.ca

Federal/Provincial/Territorial CPP Consultations Secretariat. 1996. *Report on the Canada Pension Plan Consultations.* Ottawa: Department of Finance.

Federal/Provincial/Territorial Governments of Canada. 1996. *Information Paper for Consultations on the Canada Pension Plan.* Ottawa: Department of Finance.

Federal/Provincial/Territorial Ministers Responsible for the Status of Women. 1997. *Economic Gender Equality Indicators.* Ottawa: Status of Women Canada.

Ferber, Marianne A., and Julie A. Nelson, eds. 1993a. *Beyond Economic Man: Feminist Theory and Economics.* Chicago: University of Chicago Press.

– 1993b. 'Introduction: The Social Construction of Economics and the Social Construction of Gender.' In Marianne A. Ferber and Julie A. Nelson, eds., *Beyond Economic Man: Feminist Theory and Economics.* Chicago: University of Chicago Press, 1–22.

Fergusson, Robb. 1999. 'Equity Ignores the Oldest Law Right Here.' *Calgary Sun,* 28 October, A15.

Ferris, L. et al. 1998. 'Factors Influencing the Delivery of Abortion Services in Ontario: A Descriptive Study.' *Family Planning Perspectives* 30, 134–8.

– 1995. 'Small Area Variations in Utilization of Abortion Services in Ontario from 1985–1992.' *Canadian Medical Association Journal* 152(11), 1801–7.

Fife, Robert, and Sheldon Alberts. 1999. 'Liberals Unlikely to Appeal Pay Equity Ruling.' *National Post,* 21 October, A7.

Findlay, J. Richard. 1997. 'Town's Lust to Host Jails Is Desperate.' *Toronto Star,* 20 August, A23.

Findlay, Sue. 1987. 'Facing the State: The Politics of the Women's Movement Recommended.' In Heather Jon Maroney and Meg Luxton, eds., *Feminism and Political Economy: Women's Work, Women's Struggles*. Toronto: Methuen, 31–50.

Fine, Bob. 1984. *Democracy and the Rule of Law: Liberal Ideals and Marxist Critiques*. London: Pluto Press.

Finnie, Ross. 1993. 'Women, Men and the Economic Consequences of Divorce: Evidence from Canadian Longitudinal Data.' *Canadian Review of Sociology and Anthropology* 30, 205–41.

Fleischman, J. 1996. *Violence against Street Prostitutes in Halifax (1980–1994)*. Ottawa: Department of Justice Canada, Technical Report No. TR1996-17F.

Flood, Colleen, and Tom Archibald. 2001. 'Legal Constraints on Privately-Financed Health Care in Canada: A Review of the Ten Provinces.' April. http://www.utoronto.ca/hlthadmin/dhr.

Flood, Elspeth. 2000. 'DC Plan Dilemma: To Give, or Not to Give Advice? That Is the Question.' *Benefits Canada*, February, 12.

Floyd, Gordon. 1996. 'The Voluntary Sector in Canada's New Social Contract: More Responsibility But No Voice?' *Philanthropist* 13(2), 39–45.

Folbre, Nancy. 1994. *Who Pays for the Kids? Gender and the Structures of Constraint*. London: Routledge.

Folbre, Nancy, and Heidi Hartmann. 1988. 'The Rhetoric of Self-Interest and the Ideology of Gender.' In Arjo Klamer, Donald N. McCloskey, and Robert M. Solow, eds., *The Consequences of Economic Rhetoric*. Cambridge: Cambridge University Press, 184–203.

Forbes, Ian. 1996. 'The Privatization of Sex Equality Policy.' *Parliamentary Affairs* 49, 143–60.

Fox, Nicholas. 1993. *Postmodernism, Sociology and Health*. Buckingham: Open University Press.

Frader, Laura L., and Sonya O. Rose. 1996. 'Introduction: Gender and the Reconstruction of European Working-Class History.' In Laura L. Frader and Sonya O. Rose, eds., *Gender and Class in Modern Europe*. Ithaca, NY: Cornell University Press, 1–33.

Francis, Johanna, and Jason Clemens. 1999. 'Public and Private Charities: Ontario as a Case Study.' *Fraser Forum*, June, online: Fraser Institute Homepage http://www.fraserinstitute.ca/publications/forum/1999/06/02_public_private.htm (13 August 1999).

Franklin, Sarah. 1995. 'Postmodern Procreation: A Cultural Account of Assisted Reproduction.' In Faye D. Ginseberg and Rayna Rapp, eds., *Conceiving the New World Order: The Global Politics of Reproduction*. Berkeley: University of California Press, 323–345.

Franklin, Sarah, Celia Lury, and Jackie Stacey, eds. 1991. *Off-Centre: Feminism and Cultural Studies*. London: HarperCollins Academic.

Franklin, Sarah, and Helena Ragone, eds. 1998. *Reproducing Reproduction: Kinship, Power and Technological Innovation*. Philadelphia: University of Pennsylvania Press.

Fraser, Graham. 1991. 'Prostitutes Walking Dead-end Street.' *Globe and Mail*, 19 December, A5.

Fraser, Nancy. 1998. 'Social Justice.' *Tanner Lectures on Human Values* 19, 1–67.

– 1997a. *Justice Interruptus: Critical Reflections on the 'Post-socialist' Condition*. New York: Routledge.

– 1997b. 'After the Family Wage: A Postindustrial Thought Experiment.' In Nancy Fraser, ed., *Justice Interruptus: Critical Reflections on the 'Postsocialist' Condition*. Routledge: New York, 41–66.

– 1994. 'Rethinking the Public Sphere: A Contribution to Actually Existing Democracy.' In Craig Calhoun, ed., *Habermas and the Public Sphere*. Cambridge, MA: MIT Press.

– 1993. 'Clintonism, Welfare, and the Antisocial Wage: The Emergence of a Neoliberal Political Imaginary.' *Rethinking Marxism* 6(1), 9–23.

– 1989. *Unruly Practices: Power, Discourse, and Gender in Contemporary Social Theory*. Minneapolis: University of Minnesota Press.

– 1987. What's Critical about Critical Theory? The Case of Habermas and Gender.' In Seyla Benhabib and Drucilla Cornell, eds., *Feminism as Critique: On the Politics of Gender*. Minneapolis: University of Minnesota Press, 31–56.

Fraser, Nancy, and Linda Gordon. 1997. 'A Genealogy of Dependency: Tracing a Keyword of the U.S. Welfare State.' In Nancy Fraser, ed., *Justice Interruptus: Critical Reflections on the 'Postsocialist' Condition*. New York: Routledge, 121–49.

Freiberg, Arie. 1996. 'Bang Bang Maxwell's Silver Hammer? Superannuation Crime in the 1990s.' *Australian Business Law Review* 24, 217–35.

Frug, Mary Joe. 1992. 'A Postmodern Feminist Legal Manifesto.' In Mary Joe Frug, *Postmodern Legal Feminism*. New York: Routledge, 125–53.

Fudge, Judy. 2001. 'Consumers to the Rescue? Corporate Campaigns Against Labour Abuse.' In Susan B. Boyd, Dorothy Chunn, and Bob Menzies, eds., *Abusing Power*. Halifax: Fernwood, 146–59.

– 2000. 'The Paradoxes of Pay Equity: Reflections on the Law and the Market in *Bell Canada* and the *Public Service Alliance of Canada*.' *Canadian Journal of Women and the Law* 12, 313–44.

– 1999. 'Legal Forms and Social Norms: Class, Gender, and the Legal Regulation of Women's Work in Canada from 1870 to 1920.' In Elizabeth Comack, ed., *Locating Law: Race/Class/Gender Connections*. Halifax: Fernwood, 160–82.

– 1997. 'Precarious Work and Families.' In *Working Paper for the Centre for Research on Work and Society*. North York, ON: Centre for Research on Work and Society.

- 1996a. 'Rungs on the Labour Law Ladder: Using Gender to Challenge Hierarchy.' *Saskatchewan Law Review* 60(2), 237–63.
- 1996b. 'Fragmentation and Feminization: The Challenge of Equity for Labour Relations Policy.' In Janine Brodie, ed., *Women and Canadian Public Policy*. Toronto: Harcourt Brace, 57–87.
- 1993. 'Fashioning the Patterns: Homeworkers in the Garment Industry.' Unpublished.
- 1989. 'The Efficacy of Entrenching a Bill of Rights Upon Political Discourse.' *International Journal of the Sociology of Law* 17, 445.
- 1987. 'The Public/Private Distinction: The Possibilities and Limits to the Use of Charter Litigation to Further Feminist Struggles.' *Osgoode Hall Law Journal* 25, 485–554.

Fudge, Judy, and Patricia McDermott. 1991. *Just Wages: A Feminist Assessment of Pay Equity*. Toronto: University of Toronto.

Fudge, Judy, and Leah Vosko. 2001. 'Gender, Segmentation and the Standard Employment Relationship in Canadian Labour Law and Policy.' *Economic and Industrial Democracy* 22, 271–310.

Fuller, Colleen. 1998. *Caring for Profit: How Corporations are Taking Over Canada's Health Care System*. Vancouver: New Star Books.

Gabriel, Christina. 1996. 'One or the Other? "Race," Gender and the Limits of Official Multiculturalism.' In Janine Brodie, ed., *Women and Public Policy*. Toronto: Harcourt, 173–98.

Gabriel, Christina, and Laura Macdonald. 1996. 'NAFTA and Economic Restructuring: Some Gender Implications.' In Isabella Bakker, ed., *Rethinking Restructuring: Gender and Change in Canada*. Toronto: University of Toronto Press, 165–86.

Gallagher, J. 1997. 'Religious Freedom, Reproductive Health Care, and Hospital Mergers.' *Journal of the American Medical Women's Association* 52(2), 65–8.

Galloway, Donald. 1991. 'The Extraterritorial Application of the Charter to Visa Applicants.' *Ottawa Law Review* 23, 335.

Gal-Or, Noemi. 1998. 'Labor Mobility under NAFTA: Regulatory Policy Spearheading the Social Supplement to the International Trade Regime.' *Arizona Journal of International and Comparative Law* 15, 365.

Gandy, J.M. 1970. 'The Exercise of Discretion by Police as a Decision-Making Process in the Disposition of Juvenile Offenders.' *Osgoode Hall Law Journal* 8(2), 329.

Gannon, Philippa. 1997. 'The Science of Biotechnology: Present, Past and Future Quagmires.' In Kerry Petersen, ed., *Intersections: Women on Law, Medicine and Technology*. Aldershot: Dartmouth Publishing Company, 201–20.

Garrett, Elizabeth. 1997. 'Who Directs Direct Democracy?' *University of Chicago Law School Roundtable* 4, 17–36.

Gatens, Moira. 1996. *Imaginary Bodies: Ethics, Power and Corporeality*. New York: Routledge.

– 1992. 'Power, Bodies and Difference.' In Michele Barrett and Anne Phillips, eds., *Destabilizing Theory: Contemporary Feminist Debates*. Stanford: Stanford University Press.

Gavigan, Shelley. 1999. 'Legal Forms, Family Forms, Gendered Norms: What Is a Spouse?' *Canadian Journal of Law and Society* 14(1), 127–57.

– 1993. 'Paradise Lost, Paradox Revisited: The Implications of Feminist, Lesbian and Gay Engagement to Law.' *Osgoode Hall Law Journal* 31, 589–624.

– 1992. '*Morgentaler* and Beyond: Abortion, Reproduction, and the Courts.' In Janine Brodie, ed., *The Politics of Abortion*. Toronto: Oxford University Press.

Gee, Marcus. 2000. 'Health Care is No. 1 Concern.' *Globe and Mail*, 7 February, A5.

Gemme, R., A. Murphy, M. Bourque, M.A. Nemeh, and N. Payment. 1984. 'A Report on Prostitution in Quebec.' Ottawa: Department of Justice, Working Papers on Pornography and Prostitution. Report No. 11.

Gemme, R., N. Payment, and L. Malenfant. 1989. *Street Prostitution: Assessing the Impact of the Law, Montreal*. Ottawa: Minister of Supply and Services.

Gerson, Giles. 1999. 'Government Considering Major Pay Equity Reforms.' *National Post*, 28 October, A9.

Giacomini, M., J. Hurley, and G. Stoddart. 2000. 'The Many Meanings of Deinsuring a Health Service: The Case of In Vitro Fertilization in Ontario.' *Social Science and Medicine* 50, 1485–1500.

Gill, Stephen, and David Law. 1988. *The Global Political Economy*. Baltimore: Johns Hopkins University Press.

Girard, Daniel. 1998. 'Firms to Bid on Offender Centres: Government Seeks New Youth Facility Operators.' *Toronto Star*, 6 February, A4.

Global Survival Network (Gillian Caldwell, Steven Galster, and Nadia Steinzor). 1997. *Crime and Servitude: An Expose of the Traffic in Women for Prostitution from the Newly Independent States*. Washington: Global Survival Network.

Globe and Mail. 1999a. 'Child Development More Affected by Parenting than Social Class.' *Globe and Mail*, 4 October.

– 1999b. 'Study Finds Workfare Not Working: Shortage of Child-care Spaces Pulls Job Seekers Back to Welfare, It Says.' *Globe and Mail*, 25 September.

– 1998a. 'Where Have All the Smart Men Gone.' *Globe and Mail*, 28 December, A18.

– 1998b. 'Time to Pay Equity's Piper.' *Globe and Mail*, 19 November, A28.

– 1998c. 'Equity Doesn't Compute.' *Globe and Mail*, 17 October.

- 1998d. 'Pay Equity: The Casino Is Open?' *Globe and Mail*, 1 August, D6.
- 1998e. 'St. Michael's Won't Budge on Birth Control.' *Globe and Mail*, 11 April, A5.
- 1998f. 'Strippers Chilled by Immigration Rules.' *Globe and Mail*, 31 July.
- 1998g. 'Helping Parents Kid Around.' *Globe and Mail*, 19 Feb.
- 1997a. 'Child Support Bill May Be Killed: Renegade Liberal Senator Cools Joins with Conservatives to Fight Changes in Payments.' *Globe and Mail*, 30 January, A1.
- 1997b. 'Teenager Gets Nine Years in Stabbing – Case Tried in Adult Court after Judge Finds Provisions of Young Offenders Act Insufficient.' *Globe and Mail*. 19 March, A10.
Godfrey, Tom. 2000a. 'Foreign Peelers Crucial, Say Clubs.' *Toronto Sun*, 10 May, 7.
- 2000b. 'Strippers Get the Boot.' *Toronto Sun*. 17 March.
- 2000c. 'Canada Tries to Break the Habit – Foreign Strippers are Posing as Nuns, Officials Say.' *Toronto Sun*, 9 May, 5.
Gollom, Mark. 1998. 'Tribunal Member Supports Pay Equity Appeal.' *Ottawa Citizen*, 4 October, A6.
Gordon, Linda, et al. 1988. 'What Does Welfare Regulate?' *Social Research* 55(4), 609–47.
Gordon, Robert. 1987. 'Unfreezing Legal Reality: Critical Approaches to Law.' *Florida State University Law Review* 15, 195–220.
Grant, Isabel, and Judith Mosoff. 1998. 'Hearing Claims of Inequality: *Eldridge v. British Columbia (A.G.)*. *Canadian Journal of Women and the Law* 10, 229–43.
Greenspon, Edward. 1998a. 'Pay-Equity Costs too High: Chrétien.' *Globe and Mail*, 18 August.
- 1998b. 'Ottawa Plans Pay-Equity Appeal.' *Globe and Mail*, 15 August.
Greschner, Donna. 1989. 'Feminist Concerns with the New Communitarians: We Don't Need Another Hero.' In Allan C. Hutchinson and Leslie J.M. Green, eds., *Law and the Community: The End of Individualism?* Toronto: Carswell, 119–50.
Grieco, Elizabeth, and Monica Boyd. 1998. *Women and Migration: Incorporating Gender into International Migration Theory.* Florida State University: Center for the Study of Population Working Paper.
Griffith, B. 2000. 'Competition and Containment in Health Care.' *International Journal of Health Services* 30(2), 257–84.
Griffiths, N.E.S. 1993. *The Splendid Vision: Centennial History of the National Council of Women, 1893–1993.* Ottawa: Carleton University Press.
Guest, Dennis. 1997. *The Emergence of Social Security in Canada.* 3rd ed. Vancouver: UBC Press.

Gunderson, Morley. 1998. *Women and the Canadian Labour Market: Transitions towards the Future*. Toronto: Nelson.

Guttormson, Kim. 2000. 'Women Lived "Like Animals."' *Winnipeg Free Press*, 5 May, A1.

Guyatt, Gordon. 2001. 'Laser Eye Surgery: A Disturbing Model for Private Health-Care Delivery.' *Annals Royal College of Physicians and Surgeons of Canada*. 34(3), 157–9.

Habermas, Jürgen. 1989. *The Structural Transformation of the Public Sphere*. Trans. Thomas Burger and Frederick Lawrence. Cambridge, MA: MIT Press.

Hall, Michael, Tamara Knighton, Paul Reed, Patrick Bussiere, Don McRae, and Paddy Bowen. 1998. *Caring Canadians, Involved Canadians: Highlights from the 1997 National Survey of Giving, Volunteering and Participating*. Ottawa: Minister of Industry.

Hall, Michael H., and Paul B. Reed. 1998. 'Shifting the Burden: How Much Can Government Download to the Non-profit Sector?' *Canadian Public Administration* 41(1), 1–20.

Hall, Stuart, Chas Critcher, Tony Jefferson, John Clarke, and Brian Roberts. 1978. *Policing the Crisis: Mugging, The State, and Law and Order*. London: Macmillan.

Hamilton Spectator. 1998. 'Harris Apologizes for Comment on Pregnant Welfare Mothers: Said Allowance Cut as They Might Spend the Money on Beer.' *Hamilton Spectator*, 17 April, C4.

Hancock, Linda. 1985. *The Involvement of Young Persons in Prostitution*. Melbourne: Crown Law Office.

Hannah-Moffat, Kelly. 1999. 'Moral Agent or Actuarial Subject: Risk and Canadian Women's Imprisonment.' *Theoretical Criminology* 3(1), 71–94.

Haraway, Donna. 1991. *Simians, Cyborgs and Women: The Reinvention of Nature*. New York: Routledge.

Harmes, Adam. 1998. 'Institutional Investors and the Reproduction of Neo-liberalism.' *Review of International Political Economy* 5(1), 92–121.

Harper, P.S. 1995. 'Direct Marketing of Cystic Fibrosis Carrier Screening: Commercial Push or Population Need?' *Journal of Medical Genetics* 32(4), 249–50.

Harper, Tim. 2000. 'Ottawa to Warn Klein over Bill 11.' *Toronto Star*, 11 May, A12.

Harris, Michael. 2000. 'Walkerton Won't End My Career: Harris.' *National Post*, 6 June, A1.

Harris, Patricia. 1999. 'Public Welfare and Liberal Governance.' In Alan Petersen, Ian Barns, Janice Dudley, and Patricia Harris. *Poststructuralism, Citizenship and Social Policy*. New York: Routledge, 25–64.

Harvey, David. 1989. *The Condition of Postmodernity: An Enquiry into the Origins of Cultural Change.* Oxford: Blackwell Press.

Harvey, Robin. 1999. 'Program to Stop Runaways Chopped: Children's Aid Blames Provincial Changes in Welfare Funding.' *Toronto Star,* 8 April.

Hatch, A.J., and C.T. Griffiths. 1991. 'Child Saving Postponed: The Impact of the Juvenile Delinquents Act on the Processing of Young Offenders in Vancouver.' In R. Smandych, G. Dodds, and A. Esau, eds., *Dimensions of Childhood: Essays on the History of Children and Youth in Canada.* Winnipeg: Legal Research Institute of the University of Manitoba.

Hathaway, James. 1994. *Report of the National Consultation on Family Class Immigration.* North York, ON: Department of Citizenship and Immigration and Refugee Law Research Unit, Centre for Refugee Studies, York University, 20 June.

Hay, Douglas. 1992. 'Time, Inequality, and Law's Violence.' In Austin Sarat and Thomas R. Kearns, eds., *Law's Violence.* Ann Arbor: University of Michigan Press, 141–73.

– 1975. 'Property, Authority and the Criminal Law.' In Douglas Hay et al., eds., *Albion's Fatal Tree: Crime and Society in Eighteenth-Century England.* New York: Pantheon Books, 17–63.

Health Action Lobby. 1994. 'Getting to the Core of Comprehensiveness.' March.

Health Canada. 1999. *Reproductive and Genetic Technologies – Overview Paper.* http://www.hc-sc.gc.ca/english/protection/biologies/-genetics/reproduction/rgt/overview.html

– 1998a. *Health Protection Branch Information.* http://www.hc-sc.gc.ca/hpb/transition/index.html

– 1998b. *Health Protection for the 21st Century: Renewing the Federal Health Protection Program.* http://www.hc-sc.gc.ca/hpb/transition/index.html

–1998c. *Shared Responsibilities, Shared Vision: Renewing the Federal Health Protection Legislation.* http://www.hc-sc.gc.ca/hpb/transition/index.html

– 1998d. *Health Protection Branch Transition: Legislative Renewal.* http://www.hc-sc.gc.ca/hpb/transition/index.html

– 1996. *Health Canada News Release 1996–44.* Ottawa. http://www.hc-sc.gc.ca/hpb/transition/index.html

Health Services Restructuring Commission (Ontario). December 1999. 'Primary Health Care Strategy.' *Health Services Restructuring Commission.* http://www.hsrc-crss.org/hsrc/phase2/rr‸phc‸final.doc

Health Services Restructuring Commission (Ontario) (HSRC). 1998. 'Stormont, Dundas & Glengarry, Prescott & Russell Counties Health Services Restructuring Report.' August.

– 1997a. 'News Release.' July.

– 1997b. 'Direction to Wellesley Central Hospital.' July.

- 1997c. 'Fact Sheet: Metropolitan Toronto Community and Teaching Hospitals.' 23 July.
- 1997d. 'Pembroke Health Services Restructuring Report of the Facilitator Hugh Kelly.' June.
- 1997e. 'Metropolitan Toronto Health Services Restructuring Report: Wellesley Central Hospital.' March.
- 1997f. 'Pembroke Health Services Restructuring Report.' February.

Hein, Gregory. 2000. *Interest Group Litigation and Canadian Democracy*. Montreal: Institute In Research on Public Policy.

Held, David, et al. 1999. *Global Transformations*. Stanford: Stanford University Press.

Herman, Didi. 1997. *The Anti-Gay Agenda: Orthodox Vision and the Christian Right*. Chicago: University of Chicago Press.

Highcrest, Alexandra. 1992. 'Prostitution Is Business and Business Is Tough.' *Globe and Mail*, 29 September.

Himmelstein, David, et al. 1999. 'Quality of Care in Investor-Owned vs. Not-for-Profit HMOs.' *Journal of the American Medical Association* 282(2), 159–63.

Hobbs, Margaret. 1993a. 'Equality and Difference: Feminism and the Defence of Women Workers during the Great Depression.' *Labour/Le Travail* 32, 201–23.

- 1993b. 'Rethinking Anti-Feminism in the 1930s: Gender Crisis or Workplace Justice?' *Gender and Society* 5(1), 4.

Hochberg, J. 1996. 'The Sacred Heart Story: Hospital Mergers and Their Effects on Reproductive Rights.' *Oregon Law Review* 75, 945–67.

Hodgetts, J.E., William McCloskey, Reginald Whitacker, and Seymour Wilson. 1972. *The Biography of an Institution: The Civil Commission of Canada, 1908–1967*. Montreal: McGill-Queen's University Press.

Hogg, Peter W., Joanne E. Magee, and Ted Cook. 1999. *Principles of Canadian Income Tax Law*. 3rd ed. Scarborough, ON: Carswell.

Hollifield, James. 1998. 'Migration, Trade and the Nation-State: The Myth of Globalization.' *University of California at Los Angeles Journal of International Law and Foreign Affairs* 3, 595.

House of Commons. 1999a. *Debates*. (20 October) at 1415 (exchange between Prime Minister Chrétien and Preston Manning, the leader of the reform party). http://www.parl.gc.ca (9 November).

- 1999b. *Debates*. (22 October) at 1135 (exchange between Lucienne Robillard and Philip Mayfield). http://www.parl.gc.ca (9 November).

- 1999c. *Debates of the House of Commons of Canada (Hansard) 37th Parliament, 1st Session*, 27 February.

- 1999d. Standing Committee on Finance. *For the Benefit of the Children: Improving Tax Fairness (Nineteenth Report of the Standing Committee on Finance, Sub-Committee* on *Tax Equity for Canadian Families with Dependent Children)*. Ottawa: Queen's Printer.

– 1999e. *Debates of the House of Commons of Canada (Hansard), 36th Parliament, 1st Session*, 4 March.

– 1997b. *Debates of the House of Commons of Canada (Hansard) 36th Parliament, 1st Session*, 6 October.

– 1997b. *Debates of the House of Commons of Canada (Hansard) 36th Parliament, 1st Session*, 24 November.

– 1997c. *Debates of the House of Commons of Canada (Hansard) 36th Parliament, 2nd Session*, 4 December.

– 1997d. Standing Committee on Finance. *Evidence*. 18 November, online: Parliamentary Internet http://www.parl.gc.ca/InfoComDoc/36/1/FINA/Meetings/Evidence/finaev47-e.htm (21 July 2000).

– 1997e. Standing Committee on Finance. *Evidence*. 19 November, online: Parliamentary Internet http://www.parl.gc.ca/InfoComDoc/36/1/FINA/Meetings/Evidence/finaev54-e.htm (21 July 2000).

– 1990. Standing Committee on Justice and the Solicitor General. *Fourth Report of the Standing Committee on Justice and the Solicitor General on Section 213 of the Criminal Code (Prostitution-Soliciting)*. Ottawa: Minister of Supply and Services Canada.

– 1985. Special Committee on Prostitution and Pornography (Fraser Committee). *Report of the Special Committee on Prostitution and Pornography*. Ottawa: Minister of Supply and Services Canada.

– 1984. Special Committee on Sexual Offences against Children and Youth (Badgley Committee). *Report of the Special Committee on Sexual Offences Against Children and Youth*. Ottawa: Minister of Supply and Services Canada.

Houstan, S.E. 1972. 'Victorian Origins of Juvenile Delinquency: A Canadian Experience.' *History of Education Quarterly* (fall), 255.

Howard, R., G.C. Ruggeri, and D. Van Wart. 1995. 'Federal Tax Changes and Marginal Tax Rates, 1986 and 1993.' *Canadian Tax Journal* 43(4), 906–22.

Hubbard, Ruth, and Elijah Wald. 1993. *Exploding the Gene Myth: How Genetic Information Is Produced and Manipulated by Scientists, Physicians, Employers, Insurance Companies, Educators, and Law Enforcers*. Boston: Beacon Press.

Hughes, Patricia. 2000. 'P.S.A.C. v. *Canada (Treasury Board)*: The Long and Winding Road to Equity.' *Canadian Labour and Employment Law Journal* 8, 55–77.

– 1998. 'A Model for Future Challenges to Government Action?' *Canadian Labour and Employment Law Journal* 6, 77–97.

Hunt, Alan. 2000. *Legal Governance and Social Relations: Empowering Agents and the Limits of Law*. Ottawa: Law Commission of Canada.

– 1999. *Governing Morals: A Social History of Moral Regulation.* Cambridge: Cambridge University Press.

– 1993. *Explorations in Law and Society: Toward a Constitutive Theory of Law.* New York: Routledge.

Ikemoto, Lisa. 1996. 'When a Hospital Becomes Catholic.' *Mercer Law Review* 47, 1087–1134.

Immigration Legislative Review Advisory Group (ILRAG). 1997. *Not Just Numbers: A Canadian Framework for Future Immigration.* Ottawa: Minister of Public Works and Government Services Canada.

International Labour Organization (ILO). 1995. *297th Report of the Committee on Freedom of Association,* 282nd Session, Geneva, March–April, Case No. 1758, 53–65.

International Organization for Migration. 1999. 'Irregular Migration in Canada.' *Trafficking in Migrants,* July, 2.

International Trade Reporter. 1999. 'WTO: U.S., Canada Lodge Complaints over Rapid Rise in Genetic Labeling Measures.' *International Trade Reporter* 16(24), 1006.

Ismael, Jacqueline S., and Yves Vaillancourt, eds. 1988. *Privatization and Provincial Social Services in Canada: Policy, Administration and Service Delivery.* Edmonton: University of Alberta Press.

Israelite, Neita Kay, Arlene Herman, Yasmin Khan, Rosamaria Andino and Veronica Pacini-Ketchabaw. 1999. *Voices of Recent Latina Immigrants and Refugees: Effects of Budget Cuts on Their Settlement Experiences.* Toronto: Joint Centre for Excellence for Research on Immigration and Settlement.

Iyer, Nitya. 1997. 'Some Mothers Are Better than Others: A Re-examination of Maternity Benefits.' In Susan B. Boyd, ed., *Challenging the Public/Private Divide: Feminism, Law and Public Policy.* Toronto: University of Toronto Press, 168–94.

Jackman, Martha. 1996. 'The Constitutional Basis for Federal Health Regulation.' *Health Law Review* 5(2), 3–10.

Jackson, Chris. 1996. 'The Valuation of Unpaid Work at Statistics Canada.' *Feminist Economics* 2(3), 145–9.

Jacoby, Daniel. 1998. *Immigrant Sponsorship: For a Fair System.* Summary Report of the Quebec Ombudsman, May.

Jacot, Henri. 2000. 'An Unsuspected Collectivism?' *New Left Review* 1, 122–9.

Jaggar, Alison M. 1994. 'Prostitution.' In M. Jaggar, ed., *Living with Contradictions in Feminist Social Ethic.* Boulder, CO: Westview Press.

Jakubowski, Lisa Marie. 1999. '"Managing" Canadian Immigration: Racism, Ethnic Selectivity, and the Law.' In Elizabeth Comack, ed., *Locating Law: Race/Class/Gender Connections.* Halifax: Fernwood, 98–123.

Janzen, Leah. 1999a. 'Chinese Workers Unwelcome.' *Winnipeg Free Press*, 15 June, A1.

– 1999b. 'Axworthy Probes Garment Case.' *Winnipeg Free Press*, 16 June, A3.

Jenson, Jane. 1998. *Mapping Social Cohesion: The State of Canadian Research.* Ottawa: CPRN Study No. F/03.

– 1997. 'Fated to Live in Interesting Times: Canada's Changing Citizenship Regimes.' *Canadian Journal of Political Science* 30(4), 627–44.

– 1996. 'Part-Time Employment and Women: A Range of Strategies.' In Isabella Bakker, ed., *Rethinking Restructuring: Gender and Change in Canada.* Toronto: University of Toronto Press, 92–110.

– 1989. '"Different" but not "Exceptional": Permeable Fordism in Canada.' *Canadian Review of Sociology and Anthropology* 26(1), 69–94.

– 1986. 'Gender and Reproduction: Or, Babies and the State.' *Studies in Political Economy* 20, 9–46.

Jenson, Jane, and Judith Maxwell. 1999. 'Parents Need More and Better Choices.' *Globe and Mail*, 17 September.

Jessop, Bob. 1993. 'Towards a Schumpeterian Workfare State? Preliminary Remarks on Post-Fordist Political Economy.' *Studies in Political Economy* 40, 7–39.

Jhappan, Rhadha, ed. 2001. *Women's Legal Strategies in Canada: A Friendly Assessment.* Toronto: University of Toronto Press

– 1998. 'The Equality Pit or the Rehabilitation of Justice.' *Canadian Journal of Women and the Law* 10, 60–107.

Johnson, Rebecca. 2000. 'Power and Wound: A Study of the Interaction of Privilege and Disadvantage in *Symes v. Canada*.' SJD Dissertation, Univ. of Michigan Law School.

Johnston, Nicole. 2000. 'Gene Therapy: Hope or Hype?' *Globe and Mail*, 18 April.

Joppke, Christian. 1999. *Immigration and the Nation-State: The United States, Germany and Great Britain.* New York: Oxford University Press.

Judek, Stanislaw. 1968. *Women in the Public Service: Their Utilization and Employment.* Ottawa: Canada Department of Labour.

Kapur, Ratna, and Brenda Cossman. 1996. *Subversive Sites: Feminist Engagements with Law in India.* New Delhi: Sage.

Kavanagh, Anne M., and Dorothy H. Broom. 1998. 'Embodied Risk: My Body, Myself?' *Social Science Medicine* 46(3), 437–44.

Kay, Fiona. 1997. 'Balancing Acts: Career and Family Among Lawyers.' In Susan B. Boyd, ed., *Challenging the Public Private Divide: Feminism, Law and Public Policy.* Toronto: University of Toronto Press, 195–224.

Kay, Fiona, and Joan Brockman. 2000. 'Barriers to Gender Equality in the Canadian Legal Establishment.' *Feminist Legal Studies* 8, 169–98.

Keane, Carl. 1995. 'Victimization and Fear: Assessing the Role of Offender and Offence.' *Canadian Journal of Criminology* 37(3), 431–56.

Kelley, Ninette, and Michael Trebilcock. 1999. *The Making of the Mosaic: A History of Canadian Immigration Policy.* Toronto: University of Toronto Press.

Kennedy, Duncan. 1993, 'The Stakes of Law, or Hale and Foucault!' In Duncan Kennedy, *Sexy Dressing Etc.* Cambridge: Harvard University Press, 83–125.

Kesselman, Jonathan. 2000. *Flat Taxes, Dual Taxes, Smart Taxes: Making the Best Choices. Policy Matters.* Montreal: Institute for Research on Public Policy.

King, Anthony, ed. 1997. *Culture, Globalization and the World-System: Contemporary Conditions for the Representation of Identity.* Minneapolis: University of Minneapolis Press.

King, D. 1995. 'The State of Eugenics.' *New Statesman and Society,* 25 August, 25–6.

King, Michael, and Christine Piper. 1995. *How the Law Thinks about Children.* 2nd ed. Aldershot: Ashgate Publishing.

Kingsford Smith, Dimity. 1999. 'Contrasts with Canada: Women and Retirement Income in Australia.' Notes for Paper Delivered at the Women and Retirement Income Continuing Legal Education Seminar, University of Sydney, Faculty of Law, Australia, March 29. Copy on file with the author.

Kirk, M. 1997. 'Commercial Gene Testing: The Need for Professional and Public Debate.' *British Journal of Nursing* 6, 1043–47.

Klatch, Rebecca. 1988. 'Coalition and Conflict among Women of the New Right.' *Signs: Journal of Women in Culture and Society* 13(4), 671–94.

Klein, Naomi. 2000. *No Logo, No Space, No Choice, No Job: Taking Aim at the Brand Bullies.* Toronto: A.A. Knopf.

Klein, Ralph. 1999. 'Why I Want to Privatize Surgical Services.' *Time,* 6 December, 52.

Kline, Marlee. 1997. 'Blue Meanies in Alberta: Tory Tactics and the Privatization of Child Welfare.' In Susan B. Boyd ed., *Challenging the Public/Private Divide: Feminism, Law and Public Policy.* Toronto: University of Toronto Press, 330–59.

– 1994. 'The Colour of Law: Ideological Representation of First Nations in Legal Discourse.' *Social and Legal Studies* 3, 421–76.

Knopff, Rainer. 1989. *Human Rights and Social Technology: The New War on Discrimination.* Ottawa: Carleton University Press.

Kofman, Eleonore. 1999. 'Female "Birds of Passage" a Decade Later: Gender and Immigration in the European Union.' *International Migration Review* 33, 269.

Korpi, Walter. 1998. 'The Iceberg of Power below the Surface: A Preface to Power Resources Theory.' In Julia S. O'Connor and Gregg M. Olsen, eds., *Power Resources Theory: A Critical Approach.* Toronto: University of Toronto Press, vii–xiv.

Krever, Richard. 1981. 'The Origin of Federal Income Taxation in Canada.' *Canadian Taxation* 3(4), 170–88.

La Novara, Pina. 1993. *A Portrait of Families in Canada.* Ottawa: Statistics Canada, Housing, Family and Social Statistics Division, Target Groups Project (Cat.No.89-523E).

Laghi, Brian. 1997. 'Alberta's Abused Children Wait-listed for Aid.' *Globe and Mail*, 17 October, A6.

Lahey, Kathleen. 1999. *Are We 'Persons' Yet? Law and Sexuality in Canada.* Toronto: University of Toronto Press.

– 1998. *The Political Economies of 'Sex' and Canadian Income Tax Policy.* Kingston, ON: Faculty of Law, Queen's University.

– 1985. 'The Tax Unit in Income Tax Theory.' In E. Diane Pask, Kathleen E. Mahoney, and Catherine A. Brown, eds., *Women, the Law and the Economy.* Toronto: Butterworths, 277–310.

Lalonde, Marc. 1974. *A New Perspective on the Health of Canadians: A Working Document.* Ottawa: Health and Welfare Canada.

Laslett, Barbara, and Johanna Brenner. 1989. 'Gender and Social Reproduction: Historical Perspective.' *Annual Review of Sociology* 15, 381–404.

Lautt, M.A. 1984. 'Report on Prostitution in the Prairie Provinces.' *Working Papers on Pornography and Prostitution Report No. 9.* Ottawa: Department of Justice.

Lavis, J., J. Lomas, G. Anderson, A. Donner, N. Iscoe, G. Gold, and J. Craighead. 1998. 'Free-Standing Health Care Facilities: Financial Arrangements, Quality Assurance and a Pilot Study.' *Canadian Medical Association Journal* 158(3), 359–63.

Law Reform Commission of Canada. 1979. *Sterilization: Implications for Mentally Retarded and Mentally Ill Persons* (Working Paper No. 24.). Ottawa: Minister of Supply and Services Canada.

Laxer, James. 1999. 'How Bell Treats Its Operators.' *Globe and Mail*, 14 January, A1.

Leblanc, Daniel. 1999a. 'Civil Servants to Get $3.6 Billion.' *Globe and Mail*, 20 October.

– 1999b. 'Civil Servants Win on Pay Equity.' *Globe and Mail*, 20 October, A1, A6.

– 1999c. 'Top Court Denies Bell's Appeal: Operators' Case Goes Back to Rights Tribunal.' *Globe and Mail*, 9 July, A1.

– 1999d. 'Bell to Appeal Pay-equity Ruling to Supreme Court.' *Globe and Mail*, 16 January, A2.

– 1999e. 'Bell Canada Dumps 2,400 Phone Operators.' *Globe and Mail*, 12 January, A1.

– 1998a. 'Many Feel Pay-equity Award too High: Poll.' *Globe and Mail*, 5 December, A16.

- 1998b. 'Bell Pay-equity Ruling a Setback for Ottawa.' *Globe and Mail,* 18 November, A1, A4.
- 1998c. 'Ottawa to Sweeten Pay-equity Offer.' *Globe and Mail,* 12 September.
- 1998d. 'Union Greets Liberal Appeal with Protests.' *Globe and Mail,* 28 August, A9.
- 1998e. 'Chrétien Regrets Promise to Observe Pay Equity Ruling.' *Globe and Mail,* 27 August, A21.

Lee, Ian, and Clem Hobbs. 1996. 'Pink Slips and Running Shoes: The Liberal Government's Downsizing of the Public Service.' In Gene Swimmer, ed., *How Ottawa Spends, 1996–97: Life under the Knife.* Ottawa: Carleton University Press, 337.

Lee, Jo-Anne. 1999. 'Immigrant Women Workers in the Immigrants Settlement Sector.' *Canadian Woman Studies,* 19(3), 97–103.

Lemelin, Maurice. 1978. *The Public Service Alliance of Canada: A Look at a Union in the Public Sector.* Los Angeles: Institute of Industrial Relations, University of California.

Leonard, Peter. 1997. *Postmodern Welfare: Reconstructing an Emancipatory Project.* London: Sage Publications.

Leonard, Peter, and Barbara Nichols. 1994. 'Introduction: The Theory and Politics of Aging.' In P. Leonard and B. Nichols, eds., *Gender, Aging and the State.* Montreal: Black Rose, 1–16.

Leone, Richard C., and Greg Anrig, Jr, eds., 1999. *Social Security: Beyond the Basics.* New York: Century Foundation Press.

Lerner, Gerda. 1997. *Why History Matters: Life and Thought.* New York: Oxford University Press.

Lero, Donna, and Karen Johnson. 1994. *110 Canadian Statistics on Work and Family.* Ottawa: Canadian Advisory Council on the Status of Women.

Lesbian and Gay Immigration Task Force – Vancouver. 1998. *Beyond Borders: The Journey Towards Equal Immigration Rights for Lesbian and Gay Canadians.* Vancouver: LEGIT. May.

Leschied, Alan. 1995. 'The Young Offenders Act: Law of Retribution or Restoration?' *Education and Law Journal,* 329–33.

Lessard, Hester. 1997. 'Creation Stories: Social Rights and Canada's Constitution.' In Patricia Evans and Gerda Wekerle, eds., *Women and the Canadian Welfare State.* Toronto: University of Toronto Press, 71–90.

- 1993. 'The Construction of Health Care and the Ideology of the Private in Canadian Constitution Law.' *Annals of Health Law* 3, 121–59.

Lewis, Jane. 1998. 'Gender and The Development of Welfare Regimes.' In Julia S. O'Conner and Gregg M. Olsen, eds., *Power, Resources Theory and the Welfare State.* Toronto: University of Toronto Press.

Lewis, Michael. 1999. 'Bell Partly Relents in Operator Fight.' *National Post*, 19 January, C1.

Light, D. 1996. 'Betrayed by the Surgeons.' *Lancet* 347, 812–13.

Lindberg, Caroline. 1999. 'Who Gets What: Access to Services in Ontario for Persons without Permanent Status in Canada – An Overview.' *Entering 2000: New Immigration/Citizenship Policy and Practice*. Ottawa: Canadian Bar Association. April (rev. November 1999).

Lines, Liz. 1998. *Toronto Roundtable on Prostitution Involving Children and Youth*. Toronto: Board of Health. http://www.city.toronto.on.ca/legdocs/agendas/ committees/ (17 July 2000).

Lippman, Abby. 2000. 'Draft Paper for the CBS Workshop.' Proceedings of the National Strategic Workshop on the Canadian Biotechnology Strategy: Assessing its Effects on Women and Health.' In F. Miller, L. Weir nd R. Mykitiuk. 2000. *The Gender of Genetic Futures*. Toronto: NNEWH Working Paper Series, 32–9.

– 1998. 'The Politics of Health: Geneticization v. Health Promotion.' In Susan Sherwin et al., eds., *The Politics of Women's Health: Exploring Agency and Autonomy*. Philadelphia: Temple University Press, 64–82.

– 1990. 'Prenatal Genetic Testing and Screening: Constructing Needs and Reinforcing Inequities.' *American Journal of Law and Medicine* 17, 15–73.

Lipset, Martin, and Earl Raab. 1970. *The Politics of Unreason: Right-Wing Extremism in America, 1790–1970*. New York: Harper and Row.

Lipsett, B., and M. Reesor. 1997. *Flexible Work Arrangements: Evidence from the 1991 and 1995 Survey of Work Arrangements*. Ottawa: Human Resources and Development Canada.

Lister, Ruth. 1990. 'Women, Economic Dependency and Citizenship.' *Journal of Social Policy* 19(4), 445–67.

Little, Bruce. 2000a. 'Canada Leads the Way in G7 Deficit Battle.' *Globe and Mail*, 29 February.

– 2000b. 'A Trillion-dollar Economy.' *Globe and Mail*, 1 June.

– 1999. 'Pay-equity Ruling Unlikely to Break Federal Piggy Bank.' *Globe and Mail*, 25 October.

– 1998. 'Federal Cutbacks Eased by Private Sector.' *Globe and Mail*, 13 July, A7.

Little, Margaret. 1998. *'No Car, No Radio, No Liquor Permit': The Moral Regulation of Single Mothers in Ontario, 1920–1997*. Toronto: Oxford University Press.

Lochhead, Clarence, and Katherine Scott. 2000. *The Dynamics of Women's Poverty in Canada*. Ottawa: Status of Women Canada.

Lock, Margaret. 1998. 'Situating Women in the Politics of Health.' In Susan Sherwin, coord., *The Politics of Women's Health: Exploring Agency and Autonomy*. Philadelphia: Temple University Press, 48–63.

Lock, Margaret, and Patricia Kaufert, eds. 1998. *Pragmatic Women and Body Politics.* Cambridge: Cambridge University Press.

Loeppky, Rodney. 1999. 'Gene Production.' *Studies in Political Economy* 60, 29.

Loney, Martin. 1999. 'Equity Ruling Shows Courts in Grip of Radical Feminism.' *Financial Post (National Post),* 20 October, C7.

– 1998. *The Pursuit of Division: Race, Gender and Preferential Hiring in Canada.* Montreal: McGill-Queen's University Press.

Lowe, Graham S. 1987. *Women in the Administrative Revolution.* Toronto: University of Toronto Press.

Lowman, J., C. Atchison, and L. Fraser. 1996. *Men Who Buy Sex: Summary of Phase 1 Report.* Victoria: Ministry of the Attorney-General.

Lowman, J., and L. Fraser. 1995. *Violence against Persons Who Prostitute: The Experience in British Columbia.* Ottawa: Department of Justice Canada.

– 1989. *Street Prostitution: Assessing the Impact of the Law, Vancouver.* Ottawa: Minister of Supply and Services Canada.

Lupton, Deborah. 1995. *The Imperative of Health: Public Health and the Regulated Body.* London: Sage Publications.

Lutz, Helma. 1997. 'The Limits of European-ness: Immigrant Women in Fortress Europe.' *Feminist Review* 57, 93–111.

Luxton, Meg. 1997a. 'Feminism and Families: The Challenge of Neo-Conservatism.' In Meg Luxton, ed., *Feminism and Families: Critical Policies and Changing Practices.* Halifax: Fernwood.

– 1997b. 'The UN, Women, and Household Labour: Measuring and Valuing Unpaid Work.' *Women's Studies International Forum* 20(3), 431–9.

Luxton, Meg, and Ester Reiter. 1997. 'Double, Double, Toil and Trouble ... Women's Experience of Work and Family in Canada 1980–1995.' In Patricia M. Evans and Gerda R. Wekerle, eds., *Women and the Canadian Welfare State.* Toronto: University of Toronto Press, 197–221.

Luxton, Meg, and Leah Vosko. 1998. 'Where Women's Efforts Count: The 1996 Census Campaign and "Family Politics" in Canada.' *Studies in Political Economy* 56, 49–82.

MacDaniel, Susan A. 1997. 'Serial Employment and Skinny Government: Reforming Caring and Sharing Among Generations.' *Canadian Journal on Aging* 16, 465–84.

MacDonald, Martha. 1998. 'Gender and Social Security Policy: Pitfalls and Possibilities.' *Feminist Economics* 4(1), 1–25.

– 1995. 'Economic Restructuring and Gender in Canada: Feminist Policy Initiatives.' *World Development* 23(11), 2005–17.

MacIntosh, Constance. 1999. *Shifting Connections: A Report on Emerging Federal Policy Relating to Women's Health, the New Genetics and Biotechnology.* For The Working Group on Women and the New Genetics. Toronto: National Network on Environments and Women's Health.

MacIntosh, Jeffrey. 1993. 'The Role of Institutional and Retail Investors in Canadian Capital Markets.' *Osgoode Hall Law Journal* 31(2), 371–472.

MacKenzie, Hugh. 2000. 'The Lottery in Which Everyone Wins?' *Behind the Numbers* 3(1), 1 November, 1–3.

Mackie, Richard. 2001. 'More Private Health Care in Store.' *Globe and Mail*, 20 March, A9.

– 2000. 'Study Finds Workfare Not Working.' *Globe and Mail*, 25 September.

– 1998. 'Fee Cap on Abortions Called Threat to Access.' *Globe and Mail*, 20 October, A3.

MacKinnon, Catharine. 1989. *Toward a Feminist Theory of the State*. Cambridge: Harvard University Press.

– 1987. *Feminism Unmodified: Discourses on Life and Law*. Cambridge: Harvard University Press.

Macklin, Audrey. 1994. 'On the Inside Looking In: Foreign Domestic Workers in Canada.' In Winona Giles and Sedef Arat-Koc, eds., *Maid in the Market: Women's Paid Domestic Labour*. Halifax: Fernwood.

– 1992a. 'Foreign Domestic Worker: Imported Housewife or Mail-Order Servant?' *McGill Law Journal* 37, 681–760.

– 1992b. '*Symes* v. *M.N.R.*: Where Sex Meets Class.' *Canadian Journal of Women and the Law* 5(2), 498–517.

Maclean's Magazine. 1996. 'Cutting Back.' 1 July.

MacMillan, Robert, and Marsha Barnes. 1991. '*The Independent Health Facilities Act*: A First for North America.' *Health Law in Canada* 11(3), 59–64.

Macnaughton, Alan, Thomas Matthews, and Jeffrey Pittman. 1998. 'Stealth Tax Rates: Effective versus Statutory Personal Marginal Tax Rates.' *Canadian Tax Journal* 46(5), 1029–66.

MacNaughton, John A. 1999. 'The CPP Investment Board: Remarks by John MacNaughton.' October/November, online: Canada Pension Plan Investment Board Homepage http://www.cppib.ca/media/101999_SP.htm (21 August 2000).

MacPherson, C.B. 1965. *The Real World of Democracy*. Toronto: CBC Learning Systems.

Madore, O. 1995. 'The Canada Health and Social Transfer: Operation and Possible Repercussions on the Health Care Sector.' In *Current Issue Review 95–2E*. Ottawa, Research Branch, Library of Parliament, 1–12

Mahoney, Jill. 2000a. 'Alberta Law on Child Prostitution Struck Down: "Draconian" Measure Lacks Safeguards, Judge Says.' *Globe and Mail*. 29 July, A1.

– 2000b. 'Alberta Defies Court on Prostitution: Will Continue to Enforce Disputed Law as It Appeals, Says Young Sex Workers Need Protection.' *Globe and Mail*, 1 August, A2.

Mahowald, Mary E. 1996. 'Genetic Technologies and Their Implications for Women.' *University of Chicago Roundtable* 3(2), 439–63.

Majone, Giandomenico. 1990. 'Introduction.' In Giandomenic Majone, ed., *Deregulation or Reregulation? Regulatory Reform in Europe and the United States*. London: Pinter Publishers, 1–6.

Mallan, Caroline. 2000. '"Brian's Law" Passes Hurdle: Health Act Changes Could Force Treatment for Mentally Ill.' *Toronto Star*, 8 June, A12.

– 1992. 'Hookers, Residents Battle in Parkdale.' *Toronto Star*, 26 September, A4.

Maloney, Maureen A. 1994. 'What Is the Appropriate Tax Unit for the 1990s and Beyond.' In Allan M. Maslove, ed., *Issues in the Taxation of Individuals*. Toronto: University of Toronto Press, 116–54.

– 1989. 'Women and the Income Tax Act: Marriage, Motherhood and Divorce.' *Canadian Journal of Women and the Law* 3, 182–210.

Mandel, Michael. 1994. *The Charter of Rights and the Legalization of Politics in Canada*. Rev. ed. Toronto: Thompson.

Manning, Preston. 1997. *A Fresh Start for Canadians*. Calgary: Reform Party of Canada.

Marsden, Lorna. 1980. 'The Role of the National Action Committee on the Status of Women in Equal Pay Policy in Canada.' In Ronnie Steinberg Ratner, ed., *Equal Employment Policy for Women: Strategies for Implementation in the United States, Canada and Western Europe*. Philadelphia: Temple University Press, 242–60.

Marshall, Robert. 1999. 'Autonomy and Sovereignty in the Era of Global Restructuring.' *Studies in Political Economy* 59 (summer), 115–47.

Marshall, Thomas H. 1977. *Class, Citizenship and Social Democracy*. Chicago: University of Chicago Press.

– 1963. *Sociology at the Crossroads and Other Essays*. London: Heineman.

Martin, Dianne L. 1998. 'Retribution Revisited: A Reconsideration of Feminist Criminal Law Reform Strategies.' *Osgoode Hall Law Journal* 36, 151–88.

– 1992. 'Passing the Buck: Prosecution of Welfare Fraud, Preservation of Stereotypes.' *Windsor Yearbook of Access to Justice* 12, 52–97.

Martin, Dianne L., and Ray Kuszelewski. 1997. 'The Perils of Poverty: Prostitutes' Rights, Police Misconduct and Poverty Law.' *Osgoode Hall Law Journal* 35, 835–63.

Martin, Dianne L., and Janet Mosher. 1995. 'Unkept Promises: Experiences of Immigrant Women with the Neo-criminalization of Wife Assault.' *Canadian Journal of Women and Law* 8, 3–44.

Martin, Emily. 1997. 'The End of the Body?' In Roger N. Lancaster and Micaela di Leonardo, eds., *The Gender/Sexuality Reader: Culture, History, Political Economy*. New York: Routledge, 543–58.

Martin, Sheilah L. 1989. *Women's Reproductive Health, the Canadian Charter of Rights and Freedoms, and the Canada Health Act*. Calgary: Canadian Advisory Council on the Status of Women.

Maslove, Allan M. 1995. *National Goals and the Federal Role in Health Care*. Prepared for the National Forum on Health. Ottawa: National Forum on Health.

Maslove, Allan M., and Gene Swimmer. 1980. *Wage Controls in Canada, 1975–1978*. Montreal: Institute for Research on Public Policy.

Matas, Robert. 1999. 'Child Prostitution Booming in B.C., Report Finds.' *Globe and Mail*, 21 June, A7.

– 1997. 'Child Sex Trade Curbs in Vain, Study Says. Vancouver Report Indicates Juveniles Charged More Often Than Those Who Hire Them.' *Globe and Mail*, 25 September, A5.

Matloff, Norman. 2000. 'Debunking the Myth of a Desperate Software Labor Shortage.' Testimony to the US House Judiciary Committee Sub-Committee on Immigration (21 April). Available online at http://heather.cs.ucdavis.edu/itaa.real.html#tth_sEc11.

Mawer, Virginia L. 1997. 'Philanthropy and Life Insurance for High Net Worth Clients.' Paper delivered to the Profiles in Wealth Conference, Toronto, 23–24 October.

Maxwell, Judith. 2000a. 'Globalization – Who Will Be the Guardians of the Public Interest.' *Toronto Star*, 9 January.

– 2000b. 'Managing Interdependence.' *Network News* 8, 13.

May, Kathyrn. 1999a. 'Pay-equity Talks Shrouded in Secrecy.' *Ottawa Citizen*, 26 October, A3.

– 1999b. 'PS, Government Set for Showdowns: Pay Equity in Court, Pension Fight in Senate.' *Ottawa Citizen*, 31 May A3.

– 1998. 'Pay Equity: Chrétien Promised to Pay.' *Ottawa Citizen*, 6 August, A1, A2.

Mays, Shirley L. 1995. 'Privatization of Municipal Services: A Contagion in the Body Politic.' *Duquesne Law Review* 34, 41–70.

McBride, Stephen. 1992. *Not Working: State, Unemployment and Neo-Conservatism in Canada*. Toronto: University of Toronto Press.

McBride, Stephen, and John Shields. 1993. *Dismantling a Nation: Canada and the New World Order*. Halifax: Fernwood Publishing.

McCaffery, Edward J. 1997. *Taxing Women*. Chicago: University of Chicago Press.

McCann, Michael. 1994. *Rights at Work: Pay Equity Reform and the Politics of Legal Mobilization*. Chicago: University of Chicago Press.

McCarthy, S. 1999. 'Tax Act to Recognize Same-sex Couples.'*Globe and Mail*, 29 March.

McCarthy, S., and R. Mackie. 2000. 'Health Deal Points to Election.' *Globe and Mail*, 12 September, A1, A4.

McCarthy, S., and M. McKinnon. 2000. 'One-time Cash Boost Planned for Health Care.' *Globe and Mail*, 2 February, A1, A2.

McCarthy, S., and J. Sallot. 1998. 'Pay-equity Bill at Least $3 Billion.' *Globe and Mail*, 30 July 1998, A1.

McCarthy, William. 1995. *On the Streets: Youth in Vancouver, Province of British Columbia*. Victoria: Ministry of Social Services, Research, Evaluation and Statistics Branch.

McColgan, Aileen. 1997. *Just Wages for Women*. Oxford: Claredon Press.

McDaniel, C.-G. 2000. 'Contraceptive Rights Put Ahead of Religion.' *Medical Post*, 18 July, 45.

McDermott, Patricia. 1992. 'Employment Equity and Pay Equity: And Never the Twain Shall Meet?' *Canadian Woman Studies* 12(3), 24.

McDonald, Lynn. 1997a. 'Editorial: Pension Questions That Are Politically Out-of-the-Question.' *Canadian Journal on Aging* 16, 393–406.

– 1997b. *Widowhood and Retirement: Women on the Margin*. Toronto: Centre for Applied Social Research.

McDowell, Linda. 1991. 'Life without Father and Ford: The New Gender Order of Post-Fordism.' *Transactions of the Institute of British Geographers* 16, 100–19.

McFetridge, Donald. 1997. *The Economics of Privatization*. Toronto: C.D. Howe Institute.

McGee, Glenn. 1997. *The Perfect Baby: A Pragmatic Approach to Genetics*. New York: Rowan and Littlefield Publishers.

McGinnis, Janice Dickin. 1994. 'Whores and Worthies: Feminism and Prostitution,' *Canadian Journal of Law and Society* 9(1), 105–22.

Mcguire, Maureen. 1997. '"Getting Tougher?": An Act to Amend the Young Offenders Act and the Criminal.' *Canadian Journal of Criminology* 39, 185–214.

McIlroy, Anne. 2000a. 'Provinces Given $2.5 Billion Infusion.' *Globe and Mail*, 29 February, F3.

– 2000b. 'Children's Agenda Gets Kick-start.' *National Post*, 8 June.

McKusick, Victor A. 1993. 'Medical Genetics: A 40-Year Perspective on the Evolution of a Medical Speciality From a Basic Science.' *Journal of the American Medical Association* 270, 2351–6.

McMichael, P. 1999. 'The Global Crisis of Wage Labour.' *Studies in Political Economy* 58, 11.

Medicine Hat News. 1928. 'Hoadley Sterilization Bill Occupies Attention of Legislatures.' *Medicine Hat News*, 24 February.

Mehlman, Maxwell, and Jeffrey Botkin, eds. 1998. *Access to the Genome: The Challenge to Equality.* Washington: Georgetown University Press.

Michell, Paul. 1995. 'The Political Purposes Doctrine in Canadian Charities Law.' *Philanthropist* 12(4), 3–32.

Miles, Robert. 1993. *Racism after 'Race' Relations.* London: Routledge Books.

Miller, Peter, and Nikolas Rose. 1990. 'Governing Economic Life.' *Economy and Society* 19, 1–31.

Milne, Celia. 2000a. 'The Balance between Church and Hospital.' *Medical Post,* 5 December, 38–9.

– 2000b. 'The Salvation Army's Fall from Grace.' *Medical Post,* 5 December, 38.

Mohr, Renate M. 1990. 'Sentencing as a Gendered Process.' *Canadian Journal of Criminology* 32(3), 479–85.

Mooers, Colin. 1998. 'And We Still Resist? Globalization, Citizenship and Class Formation.' *Social Studies Bulletin* 53.

Moran, Mayo. Forthcoming. 'Rethinking Public Benefit: The Definition of Charity in the Era of the *Charter.*' In Bruce Chapman, Jim Phillips, and David Stevens, eds., *Charities: Between State and Market.* Montreal: McGill-Queen's University Press (draft on file with the author).

Morgan, Nicole. 1988. *The Equality Game: Women in the Federal Public Service (1908–1987).* Ottawa: Canadian Advisory Council on the Status of Women.

– 1986. *Implosion: An Analysis of the Growth of the Federal Public Service in Canada (1945–1985).* Montreal: Institute for Research on Public Policy.

– 1981. *Nowhere to Go? Possible Consequences of the Demographic Imbalance in Decision-Making Groups of the Federal Public Service.* Montreal: Institute for Research on Public Policy.

Morissette, René, and Marie Drolet. 1999. *The Evolution of Pension Coverage of Young and Prime-Aged Workers in Canada.* Ottawa: Statistics Canada.

Morrissey, Christine. 1999. Personal Interview. August 1999.

Morris, Marika, Jane Robinson, and Janet Simpson, et al. 1999. *The Changing Nature of Home Care and Its Impact on Women's Vulnerability to Poverty.* Ottawa: Status of Women Canada.

Morton, Millie. 1999. 'The Legal Position of Migrant Workers in Canada.' *Speaking About Rights* 14, 10.

Mosher, Janet. 2000. 'Managing the Disentitlement of Women: Glorified Markets, the Idealized Family, and the Undeserving Other.' In Sheila Neysmith, ed., *Restructuring Caring Labour: Discourse, State Practice, and Everyday Life.* Toronto: Oxford University Press.

Mossman, Mary Jane. 1997. 'Child Support or Support for Children? Rethinking "Public" and "Private" in Family Law.' *University of New Brunswick Law Journal* 46, 63–85.

– 1994. 'Feminism and Legal Method: The Difference It Makes.' In Tina Loo
   and Lorna R. McLean, eds., *Historical Perspectives in Law and Society in Canada.*
   Toronto: Copp Clark Longman, 321–38.
Mossman, Mary Jane, and Morag MacLean. 1997. 'Family Law and Social Assis-
   tance Programs: Rethinking Equality.' In Patricia Evans and Gerda Wekerle,
   eds., *Women and the Canadian Welfare State.* Toronto: University of Toronto Press.
Moulton, D. 1997. 'N.S. Government Cuts Insured Services.' *Medical Post*, 25 Feb-
   ruary, title page, 42.
Moyer, S., and P.J. Carrington. 1989. *Street Prostitution: Assessing the Impact of the
   Law: Toronto.* Ottawa: Minister of Supply and Services Canada.
Mullan, David. 1999. 'The Role of the Judiciary in the Review of Administrative
   Policy Decisions: Issues of Legality.' In Mary Jane Mossman and Ghislain Otis,
   eds., *The Judiciary as Third Branch of Government: Manifestations and Challenges to
   Legitimacy.* Montreal: Les Éditions Themis, 313–76.
– 1996. *Administrative Law.* 3rd ed. Toronto: Thomson Canada.
Murphy, H.C., and J. Cool. 1990. *'Dropping Out and Dropping In': A Study of Youth
   and Literacy.* Ottawa: Canadian Youth Foundation.
Murray, Scott. 1998. *Brain Drain or Brain Gain? What Do the Data Say?* Ottawa: Sta-
   tistics Canada.
Murray, Thomas, Mark Rothstein, and Robert Murray Jr, eds. 1996. *The Human
   Genome Project and the Future of Health Care.* Bloomington: Indiana University
   Press.
Muszynski, Alicia. 1996. *Cheap Wage Labour: Race and Gender in the Fisheries of Brit-
   ish Columbia.* Montreal: McGill-Queen's Press.
Mwarigha, M.S. 1997a. *Issues and Prospects: The Funding and Delivery of Immigrant
   Services in the Context of Cutbacks, Devolution and Amalgamation.* Toronto: Joint
   Centre for Excellence for Research on Immigration and Settlement.
– 1997b. *The Impact of Cutbacks and Restructuring on the NGO Sector and the Delivery
   of Immigrant Services.* Toronto: Joint Centre for Excellence for Research on
   Immigration and Settlement.
Mwarigha, M.S., and Colette Murphy. 1997. *Merchants of Care? The Non-Profit Sec-
   tor in a Competitive Social Services Marketplace.* Toronto: Social Planning Council
   of Metropolitan Toronto.
Mykitiuk, Roxanne. 1994. 'Fragmenting the Body.' *Australian Feminist Law Jour-
   nal* 2, 63–98.
Nader, Aymen. 1997. 'Providing Essential Services: Canada's Constitutional
   Commitment under Section 36.' *Dalhousie Law Journal* 19, 306–72.
Naffine, Ngaire. 1990. *The Law and the Sexes: Explorations in Feminist Jurisprudence.*
   Sydney: Allen and Unwin.
National Action Committee for the Status of Women. 1985. *Prostitution in Can-
   ada.* Ottawa: National Action Committee for the Status of Women.

National Anti-Poverty Organization. 1996. *Monitoring the Impacts on Social Assistance Recipients of Welfare Cuts and Changes: An Overview.* Ottawa: National Anti-Poverty Organization.

National Biotechnology Advisory Committee. 1998. *Leading in the Next Millennium (Sixth Report).* Ottawa: Industry Canada.

National Council of Welfare. 1997. *Poverty Profile.* www.ncwcnbes.net/ntmdocument/reportpovertypro/ (last visited 6/26/2000).

National Forum on Health. 1997a. *Canada Health Action: Building on the Legacy.* Final Report, Vol. 2, Synthesis Reports and Issues Papers, Determinants of Health Working Group Synthesis Report. http://wwwnfh.hc-sc.gc.ca/publicat/finvol2/determin/12over.htm

– 1997b. 'Creating a Culture of Evidence-Based Decision Making in Health.' In *Canada Health Action: Building on the Legacy.* Final Report, Vol. 2, Synthesis Reports and Issues Papers. http://wwwnfh.hc-sc.gc.ca/publicat/finvol2/ebdm/intro.htm

– 1997c. 'Key Findings.' In *Canada Health Action: Building on the Legacy.* Final Report, Vol. 2, Synthesis Reports and Issues Papers, Values Working Group Synthesis Report. http://wwwnfh.hc-sc.gc.ca/publicat/finvol2/values/keyfind.htm

– 1997d. 'Rebalancing at the Societal Level.' In *Canada Health Action: Building on the Legacy.* Final Report, Vol. 2, Synthesis Reports and Issues Papers, Striking a Balance Working Group Synthesis Report. http://wwwnfh.hc-sc.gc.ca/publicat/finvol2/balance/societ.htm

– 1996a. *Maintaining a National Health Care System: A Question of Principles ... and Money.* Ottawa: National Forum on Health.

– 1996b. *Canada Health Action: Building on the Legacy.* Final Report of the National Forum on Health, Vol. I. Ottawa, Minister of Public Works and Government Services.

– 1995. *The Public and Private Financing of Canada's Health System.* Ottawa: National Forum on Health.

National Post. 1999a. 'Apples and Oranges.' *National Post,* 20 October, A19.

– 1999b. 'Don't Appeal, Abolish.' *National Post,* 1 June, A15.

– 1999c. 'Debate Still Swirls around the Drain.' *National Post,* 4 October.

Naylor, David. 1999. 'Health Care in Canada: Incrementalism under Fiscal Duress.' *Health Affairs* 18(3), 9–26.

– 1986. *Private Practice, Public Payment: Canadian Medicine and the Politics of Health Insurance.* Montreal: McGill-Queen's University Press.

Nelson, Julie A. 1996. *Feminism, Objectivity and Economics.* London: Routledge.

Nemiroff, Greta Hofmann. 1999. '"Live-in Caregiving in Canada": An Interview.' *Speaking About Rights* 24(1), 10.

Nettleton, Sarah. 1997. 'Governing the Risk Self: How to Become Healthy,

Wealthy and Wise.' In Alan Petersen and Robin Bunton, eds., *Foucault, Health and Medicine*. New York: Routledge, 207–22.

Neysmith, Sheila. 1997. 'Towards a Woman-Friendly Long-Term Care Policy.' In Patricia Evans and Gerda Wekerle, eds., *Women and the Canadian Welfare State: Challenges and Change*. Toronto: University of Toronto Press, 222–45.

Ng, Roxanne. 1990. 'Immigrant Women: The Construction of a Labour Market Category.' *Canadian Journal of Women and the Law* 4, 96.

Nicols-Heppner, Barbara. 1984. 'Women in Public Sector Unions in Quebec: Organized for Equality.' PhD thesis, School of Social Work, McGill University.

Note. 1998. 'The Trafficking of Women for Prostitution: A Growing Problem within the European Union.' *Boston College International and Comparative Law Review* 21, 183–99.

O'Connor, Julia. 1993. 'Gender, Class and Citizenship in the Comparative Analysis of Welfare State Regimes: Theoretical and Methodological Issues.' *British Journal of Sociology* 44(3), 501–18.

Oakley, Ann. 1981. 'Normal Motherhood: An Exercise in Self-Control?' In Bridget Hutter and Gilliam Williams, eds., *Controlling Women: The Normal and the Deviant*. London: Croom Helm.

– 1989. 'Welfare Expenditure and Policy Orientation in Comparative Perspective.' *Canadian Review of Sociology and Anthropology* 26(1), 127–50.

Ocran, Amanda Araba. 1997. 'Across the Home/Work Divide: Homework in Garment Manufacture and the Failure of Employment Regulation.' Susan B. Boyd, ed., *Challenging the Public/Private Divide: Feminism, Law and Public Policy*. Toronto: University of Toronto Press, 144–67.

O'Donovan, Katherine. 1985. *Sexual Divisions in Law*. London: Weidenfeld and Nicholson.

OECD. 1998a. *OECD Economic Outlook*. Paris: OECD.

– 1998b. *Maintaining Prosperity in an Ageing Society*. Paris: OECD.

– 1997. *Societal Cohesion and the Globalizing Economy*. Paris: OECD.

– 1989. *Biotechnology: Economics and Wider Impacts*. Paris: OECD.

Olsen, Frances. 1983. 'The Family and the Market: A Study of Ideology and Legal Reform.' *Harvard Law Review* 96(7), 1497–1579.

O'Malley, Pat. 1999. 'Volatile and Contradictory Punishment.' *Theoretical Criminology* 3(2), 175–96.

– 1992. 'Risk, Power and Crime Prevention.' *Economy and Society* 21, 252–75.

O'Malley, Pat, Lorna Weir, and Clifford Shearing. 1997. 'Governmentality, Criticism, Politics.' *Economy and Society* 26, 501–17.

O'Neill, Michael A. 1997. 'Stepping Forward, Stepping Back? Health Care, the Federal Government and the New Canada Health and Social Transfer.' *International Journal of Canadian Studies* 5, 169–85.

References   469

OMA/MOHLT. 2000. Ontario Medical Association/Ministry of Health and Long Term Care Agreement (on file with the author.)

Ontario Association of Children's Aid Societies. 1993–1998. *CAS Fact Sheets*. Toronto: Ontario Association of Children's Aid Societies. Interview with Diane Cresswell, Manager of Communications, 9 July 1999.

Ontario Fair Tax Commission. 1993. *Fair Taxation in a Changing World: Report of the Ontario Fair Tax Commission*. Toronto: University of Toronto Press.

Ontario Legislative Assembly. 1999. *Debates of the Ontario Legislative Assembly (Hansard) 37th Assembly, 1st Session*, 27 October.

Ontario Legislative Assembly. 1998. *Standing Committee on Social Development. Transcript of Public Hearings, Protection of Children involved in Prostitution Act, Bill 18*. Sudbury, Ontario, 17 August; London, Ontario, 18 August; Toronto, Ontario, 28, 29 September. http://www.ontla.on.ca/hansard/comproindex.htm (11 July 2000).

Ontario Ministry of Community and Social Services. 2000. 'Placements Double in Ontario's Workfare Program: Baird.' http://www.gov.on.ca/CSS/page/news/jun500.html.

– 1998. News Release, 4 September.

– 1997. *Backgrounder, Social Assistance Reform Act 1997*. Toronto: Queen's Printer for Ontario.

– 1996. 'Future Directions in Social Services.'

– 1998. 'Policy Directive 13.0 (Immigrants, Refugees and Deportees).' *Ontario Works: Making Welfare Work*. http://www.gov.on.ca/css/page/brochure/policy/dir/dir13.0.pdf

Ontario. 1998a. *Ministry of Health Bulletin 4309*, 9 April. http://www.gov.on.ca/health/english/program/ohip/bulletin/bu/4309.html

– 1998b. *Ministry of Health Bulletin 4306*, 16 March. http://www.gov.on.ca/health/english/program/ohip/bulletin/bu/4306a.html

Ontario. Ministry of Finance. 1999. *1999 Ontario Budget: Paper B*. http://www.gov.on.ca/fin/bud99/english/99papere.pdf

Ontario Ministry of Health. N.d. *Independent Health Facilities Act Fact Sheet*.

Ontario Ministry of the Attorney General. 1999. News Release, 25 October.

– 1996a. News Release, 18 July. Government Cracks Down on Child Support Defaulters.

– 1996b. Backgrounder, 18 July. Tougher Family Support Enforcement.

Ontario Secondary School Teachers. 2000. 'Underfunding of Public Education.' http://www.osstf.on.ca/www/issues/edfi/underfunding.html

Ontario Social Safety Network Backgrounder. 1998. 'Welfare Reform and Single Mothers.' prepared by Melodie Mayson, last updated 7/1/98.

www.welfarewatch.toronto.on.ca/wrkfrw/singlemo.htm (last visited 6/25/ 2000).

Orloff, Ann Shola. 1993. 'Gender and the Social Rights of Citizenship: The Comparative Analysis of Gender Relations and Welfare States.' *American Sociological Review* 58, 303–28.

Ottawa Citizen. 1998. 'Pay Equity versus the Tax Payer?' *Ottawa Citizen,* 7 August, A9.

Ottawa Sun. 1999. 'Shame.' *Ottawa Sun,* 25 October, A13.

– 1998. 'Cheque, Please.' *Ottawa Sun,* 30 July.

Owen, Timothy. 1999. 'The View from Ontario: Settlement Services in the Late 1990s.' Unpublished Paper prepared for Vancouver *Metropolis* Conference, 13 January.

Oziewicz, Estanislao. 2000a. 'Strip Club Raided, Owner Faces Prostitution-related Charges.' *Globe and Mail,* 25 February.

– 2000b. 'Canada's Bare Essential.' *Globe and Mail,* 19 February.

– 1997. 'Ottawa Eyes Curb on Entry of Strippers.' *Globe and Mail,* 7 February, A1.

Paciocco, David M. 1996. 'The Evidence of Children: Testing the Rules against What We Know.' *Queen's Law Journal* 21, 345–93.

Paine, Hollie J. 1999. 'The Catholic Merger Crusade.' *Journal of Health Care Law* 2, 371–403.

Palmer, Ingrid. 1995. 'Public Finance from a Gender Perspective.' *World Development* 23(11), 1981–6.

Palmer, Karen. 1999. 'Apology for Abuse Draws Tears.' *Toronto Star,* 17 November, A20.

Panel on Accountability and Governance in the Voluntary Sector. 1999. *Building on Strength: Improving Governance and Accountability in Canada's Voluntary Sector.* Final Report, February.

Panitch, Leo, and Donald Swartz. 1998. 'What Happened to Freedom of Association?' *Globe and Mail,* 7 April, A27.

– 1993. *The Assault on Trade Union Freedoms: From Wage Controls to Social Contract.* Rev. ed. Toronto: Garamond.

– 1988. *The Assault on Trade Union Freedoms.* Toronto: Garamond.

Parens, Erik, and Adrienne Asch. 1999. 'The Disability Rights Critique of Prenatal Genetic Testing: Reflections and Recommendations.' *Hastings Center Report,* Special Supplement 29(5), S1–S22.

Pascoe, Bradley. 1999. Citizenship and Immigration Canada. Personal Interview, 18 June.

Pascoe, Bradley, and Beverly Davis. 1999. 'Canada's Temporary Foreign Worker Program: A New Design.' Washington: Fourth International Metropolis Conference: Trade Agreements and Migration, 8–11 December.

Pateman, Carole. 1998. 'Contributing to Democracy.' *Review of Constitutional Studies* 4(2), 191–212.

- 1988. *The Sexual Contract.* Cambridge: Polity Press.

- 1983. 'Defending Prostitution: Charges against Ericsson.' *Ethics* 93, 561–65.

Patten, Steve. 1996. 'Preston Manning's Populism: Constructing the Common Sense of the Common People.' *Studies in Political Economy* 50, 95–132.

Pearce, Frank, and Laureen Snider. 1992. 'Crimes of the Powerful: Contemporary Approaches to Corporate Crime.' *Journal of Human Justice* 3(2), 1–4.

Pearce, Frank, and Steve Tombs. 1996. 'Hegemony, Risk and Governance: "Social Regulation" and the American Chemical Industry.' *Economy and Society* 25, 428–54.

Peck, J. 1996. *Work Place: The Social Regulation of Labor Markets.* New York: Guilford Press.

Pendleton, Andrew. 1997. 'What Impact Has Privatization Had on Pay and Employment? A Review of the UK Experience.' *Relations industrielles* 53, 554–82.

Perry, David B. 1999. 'Bragging Rights.' *Canadian Tax Highlights* 7(12), 90–1.

Petersen, Alan. 1999. 'Public Health, the New Genetics and Subjectivity.' In Alan Petersen, Ian Barns, Janice Dudley, and Patricia Harris. *Poststructuralism, Citizenship and Social Policy.* New York: Routledge, 114–53.

- 1998. 'The New Genetics and the Politics of Public Health.' *Critical Public Health* 8(1), 59–71.

- 1997. 'Risk, Governance and the New Public Health.' In Alan Petersen and Robin Bunton, eds., *Foucault, Health and Medicine.* New York: Routledge, 189–206.

Pettman, Jan Jindy. 1996. *Worlding Women: A Feminist International Politics.* St Leonards, *NSW* Australia: Allen and Unwin.

Pheterson, Gail, ed. 1987. *A Vindication of the Rights of Whores.* Seattle: Seal Press.

Philipps, Lisa C. 1996. 'The Rise of Balanced Budget Laws in Canada: Legislating Fiscal (Ir)responsibility.' *Osgoode Hall Law Journal* 34(4), 681–740.

Philipps, Lisa, and Margot Young. 1995. 'Sex, Tax and the *Charter*: A Review of *Thibaudeau v. Canada.*' *Review of Constitutional Studies* 2(2), 221–304.

Phillips, Anne. 1997. 'From Inequality to Difference: A Severe Case of Displacement?' *New Left Review* 224, 143–59.

Phillips, James. 1995. 'Crossing the Line from "Charitable" to "Political".' *Philanthropist* 12(4), 33–7.

Philp, Margaret. 2000. 'Bureaucratic Sea Strands Nannies.' *Globe and Mail,* 16 September, A3.

- 1998. 'Women Climbing Wage Ladder.' *Globe and Mail,* 13 May, 4.

Phizaklea, Annie. 1998. 'Migration and Globalization: A Feminist Perspective.'

In Khalid Koser and Helma Lutz, eds., *The New Migration in Europe: Social Constructions and Social Realities*. London: Macmillan, 21.

Picard, Andre. 2000. 'Health Care Not So Bad: Survey.' *Globe and Mail*, 27 November, A11.

Picchio, Antonella. 1998. 'Wages as a Reflection of Socially Embedded Production and Reproduction Processes.' In Linda Clark, Peter de Gijsel, and Jorn Jasussen, eds., *The Dynamics of Wage Relations in the New Europe*. London: Kluwer, 195–213.

– 1992. *Social Reproduction: The Political Economy of the Labour Market*. Cambridge: Cambridge University Press.

Picciotto, Sol. 1999. 'Offshore: The State as Legal Fiction.' In Mark P. Hampton and Jason P. Abbott, eds., *Offshore Finance Centers and Tax Havens: The Rise of Global Capital*. West Lafayette: Purdue University Press, 43–79.

– 1998. 'Linkages in International Investment Regulation: The Antimonies of the Multilateral Agreement on Investment.' *University of Pennsylvania Journal of International Economics and Law* 19(3), 731–68.

Picot, Garnett. 1998. *What Is Happening to Earnings in Equity and Youth Wages in the 1990's?* Research Paper Series, Analytical Studies Research, No. 116. Ottawa: Statistics Canada.

Picot, Garnet, and Andrew Heisz. 2000. *The Performance of the 1990s Canadian Labour Market*. Business and Labour Market Analysis Division, No. 148. Ottawa: Statistics Canada.

Picot, G., M. Zyblock, and W. Pyper. 1999. *Why Do Children Move into and out of Low Income: Changing Labour Market Conditions or Marriage and Divorce?'* Research Paper Series, Analytical Studies Branch, No. 132. Ottawa: Statistics Canada.

Pierson, Ruth Roach. 1990. 'Gender and the Unemployment Insurance Debates in Canada, 1934–1940.' *Labour/Le Travail* 25, 77–103.

– 1986. *'They're Still Women After All': The Second World War and Canadian Womanhood*. Toronto: McClelland and Stewart.

Piper, Christine. 1999. 'Moral Campaigns for Children's Welfare in the Nineteenth Century.' In Michael King, ed., *Moral Agendas for Children's Welfare*. London: Routledge.

Policy Options. 1999. 'The Brain Drain.' *Policy Options*, September, 6–43.

– 1998. 'A Tax–Cutting Strategy for Canada.' *Policy Options*, December 3–48.

Porter, Ann. Forthcoming. Gender, Unemployment Insurance and the Political Economy of the Canadian Welfare State. Toronto: University of Toronto Press.

– 1998. 'Gender, Class and the State: The Case of Unemployment Insurance in Canada.' PhD diss., York University.

– 1993. 'Women and Income Security in the Post–War Period: The Case of Unemployment Insurance, 1945–1962.' *Labour/Le Travail* 31, 111–44.

President of the Treasury Board. 1995. *Employment Equity in the Public Service, Annual Report 1993–1994.* Ottawa: Minister of Supply and Services.

Press, Kevin. 2000. 'Editorial – The Sky Is Falling. The Sky Is Falling. The Sky Is Falling.' *Benefits Canada*, February, 7.

Press, Nancy, and Carole Browner. 1997. 'Why Women Say Yes to Prenatal Diagnosis.' *Social Science Medicine* 45(7), 979–89.

– 1995. 'The Normalization of Prenatal Diagnostic Screening.' In Faye D. Ginseberg and Rayna Rapp, eds., *Conceiving the New World Order: The Global Politics of Reproduction.* Berkeley: University of California Press, 307–22.

Priest, Lisa. 2001. 'New Brunswick Occupies Front Line in Fight for Private-clinic Abortions.' *Globe and Mail,* 5 March, A1, A5.

Pringle, Rosemary, and Sophie Watson. 1992. 'Women's Interests' and the Post-Structuralist State.' In Michelle Barrett and Anne Phillips, eds., *Destabilizing Theory: Contemporary Feminist Debates.* Stanford: Stanford University Press, 53–73.

Progressive Conservative Party of Canada. 1999. *Unlocking Canada's Potential: The Progressive Conservative Budget Plan.* Ottawa: Progressive Conservative Party of Canada.

– 1997. *Designing a Blueprint for Canadians.* Ottawa: Progressive Conservative Party of Canada.

Pron, Nick. 2000. 'Man Gets 8 Years for Pimping 12 Year Old: Youngest Prostitute Ever Investigated by Juvenile Task Force.' *Toronto Star,* 23 June, B9.

Provincial and Territorial Ministers of Health. 2000. 'Understanding Canada's Health Care Costs, Interim Report.' (June, 2000) http://www.premier. gov.on.ca./English/news/Health Report060900.htm

Public Service Alliance of Canada. Pay Equity Page. http://www.psac.com/ payequity/new/June99/pay-e.htm (22 February 2000.)

Public Service Alliance of Canada. 1997. Presentation to National Joint Committee, Valleyfield, Quebec, September.

Public Service Commission of Canada. 1985. *Women in the Public Service of Canada: A Decade of Change.* Ottawa: Minister of Supply and Services.

Pulkingham, Jane. 1994. 'Private Troubles, Private Solutions: Poverty among Divorced Women and the Politics of Support Enforcement and Child Custody Determination.' *Canadian Journal of Law and Society* 9(2), 73–98.

Pulkingham, Jane, Ternowetsky. 1996. *Remaking Canadian Social Policy: Social Security in the Late 1990s.* Halifax: Fernwood Publishing.

Purvis, Trevor, and Alan Hunt. 1999. 'Identity versus Citizenship: Transformation in the Discourses and Practices of Citizenship.' *Social and Legal Studies* 8(4), 457–82.

- 1993. 'Discourse, Ideology, Discourse, Ideology, Discourse, Ideology ...' *British Journal of Sociology* 44(3), 473–99.

Pushkal, P., M. Garg, K. Frick, M. Diener-West, and N. Powe. 1999. 'Effect of the Ownership of Dialysis Facilities on Patients' Survival and Referral for Transplantation.' *New England Journal of Medicine* 341(22), 1653–60.

Quarter, Jack. 1992. *Canada's Social Economy.* Toronto: James Lorimer and Company.

Queisser, Monika. 1998. *The Second-Generation Pension Reforms in Latin America.* Paris: Development Centre of the OECD.

Rachlis, M. 1995. 'Defining Basic Services and De-Insuring the Rest: The Wrong Diagnosis and the Wrong Prescription.' *Canadian Medical Association Journal* 152(9), 1401–5.

Rashid, Abdul. 1993. 'Seven Decades if Wage Changes.' *Perspectives on Labour and Income* 5(2), 9–21.

Rayman, Graham. 2001. 'Smuggled for Sex: Toronto Targets Trafficking.' *Newsday*, 14 March.

Razack, Sherene. 1993. 'Exploring the Omissions and Silences in Law around Race.' In Joan Brockman and Dorothy Chunn, eds., *Investigating Gender Bias: Law, Courts and the Legal Profession.* Toronto: Thompson Educational Publishing, 37–48.

- 1991. *Canadian Feminism and the Law: The Women's Legal Education and Action Fund and the Pursuit of Equality.* Toronto: Second Story Press.

REAL Women of Canada. Undated. *Position Paper on Pension and Tax Reform.* www.realwomenca.com/html/pension_and_tax_reform.html.

- 1998. *In the Supreme Court of Canada between the Attorney General of Ontario and M and H, Factum of the Intervenor.*

Reform Party of Canada. Undated. *Blue Sheet: Principles and Policies of the Reform Party of Canada, 1996–97.* Calgary: Reform Party of Canada.

- 1997. 'Do You Think the Law Should Allow Adults to Have Sex with 14 Year Olds?' News Release, 6 March. http://www.reform.ca/garrypress/ consentl.html (June 24, 1999).

Rekart, Josephine. 1993. *Public Funds, Private Provision: The Role of the Voluntary Sector.* Vancouver: UBC Press.

Research Subgroup of the Sexually Exploited Youth in the Capital Regional District. 1997. *A Consultation with 75 Youth Involved in the Sex Trade in the Capital Regional District.* Ottawa: Capital Regional District.

Reuter. 1993. 'China to Pass Eugenics Law.' *Globe and Mail*, A1.

Revenue Canada. Undated. *Registered Charities: Education, Advocacy, and Political Activities (RC4107E Draft).* Ottawa: Minister of National Revenue.

Richmond, C. 1996. 'NHS Waiting Lists Have Been a Boon for Private Medicine in the UK.' *Canadian Medical Association Journal* 154(3), 378–81.

Richmond, Ted. 1996. 'Effects of Cutbacks on Immigrant Service Agencies.' Toronto: Joint Centre of Excellence for Research on Immigration and Settlement.

Rittich, Kerry. 1998. 'Recharacterizing Restructuring: Gender and Distribution in the Legal Structure of Market Reform.' SJD diss., Harvard Law School.

Roach, Kent. 1999. *Due Process and Victim's Rights: The New Law and Politics of Criminal Justice.* Toronto: University of Toronto Press.

Roberts, Dorothy E. 1996. 'Biology, Justice, and Women's Fate.' *University of Chicago Roundtable* 3(2), 465–71.

Roberts, Julian V., and Anthony N. Doob. 1990. 'News Media Influences on Public Views of Sentencing.' *Law and Human Behaviour* 14, 451–68.

Robertson, Ann. 2000. 'Risk, Biotechnology and Political Rationality: Lessons from Women's Accounts of Breast Cancer Risks.' In F. Miller, L. Weir, and R. Mykitiuk, *The Gender of Genetic Futures.* Toronto: NNEWH Working Paper Series, 63–75.

Robinson, Art. 1992. '"Johns" Get Harrassed by Riversdale Residents: Embarrassed Men Caught by Cameras.' *Star Phoenix,* 13 June, A7.

Robinson, Sara. 2000. 'High-Tech Workers Are Trapped in Limbo by I.N.S.' *New York Times,* 28 February.

Robinson, W.G. 1983. 'Illegal Migrants in Canada.' Report to Minister of Employment and Immigration Lloyd Axworthy. Ottawa: Minister of Supply and Services.

Robson, Bill. 1996. 'Keeping Mistakes "Honest": A Plea for Straight Talk about the CPP.' In *Experts' Forum on Canada Pension Plan Reform.* Ottawa: Caledon Institute of Social Policy, 21–7.

Rose, Nikolas. 1999. *Powers of Freedom: Reframing Political Thought.* Cambridge: Cambridge University Press.

– 1996a. 'The Death of the Social? Re-figuring the Territory of Government.' *Economy and Society* 25, 327–56.

– 1996b. 'Governing "Advanced" Liberal Democracies.' In Andrew Barry, Thomas Osborne, and Nikolas Rose, eds., *Foucault and Political Reason: Liberalism, Neo-liberalism and Rationalities of Government.* Chicago: University of Chicago Press, 37–64.

– 1994. 'Expertise and the Government of Conduct.' In Austin Sarat and Susan Silbey, eds., *Studies in Law, Politics and Society,* vol. 14. Greenwich, Conn.: JAI Press.

– 1987. 'Beyond the Public/Private Division: Law, Power and the Family.' *Journal of Law and Society* 14, 61.

Rosen, Hanna. 1996. 'Separation Anxiety: The Movement to Save Marriage: Repealing No-Fault Divorce Laws.' *The New Republic* 214(19), 14.

Ross, Ellen, and Rayna Rapp. 1997. 'Sex and Society: A Research Note from

Social History and Anthropology.' In Roger N. Lancaster and Micaela di Leonardo, eds., *The Gender/Sexuality Reader: Culture, History, Political Economy.* New York: Routledge, 153–68.

Rothman, Barbara Katz. 1998. *Genetic Maps and Human Imaginations: The Limits of Science in Understanding Who We Are.* New York: W.W. Norton.

– 1989. *Recreating Motherhood: Ideology and Technology in a Patriarchal Society.* New York: W.W. Norton.

Roy, Arun. 1997. 'Job Displacement Effects of Canadian Immigrants by Country of Origin and Occupation.' *International Migration Review* 31(1), 150–62.

Roy, David J., John R. Williams, and Bernard M. Dickens. 1994. *Bioethics in Canada.* Scarborough, ON: Prentice-Hall.

Royal College of Obstetricians and Gynecologists (UK). 2000. 'The Care of Women Requesting Induced Abortion.' http://www.rocg.org.uk/guidelines/induced_abortion.html

Royal Commission on New Reproductive Technologies. 1993. *Proceed with Care: Final Report of the Royal Commission on New Reproductive Technologies.* Ottawa: Minister of Government Services Canada.

Royal Commission on Taxation. 1966. *Report of the Royal Commission on Taxation.* Ottawa: Queen's Printer.

Royal Commission on the Economic Union and Development Prospects for Canada. 1985. *Report of the Royal Commission on the Economic Union and Development Prospects for Canada.* Ottawa: Minister of Supply and Services.

Royal Commission on the Status of Women in Canada. 1970. *Report of the Royal Commission on the Status of Women in Canada.* Ottawa: Information Canada.

Rubin, Gayle. 1984. 'Thinking Sex: Notes for a Radical Theory of the Politics of Sexuality.' In Carole S. Vance, ed., *Pleasure and Danger: Exploring Female Sexuality.* London: Routledge and Kegan Paul.

Rudolph, Hedwig, and Mirjana Morokvasic, eds. 1993. *Bridging States and Markets: International Migration in the Early 1990s.* Berlin: Edition Sigma.

Ruggeri, G.C., D. Van Wart, and R. Howard. 1994. 'The Redistributional Impact of Taxation in Canada.' *Canadian Tax Journal* 42(2), 417–51.

Ruimy, Joel. 1998. 'Tough Stand Taken on Youth Crime. Panel of MPPs to Recommend Initiatives.' *Toronto Star,* 31 January, A6.

Rusk, James. 1998. 'Tory Panel Wants to Crack Down on Ontario's Youth Crime: Tough Position May Be Sound Election Strategy, Pollster Says.' *Globe and Mail,* 2 June, A7.

– 1993. 'Ontario Reviews OHIP Coverage.' *Globe and Mail,* 1 December, A4.

Ryan, Mary. 1994. 'Gender and Public Access: Women's Politics in Nineteenth Century America.' In Craig Calhoun, ed., *Habermas and the Public Sphere.* Cambrige, Mass: MIT Press.

Salamon, Lester M. 1995. *Partners in Public Service: Government-Nonprofit Relations in the Modern Welfare State*. Baltimore: Johns Hopkins University Press.

– 1994. 'The Rise of the Nonprofit Sector.' *Foreign Affairs* 73(4), 109–22.

Sandelowski, Margarete, and Linda Corson Jones. 1996. 'Couples' Evaluations of Foreknowledge of Fetal Impairment.' *Clinical Nursing Research* 5(1), 81–97.

Sanders, Douglas. 1997. 'Does Canadian Law Support Us?' 2 November. Unpublished.

Sarick, Lila. 1997. 'Spousal Rejection Rate Queried.' *Globe and Mail*. 4 November, A8.

Sarlo, Chris. 1999. 'Taxes and the Single Earner Family.' *Fraser Forum*, March, online: Fraser Institute Homepage http://www.fraserinstitute.ca/publications/forum/1999/03/taxes.htm (29 June 2000).

Sas, L., and P. Hurley. 1997. *Project 'Guardian': The Sexual Exploitation of Male Youth in London*. London: London Family Court Clinic.

Sassen, Saskia. 1998. *Globalization and Its Discontents*. New York: New Press.

– 1996. *Losing Control? Sovereignty in an Age of Globalization*. New York: Columbia University Press.

Satzewich, Vic. 1991. *Racism and the Incorporation of Foreign Labour: Farm Labour Migration to Canada since 1945*. London: Routledge.

Savoie, Donald J. 1999. 'The Rise of Court Government in Canada.' *Canadian Journal of Political Science* 32(4), 635–64.

Scambler, Graham, and Annette Scambler. 1997. *Rethinking Prostitution: Purchasing Sex in the 1990s*. London: Routledge.

Scharf, Kimberley, Ben Cherniavsky, and Roy Hogg. 1997. *Tax Incentives for Charities in Canada*. Ottawa: Canadian Policy Research Networks Inc.

Schreader, Alicia. 1990. 'The State Funded Women's Movement: A Case of Two Political Agendas.' In Roxana Ng, Gillian Walker, and Jacob Muller, eds., *Community Organization and the Canadian State*. Toronto: Garamond Press, 184–99.

Schwartz, B. 1997. 'NAFTA Reservations in the Area of Health Care.' *Health Law Journal* 5, 99–117.

Science Advisory Board. 2000. *Report of the Committee on the Drug Review Process*. Ottawa: Health Canada.

Scott, Joan. 1986. 'Gender: A Useful Category of Historical Analysis.' *American Historical Review* 93, 1053–73.

Scott, Katherine. 1996. 'The Dilemma of Liberal Citizenship: Women and Social Assistance Reform in the 1990s.' *Studies in Political Economy* 50, 7–36.

Scott, Katherine, and Clarence Lochhead. 1997. *Are Women Catching Up in the Earnings Race?* Social Research Series, Paper No. 3. Ottawa: Canadian Council on Social Development.

Sears, Alan. 1999. 'The Lean State and Capitalist Restructuring: Towards a The-
    oretical Account.' *Studies in Political Economy* 59, 91–114.
Seccombe, Wally. 1992. *A Millennium of Family Change.* London: Verso.
Senate. 1997a. Standing Senate Committee on Banking, Trade and Commerce.
    Examination of the Present State of the Financial System in Canada – Evidence.
    18 November, online: Parliamentary Internet http://www.parl.gc.ca/36/1/
    parlbus/commbus/senate/com-e/bank-e/05eva-e.htm (21 July 2000).
– 1997b. Standing Senate Committee on Banking, Trade and Commerce. *Exam-
    ination of the Present State of the Financial System in Canada – Evidence.* 19 Novem-
    ber, online: Parliamentary Internet http://www.parl.gc.ca/36/1/parlbus/
    commbus/senate/com-e/bank-e/05evb-e.htm (21 July 2000).
– 1997c. Standing Committee on Social Affairs, Science and Technology.
    28 January, 18:45.
– 1996. Standing Committee on Social Affairs, Science and Technology.
    10 December, 16:30.
Shamsuddin, Abul. 1997. *The Double-Negative Effect on the Earnings of Foreign-born
    Females in Canada.* Vancouver: Vancouver Centre of Excellence Research on
    Immigration and Integration in the Metropolis.
Sharma, Nandita. 2000. 'Race, Class, Gender and the Making of Difference: The
    Social Organization of "Migrant Workers" in Canada.' *Atlantis* 24(2), 5–15.
Sharpe, G., and D. Weisstub. 1996. 'Bill 26: Towards the Restructuring of
    Ontario's Health Care System.' *Health Law in Canada* 17(2), 31–41.
Shaver, Francis. 1994. 'The Regulation of Prostitution: Avoiding the Morality
    Traps.' *Canadian Journal of Law and Society*, 9(1), 123–41.
– 1993. 'Prostitution: A Female Crime?' In E. Adelberg and C. Currie, eds.,
    Women and the Canadian Justice System. Vancouver: Press Gang.
– 1985. 'Prostitution: A Critical Analysis of Three Policy Approaches.' *Canadian
    Public Policy* 11(3), 493–503.
Shephard, Michelle. 1999a. '72-hour Rescue for Child Prostitutes. Toronto
    Studying Calgary "Safe Haven" Plan to Aid Street Kids.' *Toronto Star*, 18 April,
    A1.
– 1999b. 'Girls above Law – and Beyond Help: Police Frustrated by Restrictive
    Laws on Teen Hookers.' *Toronto Star*, 18 April, A12.
– 1999c. 'How All the Right Words Lured Girl into Street Life: Toronto Man
    Jailed on Charges of Prostitution.' *Toronto Star*, 9 March, B1.
Sherwin, Susan. 1998a. 'Biotechnology and Health: The Place of Ethics in a
    National Strategy.' Unpublished MS.
– 1998b. 'Response from the Maritime Centre of Excellence for Women's
    Health (MCEWH) to Health Protection Branch Discussion Papers.' Unpub-
    lished MS.

Sherwin, Susan, and Christy Simpson. 1999. 'Ethical Questions in the Pursuit of Genetic Information: Geneticization and BRCA1.' In A. Thompson and R. Chadwick, eds., *Genetic Information: Acquisition, Access and Control.* New York: Kluwer Academic/Plenum Publishers, 121.

Shrage, L. 1994. *Moral Dilemmas of Feminism: Prostitution, Adultery and Abortion.* London: Routledge, 1994.

– 1989. 'Should Feminists Oppose Prostitution?' *Ethics* 99, 347–61.

Silbert, T., and A. Pines. 1982. 'Entrance into Prostitution.' *Youth and Society* 13, 471–500.

Silk Klein, Suzanne. 1985. 'Individualism, Liberalism, and the New Family Law.' *University of Toronto Faculty of Law Review* 116–35.

Sillars, Les. 1995. 'A New Player in the Game.' *Alberta Report / Western Report* 22, 11–20.

Silver, Allan. 1992. 'The Demand for Order in Civil Society: A Review of Some Themes in the History of Urban Crime, Police and Riot.' In K. McCormick and L. Visano, eds., *Understanding Policing.* Toronto: Canadian Scholars Press.

Simand, Harriet. 1998. 'Women's Health Protection.' *Canadian Women's Health Network* 1(4), 1–3.

Simmons, Alan. 1999. 'Economic Integration and Designer Immigrants: Canadian Policy in the 1990s.' In *Free Markets, Open Societies, Closed Borders?* Miami: North-South Center Press, 53–69.

– 1996. *International Migration Flows and Human Rights in North America: The Impact of Trade and Restructuring.* New York: Center for Migration Studies.

Simon, Jonathan. 1999. 'Law after Society.' *Law and Social Inquiry* 24, 143–94.

Simpson, Jeffrey. 1999. 'The Politics of Redress.' *Globe and Mail,* 20 October, A23.

Singer, Linda. 1993. *Erotic Welfare: Sexual Theory and Politics in the Age of Epidemic.* New York: Routledge.

Skurka, Steven. 1993. 'Two Scales of Justice: The Victim as Adversary.' *Criminal Law Quarterly* 35, 334–54.

Smart, Carol. 1992. 'The Woman of Legal Discourse.' *Social and Legal Studies* 1(1), 29–44.

– 1989. *Feminism and the Power of Law.* London: Routledge.

Smith, Daniel A. 1998. *Tax Crusaders and the Politics of Direct Democracy.* New York: Routledge.

Smith, Roger S. 1995. 'The Personal Income Tax: Average and Marginal Rates in the Post-War Period.' *Canadian Tax Journal* 43(5), 1055–76.

Smith, Steven, and Michael Lipsky. 1993. *Non profits for Hire: The Welfare State in the Age of Contracting.* Cambridge: Harvard University Press.

Snider, Laureen. 1994. 'Feminism, Punishment and the Potential of Empower-
    ment.' *Canadian Journal of Law and Society* 9, 75–104.
– 1990. 'The Potential of the Criminal Justice System to Promote Feminist Con-
    cerns.' *Studies in Law, Politics and Society* 10, 143–72.
Sohrab, Julia. 1996. *Sexing the Benefit: Women, Social Security and Financial Indepen-
    dence in EU Sex Equality Law.* Dartmouth: Aldershot.
Solinger, Rickie. 1998. 'Dependency and Choice: The Two Faces of Eve.' *Social
    Justice* 25(1), 1.
Solomon, Williams. 2000. 'Press Coverage of the WTO protests in Seattle.'
    Monthly Review 52(1), 12–20.
Somerville, Jennifer. 1992. 'The New Right and Family Politics.' *Economy and
    Society* 21(2), 93–128.
Sonnen, C., and M. McCracken. 1999. 'Downsizing, Passive Privatization and Fis-
    cal Arrangements.' In Daniel Drache and Terry Sullivan, eds., *Market Limits in
    Health Reform: Public Success, Private Failure.* New York: Routledge, 225–44.
Sossin, Lorne. 1998. 'Salvaging the Welfare State? The Prospects for Judicial
    Review of the Canada Health and Social Transfer.' *Dalhousie Law Journal* 21,
    141–98.
Soysal, Yasmin. 1994. *Limits of Citizenship: Migrants and Postnational Membership in
    Europe.* Chicago: University of Chicago Press.
Spears, John. 1999. 'No Room for Refugees, Mayor Says.' *Toronto Star*, 13 Octo-
    ber.
Special Joint Committee on Custody and Access. 1999. *For the Sake of the Children.*
    Ottawa: Queen's Printer.
Spector, Michael. 1998. '"Traffickers" New Cargo: Naïve Slavic Women.' *New
    York Times*, 11 January, 1.
Stacey, Meg. 1996. 'The New Genetics: A Feminist View.' In Theresa Marteau
    and Martin Richards, eds., *The Troubled Helix: Social and Psychological Implica-
    tions of the New Human Genetics.* Cambridge: Cambridge University Press, 331–
    49.
Stackhouse, John. 2000. 'Brain Dead: Why Canada Just Doesn't Cut It Anymore
    for the World's Best and Brightest.' *Globe and Mail* (Toronto), 18 March.
Stainton Rogers, Wendy, and Rex Stainton Rogers. 1999. *What Is Good and Bad
    Sex for Children?* In Michael King, ed., *Moral Agendas for Children's Welfare.* Lon-
    don: Routledge.
Standing Committee on the Legislative Assembly. 1997. *Final Report on Referenda.*
    June. Legislative Assembly of Ontario.
Stanford, Jim. 1996. 'Discipline, Insecurity and Productivity: The Economics
    between Labour Market "Flexibility."' In Jane Pulkingham and Gordon Ter-
    nowetsky, eds., *Remaking Canadian Social Policy.* Halifax: Fernwood.

Starr, P. 1989. 'The Meaning of Privatization.' In Sheila B. Kamerman and Alfred J. Kahn, eds., *Privatization and the Welfare State*. Princeton, NJ: Princeton University Press.

– 1982. *The Social Transformation of American Medicine*. New York: Basic Books.

Statistics Canada. 2000a. *Women in Canada 2000: A Gender-based Statistical Report*. Ottawa: Statistics Canada.

– 2000b. *The Daily*, 7 April. http://www.statcan.ca/Daily/English/000407/d000407c.htm.

– 1999. *Retirement Savings Through RPPs and RRSP 1991–1997*. Ottawa: Minister of Industry.

– 1998. *Pensions Plans in Canada Statistical Highlights and Key Tables January 1, 1997*. Ottawa: Minister of Industry.

– Canada. 1997. *Pension Plans in Canada January 1, 1996*. Ottawa: Minister of Industry.

– 1996. *Census Families in Private Households by Family Structure, 1991 and 1996 Censuses*. Ottawa: Statistic Canada.

– 1995. *Women in Canada: A Statistical Report*. Ottawa: Minister of Industry.

– 1992. *Lone Parent Families in Canada*. Target Groups Project. Ottawa: Statistics Canada.

Status of Women Canada. 2001. News Release. *Women Still Work More Than Men*. 12 March.

– 1998. *Gender-Based Analysis: A Guide for Policy-Making, Working Paper*. www.swc-cfc.gc.ca/publish/gbagid-e.html.

– 1996. *Gender-based Analysis*. Ottawa: Status of Women Canada.

Staudt, Nancy C. 1996a. 'The Political Economy of Taxation: A Critical Review of a Classic.' *Law and Society Review* 30(3), 651–66.

– 1996b. 'Taxing Housework.' *Georgetown Law Journal* 84, 1571–1647.

Steedman, Mercedes. 1997. *Angels of the Workplace: Women and the Construction of Gender in the Canadian Clothing Industry, 1890–1940*. Toronto: Oxford University Press.

Stewart, Miranda. 1999. 'Domesticating Tax Reform: The Family in Australian Tax and Transfer Law.' *Sydney Law Review* 21, 453–86.

Stoddart, G., M. Barer, and R. Evans. 1994. 'User Charges, Snares and Delusions: Another Look at the Literature.' Report prepared for the Ontario Premier's Council on Health, Well-being and Social Justice. Toronto: Queen's Printer.

Stoddart, G., M. Barer, R. Evans, and V. Bhatia. 1993. 'Why Not User Charges? The Real Issues.' Report prepared for the Ontario Premier's Council on Health, Well-being and Social Justice. Toronto: Queen's Printer.

Stoffman, Daniel. 1993. *Toward a More Realistic Immigration Policy for Canada*. Toronto: C.D. Howe Institute.

Strange, Carolyn. 1995. *Toronto's Girl Problem: The Perils and Pleasures of the City, 1880–1930.* Toronto: University of Toronto Press.

Stromberg, Glorianne. 1998. *Investment Funds in Canada and Consumer Protection.* Ottawa: Office of Consumer Affairs, Industry Canada.

– 1995. *Regulatory Strategies for the Mid-90s: Recommendations for Regulating Investment Funds in Canada.* Toronto: Ontario Securities Commission.

Studies in Political Economy. 2000. 'Forum: Assessing Seattle.' *Studies in Political Economy* 62(Summer), 5–42.

Sutcliffe, Bob. 1998. 'Freedom to Move in the Age of Globalization.' In Dean Baker, Gerald Epstein, and Robert Pollin, eds., *Globalization and Progressive Economic Policy.* Cambridge: Cambridge University Press, 325.

Sutherland, S.L. 1987. 'Federal Bureaucracy: The Pinch Test.' In M. Prince, ed., *How Ottawa Spends, 1987–88.* Toronto: Methuen, 38–128.

Sutton, W. 1996. 'The Saga of the Toronto Birth Centre: An Engagement with Government.' *Health Law Journal* 4, 151–78.

Swimmer, Gene. 1995. 'Collective Bargaining in the Federal Public Service of Canada: The Last Twenty Years.' In Gene Swimmer and Mark Thompson, eds., *Public Sector Collective Bargaining in Canada.* Kingston, ON: IRC Press, 368–407.

Swimmer, Gene, and Darlene Gollesch. 1986. 'Affirmative Action for Women in the Federal Public Service.' In M. Prince, ed., *How Ottawa Spends, 1986–87.* Toronto: Methuen, 208–49.

Swimmer, Gene, Michael Hicks, and Terry Milne. 1995. 'Public Service 2000: Dead or Alive?' In Susan D. Phillips, ed., *How Ottawa Spends, 1994–1995.* Ottawa: Carleton University Press, 165–205.

Swimmer, Gene, with Kjerstin Kinaschuk. 1992. 'Staff Relations under the Conservative Government: The Singer Changes but the Song Remains the Same.' In Frances Abele, ed., *How Ottawa Spends, 1992–1993.* Ottawa: Carleton University Press, 267–316.

Swinton, Katherine. 1995. 'Accommodating Equality in the Unionized Workplace.' *Osgoode Hall Law Journal* 33, 703–47.

Szabo, Paul. 1997. Strong Families ... Make A Strong Country. (Unpublished, on file with the author).

Tabb, William. 1999a. 'Progressive Globalism: Challenging the Audacity of Capital.' *Monthly Review* 50(9), 1–18.

– 1999b. 'After Seattle.' *Monthly Review* 50(1), 1–18.

Table feministe de concertation provinciale de l'Ontario. No Date. 'Submission to the Health Services Restructuring Commission.' Ottawa: Carleton.

Taft, K., and G. Stewart. 2000. 'Private Profit or Public Good: The Economics and Politics of the Privatization of Health Care.' Edmonton: Parkland Institute.

Tam, Pauline. 1999 'Doors Open for Skilled Migrants.' *Ottawa Citizen*. 8 September.

Taylor, Barbara, and Anne Phillips. 1980. 'Sex and Skill Notes towards a Feminist Economics.' *Feminist Review* 6, 85.

Taylor, Malcolm G. 1987. *Health Insurance and Canadian Public Policy: The Seven Decisions That Created the Canadian Health Insurance System and Their Outcomes.* 2nd ed. Montreal: McGill-Queen's University Press.

Taylor, Margaret. 2000. Exotic Dancers Alliance, Personal Communication. 12 May.

Teeple, Gary. 1995. *Globalization and the Decline of Social Reform.* Toronto: Garamond Press.

Teghtsoonian, Katherine. 1997. 'Who Pays for Caring for Children? Public Policy and the Devolution of Women's Work.' In Susan B. Boyd, ed., *Challenging the Public/Private Divide: Feminism, Law, and Public Policy.* Toronto: University of Toronto Press, 113–43.

– 1995. 'Work and/or Motherhood: The Ideological Construction of Women's Options in Canadian Child Care Policy Debates.' *Canadian Journal of Women and the Law* 8, 411–39.

Testart, Jacques. 1995. 'The New Eugenics and Medicalized Reproduction.' *Cambridge Quarterly of Healthcare Ethics* 4, 304–12.

The International League of Societies for Persons with Mental Handicap. 1994. *Just Technology? From Principles to Practice in Bio-Ethical Issues.* Toronto: Roeher Institute.

Thobani, Sunera. 2000. 'Nationalizing Canadians: Bordering Immigrant Women in the Late Twentieth Century.' *Canadian Journal of Women and the Law* 12(2), 279–312.

Thompson, Allan. 1999a. 'Head Tax on Refugees a Headache.' *Toronto Star*, 17 May.

– 1999b. 'Promised Fresh Start Turns into Enslavement.' *Toronto Star*, 20 February.

Thompson, Ginger. 1999. 'Abused and Unshielded, Wives.' *New York Times* 18 April, 37.

Thornton, Margaret, ed. 1995. *Public and Private: Feminist Legal Debates.* Melbourne: Oxford University Press.

Toronto Star. 2000. 'Canada Seen through the Eyes of the Wealthy.' *Toronto Star*, 13 January, OP1.

– 1997. 'Fear in the Schoolyard: Are Teenagers Becoming More Violent.' *Toronto Star*, 12 May, A26.

– 1996. 'Child-support Law to Hunt Out Deadbeats.' *Toronto Star*, 7 November, A17.

Toulin, Alan. 2000. 'Ottawa Promotes Envy, Failure: CEOs.' *National Post*, 4 April, A1.

Townson, Monica. 2000. *A Report Card on Women and Poverty*. Ottawa: Canadian Centre for Policy Alternatives.

– 1999. *Health and Wealth: How Social and Economic Factors Affect Our Well Being*. Ottawa: Canadian Centre for Policy Alternatives.

– 1997. *Non-Standard Work: The Implications for Pension Policy and Retirement Readiness*. Ottawa: Women's Bureau, Human Resources Development Canada.

– 1996. 'What Is the Problem?' In *Experts' Forum on Canada Pension Plan Reform*. Ottawa: Caledon Institute of Social Policy, 29–43.

– 1995. *Women's Financial Futures: Mid-Life Prospects for a Secure Retirement*. Ottawa: Canadian Advisory Council on the Status of Women.

– 1977. *Women in the Public Service: Have New Directives Been Effective? A Review of Employment Statistics for 1976*. Ottawa: Advisory Council on the Status of Women.

Treasury Board Secretariat. Pay Equity Page. http://www.tbs-sct.gc.ca/wnew/PayEquity/siglist_e.html (22 February 2000).

Treff, Karin, and David B. Perry. 1998. *1998 Finances of the Nation*. Toronto: Canadian Tax Foundation.

Tshuma, Lawrence. 2000. 'Hierarchies and Government versus Networks and Government: Competing Regulatory Paradigms in Global Economics Regulation.' *Social and Legal Studies* 9(1), 115–42.

– 1999. 'The Political Economy of the World Bank's Legal Framework for Economic Development.' *Social and Legal Studies* 8(1), 75–96.

Tuohy, Carolyn J. 1999. *Accidental Logics: The Dynamics of Change in the Health Care Arena in the United States, Britain and Canada*. New York: Oxford University Press.

– 1994. 'Principles and Power in the Health Care Arena: Reflections on the Canadian Experience.' *Health Matrix* 4, 205–41.

Turnbull, Barbara. 1998. 'Young Males Losing Ground in Wage Stakes.' *Toronto Star*, 29 July, A2.

Turner, Bryan S. 1997. 'From Governmentality to Risk – Some Reflections on Foucault's Contribution to Medical Sociology.' In Alan Petersen and Robin Bunton, eds., *Foucault: Health and Medicine*. New York: Routledge, ix–xxi.

Tyner, James. A. 1996. 'The Gendering of Philippine International Labor Migration.' *Professional Geographer* 48, 405–17.

Unger, Roberto Mangabeira. 1998. *Democracy Realized: The Progressive Alternative*. London: Verso.

United Nations Development Programme (UNDP). 1999. *Human Development Report 1999*. New York and Oxford: Oxford University Press.

Ursel, Jane. 1992. *Private Lives, Public Policy: 100 Years of State Intervention in the Family*. Toronto: Women's Press.

Valpy, Michael. 1990. 'Different Urban Faces of Street Prostitution.' *Globe and Mail*, 2 August, A5.

Valverde, Marianna. 1991. *The Age of Light, Soap and Water: Moral Reform in English Canada, 1885–1925*. Toronto: McClelland and Stewart.

Valverde, Mariana, Ron Levi, Clifford Shearing, Mary Condon, and Pat O'Malley. 1999. *Democracy in Governance: A Socio-Legal Framework*. Ottawa: Law Commission of Canada.

van Walsum, Sarah. 1994. 'Mixed Metaphors: The Nation and the Family.' *Focaal* 22/23, 199.

Vanier Institute of the Family. 2000. *Profiling Canada's Families II*. Ottawa: Vanier Instiute of the Family.

– 1994. *Profiling Canada's Families*. Ottawa: Vanier Institute for the Family.

Vanwesenbeeck, Ine. 1994. *Prostitutes' Well-being and Risk*. Amsterdam: VU Uitgeverij.

Vermaeten, Frank, W. Irwin Gillespie, and Arndt Vermaeten. 1994. 'Tax Incidence in Canada.' *Canadian Tax Journal* 42(2), 348–416.

Vickers, Jill, Pauline Rankin, and Christine Appelle. 1993. *Politics as if Women Mattered: A Political Analysis of the National Action Committee on the Status of Women*. Toronto: University of Toronto Press.

Vosko, Leah. 2000. *Temporary Work: The Gendered Rise of a Precarious Employment Relationship*. Toronto: University of Toronto Press.

– 1998. 'No Jobs, Lots of Work: The Gendered Rise of the Temporary Employment Relationship in Canada, 1867–1997.' PhD thesis, York University.

Waine, Barbara. 1992. 'Workers as Owners: The Ideology and Practice of Personal Pensions.' *Economy and Society* 21(1), 27–43.

Waitzer, Edward J. 1996. 'Philanthropy and Prosperity: Rebuilding Social Capital.' *Philanthropist* 13(3), 3–9.

Walby, Sylvia. 1997. *Gender Transformations*. London: Routledge.

Walker, Gillian. 1990. *Family Violence and the Women's Movement: The Conceptual Politics of Struggle*. Toronto: University of Toronto Press.

Walker, William. 1999. 'Breakdown of Family Blamed for Child Poverty: Liberal MP Urges Return to Traditional Values.' *Toronto Star*, 23 March, A3.

Walkowitz, Judith R. 1992. *City of Dreadful Delight: Narratives of Sexual Danger in Late Victorian London*. Chicago: University of Chicago Press.

Walzer, Michael. 1984. 'Liberalism and the Art of Separation.' *Political Theory* 12(3), 315–30.

– 1983. *Spheres of Justice*. Basic Books.

Waring, Marilyn. 1988. *If Women Counted: A New Feminist Economics.* San Francisco: Harper Collins Publishers.

Warskett, Rosemary. 1997. 'Learning to Be "Uncivil": Class Formation and Feminization in the Public Service Alliance of Canada, 1966–1996.' PhD thesis, Carleton University.

– 1996. 'The Politics of Difference and Inclusiveness within the Canadian Labour Movement.' *Economic and Industrial Democracy* 17, 587–625.

– 1993. 'Can a Disappearing Pie Be Shared Equally? Unions, Women and Wage "Fairness".' In Linda Briskin and Patricia McDermott, eds., *Women Challenging Unions.* Toronto: University of Toronto Press, 249–68.

– 1991. 'Political Power, Technical Disputes, and Unequal Pay: A Federal Case.' In Judy Fudge and Pat McDermott, eds., *Just Wages: A Feminist Assessment.* Toronto: University of Toronto Press, 172–91.

– 1990. 'Wage Solidarity and Pay Equity.' *Studies in Political Economy* 32, 55–84.

Weeks, Jeffrey. 1981. *Sex, Politics and Society.* London: Longman.

Weir, Lorna. 1996. 'Recent Developments in the Government of Pregnancy.' *Economy Society* 25(3), 373–92.

Weisberg, D.K. 1985. *Children of the Night: A Study of Adolescent Prostitution.* Lexington: D.C. Heath.

Weiss, Linda. 1999. 'Managed Openness: Beyond Neo-Liberal Globalism.' *New Left Review* 238, 126–40.

Welsh, Moira, and Kevin Donovan. 1997. 'We Need Cash and Workers Not Studies, CAS Staff Say.' *Toronto Star,* 22 August, A4.

Western Report. 1995. 'No End to Doing Good: A Eugenics Lawsuit Highlights Seven Sinister Decades of Medically Selecting Who Should Live and Who Won't, Leilani Muir Case.' *Western Report* 10(24), 38–41.

White, Julie. 1993. *Sisters and Solidarity: Women and Unions in Canada.* Toronto: Thompson Educational Publishing.

– 1980. *Women and Unions.* Ottawa: Canadian Advisory Council on the Status of Women.

Whittington, Les. 2000. 'Tax Plan May Flatten Day.' *Hamilton Spectator,* 11 July, D3.

Wilkinson, Richard G. 1996. *Unhealthy Societies: The Afflictions of Inequality.* London: Routledge.

Williams-Jones, Bryn. 1999. 'Re-Framing the Discussion: Commercial Genetic Testing in Canada.' *Health Law Journal* 7, 49–67.

Wilson, Jeffrey. 1997. *Wilson on Children and the Law.* Toronto: Butterworths.

Wolfson, Michael C., and Brian B. Murphy. 1998. 'New Views on Inequality Trends in Canada and the United States.' *Monthly Labor Review,* April, 3–23.

Wolpert, Julian. 1993. *Patterns of Generosity in America: Who's Holding the Safety Net?* New York: Twentieth Century Fund Press.

Women and Taxation Working Group. 1992. *Report.* Toronto: Ontario Fair Tax Commission.

Woodiwiss, Anthony. 1990. *Social Theory after Post-Modernism: Rethinking Production, Law and Class.* London: Pluto Press.

Woodman, Faye L. 1988. 'The Tax Treatment of Charities and Charitable Donations since the Carter Commission: Past Reforms and Present Problems.' *Osgoode Hall Law Journal* 26(3), 537–76.

Woolley, Francis R. 1993. 'The Feminist Challenge to Neoclassical Economics.' *Cambridge Journal of Economics* 17, 485–500.

Working Group on Women and Health Protection – Health Protection Branch Transition Project. 1999. *'To Do No Harm' – Why Women Are Concerned about the Dismantling of Health Protection Legislation in Canada.*

Workman, Thom. 1999. 'Hegemonic Modulation and the Discourse of Fiscal Crisis.' *Studies in Political Economy*, 61–90.

Wright, Michael. 1993. 'A Critique of the Public Choice Theory Case for Privatization: Rhetoric and Reality.' *Ottawa Law Review* 25(1), 1–38.

Wysong, P. 1999. 'Non-profit Centres Delivered Better Dialysis.' *Medical Post*, 21 December, cover, 49.

Yanz, Linda, Bob Jeffcott, Deena Ladd, Joan Atlin, and Maquila Solidarity Network (Canada). 1999. *Policy Options to Improve Standards for Women Garment Workers in Canada and Internationally.* Ottawa: Status of Women Canada.

Yeatman, Anna. 1990. *Bureaucrats, Technocrats, Femocrats: Essays on the Contemporary Australian State.* Sydney: Allen and Unwin.

York, Geoffrey. 1992. 'Family Life: Not Enough Money, Too Much Stress.' *Globe and Mail*, 3 June, A1, A4.

Young, Claire F.L. 2000a. *What's Sex Got to Do with It? Tax and The 'Family.'* Ottawa: Law Commission of Canada.

– 2000b. *Women, Tax and Social Programs: The Gendered Impact of Funding Social Programs through the Tax System.* Ottawa: Status of Women Canada.

– 1999. '"Aging and Retirement Are Not Unique to Heterosexuals": *Rosenberg v. Canada.'* Paper Delivered at the Feminist Legal Academics Workshop Conference, Sydney, Australia, 24–6 February. Copy on file with the author.

– 1997. 'Public Taxes, Privatizing Effects, and Gender Inequality' In Susan B. Boyd, ed., *Challenging the Public/Private Divide: Feminism, Law and Public Policy.* Toronto: University of Toronto Press, 307–29.

– 1994a. 'Child Care: A Taxing Issue.' *McGill Law Journal* 39(3), 539–67.

– 1994b. 'Taxing Times for Lesbians and Gay Men: Equality at What Cost?' *Dalhousie Law Journal* 17(2), 533–59.

Youth Services Bureau. 1991. *Ottawa Street Prostitutes: A Survey*. Ottawa, 1991.

Zhao, John, Doug Drew, and T. Scott Murray. 2000. 'Brain Drain and Brain Gain: The Migration of Knowledge Workers from and to Canada.' *Education Quarterly Review* 6(3), 8–35.

Zweibel, Ellen. 1993. 'Child Support Policy and Child Support Guidelines: Broadening the Agenda.' *Canadian Journal of Women and the Law* 6, 371–401.

Zyblock, M. 1996. 'Why Is Family Market Inequality Increasing in Canada?' *Applied Research Branch Working Paper* W–96-11E. Ottawa: Human Resources Development Canada.

Legislation

Abortion Services Statues Amendment Act, S.B.C. 2001.

Alberta Personal Income Tax Act, S.A. 2000, c. A-35.03.

An Act to Amend Certain Statutes Because of the Supreme Court Canada Decision in M. v. H., S.O. 1999, c. 6.

An Act to Protect Children Involved in Prostitution, Bill 6 (first reading 12 May 1998, a private member's bill. Died after 3rd reading when Legislature prorogued December 1998. Reintroduced as Bill 18. 2nd reading on 11 May 2000, referred to the Standing Committee on General Government).

Anti-Inflation Act, S.C. 1974–75–76, c. 75.

Budget Implementation Act, 1991, S.C. 1991, c. 51.

Canada Health Act, R.S.C. 1985, c. C-6

Canada Labour Code, R.S.C. 1970, c. L-1.

Canada Pension Plan Investment Board Act, S.C. 1997, c. 40, as am.

Canadian Bill of Rights, S.C. 1960, c. 44, repr. in R.S.C. 1985, App. III.

Canadian Charter of Rights and Freedoms, Part 1 of the Constitution Act, 1982, Being Schedule B to the Canada Act 1982 (U.K.), 1982, c. 11.

Canadian Human Rights Act, R.S.C. 1970, c. H-9.5.

Child and Family Services Act, R.S.O. 1990, c.11; am. 1992, 1993, 1994, 1996, 1999.

Child and Family Services Authorities Act, S.A. 1997, c. C-73.

Child Welfare Act, S.A. 1984, c-8.1.

Child Welfare Amendment Act, S.A. 1997, c. 6.

Citizenship Act, R.S.C. 1985, c. C-27

Civil Service Act, R.S.C. 1906, c. 17.

Civil Service Amendment Act, S.C. 1908, c. 15.

Criminal Code, R.S.C. 1985, c. C-46.

Divorce Act, R.S.C. 1985 c. 3.

Divorce Act, S.C. 1967–68, c. 24.

Employment Equity Act, R.S.C. 1985, c. 23 (2nd Supp.).

Family Benefits Act, O. Reg. 409/95.

Family Law Act, R.S.O. 1990, c. F.3.

Family Responsibility and Support Arrears Enforcement Act, S.O. 1996, c. 31.

Family Support Plan Act, 1992. R.S.O. 1990, c. S.28.

Federal-Provincial Fiscal Arrangements and Federal Post-Secondary Education and Health Contribution Act, S.C. 1977, c. 10.

Food and Drugs Act, R.S.C. 1985, c. F-27.

General Welfare Assistance Act, R.S.O. 1990, c. G.6, repealed by S.O. 1997, c. 25.

Health Care Accessibility Act, 1986, R.S.O. 1990, c. H.3.

Health Care Protection Act, 2000, S.A. 2000, c. H-3.3

Health Insurance Act, R.S.O. 1990, c. H.6.

Hospital Insurance and Diagnostic Services Act, S.C. 1957, c. 28.

Immigration Act, R.S. 1952, c. 93.

Immigration Act, R.S. 1976, c. 52.

Immigration Act, R.S.C. 1985, c. I-2.

Immigration Regulations, SOR/78-172.

Immigration and Refugee Protection Act, S.C. 2001.

Income Tax Act, R.S.C. 1985, c. 1 (5th Supp.), as am.

Income War Tax Act, S.C. 1917, c. 28.

Independent Health Facilities Act, S.O. 1989, c. 59.

Juvenile Delinquents Act, 1929, S.C. 1929, c. 46.

Medical Care Act, S.C. 1966, c. 64.

Ministry of Health Act, R.S.O. 1990, c. M.26.

Ministry of Health and Long Term Care Statutes Law Amendment Act, S.O. 1999, c. 10.

Ontario Disability Support Program Act, S.O. 1997 c. 25, s. 2 (Schedule B).

Ontario Human Rights Code, R.S.O. 1990, c. H.19.

Ontario Income Tax Act, R.S.O. 1990, c. I.2, as am.

Ontario Works Act, 1997, S.O. 1997, c. 25.

Patent Act, R.S.C. 1985, c. P-4.

Patent Act Amendment Act 1992, R.S. 1992, c. 1.

Protecting Children from Sexual Exploitation Act, S.O.

Protection of Children Involved in Prostitution Act, S.A. 1999, c. P-19.3.

Public Hospitals Act, R.S.O. 1990, c. P.40.

Public Service Employment Act, S.C. 1966–67, c. 71.

Public Service Relations Act, S.C. 1966–67, c. 72.

Safe Streets Act, 1999, S.O. 1999, Ch.8.

Savings and Restructuring Act, S.O. 1996, c. 1.

Sexual Sterilization Act, S.A. 1928, c. 37, as am. S.A. 1937, c. 47, and S.A. 1942, c.194

Social Assistance Reform Act, S.O. 1997, c. 25.

Young Offenders Act, R.S.C. 1985, c. Y-1.

Youth Criminal Justice Act, Bill C-68 (first reading 11 March 1999. Died on the order paper when the 1st session of the 36th Parliament ended on 18 September 1999).

Intergovernmental Agreements

A Framework to Improve the Social Union for Canadians – An Agreement between the Government of Canada and the Governments of the Provinces and Territories (4 February 1999). Online: Government of Canada http://socialunion.gc.ca/news/020499_e.html

Cases

Alberta v. K.B., 28 July 2000, Calgary Docket N17871 and N17178, [2000] A.J. No. 876 (Prov. Ct. Fam. Div.).

Alpha Laboratories Inc. v. Ontario, [1999] O.J. No. 552, (1999) 121 O.A.C. 277 (Div. Ct.).

Association of Optometrists (B.C.) v. B.C. (1996), 38 Admin. L.R. (2d) 22 (B.C.S.C.).

Auton (Guardian ad litem of) v. British Columbia (Minister of Health), [2000] 8 W.W.R. 227, (2000) B.C.L.R. (3d) 55 (B.C.S.C.).

B.C. Civil Liberties Association v. B.C. (A.G.) (1988), 24 B.C.L.R. (2d) 189, [1988] 4 W.W.R. 100 (B.C.S.C.).

B.C. Government and Services Employees Union v. B.C. (Public Services Employees Relations Commission), [1999] 3 S.C.R. 3.

B.C. (Superintendent of Motor Vehicles) v. B.C. (Council of Human Rights), [1999] 3 S.C.R. 868.

Baker v. Canada (Minister of Citizenship and Immigration), [1999] 2 S.C.R. 817.

Blencoe v. B.C. (Human Rights Commission), [2000] S.C.J. No. 44, 2000 S.C.C. 44.

Brown v. B.C. (A.G.) (1998), 41 B.C.L.R. (3d) 265 (B.C.S.C.).

Brown v. B.C. (Minister of Health) (1990), 66 D.L.R. (4th) 444 (B.C.S.C.).

Cameron v. Nova Scotia. (A.G.) (1999), 177 D.L.R. (4th) 611 (N.S.C.A.); leave to appeal denied 29 June 2000, [1999] S.C.C.A. No. 531.

Canada (Minister of Finance) v. Finlay, [1986] 2 S.C.R. 607.

Canadian AIDS Society v. Ontario (1995), 25 O.R. (3d) 388 (Gen. Div.); aff'd (1996), 31 O.R. (3d) 798 (C.A.).

Canadian Union of Public Employees (CUPE) v. Ontario (Minister of Labour) (2000), 51 O.R. (3d) 417 (C.A.)

Chartier v. Chartier, [1998] S.C.J. No.79.

Collett v. Ontario (A.G.) (1995), 81 O.A.C. 85 (Div. Ct.).

Dartmouth/Halifax City Regional Housing Authority v. Sparks (1993), 119 N.S.R. (2d) 91, 330 A.P.R. 91 (N.S.C.A.).

Dunmore v. Ontario (A.G.) (1997), 37 O.R. (3d) 287 (Gen. Div.); aff'd (1999), 182 D.L.R. (4th) 471, 49 C.C.E.L. (2d) 29 (C.A.); leave to appeal granted [1999] S.C.C.A. No. 196.

Egan v. Canada, [1995] 2 S.C.R. 513.

Eldridge v. B.C. (A.G.), [1997] 3 S.C.R. 624.

Falkiner et al. v. Attorney General (Ontario) (1996), 140 D.L.R. (4th) 115.

Falkiner et al. v. Attorney General (Ontario) (2000), Ontario Divisional Court, 28 June 2000, court file 557/98.

Family and Children's Services of Kings County v. T.G. and R.G. (30 October 1998), No. F-CSK-97-22, [1998] N.S.J. No. 570 (N.S. Fam. Ct.).

Federated Anti-Poverty Groups v. B.C. (A.G.) (1991), 70 B.C.L.R. (2d) 325 (S.C.).

Ferrel v. Ontario (A.G.) (1998), 42 O.R. (3d) 97 (C.A.); leave to appeal refused (6 December 1999, S.C.C.); [1999] S.C.C.A. No. 79.

Finlay v. Canada (Minister of Finance), [1993] 1 S.C.R. 1080.

Francis v. Baker, [1999] 3 S.C.R. 250.

Granovsky v. Canada (Minister of Employment and Immigration), [2000] S.C.J. No. 29, [2001] 1 S.C.R. 703.

Hill v. Church of Scientology, [1995] 2 S.C.R. 1130.

Hodgkinson v. Simms, [1994] 3 S.C.R. 377.

Hughes v. Canada (A.G.) (1994), 80 F.T.R. 300 (T.D.).

Hutt v. The Queen, [1978] 2 S.C.R. 476.

Irshad (Litigation guardian of) v. Ontario (Minister of Health) (1999), 88 O.T.C. 321, 60 C.R.R. 231 (Ont. Gen. Div.); appeal dismissed, [2001] O.J. No. 648 (Ont. C.A.), 28 February 2001; [2001] S.C.C.A. No. 218 (S.C.C.)

Jabs Construction Limited v. The Queen, 99 D.T.C. 729 (T.C.C.)

Knodel v. B.C. (Medical Services Commission), [1991] B.C.J. No. 2588 (B.C.S.C.).

Laflamme v. Prudential-Bache Commodities Canada Ltd., [2000] S.C.J. No. 25 online: QL (SCJ).

Lalonde v. Ontario (HSRC) (2000), 181 D.L.R. (4th) 263, 48 O.R. (3d) 50 (Div. Ct.); [2001] O.J. No 4767 (Ont. C.A.)

Law v. Canada (Minister of Employment and Immigration), [1999] 1 S.C.R. 497.

Lexogest Inc. v. Manitoba (A.G.) (1993), 101 D.L.R. (4th) 523, 85 Man. R. (2d) 8 (Man. C.A.).

Lovelace v. Ontario, [2000] S.C.J. No. 36, 2000 S.C.C. 37; [2000] 1 S.C.R. 950.

M. v. H., [1999] 2 S.C.R. 3.

Masse v. Ontario (Minister of Community and Social Services) (1996), 134 D.L.R.
(4th) 20 (Gen. Div.); leave to appeal refused [1996] O.J. No. 1526 (C.A.).

McKinney v. University of Guelph, [1990] 3 S.C.R. 229.

Minister of Community Services and A.A., 4 May 1995, No. CFSA94-72, [1995] N.S.J.
No. 590 (N.S. Fam. Ct.).

Morgentaler v. P.E.I. (Minister of Health and Social Services) (1995), 122 D.L.R. (4th)
728 (P.E.I .S.C.)

N.B. (Minister of Health and Community Services) v. G.C.J., [1999] 3 S.C.R. 46.

Nova Scotia (Minister of Community Services) v. T.M. (1992), 119 N.S.R. (2d) 163,
330 A.P.R. 163 (N.S.Fam.Ct).

Ontario (A.G.) v. Dieleman (1994), 20 O.R. (3d) 229 (Gen. Div.).

Ontario Human Rights Commission v. Ontario (1994), 19 O.R. (3d) 387 (C.A.).

Ottawa Carleton Dialysis Services v. Ontario (Minister of Health), [1996] O.J. 2721
(Div. Ct.).

Pelech v. Pelech (1987), 7 R.L.F. (3d) 225.

Pembroke Civic Hospital v. Ontario (Health Services Restructuring Commission) (1997),
36 O.R. (3d) 41 (Div. Ct.).

*Quebec (Commission des droits de la personne et des droits de la jeunesse) v. Montreal;
Quebec v. Boisbriand,* [2000] S.C.J. No. 24, [2001] 1 S.C.R. 665.

R. v. Ashok Kumar Dua, 5 May 1999, London File No. 4756 (Ont. Ct. Gen. Div.).

R. v. Burt (2000), 258 A.R. 334 (Q.B.).

R. v. C.(T.), 14 January 1988, Kitchener [1988] O.J. No. 547 (Ont. Dist. Ct.).

R. v. D.E.M., [1984] O.J. No. 678.

R. v. Downey (1992), 72 C.C.C. (3d) 1 (S.C.C.).

R. v. Dyment, [1988] 2 S.C.R. 417.

R. v. Foster (1984), 13 C.C.C. (3d) 435 (Alta. C.A.).

R. v. I.C.V. (6 August 1985), Toronto Registry Y-573/85 (Ont. Prov. Ct. Fam.
Div.), [1985] O.J. No. 787.

R. v. L.K.T., 27 January 1998, DRS 98-07771, [1998] A.J. No. 97 (Alta. Prov. Ct., Y.
Div.).

R. v. Leo (1993), 144 A.R. 98 (Prov. Ct. Crim. Div.).

R. v. Mark Richard Morgan, 5 February 1986 (Ont. Dist. Ct.).

R. v. Mills, [1999] 3 S.C.R. 668.

R. v. Morgentaler, [1993] 3 S.C.R. 463.

R. v. Morgentaler, [1988] 1 S.C.R. 30.

R. v. Pelley (1990), 82 Nfld. & P.E.I.R. 293 (Nfld. S.C.T.D.).

R. v. S. S., [1990] 2 S.C.R. 254.

R. v. Skinner (1990), 56 C.C.C. (3d) 1 (S.C.C.).

R. v. Stagnitta (1990), 56 C.C.C. (3d) 17 (S.C.C.).

Re A.C., 3 April 1990, Edmonton, [1990] A.J. No. 331 (Alta. Prov. Ct., Fam. Div.).

Re Dele Ilis (1998), 21 O.S.C.B. 305

Re Doctors Hospital and Minister of Health et al. (1976), 12 O.R. (2d) 164.

Re Eve (1986), 31 D.L.R. (4th) 1 (S.C.C.).

Re Isabey and Manitoba Medical Services Comm'n (1986), 28 D.L.R. (4th) 735 (Man. C.A.).

Re Koonar and Minister of Health (1982), 133 D.L.R. (3d) 396 (Ont. Div. Ct.).

Re Mersch (1998), 21 O.S.C.B. 3805

Re M.G. (1980), 18 R.F.L. (2d) 355 (B.C. Prov. Ct.).

Re Metropolitan General Hospital and Minister of Health (1979), 25 O.R. (2d) 699 (H.C.).

Re Multi-Malls and Minister of Transportation & Communications (1977), 14 O.R. (2d) 49 (C.A.).

Re Wittman and Medical Services Commission (1990), 71 D.L.R. (4th) 140 (B.C.S.C.).

Reference re Sections 193 & 195 of the Criminal Code (1990), 56 C.C.C. (3d) 65 (S.C.C.).

Retail, Wholesale and Department Store Union v. Dolphin Delivery, [1986] 2 S.C.R. 573.

Rombaut v. N.B. (Minister of Health and Community Services) (2000), 225 N.B.R. (2d) 298 (Q.B.); [2001] N.B.J. No. 243 (N.B.C.A.).

Rosenberg v. Canada (Attorney General) (1998), 38 O.R. (3d) 577.

Russell v. Ontario (Health Services Restructing Commission) (1998), 114 O.A.C. 280 (Div. Ct.); aff'd (1999), 175 D.L.R. (4th) 185 (Ont. C.A.).

S.E.I.U. Local 204 v. Ontario (1997), 35 O.R. (3d) 508 (Div. Ct.).

Silion v. Canada (Minister of Citizenship and Immigration) (1999), 173 F.T.R. 302 (T.D.).

Stein v. Quebec (Regie de l'Assurance-maladie), [1999] Q.J. No. 2724 (S.C.).

Stoffman v. Vancouver General Hospital, [1990] 3 S.C.R. 483.

Thibaudeau v. Canada (Minister of National Revenue), [1995] 2 S.C.R. 627.

Toronto Birth Centre Inc. v. Minister of Health (1996), 92 O.A.C. 74 (Div. Ct.).

Vancouver Society of Immigrant and Visible Minority Women v. M.N.R., [1999] 1 S.C.R. 10.

Vriend v. Alberta (1998), 156 D.L.R. (4th) 385 (S.C.C.).

Waldman v. British Columbia (Medical Services Commission) (1999), 177 D.L.R. (4th) 321; [1999] 12 W.W.R. 542 (B.C.C.A.).

Wellesley Central Hospital v. Ontario (HSRC) (1997), 151 D.L.R. (4th) 706 (Div. Ct.).